Transforming Humanities and Social Sciences Through AI

Salmane Bourekkadi
Ibn Tofail University, Morocco

IGI Global
Scientific Publishing
Publishing Tomorrow's Research Today

Published in the United States of America by
IGI Global Scientific Publishing
701 East Chocolate Avenue
Hershey, PA, 17033, USA
Tel: 717-533-8845 | Fax: 717-533-7115
Website: https://www.igi-global.com E-mail: cust@igi-global.com

Library of Congress Cataloging-in-Publication Data

Names: Bourekkadi, Salmane, 1988- editor
Title: Transforming humanities and social sciences through AI / [edited by] Salmane Bourekkadi.
Description: Hershey, PA : IGI Global Scientific Publishing, [2026] | Includes bibliographical references and index. | Summary: "This book aims to explore how artificial intelligence is reshaping traditional disciplines by enhancing research methodologies, fostering interdisciplinary collaboration, and addressing ethical challenges"-- Provided by publisher.
Identifiers: LCCN 2025017533 (print) | LCCN 2025017534 (ebook) | ISBN 9798337334363 hardcover | ISBN 9798337334370 paperback | ISBN 9798337334387 ebook
Subjects: LCSH: Artificial intelligence--Educational applications | Humanities--Technological innovations | Social sciences--Technological innovations
Classification: LCC LB1028.43 .T75 2026 (print) | LCC LB1028.43 (ebook)
LC record available at https://lccn.loc.gov/2025017533
LC ebook record available at https://lccn.loc.gov/2025017534

British Cataloguing in Publication Data
A Cataloguing in Publication record for this book is available from the British Library.

Table of Contents

Detailed Table of Contents

their capabilities and improve the quality of medical care offered to patients. However, the study emphasises the need to maintain human and ethical oversight in the use of these technologies to ensure the protection and fairness of patients.

The development of artificial intelligence (AI) is becoming increasingly important. As the healthcare field evolves and becomes more complex, nursing education must also transform to keep pace with this changing landscape. The integration of AI into nursing training represents a significant advancement in how healthcare professionals are educated, with the primary goal of improving teaching, learning, and critical thinking among students. Realistic AI-powered simulations give students the opportunity to practice clinical skills in safe virtual environments, increasing their confidence and preparing them for real-world professional situations. Furthermore, AI-supported learning can also foster the development of critical thinking, enhance clinical reasoning skills, and strengthen teamwork among nursing students. In conclusion, integrating AI into nursing education offers great opportunities to improve learning and prepare future nurses for the healthcare of tomorrow while encouraging responsible and innovative use of this technology.

The integration of artificial intelligence (AI) into social and solidarity economy (SSE) organizations offers both opportunities and challenges for the sector's core values of solidarity, democracy, and social justice. While AI can enhance innovation, efficiency, and social inclusion, it also raises questions about its alignment with SSE principles. This chapter uses a multilevel quantitative approach and hierarchical linear modeling to analyze AI adoption in a representative sample of SSE organizations, considering both organizational and contextual factors. The findings indicate that

This study examines the extent of acoustic similarity between artificial and human speech within the framework of Korean language education for non-native learners. The main objective is to ascertain whether the speech patterns of language learners resemble those of native speakers or those produced by artificial intelligence (AI) text-to-speech (TTS) systems. Utilizing a mixed-methods approach, fifteen experimental teams—consisting of native Korean speakers, Korean language learners from Universiti Malaysia Sabah, and five Korean TTS engines—generated a corpus of forty-five recorded utterances. Each sample was changed into spectral data and analyzed with Dynamic Time Warping (DTW) to find differences in timing and frequency.

This article explores the use of artificial intelligence (AI) tools among doctoral students at Ibn Tofail University, focusing on their perceived impact on research quality and training needs. A quantitative survey of 30 students revealed high AI adoption: 93.3% use ChatGPT, 50% Grammarly, and 20% QuillBot. Despite these figures, all respondents expressed a strong need for structured training to develop digital literacy and responsible usage. While AI tools assist in writing, paraphrasing, and content generation, their potential is limited by ethical concerns and lack of formal guidance. The study highlights the importance of implementing targeted, discipline-specific programs to ensure effective and ethical integration of AI in doctoral education. These findings contribute to the broader discussion on digital transformation in higher education and illustrate how AI is beginning to reshape academic research practices.

This chapter examines the evolution of conceptions of language within the framework of cognitive science, focusing on the shift from a computational paradigm to an embodied approach to cognition. Grounded in a central question — how the mind-as-computer metaphor was gradually replaced by a view of language rooted in lived experience and body–environment interaction — the study adopts a historical, comparative, and critical methodology. The analysis traces major paradigms and compares linguistic models, from Chomskyan formalism to cognitive linguistics. It draws on insights from the philosophy of mind, cognitive psychology, and linguistics to shed light on the epistemological transformations at stake. This chapter, through its historical, theoretical, and practical sections, aims to highlight the continuities, ruptures, and conceptual contributions that have led to a reconfiguration of language as a phenomenon that is at once cognitive, physical, and contextual, from a resolutely interdisciplinary perspective.

This work studies the incorporation of artificial intelligence (AI) as a vector of pedagogical innovation in the teaching/learning of physical education and sports (PE). Based on a systematic literature review of recently published work (2023-2024), this chapter highlights three major advantages of AI devices in PE teaching, including the individualization of educational pathways, the objectivity of evaluation and the development of learners' motivation and commitment, including those with disabilities. The critical analysis highlights challenges to be overcome, namely teacher training, data privacy and educational equity for all. An interdisciplinary conceptual framework is proposed as well as recommendations regarding education policies, digital investment and institutional cooperation. This study aims to establish the foundations for a deontological and continuous integration of AI tools in PE, for innovative, inclusive pedagogical practices adapted to the individual needs of learners.

The translation of environmental terms from French to Arabic poses significant challenges due to linguistic, cultural, and conceptual differences. These challenges are compounded by the complexity of environmental terminology, which often involves specialized vocabulary related to ecology, climate change, sustainability, and conservation. Common errors in translation include misinterpretations of technical terms. Artificial Intelligence offers a promising solution to these translation challenges. AI can also assist in creating more culturally relevant translations, ensuring that the environmental message is conveyed correctly across linguistic and cultural boundaries. This study explores how AI can improve the translation of environmental terms from French to Arabic, addressing both linguistic and cultural barriers. By applying AI in the translation process, it is possible to bridge gaps between languages and enhance cross-cultural communication on environmental issues, thus contributing to more effective global environmental discourse.

This chapter explores the intersection of machine learning and psychology, highlighting how machine learning technologies are transforming both empirical research and the practice of psychology. We provide a comprehensive overview of the innovative applications of machine learning within the field of psychology, including areas such as predictive behavioral analysis and the use of natural language processing techniques to identify emotional indicators in interpersonal communications. This chapter explores sophisticated methodologies, to demonstrate the efficacy of these instruments in the diagnosis of mental health disorders, thereby augmenting objectivity in evaluations and refining intervention strategies. Additionally, we address ethical considerations and concerns related to data confidentiality and interpretation while offering insights into the future development of this interdisciplinary field. This manuscript is designed for scholars and practitioners aiming to comprehend the potentials and constraints of machine learning in the analysis of human behavior.

Citizens' awareness of environmental problems has been strengthened over the past two decades by the publication of a wide dissemination of information and data on the real state of the environment and the dangers likely to arise if corrective actions and measures are not put in place. The integration of AI makes it possible to stimulate personalized solutions adapted to each individual by offering promising prospects and promoting a sustainable lifestyle within Smart Cities. The success of individual awareness programs is related to the growth of the interest in sustainable development in society in order to increase ecological and environmentally friendly behavior. Our study aims to highlight the importance of the integration and motivation of the citizen to use renewable energies in addition to other stakeholders in order to support the smart city project.

This article investigates the expanding role of artificial intelligence (AI) in value co-creation within service industries. Through a narrative literature review, it highlights four key contributions of AI: enhancing customer engagement through interactive experiences, enabling intelligent automation in collaborative processes, hyper-personalizing offerings via real-time data analytics, and creating new co-creation opportunities with innovative interfaces. Sector-specific examples from hospitality, healthcare, education, and finance illustrate these aspects. Theoretically, the article proposes expanding the co-creation model to include intelligent agents and redefines roles within service systems. Managerially, it stresses the need for hybrid human-AI frameworks and redesigning customer journeys. Limitations include the exploratory nature and reliance on secondary data, pointing to future research on empirical studies, ethical and cultural dimensions, and cross-sector comparisons.

Preface

INTRODUCTION

At the dawn of the twenty-first century, the humanities and social sciences stand at a crossroads: on one side, the enduring legacy of disciplines grounded in centuries of humanistic inquiry, reflection, and interpretation; on the other, a rapidly evolving future driven by digital technologies, artificial intelligence, data analytics, and connected infrastructures. Transforming Humanities and Social Sciences Through Digital Technologies emerges as a timely and necessary exploration of this intersection.

This volume embodies an ambitious intellectual endeavor to demonstrate that digital tools are not mere technical supplements but true catalysts of epistemological transformation. It reflects a deep commitment to thinking with technologies not as an external aid, but as an invitation to reimagine the very objects, methods, and paradigms of research in the humanities and social sciences.

The chapters collected here navigate between theory and practice, between critique and innovation. Each contribution shows how digital methodologies reshape archives, data visualization, knowledge interfaces, cultural mediation, interdisciplinary collaboration, and the ethical dimensions of technology. Together, they form bridges between the digital and the human, between data and meaning, between technique and critique.

Yet, transformation is never without challenge. The authors also examine the risks and limitations of this shift: algorithmic surveillance, data bias, digital divides, methodological standardization, platform dependency, and long-term preservation of digital artifacts. Thus, this book serves both as a guide to opportunities and as a thoughtful alert to potential pitfalls.

OVERVIEW OF CHAPTERS

Chapter 1: AI-Driven Innovation and Corporate Social Responsibility Governance in Morocco's Digital-Intelligence Era

This chapter explores in depth recent developments in CSR governance practices in the specific context of Morocco in the era of smart digitalization. Over the past decade, the widespread adoption of technologies such as artificial AI, big data, IoT, and digital platforms has profoundly reshaped modes of production, governance, and interaction between companies and their stakeholders. This digital transformation, integrated into national strategies such as "Digital Morocco 2030," aims to position Morocco as an African hub for innovation, modernize the productive apparatus, and stimulate innovative entrepreneurship. The central concept of algorithmic governance is introduced as a new hybrid form of governance, involving automated technological mechanisms that redefine traditional models of organizational control and raise new challenges in terms of ethics, transparency, and fairness. In the Moroccan context, these challenges are exacerbated by specific structural and institutional constraints, such as the hybridization of imported formal standards and local informal practices.

Chapter 2: Analysis of Perceptions and Challenges of Telemedicine Implementation in Rural Areas and IA

Access to healthcare in rural areas remains a challenge in Morocco; telemedicine offers a new approach to primary care; however, its integration faces challenges; our study aims to explore how these challenges are perceived by institutional stakeholders in Morocco; this is a retrospective qualitative study of a pilot project; The study showed that there is a very positive perception of the usefulness of telemedicine in terms of improving accessibility, technological development, service quality, and human resource optimization. However, its integration is conditioned by several factors, including human factors, organizational conditions, and contextual factors. AI offers several advantages and can help overcome certain challenges. The integration of telemedicine requires a multidimensional approach that takes into account the complexity of the Moroccan healthcare system and leverages the advantages of AI.

Chapter 3: Artificial Intelligence and Augmented Reality for Optimized Sensory Development in Preschool Children With Autism Disorders

Inclusive education in preschool is a fundamental requirement in education systems, especially for children with autism disorders (ETSA), who often have sensory peculiarities and difficulties in social interactions, requiring adapted and innovative pedagogical approaches. Artificial intelligence (AI) and augmented reality (AR) would offer immersive and interactive environments, capable of meeting the individual needs of children regardless of their skills, by simulating social situations, modulating sensory stimuli, and providing real-time feedback. This study adopts a mixed approach (questionnaire, observations in inclusive classrooms and interviews with educators), to analyze the impact of these technologies on sensory development and the inclusion of ETSAs in preschool education. It identifies the opportunities and limits of their integration into Moroccan preschool pedagogical practices, and proposes concrete avenues for educational development for a more effective inclusion through digital technology.

Chapter 4: Artificial Intelligence and Digital Health Applications: Field Study from the Perspective of the Sociology of Health and Disease: Doctors as a Model

This study deals with uncovering the increasing role of artificial intelligence in the medical field with special attention to its applications and how doctors benefit from it. The study used the descriptive method on a random sample of 50 doctors, and collected the study data on the questionnaire technique. In the end, the study concluded that artificial intelligence receives great attention in medical affairs and has a high impact on doctors through medical awareness, professional development, and medical diagnosis. At the conclusion of the study, it was emphasised that artificial intelligence does not replace doctors, but rather is an auxiliary tool that can develop their capabilities and improve the quality of medical care offered to patients. However, the study emphasises the need to maintain human and ethical oversight in the use of these technologies to ensure the protection and fairness of patients.

Chapter 5: Artificial Intelligence and Nursing Education, Enhancing Teaching, Learning and Critical Thinking: Artificial Intelligence and Nursing Education

The development of artificial intelligence (AI) is becoming increasingly important. As the healthcare field evolves and becomes more complex, nursing education must also transform to keep pace with this changing landscape. The integration of AI into nursing training represents a significant advancement in how healthcare professionals are educated, with the primary goal of improving teaching, learning, and critical thinking among students. Realistic AI-powered simulations give students the opportunity to practice clinical skills in safe virtual environments, increasing their confidence and preparing them for real-world professional situations. Furthermore, AI-supported learning can also foster the development of critical thinking, enhance clinical reasoning skills, and strengthen teamwork among nursing students. In conclusion, integrating AI into nursing education offers great opportunities to improve learning and prepare future nurses for the healthcare of tomorrow while encouraging responsible and innovative use of this technology.

Chapter 6: Artificial Intelligence and Social Economy: Towards a Critical Epistemology of Solidarity Transformation

The integration of artificial intelligence (AI) into social and solidarity economy (SSE) organizations offers both opportunities and challenges for the sector's core values of solidarity, democracy, and social justice. While AI can enhance innovation, efficiency, and social inclusion, it also raises questions about its alignment with SSE principles. This chapter uses a multilevel quantitative approach and hierarchical linear modeling to analyze AI adoption in a representative sample of SSE organizations, considering both organizational and contextual factors. The findings indicate that AI's positive impact on efficiency and social innovation is real, but its ability to advance a solidarity-based transformation depends on internal resources, leadership, institutional support, and inclusive practices. AI strengthens the SSE's social mission only when embedded in participatory and democratic frameworks.

Chapter 7: Artificial Intelligence, Humanity, and Sustainability: Trends and Opportunities

Artificial intelligence (AI), humanity, and sustainability issues are among the important issues that need to be considered together and that attract the attention of people from almost every segment of society. This chapter aims to conduct trends and opportunities analysis on the AI, humanity, and sustainability issue. For this purpose, a trends and opportunities analysis was conducted on publications on the AI, humanity, and sustainability issue in the Web of Science (WoS) database using the Biblioshiny application. The trend and opportunities analysis was conducted within the scope of some descriptive and, three field plot, country collaboration analysis, most frequently used word, word cloud, thematic map, thematic evolution and trend topics analyses. This chapter is thought to provide useful information for researchers and practitioners on the AI, humanity, and sustainability issue.

Chapter 8: Environments Detreminants of Tuberculosis: AI as an Innovative Solution

Tuberculosis (TB) continues to be a major public health issue worldwide, with its prevalence heavily influenced by environmental determinants such as poor living conditions, air pollution, and limited healthcare access. These factors contribute to the spread and persistence of TB, particularly in under-resourced and vulnerable communities. Understanding the environmental influences on TB transmission is key to developing effective prevention and intervention strategies. Artificial Intelligence (AI) offers a groundbreaking solution for analyzing the complex relationships between environmental determinants and TB. This study explores the potential of AI in addressing the environmental determinants of tuberculosis, showcasing how AI can be applied to enhance disease monitoring, improve resource allocation, and support effective policy-making. Integrating AI into public health strategies offers the opportunity to transform the approach to TB control, enabling a more proactive and data-driven response to this global health challenge.

Chapter 9: Examining Acoustic Correspondence Between Artificial and Human Speech Patterns in Korean Language Instruction for Non-Native Speakers

This study examines the extent of acoustic similarity between artificial and human speech within the framework of Korean language education for non-native learners. The main objective is to ascertain whether the speech patterns of language learners resemble those of native speakers or those produced by artificial intelligence (AI) text-to-speech (TTS) systems. Utilizing a mixed-methods approach, fifteen experimental teams—consisting of native Korean speakers, Korean language learners from Universiti Malaysia Sabah, and five Korean TTS engines—generated a corpus of forty-five recorded utterances. Each sample was changed into spectral data and analyzed with Dynamic Time Warping (DTW) to find differences in timing and frequency.

Chapter 10: Exploring the Adoption of AI Tools Among PhD Students at Ibn Tofail University: A Quantitative Study

This article explores the use of artificial intelligence (AI) tools among doctoral students at Ibn Tofail University, focusing on their perceived impact on research quality and training needs. A quantitative survey of 30 students revealed high AI adoption: 93.3% use ChatGPT, 50% Grammarly, and 20% QuillBot. Despite these figures, all respondents expressed a strong need for structured training to develop digital literacy and responsible usage. While AI tools assist in writing, paraphrasing, and content generation, their potential is limited by ethical concerns and lack of formal guidance. The study highlights the importance of implementing targeted, discipline-specific programs to ensure effective and ethical integration of AI in doctoral education. These findings contribute to the broader discussion on digital transformation in higher education and illustrate how AI is beginning to reshape academic research practices.

Chapter 11: From Machine Language to Embodied Cognition: A Paradigmatic Shift in Cognitive Linguistics

This chapter examines the evolution of conceptions of language within the framework of cognitive science, focusing on the shift from a computational paradigm to an embodied approach to cognition. Grounded in a central question — how the mind-as-computer metaphor was gradually replaced by a view of language rooted in lived experience and body–environment interaction — the study adopts a historical, comparative, and critical methodology. The analysis traces major paradigms and compares linguistic models, from Chomskyan formalism to cognitive linguistics. It draws on insights from the philosophy of mind, cognitive psychology, and linguistics to shed light on the epistemological transformations at stake. This chapter, through its historical, theoretical, and practical sections, aims to highlight the continuities, ruptures, and conceptual contributions that have led to a reconfiguration of language as a phenomenon that is at once cognitive, physical, and contextual, from a resolutely interdisciplinary perspective.

Chapter 12: Inclusive Pedagogy and Artificial Intelligence in the Teaching of Physical Education and Sports

This work studies the incorporation of artificial intelligence (AI) as a vector of pedagogical innovation in the teaching/learning of physical education and sports (PE). Based on a systematic literature review of recently published work (2023-2024), this chapter highlights three major advantages of AI devices in PE teaching, including the individualization of educational pathways, the objectivity of evaluation and the development of learners' motivation and commitment, including those with disabilities. The critical analysis highlights challenges to be overcome, namely teacher training, data privacy and educational equity for all. An interdisciplinary conceptual framework is proposed as well as recommendations regarding education policies, digital investment and institutional cooperation. This study aims to establish the foundations for a deontological and continuous integration of AI tools in PE, for innovative, inclusive pedagogical practices adapted to the individual needs of learners.

Chapter 13: Integrating Social AI Into French–Arabic Environmental Translation: Common Challenges and Solutions

The translation of environmental terms from French to Arabic poses significant challenges due to linguistic, cultural, and conceptual differences. These challenges are compounded by the complexity of environmental terminology, which often involves specialized vocabulary related to ecology, climate change, sustainability, and conservation. Common errors in translation include misinterpretations of technical terms. Artificial Intelligence offers a promising solution to these translation challenges. AI can also assist in creating more culturally relevant translations, ensuring that the environmental message is conveyed correctly across linguistic and cultural boundaries. This study explores how AI can improve the translation of environmental terms from French to Arabic, addressing both linguistic and cultural barriers. By applying AI in the translation process, it is possible to bridge gaps between languages and enhance cross-cultural communication on environmental issues, thus contributing to more effective global environmental discourse.

Chapter 14: Revolutionizing Psychological Methods through Machine Learning

This chapter explores the intersection of machine learning and psychology, highlighting how machine learning technologies are transforming both empirical research and the practice of psychology. We provide a comprehensive overview of the innovative applications of machine learning within the field of psychology, including areas such as predictive behavioral analysis and the use of natural language processing techniques to identify emotional indicators in interpersonal communications. This chapter explores sophisticated methodologies, to demonstrate the efficacy of these instruments in the diagnosis of mental health disorders, thereby augmenting objectivity in evaluations and refining intervention strategies. Additionally, we address ethical considerations and concerns related to data confidentiality and interpretation while offering insights into the future development of this interdisciplinary field. This manuscript is designed for scholars and practitioners aiming to comprehend the potentials and constraints of machine learning in the analysis of human behavior.

Chapter 15: The integration of AI and stakeholders in citizen motivation towards a sustainable energy transition in the context of a Smart City

Citizens' awareness of environmental problems has been strengthened over the past two decades by the publication of a wide dissemination of information and data on the real state of the environment and the dangers likely to arise if corrective actions and measures are not put in place. The integration of AI makes it possible to stimulate personalized solutions adapted to each individual by offering promising prospects and promoting a sustainable lifestyle within Smart Cities. The success of individual awareness programs is related to the growth of the interest in sustainable development in society in order to increase ecological and environmentally friendly behavior. Our study aims to highlight the importance of the integration and motivation of the citizen to use renewable energies in addition to other stakeholders in order to support the smart city project.

Chapter 16: The Role of AI in Facilitating Value Co-Creation in Service Industries

This article investigates the expanding role of artificial intelligence (AI) in value co-creation within service industries. Through a narrative literature review, it highlights four key contributions of AI: enhancing customer engagement through interactive experiences, enabling intelligent automation in collaborative processes, hyper-personalizing offerings via real-time data analytics, and creating new co-creation opportunities with innovative interfaces. Sector-specific examples from hospitality, healthcare, education, and finance illustrate these aspects. Theoretically, the article proposes expanding the co-creation model to include intelligent agents and redefines roles within service systems. Managerially, it stresses the need for hybrid human-AI frameworks and redesigning customer journeys. Limitations include the exploratory nature and reliance on secondary data, pointing to future research on empirical studies, ethical and cultural dimensions, and cross-sector comparisons.

Chapter 17: Transforming Education with Artificial Intelligence: Tools, Challenges, and Future Directions

Artificial intelligence (AI) is rapidly reshaping education by enhancing teaching methods, personalizing learning experiences, and fostering critical thinking skills. This chapter reviews key AI technologies such as intelligent tutoring systems, adaptive learning platforms, and natural language processing tools and their applications in improving instruction, assessment, and learner engagement. It also examines AI's role in developing higher-order cognitive skills through collaborative learning and argumentation support. The chapter discusses challenges including data privacy, algorithmic bias, and equitable access, alongside ethical considerations vital for responsible AI integration. Finally, it outlines future research directions, emphasizing emerging technologies and interdisciplinary collaboration. This comprehensive overview highlights AI's transformative potential to create inclusive, personalized, and effective educational environments that prepare learners for complex real-world challenges.

Chapter 18: Unfolding the Ethical and Philosophical Implications of AI in Shaping Human-Centered Fields

The integration of Artificial Intelligence (AI) into humanist areas in the profession such as healthcare, education, law, and arts provokes significant ethical and philosophical dilemmas. The use of AI in human centered disciplines has a significant contribution in the fast-evolving environment. The philosophical and ethical issues of the implementation of AI as well as human-centered sciences are problematic and multidimensional. Ethics is one of the most urgent philosophical problems of AI in the anthropocentric fields. In AI systems, especially in the health and legal decision-making processes, some ethical issues should be included in the programming of AI systems as it is the bias in the AI decision-making that is responsible of the AI-driven results. Morally, in the delicate and supreme consideration that should take place in these areas, the input of AI causes influence on human creativity, and raises issues regarding the essence of intelligence and authorship; it lessens human reasoning, and decision-making.

One of the great strengths of this volume lies in its dual perspective diagnostic and prospective. It not only analyzes what is changing but also envisions what an "augmented humanity" could and should be: a humanity illuminated by technology yet vigilant about values, inclusion, and plurality.

For educators, researchers, students, librarians, developers, and anyone engaged in reflecting on the relationship between knowledge, technology, and society, this book offers a stimulating companion. It invites careful reflection, ethical awareness, and bold experimentation.

May the following pages inspire new dialogues, innovative research, and a generation of scholars who will not merely use technologies but will make them genuine partners in thought.

Acknowledgment

The realization of Transforming Humanities and Social Sciences Through Digital Technologies would not have been possible without the dedication, collaboration, and vision of many individuals and institutions.

First and foremost, I extend my sincere gratitude to the contributing authors, whose intellectual rigor, creativity, and commitment to advancing interdisciplinary knowledge made this volume a reality. Each chapter reflects their deep engagement with the evolving dialogue between technology and the human sciences, offering innovative perspectives that enrich both scholarship and practice.

My heartfelt appreciation goes to the editorial and development team at IGI Global, particularly Melissa, whose guidance, patience, and professionalism ensured that every stage of the editorial process was conducted with clarity and excellence. Their support, from initial proposal to final production, was invaluable in shaping this collective endeavor.

I am equally indebted to the peer reviewers for their thoughtful evaluations, constructive feedback, and scholarly generosity. Their expertise strengthened the quality, depth, and coherence of the book, helping authors refine their contributions and align them with the highest academic standards.

Special thanks are due to my co-editors and collaborators, whose insights and encouragement were instrumental throughout this journey. Our shared discussions about the transformative power of digital technologies in reshaping education, research, and social thought were both inspiring and enlightening.

Chapter 1
AI-Driven Innovation and Corporate Social Responsibility Governance in Morocco's Digital-Intelligence Era

Fadila El Hazbi
https://orcid.org/0009-0000-8721-6688
Ibn Zohr University, Morocco

Mounir Younes
https://orcid.org/0009-0006-6741-2044
Faculty of Law, Economics, and Social Sciences, Ibn Zohr University, Morocco

ABSTRACT

This chapter explores in depth recent developments in CSR governance practices in the specific context of Morocco in the era of smart digitalization. Over the past decade, the widespread adoption of technologies such as artificial AI, big data, IoT, and digital platforms has profoundly reshaped modes of production, governance, and interaction between companies and their stakeholders. This digital transformation, integrated into national strategies such as "Digital Morocco 2030," aims to position Morocco as an African hub for innovation, modernize the productive apparatus, and stimulate innovative entrepreneurship. The central concept of algorithmic governance is introduced as a new hybrid form of governance, involving automated technological mechanisms that redefine traditional models of organizational control and raise new challenges in terms of ethics, transparency, and fairness. In

DOI: 10.4018/979-8-3373-3436-3.ch001

the Moroccan context, these challenges are exacerbated by specific structural and institutional constraints, such as the hybridization of imported formal standards and local informal practices.

INTRODUCTION

Over the past decade, digital transformation has fundamentally reshaped production processes, governance frameworks, and modes of interaction between corporations and their stakeholders. Driven by advances in artificial intelligence (AI), big data analytics, the Internet of Things (IoT), and digital platforms, this shift has unfolded within the broader context of what scholars have termed "intelligent digitalization" (Xiao & Yang, 2019). In this paradigm, data emerges not merely as an input for production, but as a strategic asset that redefines value creation and restructures social relations.

At its core, intelligent digitalization has propelled organizations to fundamentally rethink traditional models of governance and management. Through algorithmic governance, AI-driven tools facilitate more efficient, transparent, and responsive decision-making processes, enabling real-time adjustments and predictive analyses that enhance both operational efficiency and stakeholder engagement. Big data analytics, by providing unprecedented insight into consumer behavior, operational effectiveness, and market dynamics, empower companies to personalize their offerings, anticipate customer needs, and significantly enhance their competitiveness.

Moreover, the integration of IoT technology within production and operational processes enables enhanced connectivity across organizational functions, resulting in smarter logistics, improved resource allocation, and reduced environmental footprints. For instance, IoT sensors embedded in supply chains not only monitor and optimize the flow of goods but also ensure compliance with sustainability standards and ethical sourcing practices, thereby enhancing the CSR profile of businesses.

Digital platforms have emerged as central components of this intelligent digitalization wave, reshaping not only economic exchanges but also social interactions among stakeholders. Platform-based ecosystems foster greater collaboration, innovation, and co-creation between businesses, consumers, regulators, and communities. By leveraging network effects, these platforms stimulate continuous innovation cycles, democratize access to resources, and cultivate new forms of social capital, significantly reshaping how value is perceived, created, and distributed

This technological evolution has brought about a profound reconfiguration of CSR, both in terms of implementation modalities and the legitimizing discourses that underpin it. This is particularly salient in developing countries, where the socio-tech impact of digital technologies is often intensified by institutional asymmetrical and structural constraints. In the Moroccan context, digital transition is taking shape within a transforming political-economic landscape, underpinned by a state-led ambition to position the country as a regional hub for innovation and digital technologies. This is evidenced by national strategies such as "Maroc Digital 2020" and the more recent "Digital Morocco 2030", which seek to modernize productive systems, enhance social inclusion, and foster innovative entrepreneurship.

However, this transformation cannot be reduced to a mere technical shift. Rather, it raises far- reaching questions related to governance, algorithmic regulation, and corporate accountability, as emerging technologies redefine the boundaries between organizations, individuals, and society. Within this evolving landscape, algorithmic governance, understood as the constellation of norms, mechanisms, procedures, and actors engaged in regulating automated decision-making technologies (Zouridis et al., 2020), has emerged as a pivotal concern. This nascent, hybrid, and distributed mode of governance challenges conventional organizational control structures and introduces new tensions among efficiency, transparency, fairness, and ethical integrity.

In the CSR domain, algorithmic governance directly interrogates how firms design, execute, evaluate, and communicate their environmental and social commitments. Academic literature has traditionally approached CSR through normative and strategic lenses. From Carroll's foundational typologies (1979, 1991) and Freeman's stakeholder theory (1984) to Porter and Kramer's framework of shared value creation (2011), corporate responsibility has been largely framed as a voluntary engagement, guided either by entrepreneurial ethics, institutional legitimacy (Suchman, 1995), or competitive advantage.

Yet, these established frameworks struggle to fully capture the dynamics introduced by intelligent digitalization. The processes by which legitimacy is constructed, regulation is enacted, and actors interact are undergoing rapid transformation. On one hand, AI systems can enhance CSR effectiveness, for instance, by automating ESG report analysis or optimizing supply chains according to sustainability criteria. On the other hand, they raise critical ethical concerns such as algorithmic bias, decision-making opacity, and discriminatory exclusions.

This duality necessitates a reconsideration of existing governance architectures. Scholars such as Floridi et al. (2018) advocate for ethical AI grounded in principles of transparency, accountability, and social justice. Their perspective aligns with the responsible innovation paradigm (Stilgoe et al., 2013), which emphasizes the need to embed societal values within the design processes of emerging technologies.

In the Global South, and in Morocco in particular, these debates acquire distinct significance. The regulatory landscape is often characterized by a coexistence of imported formal rules and endogenous informal practices (Jamali & Karam, 2018), which complicate both technological governance and the operationalization of CSR initiatives. Moreover, the rapid diffusion of mobile technologies and digital platforms is generating new markets, while simultaneously exacerbating social vulnerabilities such as digital exclusion, algorithmic opacity, and precarious platform labor (Fairwork, 2023).

Against this backdrop, this Chapter explicitly addresses a critical research gap: while extensive literature explores the *impact* of digital transformation on CSR, and a separate body of work examines algorithmic governance, there is a distinct lack of empirical research exploring how these two streams converge—specifically, how CSR itself is being *reconfigured* as a form of algorithmic co-governance within the unique institutional context of an emerging economy like Morocco.

To investigate this, the study adopts a hybrid theoretical framework that integrates the Multi-Stakeholder Governance Theory (Scherer & Palazzo, 2011), which views corporations as political actors, with the principles of Responsible Innovation (Stilgoe et al., 2013). This lens allows us to analyze CSR not as a simple voluntary add-on, but as a deeply embedded, contested, and technologically mediated governance process.

More specifically, the study seeks to address the following questions: How are Moroccan companies integrating digital technologies and AI into their CSR strategies? What new organizational, institutional, and ethical frameworks are emerging to support this integration? To what extent does algorithmic governance strengthen, or undermine, the legitimacy and effectiveness of CSR commitments?

To investigate these issues, the Chapter draws on a contextual analysis of the Moroccan case, complemented by sectoral case studies (including industry, agriculture, and fintech) and empirical data collected through recent surveys with corporate and public-sector actors. By bridging these theoretical frameworks with grounded insights, this study aims to develop a novel analytical model for conceptualizing CSR as a form of algorithmic co-governance.

The contribution of this Chapter is therefore twofold. Theoretically, it reconfigures CSR by anchoring it within the dynamics of algorithmic governance, moving beyond descriptive accounts of "digital CSR" to offer a critical governance perspective. It illuminates the inherent tensions between technological innovation and social responsibility, between automation and ethical imperatives, and between decision-making efficiency and stakeholder inclusion. Empirically, the Chapter provides a unique analysis of the specificities of Morocco's digital transformation, offering valuable, context-specific insights for scholars, policymakers, and practitioners.

The structure of the Chapter is organized into four thematic sections. It begins by reviewing the theoretical foundations of CSR governance in the digital era. It then analyzes the major economic transformations and emergent social challenges associated with Morocco's digital transition. The third section focuses on innovations in CSR implementation, organizational vectors, and conceptual paradigms influenced by intelligent technologies. The final section examines new models of algorithmic governance, conceptualized as distributed CSR governance within Moroccan enterprises.

1. THEORETICAL FOUNDATIONS OF CSR GOVERNANCE

Since Sheldon (1923) introduced the concept of CSR, its evolution has followed a progressive trajectory. Initially framed as the moral duty of individual entrepreneurs, CSR gradually shifted toward a stakeholder-oriented approach (Freeman & McVea, 2001), evolved into a competitive strategic integration model (Porter & Kramer, 2006), and more recently, transformed into a platform-based paradigm emphasizing co-creation and shared value (Schaltegger et al., 2016). Within this evolving framework, CSR has become increasingly embedded in strategic formulation, operational management, and corporate implementation processes through three primary modes of integration: cognitive integration (Gond et al., 2012), managerial integration (Hahn et al., 2014), and thematic integration (Carroll & Shabana, 2010). This transition marks a departure from the neoclassical paradigm focused on shareholder profit maximization toward a more holistic CSR management model emphasizing global value creation (Mubushar et al, 2021; Garriga & Melé, 2004).

However, despite its integrated structure, the enterprise-centered CSR model exhibits notable limitations. It fails to prevent social disconnection between corporations and broader society (Matten & Moon, 2020; Xu et al., 2024), leading to various forms of deviant corporate behavior, including superficial CSR engagement (Wickert & de Bakker, 2018), performative social responsibility or “greenwashing” (Delmas & Burbano, 2011), and opportunistic instrumentalization of CSR for economic rent-seeking (Marquis & Qian, 2014). These shortcomings necessitate a reevaluation of CSR through a broader governance perspective, emphasizing collaborative governance involving multiple external stakeholders (Soundararajan et al., 2019; Bowen et al., 2017).

In response to these deficiencies, scholars have progressively reframed CSR through the lens of governance (Aguilera et al., 2006; Rasche et al., 2013). This perspective seeks to ensure the longevity of responsible practices by embedding corporations within a multi-stakeholder governance framework, facilitating active collaboration among businesses, public authorities, civil society, and individual citizens (Freeman, Harrison, & Wicks, 2007; Scherer & Palazzo, 2011). Within this governance structure, stakeholders collectively implement formal and informal regulatory mechanisms to shape corporate management practices, influence internal corporate perspectives, and mitigate opportunistic behaviors (Mena & Palazzo, 2012).

Furthermore, institutional transformations, characterized by heightened attention to social and environmental responsibility, have fostered the international diffusion of increasingly stringent, legitimate, and widely accepted governance norms (Matten & Moon, 2008; Jamali, Karam, Yin, & Soundararajan, 2017). These institutional developments have gradually established themselves as the dominant global model for CSR governance, driving convergence in responsible business practices across national and sectoral boundaries (Jackson & Apostolakou, 2010).

This shift creates a fundamental tension, central to this chapter's analysis: a conflict between the traditional, voluntary, and firm-centric view of CSR and the emerging reality of an embedded, semi-automated, and non-voluntary "algorithmic governance" of responsibility, where ethical standards are increasingly encoded directly into the technologies firms deploy.

2. MAJOR ECONOMIC TRANSFORMATIONS AND EMERGING SOCIAL CHALLENGES IN THE ERA OF INTELLIGENT DIGITALIZATION

2.1. Restructuring of Traditional Industries and the Emergence of Novel Economic Models

Intelligent digitalization, a multidimensional concept combining advanced digital technologies (big data, artificial intelligence, cloud computing) with adaptive organizational capabilities, has emerged as a principal driver of economic transformation (Schwab, 2016). This shift represents a new industrial transition, succeeding three major technological revolutions: steam-powered mechanization, electricity, and automation (Brynjolfsson & McAfee, 2017; Perez, 2009).

Although countries have integrated these phases at varying paces, Morocco is currently undergoing a sustained digital transition, facilitated by public policies such as *Maroc Digital 2020* (World Bank, 2022; OECD, 2021). Recent studies indicate that Morocco exhibits distinct regional characteristics, exemplified by local smart-city initiatives such as *Casablanca Smart City*, which integrate digital technologies to enhance urban efficiency and citizen well-being.

This phase, marked by the cross-sectoral integration of digital technologies into value chains, has profoundly reshaped productive models. AI enables large-scale personalization, redefining the relationship between productivity and individual adaptation. Research highlights that this personalization relies heavily on the extensive use of user-generated big data, fundamentally altering corporate market forecasting and responsiveness (Agrawal et al., 2018; Autor et al., 2020).

Moreover, the integration of artificial intelligence and cloud computing has fostered advanced automation and process optimization, enhanced organizational flexibility while reduced operational costs (Manyika et al., 2017). Empirical studies underscore significant efficiency gains in manufacturing and logistics, where AI facilitates predictive planning and resource optimization (Bughin et al., 2018; Trajtenberg, 2018).

In Morocco, this transformation is manifesting through accelerated modernization of traditional industries. For instance, agriculture, a cornerstone of the national economy, is undergoing substantial innovation through Agri Tech solutions. These technologies enhance resource management, particularly water conservation, amid mounting environmental pressures. Precision irrigation systems, IoT soil moisture sensors, and meteorological forecasting applications optimize agricultural production and facilitate climate-adaptive farming practices. The *Digital Agriculture Morocco* program, supported by the World Bank, assists farmers in this technological transition by providing digital decision-support tools (World Bank, 2022).

The industrial sector is also advancing through large-scale digitalization efforts. The OCP Group, a leading player in phosphate production, exemplifies this transformation with its *Smart Mining* strategy. Through AI-driven automation, IoT connectivity, and robotics, OCP enhances operational efficiency, mitigates environmental risks, and optimizes resource utilization (OCP Group, 2022). This initiative aligns with the *industry 4.0* vision, fostering interconnected intelligent production systems.

Similarly, the logistics sector has undergone significant digital adaptation, particularly through predictive analytics and AI-driven optimization. Companies such as *Barid Al-Maghrib* leverage digital platforms for real-time parcel tracking, distribution network optimization, and demand forecasting. Meanwhile, *Tanger Med*, Africa's top-ranked maritime port, utilizes advanced technologies to manage logistics flows and streamline international trade (UNCTAD, 2023).

Beyond industry-specific transformations, digitalization has profoundly reshaped Moroccan market dynamics by mitigating information asymmetries among businesses, consumers, and regulatory institutions. The use of big data enables precise customer segmentation, predictive behavioral analysis, and real-time market adaptation, fostering greater transparency, reduced uncertainty, and enhanced competitiveness. In response, the *National Commission for the Protection of Personal Data Protection (CNDP)* has launched *Data-Tika*, an initiative aimed at establishing a secure and ethical data governance ecosystem (Ferrouhi & Sliman, 2023).

Recent academic studies confirm that the enhancement of digital skills among Moroccan professionals now serves as a genuine lever for productivity. Empirical research conducted on Moroccan SMEs reveals a significant correlation between the intensity of digital transformation and the increase in value added per employee, with the effect being particularly pronounced when companies invest in continuous training programs for their workforce.

At the university level, UM6P exemplifies this dynamic: a recent case study demonstrates that an AI-driven personalized learning platform has improved academic performance in STEM (Science, Technology, Engineering, and Mathematics) modules by 18%, while also strengthening students' cognitive autonomy (Baba et al., 2024). These findings align with the conclusions of Frey & Osborne (2017), who argue that human capital oriented toward “AI-complementary skills” is becoming critical for sustaining economic growth in the era of automation.

Simultaneously, Morocco’s *Technopark* ecosystem, expanded to Casablanca, Rabat, and Tangier, plays a crucial role in knowledge production and technological transfer. An analysis published in *Administrative Sciences* shows that interactions between startups, universities, and large enterprises within this technological hub promote patent generation and the dissemination of innovation management practices, partly facilitated by targeted mentorship and seed-funding initiatives. This organizational permeability contributes to the emergence of a “cognitive workforce” capable of co-creating value alongside intelligent systems.

The transition from a closed R&D model to open innovation is further illustrated by the proliferation of university-integrated FabLabs and industrial makerspaces. A recent survey of Moroccan students indicates that regular participation in these spaces significantly enhances their prototyping capabilities and increases their propensity to launch entrepreneurial ventures. In a similar vein, the B2B platform *Chari* is frequently cited in academic literature as an exemplary startup that has leveraged platform economics and fintech principles to reinvent the distribution of FMCG (Fast-Moving Consumer Goods), while successfully attracting international venture capital. These initiatives demonstrate that open innovation processes, combined with robust digital infrastructure, accelerate the emergence of novel business models.

The ripple effects extend to Morocco’s SME sector. A study published in *TEM Journal* (2025) finds that companies integrating internal digital competencies, external collaborations (incubators, clusters), and technology investments simultaneously exhibit a revenue growth rate 12% higher than their counterparts less engaged in open innovation (Bennacer et al., 2025). These findings reinforce the notion that beyond large firms, the combination of “digital human capital + collaborative ecosystems” constitutes a key driver of Morocco’s competitiveness in the age of intelligent systems.

The dynamics of the digital economy are built upon an inseparable triad: algorithms, which encode optimization rules; computational power, which has evolved into an autonomous production factor; and data, now considered a strategic asset subject to regulations such as the GDPR (General Data Protection Regulation). The research of Brynjolfsson & McElheran (2016) highlights that value creation increasingly depends on firms' ability to orchestrate these three resources within real-time decision chains driven by artificial intelligence and predictive analytics.

This technological convergence is blurring traditional sectoral boundaries. The OECD (2020) observes that agricultural, industrial, and logistics sectors are progressively hybridizing with digital services, forming complex and transversal value chains that defy legacy statistical classifications from the industrial era.

Within academic literature, the very definition of the digital economy remains a subject of debate. Bukht & Heeks (2017) categorize it into three levels: a core domain centered on ICT, an intermediate domain dominated by platforms, and an expanded domain reflecting the diffusion of digital technologies across all productive activities. While widely adopted, this taxonomy illustrates the difficulty of establishing a universally accepted measurement framework across nations.

To address this uncertainty, the OECD has proposed a functional definition based on three criteria: reliance on digital information as a key input, utilization of platforms as transactional channels, and the digital delivery of goods or services. This framework, updated in *Measuring the Digital Transformation* (OECD, 2021), serves as a foundation for harmonizing national statistical data, such as satellite accounts and digital input-output tables, with standardized indicators.

Despite progress, measurement challenges persist. Ahmad et al. (2017) argue that intangible assets such as data and algorithms remain undervalued in national accounting systems, while Bridgman et al. (2024) demonstrate, using the U.S. BEA's digital satellite account, that a reevaluation of these assets significantly enhances the digital sector's contribution to GDP.

In Morocco, quantification remains partial. A survey of 420 SMEs reveals that firms employing a dual strategy of internal training and technology investment experience an average increase in value added per employee of 9-12% (Bennacer et al., 2025). However, the *High Commission for Planning* has yet to disaggregate the digital economy as an autonomous aggregate, limiting its macroeconomic visibility.

Studies by Mahboub & Sadok (2024) indicate that over 70% of large Moroccan enterprises recognize digitalization as a strategic lever, yet they continue to face governance and internal competency challenges related to data management.

Meanwhile, Morocco's internet penetration rate has surged from 71% in 2019 to 92.2% by early 2025, representing over 35 million users, driven by rapid mobile network expansion and widespread adoption of online platforms. This trend is also reflected in subscription figures: the *National Telecommunications Regulatory Authority (ANRT)* recorded 42.13 million active mobile subscriptions by September 2024, bringing the SIM card penetration rate to 112.7%, a level indicative of multi-connectivity across voice, data, and IoT services (ANRT, 2023).

While coverage is nearly universal, broadband performance remains suboptimal. According to *Speedtest* rankings as of March 2024, Morocco ranks 67th globally for mobile internet (39.0 Mbps average download speed) and 129th for fixed broadband (26.9 Mbps), trailing the standards of advanced economies.

Smartphone proliferation has fueled an explosion in mobile connectivity: as of early 2025, Morocco counted 54.9 million active cellular connections, representing 143% of the population, facilitating widespread adoption of fintech and OTT (Over-the-Top) content services. Bennacer et al. (2025) note that SMEs investing in digital training see a 9-12% increase in per-employee value added, while Ouzif et al. (2024) confirm, through the TAM model framework, the catalytic role of technology acceptance on SME competitiveness.

The most visible transformation has occurred in financial transactions. The *Interbank Electronic Banking Center* reports 25.2 million online transactions totaling 8.7 billion MAD over the first nine months of 2023, reflecting respective annual increases of 23% and 24%. Contactless payments accounted for 53.3% of all operations in 2023, with mobile payment solutions such as Apple Pay and Google Pay driving three-digit growth rates; some segments, such as *Tap-to-Mobile*, recorded a 346% year-over-year transaction increase (Ferrouhi & Sliman, 2023).

Ultimately, the rapid spread of connectivity and digital financial tools signals a lasting shift in consumer behavior, reinforced by telecommuting, online education, and financial inclusion strategies. To fully harness the potential of this digital capital for productivity gains, Morocco must accelerate nationwide fiber broadband deployment and foster innovation in data-intensive services to maximize the growth dividends identified by both national and international research.

2.2. Emerging Social Challenges in the Era of Intelligent Digitalization

The accelerated digital transformation of modern societies, driven by technologies such as artificial intelligence (AI), big data, and digital platforms, has profoundly reconfigured social dynamics. While intelligent digitalization enhances economic vitality and service efficiency, it also raises new societal challenges across three interdependent dimensions: individual, organizational, and societal.

- **Individual level: privacy and algorithmic surveillance**

The widespread use of smartphones, e-wallets, and social networks has led to extensive data collection, including geolocation information, purchase histories, and social interactions. In Morocco, the *Commission Nationale de Contrôle de la Protection des Données à Caractère Personnel (CNDP)* has launched the *Data-Tika* and *Koun3labal* programs to promote digital sovereignty and information rights education (CNDP, 2022). Despite these initiatives, significant information asymmetries persist, many users remain unaware of the extent of automated data processing, reinforcing dependence on algorithmic recommendations as theorized in *Surveillance Capitalism* (Mendoza, 2022).

Although *Law 09-08* on data protection mandates informed consent and explicit processing purposes, its enforcement remains inconsistent within platform environments (Gaagouch, 2024). Recent studies highlight how biased data collection may reproduce, or even exacerbate, socioeconomic inequalities when predictive models are trained on unrepresentative datasets (Pasipamire & Muroyiwa, 2024). Given these risks, CNDP must strengthen algorithmic auditing, particularly in credit scoring, targeted advertising, and facial recognition, while reinforcing ex-ante transparency through *Algorithmic Impact Assessments*.

- **Organizational level: algorithmic accountability and corporate ethics**

Financial institutions, including banks, insurers, and fintech firms, increasingly rely on AI models for credit allocation and fraud detection. Studies on automated credit scoring reveal that proxy variables (e.g., postal codes, mobile billing history) may inadvertently generate discriminatory outcomes, necessitating statistical and causal fairness safeguards (Garcia et al., 2024). The complexity of accountability is further compounded by the multi-stakeholder structure of AI systems, involving developers, integrators, and cloud service providers. In cases of harm, legal attribution becomes ambiguous, fueling calls for new *strict liability* frameworks tailored to autonomous systems (Marchisio, 2021).

In response to these challenges, pioneering firms are establishing *data governance committees*, adopting frameworks such as *ISO/IEC 42001* or *NIST AI RMF*, and publishing *Responsible AI Charters*. Moroccan scholars advocate for a *holistic, ethical, and accountable* national AI strategy that integrates technical standards, human oversight, and independent impact evaluations (Lafram & Bahji, 2024). Meanwhile, CNDP is piloting an algorithmic compliance label inspired by European *privacy seals*, aiming to encourage sectoral self-regulation while mitigating both inadvertent failures (coding errors, model drift) and deliberate manipulations (profit-driven discriminatory optimization).

- **Societal level: digital inequality and social fragmentation**

Despite high overall connectivity levels, significant disparities remain between urban and rural areas, educated and less-educated populations, and between genders (World Bank, 2022). Limited fiber-optic access and insufficient digital literacy hinder the expansion of remote work and e-governance services in peripheral regions, exacerbating the exclusion from essential rights such as online education and digital healthcare.

In labor markets, AI and automation are driving skill polarization: repetitive jobs, primarily held by low-skilled workers, face increasing automation risks, while demand surges for expertise in data science and AI. The *International Labour Organization (ILO)* warns that digital platforms disproportionately redistribute value at the expense of unskilled labor, absent adequate requalification programs (ILO, 2021). Therefore, continuous professional training, digital skill certification, and portable social protection schemes are essential to prevent widespread job obsolescence.

Finally, algorithmically personalized information flows intensify cognitive fragmentation, recommendation systems reinforce user preferences, limiting exposure to diverse viewpoints and weakening public discourse (Flaxman et al., 2016). Experimental research demonstrates that even minor algorithmic adjustments can exacerbate polarization on social networks. Media literacy initiatives and expanded sorting mechanisms (e.g., chronological feeds, reliability indicators) have been tested in various countries and offer viable countermeasures for the Moroccan context.

3. INNOVATION AND THE TRANSFORMATION OF CSR IN THE ERA OF INTELLIGENT DIGITALIZATION

The increasing diffusion of digital and intelligent technologies, such as big data, artificial intelligence (AI), digital platforms, and blockchain, is fundamentally reshaping the foundations of economic growth and redefining the relationship between businesses and society. This transformation introduces new ethical and legal dilemmas, including concerns related to privacy, platform concentration, and debates surrounding machine autonomy in decision-making (Floridi et al., 2018). Within this context, CSR is evolving and innovating in close alignment with the technological capabilities of organizations.

The rise of *algorithmic rationality*, defined as AI systems' ability to continuously extract, correlate, and interpret vast datasets to inform decision-making, now complements traditional human rationality (Mittelstadt et al., 2016). In practice, this rationality manifests in automated ESG scoring, where natural language processing algorithms analyze annual reports, identify socially and environmentally material information, and generate near-instantaneous scores, reducing reporting delays by approximately 30% compared to manual methods (Calvano et al., 2019). Predictive models also facilitate dynamic environmental monitoring across supply chains, forecasting energy consumption and carbon footprints across key operational nodes and recommending adjustments before significant deviations occur (Dwivedi et al., 2021).

In Morocco, this shift is already evident. Financial institutions such as *Attijariwafa Bank* and *Bank of Africa* employ machine learning-based CSR scoring engines to condition green finance allocations. Meanwhile, emerging startups such as *DataPathology* (healthcare) and *DeepEcho* (industry) leverage computer vision to track environmental footprints comprehensively, improving transparency for stakeholders while generating reported energy savings of between 12% and 18% (Abdallah-Ou-Moussa et al., 2024).

However, delegating CSR-related decisions to AI systems raises several governance challenges. First, the opacity of complex models (*black-box algorithms*) constrains corporate leadership's ability to justify decisions, potentially undermining the legitimacy of responsible business actions. Second, data biases may lead to service exclusions, discriminatory selections, or differential pricing, as highlighted by literature examining automation risks (Malgieri, 2020). Lastly, Morocco's regulatory framework remains under development, while the *CNDP* draws inspiration from the European *GDPR*, the mandate for *meaningful human oversight* is not yet fully operational across all sectors.

To address these issues, *OCP Group*, *Maroc Telecom*, and *Inwi* have established *algorithmic ethics committees*, composed of legal experts, data scientists, and stakeholder representatives, in alignment with *AI4People* guidelines (Floridi et al., 2018). These multidisciplinary governance structures aim to ensure data traceability, model verifiability through regular audits, and accountability mechanisms enabling affected stakeholders to seek redress.

When appropriately regulated, AI-driven algorithms can serve as catalysts for CSR. Intelligent energy management systems (*smart grids* or *digital twins*) reduce industrial electricity consumption by up to 20% (Chatterji et al., 2016). Alternative credit-scoring engines leveraging digital footprints expand microcredit access for women-led small businesses in urban peripheries such as Casablanca and Fez while maintaining below-average default rates (Abbass & Benjelloun Andaloussi, 2022). Similarly, UM6P's *Green Tech Valley* program in Benguérir exemplifies the convergence of innovation and sustainability, applying AI models to phosphate waste recycling and water consumption optimization, driving Moroccan research toward a more inclusive circular economy (Abdallah-Ou-Moussa et al., 2024).

The literature supports the notion that responsible technological integration within CSR strategies enhances both social impact and financial performance, provided that companies combine *robust algorithmic governance* with explicit stakeholder engagement (Dwivedi et al., 2021; Floridi et al., 2018).

The widespread adoption of digital platforms has positioned real-time data connectivity and algorithmic analytics at the core of value creation in Morocco's economy. Companies such as *Glovo, Jumia, Chari.ma,* and *Heetch Maroc* function as *two-sided markets*, their asymmetric pricing models and cross-network effects reflect the mechanisms identified by Rochet & Tirole (2003), Evans (2003), and Hagiu & Wright (2015). Since the number of sellers determines buyer utility, and vice versa, these platforms act as systemic hubs whose algorithmic decisions (e.g., worker compensation, ranking mechanisms, visibility allocation) shape workplace safety, equity, and data protection. *Fairwork* evaluations indicate that none of the platforms operating in Morocco yet meet all five principles of *fair labor*.

Simultaneously, AI-driven enterprises (*SmartPredict, DataPathology, DeepEcho, Atlan Space*) are embedding predictive algorithms for sales forecasting, medical diagnostics, and anomaly detection within decision-making chains. This unprecedented technological influence revives concerns about opacity and developer accountability (Morley et al., 2021). In response, Morocco's *CNDP* incorporated *accountability* and *fundamental rights protection* principles into its *Data-Tika* framework in 2021, prompting major corporations, including *OCP Group, Maroc Telecom,* and *Inwi*, to establish algorithmic ethics committees inspired by *AI4People* guidelines (Floridi et al., 2018).

4. ALGORITHMIC GOVERNANCE PARADIGMS IN THE ERA OF INTELLIGENT DIGITALIZATION: A CSR GOVERNANCE PERSPECTIVE

In emerging economies, individualized CSR approaches have gradually given way to multi-actor configurations, integrating CSR into value chains, territorial clusters, or sectoral coalitions. Jamali & Karam (2018) demonstrate that such collective anchoring enhances institutional legitimacy while extending positive externalities. Midttun (2018), in comparing Nordic-model flexibility, argues that the alignment of public standards with voluntary commitments fosters *networked CSR*, enabling *co-regulation* (Midttun, 2018).

The rise of digital platforms introduces a third phase: *ecosystemic CSR*. Chen et al. (2022) describe how platform governance and design inherently embed responsibility functions, blockchain traceability, ecological nudges, and carbon offset modules, thus integrating social performance directly into algorithmic architecture. Cutolo & Kenney (2021) further highlights that these *meta-organizations* redistribute decision-making power between operators and complementors, establishing new accountability structures (Cutolo & Kenney, 2021).

In Morocco, the *Digital Morocco 2030* strategy commits $1.1 billion to economic transformation, digital inclusion, and positioning the nation as an African innovation hub. This transformation is driven by a connectivity rate exceeding 90% and strengthened through public-private partnerships focused on deploying artificial intelligence (AI), 5G networks, and cloud computing, technologies that are reshaping CSR practices (Elhazziti et al., 2023).

This trajectory fosters ecosystems where CSR is intrinsically linked to digital projects. A recent panel study on Casablanca-listed firms reveals a positive correlation between digital transformation intensity and published CSR scores, confirming the catalytic effect of technology on corporate responsibility (Assarraj & Maache, 2024).

In the automotive insurance sector, digitized claims processing and telematics simultaneously reduce carbon footprints and operational costs (Abdallah-Ou-Moussa et al., 2024). Ultimately, the societal legitimacy of platforms and AI solutions will depend not solely on technological sophistication but on the robustness of governance frameworks ensuring responsible deployment.

E-commerce platforms such as *Jumia Maroc, Avito,* and *Chari* leverage their digital interfaces to support educational and environmental initiatives while simultaneously offering green incentives to vendors. The study conducted by Awuah Peprah et al. (2024) on Jumia's strategic legitimation within an institutionally fragmented context illustrates this convergence between social acceptability and growth imperatives.

In parallel, the adoption of e-commerce among small and medium-sized enterprises (SMEs) accelerates when firms possess both digital competencies and an innovation-oriented organizational culture, a phenomenon substantiated by research from Ben Youssef & Dahmani (2023). This momentum is further reinforced by Morocco's social entrepreneurship ecosystem. Kabbaj et al. (2016) demonstrate that initiatives such as *Injaz Al Maghrib* and social innovation labs foster collaborative solution development by engaging businesses, non-governmental organizations (NGOs), and academic institutions. Public administration has also expedited the digitization of service delivery during the pandemic, revealing the potential of *data-driven CSR* in the public sector (Nachit & Belhcen, 2020).

Also, Algorithmic governance, defined as the application of algorithms and big data in regulation, coordination, and oversight processes, is redefining the ability of corporations and stakeholders to create and manage social and environmental value (Zouridis et al., 2020).

Several major Moroccan corporations have already adopted this approach. The OCP Group's I-Sense program leverages machine learning for predictive maintenance at mining sites, optimizing water and energy consumption in alignment with the conglomerate's 2040 carbon neutrality plan. Engineers retain the authority to deactivate models generating adverse externalities, illustrating the "ethical kill switch" principle advocated in responsible innovation frameworks (OCP, 2023).

Corporations are increasingly deploying algorithmic dashboards to continuously monitor their Environmental, Social, and Governance (ESG) metrics. A study on Morocco's automobile insurance sector revealed that digitalizing customer interactions reduced paper consumption by 37% while enhancing transparency in compensation processes, thereby strengthening the social dimension of CSR (El Idrissi & Bennani, 2024). Similarly, a structured analysis of CSR reports from 68 publicly listed companies in Casablanca indicated a positive correlation between analytical intelligence and CGEM-RSE scores (Saida et al., 2024).

Given the proliferation of algorithms in sensitive domains such as credit evaluation, hiring, and security, distributed governance has become imperative. Regulators, civil society actors, employees, and customers collaboratively develop audit protocols. The CGEM CSR Label, updated in 2024, introduced a "algorithmic transparency" criterion, requiring firms to publish AI registries and impact assessments. Recent research has shown that companies holding this label have reduced reputational risks linked to algorithmic bias by 12% (El Haddach, 2024). The National Commission for the Protection of Personal Data (CNDP) is supporting these developments with sector-specific guidelines on video surveillance and telehealth, positioning itself as a trusted digital intermediary.

Regulatory frameworks are also advancing at the international level. The European Union's Artificial Intelligence Act, enacted in June 2024, mandates traceability requirements for high-risk AI systems. This extraterritorial effect compels Moroccan export-driven enterprises to align their practices accordingly. In response, Morocco's Ministry of Digital Transition signed a memorandum of understanding with Nokia in April 2025 to pilot AI solutions within regulatory sandboxes before commercial deployment (El Haddach, 2024).

Overall, AI's growing influence is positioning Moroccan CSR within a polycentric governance ecosystem: responsible innovation fosters low-carbon solutions, algorithmic self-governance enhances ESG monitoring, co-governance strengthens societal legitimacy, and public regulation ensures international harmonization. By strategically integrating these dimensions, Moroccan enterprises can transform algorithmic governance into a sustainable competitive advantage while actively contributing to national development objectives.

5. PERSPECTIVES OF STUDY

A thorough examination of the evolution of CSR practices in the era of intelligent digitalization reveals a wide array of theoretical, empirical, and operational perspectives. These avenues for further inquiry emerge at the intersection of technological innovation, institutional configurations, and evolving social expectations. As algorithmic technologies increasingly permeate decision-making processes, regulatory instruments, and interaction mechanisms between firms and stakeholders, there is an urgent need to reconfigure analytical and intervention frameworks, both in advanced economies and in emerging contexts. In Morocco, which has embarked on an ambitious digital transformation agenda, the current juncture is particularly critical: the governance choices made about algorithmic systems will have long-lasting implications for social legitimacy, sustainable performance, and organizational justice.

From an academic standpoint, algorithmic governance applied to CSR remains an underexplored field, one that calls for structured inquiry through interdisciplinary approaches combining management sciences, organizational sociology, political theories of regulation, and applied ethics. A promising research trajectory involves the development of hybrid conceptual frameworks that allow for the analysis of algorithmic systems not merely as technical tools, but as socio-technical assemblages embedded with power dynamics, and normative orientations. In this regard, the work of Zuboff (2019), and Eubanks (2018) provides critical foundations for interrogating the dynamics of control, opacity, and surveillance in digital environments. Integrating these critical perspectives into the study of algorithmic CSR would move the field beyond performance-centric and positivist approaches, enabling a deeper engagement with issues of legitimacy, accountability, and stakeholder resistance.

Empirically, examining algorithmic governance practices within Moroccan firms requires the adoption of qualitative and mixed-method research designs. While quantitative surveys can identify general trends in digital adoption or CSR perceptions, they often fall short of capturing the nuanced interplay between technology, institutional norms, and managerial agency. In-depth case studies involving semi-structured interviews, participant observation, and documentary analysis are essential to uncover the actors' logics, ethical trade-offs, and emergent forms of endogenous regulation in specific organizational settings. Research might, for example, explore the role of newly established algorithmic ethics committees in Moroccan corporations, the implementation of transparency protocols in the banking sector, or the deployment of intelligent technologies in national energy transition policies.

In a comparative vein, it would be fruitful to initiate cross-contextual studies in the Global South to investigate how international standards of digital governance are interpreted, localized, or contested across diverse institutional environments. Morocco, as an emerging country with a clear digital ambition, constitutes a particularly valuable case for analyzing the frictions between global regulatory harmonization and local practice. Such an approach would enable a productive dialogue between digital governance literature and fields such as intercultural management, institutional economics, and the anthropology of technology.

From a managerial perspective, emerging imperatives call on Moroccan firms to strengthen their internal governance capacities in response to the challenges posed by decision-making automation. The focus must now extend beyond digitalizing operations or optimizing ESG metrics via algorithms; instead, it should encompass the construction of robust governance architectures capable of overseeing technological applications, ensuring ethical compliance, and involving stakeholders in strategic decision-making processes. This entails the integration of new cross-functional roles, such as digital ethics officers, algorithm auditors, or data transparency coordinators, tasked with aligning performance goals with demands for justice and accountability.

The transformation of organizational models also necessitates a comprehensive overhaul of training and capacity-building processes. It is increasingly essential to equip managers with critical literacies in algorithmic systems, including awareness of embedded biases, data governance challenges, and stakeholder negotiation in digitized environments. This transition cannot succeed without the active engagement of higher education institutions, which must embed algorithmic governance issues into management, engineering, and legal curricula. In this regard, institutions such as the Mohammed VI Polytechnic University and engineering schools in Rabat and Casablanca are well positioned to spearhead interdisciplinary training programs in intelligent CSR and digital governance.

On the policy front, medium-term prospects require the consolidation of a coherent normative framework to regulate algorithmic applications within business environments. While notable progress has been made, particularly through the initiatives of the CNDP, sector-specific guidelines, and draft legislation, there remains a lack of an integrated vision linking algorithmic governance to Morocco's national sustainable development strategy. The formulation of a legal framework for responsible artificial intelligence, grounded in principles of fairness, transparency, human oversight, and proportionality, would be a critical step forward. Such a framework could draw inspiration from the European Union's AI Act while being tailored to Morocco's institutional, socio-cultural, and economic particularities.

Additionally, the establishment of independent oversight bodies with both technical and ethical competencies would enhance accountability in the use of AI in sensitive sectors such as finance, healthcare, insurance, and human resources. These entities could serve as trusted intermediaries, supporting existing regulatory agencies by ensuring algorithmic traceability, accountability, and participatory evaluation. In parallel, CSR certification schemes, such as those administered by the General Confederation of Moroccan Enterprises (CGEM), could be enhanced by incorporating criteria related to algorithmic governance, data sensitivity management, and social impacts of deployed technologies.

More broadly, this research underscores the necessity of empowering civil society actors, NGOs, labor unions, consumer associations, and citizen collectives, with the tools and resources to monitor and advocate around issues of digital governance. The increasing opacity and technocratic nature of algorithmic decision-making risk alienating citizens from actual lack of power. Thus, it is imperative to develop educational resources, participatory platforms, and deliberate mechanisms that facilitate public understanding and engagement with digital governance. Such democratization of technology is essential to preserving the inclusive and pluralistic character of CSR in the digital age.

Finally, at the theoretical level, this research calls for a reassessment of foundational CSR paradigms in light of transformations induced by intelligent digitalization. Traditional models, which posited rational actors balancing responsibility and performance, are now being disrupted by technologies that obscure the boundaries between intentionality, automation, and accountability. There is, therefore, a pressing need to articulate a new grammar of organizational responsibility, one that accommodates algorithmic delegation, distributed accountability, and the co-production of norms by hybrid actors (human, technical, and institutional). This theoretical renewal invites scholars to rethink notions such as responsibility, immutability, and legitimacy in environments where decisions are no longer solely enacted by human subjects but emerge from interconnected, distributed networks.

In this sense, algorithmic CSR governance should not be viewed as a mere technological adjustment of existing practices. Rather, it signals a conceptual and operational turning point, one that fundamentally redefines the relationship between business, society, and technology. Future inquiry must continue to interrogate these zones of indeterminacy, develop context- sensitive analytical tools, and support the implementation of ethical, sustainable, and inclusive technological solutions. This endeavor, however, can only succeed through collective action, at the intersection of academic research, public policy, corporate governance, and civic engagement.

GENERAL CONCLUSION

This chapter has explored the profound and multidimensional reconfiguration of Corporate Social Responsibility (CSR) in Morocco, situated at the intersection of intelligent digitalization and the emergence of algorithmic governance. Our analysis has endeavored to move beyond traditional frameworks that treat CSR as a voluntary engagement. We demonstrate that CSR is, in fact, becoming an embedded, distributed, and fundamentally technologically-mediated function. The integration of artificial intelligence, big data, and digital platforms is not merely providing new tools to optimize CSR practices; it is fundamentally altering the very governance structures that define, monitor, and enforce corporate accountability.

The Moroccan context, characterized by a strong state-led ambition embodied in the "Digital Morocco 2030" strategy and a hybrid regulatory landscape (Jamali & Karam, 2018), provides a unique laboratory for observing these dynamics. We identify a central paradox: while AI offers considerable opportunities to enhance CSR efficiency, such as resource optimization in industry (OCP Group) or the expansion of financial inclusion (fintech), it simultaneously introduces critical systemic risks. These risks include algorithmic bias, decisional opacity (the "black box" phenomenon), and the creation of new forms of social fragmentation.

The primary finding of this study is that achieving and maintaining legitimacy in this new technological era demands both a conceptual and practical shift. A move is required from a firm-centric view of CSR to a more complex and negotiated model of multi-stakeholder "algorithmic co-governance." The recent creation of corporate ethics committees, the launch of the CNDP's "Data-Tika" initiative for digital trust, and the explicit integration of the "algorithmic transparency" criterion into the CGEM's CSR Label are not anecdotal developments. They represent the initial foundations of a new governance architecture where responsibility is shared among the corporation, regulators, and civil society, mediated through the interface of technology.

The implications of this transformation are profound and shared. For policy-makers and regulators, the simple protection of personal data, while necessary, is no longer sufficient. The strategic challenge is to develop agile regulation capable of anticipating and overseeing high-risk AI systems, notably by mandating robust Algorithmic Impact Assessments (AIAs) in critical sectors like finance, healthcare, and employment. However, such regulation will remain ineffective without a substantial strengthening of institutional capacity, including the technical competence to audit complex algorithms and ensure that "accountability" becomes a practical, verifiable reality, not just a legal principle.

For business leaders and managers, responsibility no longer begins at the moment of deployment, but long before, during the design phase. They must imperatively adopt "Governance by Design," integrating ethical and social imperatives from the earliest stages of technological development. In practice, this involves establishing multi-disciplinary data governance committees (comprising legal, ethical, and technical experts) and adopting emerging international standards, such as ISO/IEC 42001 on AI management systems. Furthermore, investing in the algorithmic literacy of *all* decision-makers, not just technical teams, is crucial. This is the only way to mitigate the "black box" risk and ensure that automated strategic choices remain aligned with corporate values. Managerial involvement in AI governance is therefore no longer an option, but the very condition for social acceptability and sustainable innovation.

While this study offers a critical analysis of these emerging trends, it has limitations that open essential avenues for future research. Our approach, which relies significantly on qualitative analysis and sectoral case studies, would benefit from being complemented by large-scale quantitative research. It would be particularly relevant to develop models to statistically measure the correlation, and perhaps even the causality, between the adoption of specific AI solutions and the measurable evolution of ESG (Environmental, Social, and Governance) performance and scores within Moroccan firms, both listed and unlisted.

Moreover, our analytical scope logically focused on large, structured corporations and high-growth sectors (industry, finance, technology), which are the early adopters of these technologies. A crucial future research perspective would thus be to study these same dynamics within the informal economy and the vast network of small and medium-sized enterprises (SMEs), which form the backbone of the Moroccan economy. Understanding how "algorithmic governance" is deployed within them—or, conversely, how its absence widens inequalities—is fundamental to assessing the risk of a two-speed CSR emerging, disconnected from the country's social realities.

Finally, this chapter is, by necessity, centered on the Moroccan case. A rigorous comparative analysis would be extremely valuable to the academic community. Such a study could examine how this algorithmic co-governance of CSR is evolving differently in other MENA (Middle East and North Africa) countries, such as Egypt, Tunisia, or the Gulf nations, which possess distinct digital infrastructures, regulatory traditions, and institutional contexts.

In closing, the permanent dialectic between the technological promise of efficiency and the ethical imperative of responsibility remains the central question of our time. As Moroccan companies continue their inevitable digital transition, their long-term sustainability and social legitimacy will not be defined by the intelligence of their systems alone, but by the wisdom, transparency, and inclusivity of their governance.

REFERENCES

Abdallah-Ou-Moussa, S., Wynn, M., Kharbouch, O., & Rouaine, Z. (2024). Digitalization and corporate social responsibility: A case study of the Moroccan auto-insurance sector. *Administrative Sciences, 14*(11), 282. DOI: 10.3390/admsci14110282

Agrawal, A., Gans, J., & Goldfarb, A. (2018). *Prediction machines: The simple economics of artificial intelligence*. Harvard Business Review Press.

Aguilera, R. V., Williams, C. A., Conley, J. M., & Rupp, D. E. (2006). Corporate governance and social responsibility: A comparative analysis of the UK and the US. *Corporate Governance, 15*(4), 476–495. DOI: 10.1111/j.1467-8683.2006.00495.x

Ahmad, N., Ribarsky, J., & Reinsdorf, M. (2017). *Can potential mismeasurement of the digital economy explain the post-crisis slowdown in GDP and productivity growth?* (OECD Statistics Working Paper No. 2017/09). OECD Publishing.

Assarraj, I., & Maache, M. (2024). The impact of digital transformation on CSR: An empirical study of Casablanca-listed firms. Manuscrit inédit.

Autor, D., Mindell, D., & Reynolds, E. (2020). *The work of the future: Building better jobs in an age of intelligent machines*. MIT Task Force on the Work of the Future.

Autorité Nationale de Réglementation des Télécommunications (ANRT). (2023). *Annual report 2022*.

Baba, K., El Faddouli, N.-E., & Cheimanoff, N. (2024). Mobile-optimized AI-driven personalized learning: A case study at Mohammed VI Polytechnic University. *International Journal of Interactive Mobile Technologies, 18*(4), 81–96. DOI: 10.3991/ijim.v18i04.46547

Ben Youssef, A., & Dahmani, M. (2023). Examining the drivers of e-commerce adoption by Moroccan firms: A multi-model analysis.

Bennacer, M., El Mahdi, E. M., & El Massaoudi, M. (2025). Digital transformation in Moroccan SMEs: Overcoming barriers and achieving growth. *TEM Journal, 14*(2), 1269–1278. DOI: 10.18421/TEM142-28

Bowen, K. J., Cradock-Henry, N. A., Koch, F., Patterson, J., Häyhä, T., Vogt, J., & Barbi, F. (2017). Implementing the Sustainable Development Goals: Addressing collective action, trade-offs, and accountability. *Current Opinion in Environmental Sustainability, 26–27*, 90–96. DOI: 10.1016/j.cosust.2017.05.002

Bridgman, B., Highfill, T., & Samuels, J. (2024). Introducing consumer durable digital services into the BEA Digital Economy Satellite Account. *Telecommunications Policy*, *48*(1), 102618. DOI: 10.1016/j.telpol.2023.102618

Brynjolfsson, E., & McAfee, A. (2017). *Race against the machine*. Digital Frontier Press.

Brynjolfsson, E., & McElheran, K. (2016). *Data in action: Data-driven decision making in U.S. manufacturing* (NBER Working Paper).

Bughin, J., Seong, J., Manyika, J., Chui, M., & Joshi, R. (2018). *Notes from the AI frontier: Modeling the impact of AI on the world economy* (McKinsey Global Institute Discussion Paper).

Bukht, R., & Heeks, R. (2017). *Defining, conceptualising and measuring the digital economy* (Development Informatics Working Paper No. 68). University of Manchester.

Calvano, E., Calzolari, G., Denicolò, V., & Pastorello, S. (2019). Artificial intelligence, algorithmic pricing and collusion. Manuscrit de travail.

Carroll, A. B. (1979). A three-dimensional conceptual model of corporate social performance. *Academy of Management Review*, *4*(4), 497–505. DOI: 10.2307/257850

Carroll, A. B. (1991). The pyramid of corporate social responsibility: Toward the moral management of organizational stakeholders. *Business Horizons*, *34*(4), 39–48. DOI: 10.1016/0007-6813(91)90005-G

Carroll, A. B., & Shabana, K. M. (2010). The business case for corporate social responsibility: A review of concepts, research and practice. *International Journal of Management Reviews, 12*(1), 85–105.* DOI: 10.1111/j.1468-2370.2009.00275.x

Chatterji, A. K., Levine, D. I., & Toffel, M. W. (2016). Do ratings of firms converge? Implications for managers, investors and strategy researchers. *Strategic Management Journal*, *37*(9), 1597–1614. DOI: 10.1002/smj.2407

Delmas, M. A., & Burbano, V. C. (2011). The drivers of greenwashing. *California Management Review, 54*(1), 64–87.* DOI: 10.1525/cmr.2011.54.1.64

Dwivedi, Y. K., Hughes, L., Ismagilova, E., Aarts, G., Coombs, C., Crick, T., Duan, Y., Dwivedi, R., Edwards, J., Eirug, A., Galanos, V., Ilavarasan, P. V., Janssen, M., Jones, P., Kar, A. K., Kizgin, H., Kronemann, B., Lal, B., Lucini, B., & Williams, M. D. (2021). Artificial intelligence (AI): Multidisciplinary perspectives on emerging challenges, opportunities, and agenda for research, practice, and policy. *International Journal of Information Management*, *57*, 101994. DOI: 10.1016/j.ijinfomgt.2019.08.002

Elhazziti, M. A., Ferraz, D., Elazzouzi, E., et al. (2023). *Digital transformation in Morocco: Challenges and perspectives.*

Eubanks, V. (2018). *Automating inequality: How high-tech tools profile, police, and punish the poor.* St. Martin's Press.

European Union. (2024). *Regulation (EU) 2024/1689: Artificial Intelligence Act.*

Fairwork. (2023). *Fairwork annual report 2023: The state of platform work.* https://fair.work/en/fw/publications/fairwork-annual-report-2023

Ferrouhi, E. M., & Sliman, M. (2023). Determinants of mobile payment and mobile wallet adoption in Morocco. SSRN *Electronic Journal.* /DOI: 10.2139/ssrn.4604910

Flaxman, S., Goel, S., & Rao, J. M. (2016). Filter bubbles, echo chambers, and online news consumption. *Public Opinion Quarterly, 80*(S1), 298–320. DOI: 10.1093/poq/nfw006

Floridi, L., & Cowls, J. (2018). A unified framework of five principles for AI in society. *Harvard Data Science Review, 1*(1). Advance online publication. DOI: 10.1162/99608f92.8cd550d1

Freeman, R. E., Harrison, J. S., & Wicks, A. C. (2007). *Managing for stakeholders: Survival, reputation, and success.* Yale University Press.

Freeman, R. E., & McVea, J. F. (2001). A stakeholder approach to strategic management. SSRN *Electronic Journal.* DOI: 10.2139/ssrn.263511

Frey, C., & Osborne, M. (2017). The future of employment: How susceptible are jobs to computerization? *Technological Forecasting and Social Change, 114*, 254–280. DOI: 10.1016/j.techfore.2016.08.019

Friedman, M. (1970). The social responsibility of business is to increase its profits. The New York Times Magazine.

Gaagouch, A. (2024). The protection of personal data according to the civil and criminal Moroccan laws in light of jurisprudence. *Journal of Data Protection & Privacy, 6*(3), 240–255. DOI: 10.69554/WZUI7344

Garcia, A. C. B., Garcia, M. G. P., & Rigobon, R. (2024). Algorithmic discrimination in the credit domain: What do we know about it? *AI & Society, 39*(4), 2059–2098. DOI: 10.1007/s00146-023-01676-3

Garriga, E., & Melé, D. (2004). Corporate social responsibility theories: Mapping the territory. *Journal of Business Ethics, 53*(1–2), 51–71.* DOI: 10.1023/B:BUSI.0000039399.90587.34

Gond, J.-P., Grubnic, S., Herzig, C., & Moon, J. (2012). Configuring management control systems: Theorizing the integration of strategy and sustainability. *Management Accounting Research, 23*(3), 205–223.* https://doi.org/DOI: 10.1108/09513571211225069

OCP Group. (2022). *Integrated sustainability report 2021/2022.*

OCP Group. (2023). *I-Sense®: AI-powered Maintenance 5.0 solutions for industry.*

Hahn, T., Figge, F., Pinkse, J., & Preuss, L. (2014). Cognitive frames in corporate sustainability: Managerial sensemaking with paradoxical and business-case frames. *Academy of Management Review, 39*(4), 463–487.* DOI: 10.5465/amr.2012.0341

Haut-Commissariat au Plan (HCP). (2020). *National survey on ICT use by enterprises.*

International Labour Organization. (2021). [*The role of digital labour platforms in transforming the world of work.*]. *World Employment and Social Outlook*, •••, 2021.

International Telecommunication Union. (2022). *Measuring digital development: Facts and figures 2022 – Africa.*

Jackson, G., & Apostolakou, A. (2010). CSR in Western Europe: An institutional mirror or substitute? *Journal of Business Ethics, 94*(3), 371–394.* DOI: 10.1007/s10551-009-0269-8

Jamali, D., Karam, C., Yin, J., & Soundararajan, V. (2017). CSR logics in developing countries: Translation, adaptation and stalled development. *Journal of World Business, 52*(3), 343–359.* DOI: 10.1016/j.jwb.2017.02.001

Jamali, D., & Karam, C. M. (2018). CSR in developing countries as an emerging field of study. *International Journal of Management Reviews, 20*(1), 32–61. DOI: 10.1111/ijmr.12112

Kabbaj, M., El Ouazzani, K., Elamrani, J., & Lemtaoui, M. (2016). A study of the social entrepreneurship ecosystem: The case of Morocco. *Journal of Developmental Entrepreneurship, 21*(4), 1650021. DOI: 10.1142/S1084946716500217

Kolk, A., & Pinkse, J. (2010). The integration of corporate governance in CSR disclosures. *Corporate Social Responsibility and Environmental Management, 17*(1), 15–26.* DOI: 10.1002/csr.204

Lafram, A., & Bahji, S. E. (2024). Artificial intelligence in Morocco: Towards a holistic, responsible and ethical national AI strategy for Moroccan competitiveness and strategic intelligence. In *Proceedings of the 20th European Conference on Management, Leadership & Governance* (pp. 255–263). Academic Conferences International. DOI: 10.34190/ecmlg.20.1.2909

Mahboub, H., & Sadok, H. (2024). Digital transformation of the Moroccan economy: A performance comparative approach. *Journal of Digital Economy Studies, 5*(2), 55–74.

Manyika, J., Lund, S., Chui, M., Bughin, J., Woetzel, J., Batra, P., Ko, R., & Sanghvi, S. (2017). *Jobs lost, jobs gained: What the future of work will mean for jobs, skills, and wages*. McKinsey Global Institute.

Marchisio, E. (2021). In support of "no-fault" civil-liability rules for artificial intelligence. *SN Social Sciences, 1*(2), 54. DOI: 10.1007/s43545-020-00043-z

Marquis, C., & Qian, C. (2014). CSR reporting in China: Symbol or substance? *Organization Science, 25*(1), 127–148. DOI: 10.1287/orsc.2013.0837

Matten, D., & Moon, J. (2008). "Implicit" and "explicit" CSR: A conceptual framework for a comparative understanding of corporate social responsibility. *Academy of Management Review, 33*(2), 404–424. DOI: 10.5465/amr.2008.31193458

Matten, D., & Moon, J. (2020). Reflections on the 2018 Decade Award: The meaning and dynamics of corporate social responsibility. *Academy of Management Review, 45*(1), 7–28. DOI: 10.5465/amr.2019.0348

Mena, S., & Palazzo, G. (2012). Input and output legitimacy of multi-stakeholder initiatives. *Business Ethics Quarterly, 22*(3), 527–556. DOI: 10.5840/beq201222333

Mendoza, C. (2022). Review of *The age of surveillance capitalism* by S. Zuboff. *Church. Communication and Culture, 7*(2), 452–455. DOI: 10.1080/23753234.2022.2086891

Meyer, J. W., & Rowan, B. (1977). Institutionalized organizations: Formal structure as myth and ceremony. *American Journal of Sociology, 83*(2), 340–363. DOI: 10.1086/226550

Ministry of Digital Transition. (2024). *Digital Morocco 2030*. https://www.mmsp.gov.ma/sites/default/files/202409/PlaquetteInstitutionnel_18092024_Ang.pdf

Mittelstadt, B. D., Allo, P., Taddeo, M., Wachter, S., & Floridi, L. (2016). The ethics of algorithms: Mapping the debate. *Big Data & Society, 3*(2), 2053951716679679. DOI: 10.1177/2053951716679679

Morocco, E. Y. (2022). *Digital transformation of Moroccan enterprises: Current status and outlook*. Ernst & Young Morocco.

Mubushar, M., Rasool, S., Haider, M. I., & Cerchione, R. (2021). The impact of CSR activities on stakeholders' value co-creation behaviour. *Corporate Social Responsibility and Environmental Management, 28*(6), 1906–1920. DOI: 10.1002/csr.2168

Nachit, H., & Belhcen, L. (2020). Digital transformation in times of COVID-19 pandemic: The case of Morocco. Manuscrit de travail.

National Commission for the Control of Personal Data (CNDP). (2021). *DATA-TIKA program.* https://www.cndp.ma/wp-content/uploads/2023/12/CNDP-MDJS-DATA_TIKA-Press_release-EN-20211224.pdf

Organisation for Economic Co-operation and Development (OECD). (2014). *Measuring the digital economy: A new perspective.*

Organisation for Economic Co-operation and Development (OECD). (2017). *Algorithms and collusion: Competition policy in the digital age.*

Ouzif, H., Hai, I., El Boukhari, H., & Abdellaoui, M. (2024). The impact of information and communication technologies on the competitiveness of SMEs in Morocco: An approach based on the technology acceptance model. *International Journal of Social Science and Human Research, 7*(11), 8122–8135. DOI: 10.47191/ijsshr/v7-i11-01

Pasipamire, N., & Muroyiwa, A. (2024). Navigating algorithm bias in AI: Ensuring fairness and trust in Africa. [Harvard University Press.]. *Frontiers in Research Metrics and Analytics, 9*, 9. DOI: 10.3389/frma.2024.1486600

Perez, C. (2009). Technological revolutions and techno-economic paradigms. *Cambridge Journal of Economics, 34*(1), 185–202. DOI: 10.1093/cje/bep051

Porter, M. E., & Kramer, M. R. (2006). Strategy and society: The link between competitive advantage and corporate social responsibility. *Harvard Business Review, 84*(12), 78–92.

Porter, M. E., & Kramer, M. R. (2011). Creating shared value: How to reinvent capitalism and unleash a wave of innovation and growth. *Harvard Business Review, 89*(1/2), 62–77.

Rasche, A., de Bakker, F. G. A., & Moon, J. (2013). Complete and partial organizing for corporate social responsibility. *Journal of Business Ethics, 115*(4), 651–663.* DOI: 10.1007/s10551-013-1824-x

Schaltegger, S., Hansen, E. G., & Lüdeke-Freund, F. (2016). Business models for sustainability: Origins, present research, and future avenues. *Organization & Environment, 29*(1), 3–10.* DOI: 10.1177/1086026615599806

Scherer, A. G., & Palazzo, G. (2011). The new political role of business in a globalized world: A review of a new perspective on CSR. *Journal of Management Studies, 48*(4), 899–931.* DOI: 10.1111/j.1467-6486.2010.00950.x

Schwab, K. (2016). *The fourth industrial revolution.* World Economic Forum.

Scott, W. R. (2001). *Institutions and organizations* (2nd ed.). Sage Publications.

Sheldon, O. (1923). *The philosophy of management.* Sir Isaac Pitman & Sons.

Soundararajan, V., Brown, J. A., & Wicks, A. C. (2019). Can multistakeholder initiatives foster inclusive global supply chains? Improving deliberative capacity with a stakeholder orientation. *Business Ethics Quarterly, 29*(3), 1–28. DOI: 10.1017/beq.2018.38

Stilgoe, J., Owen, R., & Macnaghten, P. (2013). Developing a framework for responsible innovation. *Research Policy, 42*(9), 1568–1580. DOI: 10.1016/j.respol.2013.05.008

Suchman, M. C. (1995). Managing legitimacy: Strategic and institutional approaches. *Academy of Management Review, 20*(3), 571–610. DOI: 10.2307/258788

Trajtenberg, M. (2018). Artificial intelligence as the next GPT: A political-economy perspective (NBER Working Paper No. 24245). National Bureau of Economic Research. DOI: 10.3386/w24245

United Nations Conference on Trade and Development (UNCTAD). (2023). *Review of maritime transport 2023.*

United Nations Educational, Scientific and Cultural Organization (UNESCO). (2021). *Recommendation on the ethics of artificial intelligence.*

United States Agency for International Development (USAID). (2021). *Digital agriculture profile.*

Wachter, S., Mittelstadt, B., & Floridi, L. (2017). Why a right to explanation of automated decision-making does not exist in the General Data Protection Regulation. *International Data Privacy Law, 7*(2), 76–99. DOI: 10.1093/idpl/ipx005

Wickert, C., & de Bakker, F. G. A. (2018). Pitching for social change: Toward a relational approach to selling and buying social issues. *Academy of Management Discoveries, 4*(1), 50–73.* DOI: 10.5465/amd.2017.0021

World Bank. (2022). *Morocco: Second financial and digital inclusion development policy financing* (Report No. P174004).

Xiao, H., & Yang, Z. (2019). 70 : [The evolution of corporate–society relations in New China over the past 70 years: Process, logic, and prospects]. *Reform, 2019*(06), 5–19.

Xu, L., Xie, L., Mei, S., Hao, J., Zhang, Y., & Song, Y. (2024). Corporate sustainability reporting and stakeholders' interests: Evidence from China. *Sustainability (Basel)*, *16*(8), 3443. DOI: 10.3390/su16083443

Zouridis, S., Van Eck, M., & Bovens, M. (2020). Automated discretion. In Evans, T., & Hupe, P. (Eds.), *Discretion and the quest for controlled freedom*. Palgrave Macmillan. DOI: 10.1007/978-3-030-19566-3_20

Zuboff, S. (2019). *The age of surveillance capitalism: The fight for a human future at the new frontier of power*. PublicAffairs.

Zuiderveen Borgesius, F. J. (2020). Strengthening legal protection against discrimination by algorithms and artificial intelligence. *International Journal of Human Rights*, *24*(10), 1–22. DOI: 10.1080/13642987.2020.1743976

Chapter 2
Analysis of Perceptions and Challenges of Telemedicine Implementation in Rural Areas and IA

Najoua Eloualhani
https://orcid.org/0009-0005-9458-2797
University Abdelmalek Esaadi Tetouan, Morocco

Ahmed Maghni
University Abdelmalek Esaadi Tetouan, Morocco

ABSTRACT

Access to healthcare in rural areas remains a challenge in Morocco; telemedicine offers a new approach to primary care; however, its integration faces challenges; our study aims to explore how these challenges are perceived by institutional stakeholders in Morocco; this is a retrospective qualitative study of a pilot project; The study showed that there is a very positive perception of the usefulness of telemedicine in terms of improving accessibility, technological development, service quality, and human resource optimization. However, its integration is conditioned by several factors, including human factors, organizational conditions, and contextual factors. AI offers several advantages and can help overcome certain challenges. The integration of telemedicine requires a multidimensional approach that takes into account the complexity of the Moroccan healthcare system and leverages the advantages of AI.

DOI: 10.4018/979-8-3373-3436-3.ch002

INTRODUCTION

Health care in rural areas of Morocco is a major concern, and equitable access to it is a sector priority and a fundamental pillar in guaranteeing social justice in a state governed by the rule of law. Indeed, territorial disparities in healthcare in Morocco represent a structural challenge, with only 79.6% of the rural population being cared for by healthcare professionals, and only 73.7% visiting a healthcare facility (MSPS, 2022).Moreover, this disparity is clearly demonstrated by the distribution of nursing care and medical consultations, which show an imbalance between urban and rural areas: the percentage of patients receiving nursing care is only 44.63% and 29.68% for medical consultations, compared with 55.36% and 70.31% respectively in urban areas (MSPS, 2022)

These figures are corroborated by the existence of accessibility problems, with the inhabitants of remote or enclave areas facing geographical and financial difficulties of access to healthcare structures, which are mainly concentrated in urban areas (Radi, 2023).In this context, telemedicine represents an innovative solution capable of transforming practices and interventions in rural areas. By facilitating access to specialized consultations, early diagnosis of certain diseases and personalized medical follow-up, this technological solution overcomes geographical barriers and offers a new model for healthcare development.

In India, the introduction of telemedicine has reduced waiting times for patients in rural areas by 40% (Goyal & Kumar, 2021) Morocco, faced with the same challenges, is seeking to adapt this approach. Nevertheless, its adoption has not been easy to design and integrate into such a complex system. It is also a question of facilitating its appropriation by healthcare professionals. Its adoption depends on a number of factors, including the recognition and commitment of institutional leaders (Broens et al., 2007).

Telemedicine, as a means of improving access to care, has demonstrated its effectiveness in several countries around the world. According to previous work, few studies have examined the perceptions of institutional actor on the use of telemedicine and the challenges encountered. Our study aims to shed light on the perceptions of institutional actor who have witnessed the experimentation of telemedicine in rural Morocco. It has two research objectives:

1- To analyze institutional managers' perceptions of the usefulness of telemedicine (TM) in primary Healthcare Establishment (PHE).
2- Explore the challenges of implementation

Our study is positioned in a rather special context, that of healthcare sector reform, including the digitalization component, which represents an essential pillar of healthcare provision. In this respect, our aim is to answer our research question: How can telemedicine improve access to healthcare in rural areas, while overcoming institutional and technological challenges? To answer our research question, we adopted a rigorous methodology based on a literature review on the adoption of telemedicine in primary healthcare Establishment (PHE) and a qualitative study conducted with officials from the Ministry of Health and Social protection.

CONCEPTUEL BACKGROUND AND TELEMEDICINE

The first definitions date back to 1998, when the WHO defined telemedicine as "a professional activity that uses digital telecommunication resources to enable physicians and other medical personnel to perform medical procedures for patients at a distance".

In 2010, the WHO defined telemedicine as the practice of medicine via information and communication technologies; It represents a major innovation in the organization of healthcare systems. It encompasses several acts such as teleconsultation remote monitoring; remote expertise, remote regulation and remote assistance; telemedicine is evolving with the development of the field of e-health, which marks an increasing digitalization of medical practices (Bashshur et al., 2016) ;

At the end of the Ottawa conference on artificial intelligence and ethics held in 2019, the consensus was that telemedicine is the combined use of care and computer or communication vectors to help bridge the gap between caregivers and patients.

The historical evolution of telemedicine can be divided into four phases: Preliminary phase when the Radio and telephony were widely used to transmit medical information, either for military reasons during wars, or to disseminate information to remote areas such as Alaska and Australia (Bashshur & Shannon, 2010); the second phase (1960-1990) when the first applications appeared; and thanks to NASA's program, doctors were able to monitor physiological parameters from space suits for the first time in human history (Bashshur, 2016), telemedicine was seen as a solution to the problems of geographical and economic accessibility in rural areas of the United States and in Nordic countries, which suffer from; the third phase (2000-2019) is marked by heterogeneous development marked by regulatory support for the practice of technological innovation, as recognized in France's *Hospital-Patient-Sante-Territoire* 2009 law; and the fourth phase (Period 2019- to present day) during which the Covid19 pandemic period was a global catalyst marked by massive use of telemedicine applications and the adoption of this practice in several countries around the world; it has become a pillar of the healthcare system; creating professionals specialized in digitalized care pathways and the use of artificial intelligence such as predictive disease monitoring algorithms (Moulin et al., 2022) ;

Today, the use of technology in healthcare is becoming increasingly important, with the development of artificial intelligence (AI) in medical practice, machine learning, natural language processing (NLP) and robotics contributing to the development of care and improving therapeutic outcomes by ensuring remote monitoring and involving travel costs (Desveaud, 2024)

Indeed, AI-based telemedicine systems analyze patient data to suggest suitable care options, optimizing healthcare system efficiency and patient satisfaction (Gorincour et al., 2021) ; they generate faster and more accurate diagnoses, reducing the need for face-to-face consultations (RADAH & ELHIA, 2025) .In radiology, for example, it improves workflow efficiency, facilitates examination interpretation and enhances the quality and safety of care (HAIDAR AHMAD et al., 2022).

ChatGPT, a sub-application of AI, is an advanced text-generating language and dialogue model; its use in healthcare improves prevention and patient education through its explanations of medical information. According to research published in JAMA (Journal of the American Medical Association), the use of ChatGPT in cardiovascular disease prevention has shown promising potential as a cardiovascular health education tool, thanks to the simplified explanations and coherent information it provides to patients (Ghanimi, 2024).

These technologies are particularly advantageous in rural areas, where they can overcome geographical constraints and the lack of medical resources (Raphael & Ngaha, 2024) by facilitating decision-making, automating certain administrative tasks and improving the delivery of care (Mignot & Schultz, 2022), and thanks to these advantages, AI contributes to reinforcing accessibility to healthcare services and consequently ensuring equity and equality of access to care for the population in landlocked areas.

LITERATURE REVIEW AND THEORETICAL FRAMWORK OF THE RESEARCH

1. LITERATURE REVIEW

Internationally, few studies have looked specifically at telemedicine practices in primary care structures, and fewer in rural areas in Morocco.

To establish a review of the literature, we based ourselves on studies published over the last five years that have dealt with the practice of telemedicine in primary care or for general consultations, among which telemedicine and teleconsultation have the potential to offer safe, efficient and cost-effective means of improving healthcare in isolated and remote areas (Carrillo De Albornoz et al., 2022a). Indeed, telemedicine offers the possibility of reacting immediately to a medical emergency, giving advice and making decisions before patients are transferred to hospital emergency departments, (Jiménez-Rodríguez et al., 2020)

Indeed, telemedicine and more specifically teleconsultation offer the possibility of contacting expert and competent professionals from remote areas (Bashshur et al., 2000), according to (Carrillo De Albornoz et al., 2022b; Nasir et al., 2024) telemedicine in primary care reduces the use of equipment and drugs, which could influence primary care costs.

With this in mind, several countries have turned to telemedicine to ensure accessibility to care; at the time of Covid19 the eSanjeevani mobile telemedicine program in remote rural areas in India was able to carry out over 276 million consultations; with a frequency of 300,000 consultations per day (Dastidar et al., 2024) ; also in Brazil, the deployment of a national network connecting rural hospitals to specialized health centers between 2023 enabled over 6312 consultations in 8 months, with an 85% patient satisfaction rate (Lamas et al., 2025).

Even the Moroccan government undertook telemedicine experiments in 2018 in certain pilot sites with the aim of demonstrating the effectiveness of the device in 6 sites in rural areas and improving local healthcare provision (M.mounchayane, 2019) ; and following practical experimentation and demonstration of the system's effectiveness, this initiative was extended by a program of connected mobile medical units with the aim of improving access to care for populations living in remote areas in Morocco

Although the benefits of telemedicine are considerable, and it reduces many health problems, its widespread use is limited by a number of challenges that can be categorized into four areas: technological, organizational, human and economic. In other studies, barriers are discussed independently of any classification (Saigí-Rubió et al., 2022)

Infrastructural and technological barriers have been identified as the most important barriers in rural areas. (Dudit & Ferlazzo, 2022) have shown that technological limitations are linked to the lack of basic tools and equipment for communication, lower Internet use and the lack of necessary standards (Schwamm et al., 2020) . In France, 30% of rural areas are not connected or have a limited connection, which penalizes access to telemedicine services (ARCEP, 2023) ;

In addition to the obstacles mentioned above, other ethical issues need to be taken into consideration when using AI-assisted telemedicine; notably in terms of confidentiality, transparency and informed consent of patients (Morley et al., 2020) ; the use of ChatGPT must be used with discernment, avoiding any misinformation or drift, which requires adverse governance (Currie, 2023)

In Morocco, telemedicine offers a solution to the problem of access to healthcare, particularly in rural areas. This makes it possible to reduce disparities in access to care and remedy the shortage of human resources (M.mounchayane, 2019) ; however, several barriers hinder the sustainability of the projects undertaken (Rouidi et al., 2023) ; the literature reviewed suggests that the majority of studies (ELOUADI et al., 2020; M.mounchayane, 2019; RADAH & ELHIA, 2025; Rouidi, Elouadi, Hamdoune, et al., 2022; Rouidi et al., 2023) have been conducted with end-users, while the perceived usefulness and challenges of institutional actor are under-explored;

Also; the debate on technology acceptance factors in healthcare still remains a fertile area for scientific research; the theoretical model of TAM technology acceptance often used in healthcare remains insufficient to explain the factors influencing telemedicine use; further research to improve this framework is still needed (Tao et al., 2020) .the proposed theoretical framework combining the TAM model and the Barrier model (Gagnon et al., 2012) adds potential factors influencing acceptance of telemedicine use in primary care in Morocco

This study aims to contribute to a better understanding of managers' perceptions of the usefulness and challenges of implementing telemedicine in rural Morocco, and is being carried out in a particular context of structural reform of the health and social protection system in Morocco; of which the digitization of the health system is a fundamental axis; its conclusions will make it possible to give operational recommendations to Moroccan institutional decision-makers.

2. THEORETICAL FRAMEWORK

In this study, we chose to use the Technology Acceptance Model (TAM) proposed by Davis in 1986, This model has been tested in several contexts to predict individual behavior towards telemedicine adoption(AlQudah et al., 2021; Arfi et al., 2021; Atarodi et al., 2019; Garavand et al., 2022).

According to a systemic review aimed at identifying telemedicine acceptance factors the TAM model is the most suitable and used model in the healthcare context (Rouidi, Elouadi, Hamdoune, et al., 2022) ; the basic technology acceptance model (TAM), positions user attitude and intention as the determinant of actual technology use; and this attitude is influenced by two variables: perceived usefulness (PU),, and ease of use (EU).This model has been extended by other theories (TAM2, TAM3 and the Unified Theory of Technology Acceptance and Use (UTAUT 1 and UTAUT 2)).

In addition to this framework, we based ourselves on the barrier model proposed by (Gagnon et al., 2012) which identifies four types of barrier: Barriers related to technology (design issues and lack of compatibility and interoperability); barriers related to individuals (work overload and resistance to change); barriers related to the human environment (disruption of the caregiver-care receiver relationship, lack of application to patient characteristics), barriers related to the organizational environment (lack of a strategic plan and administrative support); professional divide (interdisciplinary resistance, role change) (Gagnon et al., 2012).

METHODOLOGY

Our study focused on projects undertaken at national level by the Moroccan Society of Telemedicine SMT during the period 2018-2023 to ensure accessibility to healthcare services in rural areas and solve the problem of doctor shortage in landlocked areas.

The pilot telemedicine service was deployed in synchronous mode, with healthcare professionals working directly with patients during telemedicine sessions scheduled by the project management center at the Mohammed VI University of Health Sciences in Casablanca, in liaison with rural health centers. The service requires a camera, a computer, software, a stable Internet connection and an equipment suitcase.

This is a descriptive, qualitative, exploratory and retrospective study, carried out after the implementation of telemedicine in primary health care structures in Morocco. The choice of this method is justified firstly by the limited number of cases involved in the experimentation process. Secondly, because of its ability to deepen knowledge of the research object, explore different perceptions, and understand individual events and behaviors. The strength of this method lies in its ability to interpret reality, taking into account the complexity of the phenomenon under study (Mukamurera et al., 2006).

To carry out this study on perceptions of usefulness and challenges, we targeted managers who had experienced the implementation of telemedicine or had participated in meetings to evaluate the pilot experience. The principle of participant selection was based on the knowledge network, with the network effect: each participant recommending another participant at the end of the interview.

The study involved a total of 20 participants: 6 managers from the central departments of the Ministry of Health; 6 managers from regional health structures; 8 managers at local level. Interviews lasted between 20 and 30 minutes. To present the verbatims, managers are identified by their level (central, regional, local).

Data collection was based on a rigorous methodology to ensure the relevance of the information obtained. To this end, an interview guide (Appendix 1) was drawn up, based on the literature review and the theoretical framework of our study;

The grid comprises 7 questions designed to gather information on the use of telemedicine.

The interview questions were designed to meet the following objectives:

1- The 1st question concerns respondents' perception of telemedicine use;
2- The 2nd question asks about implementation methods;
3- The 3rd and 4th questions focus on user reactions and difficulties encountered;
4- The 5th question looks at the situation of the practice in Morocco;

5- The 6th and 7th questions aim to identify the success and failure factors of the experiment, and to gather practical recommendations to ensure successful implementation of the system.

This guide was validated by 5 experts by calculating the CVI content validity index (Polit and Beck 2006), which assesses the relevance of the instrument's items to the research objectives; The experts were mainly healthcare professionals who had participated in the telemedicine project and had the necessary skills to check the relevance of the questions; The results enabled us to simplify the questions and guarantee maximum validity (Appendix 2); Our guide obtained a score of 0.82, which is the recommended score for content validity.

Interviews were planned in advance and appointments were agreed; five people preferred face-to-face interviews with an agreement to record; the remaining interviewees preferred remote interviews by telephone; interviews lasted between 15 and 20 minutes; some interviewees agreed to be recorded, while others were reluctant; responses were recorded by Dictaphone and transcribed manually.

In this article, we have used the human resources results, i.e. the questions that meet the objectives of our study.

The interviews were transcribed in full. They were subjected to a manual thematic content analysis. A propositional analysis was used to generate initial codes; and to categorize perceptions and challenges, we followed a systematic process based on Miles and Huberman 2003, first segmenting and organizing the data, then reducing them by searching for similarities; this approach enabled us to structure and make sense of the data and group them into coherent categories.

However, the study of the perception and challenges of using telemedicine in primary health care structures in Morocco presented certain technical limitations; finding participants was the most apparent obstacle; the experiment brought together a limited set of actors from the Ministry of Health and Social Protection; and most of the executives who lived through the experiment were transferred from their posts.

RESULTS

1. IMPLEMENTING TELEMEDICINE IN PILOT SITES

The telemedicine project, piloted by the Department of Hospitals and Ambulatory Care and managed by the Moroccan society of Telemedicine (SMT) based at the Université Mohammed VI des Sciences de la Santé, where the simulation room and telemedicine platforms are connected to sites already identified in coordination with the Ministry of Health and Social Protection (Figure 1). A review of the documentation provided by SMT shows that the projects have been planned for 3 horizons:

Figure 1. Phases of the telemedicine implementation project in pilot sites of primary health care

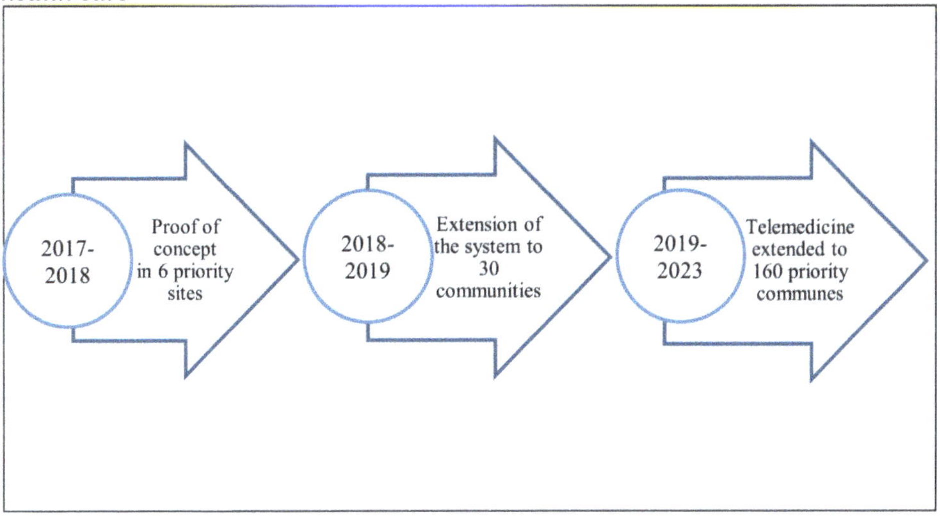

Source: Authors' Original Creation

"Well, it started in 2018; it coincided with the vision of the reform, so the 2018 period was a period of reflection." Central manager

Consensus on certain sites in coordination with the Ministry of Health; Moroccan society of Telemedicine ensured the installation of equipment and training of local teams "*We were accompanied by the project leaders from the start; and we underwent training at Casablanca level, and then we started the project at provincial level. In the beginning, there were a few equipment problems, but afterwards, the center was equipped with good equipment and it's being put to good use*". Regional manager

2. PERCEIVED BENEFITS OF TELEMDEICINE

Improving access to specialist care: Telemedicine experimentation in rural primary care structures has been underway for some time, and came to fruition in 2018 with the conclusion of an agreement between the Ministry of Health, the Moroccan telemedicine company SMT and other stakeholders to cover 160 rural localities by 2023. "*The experiment began in the EMILSHIL center, then in 2018 the experiment was extended to other sites*." regional manager

19 out of 20 managers have a positive perception of the use of telemedicine in primary care medicine in rural areas, according to a manager in the human resources department: "*For me, the integration of any form of technology can only be beneficial for any structure*." Central manager

Most of those interviewed believe that telemedicine is highly beneficial not only for the healthcare system, but also for patients: "*Telemedicine in primary care offers several advantages and opportunities. Telemedicine improves access to care for rural and isolated populations*".

On the other hand, some officials feel that the experiment has not served the population in rural areas: "*the objective has not always been achieved, since this is still true in 2024*", says a central official, and that the experiments carried out have not been sustained: "*We are in a context of change, and we need to stabilize the system first before we can take any initiatives*". Central manager

The lack of follow-up, evaluation and documentation of past experiences has a negative impact on the perception of some managers, who feel that the delay in implementing telemedicine in rural areas is due to isolated initiatives, without an integrating framework or long-term vision: "*For me, the delay is due to these somewhat isolated initiatives. The first initiative, I believe, dates back to 2011. We've set up the initiatives, there's the telemedicine association [...] But this somewhat fragmented approach is causing us to lag behind* [...]." Central manager

Furthermore, the lack of implementation conditions and the challenges encountered are themselves obstacles to the project's success: "We need to check what the conditions are, because these are the conditions that have not been met to make the experiment a success and generalize the practice.

18 of the 20 managers questioned on the usefulness of telemedicine for primary healthcare confirmed its positive contribution. The (Table 1) below shows the contribution of telemedicine in primary healthcare.

Table 1. The contribution of telemedicine in Primary Healthcare

Theme			Total	Frequency R
Access to care			38	33,34
Support for care strategy			28	24,56
Human resources optimization			22	19,29
Quality of care			11	9,65
Patient satisfaction			8	7,02

continued on following page

Table 1. Continued

Theme			Total	Frequency R
Economic benefits			6	5,26
Technological development in rural areas			1	0,88
Total			114	100%

Source: Authors' Original Creation

Accessibility to specialized care is one of the main advantages. The use of technology in patient monitoring has proved effective, particularly for patients living in remote areas. According to a manager from the Department of Regulation and Litigation, "*it also enables the provision of local specialist services for remote and isolated areas*".

According to an official from the Department of Hospitals and Ambulatory Care, the use of telemedicine in primary care has been shown to be effective by international literature: "*It is useful for primary care, as literature and experiences from other countries have shown results. In the case of Morocco, with its inadequate coverage and shortage of healthcare staff, if it ever materializes, it will certainly have an impact*".

In the same perspective, telemedicine is seen as a complement to the "fixed" coverage strategy provided by health centers and to the mobile coverage mode, which consists of field visits by mobile medical units and specialized medical caravans. According to a regional health care manager in Morocco: "*Telemedicine can be seen as a health coverage strategy. It's a mechanism or a tool that enables us to complement the health coverage strategy. Of course, it complements other strategies, whether fixed or mobile*".

Telemedicine brings specialist consultations closer to people living in remote areas, eliminating the cost and time involved in travelling to the local or provincial hospital, which is the second level of healthcare provision.

Telemedicine is a tool that can be used to: strengthen health initiatives in a given area, while guaranteeing accessibility to care; strengthen the prevention of epidemics and communicable diseases; and monitor diseases, according to a regulatory and legal department manager: "*Support for health programs [...]. Telemedicine is an alternative for conferring the right to healthcare without discrimination and with the same level of quality between urban and rural areas*".

Optimizing human and medical resources: Telemedicine is a promising solution to the problem of the shortage of human resources, particularly specialist doctors; telemedicine enables specialist doctors to extend their field of action by providing specialist consultations, diagnosis or care to a remote population via telemedicine platforms, according to a manager from the Draa Tafilalt region: "*For us, Telemed-*

icine is an alternative to solve the problem of the shortage of human resources and serve the population in landlocked areas."

Telemedicine plays a very important role in improving training, particularly for nurses working in primary care centers. A telemedicine session with a professor from a university hospital or a specialist doctor from a hospital can be a training opportunity, according to a manager in the Department of Hospitals and Ambulatory Care: "*Indeed, when I do telemedicine with a specialist, I learn at the same time. So the nurse who does telemedicine with the doctor also learns a lot*".

The use of telemedicine can also help improve working conditions for healthcare professionals, enabling them to organize their time more efficiently by coordinating with specialist doctors in consultation centers, and eliminating travel costs. According to one regional manager: "[...] *Doctors can manage their time more efficiently, reducing travel and optimizing consultations. For patients, telemedicine reduces travel costs*".

Telemedicine improves the quality of care by ensuring continuous monitoring of patients suffering from illnesses, as well as improving access to specialist consultations (quickly and without waiting for an appointment). Added to these benefits are better emergency management and reduced risk of exposure to infections. According to one key manager, "*several studies have demonstrated the added value and positive impact that adopting technology can have on the quality of healthcare services*".

Reducing geographical health inequalities: The introduction of telemedicine in rural areas requires the development of technological infrastructures, in particular the extension of Internet coverage and digital connectivity, as well as the familiarization of the rural population with digital tools. According to one regional manager, "[...] *Of course, telemedicine offers the opportunity to train and sensitize healthcare professionals and patients to new technologies. In addition, the deployment of telemedicine can encourage the development of technological infrastructures in rural areas*".

3. CHALLENGES OF IMPLEMENTIG TELEMEDICINE IN PHE

Based on the experience of telemedicine in the pilot sites, several challenges have hindered the use of telemedicine in PHE; according to the analysis carried out, these challenges can be classified into 8 categories. The analysis of theme occurrences has enabled us to determine the weight of the challenges, as shown in the Figure 2 below:

Figure 2. The challenges of implementing TM-PHE

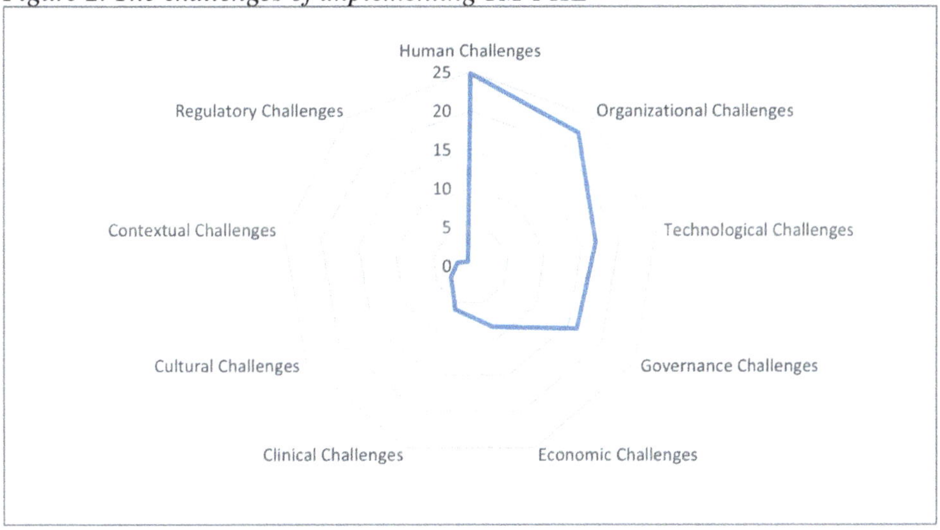

Source: Authors' Original Creation

This figure shows the frequency of themes relating to challenges raised by managers when experimenting with the practice of telemedicine in primary care structures. Following our theoretical framework, these challenges can be structured around four dimensions: human factors, organizational factors, technological factors and contextual factors.

The following presentation highlights the preponderance of each emerging sub-dimension

Human challenges (Figure 3): represent the greatest challenge, with a relative frequency of 24.69%. Respondents believe that telemedicine can help overcome the problem of lack of resources. However, other human resources-related issues emerge, such as the availability of human resources, the acceptability of specialist physicians, the stability of human resources, the skills of professionals, the training of healthcare professionals, resistance to change and the lack of incentives.

Figure 3. The human challenges of implementing telemedicine in PHE

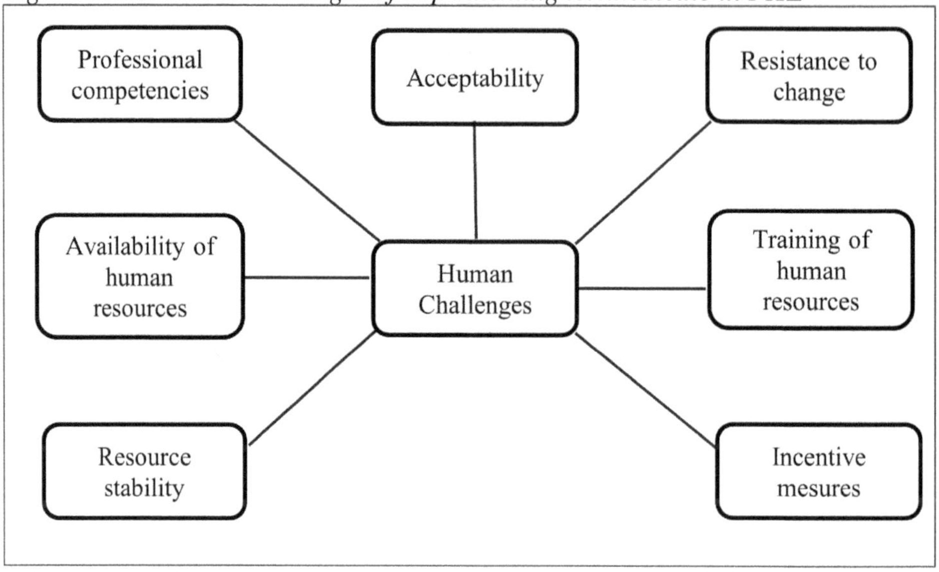

Source: Authors' Original Creation

According to an official from the Ministry of Health and protection. According to manager in the regulatory and litigation department, "*.....we introduced telemedicine to solve the human resources problem, but this brought to light other problems linked to human resources, linked to incentives, linked to improvement, linked to departure, linked to training, linked to awareness,*".

The problem of acceptability too: "*The failures are mainly due to the involvement of specialists. They get involved in the first few days, the second few days, the first few weeks and the second few weeks. Then they relax. Maybe it's because they can't find themselves, maybe it's a workload for them, maybe it's because they don't get paid, maybe it's because of the technology or the connection*". central manager

Similarly, it should be stressed that primary healthcare structures in rural areas suffer from an instability of healthcare professionals. It's a transition zone: "*at first, nobody wanted to do the training and get involved in this work; then each province committed to providing a nurse and a doctor, and they were trained by the SMT*". regional manager.

In addition to the challenges mentioned, there is the problem of competence: "*healthcare professionals and patients may lack the training and technical skills to use teleconsultation platforms effectively*", regional manager

Resistance to change: "*at the time of the experiment, there was a reluctance to change and the difficulty of using teleconsultation*".

And the lack of incentives such as fee-for-service "[...] *the problem with the success of the experiment beyond what has been done, I think it's the staff incentives* [...]".

Organizational challenges (Figure 4): that arose during the telemedicine experiment with a frequency of 22.28%, such as the choice of implementation sites that had to meet certain objective criteria guaranteeing the success of the telemedicine experiment.

Figure 4. Organizational challenges related to the implementation of TM in PHE

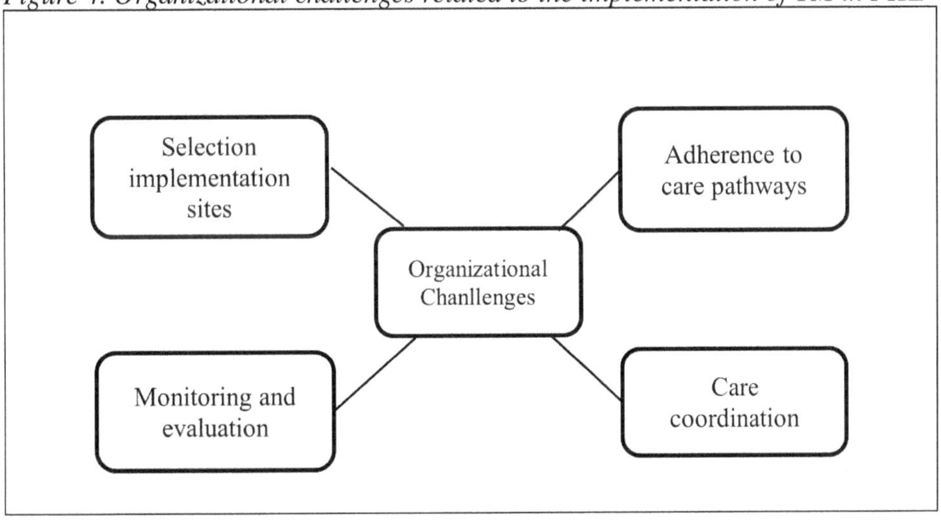

Source: Authors' Original Creation

One of the points raised was the need to respect the patient's care pathway, especially as the direct link between the health center and the third level of care created a kind of "overshoot" of the all-important secondary level. It would have been wiser to establish a link with the second level rather than the third, which brings us back to the question of coordination, which emerged as a major problem, particularly with regard to planning work with third-level specialists. According to one regional manager: "*There are also difficulties in terms of coordination, making appointments, ensuring that the patient is present at the same time as the specialist on the day and at the time scheduled for telemedicine, either because the patient is absent, or because of the availability of doctor, and also the problem of skills*".

Also monitoring and evaluation the pilot experiment because most of those interviewed felt that the experiment had not been properly monitored and evaluated, which meant that the necessary lessons could not be learned. "*The third element of failure is the evaluation of the pilot experiment. The evaluation of the pilot experiment had to be done: is it effective or not*?" said the central manager.

Governance problems were reflected in the lack of leadership to define a clear telemedicine strategy. "*We don't have a departmental strategy that capitalizes on all the technical activities, but there are private activities [...], public [...], but a national overview, no*. "central manager

There is also disagreement on priorities between project stakeholders, which highlighted a governance problem with a frequency of 16.26%. According to one central stakeholder: "*We don't have a departmental strategy that capitalizes around all the technical activities, but there are private [...], public [...] activities, but a national overview, no.*"

The absence of a clear regulatory framework for the practice of telemedicine is also a challenge. Most respondents called for a clearer framework that delineates responsibilities, integrates telemedicine acts and their recognition in the nomenclature of acts "*The absence of a clear and appropriate legal framework for teleconsultation can create uncertainty and obstacles to its deployment*" Regional manager

Technological challenges (Figure 5): its represent a major challenge encountered when implementing telemedicine in PHE, with a relative frequency of 16.86%. The availability of a technological infrastructure is seen as an essential and crucial element in the challenges raised.

Figure 5. Technological challenges related to the implementation of TM in PHE

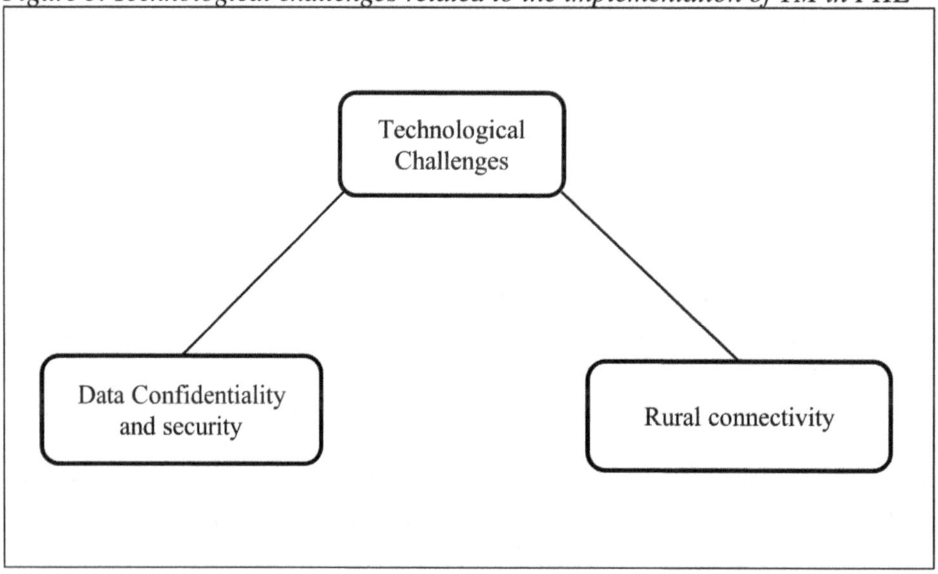

Source: Authors' Original Creation

Most respondents focused on the connectivity of the rural world with good quality, high-speed Internet networks, the equipment used and the technological environment in which the consultation takes place. The institutional managers interviewed felt that quality was deplorable, with many interruptions and disconnections during virtual consultations. Technical problems were also reported, leading to loss of concentration, demotivation and frustration among healthcare professionals. "*.... One of the challenges is to install the Internet and connect rural populations to it. That's a challenge we have to face too.*" Regional Director

And although consultations were carried out in synchronous mode, most managers felt that confidentiality and data security were among the major concerns during these telemedicine sessions, with a view to respecting privacy and the confidentiality of medical data in line with medical ethics "*As I said before, there are ethical, legal and regulatory constraints, because when we don't have our patients, we are in direct contact with the caregiver. Of course, respect for privacy, respect for professional secrecy; when this service is provided at a distance, there are risks. And of course, we have to reduce these risks by taking a series of measures in terms of information security*", regional manager.

Contextual challenges (Environment): Other challenges raised by managers include economic challenges, with a frequency of 8.43%; lack of funding can hinder the implementation and sustainability of the practice. "*The first thing to do was to decide how to fund the project: should we do it through a partnership or existing partnership funds? This was difficult, if not impossible, because partnerships, given the current law, public-private partnerships, don't allow this type of funding. And the Ministry had no funding forecasts*" central manager

Similarly, there was a lack of financial sustainability for the project "*The project budget was a challenge; in fact, the budget that was presented was huge. Because the practice of medicine, in relation to patients, in relation to the number of visits, in relation to costs, was unjustified and excessive in relation to normal practice. So automatically, the feasibility of the projects, of the generalization of telemedicine, was a question*". central manager

Clinical challenges accounted for a significant proportion of the challenges raised, with a frequency of 6.02%. Some managers feel that the relationship between caregiver and patient is a major issue in this remote consultation: the therapeutic bond is based on trust and empathy, while the non-materialization of the relationship can influence medical questioning. According to one regional manager, "*But the particularity of telemedicine is that there is no direct contact between the caregiver and the patient, and this particularity means that telemedicine is also a little special in technical, scientific and cultural terms*".

Similarly, the nature of the pathology to be treated is important, as some pathologies require explorations to deliver the treatment, leading to the postponement of consultation appointments, and sometimes the non-return of patients; Cultural issues, notably the acceptability of the population, depend closely on a number of factors, not the least of which is the embodied culture. Medicine is essentially based on direct exchanges, and distance can create a climate of mistrust and a lack of mutual understanding between the healthcare professionals and the patient, not to mention the population's perception of technology, whether good or bad. Added to this are language barriers, cultural and religious habits and beliefs: "*There may be a cultural reluctance to adopt remote consultations, with some patients preferring face-to-face interactions. Patients may have doubts about the effectiveness and quality of remote care compared to face-to-face consultations*", regional manager.

Finally, the health context in which the experimentation took place, with a frequency of 1.80%, minimal but not negligible. The experimentation was interrupted in the particular circumstances of the Covid-19 pandemic, which called into question the whole practice and caused a temporary halt to the projects undertaken. "*experimentation was interrupted between 2020 and 2021 due to the Covid-19 health crisis, which upset priorities. but thanks to these practices, we were able to identify the obstacles to be overcome*". local manager

DISCUSSION

The positive perception of institutional managers testifies to a growing openness to technology in healthcare and a recognition of the positive impact it can have, particularly in underserved areas; of the 20 managers interviewed, 19 affirmed the usefulness of the practice in terms of improving accessibility to care, optimizing human resources management, saving money for patients and improving the quality of services (Bashshur et al., 2000).

This positive perception testifies to the openness of Moroccan managers to new care practices and a willingness to follow the global consensus demonstrated by scientific work carried out notably during the Covid-19 pandemic (Smith et al., 2022) ;According to another study carried out in the province of Tétouan, general practitioners recognize the potential offered by telemedicine to improve local care and the quality of care offered to citizens, despite the lack of training and information in this area (H.ELBOUNI & H CHRIFI, 2021).

Telemedicine worldwide has helped reduce territorial inequalities in healthcare provision (Jardé et al., 2019) . However, international experience has shown difficulties in adoption and implementation. According to a systematic review of 98 studies dedicated to the effectiveness of telemedicine, (da Silva Mattos et al., 2015) certain challenges related to technological infrastructure, the cost of technology, the availability of qualified professionals and confidentiality call into question certain telemedicine practices and hinder its adoption in several OECD countries.

The results of our research are in line with previous studies (Broens et al., 2007; Durupt et al., 2016a; Jardé et al., 2019; Simon & Gayrard, 2017; Van Tilburg et al., 2024) subject to certain specificities linked to the Moroccan context.

Practice tests in rural Moroccan PHE have shown that human challenges constitute a major challenge, with the highest frequency of 30.17%. These challenges are mainly explained by lack of training and technical skills, resistance to change and work overload. These findings corroborate those of work on the use of technology in rural healthcare, which has shown that the skills and strong commitment of end-users condition technology adoption (Durupt et al., 2016a; Mbemba et al., 2017).

According to a study of Moroccan doctors on acceptability factors for healthcare professionals, compatibility between the task and the technology, the usefulness of the device, the influence of superiors and the availability of technical support are key acceptability factors, which is in line with the findings of work carried out by (Filali et al., 2023).

Technological challenges rank with a frequency of 19.82%, and are essentially reflected in the problem of digital infrastructure, which conditions the quality of the connection and consequently the quality of the diagnosis made by healthcare professionals, and the high cost of equipment and technological facilities, which can act as a brake on the widespread use of telemedicine. These findings concur with those of Bashshur et al. 2022, who emphasize the need to address digital disparities in access.

Organizational challenges (18.96%) concern deficient organizational processes, insufficient coordination between different levels of care, the absence of remote care protocols and the integration of the practice into the daily acts of healthcare professionals, which is in line with the results of previous studies (Broens et al., 2007; Gagnon et al., 2012; Rashid L. Bashshur, Gary W. Shannon, 2010).

Governance challenges (9.42%) demonstrate the importance of coordination between the various people responsible for the healthcare system. The involvement of all stakeholders - healthcare professionals, patients and local authorities - is key to the success of telemedicine projects.

Lack of commitment can be due to a lack of communication around the practice or ignorance of the benefits on offer, but also to fear of a profound change in working methods (Tchakomi, 2017) Integrating telemedicine requires a reorganization of processes. The lack of clear guidelines and national leadership, relayed to regional and local levels, are obstacles to implementation and sustainability.

Clinical challenges (8.62%) concern the quality of diagnoses established remotely, mainly for pathologies requiring physical assessment, which has also been confirmed by doctors who wish to preserve their role as primary actor (Durupt et al., 2016b).

Economic challenges (7.75%) reflect concerns about the costs of technology, equipment (acquisition and maintenance costs) (Jardé et al., 2019) Developing a funding model for the practice and its sustainability is a challenge and calls for consideration of how the procedure could be reimbursed by insurance or public-private partnership funds. (Durupt et al., 2016a)

Cultural challenges (4.31%): this minimal representation demonstrates the great openness of Moroccan managers to new technologies. Language and cultural barriers will need to be addressed to successfully integrate telemedicine into healthcare professionals practice. (Van Tilburg et al., 2024) (Alodhialah et al., 2024)

Regulatory challenges do not represent a major issue for institutional managers, as the Moroccan legislator has already put in place a legal framework conducive to the development of the practice. Notably through the promulgation of decree number 2-18-378 of 11 kaada 1439 (July 25, 2018) relating to the procedures for obtaining authorization to practice and the procedures for organizing practice; and decree no. 2-20-675 of 8 joumada II 1422 (January 22, 2021) amending and supplementing decree number 2-18-378 by easing the conditions for healthcare professionals to practice telemedicine with a view to promoting its practice. The concerns of healthcare professionals focus more on the security and confidentiality of medical information (ELOUADI et al., 2020). by creating a strict legislative framework guaranteeing the confidentiality of medical information; the security and quality of care; such as the case of the United States, which has the HIPAA law, and the GDPR standards in France, which impose encryption and confidentiality requirements for medical communications (Keesara et al., 2020) .

To overcome all these challenges, the Ministry of Health must prioritize the strengthening of digital infrastructures in the rural world in order to optimize the use of ICT, by healthcare professionals (Radi, 2023) . This requires the establishment of a regulatory framework to protect medical data, with the effective participation of stakeholders to ensure the success of the project.

From the same perspective, the integration of artificial intelligence (AI) into remote healthcare practice makes sense, as this technology offers particular advantages in terms of accuracy and acceleration of the diagnosis and management process. Indeed, in the context of diagnosis, algorithms powered by artificial intelligence (AI) improve the quality of medical images (Shaheen, 2021), automate measurements and facilitate the identification of various pathologies including cardiovascular disease and cancer ((Yousefi & Gagnon, 2024)).

These algorithms go beyond individual performance and facilitate the interpretation of medical images, reducing interpretation errors, improving the consistency of analyses and enabling early detection and intervention. In addition, AI accelerates patient prioritization and the development of personalized treatment protocols (Gosselin et al., 2021), contributing to improved clinical outcomes and more efficient workflow management.

Through real-time remote analysis and continuous patient monitoring, AI also improves accessibility to care (Bergeron & Carroué, 2025), particularly in rural and remote areas where access to healthcare professionals is limited.

Beyond diagnosis, AI's ability to analyze large amounts of complex medical data improves clinical decision-making, optimizes hospital operations and accelerates medical discoveries (Manaouil et al., 2024) The integration of AI has fostered the development of predictive analytics, early disease detection and workflow optimization, contributing significantly to the quality of healthcare delivery (Osei-Tutu, 2024).

In Morocco, AI in the healthcare sector offers many benefits in terms of accurate diagnosis and medical treatment, optimizing resources and facilitating access to care for populations in rural and remote areas. However, it is still at a relatively early stage, and efforts will need to be made by health authorities to encourage its development; and obviously this can only be achieved through the development of technological infrastructure in rural areas; the training of health professionals who are able to align with the new digitalization strategies of the health sector; but also to have patients who are able to use these new technologies and accept the new form of care system.

CONCLUSION

The development of telemedicine in rural areas represents a major step forward in improving access to healthcare. However, integrating telemedicine into healthcare systems requires more than just technological implementation.

Our study has shown that the success of a project depends on a multidisciplinary approach, taking into account human, organizational, contextual and clinical dimensions. The complexity of the Moroccan healthcare system calls for careful thought right from the design phase, in order to anticipate challenges and ensure the sustainability of telemedicine adoption initiatives.

Our findings underline the importance of a participatory approach involving all stakeholders: healthcare professionals, decision-makers, digital health engineers, and above all the patients themselves. Indeed, while technological infrastructure is a sine qua non, it will not suffice without in-depth work on change management, initial and continuing training for healthcare professionals, raising patient awareness and integrating telemedicine into a coherent, inclusive public health policy.

Empirical experimentation reveals that the implementation of telemedicine in rural areas comes up against numerous obstacles: cultural barriers, lack of digital skills on the part of certain professionals, limited acceptability by patients, and so on. In addition, regulatory constraints and funding issues can slow the adoption of telemedicine.

Faced with these challenges, we need to develop appropriate strategies, based on ongoing evaluation of existing systems and practical feedback, in order to adjust our actions in line with local realities.

In view of the results obtained, several avenues of research deserve to be explored in greater depth to promote better integration of telemedicine in rural areas:

Assessing the impact of participatory models: It would be relevant to analyze how the involvement of stakeholders right from the design stage of telemedicine projects influences their success and sustainability.

Studying the determinants of telemedicine acceptability: understanding the factors influencing acceptance by professionals and patients would enable implementation strategies to be adapted to improve telemedicine uptake.

Analyzing the effects of telemedicine on quality of care and the reduction of health inequalities: A longitudinal approach could enable us to measure the real impact of these systems on patient care in rural areas.

Integrating telemedicine into public health policies: This involves studying how regulatory frameworks and national health strategies can better support the growth of telemedicine by guaranteeing its funding and accessibility.

Leveraging artificial intelligence Artificial intelligence in telemedicine brings many benefits in terms of personalizing treatments, optimizing the patient pathway and improving clinical outcomes.

In conclusion, telemedicine is a powerful lever for improving access to health-care in rural areas, but its deployment requires a global and systemic approach. The provision of technological tools is not enough; it must be part of a process of transforming practices, reinforcing skills and putting in place a legislative and regulatory framework to protect the confidentiality of medical information and the ethics of care. The future of telemedicine will therefore depend on the ability of decision-makers and healthcare professionals to integrate these dimensions, and to accompany this change in a progressive and inclusive way.

REFERENCES

Alodhialah, A. M., Almutairi, A. A., & Almutairi, M. (2024). Telehealth Adoption Among Saudi Older Adults : A Qualitative Analysis of Utilization and Barriers. *Health Care*, *12*(23), 2470. DOI: 10.3390/healthcare12232470 PMID: 39685092

AlQudah, A. A., Al-Emran, M., & Shaalan, K. (2021). Technology Acceptance in Healthcare : A Systematic Review. *Applied Sciences (Basel, Switzerland)*, *11*(22), 10537. DOI: 10.3390/app112210537

ARCEP. (2023).

Arfi, W. B., Nasr, I. B., Kondrateva, G., & Hikkerova, L. (2021). The role of trust in intention to use the IoT in eHealth : Application of the modified UTAUT in a consumer context. *Technological Forecasting and Social Change*, *167*, 120688. DOI: 10.1016/j.techfore.2021.120688

Atarodi, S., Berardi, A. M., & Toniolo, A.-M. (2019). Le modèle d'acceptation des technologies depuis 1986 : 30 ans de développement. *Psychologie du Travail et des Organisations*, *25*(3), 191–207. DOI: 10.1016/j.pto.2018.08.001

Bashshur, R. L., Howell, J. D., Krupinski, E. A., Harms, K. M., Bashshur, N., & Doarn, C. R. (2016). The Empirical Foundations of Telemedicine Interventions in Primary Care. *Telemedicine Journal and e-Health*, *22*(5), 342–375. DOI: 10.1089/tmj.2016.0045 PMID: 27128779

Bashshur, R. L., Reardon, T. G., & Shannon, G. W. (2000). Telemedicine : A New Health Care Delivery System. *Annual Review of Public Health*, *21*(1), 613–637. DOI: 10.1146/annurev.publhealth.21.1.613 PMID: 10884967

Bashshur, R. L., & Shannon, G. W. (2010). History of Telemedicine : Evolution, Context, and Transformation. *Healthcare Informatics Research*, *16*(1), 65. DOI: 10.4258/hir.2010.16.1.65

Bergeron, H., & Carroué, L. (2025). *Enjeux de l'intelligence artificielle en santé.* Portail HAL Sciences Po.

Broens, T. H. F., Huis in't Veld, R. M. H. A., Vollenbroek-Hutten, M. M. R., Hermens, H. J., van Halteren, A. T., & Nieuwenhuis, L. J. M. (2007). Determinants of successful telemedicine implementations : A literature study. *Journal ofTelemedicine and Telecare*, *13*(6), 303–309. DOI: 10.1258/135763307781644951 PMID: 17785027

Carrillo De Albornoz, S., Sia, K.-L., & Harris, A. (2022a). The effectiveness of teleconsultations in primary care : Systematic review. *Family Practice, 39*(1), 168–182. DOI: 10.1093/fampra/cmab077 PMID: 34278421

Carrillo De Albornoz, S., Sia, K.-L., & Harris, A. (2022b). The effectiveness of teleconsultations in primary care : Systematic review. *Family Practice, 39*(1), 168–182. DOI: 10.1093/fampra/cmab077 PMID: 34278421

Currie, G. M. (2023). Academic integrity and artificial intelligence : Is ChatGPT hype, hero or heresy? *Seminars in Nuclear Medicine, 53*(5), 719–730. DOI: 10.1053/j.semnuclmed.2023.04.008 PMID: 37225599

da Silva Mattos, S., Hazin, S. M. V., Regis, C. T., de Araújo, J. S. S., de Lira Albuquerque, F. C., Moser, L. R. D. N., de Paula Hatem, T., de Freitas, C. P. G., Mourato, F. A., Tavares, T. R., Gomes, R. G. S., Severi, R., Santos, C. R., da Silva, J. F., Rezende, J. L., Vieira, P. C., & de Lima Filho, J. L. (2015). A telemedicine network for remote paediatric cardiology services in north-east Brazil. Bulletin of the World Health Organization, 93(12), 881-887. Scopus. DOI: 10.2471/BLT.14.148874

Dastidar, B. G., Jani, A. R., Suri, S., & Nagaraja, V. H. (2024). Reimagining India's National Telemedicine Service to improve access to care. *The Lancet Regional Health. Southeast Asia, 30*, 100480. DOI: 10.1016/j.lansea.2024.100480 PMID: 39323563

Desveaud, K. (2024). L'intelligence artificielle décryptée. Comprendre les enjeux et risques éthiques de l'IA pour mieux l'appréhender. EMS Éditions; Cairn.info. https://shs.cairn.info/intelligence-artificielle-decryptee--9782376879602?lang=fr

Dudit, L., & Ferlazzo, E. (2022). Télémédecine et urgences : Pertinence de la réponse d'un centre de réception et de régulation des appels. Paul Georges Reuter. Action publique. Recherche et pratiques, N° 15(3), 52-52. Cairn.info. DOI: 10.3917/aprp.015.0052

Durupt, M., Bouchy, O., Christophe, S., Kivits, J., & Boivin, J.-M. (2016a). La télémédecine en zones rurales : Représentations et expériences de médecins généralistes. *Santé Publique (Vandoeuvre-Les-Nancy, France), 28*(4), 487–497. DOI: 10.3917/spub.164.0487 PMID: 28155753

Durupt, M., Bouchy, O., Christophe, S., Kivits, J., & Boivin, J.-M. (2016b). Telemedicine in rural areas : General practitioners' representations and experiences. Sante Publique, 28(4), 487-497. *Scopus.* Advance online publication. DOI: 10.3917/spub.164.0487

ELOUADI, A. elmajid, HAMDOUNE, A., & ROUIDI, M. (2020). L'acceptation de la télémédecine chez les médecins marocains : Étude qualitative en utilisant le modèle UTAUT.

Filali, S., Markaoui, K., & Ouchni, A. (2023). Transformation digitale des organisations de soins : Facteurs d'adoptions et scenario d'intégration: Revue Congolaise de Gestion. *Numéro, 36*(2), 65–91. DOI: 10.3917/rcg.036.0065

Gagnon, M.-P., Desmartis, M., Labrecque, M., Car, J., Pagliari, C., Pluye, P., Frémont, P., Gagnon, J., Tremblay, N., & Légaré, F. (2012). Systematic Review of Factors Influencing the Adoption of Information and Communication Technologies by Healthcare Professionals. *Journal of Medical Systems, 36*(1), 241–277. DOI: 10.1007/s10916-010-9473-4 PMID: 20703721

Garavand, A., Aslani, N., Nadri, H., Abedini, S., & Dehghan, S. (2022). Acceptance of telemedicine technology among physicians : A systematic review. *Informatics in Medicine Unlocked, 30*, 100943. DOI: 10.1016/j.imu.2022.100943

Ghanimi, R. (2024). *ChatGPT dans les soins de santé : OPPORTUNITÉS ET RESPONSABILITÉS*. Chronique.

Gorincour, G., Monneuse, O., Ben Cheikh, A., Avondo, J., Chaillot, P.-F., Journe, C., Youssof, É., Lecomte, J.-C., & Thomson, V. (2021). La gestion des urgences abdominales de l'adulte à l'aide de la télémédecine et de l'intelligence artificielle. *Journal de Chirurgie Viscerale, 158*(3), S28–S33. DOI: 10.1016/j.jchirv.2021.01.006

Gosselin, L., Thibault, M., Lebel, D., & Bussières, J.-F. (2021). Utilisation de l'intelligence artificielle en pharmacie : Une revue narrative. *The Canadian Journal of Hospital Pharmacy, 74*(2). Advance online publication. DOI: 10.4212/cjhp.v74i2.3100 PMID: 33896953

Goyal, J. P., & Kumar, P. (2021). Telemedicine During the COVID-19 Pandemic : Moving from Physical to Virtual Outpatient Care. *Indian Journal of Pediatrics, 88*(10), 959–960. DOI: 10.1007/s12098-021-03924-0 PMID: 34449026

HAIDAR AHMAD. H., HAMID SALIH, M. A., LUANGRATH, A., SEDE, T., & ZUGAJ, L. (2022). Evaluation des Applications d'intelligence artificielle au service de l'imagerie médicale [PDF,PowerPoint]. Universite de Technologie de Compiegne. DOI: 10.34746/KBKC-CD39

H.ELBOUNI, & H CHRIFI. (2021). Perception et attente des medecins generaliste de tetouan.

Jardé, O., Delescluse, S., Yzet, T., Binda, T., Gignon, M., & Manaouil, C. (2019). Le déploiement de la télémédecine pour répondre aux enjeux du XXIe siècle : Exemples d'expérimentation en Picardie. *Bulletin de l'Académie Nationale de Médecine, 203*(3-4), 209–214. DOI: 10.1016/j.banm.2018.06.001

Jiménez-Rodríguez, D., Santillán García, A., Montoro Robles, J., Rodríguez Salvador, M. D. M., Muñoz Ronda, F. J., & Arrogante, O. (2020). Increase in Video Consultations During the COVID-19 Pandemic : Healthcare Professionals' Perceptions about Their Implementation and Adequate Management. *International Journal of Environmental Research and Public Health, 17*(14), 5112. DOI: 10.3390/ijerph17145112 PMID: 32679848

Keesara, S., Jonas, A., & Schulman, K. (2020). Covid-19 and Health Care's Digital Revolution. *The New England Journal of Medicine, 382*(23). Advance online publication. DOI: 10.1056/NEJMp2005835 PMID: 32240581

Lamas, C. D. A., Santana Alves, P. G., Nader De Araújo, L., De Souza Paes, A. B., Cielo, A. C., Maciel De Almeida Lopes, L., Longo Araújo De Melo, A., Yokoyama, T., Pagani Savastano, C., Gobi Scudeller, P., & Carvalho, C.Digital Primary Health Unit HCFMUSP Study Group. (2025). Telehealth Initiative to Enhance Primary Care Access in Brazil (UBS+Digital Project) : Multicenter Prospective Study. *Journal of Medical Internet Research, 27*, e68434. DOI: 10.2196/68434 PMID: 40299477

Manaouil, C., Chamot, S., & Petit, P. (2024). Le médecin confronté à l'IA (Intelligence artificielle) : Éthique et responsabilité. *Médecine & Droit, 2024*(186), 50–66. DOI: 10.1016/j.meddro.2024.02.001

Mbemba, G. I. C., Hamelin-Brabant, L., Gagnon, M.-P., Ngangue, P. A., & Bagayoko, C. O. (2017). Utilisation et perceptions de la télésanté par les professionnels de la santé des zones rurales au Mali. European Research in Telemedicine / La Recherche Européenne en Télémédecine, 6(3-4), 165-172. DOI: 10.1016/j.eurtel.2017.10.001

Mignot, L., & Schultz, É. (2022). Les innovations d'intelligence artificielle en radiologie à l'épreuve des régulations du système de santé. Réseaux, N° 232-233(2), 65-97. Cairn.info. DOI: 10.3917/res.232.0065

M.mounchayane, F. E. (2019). Télémédecine pour améliorer l'offre de soin de proximité:

Morley, J., Machado, C. C. V., Burr, C., Cowls, J., Joshi, I., Taddeo, M., & Floridi, L. (2020). The ethics of AI in health care : A mapping review. *Social Science & Medicine, 260*, 113172. DOI: 10.1016/j.socscimed.2020.113172 PMID: 32702587

Moulin, T., Simon, P., Staccini, P., Sibilia, J., & Diot, P. (2022). Santé numérique – télémédecine : L'évidence d'une formation universitaire pour tous les professionnels de santé. *Bulletin de l'Académie Nationale de Médecine, 206*(5), 648–656. DOI: 10.1016/j.banm.2022.04.011

MSPS. (2022). MSPS santé en chiffre.

Mukamurera, J., Lacourse, F., & Couturier, Y. (2006). Des avancées en analyse qualitative : Pour une transparence et une systématisation des pratiques. Recherches qualitatives, 26(1), 110-138. Érudit. DOI: 10.7202/1085400ar

Nasir, B. F., Leedie, F., Fox, J., Martin, P., Alam, K., Wallis, K., McGrail, M. R., & Kondalsamy-Chennakesavan, S. (2024). Can digital innovation transform rural primary health care? A systematic review protocol. BMJ Open, 14(6). *BMJ Open, 14*(6), e083152. Advance online publication. DOI: 10.1136/bmjopen-2023-083152 PMID: 38890142

OMS. (1998). RAPPORT OMS.

OMS. (2010)... *Rapport sur la Santé dans le Monde.*

Osei-Tutu, K. (2024). Redéfinir l'excellence des soins de santé en intégrant la compassion inclusive et l'humanité partagée dans un schéma de compétences médicales transformateur. *Canadian Medical Association Journal, 196*(19), E681–E684. DOI: 10.1503/cmaj.231273-f PMID: 38772609

RADAH, A., & ELHIA, M. (2025). Intelligence artificielle et amélioration de l'offre de soins au Maroc défis et perspectives. Journal of Integrated Studies In Economics, Law, Technical Sciences & Communication.

Radi, Y. (2023). *L'accès aux soins de santé en milieu rural au Maroc : Une étude de la gouvernance et de l'instrumentation de l'action publique dans le cadre de l'Initiative Nationale pour le Développement Humain.* INDH.

Raphael, K., & Ngaha, T. Y. S. (2024). L'Intelligence Artificielle comme levier pour le diagnostic rapide des maladies dans les zones reculées d'Afrique : Une approche basée sur des données et des simulations. HAL science ouverte.

Rouidi, M., Abd Elmajid, E., Hamdoune, A., & Choujtani, K. (2023). Acceptance factors of telemedicine technology during Covid-19 pandemic among health professionals : A qualitative study.

Rouidi, M., Elouadi, A. E., Hamdoune, A., Choujtani, K., & Chati, A. (2022). TAM-UTAUT and the acceptance of remote healthcare technologies by healthcare professionals : A systematic review. *Informatics in Medicine Unlocked, 32*, 101008. DOI: 10.1016/j.imu.2022.101008

Russell, S., & Norvig, P. (2021). *Artificial Intelligence : A Modern Approach.* PEARSON SERIES IN ARTIFICIAL INTELLIGENCE.

Saigí-Rubió, F., Borges Do Nascimento, I. J., Robles, N., Ivanovska, K., Katz, C., Azzopardi-Muscat, N., & Novillo Ortiz, D. (2022). The Current Status of Telemedicine Technology Use Across the World Health Organization European Region : An Overview of Systematic Reviews. *Journal of Medical Internet Research, 24*(10), e40877. DOI: 10.2196/40877 PMID: 36301602

Schwamm, L. H., Erskine, A., & Licurse, A. (2020). A digital embrace to blunt the curve of COVID19 pandemic. *NPJ Digital Medicine, 3*(1), 64. Advance online publication. DOI: 10.1038/s41746-020-0279-6 PMID: 32377575

Shaheen, M. Y. (2021). Applications of Artificial Intelligence (AI) in healthcare. *RE:view*. Advance online publication. DOI: 10.14293/S2199-1006.1.SOR-.PPVRY8K.v1

Simon, P., & Gayrard, P. (2017). Télémédecine. Des pratiques innovantes pour l'accès aux soins.

Tao, D., Wang, T., Wang, T., Zhang, T., Zhang, X., & Qu, X. (2020). A systematic review and meta-analysis of user acceptance of consumer-oriented health information technologies. *Computers in Human Behavior, 104*, 106147. DOI: 10.1016/j.chb.2019.09.023

Tchakomi, Y. (2017). La santé mobile : Défis et opportunités pour les systèmes de soins.

Van Tilburg, M. L., Spin, I., Pisters, M. F., Staal, J. B., Ostelo, R. W., Van Der Velde, M., Veenhof, C., & Kloek, C. J. (2024). Barriers and Facilitators to the Implementation of Digital Health Services for People With Musculoskeletal Conditions in the Primary Health Care Setting : Systematic Review. *Journal of Medical Internet Research, 26*, e49868. DOI: 10.2196/49868 PMID: 39190440

Yousefi, F., & Gagnon, M.-P. (2024). L'intelligence artificielle (IA) pour la promotion de la santé et la réduction de la maladie : Synthèse des connaissances. Observatoire international sur les impacts sociétaux de l'intelligence artificielle et du numérique. DOI: 10.61737/PJLD3032

KEY TERMS AND DEFINITIONS

Artificial Intelligence: AI is an interdisciplinary field creating a system capable of performing operations such as learning; reasoning; analysis; interpretation and decision-making (Russell & Norvig, 2021)

Caregiver-Care Receiver Relationship: is a therapeutic bond between health-care professionals and their patients. These bonds are established with the aim of maintaining, restoring, or promoting the patient's health.

Primary Health Care: A societal approach to health that aims to ensure the highest possible level of health and well-being and its equitable distribution by prioritizing the needs of populations as early as possible throughout the care chain, from health promotion and disease prevention to treatment, rehabilitation, and palliative care, while remaining as close as possible to the everyday environment of populations (OMS 2023)

Technology Acceptance Model (TAM): is a theoretical model for studying the factors influencing the use of technology and is based on two major constructs: perceived usefulness and ease of use.

Teleconsultation: Teleconsultation is a form of telemedicine; it is a medical practice that connects a healthcare professional to a patient via technological means for the purpose of diagnosis, treatment, or consultation

Chapter 3
Artificial Intelligence and Augmented Reality for Optimized Sensory Development in Preschool Children With Autism Disorders

Lamiae Bezzaz
https://orcid.org/0009-0003-9802-2549
Faculty of Letters and Human Sciences, Ibn Tofail University, Morocco

Mohamed Meliani
https://orcid.org/0009-0008-5532-0454
Faculty of Letters and Human Sciences, Ibn Tofail University, Morocco

ABSTRACT

Inclusive education in preschool is a fundamental requirement in education systems, especially for children with autism disorders (ETSA), who often have sensory peculiarities and difficulties in social interactions, requiring adapted and innovative pedagogical approaches. Artificial intelligence (AI) and augmented reality (AR) would offer immersive and interactive environments, capable of meeting the individual needs of children regardless of their skills, by simulating social situations, modulating sensory stimuli, and providing real-time feedback. This study adopts a mixed approach (questionnaire, observations in inclusive classrooms and interviews with educators), to analyze the impact of these technologies on sensory development and the inclusion of ETSAs in preschool education. It identifies the opportunities

DOI: 10.4018/979-8-3373-3436-3.ch003

and limits of their integration into Moroccan preschool pedagogical practices, and proposes concrete avenues for educational development for a more effective inclusion through digital technology.

INTRODUCTION

Inclusive education presents a universal requirement in education policies, playing a leading role in equitable and successful access to learning for all, including children with disabilities (SWD). In the Moroccan educational context, the reforms undertaken in recent decades reflect a strong desire to guarantee access to quality education for all children from an early age. This orientation is part of the Strategic Vision 2015-2030 for the reform of education carried out by the Higher Council for Education, Training and Scientific Research (CSEFRS, 2015) which emphasizes inclusive education from preschool. The generalization of preschool education is a national priority, with the aim of ensuring equitable and appropriate schooling conditions for all school-age children (CSEFRS, 2015). Equity and equal opportunities are highlighted as major political and societal issues in the consolidation of an inclusive and democratic school, with the generalization of education constituting a central lever for the achievement of equity (CSEFRS, 2015). The commitment to quality education is also a fundamental axis of this reform dynamic. Educational quality is defined by the learner's ability to fully acquire cognitive, practical, affective, expressive and creative skills (CSEFRS, 2015) reflecting a holistic approach to education. The implementation of this vision was supported by the launch of the National Program for the Generalization and Development of Preschool (PNGDP) in 2018 by the Ministry of National Education. Spanning a ten-year period, the program aims to achieve a 100% pre-school enrolment rate by 2027-2028 for children aged 4 and 5, making pre-school education not only accessible to all, but also integrated into compulsory education. Indeed, the PNGDP seeks to improve the quality of teaching, to strengthen the training of educators and to gradually rehabilitate traditional preschool practices by making children aged 3 years old adhere to them at the end, it is a fundamental lever in the democratization of preschool in Morocco, meeting the imperatives of equity and equal opportunities. At the same time, the adoption of Ministerial Note No. 19-047 on inclusive education highlighted a major and decisive step in favor of the schooling of ESH (Ministry of National Education, 2019). This circular generates a framework for action to guarantee the right to inclusive, equitable and quality education for all children, in line with Morocco's international commitments on the rights of the child and persons with disabilities. In this context, the effective inclusion of children with autism spectrum disorder (CASD) in preschool poses considerable challenges, particularly those relating to pedagogical adaptation, the management of sensory particularities and the improvement of social communication. ASD in early childhood is a neurodevelopmental disorder characterized by alterations in social communication, repetitive behaviors, and emotional dysregulation, affecting approximately 1/36 8-year-old children. Emotional dysregulation (ED) is common in preschool CASDs, 30% of whom have severe or moderate dysregulation, associated with increased emotional-behavioral difficulties, especially in boys (Conti et al., 2024). The school placement of CASDs in early childhood is influenced by their cognitive and language development, with impaired cognitive development being a strong predictor of certain school modalities (Lirola & Sánchez, 2024). The developmental trajectories of these children are very heterogeneous, with marked psychomotor deficits compared to other neurodevelopmental disorders. This reveals the importance of in-depth evaluations and taking into account the point of view of caregivers in the understanding of these profiles (Martelli et al., 2025). The inclusion of CASDs in the Moroccan preschool environment raises complex issues, namely the management of sensory hypersensitivity or hyposensitivity, difficulties in emotional regulation and limitations in verbal and/or non-verbal communication. The work of Martelli et al. (2025) highlights the great heterogeneity of developmental trajectories in these children, requiring in-depth assessments and differentiated pedagogical strategies.

In addition, Lirola and Sánchez (2024) state that cognitive and language skills are major predictors of early childhood schooling arrangements. A significant alteration in the child's cognitive development influences not only the type of educational device proposed, but also the appropriateness of its integration into ordinary classes.

In the Moroccan context, despite remarkable progress, the education system still faces significant structural challenges: lack of specialized initial and continuing training for educators, insufficient material resources, lack of appropriate technological tools, and socio-cultural resistance to welcoming SWDs (Bezzaz and Meliani, 2024). As such, it is essential to design and implement innovative, personalized and scientifically based educational strategies, taking into account the individualized needs of CASDs. These approaches must aim to improve their developmental trajectories, in particular by supporting sensory, emotional and communication skills. Such individualized support is an essential lever to ensure real and sustainable educational and social inclusion. In this perspective, the integration of emerging technologies such as Artificial Intelligence (AI) and Augmented Reality (AR) within the educational process offers new perspectives. AI is increasingly being used in educational settings, enabling personalized learning environments. This system can be adapted to the individualized needs of school-age children, including CASDs. It offers adapted activities and interventions. AI-guided platforms can analyze a child's progress and adjust the difficulty level of tasks accordingly, ensuring a learning experience that is both challenging and effective (Atturu & Naraganti, 2024) (Maulidin, 2024). In addition, AI systems provide immediate, real-time feedback, which helps children understand their progress and perceive their improvement. This characteristic is indispensable in the development of their self-regulatory skills. (Mehta et al., 2023). In addition, AI-powered tools, such as interactive games and animated characters, can improve a child's level of engagement and motivation to learn, especially one whose individualized needs are not fully addressed by traditional teaching methods (Porayska-Pomsta et al., 2018) (Ranaweera et al., 2023). In the same vein, AR has become a powerful tool for improving sensory development and promoting the inclusion of CASDs. Creating interactive and immersive environments, it can simulate real-world scenarios and help children better understand and navigate social situations. AR can offer the opportunity to design controlled immersive experiences. For example, AR-based games can help CASDs learn about new environments in a progressive, playful way, reducing anxiety and fear (Mammalogy, 2023). It also facilitates alternative communication by providing interactive visual and auditory supports, adapted to the perceptual particularities of these children with special needs (Avan & Kalenderoğlu, 2024). In this context, a central question emerges:

How can AI and RA be used to optimize the sensory development and inclusion of children with ASD in preschool education in Morocco? This question is part of a twofold problem: on the one hand, that of adapting pedagogical tools to the specific sensory needs of CASDs, and on the other hand, that of the effective integration of these tools in a Moroccan educational context marked by structural and cultural constraints. This chapter aims to systematically explore the role of AI and AR in optimizing sensory development and early school inclusion of CASDs, based on the latest scientific advances and field surveys in a Moroccan context. The main contribution lies in a cross-analysis of the potentialities offered by these immersive technologies, the specific challenges related to their implementation in Moroccan preschool classes and practical recommendations for an adapted and culturally relevant integration. Thus, this chapter seeks to enrich the debate on inclusive pedagogical innovation in Morocco, by focusing on the effective inclusion of CASDs in preschool education. Through a cross-analysis between the contributions of AI and AR, concrete avenues are proposed for the development of differentiated and innovative educational practices, based on the integration of new immersive technologies. In order to answer the research question above, this chapter is structured as follows:

- The methodology details the approach adopted, based on a literature review, field observations and a questionnaire with preschool educators in Morocco.
- The results section presents the main observations and analyses from the data collected.

- The discussion analyzes the results obtained in the light of educational, pedagogical and technological issues, in a Moroccan context, in connection with the inclusion of CASDs in the era of AI/AR use.
- The conclusion offers research perspectives and recommendations for inclusive education policy in Morocco.

METHODOLOGY: A MIXED APPROACH AT THE CROSSROADS OF FIELD AND INNOVATION

Nature of the Research

This study subscribes to an exploratory mixed methodological approach, whose ambition is the articulation between emerging technologies (AI/AR) and the inclusion of ESH, mainly CASDs in Moroccan preschool. It combines:

- A systematic literature review to identify key concepts, theoretical frameworks, and recent work on the use of AI and AR in inclusive education practices, including in the context of pre-primary education.
- Field surveys were carried out using the observation technique, particularly in preschool structures hosting CASDs, in this case the Med VI National Center for Disabilities in Sala Al Jadida and two schools in the city of Salé. This fieldwork made it possible to collect qualitative data on pedagogical practices, educational interactions and care modalities.
- A survey conducted using an online questionnaire with a sample of 39 Moroccan preschool educators. The aim of this questionnaire is to collect respondents' perceptions, knowledge and experiences on the use of AI and AR in educational practices in inclusive classrooms integrating CASDs. It includes both closed-ended and open-ended questions about informants' career paths, their familiarity with these technologies, and their view of their inclusive potential.

The proposed analysis is based on the ability to explore in depth the phenomena related to the subjective experience of educational actors and the contextual impact of innovative educational technologies (Guizado-Barrientos et al., 2023).

Source Selection

The literature review is based exclusively on recent studies, published between 2018 and 2025, mainly from indexed scientific journals and validated papers at international conferences. It seeks to update knowledge in a field through the collection of field data. The exploratory phase is structured around three modalities:

Observations conducted in preschool classes hosting CASDs, semi-structured interviews with specialized educators and pedagogical managers during visits to the Med VI National Center for Disabilities (Sala Al Jadida) and an online questionnaire piloted with preschool educators in Morocco.

1 Direct Observations in the Classroom

In order to select the direct observation samples, the choice was made of three preschool classes from two different schools located in the city of Salé. The objective is to raise pedagogical practices and inclusive dynamics in the field in real learning situations. The observations focus on the technological tools used and educational interactions.

In the framework of this study, two schools located in distinct urban districts of the city of Salé are chosen for field observations. The choice is based on criteria of socio-economic diversity and accessibility, and on the presence of children identified or presumed to have ASD integrated into preschool classes.

a. School 1

The first school observed was located in the urban district of Tabriquet, precisely in the working-class district of Frougui. The school does not have a resource room, and the material resources available to the educators are limited. However, it is part of national efforts for the generalization of preschool and inclusive education.

A preschool class observed in this establishment includes about 22 children, including a boy with characteristic signs of ASD. Unlike other similar cases, this child does not benefit from any specialized follow-up.

b. School 2

The second school is located in the district of Hssain, precisely in Sala Al-Jadida, an urbanized area with an average socio-economic level. This school has a resource room and a multipurpose space, and offers reception conditions that are more favourable to inclusive education.

Two classes were observed, bringing together about 40 children. A boy with ASD attends one of them. At the same time, he is enrolled and monitored in the preschool unit of the autism unit at the Mohammed VI National Center for People with Disabilities. However, the educators were not informed of his diagnosis at the time of the observations (according to their testimonies). The child's mother only mentions a “slight language delay”, for fear of stigmatization or refusal to integrate him into a regular school. This parental silence is a significant obstacle to the implementation of relevant support.

The observations were conducted between February 15 and March 25, 2025, at a rate of two sessions per class with an average duration of 60 minutes. The sessions are chosen for their evaluative potential.

1 Visit of the Preschool Unit Within the Autism Unit at the Med VI National Center for the Disabled (Sala Al Jadida)

In a complementary approach to classroom observation, a series of visits was carried out in the preschool unit attached to the autism unit of the Mohammed VI National Center for People with Disabilities in Sala Al Jadida. These visits, spread over a period of one month (January 24 to February 24, 2025) at a rate of one to two sessions per week, made it possible to observe in a regular and in-depth manner the educational support modalities offered to CASD.

The analysis of the functioning of this specialized structure provides valuable insights into differentiated pedagogical practices, the tools mobilized and the coordination between educators and other stakeholders.

2 Exploratory Questionnaire

As an extension of the field observations, a structured exploratory questionnaire is piloted online with preschool educators in Morocco (39 participants). This tool aims to collect additional data on their representations, knowledge and experiences regarding the use of emerging technologies, in particular AI and AR, in a context of inclusive teaching, CASD cases. This questionnaire contains closed and open questions on several dimensions: level of familiarity with technological tools, current or potential use in the classroom, recognized obstacles and needs expressed in terms of training or institutional support.

Figure 1. Questionnaire

Elements	Details
Number of participants	39 Moroccan preschool educators
Format	Online questionnaire (Google Forms)
Average response time	Approximately 10 minutes
Total number of questions	17 questions
Topics covered	Familiarity with AI and AR Current or Proposed Uses Perceived obstacles Training and support needs
Broadcast period	April 2025

The analysis of the data is based on a triangulation logic: the characterized data (from interviews and observations) are related to the statistical data (from the questionnaires) to identify convergences, gaps and areas for improvement. This approach makes it possible to provoke contextualized recommendations, co-constructed with stakeholders and adapted to the realities on the ground.

Methodological Limitations

Like any exploratory study in a real context, it is confronted with a number of limitations, including:

- The small and targeted sample: the limited number of schools observed, although selected for their contextual diversity (specialized centers, public schools), does not allow for a generalization of the results to the whole of Moroccan preschool.
- Limited access to AI/AR tools in real use: with the absence of truly operational technological devices in the classes observed, the study had to rely on the perceptions, projections and expectations of professionals, rather than on the analysis of actual practices integrating these emerging technologies. This restricts the direct empirical scope and anchors the reflection in an exploratory and prospective logic.

RESULTS: PERCEPTION, PRACTICES AND BARRIERS TO THE INTEGRATION OF AI AND AR

This research led to the following results in three main areas:

- Direct observations in three preschool classes of two different schools located in the city of Salé (Rabat-Salé-Kenitra Region, Morocco).
- Semi-structured interviews conducted with specialized educators and pedagogical managers.
- A structured questionnaire administered to a sample of Moroccan preschool educators.

These three sources are mobilized in order to analyze the representations, practices and expectations regarding the inclusion of CASDs in preschool education and the potentials of AI and AR as tools for sensory, social and cognitive support for these children.

The analysis of the collected corpus is established around thematic axes, namely current practices concerning the evaluation and inclusion of CASDs, the impact of AI on pedagogical adaptation for the benefit of CASDs, the contributions of AR to sensory development, the systematic, cultural and professional challenges and obstacles to the integration of emerging technologies, and a synthesis of the results proposing concrete courses of action.

Evaluation and Inclusive Practices of CASDs

This chapter presents the results of direct observations conducted in the two schools with preschool classes, interviews with educators, and the online questionnaire with educators.

1 Preschool Observations

Field observations conducted between February and March 2025, in two schools located in the city of Salé in Morocco, highlight differentiated dynamics in terms of equipment, inclusive teaching practices and the frequency and quality of the follow-up provided by specialists: two schools sampled on the basis of their socio-economic diversity and their reception of CASD.

Figure 2. Characteristics of the two schools observed

Criterion	School 1	School 2
Urban area	Popular urban area	Middle to Upper Urban Area
Available Resources	Low (no resource room)	Resource room + room manager
CASD medical follow-up	No follow-up	Follow-up at the Med VI centre
Knowledge of the diagnosis	Not disclosed	Ignored by educators
Class size	22	20
Specific training focused on inclusion	Yes	Yes
Adapted technological equipment	Nothingness	Existing

The educator in charge of class A in school 1 has received basic training on inclusive education, which is reflected in some spontaneous practices of adaptation to the case of the CASD welcomed. However, no digital tools, let alone devices based on AI or AR, are used in the classroom observed. This absence is explained by a lack of specific training and adapted technological resources. Also, the lack of specialized human resources within the institution hinders the implementation of an integration of these emerging technologies in the service of truly differentiated and inclusive assessment and/or learning.

The educator in charge of class B in school 2 also benefited from a short training course on inclusion. Although some spontaneous adaptations are visible in her practices, the digital tools she uses in the classroom remain generic (PC, video projector, Bluetooth speaker), and do not fall under immersive or intelligent technologies. The lack of integration of AI and/or AR-based solutions, coupled with a lack of coordination with specialized professionals, significantly limits the effectiveness of the evaluation and the implementation of support tailored to the specific needs of CASDs.

Within the two establishments, no assessment tool adapted to the specific needs of CASDs was identified. The educators use observation boards or generic grids that are not differentiated and without taking into account the sensory or behavioral needs of these children.

The educational activities are essentially based on oral communication, based on listening to instructions, verbal responses and/or free drawings. This standardization of media and modes of interaction automatically excludes children with impaired language and sensory abilities.

These data compare the observations of Martelli et al. (2025) on the heterogeneity of developmental trajectories in CASDs and the need for pedagogical differentiation from preschool education.

2 Results of Semi-Structured Interviews

Seven interviews were conducted, four with preschool educators, two with specialized educators from the Med VI National Center, and one with a pedagogical manager from the same center. These interviews were to explore current practices, representations of inclusion and perceptions of immersive educational technologies.

In order to allow a freer use of the data, the questions planned for the interviews with the centre's professionals have been reformulated in the form of a structured questionnaire. This format allowed for direct responses while maintaining the depth of their expertise.

The recurring themes highlighted through the combined analysis of the interviews and the questionnaire are as follows:

Figure 3. Major themes from the interviews

Themes	Frequency of occurrence	Questionnaire results (N=3)
Lack of hands-on training	6/7	2/3 have received specific training, often basic
Lack of ASD assessment tools	6/7	The most cited tools are traditional visual aids, few use specialized digital tools
Difficulties in communicating with family and school	5/7	2/3 mentioned them as a recurring issue
Interest in visual tools	4/7	3/3 use pictograms, visual routines, structured supports and sequential images.
Fear of doing wrong	4/7	2/3 express uncertainty in the appropriate pedagogical implementation, they consider themselves little or moderately capable of adapting their practices.
Knowledge of AI and AR-based educational tools	4/7	2/3 are familiar with AI-based tools and applications
Openness to emerging technologies	5/7	3/3 in favor of the use of AI and AR in the classroom.

These results highlight a strong demand for professionalism, particularly regarding the differentiation and adaptation of assessments, the management of sensory heterogeneity, the understanding of autistic disorder and the knowledge and use of AI and AR for the benefit of CASDs.

The educators at the specialized center emphasize the value of structured routines, visual aids, and progressive sensory adaptations. They encourage the rapprochement between ordinary schools and specialized structures in order to avoid breaks in the educational path of CASDs. They also reveal a significant gap between enthusiasm for technological innovation and real mastery of the tools available.

3 Results of the Questionnaire

The questionnaire administered online to Moroccan preschool educators collected data on educators' practices, attitudes and representations towards CASDs and immersive educational technologies.

a. Socio-Demographic and Occupational Profile of Respondents

All the informants are women, aged between 35 and 44 and working as educators in ordinary preschool classes. Their level of education varies from bachelor's to master's degree. Cumulative professional experience covers a wide spectrum, from less than two years to more than ten years: the majority (60%) is between two and ten years.

This profile reflects a female professional population, from a variety of training backgrounds and relatively experienced.

b. Inclusion Practices

In order to rigorously assess the degree of preparedness of preschool educators to deal with CASDs, a set of indicators was mobilized. The table above presents the results collected.

Figure 4. Inclusion Practices

Item Rated	Responses and results			
Have you taken any specific training on the inclusion of children with disabilities?	Yes, in-depth training	Yes, basic training	No	
	4 (10.3 %)	15 (38.5 %)	22 (56.4 %)	
How do you assess your current ability to adapt your teaching practices to the specific sensory needs of children with ASD?	Very good	Average	Weak	
	6 (15.4 %)	23 (59 %)	10 (25.6 %)	
Do you currently have one or more CASD (ASD) in your class?	Yes		No	
	29 (74.4 %)		10 (25.6 %)	
If a child with ASD were to be integrated into your class, how would you rate your degree of preparation and acceptance to welcome them?	Very supportive and well prepared	Favourable but unprepared	Mixed or hesitant	Reluctant or unfavourable
	9 (23.1 %)	21 (53.8 %)	7 (17.9 %)	2 (5.1 %)
What kinds of tools are you currently using to support learning for children with ASD? (multiple choice possible)	Classic visual aids	Classic educational tablets	TSA-specific software or applications	No specific tools used
	17(43.6 %)	6 (15.4 %)	3 (7.7 %)	19(48.7 %)

c. Formation

Only 10.3% of participants report having received extensive training on inclusion, while 38.5% reveal having received basic training. This figure is still encouraging but highlights a structural lack in specialised continuing education, since more than half (56.4%) have not received any training focused on inclusion.

This situation confirms the observations made during field observations: teachers deploy practices that are mostly intuitive or generalist, due to the lack of differentiated teaching tools. It also joins the work of Bezzaz and Meliani (2024), who call for the institutionalization of specialized, contextualized and sustainable training to meet the needs of all children, including CASDs.

d. Pedagogical Adaptation

When asked about the ability of educators to adapt their teaching practices to the individualized sensory needs of CASDs, only 15.4% of them said they were very competent, while 59% considered themselves moderately competent, and 25.6% admitted to having great difficulties at this level. These data confirm the existence of professional uncertainty, aggravated by the lack of tools, training, feedback and support mechanisms.

And it is very worrying that this lack of trust coexists with a strong presence of CASDs in preschool classes, nearly 74.4% of respondents say that they welcome at least one CASD in their classes. This clearly underlines the gap between the reality of inclusion and the preparation of teaching teams.

e. Preparation for the Welcome

As for the integration of a child with ASD into the classroom, nearly 77% say they are ready to welcome them. However, more than half of them (53.8%) admit that they do not feel sufficiently prepared, and only 23.1% see themselves as being able to provide truly appropriate support. This imbalance revealed between the ethical posture of openness and insufficient professional preparation reveals a major paradox of the educational inclusion of ESH in Morocco. It testifies to a strong pedagogical will, hampered by training systems and working conditions that are not adapted to the requirements of an inclusive, equitable and successful education.

f. Available Educational Resources

The tools used reveal a massive use of traditional media, 43.6% use standard visual aids often not adapted to CASDs. Only 15.4% of participants use conventional educational tablets and 7.7% use apps designed for CASDs. The most worrying figure is that of educators who do not use any specific tools (48.7%), which indicates a virtual absence of real pedagogical adaptations despite the actual presence of atypical profiles.

These results corroborate the direct observations made in the field by the present work and the findings of Martelli et al. (2025), highlighting that the lack of differentiated tools is a factor aggravating the developmental difficulties of CASDs at school.

The analysis of the reported practices highlights a significant gap between the growing presence of CASDs in Moroccan preschool classes and the level of preparation of educators to respond to them in an appropriate and differentiated way. In this context, AI and AR offer a major opportunity to support the expected pedagogical transformation.

g. Uses and Knowledge of AI and AR Technologies

Faced with the limits of current approaches, immersive technologies such as AI and AR represent an original potential for pedagogical innovation. However, their integration depends closely on the acceptability and familiarity of educators.

Figure 5. Uses and Knowledge of Emerging Technologies

	Items	Answers and results		
Use of emerging technologies	Do you use AI-based apps or tools in your daily life?	Yes, regularly	Yes, occasionally	No, never
		7 (17.9 %)	18 (46.9 %)	14 (35.9 %)
	Have you ever used AR applications (games, photo filters, virtual tours, etc.) in your daily life?	Yes, regularly	Yes, occasionally	No, never
		2 (5.1 %)	17 (43.6 %)	20 (51.3 %)
Knowledge of emerging technologies	Are you familiar with AI-based educational tools?	Yes, I'm already using them	Yes, but I don't use them	No, I don't know
		7 (17.9 %)	13 (33.3 %)	19 (48.7 %)
	Are you familiar with AR-based tools?	Yes, I'm already using them	Yes, but I don't use them	No, I don't know
		3 (7.7 %)	11 (28.2 %)	25 (64.1 %)

Understanding educators' familiarity with immersive technologies, both in their personal lives and in their professional practice, is a key indicator to assess their level of readiness for successful educational integration. The results collected highlight a gap between the informal use of technologies and their mobilization in a structured educational context.

h. Use of Immersive Technologies

Nearly 65% of respondents say they use AI in their daily lives, including 17.9% on a regular basis. This rate, although modest, reflects the gradual anchoring of AI in the usual digital practices of educators, in particular through translation tools, voice assistance and/or personalized recommendation. Conversely, AR remains largely marginalized: 51.3% of participants have never used it, and only 5.1% use it regularly. This disparity in adoption is partly explained by differences in accessibility, as AI is massively integrated into common digital devices (smartphones, tablets, etc.), while AR often requires specific equipment (headsets, dedicated applications, etc.) that is still unfamiliar in standard environments.

i. Level of Knowledge of AI and AR-Based Educational Tools

The mastery of AI-based educational tools is still limited: only 17.9% of respondents are already using it, while 48.7% say they are not aware of it. Similarly, 64.1% of participants are not aware of AR-based educational devices. These data reveal a deficit in exposure and professional initiation and a high potential for acculturation.

The fact that 33.3% of education officers have heard of AI-based tools, and that 28.2% have become aware of AR-based tools without using them, suggests a fertile ground for the emergence of acculturation, training or supervised experimentation devices with pilot projects.

These results corroborate the findings from the field: despite the fact that educators express a latent curiosity about these technologies, which do not spontaneously translate into effective use due to a lack of support, awareness, adapted training and technical support.

In this sense, favorable perceptions are not enough to guarantee a transformation of practices: rather, they underline a need to structure the inclusive digital transition, as suggested by Mehta et al. (2023), according to whom the success of technological innovations is based first and foremost on human and institutional investment.

j. Cross-Analysis: Potential for Appropriation and Difficulties to Overcome

The comparison of the results received indicates the existence of a core of "pioneer" educators, already familiar with AI-based tools, and ready to experiment with their pedagogical applications. This group can play a major role as a lever for dissemination in a strategy of "peer training" or "digital mentoring". However, most educators preserve the posture of observer, or even critical distance, which requires a gradual contextualized entry accompanied by emerging educational technologies.

These findings are in line with the conclusions of Lyu et al. (2024) and Bhatt et al. (2024), who insist on the need to articulate technological development with strategies of continuing education, technical support and pedagogical co-construction.

k. Educators' Stated Perceptions of the Educational Potential of AI and AR Technologies

The accessibility of a technology depends not only on its functionality, but also on the representations that these users have of it. For this reason, the questionnaire was not limited to the use and knowledge of immersive technologies by educators, but also explored their perceptions of the pedagogical usefulness of these devices and the perceived obstacles to their integration.

Figure 6. Educators' Perceptions of the Educational Potential of AI and AR

	Items	Answers and results				
Perceptions	Do you think AI could help to better personalize the educational support of children with ASD?	Yes		No		
		25 (64.1 %)		14 (35.9 %)		
	Do you think AR could help improve sensory and social skills in children with ASD?	Yes		No		
		29 (74.4 %)		10 (25.6 %)		
	What do you see as the main barriers to integrating AI/AR tools into your classroom?	Lack of technological equipment	Lack of appropriate training	High cost of tools	Difficulty in adapting to the Moroccan educational context	Institutional or cultural resistance
		33 (84.6 %)	28 (71.8 %)	13 (33.3 %)	17 (43.6 %)	6 (15.4 %)

l. Artificial Intelligence: a Promising Technology, but Still in Search of Legitimacy

A majority of 64.1% of the educators surveyed believe that AI could contribute to the personalization of the educational support of CASDs. This result suggests that, despite the lack of concrete use, AI is perceived by the majority as a potentially relevant solution to the diversity of cognitive and sensory profiles.

However, a significant number of educators expressing cautious reservations (35.9%) reveal an insistent caution with regard to this "hard-skill" technology

This reluctance reflects a tension between the recognition of technological potential and the uncertainties related to its pedagogical integration, the necessary training, or its impact on the educational relationship.

These results converge with the analyses of Porayska-Pomsta et al. (2018) who highlight the risks of technological instrumentalization devoid of ethical reflection and adapted human mediation.

m. Augmented Reality: a Majority Craze Linked to Sensory Dimensions

74.4% of participants believe that AR could help develop the sensory and social skills of CASDs. This perception reflects a recognition of the immersive assets offered by AR, particularly with regard to its ability to propose controlled sensory gradations, model interactions and simulate social scenarios.

This perception is in line with the findings of Avan and Kalenderoğlu (2024) who highlight the potential of AR to make abstract concepts tangible, reduce anxiety about change, and strengthen spatio-temporal cues in young learners.

n. Difficulties to be Overcome: Material Constraints and Institutional Barriers

When asked about the main obstacles to the integration of AI and AR-based tools into their teaching practices, educators highlighted several challenges: The lack of technological equipment closely followed by the lack of adapted training was raised by 84.6% and 71.8% of educators, respectively. Then come the difficulties of adapting to the Moroccan educational context (43.6%), followed by the high cost of tools (33.3%) and finally institutional or cultural resistance (15.4%)

These data highlight a clear hierarchy of perceived barriers. Firstly, the lack of infrastructure and equipment is a major obstacle, which is confirmed by the observations made in the two schools covered by this research. The need for adapted training appears to be a crucial and equally critical challenge. The latter is not limited to a technical deficit but also reflects a need for psychopedagogical support linked to a lack of confidence of educators in their ability to effectively use these tools in the classroom. The difficulties of adapting to the local and national context and the cost of the devices underline the urgency of cultural and economic anchoring in the development of these technologies. Finally, although less frequently mentioned, cultural or institutional resistance should not be neglected, because it can represent a latent obstacle, especially if innovations are perceived as vertically imposed or disconnected from the daily realities of educational actors.

o. Openness to Invention Conditioned by Structural Support

The analysis of the perceptions collected confirms a cross-sectional trend observed throughout this study: educators are generally receptive to techno-pedagogical innovation and spontaneously identify relevant applications for the benefit of CASDs. However, this favourable provision is rarely translated into actual use on the ground. Three conditions appear to be decisive:

- The availability of adequate technological equipment;
- The presence of contextualized and culturally appropriate educational content;
- Sustained and continuous professional support.

These conclusions resonate with the recommendations made by Mehta et al (2023), according to which AI as an educational lever can only produce real pedagogical values if it is part of a secure framework, supported by structured training and driven by a dynamic of collective commitment.

The results obtained through the observations, interviews and questionnaire provide a global view of the Moroccan preschool system's readiness to integrate immersive technologies in an early inclusive perspective.

DISCUSSION: TOWARDS INCREASED INCLUSION: WHAT ARE THE CONDITIONS FOR SUCCESS?

The cross-interpretation of the results obtained brings out several major issues, both in terms of evaluation practices and the conditions of appropriation of immersive technologies. The following discussion explores these issues in light of recent research in inclusive education and pedagogical innovation.

The discussion is organized around four axes:

- The questioning of current evaluation practices in the face of the individualized needs of CASDs;
- The real but under-exploited potential of immersive technologies;
- Structural, cultural and human constraints hindering inclusive innovation;
- Summary of the main contributions of the study

Limitations of Current Evaluation Practices

The results highlighted a predominance of standardized evaluative tools, focused on the expected developmental norms of so-called "typical" children. The universality of this approach clashes with the neurodevelopmental realities of CASDs, whose sensory, language and behavioural profiles differ greatly (Martelli et al., 2025).

The obligation to produce a differentiated assessment is nevertheless anchored in the principles of inclusive education, as defined by the Convention on the Rights of Persons with Disabilities (UN, 2006) and taken up in Morocco's Strategic Vision 2015-2030. The lack of suitable assessment tools for CASDs is therefore a major flaw that could lead to misdiagnoses and inappropriate pedagogical decisions, or even systematic exclusion.

As several educators have pointed out, the current assessment often penalizes silent or non-verbal CASDs, especially in the recognition of their micro-progress. This finding, corroborated by Bezzaz and Meliani (2024), highlights an education system that is still normative and rigid where the standardization of assessments hinders adaptation to neurodivergent needs, accentuating educational inequalities.

Potential of Immersive Technologies for Inclusion

The integration of immersive technologies in Moroccan preschool education appears, in light of the data collected, to be a pedagogical necessity. AI systems now promote promising levers for an effective individualization of assessment systems, by offering functionalities adapted to the individual needs of each child, through:

- The automatic and continuous adaptation of educational activities, according to the needs, level and individualized pace of learning of the child;
- The detection of weak signals (fatigue, stress), the visual restitution of progress (dynamic feedback) and the learner's commitment to a reflective approach;
- The identification and interpretation of non-verbal manifestations or atypical responses, often invisible by conventional assessment methods, but revealing the cognitive and communicative potential of some CASDs.

Recent research confirms these contributions. Atturu and Naraganti (2024) and Mehta et al. (2023) have shown that AI makes it possible to design adaptive educational pathways, promoting the child's autonomy, in particular through the self-regulation of emotions and behaviors.

AR, on the other hand, is an ideal sensory interface for CASDs by offering them:

- Immersive environments for graduated exposure to stressful social contexts (transport, schools, markets, etc.);
- Interactive visual aids for alternative communication (dynamic pictograms, avatars);
- Immersive narrative scenarios promoting the structuring of time and the understanding of emotions (López-Bouzas et al, (2023)).

These tools can thus contribute to overcoming some of the major barriers faced by CASDs in the education system, such as anxiety related to transitions, misunderstanding of social codes or sensory overload. By mitigating these difficulties, they promote the development of students' autonomy and support their inclusion (Mehta et al., (2023)).

The triangulation of the data between observations, interviews and questionnaires confirms the paradox of aspiration/appropriation.

Despite the strong interest of educators in these technologies (86% in favor of AI and 71% in favor of AR), their use remains marginal due to structural (lack of equipment), cultural (stigmatization of disability) and human (insufficient training) constraints. This observation, observed in Salé, reflects the challenges of a

Moroccan education system confronted with territorial inequalities, the absence of digital equipment and/or training limiting innovation. This gap between inclusive intentions and practical realities confirms international findings on the integration of educational technologies in resource-limited contexts (Bhatt et al., (2024), Lyu et al., (2024)).

Obstacles to Inclusive Innovation

The study highlights several obstacles hindering the adoption of immersive technologies in Moroccan preschool:

- Material shortcomings: the lack of resource rooms and digital equipment in public schools limits innovation
- Inadequate training: 71.8% of educators report a lack of training on the pedagogical uses of AI and/or AR.
- Lack of coordination: the lack of dialogue between schools, families, and medical facilities hinders the implementation of appropriate measures.
- Cultural barriers: parental reluctance to recognize an ASD diagnosis, for fear of stigmatization, limits pedagogical adaptation.

The parental silence around ASD, observed in particular in school 2, prevents an objective evaluation and the establishment of personalized devices: the social imagination inhibits disability and retains a patent invisibilization of it.

This reluctance reflects the presence of a still negative social representation of disability in the Moroccan context despite legal advances. This taboo slows down the dialogue between family and school and makes any co-constructed approach to inclusion difficult.

It therefore seems essential to support families in understanding autistic disorders, by developing cultural mediation, listening and awareness-raising systems within the establishments.

SUMMARY OF THE MAIN CONTRIBUTIONS OF THE STUDY

The objective of this study is to explore the conditions for optimizing sensory development and preschool inclusion of CASDs in Morocco, through the integration of AI and AR technologies. The study is part of a national context where inclusive education is promoted at the discursive and institutional level (Strategic Vision 2015-2030, PNGDP 2018-2028, ministerial note 047-19), but where effective implementation remains unevenly distributed and faces structural, pedagogical and cultural obstacles.

The results obtained, resulting from a methodological triangulation combining direct observations, semi-structured interviews and a structured questionnaire, allow us to draw a nuanced picture of the current situation, professional aspirations and technological opportunities.

Observation 1: Evaluation Practices That are not Very Differentiated and not Very Inclusive

Field observations in three preschool classes from two different schools in the city of Salé revealed a dominance of standardized evaluation practices and a weak adaptation to neurodivergent profiles. No specific tools for the sensory or behavioural assessment of CASDs were observed in the two schools visited. The use of standard, non-contextualized tools tends to make the specific skills of CASDs invisible and to reinforce their silent exclusion.

These results are in line with the analyses of Conti et al. (2024) and Martelli et al. (2025), who highlight that CASDs have heterogeneous profiles, whose skills can only be effectively measured by flexible, multisensory and interactive devices.

Observation 2: a Positive Perception, but a Low Appropriation of Immersive Technologies

86% of Moroccan preschool educators, or nearly 9/10, emphasize that they are ready to use AI in the classroom and 71%, or about 7/10, are in favor of the use of AR. However, their actual use is almost non-existent, which highlights a gap between intentions and implementation capacities. Interviews confirm that educators perceive technologies as potentially useful, but they see them as complex and inaccessible, or even high-risk without training.

This discrepancy is symptomatic of what Bhatt et al. (2024) consider to be the paradox of technological accessibility in resource-limited contexts: the tools exist, but their appropriation is conditioned by contextualized support.

Observation 3: Strong Tensions Between Families, School and Diagnosis

One of the most striking results concerns the parental reluctance and silence around the ASD diagnosis. In one of the cases observed, the mother refuses to report the diagnosis, for fear of exclusion or stigmatization by the system. This phenomenon, which has been fairly documented by Bezzaz and Meliani (2024), slows down the implementation of differentiated pedagogical practices and reinforces the feeling of powerlessness of educators.

International Perspective

This diagnosis can be compared to that of other emerging countries. In Tunisia, for example, recent studies (Ben Romdahne et al., 2023 others) show that despite an inclusive legal framework, autistic children are often referred to specialized structures due to a lack of sufficient adaptations in mainstream school. In Egypt, the integration of AR in pilot schools allows for better preparation of CASDs for everyday situations (Lyu et al., 2024), but this initiative remains marginal outside the private sector.

One of the major contributions of this research is to have combined local field data, from Moroccan classrooms, with an analysis of techno-pedagogical potentialities based on recent scientific work. The result is a contextualised, nuanced and action-oriented perspective, which can feed into national reflections on digital inclusion and pedagogical innovation for children with special needs (EBS).

RECOMMENDATIONS: FOR AN INCLUSIVE STRATEGY INTEGRATING TECHNO-PEDAGOGICAL INNOVATION

This section offers recommendations to address the identified challenges and maximize the potential of inclusive immersive technologies in the Moroccan pre-school environment by addressing educators, institutions and scientific research. The proposals aim at ethical and sustainable integration, mobilizing all actors (educators, families, institutions, researchers and developers)

Conditions for an Ethical and Sustainable Integration of Emerging AI/AR Technologies

Faced with these observations, several levers appear fundamental to achieve a successful, ethical and sustainable integration of immersive technologies in Moroccan inclusive preschool classes.

1. Ecosystem and co-constructive approaches

It is necessary to think of the integration of technologies as a process of global transformation of practices, mobilizing all actors: educators, families, institutions, researchers, specialists and IT developers. Co-construction with end users (children/

educators) can guarantee better acceptability and contextual relevance of these immersive tools.

2. Contextualized continuing education

The results collected show a real demand for training on the part of educators. The aim is to go beyond the theoretical to offer concrete and contextualized modules focused on the educational uses of AI and AR, sensory management in the classroom and alternative assessment strategies for the benefit of CASDs.

3. Technological accessibility and territorial inclusion

The equipment of preschool schools and classes must be rethought for schools located in working-class, disadvantaged and rural areas, often excluded from digital innovation. Public-private partnerships can be established and explored for the financing and installation of immersive educational materials.

4. Ethical monitoring systems

The collection of data through AI, especially in an educational context, raises major ethical questions about privacy, parental consent and data security. It is essential to establish a clear legal framework for the use of AI/AR in schools in compliance with international data protection standards (the European General Data Protection Regulation (EU) 2016/679 of the European Parliament and of the Council of 27 April 2016 on the protection of natural persons with regard to the processing of personal data and on the free movement of such data, The National Commission for the Control of the Protection of Personal Data (CNDP) was created by Law No. 09-08 of 18 February 2009 on the protection of natural persons with regard to the processing of personal data (CNDP).

Towards a Moroccan Model of Inclusive Techno-Pedagogical Innovation in Preschool

The integration of immersive technologies in Moroccan preschool cannot be conceived without institutional, pedagogical and cultural anchoring. In this respect, the reflections developed in studies such as those published in the journal RISE, although generally focused on the primary and secondary levels, prove to be transposable, with adaptation, to the preschool environment, particularly in terms of techno-pedagogical innovation applied to inclusion.

The generalization of preschool in Morocco and the right to quality and equitable education, driven by the Strategic Vision 2015-2030 and the National Program for the Generalization and Development of Preschool (PNGD), require a qualitative transformation of educational practices.

The integration of technologies such as AI and/or AR is part of this logic provided that it meets the individualized needs of all, including children with ASD.

1. Training Preschool Educators in AI and AR

The challenges of technological training arouse curiosity at all levels of the education system. This is a reinforced necessity in the case of preschool, where educators are often poorly prepared for the use of digital tools and even less for their mobilization for children with special needs (EBS). Hybrid, contextualized training including AI (monitoring of cognitive and sensory progress) and AR (immersive visual aids, interactive routines) modules would allow for real pedagogical differentiation from an early age. Raising awareness of ASD through modules on the specificities of their needs (sensory deficits, alternative communication, limited social interaction, interests in repetitive activities) is imperative.

The contribution of Massiri, Ennassiri and Djemila (2023) on professional reflection insists on the need to go beyond the technical use of technological tools to question their impacts. In the case of inclusive preschool, educators must be trained to rethink their practices, to observe the sensory and emotional effects of these tools on CASD, and to continuously adjust their postures. This reflexivity is essential to transform technology into a vector of progress and not a source of exclusion or cognitive overload.

2. Promoting Practices and Collaboration

The inclusion of CASD in Moroccan preschool cannot be considered without a significant investment in the professional development of educators. The results of this study showed that despite a declared desire to welcome all profiles, the majority of the teachers questioned (72%) feel poorly equipped to effectively support CASDs. This feeling is aggravated by the lack of specialized training, the lack of educational resources and isolation from cases with special needs.

In order to break this isolation, recommendations include:

- Networking: creating local communities of practice or to share inclusive strategies proven by experienced educators.

- Cooperative collective or group work: encourage collaboration with specialized educators or assistants in inclusive classes.
- Continuous evaluation of the situation: integrate analysis of innovative inclusive practices during pedagogical meetings, thus strengthening the collaborative culture.

3. Possible Experiments and Contextual Adaptation

Moroccan preschool offers a privileged field for simple but impactful experiments, such as the simulation of social scenes through AR headsets or mobile applications (going to school, the market, the doctor, etc.), the use of intelligent voice assistants to accompany routines or promote pronunciation, the development of the Image Exchange Communication System (PECS), (it is a unique system of alternative and argumentative communication developed by Dr. Andy Bondy, PhD, and Lori Forst, speech-language pathologist, 1985) digital with AI for nonverbal children.

These tools must be adapted to the age group concerned (4-6 years old), tested through research-actions, and co-constructed taking into account the Moroccan context in terms of the languages used (dialectal/classical Arabic, Amazigh, French, English, etc.), cultural, geographical and economic diversity.

This discussion highlighted the potential of AI and AR technologies to address the challenges of inclusive education in Morocco, especially for CASDs. However, this potential can only be realised if structural, human, cultural and ethical conditions are met. Techno-pedagogical innovation should not be thought of as a miracle cure but as a lever for a fairer, more equitable educational project that respects diversity.

Institutional Actions for Digital Inclusion

At the institutional level, it is essential to create a framework conducive to the integration of immersive technologies that takes into account material deficiencies and lack of coordination.

1. Ethical Regulatory Framework

A clear framework is essential, including:

- Ministerial guidelines defining the permitted uses of AI/AR in preschool, taking into account the needs of SWDs.
- Ethical requirements guaranteeing privacy, parental consent, and data security, in compliance with the GDPR and the CNDP (Porayska-pomsta et al., (2018)).

- Digital sovereignty: developing local digital tools to avoid dependence on foreign platforms.

2. National Equipment Plan

A more developed plan is to be considered to reduce the digital divide, including:

Techno-educational kits equipping schools with tablets, AR headsets and video projectors.

Resource rooms: create mutualist spaces for schools.

Logistical support: providing internet access and open access content, validated by the Ministry, adapted to the linguistic and cultural diversity of users.

Public-private partnerships can fund the installation and even maintenance of immersive hardware, aligned with the PNGDP.

3. Adapted Local Content

The development of immersive content must include:

- Multilingual applications: produce tools in dialectal Arabic, standard Arabic, and Amazigh, such as AR simulations of daily routines.
- Participatory pedagogies involving educators in co-construction to ensure cultural relevance.

Directions for Scientific Research

Scientific research is a fundamental pillar to consolidate the empirical foundations of digital inclusion and inclusive pedagogical innovation.

1. Contextualized experiments

Micro-experiments are needed, including:

- AI/AR modules in Moroccan pilot schools.
- Behavioural assessments before and after the intervention.
- Qualitative feedback from all stakeholders (children, families, educators and specialists)

Tools such as AR simulations or AI-generated digital PECS can be adapted to the preschool age group and the Moroccan context to support nonverbal children and meet their individualized needs.

2. National Observatory

A national university observatory can be used to:

- Centralizing work on digital inclusion
- Organize interdisciplinary seminars
- Disseminating ethical guidelines

3. Longitudinal Etudes

Longitudinal protocols will be used to analyze:

- The evolution of social, sensory, cognitive and language skills
- The impact of technology on the well-being of CASDs and those around them
- Cultural perceptions of families through qualitative methods

Limitations of the Study and Research Perspectives

This exploratory study has some limitations such as: the sample size of the questionnaire which remains limited despite its online dissemination via different groups and channels, the surveys are focused on urban schools in the same city (Salé) and the technological tools could not be tested in real situations.

Indeed, future research will have to broaden the field of investigation to other regions of Morocco (rural areas, Northern, Southern, Oriental regions, etc.), concretely experiment with the use of AI and/or AR modules in different classes and preschool structures (public, private, associative, specialized centers, kindergartens, etc.) and study the longitudinal impact of these technologies on the developmental trajectories of CASDs.

In sum, the results and the discussion above show that the digital inclusion of CASDs in Moroccan preschool, through the implementation of AI and/or AR is possible, except that it is conditioned by a change requiring an alliance of complementarity between public policies, technological innovation, vocational training, scientific research and parental and social commitment.

CONCLUSION: AI AND AR AS LEVERS OF EQUITY FOR MOROCCAN PRESCHOOL

To summarize, this study presents its main contributions, proposing research perspectives and a vision for a Moroccan model of digital inclusion, in line with the Strategic Vision 2015-2030 and the PNGDP 2018-2028. The study explores the conditions for optimizing sensory development and the inclusion of CASDs in Moroccan preschool through AI and AR. Despite the institutional discourse, the operationalization of inclusive education policies in Morocco remains hampered by structural, pedagogical and cultural obstacles. The surveys conducted in the three preschool classes in the city of Salé highlight a predominance of standardized evaluation practices, unsuited to the individualized needs of CASDs, leading to an invisibilization of skills and latent exclusion (Conti et al., (2024), Martelli et al., (2025)). The lack of differentiated and contextualized tools limits the application of the inclusive principles of the Strategic Vision 2015-2030 and the ministerial note 047-19, which aggravate the gap between ambitions and actual practice. In addition, immersive technologies such as AI and AR offer promising potential. These tools allow the design of personalized learning solutions capable of overcoming the obstacles related to anxiety and sensory overload, precisely through the modulation of stimuli and the simulation of social situations. However, their low uptake, due to the lack of training and equipment, reflects a paradox of accessibility (Bhatt et al., (2024)). Socio-cultural tensions are another challenge. Parental reluctance to recognize and accept ASD diagnoses, observed during field surveys, slows down the implementation of appropriate pedagogical adaptations and increases the feeling of powerlessness of professionals (Bezzaz and Meliani, (2024)). This taboo requires cultural meditation. At the international level, Morocco's diagnosis is similar to that of other emerging countries. In Tunisia, CASDs are often referred to specialized structures due to a lack of adaptations (Ben Romdhane et al., (2023)). In Egypt, AR improves the preparation of CASDs, but it remains marginal outside the private sector (Lyu et al., (2024)). The originality of the present study lies in its dual local and techno-pedagogical roots. It offers a contextualized and action-oriented vision for the effective digital inclusion of CASDs. To build a relevant Moroccan model of digital inclusion, it is necessary to build on existing assets: a strong institutional dynamic (Strategic Vision 2015-2030, the PNGDP 2018-2028, the ministerial notes (047-19)), a committed young educator, and specialized structures such as the Mohamed VI National Center. The integration of immersive technologies is part of a global approach that mobilizes all stakeholders: educators, families, institutions, researchers and developers. The co-construction with the end users (CASD and educators) guarantees the relevance of tools such as AR simulations adapted to the Moroccan context. Our study has limitations that are reflected in the small sample (two schools), the surveys focused on urban areas and technological tools not tested in situ. Future research should broaden the field of study to rural areas and the different regions of the kingdom, experiment with AI/AR modules in public, private and associative preschool classes, and study the longitudinal impact of these technologies on the developmental trajectories of CASDs. Finally, and to conclude, it is wise to specify that techno-pedagogical innovation cannot be the miracle cure for the evil. It will just be a lever for a more equitable education that respects diversity. By reviewing pedagogical practices, didactic tools and social representations, Morocco will be able to build an inclusive preschool where each child finds his or her place in dignity.

REFERENCES

Atturu, H., & Naraganti, S. (2024). Effectiveness of AI-driven Individualized Learning Approach for Children with Autism Spectrum Disorder (ASD). *European Psychiatry : the Journal of the Association of European Psychiatrists, 67*(S1), S77. DOI: 10.1192/j.eurpsy.2024.205

Avan, Ş. K., & Kalenderoğlu, İ. (2024). AR and AI Applications Supporting Listening Skills in Early Childhood: Innovative Solutions in Language Teaching. DOI: 10.58830/ozgur.pub534.c2201

Bezzaz, L., & Meliani, M. (2024). Citoyenneté, innovation numérique et enfants autistes au préscolaire au Maroc. Communication, Colloque International Pluridisciplinaire: « L'Éducation à la Citoyenneté: Levier de la formation du développement de la jeunesse », 27-28 juin, ENCG Kénitra, Université Ibn Tofail (UIT).

Bezzaz, L., & Meliani, M. (2024). Inclusion des enfants en situation de handicap en milieu scolaire marocain: processus et impact de l'approche inclusive à l'école publique de Salé. Communication, Conférence internationale « International Conference on Innovation in Health and Education Sciences », 10-12 mai, FSJES, Université Abdelmalek Essaâdi,Tétouan.

Bhatt, S. K., Jogy, S., & Puri, A. (2024). Integration of Virtual Reality (VR) and Artificial Intelligence (AI) in Autism Therapy. *International Journal of Science and Research Archive, 12*(1), 2400–2405. DOI: 10.30574/ijsra.2024.12.1.1006

Conti, E., Calderoni, S., Guerrera, S., Guzzetta, A., Palermo, G., De Giacomo, A., Tancredi, R., Vicari, S., & Turi, M. (2024). Dysregulation Profile in Preschoolers with Autism Spectrum Disorder: An Italian Multi-Center Perspective. *Children (Basel, Switzerland), 11*(12), 1474. DOI: 10.3390/children11121474 PMID: 39767903

Guizado-Barrientos, D., Távara-Zerpa, A., & Meneses-Claudio, B. (2023). Virtual reality in communicative learning tools for children with autism spectrum disorders: A systematic literature review. *Salud, Ciencia y Tecnología, 2*, 533. Advance online publication. DOI: 10.56294/sctconf2023533

Lirola, F., & Sánchez, A. (2024). Relevant Factors in the Schooling of Children with Autism Spectrum Disorder in Early Childhood Education. *Brain Sciences, 14*(12), 1167. DOI: 10.3390/brainsci14121167 PMID: 39766366

López-Bouzas, N., & del Moral Pérez, M. E. (2023). Gamified environment supported by augmented reality for improving communicative competencies in students with ASD: Design and validation. *International Journal of Educational Research and Innovation, 19*(19), 80–93. DOI: 10.46661/ijeri.6820

López-Bouzas, N., del Moral-Pérez, M. E., & Castañeda-Fernández, J. (2023). Communicative competence in students with ASD: Interaction and immersion in a gamified augmented environment. *Education and Information Technologies*. Advance online publication. DOI: 10.1007/s10639-023-12319-x

Lyu, Y. D. L., An, P., Tong, X., Zhang, H., Katsuragawa, K., & Zhao, J. (2024). EMooly: Supporting Autistic Children in Collaborative Social-Emotional Learning with Caregiver Participation through Interactive AI-infused and AR Activities. *Proceedings of the ACM on Interactive, Mobile, Wearable and Ubiquitous Technologies*, *8*(4), 1–36. DOI: 10.1145/3699738

Mammalogy, A. (2023). Augmented Reality-Based Smart Mobile Application to Make ASD Children Accustomed to Daily Challenges. In Springer Advances in Intelligent Systems and Computing (pp. 613–625). DOI: 10.1007/978-981-19-7041-2_52

Martelli, M. E., Gigliotti, F., Giovannone, F., Lentini, G., Manti, F., & Sogos, C. (2025). Developmental Patterns in Autism and Other Neurodevelopmental Disorders in Preschool Children. *Children (Basel, Switzerland)*, *12*(2), 125. DOI: 10.3390/children12020125 PMID: 40003227

Massiri, A., Ennassiri, H., & Djemila, M. (2023). La réflexivité comme compétence professionnelle pour une formation innovante des enseignants. Dans A. Amsidder, S. Chakouk, & A. Babori (Éds.), Innovation numérique et formation des enseignants (pp. xx–xx). Revue RISE, n°4. Université Ibn Zohr.

Mehta, P., Chillarge, G. R., Sapkal, S. D., Shinde, G. R., & Kshirsagar, P. S. (2023). *Inclusion of Children With Special Needs in the Educational System, Artificial Intelligence (AI)*. IGI Global., DOI: 10.4018/979-8-3693-0378-8.ch007

Porayska-Pomsta, K., Alcorn, A., Avramides, K., Beale, S., Bernardini, S., Foster, M. E., Frauenberger, C., Good, J., Guldberg, K., Keay-Bright, W., Kossyvaki, L., Lemon, O., Mademtzi, M., Menzies, R., Pain, H., Rajendran, G., Waller, A., Wass, S. V., & Smith, T. J. (2018). Blending Human and Artificial Intelligence to Support Autistic Children's Social Communication Skills. *ACM Transactions on Computer-Human Interaction*, *25*(6), 35. DOI: 10.1145/3271484

Ranaweera, K. G., Praneetha, J., De Silva, W., Kempitiya, K. R. B. N., Gamage, I., & Thilakarthna, T. (2023). Personalized and Interactive Learning Platform for Students with Autism Spectrum Disorder. *Proceedings of the International Conference on Advanced Computing*, 828–833. DOI: 10.1109/ICAC60630.2023.10417404

KEY TERMS AND DEFINITIONS

Artificial Intelligence (AI): Artificial intelligence is a group of systems capable of simulating human intelligence: learning, adapting, solving problems. In the field of education, it allows the creation of personalized tools, such as intelligent tutors, to support all learner profiles.

Augmented Reality (AR): Augmented reality enriches the real environment with virtual elements (images, sounds, 3D objects) visible through a screen. It allows for interactive, fun learning experiences adapted to children with special needs, such as those with ASD.

Children With ASD: These are children with Autism Spectrum Disorder, which manifests itself in difficulties in social communication, particular sensory sensitivity and repetitive behaviors. Their education requires personalized approaches, tailored to their specific needs.

Immersive Technologies: These technologies, such as virtual or augmented reality, immerse the student in interactive and multisensory environments. They are especially useful for capturing the attention of children with ASD and allowing them to learn through experience.

Inclusive Education: Inclusive education aims to ensure that all children, regardless of their profile, can learn together in open, accessible and caring environments. It is based on the adaptation of teaching practices to meet the diversity of needs.

Preschool Education: This first stage of the educational pathway aims to promote the overall development of children before they enter primary school. It plays a critical role in the early detection of educational needs and the inclusion of children with developmental disabilities.

Sensory Development: Sensory development is the way a child perceives, processes, and responds to information from their senses, and in autistic children, this development can be atypical, with sometimes intense reactions to certain visual, sound, or tactile stimuli.

Techno-Pedagogical Innovation: Techno-pedagogical innovation refers to the integration of recent technologies into teaching in order to meet the varied needs of students. It helps build engagement, personalization, and inclusion.

Chapter 4

Artificial Intelligence and Digital Health Applications:

Field Study From the Perspective of the Sociology of Health and Disease – Doctors as a Model

Karim Tabaa
https://orcid.org/0009-0000-4066-0087
Faculty of Humanities and Social Sciences, Ibn Tofail University, Kenitra, Morocco

Zoubida Achahboun
Department of Sociology, Ibn Tofail University, Kenitra, Morocco

ABSTRACT

This study deals with uncovering the increasing role of artificial intelligence in the medical field with special attention to its applications and how doctors benefit from it. The study used the descriptive method on a random sample of 50 doctors, and collected the study data on the questionnaire technique. In the end, the study concluded that artificial intelligence receives great attention in medical affairs and has a high impact on doctors through medical awareness, professional development, and medical diagnosis. At the conclusion of the study, it was emphasised that artificial intelligence does not replace doctors, but rather is an auxiliary tool that can develop their capabilities and improve the quality of medical care offered to patients. However, the study emphasises the need to maintain human and ethical oversight in the use of these technologies to ensure the protection and fairness of patients.

DOI: 10.4018/979-8-3373-3436-3.ch004

1. ARTIFICIAL INTELLIGENCE IN MEDICAL PRACTICE: AN INTRODUCTION TO UNDERSTANDING DIGITAL TRANSFORMATION

The digital transformation over the past decades has brought about profound shifts in the patterns of society to the point that most events have a digital dimension, and artificial intelligence (AI) is at the centre of this process, although it is not a new practical field in achieving difficult mental and cognitive operations, which until recently was the exclusive domain of man, but the recent developments have made it an integral part of daily life, which has changed the way of work and communication with the world, and as artificial intelligence continues its progress and development, it has become an indispensable force in most fields, especially in the field of health care.

Diagnosing and treating diseases has always been the role of doctors. Today, this role is gradually disappearing or in a gradual decline of medical tasks due to the artificial intelligence revolution, which has stripped medicine of all its human characteristics, and reliance on high-tech equipment has increased over time. This has provided doctors and health actors with favourable opportunities to overcome obstacles and achieve technological innovation, which has allowed for a paradigm shift in clinical practice that has reshaped the way patients are diagnosed and treated, optimising health services and treatment plans, anticipating their course, developing medicines, and monitoring and caring for the patient through algorithms, machine learning and deep learning technologies.

In addition, patients encounter a bewildering variety of digital methods to communicate with medical providers and obtain information about healthcare issues. Through these tools, knowledge is transferred and disseminated in an awareness-raising and preventive form, with the aim of reaching as many segments of society as possible, although they sometimes collide with "Cultural deposits" that manifest themselves in the form of traditional remedies and self-treatment experiences, and this phenomenon results in a loss of awareness of the danger of these irrational practices that enter the therapeutic lexicon. Moreover, it provides answers to questions that seem embarrassing to some patients, and answers to rumours about "Taboo" diseases or those who suffer from discrimination and social stigmatisation of health due to the pressures of the dominant cultural community. In addition, sharing health guidance information from doctors that helps patients and healthy people to live a healthy lifestyle, to make informed decisions about individual patient care, and to help them prevent diseases in a codified way through the optimal and rational use of smart health tools that can benefit the career path of doctors.

Although artificial intelligence opens up promising prospects in the fields of innovation, productivity, and solving health challenges, it redraws possible boundaries and raises significant risks, raising ethical, legal, and social questions, especially with regard to the destruction of human relations between doctor and patient, thus contributing to the loss of the innate personal human touch that has a psychological and social role in providing health care to the patient. In addition, the protection of data and patient rights and the impact on the field of work and the general structure of health institutions.

From this perspective, this paper seeks to review the role of artificial intelligence at the level of health care, for a field study from the perspective of the sociology of health and illness, taking doctors as a model for this scientific study.

This paper is intended to answer the following question:

Have artificial intelligence applications been able to benefit doctors at the healthcare level ?

1.1 Hypotheses

Based on the research question, the hypotheses that the research attempts to investigate are formulated as follows:

There is a positive correlation between the use of artificial intelligence application and medical education.

There is a positive correlation between the use of artificial intelligence application and professional development.

There is a positive correlation between the use of artificial intelligence application and medical diagnosis.

1.2 Reasons for Choosing the Topic

After putting forward the hypotheses, the reasons for choosing a topic that was a response to several reasons, most notably:

- The volume of research carried out on the subject of medicine and artificial intelligence, or it can be said that it is scarce, few or nonexistent, and the lack of relevance to special needs at the local level, despite the wide recognition of the importance of the ''Social'', sociology is still underrepresented in the issue (Joyce & Cruz, 2024, p. 2), and with the growing disconnect, it represents a missed opportunity to address the complex social ills that affect the health system and its functioning and progress, which opens the way to examine how gaps emerge in the context of medical practice, and the emergence of an urgent need for critical insights or Pierre Bourdieu's ''Reflexivity'' to examine the imperialism between the interaction of smart technology with the processes that occur in the social reality of health and illness.

- In the face of the growing stakes posed by the topic of technological transformation, the emergence of a set of fundamental mutations that affected the social body, and the emergence of approaches that seek to stimulate innovation and others that aim to regulate use, which brought about radical transformations in the healthcare sector that changed the system of interaction between human and machine in a rapidly changing world, thanks to the huge potential of artificial intelligence and the adoption and implementation of its technologies on human health, it requires a careful study of the social repercussions associated with its use on the processes of diagnosis, treatment, prevention and prediction. This calls for a careful study of the social implications associated with its use on the processes of diagnosis, therapy, prevention and prediction of diseases, which makes it an important topic for sociological discussion to measure the quality and effectiveness of health care, and the extent of its penetration into the patterns of society to extend its impact to the professional performance of health workers, the organisational structure of health institutions and the relationships built between the doctor and the patient.
- The topic deals with an important group of society, namely "Doctors" and their role in legitimising the diagnosis and causes of disease and its treatment, given that the doctor's profession is characterised by a set of characteristics and features as defined by Talcott Parsons of universality, specificity, functionality, emotional neutrality and difference from other professional roles (Parsons, 1951a, p. 435). Equally important, the study deals with the variables of health, illness and medicine that constitute the first building blocks of society and all programmes and concerns concerned with development. The transformation of the health system into a digital service system is one of the priorities of public policies, and this transition brought with it changes in the professional identity of doctors that allowed reconfiguring the hierarchy in health institutions, especially with the emergence of the artificial intelligence revolution, which became a talk in medicine not only a technical discussion but a reflection of structural fluctuations and conflicts between science, technology and society, these aspects require it to understand social and cultural conditions and economic conditions that shape doctors' reactions to machine intelligence, whether positive or critical.

1.3 The Importance of the Study

Based on the reasons for choosing the topic, the importance of the research is evident in highlighting a set of important points that can contribute to achieving the objectives of the study and answering its issues, including:

- Revealing the nature of the intersection of artificial intelligence applications in the healthcare sector from the perspective of doctors, where its technologies have come to occupy a central place in the dynamics of digital health transformation and the spaces of clinics and hospitals are expanding day by day, in which many doctors and patients are exposed to "Cyborg" interactions between human and machine that penetrate the body and physiology of patients (In Ho Han et al., 2024, p.870), and have moved from the virtual world to the operating room and medical diagnosis, and imposed themselves in giving critical results that determine the patient's condition. They have exploited the gap in human resources as there is a widespread shortage of doctors locally, which has contributed to the delegation of tasks to smart tools and systems. Artificial intelligence systems are steadily reaching levels of sophistication and complexity that humans may be completely dependent on them in the near future. The results of the citizens consultation show that the contribution of artificial intelligence in the health sector is about 56.7% after education and public services, compared to other services such as cybersecurity, telecommunications, media and communication, which benefit from 19.5% (CESE, 2025, p. 16).
- Artificial intelligence is a technological revolution that is redrawing the boundaries of what is possible in many fields, whether economic, social, cultural or environmental. The adoption of artificial intelligence technologies in Morocco, with an annual growth of 15 per cent since 2018, positions the country as an emerging leader in Africa in this field, the integration of artificial intelligence into the Moroccan healthcare system presents an opportunity to address some of the challenges related to the shortage of health professionals, geographical disparities in access to care, and the need to improve the quality and reduce medical isolation, especially within marginalised geographical contexts (Haraké, 2025, p. 7). While artificial intelligence opens up promising prospects in the fields of innovation, health, medicine, productivity, and addressing the challenges of epidemics and volatile health crises, its ability to analyse large amounts of data such as medical records, case files of beneficiaries of health support programmes, social assistance, or health coverage enables forward-looking analyses. On the other hand, it raises significant risks that threaten the human being, and the widespread adoption of artificial intelligence technology beyond what is customary raises ethical, legal and social questions about the legitimacy of its use, especially with regard to the protection of personal data and the impact on the professional field of medicine.
- This study seeks to emphasize the importance of the topic in identifying the advantages, benefits, disadvantages or potential risks in the comprehensive-

ness and continuity of the use of smart applications in health care, and the extent to which this is reflected in the behaviours of patients and health actors on the ground, as well as identifying how the process of employing smart media in managing the risks of diseases, popular epidemiology and all health disorders, and how to better prepare for them before they appear, and identify appropriate interventions that can help specialists to improve patient care.

1.4 Objectives of the Study

The objectives of the research stem from the importance of the topic and seek to transform this importance into clear goals and practical means that contribute to enriching the desired benefit:

- The aim of this study is to move from a biomedical approach to a biopsychosocial approach, diagnosing the health and medical reality through the portal of digitisation and its modern applications such as artificial intelligence, virtual reality, internet of things, big data... as an individual and collective experience at the same time, focusing on disease pathways and individual patient interactions.
- Monitoring the degree of public health awareness among different social groups, nurses and patients, especially doctors, in terms of the use and impact of the introduction of artificial intelligence applications on communication dynamics and knowledge authority in the medical field, analysing the sources of information of these smart innovations and the extent of their accuracy and validity and using them to enhance health awareness, studying how users (medical staff/patients) interact with the information that leads them to adopt the health recommendations provided, decoding the cultural code of artificial intelligence and evoking the socio-cultural factors that were the cause of acceptance or rejection of the use of artificial intelligence applications in shaping the public discourse, and building social concepts of health and illness through experiences, expertise and perceptions in the actual cultural context.
- Identify where the capabilities of artificial intelligence framing the dynamics of work environment development within healthcare organisations is manifested in the automation of routine administrative tasks, resource management, improved appointment scheduling, test results, doctor workflow, and faster processing of work requests. In addition to this, measuring smart bureaucracy that is based on formal rules, regulations and laws that exclude the personal and emotional relationships of the members of the organisation. On the other hand, knowing the level of technological literacy of doctors in using these technologies to increase productivity and reduce effort, time and med-

ical errors, and assessing whether these smart tools contribute to enabling doctors to make more appropriate decisions, or whether they create new barriers and hinder the therapeutic process excessively.

- Medical diagnosis is an important measure to improve the rate of patient recovery and ensure the improvement of health status. However, thanks to artificial intelligence, collaboration has become possible, raising a number of questions that require scientific debate from the point of view of anticipating the path of its development and the risks and negative repercussions on people's health. Also, research on the confidence of doctors in the precision and reliability of the tools and the effectiveness of their algorithms in the field of medical treatment, medical education, predicting medical outcomes, diagnostics, medical robotics, medical data management, and others, which raises questions about the acceptance of patients of these machine-generated therapeutic diagnoses, which refers us to monitor the changes that have occurred in the medical profession and the usual roles, and the extent to which the human side of healthcare may be declining.

1.5 Concepts of the Study

Based on the set objectives, it is necessary to define some of the key concepts underlying the study, to ensure a specific understanding of the subject matter and the theoretical framework of the study:

- Artificial Intelligence (AI): Refers to the simulation of the human mind and the way it works, and understanding its nature through computer systems to imitate human cognitive functions, where algorithms coded in technology can learn from data so that they can perform automated tasks, is called everything that works autonomously without human intervention, without humans having to explicitly program each step of the process, and holds the promise of providing a final solution to the stubborn problems in the philosophy of the human mind and behaviour and the cognitive abilities it possesses (Bloomfield, 1988, p. 22).

Artificial Intelligence can find patterns that humans may ignore by analysing huge amounts of data, such as thinking, learning, problem solving, natural language processing, speech, image and pattern recognition, decision-making, planning... .The field of artificial intelligence is a newcomer that intersects with computer science, mathematics, neuroscience, psychology, sociology, philosophy and other scientific fields that aim to arrange intelligent behaviour in machines. Some of the most important aspects of artificial intelligence are: Algorithms, deep learning, artificial neural network, machine learning (McCarthy, 2007, p. 2).

The foundations for the creation of intelligent machines date back to the 1940s through the pioneering research of Alan Turing (Muggleton, 2014, p. 3). Since then, scientific and technological achievements in this field, especially through the development of the first computers, have contributed to fuelling the idea of intelligent machines, and contributed to the emergence of the term artificial intelligence in 1956, when researcher John McCarthy proposed the term "Artificial Intelligence" during a scientific conference in Dartmouth, USA. Since then, artificial intelligence has evolved according to advances in algorithms and the power of computing resources (McCarthy et al., 2006, p. 13).

- Health: As defined by the World Health Organisation, health is a state of complete physical, mental and social well-being, not merely the absence of disease or infirmity, and the enjoyment of the highest attainable standard of health is one of the fundamental rights of every human being without distinction as to race, religion, creed, politics, economic or social status (WHO, 1946, p. 1).

This definition shows that WHO recognises that health does not only mean freedom from disease but also includes a state of physical, psychological and social wholeness or well-being, and makes health a comprehensive system and a human right without discrimination, and that health is a criterion that determines the efficiency of human societies. The promotion of justice and equity in health has always been at the heart of the international and national community's concerns in recognition of the principle of health for all.

Talcott Parsons is regarded as one of the first sociologists to address the topic of health in his book « The Social System » published in 1951. In the tenth chapter of the book, he talks about what he calls "The sick role", from which he defines health from a functional perspective as a state of balance and as a condition of social stability, the ability to perform normal social roles in a way that falls within the parameters of the social system, adaptation to social requirements, and personal compatibility (Parsons, 1951b, p. 429).

- Digital health: Often known as telemedicine, or virtual medicine. It is a type of technological introduction to clinical practice. From the development of new health services, medicines and medical devices to their use by patients and consumers for treatment, diagnosis, prevention, disease management and monitoring, technology uses digital connectivity to improve patient care and pharmaceutical solutions. Many patients use digital technologies to search for health information, purchase prescription medicines, video, voice or email communication with health service providers and use wearable devices, enabling healthcare to be delivered in a virtual, digital environment that is different from the physical reality of health institutions, provided that its relevance is based on delivering clinical value that supports all health sector needs.

1.6 Epistemological Fields

After defining the basic concepts of the study, some fields of knowledge, whether related to the topic or in contact with it, are drawn upon in order to place these concepts in their comprehensive academic framework, and among the selected fields are: Medical Sociology and Hospital Sociology.

1.6. 1 Medical Sociology

Before diving into the field definition of this science, it is necessary to differentiate the confusion in the two terms between sociology of medicine and sociology in medicine, there is a difference in terms of meaning, role and function, the first studies medicine as a behavioural pattern (habits, traditions, rituals, beliefs ....), and its interest in a set of topics such as (social construction) and role relationships, and the social construction of disease diagnosis is a central organising theme in medical sociology, by studying how disease is socially constructed (Brown, 1995, p. 34). The second is concerned with the mutual influence between society, the individual, the body and the disease it produces, and the interactive research, methodological and theoretical principles between sociology and medicine and its context, and the integration of concepts, methods and issues related to medical practice (Nettleton, 2006, pp. 203-233).

If sociology studies social structure, and medicine focuses on health and disease issues, the branch of medical sociology represents the link between the social and medical fields, that is, it deals with the relationship between health and disease in terms of studying issues related to social, cultural, economic, digital and administrative systems, as well as the interaction between medical authority and its reflection on patients aimed at maintaining health and resisting disease.

Medical sociology emerged in both Europe and the United States as a branch of sociology in the post-Word War II period, although the actual beginning dates back to the second half of the nineteenth century, when a group of social researchers tended to study the social dimensions associated with health and illness, after being limited to specialists in the field of medical sciences, and medical sociology represents the common areas of medicine and sociology on the one hand and the field of applied research on the other. Participatory co-operation between doctors and sociologists has played its role in adopting the approach of medical science and penetrating its field to complete the road (Levine, 1987, pp. 1-4), hence (David Mechanic) defines medical sociology as, "A set of efforts that aspire to develop sociological ideas within the context of medical contexts, and to study important practical issues related to disease processes and patient care " (Mechanic, 1978a, p. 516).

In general, medical sociology can be considered the sociological study of the issues of medicine, health, illness and patients, and attention to their variables and complex concepts, and the analysis of the cultural elements spread in society in the form of values, laws, traditions, customs, norms, attitudes and lifestyles ..., which differ from one individual to another about health, illness, prevention and treatment. Including, examining the patient's relationship with medical public forces and treatment institutions.

1.6.2 Hospital Sociology

Hospital sociology is a specialised discipline within general sociology that undertakes a sociological study of the various interactions that take place within hospital settings as institutions that are important for community care and not just physical buildings (Stewart, 2019, p. 1265), and their impact on doctors, patients, nurses and staff in general. This field develops an understanding of the social aspects that influence the process of diagnosis, treatment and health care within the hospital, which is a complex environment in which people from diverse backgrounds interact as a cultural fabric (Mechanic, 1978b, p. 369).

The field of hospital sociology studies the organisational hierarchy of a medical facility, including the human-social bonds between doctors, nurses, patients and other actors, the internal competition between medical specialties and the division of labour, power and decision-making within the hospital. On the other hand, when there are homogeneous exchanges at the level of relationships and modes of action, there is an opportunity to create a collaborative mechanism for integrative engagement within the medical care team, which can lead to better patient outcomes and an acceptable level of quality of care (Coiera et al., 2002, p. 418). Conversely, a lack of understanding and ineffective communication can create dysfunction within the pathway and can have detrimental effects on patient experiences and overall health outcomes (Ghaffari, 2024, pp. 409-410), thus the primary aim of this domain is to prioritise the promotion of social communication and human interaction between the core of the group in healthcare.

Therefore, the field of hospital sociology offers insights and scientific value that enable researchers and specialists to understand the dynamics of social interactions that occur within hospital facilities and their wider impact on the health services provided to the community, through the diagnosis and exploration of social factors, which will enable the level of health care and create a more positive institutional environment for patients, staff and society in general.

1.7 Theories Explaining the Study

1.7.1 Media System Dependency

Media system dependency theory, developed by Sandra Ball-Rokeach and Melvin Defleur, is a theoretical model that arose as an extension of uses and gratifications theory, and proposed a more complex relationship between media content, social dynamics and audience behaviour rather than simply exploring individual media usage trends.

Media dependency theory is concerned with monitoring and studying the effects of media on both the individual and society, who rely on the media resources of media systems to achieve their goals of collecting, processing and disseminating information sources, including explaining the effects and dynamics of how media interact in different social contexts on emerging media environments that are more innovative, pervasive and interactive with audiences. The theory also enables it to explain what individuals do to achieve their goals and survive and expand in a media environment that depends on new media of information resources shaped by the development of more intelligent technologies than the old ones (Ball-Rokeach & DeFleur, 1976, pp. 3-10).

Media dependence theory posits that audiences use media to build social networks, access information and fulfil specific needs (Wangqu et al., 2024, p. 1), where the stronger the degree of an individual's needs for these goals, the greater the dependence, and the greater the central role that media (information systems) play in fulfilling these needs, especially in times of social change. The greater the reliance, the greater the impact on the individual's knowledge and behaviour.

This theory includes some elements whose basic ideas can be applied to analysing the relationship between actors (doctors or patients) and artificial intelligence applications in the medical field, as it helps in knowing why and how patients and doctors rely on artificial intelligence systems' information sources to meet specific needs in a medical context and societal dynamics, when multiple media options are available, as demonstrated during the COVID-19 pandemic (Ouajid, 2024, p. 4), when individuals increasingly turned to these technologies for informational support and guidance in the midst of uncertainty in decision-making processes.

1.7.2 Theories of Organisations

1.7.2.1 Human Relations Theory

The school emerged in the United States before the Second World War, drawing its roots from the ideas of Hawthorne studies conducted in Chicago. The theory seeks to understand the reasons related to workers dissatisfaction with work and the desire to reduce the importance of the role of economic motives within the workplace, emphasising the logic of feelings that govern workers' behaviour, as feelings are linked to group norms that create an informal structure that may have goals different from those of the formal structure, which are dictated by the logic of management concerned with efficiency (Mayo, 2004, pp. 1-18).

This theory is spearheaded by Elton Mayo and colleagues, who explored the relationship between physical working conditions and productivity and the construction of morale, values, attitudes and norms in influencing work behaviour, attitudes and productivity. This productivity is not only determined by material incentives, it is mainly determined by the informal norm among the work group. This informal organisation is not written on paper, is represented by mutual relationships based on love and hate, exists separate from any clearly expressed social structure, and informal organisation emerges spontaneously and fulfils the function of protecting the group from external interference by management (Sanders, 2021, p. 26).

1.7.2.2 Scientific management theory:

In contrast to the principles of the first approach, this theory is led by Frederick William Taylor and is the contemporary counterpart of the classical management theory (the theory of administrative formation) pioneered by Henri Fayol. The scientific management theory believes that organisations are (formal organisations) rational patterns with specific goals for work behaviour, based on procedures that must be followed by management to achieve organisational efficiency. It focuses on the necessity of achieving the highest degree of division of labour in order to achieve the highest level of productivity and close supervision of tasks, as well as the incentive system that motivates workers to perform their tasks better (Woolf et al., 1912, p. 473). The theory is called the mechanistic model of organisation because it considered the workers in the organisation as machines, viewed workers as units that move mechanically and ignored the human element.

Through these two theories, artificial intelligence seems to be seen as both a formal and informal regulation of doctors' processes, combining the scientific rigour of regulation with the social humanistic depth of the patient.

1.8 The Limits of the Study:

After presenting the theoretical framework that explains the scientific laws of the study, we move on to defining the boundaries of the study that outline the context of the current research, which are manifested in:

- Thematic Limitations: Limited to studying artificial intelligence applications as a model of digital health technology.
- Spatial Limitations: This study was conducted on the Tech-Med Community "Smart Apps" inside and outside the health institutions located in Rabat.
- Temporal limitations: The field study took place from the beginning of February to the end of April 2025.
- Human limitations: A group of doctors working in the urban area of Rabat and users of artificial intelligence in the field of smart medicine.

2. METHODOLOGY USED TO STUDY THE INTERACTION BETWEEN DOCTORS AND ARTIFICIAL INTELLIGENCE TECHNOLOGIES

Based on the nature of the study and its objectives, it was decided to rely on the descriptive approach as it matches the objectives of the study, as it describes the phenomenon from its various parts, providing a comprehensive understanding and interpretation of its various aspects and minute details without changing its intellectual roots, using statistical methods and theories to analyse a comprehensive perception of the reality under study. In relation to this topic concerning the applications of artificial intelligence and its relationship with doctors, it is possible to determine the degree of correlation, trends and patterns within the data and describe the nature of the underlying relationship between its variables.

2.1 Study Population and Sample

The research population includes doctors who work as general practitioners or specialists in all medical specialties that belong to the public and private sector within health institutions and who use artificial intelligence applications of various types and different contents and services in the field of health care, whether in their work or outside the walls of the institution (clinic, hospital, health centre...) and who live in Rabat at the level of the urban area (Radah & Elhia, 2025, p. 7) which was chosen because there is no significant expansion of infrastructure at the level of health centres in the rural area. After direct coordination with male and female doctors and confirming their willingness to participate and answer the study, and observing how they interact with smart media, provided that they have a degree of reliability in answering and the objectivity of their opinions. A simple random sampling method was adopted, which gives every member of the community an equal chance to be included in the sample, and the total number of the sample was about 50 individuals distributed equally between the two sexes, in order to ensure the implementation of the gender approach, and thus the socio-demographic characteristics of the research sample were as shown in the following table:

Table 1. Distribution of the study sample according to socio-demographic characteristics.

	Frequency	Percentage
Age groups		
28-33 years	16	32%
34-39 years old	12	24%
40-45 years	8	16%
46-51 years old	7	14%
52 years and above	7	14%
Employment sector		
Public Sector (Government Health)	20	40%
Private sector (private clinics and hospitals)	20	40%
Military and Security Medicine	3	6%
Medical research and education	6	12%
International Organisations and Humanitarian Work	1	2%
Professional specialization		
Primary Care Physicians (General Medicine)	20	40%
Surgeons	5	10%
Geriatricians	7	14%
Doctors of organic specialities	13	26%
Doctors of diagnostic and preventive specialities	5	10%
Years of experience in the medical field		
2 years	12	24%
5 years	17	34%
10 years	9	18%
15 years	7	14%
20 years and above	5	10%

continued on following page

Table 1. Continued

	Frequency	Percentage
Your level of knowledge about artificial intelligence in the medical field		
Beginner	4	8%
Intermediate	6	12%
Advanced	25	50%
Expert	5	10%
Professional	10	20%

2.2 Research Tool

The study relied on a standard questionnaire to collect data from respondents, due to the suitability and compatibility of the methods with the nature of the study's requirements. The questionnaire consists of sections divided into two parts. The first part includes preliminary data reflecting individual characteristics such as (gender, age groups, employment sector, Professional specialization, years of experience in the medical field, ...). The second part consists of three areas: Medical Awareness, Professional Development, and Medical Diagnosis.

The questionnaire used a 5 Likert Scale that included five levels of response, thus the values of the arithmetic averages obtained by the study were treated as follows:

Table 2. Likert scale 5 for the study themes

Interpretation	Weight	Mean Range	length of the period	level
Strongly Disagree	1	1.00 to 1.80	0.80	Low
Disagree	2	1.81 to 2.60	0.79	
Neutral	3	2.61 to 3.40	0.79	Medium
Agree	4	3.41 to 4.20	0.79	High
Strongly Agree	5	4.21 to 5.00	0.79	

The research tool was subjected to two types of testing: first, validity (apparent validity from the judges, validity of the structural consistency of the questionnaire axes), then its reliability was measured by extracting the reliability coefficient (Cronbach's Alpha) on the study sample paragraphs, as shown below:

Table 3. Alpha Cronbach's coefficients to measure the stability of the study tool

Number	Themes of the study	Number of items	Value of Stability Coefficients (Cronbach's Alpha)
1	Medical Awareness	8	0.862
2	Professional Development	8	0.730
3	Medical Diagnostics	8	0.863
Overall stability of the questionnaire		24	0.940

It was found that the total stability coefficient value for the 24 items of the questionnaire was 0.940, which is high, and its internal consistency was confirmed, making it applicable to the entire sample.

2.3 Statistical Methods Used

The Statistical Package for the Social Sciences (SPSS) and Microsoft Excel were used to process and analyse the data and use a range of statistical methods within the digital programmes: (Percentages, Frequencies, Arithmetic means, Standard deviations, Pearson's correlation coefficient, Cronbach's alpha coefficient ...)

3. RESULTS OF A CASE STUDY ON THE APPLICATION OF ARTIFICIAL INTELLIGENCE IN MEDICAL EMPOWERMENT

The transition to the next section deals with the presentation and analysis of the study results, with verification of the validity of the hypotheses put forward.

3.1 Presentation of Study Findings

In presenting the findings, two sections of the results are reviewed: usage patterns and then the themes of the study.

3.1.1 Patterns of Digital Use

Table 4. Distribution of respondents according to the use of artificial intelligence applications in medical care.

Percentage %	Frequency	Artificial Intelligence Applications
14%	7	Chatbots
26%	13	Wearable Sensors
18%	9	Smart robots
30%	15	Digital platforms
12%	6	Virtual or Augmented Reality
100%	50	Total

It can be seen from the table above that the use of artificial intelligence in medicine varies widely across the sample, with 30% of doctors preferring to use digital platforms more than other medical care applications, which is the highest percentage among all categories with a slight difference with wearable sensors, indicating that the simulation of intelligent systems is prominent in medical environments.

Table 5. Distribution of respondents according to the areas of use of artificial intelligence applications in medical care.

Percentage %	Frequency	Areas of use of artificial intelligence
12%	6	Administrative Management of Medical Practices
26%	13	Medical Research and Informatics
20%	10	Patient Health Records
32%	16	Digital Content Creation
10%	5	Patient medical support and health monitoring
100%	50	Total

It is clear from the results shown in Table (5) that the majority of doctors are inclined to the field of digital content creation, with 16 respondents (32%), which refers to the resort of some of them to publish and distribute contents with a knowledge dimension, while considering smart applications as a tool for managing health behaviours in the form of communication and interaction channels that come from the virtual doctor in the form of a digital clinic.

Table 6. Distribution of respondents according to the services of artificial intelligence applications in medical care.

Percentage %	Frequency	Artificial Intelligence Application Services
14%	7	Therapeutic development and drug discovery
24%	12	Communication between patients and healthcare providers
28%	14	Personalisation of treatment plans
12%	6	Analysing health data
22%	11	Predicting health risks and disease progression
100%	50	Total

From the data shown in Table (6), it is clear that doctors seek to tailor treatment plans for each patient based on the situation presented by 28%. By a margin of four percentage points, doctors favour communication between the patient and the healthcare provider.

3.1.2 Themes of the Study

Table 7. Axis of the use of artificial intelligence applications and medical awareness

No.	Paragraphs	Arithmetic mean	Standard Deviation	Degree	Rank
1	I see AI as useful in the process of continuing medical education, simulation-based clinical training and virtual reality environments.	3.94	1.268	Agree	2
2	Innovative artificial intelligence technologies help guide, counsel and answer patient queries.	3.24	1.117	Neutral	5
3	It offers better-than-human advice and facilitates the effective delivery of information.	3.06	1.077	Neutral	7
4	AI technologies provide up-to-date, evidence-based cultural information.	3.82	1.101	Agree	4
5	AI has a role to play in combating and warning against false or misleading information and conventional treatments.	3.18	1.207	Neutral	6
6	Artificial intelligence has helped me access the latest scientific studies, research insights, and the latest developments and discoveries in the medical arena: Videos, medical conferences, scientific papers and books.	4.46	0.788	Strongly agree	1
7	Do you think that these apps can be used by doctors in the field of patient education?	3.90	0.995	Agree	3
8	Can a patient use artificial intelligence for treatment awareness and diagnosis?	2.10	1.282	Disagree	8
The first axis: Medical Awareness		3.4625	1.104	Agree	

Table (7) shows the responses of the study participants on the first axis (the use of AI applications and medical awareness), which consists of about 8 paragraphs, where the first rank came in paragraph (6), which states: 'It benefited me to access the latest scientific studies and research insights and the latest developments and discoveries in the medical arena: Videos, medical conferences, scientific papers and books). With a standard deviation of 0.788 and an arithmetic mean of 4.46, with a total of strongly agree out of 50 items, on the contrary, the last place went to the statement (Can the patient use artificial intelligence in the field of education related to treatment and diagnosis of his health condition) With a standard deviation value of 1.282 and an arithmetic mean value of 2.10, which corresponds to a degree of disagreement in the five-point Likert scale shown earlier in Table 2, it also shows that the weighted arithmetic mean of the axis as a whole reached a value of 3.46 with a standard deviation of 1.104, which corresponds to a degree of agreement, i.e. the level of using artificial intelligence applications and medical awareness is considered high.

Table 8. Axis of utilisation of artificial intelligence applications and professional development

No.	Paragraphs	Arithmetic mean	Standard Deviation	Degree	Rank
1	Can artificial intelligence provide psychosocial support to doctors?	3.16	1.583	Neutral	7
2	AI allows me to disconnect from my social reality and focus on my daily tasks.	3.14	1.370	Neutral	8
3	Artificial intelligence reduces effort and gains more time in treatment processes and health protocols.	3.98	1.040	Agree	2
4	Artificial intelligence applications help to save costs or economic costs.	3.32	1.168	Neutral	4

continued on following page

Table 8. Continued

No.	Paragraphs	Arithmetic mean	Standard Deviation	Degree	Rank
5	AI applications optimise the work environment with rapid streamlining of administrative tasks and reduced job burnout.	3.26	1.242	Neutral	5
6	Schedule appointments, preventive reminders, alerts, patient follow-ups and optimise the management of the clinic's logistical resources.	3.22	1.418	Neutral	6
7	Provides artificial intelligence tools that help physicians improve medical care and optimise their processes to ensure maximum efficiency and deliver individualised, personalised care to all patients.	3.36	1.174	Neutral	3
8	AI applications help in analysing and evaluating medical research data and making health decisions quickly.	4.00	1.340	Agree	1
The second axis: Professional Development		3.43	1.291	Agree	

Table (8) shows the responses for the second axis (use of AI applications and professional development), where the first rank came in the first place for paragraph No. (8) which states (helps in analysing and evaluating medical research data and making health decisions quickly). With a standard deviation of 1.340 and an arithmetic mean of 4.00 with a total score of agree, while the phrase (It allows me to facilitate my social reality and devote myself to my daily tasks.) ranked last with a standard deviation of 1.370 and a mean of 3.14, which corresponds to a neutral score on the five-point Likert scale, while the weighted arithmetic mean of the axis as a whole reached a value of 3.43 with a standard deviation of 1.291, which corresponds to an agreeable score, meaning that the level of using artificial intelligence applications on professional development is considered high.

Table 9. Axis of utilisation of artificial intelligence applications and Medical Diagnostics

No.	Paragraphs	Arithmetic mean	Standard Deviation	Degree	Rank
1	AI does not apply its diagnostic techniques to all diseases and everything related to medicine.	4.26	1.065	Strongly agree	1
2	Can artificial intelligence diagnose and address the challenges of psychosocial diseases.	2.60	0.948	Disagree	8
3	AI-powered medical machines diagnose accurately and quickly, compared to traditional methods.	4.02	1.253	Agree	2
4	Can artificial intelligence be used to predict and estimate the risk of diseases and potential complications	3.86	1.278	Agree	4
5	Do you think AI is capable of interpreting and reading lab analyses medically....: Analyse medical images, such as MRI or X-ray images, diagnose and predict difficult medical conditions such as cancerous tumours, retinal diseases, pneumonia, etc.	3.96	1.009	Agree	3
6	AI applications reduce the rates of medical errors and human lapses because they are well-screened and efficiently recognised.	3.02	1.220	Neutral	6
7	In the shadow of artificial intelligence, does over-reliance on smart technology lead to the disappearance of the human and social dimension and the moral bias of the doctor.	3.04	1.049	Neutral	5
8	In your opinion, can AI applications replace medical practitioners.	2.94	1.058	Neutral	7
The third axis: medical diagnosis		3.462	1.11	Agree	

The results of Table (9) show the results of the patients' answers related to the third axis on the use of artificial intelligence applications and medical diagnostics, and the result showed that statement (1), which states (Artificial intelligence is not applied to all diseases and everything related to medicine.) On the other hand, statement No. (2), which states (Can artificial intelligence diagnose diseases of a psychological and social nature that affect the disease and address its challenges.) Ranked last with a mean value of 4.26 and a standard deviation of 1.065. As for the value of the weighted arithmetic mean of the axis as a whole, its value reached about 3.462 with a standard deviation of 1.11, which corresponds to a degree of agreement, which means that the level of use of artificial intelligence applications on medical diagnosis is also considered high.

3.2 Testing and Validating the Study's Hypotheses

Table 10. Correlation coefficients (r) values between the use of artificial intelligence and the three axes according to the study variables.

Medical Awareness	Professional Development	Medical Diagnostics	Variables
0.716 **	0.536 **	0.651 **	Professional specialization
0.638 **	0.514 **	0.513 **	Artificial Intelligence Applications
0.630 **	0.652 **	0.693 **	Areas of use of artificial intelligence
0.549 **	0.485 **	0.653 **	Artificial Intelligence Application Services

Note: (**): Correlation is statistically significant at 0.01 level.

Table (10) shows the hypothesis testing and the values of correlation coefficients (r) for the relationship between the variables of the study, through which it was found that there is a positive, direct relationship with varying degrees of proximity and distance.

4. DISCUSS AND INTERPRET THE STUDY AND HIGHLIGHT THE ETHICAL AND PROFESSIONAL CHALLENGES OF USING ARTIFICIAL INTELLIGENCE

The results of the study indicate a diversity in the use of artificial intelligence applications by doctors for health and medical purposes, moving from traditional models of care to more sophisticated, innovative, and pervasive methods. This technological integration into the medical sector is a significant change that is growing by leaps and bounds, and requires an understanding that goes beyond its technical implications to the social, cultural, and professional. This analysis seeks to explore how artificial intelligence is reconstructing new roles for doctors, and its impact on work structure changes and social relations in the health organisation.

From the data obtained, it was found that use of artificial intelligence is not limited to one type of medical specialisation in terms of practical, professional and technical expertise, but includes different types of specialisations according to different cognitive experiences, each doctor having specific goals for interactive professional practice with patients and meeting their needs. Consequently, medical professionals approach artificial intelligence systems in different ways at different career stages, resulting in unequal categories in terms of AI-based virtual medicine. Doctors with different levels of expertise may see themselves working in a synergistic and integrated manner with intelligent systems and their evolution, based on seniority, raising concerns about the autonomy of doctors in making clinical decisions.

As for artificial intelligence applications, it is noted that they are among the aids to the medical services provided by patients. Digital platforms, wearable sensors, smart robots and other innovative applications are the most responsive to the sample, they benefit from them and enable them to achieve interactions based on machine learning algorithms, processing and transferring physiological data by translating the inputted data or indicators, as artificial intelligence can read training data and send predictive alerts that enable doctors to monitor the patient's condition in case of critical changes and early detection of the patient's condition. It also helps doctors gain a new experience that simplifies the complex bureaucratic procedures around clinical decision support processes compared to traditional methods.

In terms of the use of artificial intelligence in various medical fields, digital content creation using digital communication networks was found to be more popular among doctors, as their work continues outside the walls of the health institution to give health education, follow-up or medical examination remotely through videos, photos and articles targeting patients to prevent diseases and answer their own queries, as we often find some diseases that are difficult to mention in society or "hidden diseases" circulating through the virtual world, raised by patients in complete confidentiality between the two parties, and can also be used as a tool to stop the spread of misinformation.

Artificial intelligence allows doctors to access vast amounts of information sources and extensive medical research that helps doctors in the results of the development of diseases, explore the latest medical discoveries and contribute to their dissemination through communication networks under common goals, this would develop professional relations and scientific research in the medical field, as a doctor is not a professional by his university degree but by his research experience, social skills and knowledge capabilities that he continuously develops in the field of research medicine. In addition, artificial intelligence applications use the administrative organisation of data, electronic health records, laboratory results and medical examinations of patients instead of using paper, linking the patient system with medical staff and medical monitoring equipment through multifunctional networks.

As for artificial intelligence services in healthcare, there has been a wide variety, the most important of which are the customisation of treatment plans and communication between patients and healthcare providers through patient data available on their mobile devices. Their health status and lifestyle can be monitored, and treatment plans can be provided for them specific to their diet, sleep hours, and exercise. Communication with them can be established to customise treatment plans, schedule appointments electronically, remind them to comply with the necessary instructions, and report urgent and emergency cases.

Regarding the results related to the three axes, the results of the study showed that most doctors believe that artificial intelligence helps them in providing health education, but the health practices of patients in this aspect are sometimes characterised by a large number of traditional practices and negative experiences that are included in the dictionary of alternative medicine, such as resorting to traditional medicine or healers who are termed "doctors without a suit" who delude patients about the effectiveness of their treatment, such as scholars who write amulets and talismans or herbal medicine, natural mixtures, magic and sorcery, etc. These practices are believed to be correct and effective on their body, as we often find that these actions are controlled by the "cultural deposits" that dominate the human subconscious, as from birth, the popular imagination is transmitted from one generation to another through the process of cultural inheritance as part of the process of life.

On the other hand, he believes that smart applications are more popular in the process of professional development and improving the work environment, as they contribute to reducing effort, saving time, and saving costs and resources in treatment processes. All of these simplifications allow doctors to have more time and greater benefit in supporting administrative workflows, developing personal skills, streamlining tasks, and improving their efficiency. This is sure to increase the number of treatment and diagnostic cases received by healthcare institutions.

With regard to medical diagnosis, it has been found that machine learning models are capable of interpreting laboratory tests and predicting and assessing the risk of disease, and that medical machines diagnose accurately and quickly compared to traditional methods, helping doctors to speed up the treatment process for diseases such as breast cancer (El Agouri et al., 2022, p. 1) and gastroesophageal reflux disease, atrophic gastritis, gastrointestinal bleeding, oesophageal cancer, ulcerative colitis, colorectal cancer metastases, and skin cancer (Srivastava, 2023, p. 141). There are many tests that can detect and predict its complex condition. Thus, artificial intelligence applications can greatly improve patient healthcare by creating an educational awareness template targeting patients, providing professional medical guidance, diagnosing health conditions, and making more accurate treatment decisions.

Returning to the media adoption theory, it can be applied to the results of this data to analyse, interpret and understand the topic of artificial intelligence applications and doctors in the context of digital health, and found that this technology affects the degree of its adoption and the behavioural practice of medicine, and the interactive relationship and attitudes outside the health institution with patients and the community to achieve clear goals, and the needs that machine intelligence meets from helping in providing health education, improving the work environment and helping in medical diagnosis are all potentials that are achieved according to prescribed processes and medical rules under their awareness of the comparative advantage of innovation provided that it is achieved.

By relying on innovative media in health organisations, it is also possible to rely on scientific management theory (Taylorism) Frederick Winslow Taylor as a model of automated organisation, which is based on a mechanical model of organisation because it considers doctors in the organisation to be machines and units that move automatically, and ignores the human element in the sense that it focuses on formal organisation rather than informal relationships between doctors and patients, ignores human behaviour, and considers humans to be mere machines. On the other hand, the human relations theory, led by Elton Mayo and his colleagues, believes that informal organisation increases productivity, rather than formal organisation, which does not recognise the personal interactions, communications and physical actions observed between members of the mutual group, These include feelings, emotions, affective psychological states, and reducing workers feelings of fatigue and boredom during work. Through these theories, it appears that the automated applications of smart medicine represent a field that experiences conflicts and clashes in terms of how to rely on or fully adopt the means to varying degrees.

The test to examine the study's hypotheses, which measured the relationship between its variables and determined the strength and direction of this relationship by conducting a Pearson correlation coefficient test, showed that all)r(values in the doctors responses were statistically significant at a)p value(calculated to be well below the level of (0.01) This means that the dependent variable is influenced by several variables and not just one, thus confirming the three hypotheses, meaning that there is a direct positive relationship indicating a positive correlation between the use of artificial intelligence applications and digital health, represented by health awareness, professional development and medical diagnosis. where the variable of the field of use artificial intelligence was one of the most closely related variables to the study axes, and to a strong degree compared to the other variables, which varied in degree. Therefore, it can be said that the more artificial intelligence applications are used, the more awareness, work improvement and medical diagnosis increase, This correlation is not a coincidence but rather the result of the development of smart technologies and their impact on the healthcare system and modern medical practice in particular, in multiple ways, whether by assisting medical professionals or accelerating the pace of work, which leads to efficient and accurate decision-making.

Despite the benefits and advantages of artificial intelligence in the medical field, it also involves a number of risks and challenges that should not be overlooked. The smart technology is still at the beginning of experimentation and maturity and needs more training and development within research centres, and the biggest obstacle is that artificial intelligence is absent from state policies and its ineffectiveness in this sector, as well as the limitations of artificial intelligence in some medical topics that science cannot answer (death, infection, treatment of a disease).

On another hand, there are obstacles to convincing doctors to use modern systems due to the lack of standardised technical criteria for electronic medical records. Each medical specialty must choose its own electronic software and computers from different sources, and it is difficult to determine which is best. On an ethical level, there are real risks related to cybersecurity that threaten patient privacy in terms of controlling access to personal health data, which could be misused by companies or doctors for commercial pharmaceutical purposes, given the enormous volume of data collected and held by companies and medical institutions. Traditional medical providers such as doctors, nurses and hospitals face strict regulations regarding the information they are allowed to share with other professionals, while technology companies are not subject to such requirements.

Artificial intelligence also does not guarantee equal access to health interventions, as it is limited to a certain class due to its systems requiring expensive material costs, for example, ''Robot surgery'' is not suitable for the poor class and is expensive in private clinics. In addition, some digital services and simple equipment are not available in state institutions, especially with artificial intelligence, unlike private clinics that have the latest technology.

Artificial intelligence applications may also violate legal rules that seem unacceptable or welcomed in some religions and beliefs, such as in the world of reproductive medicine with regard to the technique of fertilising eggs remotely through a robot in which artificial intelligence has succeeded in performing the fertilisation process through smart technology that assists in reproduction (Mendizabal-Ruiz et al., 2025, p. 2). Moreover, the algorithms of artificial intelligence systems can negatively affect the neutrality and objectivity of transparent, fair and reliable results, and lead to forms of algorithmic bias, ''Gender'' discrimination and class-based fairness that programmers themselves can be the source of this ethical dilemma, thereby targeting human rights principles.

Some studies call for the incorporation of the Ubuntu philosophy into a framework for strengthening the ethical governance of AI-based health research that better aligns with local and African values and context. This framework is based on four key principles: Collaboration, Openness, Harmony and Support, which are aligned with global ethical standards such as Justice, Charity, Transparency and Accountability (Odero et al., 2024, p. 1).

Hence the importance of opening up to multiple disciplines in technical training programmes, including social sciences, in order to better understand and manage the ethical and societal implications of artificial intelligence technology. Otherwise, this irrational approach could lead to the gradual decline of human skills and knowledge. Thus, technical innovations, despite their original goal of developing the health field, can cause a kind of intellectual inertia and inertia, what could be called ''Algorithmic dependency'', which is more likely to occur in health and safety fields, where the decisions made may have serious consequences.

At the professional level, although it develops work and encourages the creation of new jobs, especially in the technological and industrial sectors, it leads to the dehumanisation of the doctor-patient relationship and reduces the doctor's autonomy. This may further affect competencies and achieve a kind of defeat leading to the threat or elimination of some jobs and professions, resulting in unemployment in some tasks and layoffs of medical staff. According to the International Monetary Fund (IMF), artificial intelligence will affect 60 per cent of jobs in economically developed countries, but only 26 per cent in low-income countries. The IMF has warned of the risk of worsening social inequalities at the global level. (Cazzaniga et al., 2024, p. 2)

There is also an impact on environmental protection with the manufacture, use, and disposal of waste materials and technologies associated with health research related to artificial intelligence. This includes the consumption of large amounts of energy to power and cool data centres that store and process data, and this can lead to the redirection of electricity away from domestic use (Owoyemi et al., 2020, p. 3), especially with the impact of global warming forcing the world to conserve energy and natural resources.

In the face of all these facts, two main approaches can be deduced in understanding these transformations. The first approach is based on the idea that artificial intelligence will strengthen and develop human capabilities and help medical professionals to reach greater efficiency and reach the finest services that facilitate the healthcare process, while the second approach expects that blind trust and excessive reliance in the use of artificial intelligence can lead to human compensation, and the doctor will be forced to the decision-making authority and delegated to the machine in a defeated manner.

5. RECOMMENDATIONS AND SUGGESTIONS

Based on this diagnosis, which was shared by its various stakeholders, the call is to pay attention to strategies for the use and development of artificial intelligence that are in line with the ambitions of health actors and the relevance of the impacts of these technological innovations on the health community.

- Artificial intelligence should remain in its role as an assistant and complement, not a substitute and decision maker, and the doctor must master its legitimate use and be in line with digital developments, with the aim of achieving a beneficial balance in career paths and extracting the maximum benefit from these innovative technologies, and the human principle should be at the beginning of its cycle, as any danger or error in their use leads to the destruction of the patient's condition and the crisis of the mutual relationship between man and machine.

- Artificial intelligence does not have the ability to analyse hidden human emotions and complex social and cultural realities, as each society has a different cultural specificity that changes over time and context. In line with the demands of the times and the fluctuating challenges of health crises and pandemics, doctors must realise that digital communication is very different from in-person communication and must make time for questions and social interactions to provide quality patient care, as short visits provide an opportunity for spontaneous questions that reap important information about treatment.
- Integrate medical training in the development of a roadmap required by the potential repercussions of artificial intelligence systematically in medical and pharmacy faculties and other educational institutions, and spread awareness, education, accompaniment and proactive guidance for all health actors, whether doctors, nurses or patients, all workers in the sector, whether public or private, through social dialogue, and encourage their rational use for patients through traditional and official media and digital media.
- Prioritise the development of solutions based on artificial intelligence technologies in the health sector, which is the most important sector besides education, frame its uses and invest its potential in achieving social development, while paying attention to research, innovation and training to create a reservoir of competencies capable of advancing the health sector, which is subject to tidal fluctuations. Improving digital infrastructures and exploiting them for the health sector, from the public to the private sector, while supporting companies and small and medium-sized enterprises dedicated to innovation in the field of artificial intelligence and other advanced digital technologies.
- The need to develop an approach that meets the challenges posed and to work on proactive measures that define the limits of its use that hinder the dynamism of the progress of industrial innovation, enhance administrative governance and promote the ethics of the use of obstetric artificial intelligence that may result in medical concerns and social consequences, and aim to ensure the protection of personal data and the best interest of patients in a responsible manner that takes into account permissible medical standards.

6. CONCLUSION

The research shows that the overall use of artificial intelligence technology is constantly evolving with predictions that are currently difficult to monitor, and although it helps automate difficult and dangerous tasks, it is a black box full of mines whose boundaries are unknowable.

Artificial Intelligence can be a key enabler in the dynamics of medical change, by providing technical solutions that facilitate access to personalized and sustainable health services that take into account patients' social status and personal characteristics. When access to communication infrastructures is ensured, artificial intelligence systems become accessible to all patients, bypassing bureaucratic complexities, geographical barriers, and time and economic constraints, allowing for personalized services according to each patient's individual medical needs, promoting medical inclusion while ensuring increased equity in accessing these health innovations. However, it is currently difficult to quantify the overall impact that artificial intelligence will have on doctors. Studies on the topic have produced mixed results, but all agree that artificial intelligence will play an increasingly important role in reorganizing the physician profession in the future. However, there are still many obstacles that may arise in the future.

In conclusion, solving the puzzle of artificial intelligence and doctors requires an integrated approach that analyzes the intersections of the social, cultural, ethical, moral, value, technical, organizational, legal... dimensions of diagnostic and therapeutic behavior in a way that suits the biological nature of each patient and the physical environment in which he or she lives.

7. REFERENCES

Ball-Rokeach, S. J., & DeFleur, M. L. (1976). A dependency model of mass media effects. *Communication Research, 3*(1), 3–21. DOI: 10.1177/009365027600300101

Bloomfield, B. P. (1988). The Question of artificial intelligence: Philosophical and sociological perspectives. *Choice (Chicago, Ill.), 26*(04), 26–2117. DOI: 10.5860/CHOICE.26-2117

Brown, P. (1995). Naming and framing: The social construction of diagnosis and illness. *Journal of Health and Social Behavior, 35*(Spec No), 34–52. DOI: 10.2307/2626956 PMID: 7560848

. Cazzaniga, M., Jaumotte, F., Li, L., Melina, G., Panton, A. J., Pizzinelli, C., Rockall, E. J., & Tavares, M. M. (2024). *Gen-AI: Artificial intelligence and the future of work* (IMF Staff Discussion Note No. 2024/001). International Monetary Fund. DOI: 10.5089/9798400262548.006

Coiera, E., Jayasuriya, R., Hardy, J. L., Bannan, A. M., & Thorpe, M. E. C. (2002). Communication loads on clinical staff in the emergency department. *The Medical Journal of Australia, 176*(9), 415–418. DOI: 10.5694/j.1326-5377.2002.tb04482.x PMID: 12056992

El Agouri, H., Azizi, M., El Attar, H., El Khannoussi, M., Ibrahimi, A., Kabbaj, R., Kadiri, H., BekarSabein, S., EchCharif, S., Mounjid, C., & El Khannoussi, B. (2022). Assessment of deep learning algorithms to predict histopathological diagnosis of breast cancer: First Moroccan prospective study on a private dataset. *BMC Research Notes, 15*(1), 66. DOI: 10.1186/s13104-022-05936-1 PMID: 35183227

Ghaffari, F. (2024). Hospital Environment and Medical Sociology: User-Centered Environmental Sociology Model based on a Systematic review. HERD *Health Environments Research &. The Design Journal, 17*(3), 395–410. DOI: 10.1177/19375867241237506 PMID: 38468153

Han, I. H., Kim, D. H., Nam, K. H., Lee, J. I., Kim, K.-H., Park, J.-H., & Ahn, H. S.In Ho Han. (2024). Human-robot interaction and social robot: The emerging field of healthcare robotics and current and future perspectives for spinal care. *Neurospine, 21*(3), 868–877. DOI: 10.14245/ns.2448432.216 PMID: 39363467

Joyce, K., & Cruz, T. M. (2024). A sociology of artificial intelligence: Inequalities, power, and data justice. *Socius: Sociological Research for a Dynamic World, 10*(1), 1–6. DOI: 10.1177/23780231241275393

Levine, S. (1987). The changing terrains in medical sociology: Emergent concern with quality of life. *Journal of Health and Social Behavior*, *28*(1), 1–6. DOI: 10.2307/2137136 PMID: 3571904

Mayo, E. (2004). *The human problems of an industrial civilization.* Routledge., DOI: 10.4324/9780203487273

McCarthy, J. (2007, November 12). *What is artificial intelligence?* Stanford University. https://www-formal.stanford.edu/jmc/whatisai.pdf

McCarthy, J. J., Minsky, M., Rochester, N., & Shannon, C. E. (2006). A Proposal for the Dartmouth Summer Research Project on Artificial Intelligence. *AI Magazine*, *27*(4), 12–14. DOI: 10.1609/aimag.v27i4.1904

Mechanic, D. (1978). *Medical sociology* (2nd ed.). The Free Press.

Mendizabal-Ruiz, G., Chavez-Badiola, A., Hernández-Morales, E., Valencia-Murillo, R., Ocegueda-Hernández, V., Costa-Borges, N., Mestres, E., Acacio, M., Matia-Algué, Q., Farías, A. F., Carreon, D. S. M., Barragan, C., Silvestri, G., Martinez-Alvarado, A., Olmedo, L. M. C., Aguilar, A. V., Sánchez-González, D. J., Murray, A., Alikani, M., & Cohen, J. (2025). A digitally controlled, remotely operated ICSI system: Case report of the first live birth. *Reproductive Biomedicine Online*, *50*(5), 104943. Advance online publication. DOI: 10.1016/j.rbmo.2025.104943 PMID: 40210512

Muggleton, S. (2014). Alan Turing and the development of Artificial Intelligence. *AI Communications*, *27*(1), 3–10. DOI: 10.3233/AIC-130579

Nettleton, S. (2006). *The sociology of health and illness* (3rd ed.). Polity.

Odero, B., Nderitu, D., & Samuel, G. (2024). The Ubuntu Way: Ensuring Ethical AI Integration in Health Research. *Wellcome Open Research*, *9*, 625. DOI: 10.12688/wellcomeopenres.23021.1 PMID: 39606617

. Omari Haraké, O. (2025). Artificial intelligence in healthcare in Morocco: Potential, ethical challenges, and responsibility framework. *PM World Journal*, 14(5).

Ouajid, A. (2024). *The Impact of AI and AR in Moroccan Healthcare. Journal Name, Volume* (Issue), Article 465. DOI: 10.34874/PRSM.jidh-vol1iss1.465

Owoyemi, A., Owoyemi, J., Osiyemi, A., & Boyd, A. (2020). Artificial Intelligence for Healthcare in Africa. *Frontiers in Digital Health*, *2*, 6. DOI: 10.3389/fdgth.2020.00006 PMID: 34713019

Parsons, T. (1951). *The social system.* Free Press.

Radah, A., & Elhia, M. (2025). Artificial intelligence and improvement of healthcare provision in Morocco: Challenges and prospects. *Journal of Integrated Studies in Economics, Law, Technical Sciences & Communication, 1*(1), 1–18. https://revues.imist.ma/index.php/JISELSC/article/view/54520

Sanders, E. J. (2021). Mayo, Elton: The Fruitful Legacy of an Intellectual Explorer. In D. B. Szabla (Ed.), *The Palgrave Handbook of Organizational Change Thinkers* (2nd ed., pp. 1047–1066). Springer. DOI: 10.1007/978-3-030-38324-4_17

Srivastava, R. (2023). Applications of artificial intelligence in medicine. *Exploratory Research and Hypothesis in Medicine, 9*(2), 138–146. DOI: 10.14218/ERHM.2023.00048

Stewart, E. (2019). A sociology of public responses to hospital change and closure. *Sociology of Health & Illness, 41*(7), 1251–1269. DOI: 10.1111/1467-9566.12896 PMID: 30963595

Wangqu, J., Xue, Z., & Chen, L. (2024). Media dependency, platform-swinging, and psychological depression among young college students in the polymedia environment. *Scientific Reports, 14*(1), 1–10. DOI: 10.1038/s41598-024-82303-z PMID: 39695274

Woolf, L. S., Taylor, F. W., Scott, W. D., & Goldmark, J. (1912). The principles of scientific management. *Economic Journal (London), 22*(87), 471. DOI: 10.2307/2221959

World Health Organization. (1946). Constitution of the World Health Organization. https://apps.who.int/gb/bd/PDF/bd47/EN/constitution-en.pdf

ADDITIONAL READING

Clarke, A. (2013). *The Sociology of Healthcare*. In Routledge eBooks. DOI: 10.4324/9781315834320

Faulkner, A. (2009). *Medical technology into healthcare and society: A sociology of devices, innovation and governance*. Palgrave Macmillan., DOI: 10.1057/9780230228368

Herzlich, C. (1973). *Health and illness: A social psychological analysis* (Graham, D., Trans.). Academic Press.

Jermsittiparsert, K., & Marzo, R. R. (Eds.). (2025). *AI Technologies and Advancements for Psychological Well-Being and Healthcare*. IGI Global., DOI: 10.4018/979-8-3693-9158-7

. Rubeis, G. (2024). *Ethics of Medical AI* (The International Library of Ethics, Law and Technology, No. 24). Springer-Cham. DOI: 10.1007/978-3-031-55744-6

Spekowius, G., & Wendler, T. (Eds.). (2006). Philips Research Book Series: Vol. 6. *Advances in healthcare technology: Shaping the future of medical care*. Springer Science., DOI: 10.1007/1-4020-4384-8

White, K. N. (2002). *An introduction to the sociology of health and illness* (1st ed.). SAGE Publications., DOI: 10.4135/9781446278956

KEY TERMS AND DEFINITIONS

Alternative Medicine: A set of therapeutic practices that are based on the experiences of others, this type of medicine is not regulated by the medical profession and is therefore not considered part of modern medicine.

Bureaucracy: It is an administrative regulatory framework based on strict and complex rules and procedures that must be followed to ensure productivity, better management of institutions and organisations, efficiency and justice.

Cultural Deposits: Refers to those cultural behaviours and patterns that include inherited customs, traditions and beliefs that originated in a previous time period and were passed on from older generations to new generations through family and social upbringing.

Popular Epidemiology: A concept that refers to the health issues associated with a pandemic crisis and the health practices rooted in grassroots communities that interpret all pandemic events based on public discourses and local perceptions.

Reflexivity: A term introduced by Pierre Bourdieu that represents a key pillar in his intellectual project of what he calls "reflexive sociology". He emphasises that in order to study phenomena, the researcher must overcome prejudices and assumptions that affect the process of analysing the research and obscure a vision of the entire phenomenon.

Social Construction: This is the skeleton of society and its overall organisational framework, which defines and designs how individuals construct their actions and how they interact with institutional systems.

Ubuntu: Refers to a philosophical and ethical concept that originated primarily in sub-Saharan African societies, particularly in Zimbabwe and South Africa. In the health context, Ubuntu places great importance on community and holistic care, meaning that health is the responsibility of the whole community and not just the individual.

Virtual Medicine: It is an umbrella term that refers to digital or e-health based on the delivery of healthcare services remotely within the virtual world using the services of communication technology systems.

Chapter 5
Artificial Intelligence and Nursing Education: Enhancing Teaching, Learning, and Critical Thinking

Nezha Nacer
https://orcid.org/0000-0002-2930-4943
Institut Supérieur des Professions Infirmières et Techniques de Santé, Essaouira, Morocco

Jaouad Chouikh
Institut Supérieur des Professions Infirmières et Techniques de Santé, Essaouira, Morocco

Khadija Nacer
CHU Mohammed VI, Marrakech, Morocco

ABSTRACT

The development of artificial intelligence (AI) is becoming increasingly important. As the healthcare field evolves and becomes more complex, nursing education must also transform to keep pace with this changing landscape. The integration of AI into nursing training represents a significant advancement in how healthcare professionals are educated, with the primary goal of improving teaching, learning, and critical thinking among students. Realistic AI-powered simulations give students the opportunity to practice clinical skills in safe virtual environments, increasing their confidence and preparing them for real-world professional situations. Furthermore, AI-supported learning can also foster the development of critical thinking, enhance clinical reasoning skills, and strengthen teamwork among nursing students. In con-

DOI: 10.4018/979-8-3373-3436-3.ch005

clusion, integrating AI into nursing education offers great opportunities to improve learning and prepare future nurses for the healthcare of tomorrow while encouraging responsible and innovative use of this technology.

INTRODUCTION

In modern educational establishments, digital tools and technologies are essential in the digital age (Girier, 2024). They make learning both stimulating and enjoyable in various fields, including nursing education (Jallad et al., 2024). According to the National League for Nursing (2015), to adapt to the changing needs of patient care, enrich active and meaningful learning experiences (Montejo et al., 2024), and enable graduates to communicate effectively with patients and their caregivers in a computerized healthcare context, it is crucial to reassess the nursing education process (Jung, 2023). Thus, the use of artificial intelligence (AI) is among the most important advancements to provide students with effective learning opportunities (Bozkurt et al., 2021; Montejo et al., 2024) .

The integration of AI in nursing education is becoming increasingly important, aligning with the evolution of the healthcare landscape and the pressing demand to enhance critical thinking skills among nursing professionals. Its application goes beyond merely improving educational processes, aiming to equip future nurses with the necessary skills to provide high-quality care in a technologically advanced healthcare context (Shen et al., 2025 ; Sallam, 2023). However, this transition requires adequate training and awareness, as the adoption of AI is still in its early stages in the field of nursing, and many lack an understanding of the fundamental principles of AI (Zuhair et al., 2024).

Another crucial aspect is the ethics and data privacy when AI is integrated into nursing care. Concerns regarding data privacy, algorithm transparency, and bias prevention are central to the development and application of AI systems in healthcare (White et al., 2024). To address these challenges, it is necessary to train nurses on ethical considerations and the responsible management of AI (Cary et al., 2024).

Although AI promises to improve the delivery of care and the patient experience, it also raises concerns about a possible devaluation of human skills, as some traditional nursing tasks could be automated (Verma et al., 2024). The importance of maintaining a balance between advanced technologies and human expertise is therefore emphasized. Moreover, by providing nurses with tools to analyze complex therapeutic scenarios, AI can also free up time for more meaningful patient-nurse engagement (Verma et al., 2024; Zuhair et al., 2024).

Despite the increasing integration of AI-based systems into clinical and academic environments, current reviews lack a clear synthesis of the direct effects of AI on nursing teaching effectiveness, learning outcomes and the development of critical thinking, as well as the mechanisms by which AI can support or hinder the development of clinical reasoning. This study aims to clarify the conceptual framework linking RN, teaching, learning and critical thinking, and to identify the mechanisms and conditions conducive to efficient and ethical adoption in nursing education programs.

FOUNDATIONS AND APPLICATIONS OF AI IN HIGHER EDUCATION

1. Foundations of Artificial Intelligence

AI is defined as the ability of machines to imitate human cognitive functions, such as learning, reasoning, and problem-solving (Kouka et al., 2025). AI encompasses a range of techniques and tools that enable machines to perceive their environment, analyze information, and make decisions or trigger actions based on these analyses. The main key concepts of AI can be defined as follows:

- Machine Learning (ML): A subfield of AI that involves the use of algorithms to give computers the ability to learn from data and improve with experience without being explicitly programmed for each task (Bochaton et al., 2023).
- Natural language processing (NLP), a subcategory of AI, enables computers to understand and generate human language effectively. Its applications include text analysis and speech recognition (Zuhair et al., 2024).
- Neural Networks. These are structures inspired by the human brain, used to model complex relationships between inputs and outputs or to find structures in data. They are essential in Deep Learning, an advanced branch of ML (Omar et al., 2023).
- Natural Language Processing (NLP): A branch of AI that enables machines to understand, interpret, and respond to human language in a useful way. This includes speech recognition, text comprehension, and text generation (Leal-Junior et al., 2024).
- Computer Vision. This field of AI focuses on the understanding and interpretation of visual content in the physical world. This includes image recognition and video analysis (Van Boven et al., 2023).
- Multi-Agent Systems. These involve the coordinated interactions of multiple software agents capable of perceiving their environment and acting autonomously to achieve goals (Luo et al., 2023).

These concepts provide the foundation for the development of intelligent systems capable of adapting to new situations and operating autonomously in various environments.

2. Current Applications of AI in Higher Education

The educational system must evolve to incorporate elements of teaching related to AI, while preparing young people for a future life interacting with AI. It is imperative that the educational system equips these young people with the skills required by the future job market, so that they are competent and competitive in the relevant jobs (Jung, 2023). In response to this trend and the demands of the global professional environment, the majority of universities and vocational training institutes now offer modules related to AI as well as professional programs and courses specifically designed for AI, allowing young people to acquire relevant knowledge within the framework of their formal education and to prepare to address AI-related issues in the workplace. Research has shown that university students make significant progress in their understanding of AI-related concepts and feel capable of working with AI after taking a course on the subject (Kong et al., 2024). Faced with the challenge that AI represents in higher education, some educators are striving to establish policies addressing its use in teaching and learning. The emergence of the first digital educational tools, such as online tutorials, multimedia resources, and interactive simulations, revealed the potential of AI to enrich teaching and learning experiences. Thus, AI technology saw a growing popularity in the 1970s and 1980s (Bozkurt et al., 2021). In the 1990s, learning analytics and intelligent tutoring systems, based on data generated by AI, improved student performance and offered new opportunities for active learning (Bozkurt et al., 2021; Chang et al., 2024). According to Hwang and his collaborators (2024) as well as Han and his collaborators (2022), artificial intelligence (AI) refers to a set of methods aimed at endowing computers with the ability to imitate human cognitive functions such as learning, reasoning, communication, and decision-making. These techniques, also used in the field of patient care, enable machines to perform tasks or solve complex problems (Han et al., 2022 ; Hwang et al., 2024). In summary, it is necessary for the educational system to transform towards the incorporation of AI aspects, in order to prepare students with the required skills for their future professional lives. Many universities and vocational training institutions now offer courses and programs in AI, allowing students to acquire relevant expertise and prepare for their future careers. Similarly, the rise of digital educational resources has proven its ability to enhance teaching and knowledge acquisition experiences.

GROWING IMPORTANCE OF AI IN THE FIELD OF HEALTHCARE

AI is playing an increasingly crucial role in the field of healthcare, transforming many aspects of patient care, from diagnosis to medical research. The combination of advanced machine learning algorithms, big data analytics, and the increasing availability of health data has paved the way for artificial intelligence to make unprecedented contributions to patient care, diagnosis, and medical research (Fatima et al., 2023).

AI has become a technology capable of revolutionizing the way healthcare is delivered by analyzing large amounts of patient data, enabling early disease detection, personalized treatments, and improved patient outcomes (Zuhair et al., 2024). Machine learning algorithms, such as deep learning and natural language processing, have been effectively used to analyze medical images, predict disease progression, and support clinical decision-making (Fatima et al., 2023). In developing countries, AI plays a crucial role in improving hospital management and community care, especially in areas with high patient density and limited resources where care is often compromised. Despite the challenges, including limited adoption and high costs, AI holds a promising future in healthcare (Zuhair et al., 2024).

Moreover, AI is transforming the healthcare industry by offering opportunities for more accurate diagnostics, personalized treatments, and a reduction in administrative burdens. In parallel, AI brings significant advantages in terms of speed and efficiency, particularly in medical image analysis and drug discovery, although concerns remain regarding data security and regulation (Khan et al., 2023 ; Kitsios et al., 2023). Despite these challenges, the rapid evolution of AI continues to promise a major transformation in healthcare, improving the quality of services while ensuring the security and confidentiality of patient data (Kitsios et al., 2023). The role of AI in healthcare is not limited to care or administrative tasks; it is also transforming pedagogical methods (Birge et al., 2024 ; Girier, 2024). AI technologies in training can revolutionize the way nursing students learn by providing personalized learning experiences, adaptive tests, and realistic simulations that help bridge the gap between theoretical knowledge and practical skills (Girier, 2024). The integration of AI in educational contexts promotes the development of metacognitive skills necessary for advanced reasoning and reflective practice in clinical settings (Jallad et al., 2024).

CONTEXT OF THE EVOLUTION OF NURSING CARE

The healthcare sector is evolving rapidly, with advances in medical technology and patient care practices. AI technologies play a key role in modernizing health education, requiring innovative pedagogical approaches capable of keeping pace with these changes (Jung, 2023). Thus, over the past decade, AI has emerged as a transformative technology likely to revolutionize many sectors (Jian, 2023), including nursing education, as this training must combine academic theory and intensive clinical practice (Girier, 2024 ; Khan et al., 2023). The ability of AI to personalize learning, automate administrative tasks, and improve the accuracy of clinical decisions makes it a valuable tool for the future of nursing education (De Gagne, 2023a).

In nursing, where critical thinking and decision-making are essential, AI offers tools likely to enhance these skills by providing simulated environments for practice and feedback on decision-making processes (Tam et al., 2023; Topaz et al, 2024).

AI could significantly transform nursing education by helping to improve care outcomes, refining the student learning experience, and perfecting teaching methods. Adaptive education systems based on artificial intelligence are capable of analyzing the individual performance of each student and offering customized learning paths. These programs facilitate the detection of deficiencies, the provision of appropriate educational resources, and the tailored adaptation of teaching (Jallad et al., 2024). By using virtual reality (VR) and simulation, nursing students can benefit from immersive learning opportunities provided by VR and AI-powered simulations. In realistic virtual contexts, they have the opportunity to improve their clinical skills, decision-making ability, and critical thinking. AI systems are capable of evaluating students' performance, providing them with feedback, and supporting them in the development of their skills (Bozkurt et al., 2021).

ROLE OF AI IN IMPROVING CRITICAL THINKING AND CLINICAL REASONING IN NURSING EDUCATION

Critical thinking and clinical reasoning play a fundamental role in nursing care, allowing nurses to effectively handle complex clinical situations. Critical thinking is a cognitive process used to examine, interpret, evaluate, and respond to information in a thoughtful manner. In nursing, this includes patient assessment, clinical decision-making, and the implementation of appropriate care (Shen et al., 2025).

A study highlighted that clinical reasoning develops from scientific and professional knowledge, and is influenced by ethical decisions as well as the values of nurses. Moreover, it is essential to integrate psychosocial responses with physiological responses in educational programs to improve clinical reasoning (Birge et al., 2024).

The development of critical thinking is crucial for novice nursing students. It is considered an essential part of education at all levels, involving the analysis, evaluation, and resolution of various challenges (Yelne et al., 2023). Critical thinking plays a crucial role in shaping students' learning, cognition, analysis, and decision-making

(Tam et al., 2023). Research on students in their first clinical course has shown that they develop professional, perfectionist, caring, and self-directed learning perspectives. These students benefit from discussions in a supportive environment, fostering their critical thinking and development as reflective practitioners (Jia & Tu, 2024).

The combination of critical thinking and intuitive practice is also valid. While intuitive practice can be valuable, it requires the application of critical reflection to avoid errors based on biases. Students develop intuitive skills by practicing with critical reflection, thereby increasing their expertise and ensuring quality care (Von et al., 2022).

It is therefore essential that educational programs emphasize the strengthening of critical thinking and clinical reasoning, incorporating practices that take into account the physiological and psychosocial aspects of care, while fostering students' confidence and autonomy in their critical thinking (Birge et al., 2024). This enables us to train competent nurses capable of making informed, ethical decisions in complex clinical contexts.

Von and his colleagues assert that the integration of AI in nursing education promotes the development of clinical reasoning and critical thinking skills (Von et al., 2022). For nurses, who must make informed decisions quickly in complex clinical situations, these abilities are crucial. Thanks to a variety of educational resources, including case-based learning, interactions with simulated patients, and training in metacognitive techniques, AI can help people acquire these skills (Von et al., 2022). Furthermore, AI can resolve certain ambiguities and contradictions that currently exist in nursing education regarding the development of critical thinking (Tam et al., 2023). By integrating AI, training programs can implement more robust methods for assessing critical thinking, thanks to domain-specific tools that provide relevant feedback on student performance (Benfatah et al., 2024). The use of AI in nursing training also allows for the simulation of complex clinical scenarios, providing students with the opportunity to practice in a safe and controlled environment. These AI-based simulations can reproduce a wide variety of clinical situations, including rare or difficult cases that are hard to encounter in real practice. Moreover, AI can analyze in real-time the decisions and actions of students during these simulations, providing immediate feedback (Girier, 2024). These AI tools also allow for the personalization of learning according to the individual needs of each student, thereby optimizing their progress (Topaz et al, 2024). Moreover, the integration of AI in nursing education promotes the development of essential digital skills for practicing the profession in an increasingly technological healthcare environment. Finally, this innovative approach helps bridge the gap between theory and practice by offering students more immersive and realistic learning experiences.

OPPORTUNITIES OFFERED BY AI IN NURSING EDUCATION

The opportunities offered by artificial intelligence in the field of nursing education are numerous. In this section, we present examples illustrating these main opportunities. These elements are summarized concisely in Figure 1:

1. Personalization of Learning Paths

The personalization of learning pathways represents a transformative advancement in the field of nursing education, leveraging the power of artificial intelligence to tailor teaching to the individual needs of students (Jian, 2023). This innovative approach promises to optimize the acquisition of skills and knowledge by taking into account the learning styles, progression rates, and specific goals of each learner (Jallad et al., 2024 ; Kamalov et al., 2023). AI enables the creation of individualized learning environments by monitoring student contributions, providing appropriate tasks, and offering effective feedback (Zou et al., 2025). AI systems can continuously assess students' performance, preferences, and learning styles in order to personalize content, pace, and teaching methods (Aldwean & Tenney, 2023). This dynamic adaptability allows students to focus on the areas where they need the most help, while advanced learners can progress at their own pace, without being held back by the rest of the class (Zou et al., 2025). The inherent ability of AI systems to analyze vast datasets and generate insights offers an unprecedented way to understand learners at a granular level (Jian, 2023). Machine learning algorithms can identify knowledge gaps, predict potential difficulties, and recommend targeted learning resources, ensuring that each student receives the support they need to succeed (Aldwean & Tenney, 2023). In summary, the personalization of learning pathways in nursing education, thanks to artificial intelligence, allows for the adaptation of teaching to the individual needs of students by taking into account their style, pace, and goals. It facilitates continuous assessment and dynamic content adjustment, helping each learner progress effectively by targeting their gaps and optimizing their skills. This innovative approach offers a better understanding of students and promotes more effective learning. This learning offers significant opportunities, particularly through advanced clinical simulations.

2. Advanced Clinical Simulations

The use of AI in nursing education through advanced clinical simulations enhances realism and learner engagement, allowing for a personalization of the educational experience that adapts to the specific needs of each student (Jung, 2023). AI technologies enable the creation of interactive learning environments where students can practice clinical skills in a secure and controlled setting, which is crucial for the development of practical skills before facing real-life situations (Verma et al., 2024).

A central aspect of AI-based simulations is their ability to introduce dynamic and realistic content through virtual patients, thus offering an immersive learning method that simulates various clinical conditions. This not only strengthens the clinical reasoning of students but also their decision-making in critical situations (Jung, 2023). These simulations also give students the opportunity to make mistakes in an environment where they can receive immediate feedback, thereby promoting learning through practice and critical reflection (Verma et al., 2024).

Furthermore, AI facilitates the integration of advanced assessment tools, allowing students and instructors to obtain detailed analyses of learner performance and progress, which contributes to the continuous improvement of educational practices (Jung, 2023). However, to maximize these benefits, it is essential to establish clear guidelines for the ethical integration of AI in nursing education, while ensuring that students are prepared for the future technological and ethical challenges they will encounter in their careers (Gagne, 2023 ; Verma et al., 2024). As AI continues to transform nursing education, it becomes crucial for educational institutions to adapt their curriculum, update the skills of trainers, and promote a culture of technological learning in order to optimize the impact of advanced clinical simulations on the training of future nurses (Jallad et al., 2024 ; Verma et al., 2024).

3. Development of Critical Thinking and Clinical Reasoning

The use of AI in nursing education offers new perspectives for the development of critical thinking and clinical reasoning. These skills are essential in nursing practice where quick and precise decisions can have decisive impacts on patient health (Ramírez-Baraldes et al., 2025).

AI can be integrated into nursing education through tools such as ChatGPT, chatbots, and 3D avatars, which simulate clinical scenarios (Kouka et al., 2025 ; Ramírez-Baraldes et al., 2025). These methods enhance critical thinking and clinical reasoning by offering interactive learning experiences that assess knowledge and decision-making in increasingly severe clinical conditions (Kouka et al., 2025).

AI platforms, such as ChatGPT, serve as virtual tutors, capable of simulating realistic clinical scenarios that encourage students to apply their knowledge and exercise their clinical judgment interactively. Thus, virtual simulations and AI-driven clinical decision support systems allow students to practice clinical reasoning in safe and controlled environments, thereby improving their decision-making abilities (Verma et al., 2024).

Studies have shown that students using AI in their training have improved their ability to understand complex concepts and have developed greater competence in clinical reasoning (Huang, 2023 ; Verma et al., 2024). This interactivity allows for the personalization of learning, fostering engagement and knowledge retention.

Moreover, AI in nursing education enhances critical thinking. AI can promote the clarification of values and the critical analysis of information, essential skills for evaluating information sources and avoiding potential biases (Jung, 2023). By integrating AI into the curriculum, nursing educators can create practical activities where students effectively engage with AI-generated content, thereby enhancing critical thinking and clinical decision-making (Verma et al., 2024).

However, excessive reliance on technology risks diminishing students' critical thinking and clinical reasoning skills (Hwang et al., 2024). Therefore, educational programs must integrate AI as a complementary tool, rather than as a substitute for traditional teaching. Teachers must continue to promote critical thinking and problem-solving through practical activities and classroom discussions, to ensure that students develop the necessary skills to tackle real-world challenges (Ramírez-Baraldes et al., 2025).

4. Improvement of Collaboration and Teamwork

AI in nursing education can significantly enhance collaboration and teamwork among nursing students by fostering innovative learning environments and improving clinical decision-making (Jung, 2023). AI tools, such as virtual simulations and chatbots, offer interactive experiences that promote critical thinking and communication skills essential for effective teamwork (Zuhair et al., 2024 ; Kouka et al., 2025). Similarly, these tools can assess students' knowledge and provide immediate feedback, thereby facilitating peer discussions and collaborative learning (Kouka et al., 2025). In this environment, AI facilitates interdisciplinary collaboration, encourages the development of teaching staff, and stimulates student autonomy (Jung, 2023).

In the context of interprofessional training, particularly in nursing, the integration of AI tools can enhance students' willingness to collaborate. A study on interprofessional clinical training reveals that students trained in interprofessional environments show a greater willingness to work in teams, as measured by the Readiness for Interprofessional Learning Scale (RIPLS) (Kouka et al., 2025). This approach is also reflected in nursing education where simulation technologies reproduce real-life situations, facilitating the understanding of different roles within healthcare teams (Verma et al., 2024). Furthermore, AI can analyze patient data to help nurses and students make informed decisions, enhancing collaboration and improving the quality of care (Sun et al., 2024). It can also enhance communication by providing real-time updates and alerts, ensuring that all members of the nursing team stay informed and can collaborate effectively (Kouka et al., 2025).

These technologies enable a gradual transition towards an education that not only teaches technical skills but also encourages critical engagement and a deep understanding of interprofessional dynamics (Lane et al., 2024). Nevertheless, the future of nursing education will depend on balancing technological adoption with the maintenance of essential human skills, thereby ensuring the continuous improvement of healthcare.

Figure 1. Opportunities Offered by AI in Nursing Education

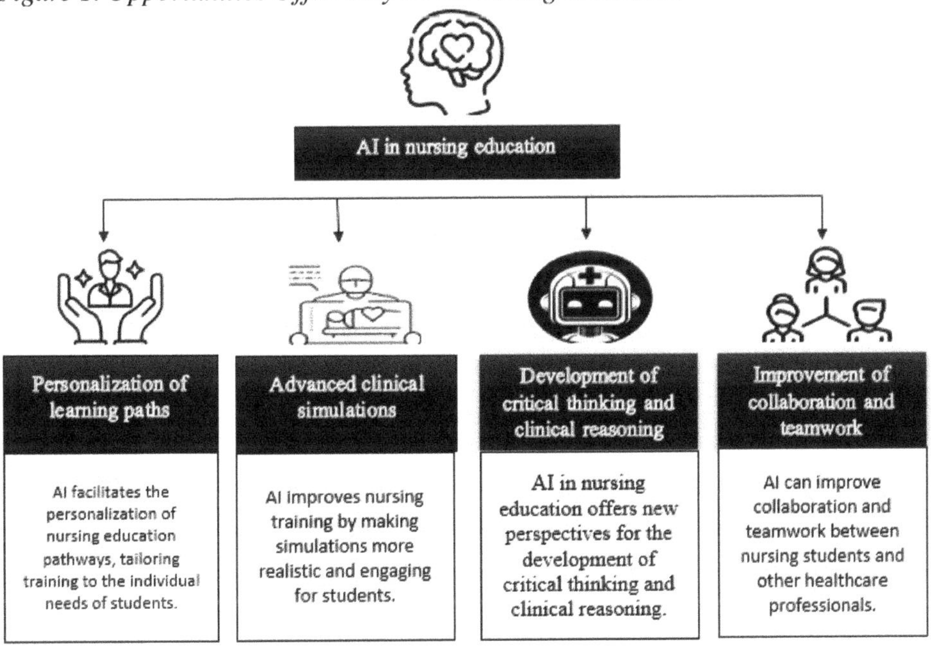

INTEGRATION OF AI IN NURSING TRAINING PROGRAMS

The integration of AI into nursing programs represents a major evolution to address contemporary health challenges. By adopting a pedagogical innovation approach, this initiative aims to prepare teachers and future nurses to effectively use these new technologies to improve the quality of care and interprofessional coordination. Examples of AI-Based Teaching Strategies are described in the following sections and summarized in Table 1.

1. Strategies for Integrating AI into Curricula

Recently, a growing number of universities and nursing faculties have sparked students' interest in using AI-based learning methods (Jallad et al., 2024). This underscores the importance of recognizing the needs in the integration of AI technical advancements into the pedagogical model of nursing education programs (Bozkurt et al., 2021 ; Chang et al., 2022).

Indeed, in nursing education, the use of technologies has recently experienced alarming growth (Gause et al., 2022). The use of applications, such as virtual reality and virtual patients, is perceived as practical, accelerating the learning of skills and creating a serene learning environment (Chang et al., 2022 ; Bozkurt et al., 2021). However, nursing trainers sometimes struggle to obtain relevant virtual audio materials to support the learning of these skills (Chang et al., 2022). Thus, equipping nurses with technological skills through the use of technology in nursing education can greatly contribute to enhancing the market value of nursing (Gause et al., 2022). This is essential, as many nursing and healthcare training institutions are gradually adopting an ecological approach and requiring technological skills from their future graduates.

Thus, integrating AI into nursing curricula requires pedagogical strategies that not only promote the adoption of these technologies but also teach students their responsible and ethical use. It is crucial to develop training aimed at clarifying fundamental values, raising awareness among future nurses about the potential impacts of AI on the patient-centered care relationship and the diversity of perspectives, in order to strengthen professional ethics (De Gagne, 2023b). Moreover, nursing educators have the opportunity to engage in continuous professional development to master these tools, thereby enabling them to effectively integrate AI into their teaching and best prepare students for their future practice (Couper, 2024). However, the integration of AI into existing programs can pose significant challenges, particularly in terms of planning, training, and managing ethical issues related to confidentiality and algorithmic biases. Ensuring compliance with regulations, while maintaining transparency and accountability, is essential to protect students' rights (Jian, 2023 ; Khan et al., 2023). Moreover, it is also important to overcome potential resistances, often related to fears of job insecurity or a misunderstanding of the technology (Couper, 2024). Clear communication about the benefits of AI, combined with training opportunities, can promote an adoption that complements the role of teachers rather than diminishes it.

2. Examples of AI-Based Teaching Strategies

In nursing education, a variety of AI-based pedagogical strategies are used, including AI-guided simulation learning, AI-enhanced teaching, and AI content and tool creation (Labrague et al., 2025). Examples of these strategies are presented in Table 1.

AI-guided simulation-based learning included and utilized AI technologies to create interactive and realistic educational scenarios. This approach leveraged AI to make the simulations closer to real clinical situations, thereby enriching learning through immersive environments. For example, Liaw et al. (2023) implemented AI-assisted virtual reality simulations using Unity 3D and Google Cloud's Dialogflow to create virtual environments allowing students to interact with virtual patients and communicate with healthcare professionals (Liaw et al., 2023). Benfatah et al. (2024a) implemented an AI-assisted debriefing, using Deepgram and Openrose to analyze audio and video data from simulation sessions in order to optimize the feedback phase after emergency scenarios involving asthma patients (Benfatah, et al., 2024a). Furthermore, in another study, Benfatah et al. (2024b) used ChatGPT as a virtual patient in Morocco, allowing students to interact with the AI as if they were attending to a real patient (Benfatah, et al., 2024b). Moreover, White et al. (2024) utilized AI-driven virtual simulations, incorporating virtual patients, wearable devices, and smart mannequins, to replicate patient interviews in a community nursing course, thereby offering students the opportunity to interact with these virtual simulators from their personal computers (White et al., 2024). For their part, Lebo and Brown (2024) implemented AI-based virtual patient simulations, incorporating evolving and complex scenarios to enrich nursing education (Lebo & Brown, 2024). Finally, Simsek-Cetinkaya and Cakir (2023) designed an interactive screen-based simulation application, assisted by AI, for breast self-examination, allowing students to interact with a female avatar in a simulated learning environment (Simsek-Cetinkaya & Cakir, 2023).

The AI-enhanced pedagogical approach involved the incorporation of AI tools into traditional educational techniques to optimize the learning process (Chang et al., 2022; Labrague et al., 2025 ; Ramírez-Baraldes et al., 2025). This method employed AI systems to enhance teaching, encourage interactive learning, and simplify task-based activities. Kowitlawakul et al. (2023) turned to Rasa, an AI learning conversational assistant, to address various course topics (Kowitlawakul et al., 2024). This allows students to interact with the tool to receive educational support and enrich their learning experience. Chang and his collaborators (2024) used the ChatGPT system, based on the CIDI model, to assist in the development of a health education module (Chang et al., 2024). They thus guided the students through a structured problem-solving process with AI interaction. Safebot, a conversational agent developed by Rodriguez-Arrastia et al. (2022), is designed to replicate acute pesticide poisoning scenarios, promoting task-based interactions to encourage practical learning (Rodriguez-Arrastia et al., 2022). Moreover, Kong et al. (2024) incorporated AI into a learning project in China, where students interacted independently with ChatGAi and ERNIE Bot, and engaged in collective discussions (Kong et al., 2024). Finally, Han et al. (2022) utilized an AI Chatbot via LandBot.io, allowing students to familiarize themselves with the program's objectives while being assessed through quizzes and personalized feedback (Han et al., 2022). During their training, the students acquired skills in nursing care management and electronic fetal monitoring, ultimately merging this knowledge.

AI is also used to design educational resources and interactive tools aimed at improving education (Akutay et al., 2024 ; Higashitsuji, 2025 ; Reed et al., 2023 ; Reed & Dodson, 2024 ; Taskiran, 2023). According to Higashitsuji et al. (2025), ChatGPT was used to develop case studies within the framework of case-based learning (CBL), which helped lighten the teachers' workload and stimulate group discussions (Higashitsuji et al., 2025). For Akutay et al. (2024), the use of DALL-E3 has enabled the creation of educational materials, which has notably contributed to improving student performance in randomized controlled trials in case management (Akutay et al., 2024). Reed & Dodson (2024) used AI-generated narratives and narrated videos to provide a detailed description of the patients' journey before the simulations, with the aim of increasing their realism and enhancing student preparation (Reed & Dodson, 2024). Finally, Reed and his collaborators (2023) used images produced by Midjourney for reflective activities focused on descriptions, thereby improving the AI's understanding of its uses (Reed et al., 2023).

Table 1. Examples of AI-Based Teaching Strategies

Simulation-based learning guided by AI	- Assisted virtual reality simulations using Unity 3D and Google Cloud's Dialogflow (Liaw et al., 2023) ; - Deepgram and Openrose for AI-assisted debriefing(Benfatah, et al., 2024a) ; - ChatGPT as a virtual patient (Benfatah, et al., 2024b) ; - Virtual simulations driven by AI (White et al., 2024) ; - Virtual patients based on AI, integrating evolving and complex scenarios (Lebo & Brown, 2024) ; - Design of an interactive screen-based simulation application, assisted by AI, for breast self-examination (Simsek-Cetinkaya & Cakir, 2023).
Incorporation of AI tools into traditional educational techniques	- Rasa, a conversational AI learning assistant, to address various course topics (Kowitlawakul et al., 2024) ; - ChatGPT, based on the CIDI model, to assist in the development of a health education module (Chang et al., 2024) ; - Safebot, a conversational agent designed to replicate acute pesticide poisoning scenarios, promoting task-based interactions to encourage practical learning (Rodriguez-Arrastia et al., 2022) ; - Use of ChatGAi and ERNIE Bot for group discussions with students (Kong et al., 2024) ; - Use of AI Chatbot via LandBot.io, allowing students to familiarize themselves with the program's objectives while being assessed through quizzes and personalized feedback (Han et al., 2022).
Design of educational resources and interactive tools by AI	- ChatGPT used to develop case studies within the framework of case-based learning (CBL) (Higashitsuji et al., 2025) ; - Use of DALL-E3 to create educational materials (Akutay et al., 2024) ; - Use of AI-generated narratives and narrated videos to prepare simulations (Reed & Dodson, 2024) ; - Use of images produced by Midjourney for reflective activities (Reed et al., 2023).

IMPACT OF AI ON THE SKILLS OF FUTURE NURSES

With the evolution of care environments thanks to AI, nursing students must adapt to these changes (Benfatah et al., 2024 ; Verma et al., 2024). Therefore, nursing education must adopt a proactive and flexible approach, carefully reviewing and modifying the curriculum to ensure that future nurses are not only well-informed about traditional nursing practices but also highly skilled in using AI technologies to improve patient outcomes and enhance the overall efficiency of healthcare delivery (Gause et al., 2022). The integration of AI in healthcare training has significant implications for the skills of future nurses (Ahmed, 2024 ; White et al., 2024), which can influence their digital and technological competencies.

Indeed, with the advent of AI and the growing complexity of the healthcare field, it is essential that nursing education reforms to equip students with advanced skills and knowledge to thrive in an environment where AI is predominant (Jian, 2023). In this sense, it is important to integrate AI technologies into training curricula to adapt to the changing demands of contemporary nursing practice (White et al., 2024). Thus, the incorporation of AI technologies into the nursing curriculum promotes the acquisition of essential digital and technological skills, optimizes academic performance, and prepares students for the complexity of current healthcare contexts (Gause et al., 2022).

CHALLENGES AND ETHICAL CONSIDERATIONS

Artificial intelligence has the capacity to revolutionize nursing education by offering opportunities to improve learning experiences, academic performance, and the preparation of students for a technologically advanced healthcare environment. However, to take advantage of these benefits, certain major obstacles must be overcome, including the costs associated with adopting technologies, ethical issues, resistance to change, and equity of access (Verma et al., 2024).

Indeed, the incorporation of artificial intelligence in nursing education requires significant investments in technology and infrastructure. Often, many educational institutions do not have the necessary resources to purchase, maintain, and update the required equipment and programs. The incorporation of AI into existing programs and teaching techniques can also prove to be complicated and time-consuming, requiring meticulous organization and coordination. It is essential to train teachers in the effective use of AI tools, and continuous support is required to address technical issues as they arise (Almagharbeh, 2025 ; Aldwean & Tenney, 2023).

Moreover, the use of AI in the educational sector raises ethical and privacy protection issues, particularly concerning the collection and exploitation of student information. Moreover, concerns remain regarding biases in AI algorithms, which could lead to unfair treatment of students based on their demographic attributes. To address these ethical issues, transparency, accountability, and robust policies are needed to protect the rights and interests of students (Zou et al., 2025 ; Bozkurt et al., 2021).

It seems that there is some resistance to the adoption of AI technologies among teachers, especially in cases of misunderstanding or fear of being laid off. Trainers might fear that AI could hinder their role or reduce the need for human trainers. It is necessary to establish a balance between technology and traditional teaching, and to provide clear communication about the benefits of AI, professional development opportunities to enhance pedagogical skills, and to ensure that AI aims to support rather than replace human teachers to overcome this resistance (Ali, 2024 ; Peng et al., 2022 ; Han et al., 2022).

Even though AI offers flexible learning opportunities, its reckless deployment could exacerbate existing inequalities. Students from disadvantaged backgrounds may not have access to the necessary technologies or a reliable internet connection, which limits their ability to enroll in AI-based educational programs. It is essential to rectify these inequalities and provide support, such as equipment loans or internet assistance, to ensure AI-powered education is accessible to all, allowing every student to benefit from it (Almagharbeh, 2025 ; Couper, 2024).

Given the rapid evolution of AI tools and technologies, the quality and effectiveness of AI-based educational resources can fluctuate. It is crucial to establish standards and best practices for the integration of AI in nursing education to ensure consistency and quality. This includes the formulation of guidelines for the application of AI in the educational sector, the evaluation of AI tool performance, and the exchange of best practices between institutions (Zou et al., 2025 ; Couper, 2024).

FUTURE PERSPECTIVES

Emerging Trends in AI for Nursing Education

The integration of AI in nursing education is marked by emerging trends that have the potential to transform the way nursing students are trained and prepared for a technology-dominated future.

1. Adaptive Learning and Personalized Tutoring

Adaptive learning and personalized tutoring assisted by AI represent a significant advancement in nursing education. These sophisticated systems analyze students' performance and interactions in real-time, allowing for a dynamic adaptation of content and teaching methods. AI can identify the areas where each student excels or encounters difficulties, thereby adjusting the pace and complexity of the lessons to optimize learning. This tailored approach fosters a deeper understanding and improved retention of essential nursing knowledge (Benfatah et al., 2024).

Moreover, these adaptive learning platforms offer considerable advantages for trainers and institutions. They provide detailed data on student progress, allowing teachers to intervene in a targeted and effective manner. AI can also suggest additional resources or specific exercises to fill the identified gaps. This personalization of learning contributes to more effective training of future nurses, ensuring that they acquire the necessary skills to excel in their profession, while potentially reducing the time and resources needed to achieve learning objectives (Hwang et al., 2024).

2. AI-Enhanced Simulations

Simulation-based education, greatly enhanced by AI, is another key trend. AI helps create an immersive and realistic learning environment that enhances student engagement and educational effectiveness. Although AI does not replace the essential educational role of nursing educators, it can enrich the learning experience through personalization and interdisciplinarity (Jung, 2023 ; Lebo & Brown, 2024 ; Liaw et al., 2023).

Education through simulation assisted by artificial intelligence (AI) represents a significant advancement in the field of nursing training. This innovative approach allows for the creation of complex and realistic clinical scenarios, giving students the opportunity to practice and refine their skills in a safe and controlled environment. AI can dynamically adapt these simulations based on each student's actions and decisions, thus providing a highly personalized learning experience. This personalization allows learners to progress at their own pace and focus on the areas where they need the most improvement (Jung, 2023 ; Liaw et al., 2023).

Furthermore, the integration of AI in education through simulation promotes interdisciplinarity by enabling the creation of scenarios that involve different medical and paramedical specialties. This holistic approach better prepares future nurses to work effectively within multidisciplinary teams. Although AI plays a crucial role in enriching the learning experience, it is important to emphasize that it does not replace the irreplaceable expertise and mentorship of nursing educators. On the contrary, it acts as a complementary tool that allows educators to focus more on developing critical skills, empathy, and clinical judgment in their students (Jung, 2023 ; Lebo & Brown, 2024 ; Liaw et al., 2023).

3. Training for Medical AI

Teaching the concept of AI in nursing curricula prepares students for the digital age. Specific courses on AI help improve students' maturity and readiness to integrate AI tools into their future clinical practices. This is crucial given the significant impact that AI is expected to have on all areas of nursing practice (Aldwean & Tenney, 2023). This training is essential to enable the nurses of tomorrow to use sophisticated AI tools effectively and responsibly in their daily clinical practice, while maintaining a patient-centered approach. The crucial importance of this training is underscored by the growing and ubiquitous impact of AI in all aspects of nursing care and medical practice, ranging from high-precision computer-assisted diagnosis to personalized and optimized treatment management, as well as the prediction of health risks and the improvement of communication between healthcare professionals and patients (Cary et al., 2024 ; Sallam, 2023).

By acquiring a solid foundation of knowledge in AI, students will be better equipped to navigate with confidence and competence in a constantly evolving healthcare environment, where technology plays an increasingly central and transformative role (Chang et al., 2022). This thorough preparation not only significantly improves the quality and efficiency of patient care but also enhances nurses' confidence, adaptability, and resilience in the face of future technological innovations in their professional field.

The integration of AI into nursing education also opens up exciting new perspectives for nursing research, allowing professionals to actively contribute to the development and improvement of AI technologies in the healthcare sector. This proactive approach prepares nurses to become key players in the design and implementation of ethical and patient-centered AI solutions, thereby strengthening their crucial role in the evolution of healthcare (Hwang et al., 2024).

4. Use of AI for the Improvement of Resources and Clinical Decisions

The use of artificial intelligence (AI) in the healthcare field represents a significant advancement for resource optimization and the improvement of clinical decisions. AI systems have the potential to radically transform the management of healthcare facilities by analyzing vast amounts of data to identify inefficiencies and propose more effective resource allocation solutions. In the clinical field, AI can assist healthcare professionals by providing rapid and accurate analyses of patient data, which can lead to earlier and more precise diagnoses, as well as personalized and optimized treatment plans (Labrague et al., 2025; Verma et al., 2024).

Moreover, AI offers promising prospects to address the growing challenges in the healthcare sector, particularly the aging population and the rise in chronic diseases. By automating certain routine tasks and providing decision support tools, AI allows healthcare professionals to focus more on the human aspects of care. This technology can also help reduce medical errors and improve patient safety by detecting anomalies or potentially dangerous drug interactions. Thus, the integration of AI into healthcare systems promises not only to improve operational efficiency but also to elevate the overall quality of care provided to patients (Verma et al., 2024).

PREPARING STUDENTS FOR AN AI-FOCUSED FUTURE

The increasing integration of AI in healthcare has a significant impact on nursing education, requiring a strategic approach to prepare nursing students for an AI-focused future. This preparation involves managing the challenges and opportunities presented by AI while aligning with the core values of the nursing profession. AI in nursing education presents a mix of challenges and opportunities (Cary et al., 2024 ; Sallam, 2023). On the one hand, AI can revolutionize nursing education by offering enriched learning experiences and more effective educational outcomes. This involves personalized learning, bridging the gap between theory and practice, and helping to manage time constraints. AI tools enhance the realism and engagement of nursing simulations, fostering interdisciplinary collaboration and autonomous learning among nursing students (Jung, 2023 ; Couper, 2024). Nevertheless, a crucial aspect of preparing nursing students for an AI-focused future is clarifying values. These exercises help reinforce fundamental nursing values such as compassion, empathy, and patient-centered care, thereby enabling students to critically assess the ethical implications of AI (De Gagne, 2023 ; Ali, 2024). The integration of an AI course into the nursing curriculum can enhance preparedness for medical AI, as research shows that students who have undergone specific AI training have achieved better results in preparedness assessments (Taskiran, 2023 ; Sun et al., 2024). Despite the promises of AI, its integration into nursing education must be approached with caution. Institutions must promote mastery of AI and encourage responsible implementation practices. This involves developing ethical guidelines and fostering an educational environment that encourages teachers and students to engage critically with AI tools (Lane et al., 2024 ; Sallam, 2023). In doing so, nursing students will be better equipped to use AI in practice, reconciling technological advantages with human-centered care values. In summary, the integration of AI into nursing education offers a promising opportunity to enhance learning and practice. However, nursing programs must carefully manage the ethical, pedagogical, and practical challenges posed by AI. By fostering an environment that values both innovation and the fundamental principles of nursing, educators can prepare students for a future where AI complements the compassionate care that is at the heart of nursing.

FUTURE STUDY DIRECTIONS

In light of the continuous evolution of artificial intelligence in the educational field, several research avenues are likely to emerge for the future. The examination of these subjects is likely to offer important perspectives on the potential, challenges, and ethical issues related to its integration. It is crucial to examine how the integration of AI fosters the confluence between technology and pedagogy, paving the way for effective and sustainable nursing education. It is also crucial to study how teachers use AI for innovative teaching methods, evaluating its influence on the engagement and understanding of future healthcare professionals. Research focused on the anticipated future scope of AI in the field of education can offer insights into its potential development, adaptation, and the changing dynamics it might introduce.

It is also crucial to study the development and effectiveness of regulations and policies addressing concerns such as plagiarism, data privacy, and AI ethics, in order to guide responsible integration. Research can focus on innovative methods for detecting and preventing plagiarism facilitated by AI-generated content, in order to preserve academic integrity. Furthermore, examining the emergence of new pedagogical methodologies leveraging AI capabilities can provide insight into the future of nursing education. The emphasis on managing ethical issues and reducing biases in AI-generated content can contribute to fair and responsible integration. Understanding how students perceive and integrate AI into their educational process, as well as the challenges and preferences they face, can guide the development of effective application strategies. We also address the difficulties related to an excessive reliance on artificial intelligence for education and the risk of reduced human interactions, proposing approaches to establish a balance. Ultimately, the exploration of these future research avenues will help illuminate the role of AI in education, thereby offering the involved parties the chance to harness its potential while managing the challenges associated with it.

CONCLUSION

The constant evolution of healthcare and nursing professions requires a transformation of traditional pedagogical methods in the training of frontline clinicians. This transformation involves the integration of technology as a catalyst for pedagogical innovation, rather than merely as a methodology. The adoption of these new technologies largely depends on the willingness of health trainers to embrace change in their educational approaches, recognizing the importance of continuous professional development to effectively integrate technology into clinical practice.

Therefore, AI represents an invaluable educational resource that, if integrated thoughtfully and ethically, can significantly enhance the development of critical thinking and clinical reasoning among nursing students. It offers innovative, engaging, and relevant methods to prepare future nurses to meet the demands of modern practice, while ensuring the maintenance of high standards of patient-centered care. However, the success of this integration depends on the ability of educators to adopt strategies that value critical reflection and establish a training framework conducive to excellence and safety in care.

REFERENCES

Ahmed, S. K. (2024). Artificial intelligence in nursing: Current trends, possibilities and pitfalls. *Journal of Medicine, Surgery, and Public Health, 3*, 100072. DOI: 10.1016/j.glmedi.2024.100072

Akutay, S., Yüceler Kaçmaz, H., & Kahraman, H. (2024). The effect of artificial intelligence supported case analysis on nursing students' case management performance and satisfaction : A randomized controlled trial. *Nurse Education in Practice, 80*, 104142. DOI: 10.1016/j.nepr.2024.104142 PMID: 39299058

Aldwean, A., & Tenney, D. (2023). Artificial Intelligence in Healthcare Sector : A Literature Review of the Adoption Challenges. *Open Journal of Business and Management, 12*(1), 1. Advance online publication. DOI: 10.4236/ojbm.2024.121009

Ali, F. N. (2024). Artificial intelligence in nursing practice: Challenges and barriers. *Helwan International Journal for Nursing Research and Practice, 3*(7), 217–230. DOI: 10.21608/hijnrp.2024.292923.1169

Almagharbeh, W. T. (2025). The impact of AI-based decision support systems on nursing workflows in critical care units. *International Nursing Review, 72*(2), e13011. DOI: 10.1111/inr.13011 PMID: 38973347

Benfatah, M., Marfak, A., Saad, E., Hilali, A., Nejjari, C., & Youlyouz-Marfak, I. (2024). Assessing the efficacy of ChatGPT as a virtual patient in nursing simulation training : A study on nursing students' experience. *Teaching and Learning in Nursing, 19*(3), e486–e493. DOI: 10.1016/j.teln.2024.02.005

Benfatah, M., Youlyouz-Marfak, I., Saad, E., Hilali, A., Nejjari, C., & Marfak, A. (2024). Impact of artificial intelligence-enhanced debriefing on clinical skills development in nursing students : A comparative study. *Teaching and Learning in Nursing, 19*(3), e574–e579. DOI: 10.1016/j.teln.2024.04.007

Birge, A. Ö., & Kutlutürkan, S. (2024). The impact of case-based education on the development of nursing students' clinical reasoning skills in managing critical illnesses: A pilot randomized controlled trial. *Journal of Education and Research in Nursing, 21*(2), 144–153. DOI: 10.14744/jern.2024.80000

Bozkurt, A., Karadeniz, A., Baneres, D., Guerrero-Roldán, A. E., & Rodríguez, M. E. (2021). Artificial Intelligence and Reflections from Educational Landscape : A Review of AI Studies in Half a Century. *Sustainability (Basel), 13*(2), 2. Advance online publication. DOI: 10.3390/su13020800

Cary, M. P.Jr, De Gagne, J. C., Kauschinger, E. D., & Carter, B. M. (2024). Advancing Health Equity Through Artificial Intelligence : An Educational Framework for Preparing Nurses in Clinical Practice and Research. *Creative Nursing*, *30*(2), 154–164. DOI: 10.1177/10784535241249193 PMID: 38689433

Chang, C.-Y., Hwang, G.-J., & Gau, M.-L. (2022). Promoting students' learning achievement and self-efficacy : A mobile chatbot approach for nursing training. *British Journal of Educational Technology*, *53*(1), 171–188. DOI: 10.1111/bjet.13158

Chang, C.-Y., Yang, C.-L., Jen, H.-J., Ogata, H., & Hwang, G.-H. (2024). Facilitating nursing and health education by incorporating ChatGPT into learning designs. *Journal of Educational Technology & Society*, *27*(1), 215–230. https://www.jstor.org/stable/48754852

Couper, A. L. (2024). Challenges and opportunities of artificial intelligence in nursing education. *Journal of Nursing Reports in Clinical Practice*, *3*(2), 213–215. DOI: 10.32598/JNRCP.2409.1177

De Gagne, J. C. (2023). The State of Artificial Intelligence in Nursing Education : Past, Present, and Future Directions. *International Journal of Environmental Research and Public Health*, *20*(6), 6. Advance online publication. DOI: 10.3390/ijerph20064884 PMID: 36981790

Fatima, I., Grover, V., Khan, I. R., Ahmad, N., & Yadav, A. (2023). Artificial Intelligence in Medical Field. *EAI Endorsed Transactions on Pervasive Health and Technology*, *9*. Advance online publication. DOI: 10.4108/eetpht.9.4713

Gause, G., Mokgaola, I. O., & Rakhudu, M. A. (2022). Technology usage for teaching and learning in nursing education : An integrative review. *Curationis*, *45*(1), 2261. DOI: 10.4102/curationis.v45i1.2261 PMID: 35792609

Girier, A. (2024). Humanities and social sciences in nursing education. Revue Education, Santé, Sociétés, Volume 10, Numéro 1, 85-100. https://doi.org/DOI: 10.17184/eac.8136

Han, J.-W., Park, J., & Lee, H. (2022). Analysis of the effect of an artificial intelligence chatbot educational program on non-face-to-face classes : A quasi-experimental study. *BMC Medical Education*, *22*(1), 830. DOI: 10.1186/s12909-022-03898-3 PMID: 36457086

Higashitsuji, A., Otsuka, T., & Watanabe, K. (2025). Impact of ChatGPT on case creation efficiency and learning quality in case-based learning for undergraduate nursing students. *Teaching and Learning in Nursing*, *20*(1), e159–e166. DOI: 10.1016/j.teln.2024.10.002

Huang, H. (2023). *Performance of ChatGPT on Registered Nurse License Exam in Taiwan : A Descriptive Study* (2023091625). *Preprints*. DOI: 10.20944/preprints202309.1625.v1

Hwang, G.-J., Tang, K.-Y., & Tu, Y.-F. (2024). How artificial intelligence (AI) supports nursing education : Profiling the roles, applications, and trends of AI in nursing education research (1993–2020). *Interactive Learning Environments, 32*(1), 373–392. DOI: 10.1080/10494820.2022.2086579

Jallad, S. T., Alsaqer, K., Albadareen, B. I., & Al-maghaireh, D. (2024). Artificial intelligence tools utilized in nursing education : Incidence and associated factors. *Nurse Education Today, 142*, 106355. DOI: 10.1016/j.nedt.2024.106355 PMID: 39163690

Jia, X.-H., & Tu, J.-C. (2024). Towards a New Conceptual Model of AI-Enhanced Learning for College Students : The Roles of Artificial Intelligence Capabilities, General Self-Efficacy, Learning Motivation, and Critical Thinking Awareness. *Systems, 12*(3), 3. Advance online publication. DOI: 10.3390/systems12030074

Jian, M. J. K. O. (2023). Personalized learning through AI. *Advances in Engineering Innovation, 5*(1), 16–19. DOI: 10.54254/2977-3903/5/2023039

Jung, S. (2023). Challenges for future directions for artificial intelligence integrated nursing simulation education. *Women's Health Nursing, 29*(3), 239–242. DOI: 10.4069/kjwhn.2023.09.06.1 PMID: 37813667

Kamalov, F., Santandreu Calonge, D., & Gurrib, I. (2023). New Era of Artificial Intelligence in Education : Towards a Sustainable Multifaceted Revolution. *Sustainability (Basel), 15*(16), 16. Advance online publication. DOI: 10.3390/su151612451

Khan, B., Fatima, H., Qureshi, A., Kumar, S., Hanan, A., Hussain, J., & Abdullah, S. (2023). Drawbacks of Artificial Intelligence and Their Potential Solutions in the Healthcare Sector. *Biomedical Materials & Devices, 1*(2), 731–738. DOI: 10.1007/s44174-023-00063-2 PMID: 36785697

Kitsios, F., Kamariotou, M., Syngelakis, A. I., & Talias, M. A. (2023). Recent Advances of Artificial Intelligence in Healthcare : A Systematic Literature Review. *Applied Sciences (Basel, Switzerland), 13*(13), 13. Advance online publication. DOI: 10.3390/app13137479

Kong, W., Ning, Y., Ma, T., Song, F., Mao, Y., Yang, C., Li, X., Guo, Y., Liu, H., Shi, J., & Liu, L. (2024). Experience of undergraduate nursing students participating in artificial intelligence+project task driven learning at different stages : A qualitative study. *BMC Nursing, 23*(1), 314. DOI: 10.1186/s12912-024-01982-1 PMID: 38720326

Kouka, A., Giannelou, E., Konstantinidis, K., & Apostolakis, I. (2025). Implementation of Artificial Intelligence in nursing education : A Narrative Review. *Health & Research Journal, 11*(1), 1. Advance online publication. DOI: 10.12681/healthresj.36795

Kowitlawakul, Y., Tan, J. J. M., Suebnukarn, S., Nguyen, H. D., Poo, D. C. C., Chai, J., Kamala, D. M., & Wang, W. (2024). Development of an Artificial Intelligence Teaching Assistant System for Undergraduate Nursing Students : A Field Testing Study. *CIN: Computers, Informatics. Computers, Informatics, Nursing, 42*(5), 334–342. DOI: 10.1097/CIN.0000000000001103 PMID: 38270543

Labrague, L. J., & Sabei, A. L. (2025). Artificial intelligence in nursing education : A review of AI-based teaching pedagogies. *Teaching and Learning in Nursing, 20*(3), 210–221. DOI: 10.1016/j.teln.2025.01.019

Lane, S. H., Haley, T., & Brackney, D. E. (2024). Tool or Tyrant : Guiding and Guarding Generative Artificial Intelligence Use in Nursing Education. *Creative Nursing, 30*(2), 125–132. DOI: 10.1177/10784535241247094 PMID: 38651267

Lebo, C., & Brown, N. (2024). Integrating Artificial Intelligence (AI) Simulations Into Undergraduate Nursing Education : An Evolving AI Patient. *Nursing Education Perspectives, 45*(1), 55–56. DOI: 10.1097/01.NEP.0000000000001081 PMID: 36728992

Liaw, S. Y., Tan, J. Z., Lim, S., Zhou, W., Yap, J., Ratan, R., Ooi, S. L., Wong, S. J., Seah, B., & Chua, W. L. (2023). Artificial intelligence in virtual reality simulation for interprofessional communication training : Mixed method study. *Nurse Education Today, 122*, 105718. DOI: 10.1016/j.nedt.2023.105718 PMID: 36669304

Montejo, L., Fenton, A., & Davis, G. (2024). Applications of artificial intelligence (AI) in healthcare and considerations for nursing education. *Nurse Education in Practice, 80*, 104158. DOI: 10.1016/j.nepr.2024.104158 PMID: 39388757

Peng, M. L., Wickersham, J. A., Altice, F. L., Shrestha, R., Azwa, I., Zhou, X., Halim, M. A. A., Ikhtiaruddin, W. M., Tee, V., Kamarulzaman, A., & Ni, Z. (2022). Formative Evaluation of the Acceptance of HIV Prevention Artificial Intelligence Chatbots By Men Who Have Sex With Men in Malaysia : Focus Group Study. *JMIR Formative Research, 6*(10), e42055. DOI: 10.2196/42055 PMID: 36201390

Ramírez-Baraldes, E., García-Gutiérrez, D., & García-Salido, C. (2025). Artificial Intelligence in Nursing : New Opportunities and Challenges. *European Journal of Education, 60*(1), e70033. DOI: 10.1111/ejed.70033

Reed, J., Alterio, B., Coblenz, H., O'Lear, T., & Metz, T. (2023). AI Image-Generation as a Teaching Strategy in Nursing Education. *Journal of Interactive Learning Research, 34*(2), 369–399. DOI: 10.70725/729255gdiorw

Reed, & Dodson, T. M. (2024). Generative AI Backstories for Simulation Preparation. *Nurse Educator, 49*(4), 184. .DOI: 10.1097/NNE.0000000000001590

Rodriguez-Arrastia, M., Martinez-Ortigosa, A., Ruiz-Gonzalez, C., Ropero-Padilla, C., Roman, P., & Sanchez-Labraca, N. (2022). Experiences and perceptions of final-year nursing students of using a chatbot in a simulated emergency situation : A qualitative study. *Journal of Nursing Management, 30*(8), 3874–3884. DOI: 10.1111/jonm.13630 PMID: 35411629

Sallam, M. (2023). Utility of ChatGPT in healthcare education, research, and practice: a systematic review of promising prospects and legitimate concerns. In *Healthcare 11(6), 887.* MDPI.

Shen, M., Shen, Y., Liu, F., & Jin, J. (2025). Prompts, privacy, and personalized learning: Integrating AI into nursing education—a qualitative study. *BMC Nursing, 24*(1), 470. DOI: 10.1186/s12912-025-03115-8 PMID: 40301862

Simsek-Cetinkaya, S., & Cakir, S. K. (2023). Evaluation of the effectiveness of artificial intelligence assisted interactive screen-based simulation in breast self-examination : An innovative approach in nursing students. *Nurse Education Today, 127*, 105857. DOI: 10.1016/j.nedt.2023.105857 PMID: 37253303

Sun, C., Zhong, Y., & Wang, L. (2024). The Application, Challenges, and Development of Artificial Intelligence in Nursing Education. *Education Reform and Development, 6*(12), 12. Advance online publication. DOI: 10.26689/erd.v6i12.9290

Tam, W., Huynh, T., Tang, A., Luong, S., Khatri, Y., & Zhou, W. (2023). La formation infirmière à l'ère des chatbots alimentés par l'intelligence artificielle (AI-Chatbots): Sommes-nous prêts? *Nurse Education Today, 129*, 105917. DOI: 10.1016/j.nedt.2023.105917 PMID: 37506622

Taskiran, N. (2023). Effect of Artificial Intelligence Course in Nursing on Students' Medical Artificial Intelligence Readiness : A Comparative Quasi-Experimental Study. *Nurse Educator, 48*(5), E147–E152. DOI: 10.1097/NNE.0000000000001446 PMID: 37133231

Topaz, M., Peltonen, L., Michalowski, M., Stiglic, G., Ronquillo, C., Pruinelli, L., Song, J., O'Connor, S., Miyagawa, S., & Fukahori, H. (2024). The ChatGPT effect: Nursing education and generative artificial intelligence. *The Journal of Nursing Education, 1*(4). Advance online publication. DOI: 10.3928/01484834-20240126-01 PMID: 38302101

Verma, R. A., Das, A. N. A., Danapure, R. H., Kosare, P. D., Moon, S. B., & Chokhare, A. G. (2024). Artificial intelligence : A huge augmentation in nursing curriculum. *IP Journal of Paediatrics and Nursing Science, 7*(4), 125–134. DOI: 10.18231/j.ijpns.2024.025

White, A., Maguire, M. B., Brown, A., & Keen, D. (2024). Impact of Artificial Intelligence on Nursing Students' Attitudes toward Older Adults : A Pre/Post-Study. *Nursing Reports, 14*(2), 2. Advance online publication. DOI: 10.3390/nursrep14020085 PMID: 38804418

Yelne, S., Chaudhary, M., Dod, K., Sayyad, A., & Sharma, R. (2023). Harnessing the power of AI: A comprehensive review of its impact and challenges in nursing science and healthcare. *Cureus, 15*. Advance online publication. DOI: 10.7759/cureus.49252 PMID: 38143615

Zou, Y., Kuek, F., Feng, W., & Cheng, X. (2025). Digital learning in the 21st century : Trends, challenges, and innovations in technology integration. *Frontiers in Education, 10*, 1562391. DOI: 10.3389/feduc.2025.1562391

Zuhair, V., Babar, A., Ali, R., Oduoye, M. O., Noor, Z., Chris, K., Okon, I. I., & Rehman, L. U. (2024). Exploring the Impact of Artificial Intelligence on Global Health and Enhancing Healthcare in Developing Nations. *Journal of Primary Care & Community Health, 15*, 21501319241245847. DOI: 10.1177/21501319241245847 PMID: 38605668

ADDITIONAL READING

Božić, V. (2024). L'intelligence artificielle dans la formation infirmière. In *Applications techniques de l'intelligence artificielle* (pp. 143–172). Springer Nature Suisse.

Chakir, A., Andry, J. F., Ullah, A., Bansal, R., & Ghazouani, M. (2024). *Applications of artificial intelligence in engineering. Summary conferences on engineering, science, and technology*. Springer. DOI: 10.1007/978-3-031-50300-9

Charow, R., Jeyakumar, T., Younus, S., Dolatabadi, E., Salhia, M., Al-Mouaswas, D., Anderson, M., Balakumar, S., Clare, M., Dhalla, A., Gillan, C., Haghzare, S., Jackson, E., Lalani, N., Mattson, J., Peteanu, W., Tripp, T., Waldorf, J., Williams, S., & Wiljer, D. (2021). Artificial intelligence education programs for health care professionals: Scoping review. *JMIR Medical Education, 7*(4), e31043. DOI: 10.2196/31043 PMID: 34898458

Jeyakumar, T., Younus, S., Zhang, M., Clare, M., Charow, R., Karsan, I., & Wiljer, D. (2023). Preparing for an AI-based future: Patient perspectives on the engagement and training of healthcare professionals for the adoption of artificial intelligence technologies in healthcare settings. *JMIR AI, 2*(1), e40973. DOI: 10.2196/40973 PMID: 38875561

Li, M. (2025). The impact of ChatGPT on teaching and learning in higher education: challenges, opportunities, and future perspectives. In M. Khosrow-Pour, DBA (Ed.), Encyclopedia of Information Science and Technology, Sixth Edition (pp. 1-20). *IGI Global Scientific Publishers*. DOI: 10.4018/978-1-6684-7366-5.ch079

Li, M. (2025). The impact of ChatGPT on teaching and learning in higher education: challenges, opportunities, and future scope. *Encyclopedia of Information Science and Technology, Sixth Edition*, 1-20. DOI: 10.4018/978-1-6684-7366-5.ch079

Opesemowo, O. A. G. (2025). Artificial Intelligence in Mathematics Education: The Pros and Cons. In Encyclopedia of Information Science and Technology, Sixth Edition (pp. 1-18). IGI Global.

Orr, L. (2025). Educational technologies in higher education: online teaching and learning. In M. Khosrow-Pour, DBA (ed.), Encyclopedia of Information Science and Technology, Sixth Edition. Early online publication. DOI: 10.4018/978-1-6684-7366-5.ch083

Sheikh, H., Prins, C., & Schrijvers, E. (2023). Artificial intelligence: definition and background. In Mission, A. I. (Ed.), *The new system technology* (pp. 15–41). Springer International Publishing., DOI: 10.1007/978-3-031-21448-6_2

Wong, K. C., & Lai, Y. C. (2025). The use of artificial intelligence applications in projects by students in vocational training. In M. Khosrow-Pour, DBA (Ed.), Encyclopedia of Information Science and Technology, Sixth Edition (pp. 1-27). IGI Global Scientific Publishers.

KEY TERMS AND DEFINITIONS

Artificial Intelligence: Artificial intelligence (AI) can be defined as software or a machine designed to automatically perform calculations and process data by following predefined algorithms. It imitates certain aspects of human intelligence, such as pattern recognition, decision-making, or language use, by employing statistical methods and machine learning models. In summary, AI reproduces intelligent behaviors through computational power, without consciousness or true understanding, but by sophisticatedly simulating human characteristics to accomplish various tasks.

Clinical Reasoning: Clinical reasoning in nursing is the process of systematic and analytical thinking that allows the nurse to interpret the collected data, assess the patient's needs, diagnose health problems, and plan, implement, and evaluate care interventions in an appropriate and effective manner.

Critical Thinking: Critical thinking in nursing is the ability to analyze, examine, and evaluate clinical situations, information, and available data in a thoughtful and objective manner, in order to make informed, ethical decisions that meet the needs of patients, while remaining open to reflection and continuous improvement.

Deep Learning: Deep learning (DL), a subset of machine learning, relies on neural networks using mathematical algorithms. These transmit information between the different nodes of the network to process complex data.

Immersive Learning: Immersive learning is an educational approach that involves immersing learners in interactive or simulated environments, often through technology. This allows them to fully engage in activities close to reality, making learning more vibrant, engaging, and memorable.

Machine Learning: Machine learning (ML) is a technology that enables computers to perform tasks or solve problems without explicit programming. Using algorithms, they extract information from data, learn, and gradually adjust their conclusions. This approach offers very flexible automatic analysis and decision-making, which can be supervised, unsupervised, semi-supervised, or reinforced, depending on the objectives and the nature of the data.

Personalized Learning: Personalized learning refers to an educational approach that tailors the learning experience to the individual needs, preferences, strengths, and pace of each student.

Simulation: This involves the integrated use of a computer model that reproduces reality within the study framework, where risk can be eliminated in the initial structured learning process.

Virtual Reality (VR): Is a simulation of a 3D image or digitally generated learning context, in which a learner can be located and with which they can interact by wearing electronic accessories such as eye glasses or gloves equipped with sensors.

Chapter 6
Artificial Intelligence and Social Economy:
Towards a Critical Epistemology of Solidarity Transformation

Layla Boulkhir
https://orcid.org/0009-0002-4288-8522
Sultan Moulay Slimane University, Morocco

Fatima Touhami
Faculty of Economics and Management, Sultan Moulay Slimane University, Morocco

Asmae Atitaou
Faculty of Legal, Economic and Social Sciences, Marrakech, Morocco

ABSTRACT

The integration of artificial intelligence (AI) into social and solidarity economy (SSE) organizations offers both opportunities and challenges for the sector's core values of solidarity, democracy, and social justice. While AI can enhance innovation, efficiency, and social inclusion, it also raises questions about its alignment with SSE principles. This chapter uses a multilevel quantitative approach and hierarchical linear modeling to analyze AI adoption in a representative sample of SSE organizations, considering both organizational and contextual factors. The findings indicate that AI's positive impact on efficiency and social innovation is real, but its ability to advance a solidarity-based transformation depends on internal resources, leadership, institutional support, and inclusive practices. AI strengthens the SSE's social mission only when embedded in participatory and democratic frameworks.

DOI: 10.4018/979-8-3373-3436-3.ch006

INTRODUCTION

Over the past decade, artificial intelligence (AI) has emerged as a major transformative force across various socio-economic domains, reshaping production methods, decision-making processes, and collective governance structures (Brynjolfsson & McAfee, 2017; Russell & Norvig, 2021). AI has now expanded well beyond the industrial sector, permeating fields such as healthcare, education, the environment, and public policy, where it promises to accelerate innovation, optimize resources, and enhance the efficiency of interventions (Haenlein & Kaplan, 2019; Bughin et al., 2018). However, this dynamic is accompanied by as many concerns as hopes, due to the risks of increasing power asymmetries, algorithmic opacity, discriminatory biases, and the marginalization of certain social groups (O'Neil, 2016; Noble, 2018; Caliskan, Bryson & Narayanan, 2017).

In this context, the social and solidarity economy (SSE) offers a particularly rich terrain for questioning the appropriation of AI in the service of the common good. SSE encompasses organizations such as cooperatives, mutuals, associations, and social enterprises that place solidarity, democratic governance, and social purpose at the heart of their activities (Defourny & Nyssens, 2012; Laville, 2015). Today, these organizations face a dual imperative: on the one hand, to seize the opportunities provided by advanced technologies to foster social innovation and collective impact (Moulaert & MacCallum, 2019); and on the other, to safeguard their foundational values in the face of the rationalization and automation logics inherent in AI (Bidet, 2021).

Despite a growing body of research on AI ethics, digital governance, and social innovation, there remains a conceptual and empirical gap concerning how AI reshapes the epistemological foundations of solidarity-based organizations. Existing studies often examine AI adoption from a technological or managerial perspective, focusing on efficiency gains, but rarely explore its implications for democratic participation, collective learning, and social justice within the SSE. This chapter addresses this shortcoming by proposing a critical and integrative framework that connects AI's algorithmic rationality with the normative principles of solidarity, inclusion, and participatory governance.

The introduction of AI in the SSE is therefore far from neutral: it raises crucial questions about the meaning of technological innovation within organizations whose primary goal is not profit maximization, but rather social emancipation, the reduction of inequalities, and the co-construction of inclusive solutions (Nicholls, Simon & Gabriel, 2015; Smith, Gonin & Besharov, 2013). Recent scholarship stresses the need to move beyond an instrumental view of AI and critically interrogate its systemic effects on democratic governance, actor participation, and social equity (Eubanks, 2018; Van Dijck, Poell & de Waal, 2018). At the same time, empirical studies indicate that AI, when critically and contextually appropriated, can serve as a catalyst for social innovation, optimization of collective resources, and amplification of solidarity-driven impact (Crawford, 2021; Boulkhir & Nafil, 2019).

Nevertheless, the academic debate remains divided: is AI a vector of emancipation, or does it risk exacerbating structural inequalities within the SSE? How can we ensure that the appropriation of AI remains aligned with the values of solidarity, inclusion, and democratic participation (Floridi et al., 2018; Morley et al., 2021)? More fundamentally, does the rise of AI call for an epistemological refoundation of social economy analysis—one that can articulate technological transformation, ethical imperatives, and social justice (Sen, 2009; Rawls, 1971)?

To address these issues, this chapter advances an original contribution by combining a critical theoretical analysis with a multilevel quantitative study of 212 SSE organizations across six Moroccan regions. The objective is to empirically assess how AI adoption affects organizational performance, innovation capacity, and participatory governance, while situating these dynamics within broader ethical and institutional contexts.

Accordingly, the chapter is structured as follows: First, it presents a critical state of the art on the interactions between AI and the SSE, highlighting current theoretical debates and research gaps. Second, it outlines the multilevel quantitative methodology used to analyze AI integration within SSE organizations, specifying the key variables, survey instruments, and analytical protocols. Finally, it discusses the main empirical findings, linking them to ethical, organizational, and social challenges, before concluding with critical perspectives and policy implications for the future transformation of the social economy in the age of AI.

BACKGROUND

1. From Technical Promise to Sociotechnical Reality

Artificial intelligence (AI) has rapidly diffused across domains beyond industry, including health, education, public administration, and social innovation (Haenlein & Kaplan, 2019; Bughin et al., 2018; Bryson, 2023). Canonical definitions emphasize AI as a set of computational techniques that simulate or augment human cognition (Russell & Norvig, 2021). Yet recent scholarship stresses that AI systems are sociotechnical—embedded in organizational routines, infrastructures, and power relations—so their effects cannot be reduced to technical performance alone (Van Dijck, Poell, & de Waal, 2018; OECD, 2023). This shift reframes evaluation criteria from accuracy and efficiency to include transparency, accountability, and distributive justice. Gap addressed. Prior literature often analyzes AI adoption in managerial or technical terms, with limited attention to participatory governance, collective learning, and equity in solidarity-oriented organizations. The present chapter responds by aligning AI analysis with the epistemic and normative commitments of the social and solidarity economy (SSE).

2. Ethical, Responsible, and Sustainable AI: Principles to Practice

Principle-based frameworks (e.g., beneficence, non-maleficence, justice, explicability) have proliferated (Floridi et al., 2018). However, principles alone do not guarantee ethical AI in practice; operationalization requires institutions, incentives, and tools for measurement and redress (Mittelstadt, 2023). Governance research therefore prioritizes explainability, contestability, impact assessments, and algorithmic audits (Morley et al., 2021; Bryson, 2023). A complementary strand interrogates bias and harm, showing how models trained on historical data can reproduce structural inequalities (Caliskan, Bryson, & Narayanan, 2017; Noble, 2018; O'Neil, 2022 updated ed.). Implication for the SSE. Because SSE organizations claim social missions—equity, inclusion, democratic control—ethical AI is not merely risk mitigation; it is mission alignment. This requires tailoring governance devices (audits, oversight boards, participatory impact assessments) to deliberative cultures and stakeholder heterogeneity typical of cooperatives, associations, and mutuals.

3. The SSE as a Distinct Governance Field

The SSE encompasses organizations that prioritize collective benefit, democratic governance, and the primacy of people over capital (Defourny & Nyssens, 2012; Laville, 2015; Bouchard & Klein, 2024). Recent comparative work documents the digital transition of the SSE, with opportunities for process transparency, co-production of services, and inclusive decision-making (OECD, 2023). At the same time, tensions emerge between technocratic optimization and participatory deliberation, echoing classic research on social-business paradoxes (Smith, Gonin, & Besharov, 2013). Gap addressed. While digitalization in the SSE is documented, the specific interplay between algorithmic rationality and solidarity-based epistemologies remains under-specified. This chapter advances a bridge by theorizing how ethical/responsible/sustainable AI can be operationalized within solidarity values (justice, equity, transparency) and by testing these links empirically.

4. AI for Social Innovation and Collective Empowerment

Evidence increasingly shows that when AI is context-sensitive and co-designed, it can enhance social outcomes: targeted public health outreach, inclusive learning pathways, resource matching, and environmental stewardship (Crawford, 2021; OECD, 2023). In SSE settings, data systems can support participatory mapping, fairer allocation of scarce resources, and accountable service delivery—provided governance mechanisms remain open to scrutiny and redress. Empirical illustrations in the Global South highlight the importance of infrastructure readiness, capacity building, and policy support to avoid deepening digital divides (Boulkhir & Nafil, 2019; OECD, 2023). Remaining gap. Many case reports lack multilevel designs capable of disentangling organizational from contextual effects (e.g., leadership vs. regional policies). Our chapter contributes by applying hierarchical linear modeling (HLM) to capture both levels simultaneously.

5. From Principles to Institutional Design in the SSE

Recent contributions argue for moving beyond ethics statements toward institutional design: how organizations embed accountability into data lifecycles, who is empowered to challenge models, and how common-good objectives are encoded in optimization targets (Bryson, 2023; Mittelstadt, 2023). In the SSE, this aligns with cooperative principles member control, transparency, and education suggesting concrete instruments:

- Algorithmic oversight boards nested in federations or consortia;
- Participatory algorithmic impact assessments integrating beneficiary voices;
- Open data/traceability strategies consistent with privacy and community consent;
- Capacity-building and peer-learning networks across SSE sectors.

Theoretical integration. Positioning AI within SSE values resonates with capability-enhancing perspectives (Sen, 2009) and with distributive-ecological frames (Raworth, 2017), recasting "responsible AI" as expansion of collective capabilities under planetary and social boundaries.

6. Synthesis and Research Agenda

The literature converges on three propositions:

1. AI's impacts are co-produced by technology, governance, and context;

2. Ethical/sustainable AI requires institutional translation (audits, participation, redress);
3. The SSE provides a privileged laboratory to test human-centered AI under conditions of democratic control and social purpose.

Contribution of this chapter. Building on these insights, we:

- articulate an integrative conceptual framework linking ethical/responsible AI to SSE values;
- test relationships between AI adoption, performance, innovation, and participatory governance using a multilevel dataset of 212 organizations across six regions;
- derive policy- and practice-oriented recommendations that translate principles into implementable governance mechanisms for SSE actors.

MAIN FOCUS OF THE CHAPTER

1. Issues, Controversies, Problems

The integration of artificial intelligence (AI) into the social and solidarity economy (SSE) raises significant and multifaceted issues that are central both to the main theme of this chapter and to the broader discourse on the digital transformation of human and social systems.

One of the core controversies lies in the potential conflict between the technocratic logic of AI and the participatory, democratic ethos of the SSE (Smith, Gonin & Besharov, 2013; Laville, 2015). AI technologies are fundamentally built on data-driven processes, optimization, and algorithmic governance, which, while offering possibilities for organizational efficiency, risk marginalizing traditional modes of collective deliberation and human judgment. This tension prompts the question: Can SSE organizations adopt AI without compromising their foundational values of inclusivity, transparency, and social justice? (Floridi et al., 2018; Eubanks, 2018). Another critical concern involves the reproduction or amplification of existing social inequalities. AI systems, when trained on biased datasets, can perpetuate or exacerbate discrimination, especially against already marginalized groups (Caliskan, Bryson & Narayanan, 2017; Noble, 2018). In the context of the SSE—which seeks to empower the most vulnerable and reduce exclusion—this presents a fundamental contradiction. Unlike profit-driven enterprises, SSE organizations are tasked not only with fostering technical innovation but also with safeguarding the ethics of care, diversity, and equity (Defourny & Nyssens, 2012; Moulaert & MacCallum, 2019).

There are also significant organizational and governance challenges. The adoption of AI demands new skills, technical infrastructure, and resources that are often limited within SSE organizations. This can lead to a technological divide between large, well-funded actors and smaller, grassroots organizations (Brynjolfsson & McAfee, 2017). Moreover, the opacity of many AI systems—often referred to as the *"black box"* problem—can undermine trust among stakeholders and erode the participatory governance that is central to the SSE (Van Dijck, Poell & de Waal, 2018). Nevertheless, emerging empirical evidence suggests that AI, if critically and inclusively implemented, can enhance social innovation, facilitate more targeted and impactful interventions, and foster new forms of collective intelligence (Crawford, 2021; Boulkhir & Nafil, 2019). Some pioneering SSE organizations are experimenting with AI tools for resource allocation, participatory mapping, and data-driven community development, showing that technological and social innovation can be mutually reinforcing when guided by shared values (Floridi et al., 2018).

2. Analytical Link: Technological Paradigms and Solidarity Values

The conceptual and epistemological bridge between artificial intelligence (AI) and the social and solidarity economy (SSE) can be understood through the dialogue between technological paradigms ethical AI, responsible AI, and sustainable AI and the normative foundations of the social economy, namely justice, equity, transparency, and democratic participation.

Recent scholarship emphasizes that ethical AI is not merely a matter of technical compliance or regulatory oversight; rather, it represents a broader social contract that requires embedding moral reasoning, inclusivity, and accountability into algorithmic systems (Mittelstadt, 2023; Bryson, 2023; Floridi et al., 2018). This perspective aligns with the epistemological principles of the SSE, which conceptualize economic action as relational, cooperative, and value-oriented (Laville, 2015; Bouchard & Klein, 2024). Both paradigms converge around the notion of collective well-being over individual optimization, suggesting that AI, when grounded in solidarity-based ethics, can operationalize the capability approach (Sen, 2009; Nussbaum, 2011) by expanding both individual and collective freedoms through technological empowerment.

From a post-humanist and socio-technical standpoint, AI can be viewed as part of an evolving assemblage of human–machine relations, requiring reflexivity in how agency and responsibility are distributed between humans, algorithms, and institutions (Latour, 2021). This critical lens challenges the dominance of instrumental rationality in AI discourse, proposing instead an ecology of intelligence grounded in cooperation and care rather than competition and control. In this light, a sustainable

AI for the SSE must not only minimize harm or bias but also actively contribute to redistributive justice, democratic co-governance, and ecological responsibility (Raworth, 2017; OECD, 2023). It implies reimagining data infrastructures as commons rather than proprietary assets, and algorithmic governance as a participatory process that reflects plural and community-based epistemologies. Consequently, the SSE can serve as both a laboratory and a regulatory counter-model for developing human-centered, solidarity-oriented AI—an epistemic space where technological innovation is re-embedded within ethical deliberation, collective empowerment, and social transformation.

3. Main Objectives of the Chapter

The main focus of this chapter is to explore these complex issues at the intersection of AI and the SSE by:

- Critically analyzing the potential and limitations of AI as a driver of social innovation within the SSE;
- Examining the organizational, ethical, and epistemological tensions that arise from the encounter between algorithmic rationality and solidarity-based practices;
- Comparing current approaches with both the traditional values of the SSE and contemporary models of digital transformation;
- Arguing for the development of frameworks and practices that reconcile technological progress with the core principles of democracy, justice, and inclusion.

Through this analytical lens, the chapter contributes to the broader debate on how the digital revolution can support—not undermine—the emancipatory potential of the social and solidarity economy.

4. Comparative Case Insights: Cross-Contextual Applications of AI in the SSE

Recent empirical developments illustrate how AI adoption within the social and solidarity economy (SSE) varies across socio-economic contexts while maintaining common principles of democratic governance and social inclusion.

4.1. Morocco – Cooperative Intelligence for Sustainable Agriculture.

In Morocco, agricultural and craft cooperatives have begun deploying simple AI-enabled decision-support tools for irrigation management, production planning, and market matching. Pilot programs supported by the *Office du Développement de la Coopération (ODCO)* and local universities integrate predictive analytics to optimize resource use under water-scarcity conditions. These initiatives demonstrate how AI can align with the SSE's sustainability mission by strengthening resilience and local autonomy (Boulkhir, 2023).

4.2. Europe – Ethical AI in Cooperative Banking.

Across Europe, cooperative financial institutions such as *Crédit Coopératif* (France) and *Raiffeisen Group* (Austria) have launched projects on algorithmic transparency and participatory oversight boards. Their aim is to balance digital efficiency with ethical accountability by embedding *explainable AI (XAI)* models in credit-scoring processes, ensuring compliance with GDPR and cooperative principles (Bryson, 2023; OECD, 2023). These cases illustrate institutionalized forms of *ethical governance* in technologically advanced environments.

4.3. Latin America – AI for Social Inclusion and Territorial Governance.

In Latin America, particularly in Brazil and Colombia, social enterprises and solidarity networks employ AI-driven mapping and data visualization to improve community planning and inclusion of informal workers. Projects supported by the *Banco do Brasil Foundation* and local universities leverage natural language processing to analyze citizen feedback and allocate resources more equitably (Bouchard & Klein, 2024). These experiments highlight the potential of AI as an enabler of participatory democracy in contexts marked by socio-economic inequality.

4.4. Comparative Analysis.

Despite contextual diversity—resource constraints in Morocco, institutional maturity in Europe, and inequality challenges in Latin America—common patterns emerge:

- Ethical alignment between technological design and social mission;
- Participatory governance as a determinant of successful AI appropriation;
- Public-policy mediation essential for bridging digital divides.

This cross-regional comparison reinforces the chapter's argument that AI's transformative capacity depends less on its technical sophistication than on the institutional and cultural embedding of algorithmic systems within solidarity-oriented governance models.

METHODOLOGY

1. Research Design

This chapter employs a multilevel quantitative research design to analyze the impact of artificial intelligence (AI) adoption within social and solidarity economy (SSE) organizations. The methodology combines primary data collected via a structured questionnaire and secondary data from institutional sources. The analytical framework distinguishes between organizational-level and contextual-level effects using hierarchical linear modeling (HLM).

2. Data Collection and Sample Characteristics

Data were collected from a stratified sample of 212 SSE organizations (cooperatives, associations, mutuals, and social enterprises) operating across six regions and three sectors (health, education, community services). The survey targeted managers and key stakeholders, ensuring diversity in organizational size, years of operation, and governance models.

Table 1. Sample characteristics of surveyed SSE organizations

Characteristic	Frequency (n=212)	Percentage (%)
Legal Form		
– Cooperative	88	41.5
– Association	71	33.5
– Mutual	31	14.6
– Social Enterprise	22	10.4
Sector		
– Health	67	31.6
– Education	61	28.8
– Community Services	84	39.6
Region	6 regions	100

continued on following page

Table 1. Continued

Characteristic	Frequency (n=212)	Percentage (%)
Size (employees)		
- 1–9	105	49.5
- 10–49	70	33.0
- 50 and more	37	17.5

3. Variables and Analytical Methods

The questionnaire measured several key variables at different levels, summarized in Table 2.

Table 2. Main variables and indicators used in the study

Level	Variable	Indicator / Measurement
Organizational (Level 1)	AI Adoption	Frequency of AI use (1=never; 5=very often)
	Social Innovation	Number of new social projects in 2 years
	Organizational Performance	Composite index (efficiency, reach, inclusion)
	Participatory Governance	Score based on stakeholder involvement
	Leadership	Transformational, Transactional (scale)
Contextual (Level 2)	Regional Policy Support	Existence of public support (0/1)
	Access to Funding	Amount (USD), Number of grants
	Digital Infrastructure	Internet speed (Mbps), digitalization index
	Sectoral Regulation	Scale (1=none; 5=very strict)

4. Analytical Framework and Conceptual Model

The multilevel analysis employs a hierarchical linear model to distinguish effects at organizational and contextual levels.

The general form of the multilevel regression model is:

$$Y_{\{ij\}} = \beta_{\{0\}} + \beta_{\{1\}X_{\{ij\}}} + \beta_{\{2\}Z_{\{j\}}} + u_j + \epsilon_{ij}$$

Where:

- Y_{ij}: Outcome variable for organization i in region$j$ (e.g., organizational performance)
- $X_{\{ij\}}$: Organizational-level predictors (AI adoption, leadership, governance)

- $Z_{\{j\}}$: Contextual-level predictors (policy support, infrastructure)
- u_j: Random effect for region jjj
- $\epsilon_{\{ij\}}$: Random error term

Figure 1. Conceptual model of AI adoption and its effects within SSE organizations

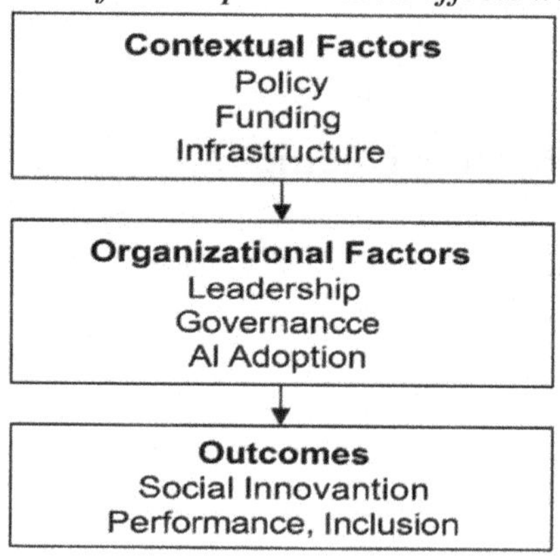

Source: Author, adapted from Smith et al. (2013) and Floridi et al. (2018)

RESULTS

1. Study Area and Sample Overview

The empirical research was conducted among social and solidarity economy (SSE) organizations in six Moroccan regions: Casablanca-Settat, Rabat-Salé-Kénitra, Marrakech-Safi, Fès-Meknès, Tanger-Tétouan-Al Hoceima, and Souss-Massa. The selected regions represent a diversity of socio-economic and digital environments, ensuring that findings reflect both urban and rural realities as well as differing levels of public policy support and infrastructure. A total of 212 organizations participated in the study. The sample included cooperatives (41.5%), associations (33.5%), mutuals (14.6%), and social enterprises (10.4%). The distribution across sectors was as follows: health (31.6%), education (28.8%), and community services (39.6%). Most organizations were small in size, with 49.5% employing fewer than ten people. Table 1 summarizes the sample characteristics.

Table 3. Sample characteristics of surveyed SSE organizations

Characteristic	Frequency (n=212)	Percentage (%)
Legal Form		
– Cooperative	88	41.5
– Association	71	33.5
– Mutual	31	14.6
– Social Enterprise	22	10.4
Sector		
– Health	67	31.6
– Education	61	28.8
– Community Services	84	39.6
Region	6 regions	100
Size (employees)		
– 1–9	105	49.5
– 10–49	70	33.0
– 50 and more	37	17.5

2. Descriptive Statistics of AI Adoption

The degree of AI adoption varied significantly among organizations. On a scale from 1 (never) to 5 (very often), the mean frequency of AI tool usage was 2.3 (SD = 1.1). Cooperatives and social enterprises reported higher average usage than associations and mutuals. Figure 2 illustrates the distribution of AI adoption levels across organization types.

Figure 2. Distribution of AI adoption levels by organization type

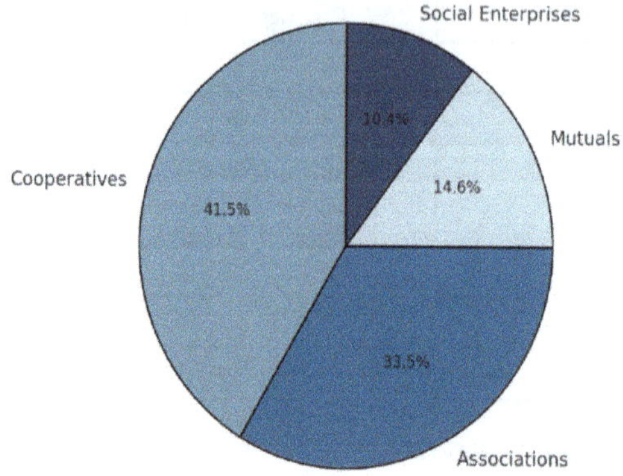

Source: Survey data, 2025

3. Organizational Performance and Social Innovation

A composite index of organizational performance (ranging from 0 to 100) was constructed based on efficiency, outreach, and inclusion scores. The mean performance index was 68.7 (SD = 14.9). Regression analysis (Table 2) showed that higher AI adoption was positively associated with higher organizational performance ($\beta = 0.31$, $p < 0.01$), controlling for size, sector, and region.

Social innovation was measured by the number of new social projects launched in the past two years. Organizations with frequent AI use reported, on average, 2.6 new projects versus 1.4 for those with little or no AI adoption ($p < 0.05$, t-test).

Table 4. Regression results: Determinants of organizational performance (HLM model)

Predictor	Coefficient (β)	Std. Error	p-value
AI Adoption	0.31	0.09	0.002**
Leadership (Transform.)	0.28	0.08	0.004**
Policy Support (Context)	0.19	0.07	0.012*
Size	0.11	0.06	0.087
Digital Infrastructure	0.13	0.05	0.035*
Constant	53.3	7.4	<0.001

Note: **p < 0.01; *p < 0.05. Model N = 212 organizations, ICC = 0.15.

4. Multilevel Effects and Contextual Factors

The hierarchical linear model indicated that 15% of the variance in performance was attributable to regional and contextual factors (intraclass correlation = 0.15). Organizations in regions with strong policy support and advanced digital infrastructure scored, on average, 8.2 points higher on the performance index than those in less supportive environments ($p < 0.01$).

Figure 3. Effect of contextual policy support on organizational performance

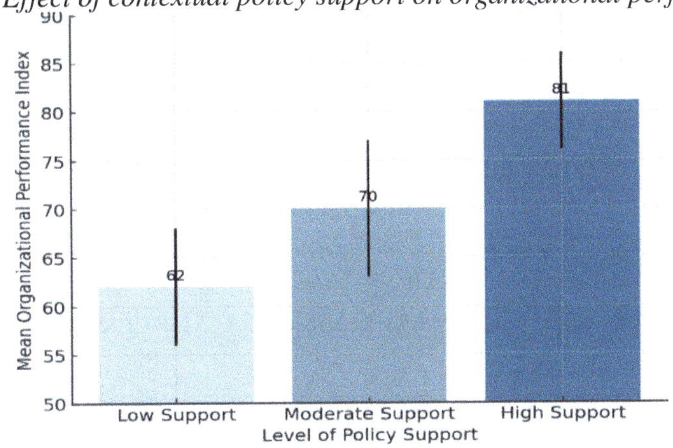

Source: Model estimates, 2025

4.1 Additional Findings

- Organizations led by women demonstrated slightly higher rates of social innovation (mean = 2.4 projects) compared to those led by men (mean = 1.9).
- Barriers most frequently cited included lack of funding for digitalization (62%), insufficient staff training (55%), and concerns about data privacy (41%).

The results highlight the importance of both organizational and contextual factors in determining the effective integration of AI in SSE organizations. AI adoption is associated with greater organizational performance and social innovation, but these benefits are contingent on supportive regional policies and digital infrastructure.

SOLUTIONS AND RECOMMENDATIONS

The empirical findings of this chapter reveal both the opportunities and the challenges associated with adopting artificial intelligence (AI) within social and solidarity economy (SSE) organizations. To address the main barriers identified—such as limited funding, skills shortages, and risks of algorithmic bias—while maximizing the social value of AI, a multi-faceted strategy is necessary.

1. Strengthening Digital Capacity and Inclusive Training

SSE organizations must prioritize digital upskilling for their members, leaders, and staff. This can be achieved through:

- Partnerships with universities, technology firms, and civil society organizations to design and deliver tailored training programs on AI fundamentals, data governance, and ethical risk assessment.
- Developing peer-to-peer knowledge-sharing networks within the SSE, enabling organizations with more experience in AI to mentor and support newcomers.

2. Promoting Participatory and Ethical AI Governance

To ensure that AI integration aligns with SSE values, it is essential to:

- Establish participatory governance structures that involve diverse stakeholders—including beneficiaries—in the design, deployment, and monitoring of AI tools.
- Create ethical guidelines and review boards within SSE federations to oversee algorithmic transparency, data protection, and fairness in decision-making.
- Adopt tools such as impact assessment checklists and algorithmic audits, drawing on frameworks like Floridi et al. (2018) and Morley et al. (2021), to regularly evaluate the social and ethical implications of AI use.

3. Leveraging Supportive Public Policies

Policy makers should:

- Design and fund dedicated grant schemes and tax incentives for digital transformation and responsible AI adoption in SSE organizations, particularly those serving marginalized communities.

- Encourage public–private–social partnerships to ensure equitable access to digital infrastructure, affordable AI tools, and open data relevant to the missions of SSE actors.
- Include SSE representatives in national and regional AI strategy boards to advocate for the sector's specific needs and ethical perspectives.

4. Facilitating Collaborative Innovation and Research

To foster inclusive and effective AI innovation:

- Support collaborative pilot projects between research institutions, technology providers, and SSE organizations to co-design, test, and scale AI applications tailored to local needs.
- Promote action research methodologies that combine empirical evaluation with participatory learning and iterative improvement, ensuring that innovation remains context-sensitive and community-driven.

5. Building Monitoring and Evaluation Frameworks

SSE organizations and policy makers should:

- Implement robust monitoring systems for tracking both the intended and unintended effects of AI adoption on organizational performance, social innovation, and inclusion.
- Use mixed-method evaluation (quantitative and qualitative) to assess outcomes, drawing on international standards and adapting metrics to the realities of the SSE.

Table 5. Summary of recommended actions for responsible AI adoption in the SSE

Strategic Area	Key Actions
Digital Capacity	Training, peer networks, digital literacy initiatives
Ethical Governance	Participatory structures, ethical boards, algorithmic audits
Policy Support	Grants, incentives, public–private–social partnerships, inclusion in strategy boards
Collaborative R&D	Pilot projects, action research, co-design with communities
Evaluation	Mixed-method monitoring, adaptive metrics, continuous feedback loops

By implementing these solutions, SSE organizations can not only overcome barriers to digital transformation but also play a leading role in developing a more inclusive, ethical, and democratically governed AI ecosystem—one that serves the common good and amplifies the social impact of the sector.

Figure 4. Key strategies for responsible AI adoption in the SSE.

Source: *Author.*

FUTURE RESEARCH DIRECTIONS

The integration of artificial intelligence (AI) within the social and solidarity economy (SSE) is a rapidly evolving field that opens numerous avenues for future research. Building on the findings and limitations of this chapter, as well as emerging global trends, several promising directions can be identified.

1. Comparative and Longitudinal Studies

a. Future research should conduct comparative analyses across different regions and legal frameworks to identify contextual factors that facilitate or hinder AI adoption in SSE organizations (Haenlein & Kaplan, 2019; Bughin et al., 2018).
   i. Such studies could reveal best practices and policy transferability (Van Dijck, Poell & de Waal, 2018).

ii. Longitudinal designs are needed to assess the medium- and long-term effects of AI on organizational performance and social innovation (Brynjolfsson & McAfee, 2017).

2. Inclusive and Participatory AI Design:

a. There is a growing need for empirical studies that examine participatory approaches in the design, deployment, and monitoring of AI systems in the SSE (Floridi et al., 2018; Morley et al., 2021).
   i. Research should explore co-design methodologies and stakeholder involvement in algorithmic governance (Eubanks, 2018).
   ii. Participatory evaluation tools and feedback loops are critical for ethical AI implementation (Smith, Gonin & Besharov, 2013).

3. Ethics, Bias, and Accountability Mechanisms:

a. Further work is required to develop, test, and validate frameworks for bias detection, fairness auditing, and accountability in AI applications (Caliskan, Bryson & Narayanan, 2017; Noble, 2018).
   i. Interdisciplinary research combining computer science, ethics, and social sciences is especially encouraged (Floridi et al., 2018).
   ii. Studies may evaluate real-world impact of ethical boards, algorithmic impact assessments, and transparency mechanisms (Morley et al., 2021).

4. AI for Social Innovation and Impact Measurement

a. Research should focus on how AI can be leveraged to create, scale, and evaluate social innovations in different sectors of the SSE (Crawford, 2021; Moulaert & MacCallum, 2019).
   i. Mixed-method metrics and indicators adapted to social impact measurement are needed (Nicholls, Simon & Gabriel, 2015).
   ii. The intersection of AI with other digital technologies (blockchain, IoT) should be further explored (Bughin et al., 2018).

5. Policy and Ecosystem Development

a. There is a need for research on the role of public policies and funding mechanisms in supporting responsible AI adoption within the SSE (Defourny & Nyssens, 2012).
   i. Studies could analyze innovation ecosystems and public–private–social collaborations (Laville, 2015).
   ii. Evaluating the scalability and sustainability of policy support programs will be crucial (Bidet, 2021).

6. Global South and Underserved Contexts

a. More research must address the challenges and opportunities of AI adoption in the SSE in the Global South and underserved regions (Boulkhir & Nafil, 2019).
   i. Attention to resource constraints, infrastructure gaps, and cultural diversity is essential (Moulaert & MacCallum, 2019).
   ii. Comparative studies may help bridge the digital divide and support inclusive, context-sensitive models (Crawford, 2021).

By pursuing these research directions, scholars and practitioners can help shape a more inclusive, ethical, and impactful future for AI in the social and solidarity economy, maximizing benefits while mitigating risks for all stakeholders.

CONCLUSION

This chapter has critically explored the complex intersections between artificial intelligence (AI) and the social and solidarity economy (SSE), demonstrating both the transformative potential and the structural challenges that emerge when algorithmic technologies are integrated into organizations guided by social, democratic, and collective values. Drawing on a multilevel quantitative analysis of 212 SSE organizations across six Moroccan regions, the results reveal that AI adoption significantly enhances organizational performance, social innovation, and collective impact—but only when embedded within ethical governance, participatory management, and supportive institutional ecosystems.

First, the findings underscore that the effects of AI adoption are multidimensional and context-dependent. Organizations that combine strong leadership, inclusive governance, and digital capabilities benefit most from AI integration. Conversely, those lacking adequate infrastructure, funding, or digital literacy face heightened risks of exclusion and dependency on external technological actors. At the contextual level, the study highlights that regional policy support and digital infrastructure play a decisive role in shaping the outcomes of AI adoption.

Second, beyond empirical contributions, this chapter offers practical recommendations for decision-makers, practitioners, and technologists seeking to harness AI for solidarity-based transformation:

- For public policy makers, there is an urgent need to design inclusive digital strategies that integrate SSE actors into national AI roadmaps through targeted funding, training, and co-creation programs. Policies should promote open data access, ethical regulation, and public–private–social partnerships that align innovation with social justice objectives.
- For SSE organizations and networks, the focus should be on developing ethical governance mechanisms—such as algorithmic oversight committees, participatory evaluation frameworks, and continuous digital upskilling initiatives—to ensure that AI adoption strengthens, rather than undermines, democratic practices.
- For technologists and researchers, designing AI systems that are explainable, context-sensitive, and socially responsible is essential. Collaborative innovation ecosystems involving universities, cooperatives, and civic organizations can serve as laboratories for co-developing inclusive and transparent digital solutions.

Third, this research is not without limitations. The cross-sectional design captures a snapshot of AI adoption but does not measure long-term organizational transformation. The sample, although regionally diverse, remains limited to six Moroccan regions, suggesting the need for comparative and longitudinal studies across different socio-economic and institutional settings. Future research should deepen understanding of the causal mechanisms linking AI adoption to social performance, explore participatory AI design methodologies, and evaluate the governance effectiveness of ethical boards and algorithmic audits in real-world SSE contexts.

Ultimately, the integration of artificial intelligence into the social and solidarity economy must not be conceived as a purely technical transition but as a collective, ethical, and epistemological project. If guided by democratic participation, inclusive innovation, and critical reflexivity, AI can become a powerful lever for renewing the emancipatory mission of the social economy—fostering a digital transformation that truly serves humanity, solidarity, and sustainable development.

ACKNOWLEDGMENT

This research received no specific grant from any funding agency in the public, commercial, or not-for-profit sectors. The authors would like to thank all participating organizations and interviewees for their time, openness, and valuable insights. Special thanks are extended to the university research team for their assistance in data collection and to the peer reviewers for their constructive comments.

REFERENCES

Bidet, E. (2021). *Social and solidarity economy: Beyond the fringe?* Edward Elgar.

Bouchard, M. J., & Klein, J. L. (2024). *Social innovation and the digital transition in the social economy*. Routledge.

Brynjolfsson, E., & McAfee, A. (2017). *Machine, platform, crowd: Harnessing our digital future*. W. W. Norton & Company.

Bryson, J. J. (2023). *The ethics of artificial intelligence: Governance, responsibility, and society*. Oxford University Press.

Bughin, J., Hazan, E., Ramaswamy, S., Chui, M., Allas, T., Dahlström, P., & Trench, M. (2018). Notes from the AI frontier: Modeling the impact of AI on the world economy. *McKinsey Global Institute*. https://doi.org/DOI: 10.2139/ssrn.3266941

Caliskan, A., Bryson, J. J., & Narayanan, A. (2017). Semantics derived automatically from language corpora contain human-like biases. *Science*, *356*(6334), 183–186. DOI: 10.1126/science.aal4230 PMID: 28408601

Crawford, K. (2021). *Atlas of AI: Power, politics, and the planetary costs of artificial intelligence*. Yale University Press., DOI: 10.12987/9780300252392

Defourny, J., & Nyssens, M. (2012). The EMES approach of social enterprise in a comparative perspective (EMES Working Paper No. 12/03). *EMES International Research Network*. https://emes.net/publications/working-papers/the-emes-approach-of-social-enterprise-in-a-comparative-perspective-emes-wp-12-03/

Eubanks, V. (2018). *Automating inequality: How high-tech tools profile, police, and punish the poor*. St. Martin's Press.

Floridi, L., Cowls, J., Beltrametti, M., Chatila, R., Chazerand, P., Dignum, V., & Schafer, B. (2018). AI4People—An ethical framework for a good AI society: Opportunities, risks, principles, and recommendations. *Minds and Machines*, *28*(4), 689–707. DOI: 10.1007/s11023-018-9482-5 PMID: 30930541

Haenlein, M., & Kaplan, A. (2019). A brief history of artificial intelligence: On the past, present, and future of artificial intelligence. *California Management Review*, *61*(4), 5–14. DOI: 10.1177/0008125619864925

Latour, B. (2021). *After lockdown: A metamorphosis*. Polity Press.

Laville, J.-L. (2015). *L'économie sociale et solidaire: Pratiques, théories, débats*. Seuil.

Mittelstadt, B. D. (2023). Principles alone cannot guarantee ethical AI. *Nature Machine Intelligence*, *5*(4), 342–350.

Morley, J., Floridi, L., Kinsey, L., & Elhalal, A. (2021). From what to how: An initial review of publicly available AI ethics tools, methods and research to translate principles into practices. *Science and Engineering Ethics*, *27*, 11. PMID: 31828533

Moulaert, F., & MacCallum, D. (2019). *Advanced introduction to social innovation*. Edward Elgar.

Nicholls, A., Simon, J., & Gabriel, M. (Eds.). (2015). *New frontiers in social innovation research*. Palgrave Macmillan. DOI: 10.1057/9781137506801

Noble, S. U. (2018). *Algorithms of oppression: How search engines reinforce racism*. NYU Press., DOI: 10.18574/nyu/9781479833641.001.0001

Nussbaum, M. C. (2011). *Creating capabilities: The human development approach*. Harvard University Press. DOI: 10.4159/harvard.9780674061200

O'Neil, C. (2016). *Weapons of math destruction: How big data increases inequality and threatens democracy*. Crown.

O'Neil, C. (2022). *Weapons of math destruction* (Updated ed.). Penguin.

OECD. (2023). *The social economy and the digital transition: Opportunities and challenges for inclusive growth*. OECD Publishing.

Rawls, J. (1971). *A theory of justice*. Harvard University Press. DOI: 10.4159/9780674042605

Raworth, K. (2017). *Doughnut economics: Seven ways to think like a 21st-century economist*. Chelsea Green Publishing.

Russell, S., & Norvig, P. (2021). *Artificial intelligence: A modern approach* (4th ed.). Pearson.

Sen, A. (2009). *The idea of justice*. Harvard University Press. Smith, W. K., Gonin, M., & Besharov, M. L. (2013). Managing social–business tensions: A review and research agenda for social enterprise. *Business Ethics Quarterly*, *23*(3), 407–442. DOI: 10.5840/beq201323327

Van Dijck, J., Poell, T., & de Waal, M. (2018). *The platform society: Public values in a connective world.* Oxford University Press. DOI: 10.1093/oso/9780190889760.001.0001

Chapter 7
Artificial Intelligence, Humanity, and Sustainability:
Trends and Opportunities

Mehmet Fatih Burak
https://orcid.org/0000-0002-9187-6491
Istanbul Beykent University, Turkey

ABSTRACT

Artificial intelligence (AI), humanity, and sustainability issues are among the important issues that need to be considered together and that attract the attention of people from almost every segment of society. This chapter aims to conduct trends and opportunities analysis on the AI, humanity, and sustainability issue. For this purpose, a trends and opportunities analysis was conducted on publications on the AI, humanity, and sustainability issue in the Web of Science (WoS) database using the Biblioshiny application. The trend and opportunities analysis was conducted within the scope of some descriptive and, three field plot, country collaboration analysis, most frequently used word, word cloud, thematic map, thematic evolution and trend topics analyses. This chapter is thought to provide useful information for researchers and practitioners on the AI, humanity, and sustainability issue.

INTRODUCTION

In the combination of AI and humans, it should be determined how the effectiveness and efficiency of humans are affected by AI or what the level of impact is. First of all, it is important to understand how the effectiveness and efficiency that

DOI: 10.4018/979-8-3373-3436-3.ch007

humans show without AI and the effectiveness and efficiency that they show with AI change (Eastwood, 2025). AI has an impact on applications we use in our daily lives, etc. Humanity can differentiate itself from AI with the human values it values. One of the most important factors in the development of AI is humanity. Humanity is the determining factor of issues such as the direction in which AI will develop and how it will be controlled (Bhandarkar et al., 2024). The AI industry continues to grow worldwide. According to research by Grand View Research (2025), the AI industry is estimated to reach 1,811,747.3 million US dollars in revenue worldwide by 2030. The AI industry is estimated to have a compound annual growth rate of 35.9% worldwide between 2025 and 2030. It can be understood that the impact of the AI industry on human life will continue to increase.

The need for sustainability is becoming more and more important every day. No matter which sector or institution it is, in order to be able to talk about success in its activities, it is important what its impact on sustainability is and how positively it can affect it. Therefore, prioritising sustainability is a strategically important issue for humanity. Humanity looks more positively at institutions and authorities that prioritise sustainability every day. For this reason, it can be understood that it may favour institutions to prioritise sustainability to gain an advantage over their competitors (Florence, 2024). The factors that are effective in making sustainability a subject of science are that it does not only concern people living today and their lifestyles, but also people and lifestyles that are expected to live in the future, that it focuses on how and to what extent people's needs today and in the future can be transformed, and that it concerns the current state and future of the world and universe we live in (Castonguay, 2025).

With bibliometric analyses, it is possible to determine what kind of change there is in the published publications on the analysed subject, what the trends and opportunities are, etc. Thus, bibliometric analyses can guide practitioners and researchers (e.g., Chusniyah et al., 2025; Quesado et al., 2025; J. Wang et al., 2025). For this reason, it is important to determine trends and opportunities related to the research topic through bibliometric and visualisation analyses.

In the literature, many studies have analysed trends, opportunities, etc. on research topics using bibliometric and visualisation analyses (e.g., Hassan et al., 2025; Liu & Chen, 2025; Ni & Abdullah, 2025). Among the bibliometric and visualization analyses on AI, there are many studies such as AI in human resource development (Benabou & Touhami, 2025), empowering student learning through AI (Yun et al., 2025), AI on branding (Hue & Hung, 2025), AI on digital marketing (Bacalhau et al., 2025), AI in energy economics (Jiao et al., 2025), AI in finance (Bayakhmetova et al., 2025), AI in education (Che Ghazali et al., 2025), AI on sustainable development and quality (Navarro & Bayona, 2025). Among the bibliometric and visualization analyses on sustainability, there are many studies such as sustainability-linked bonds

(Machado et al., 2025), environmental sustainability (Buchari et al., 2024; Shunmathy & Selvam, 2025), sustainability parameters (Biswas et al., 2025), sustainable connectivity (Priya et al., 2025), sustainability in university curricula (Garcés-Giraldo et al., 2025), sustainability of green marketing (Sumarsono et al., 2024), sustainability of digital marketing (Santamaría Ruiz et al., 2025), navigating sustainability (Crăciun et al., 2025), sustainability of blue economy (DuPrey Diederichsen et al., 2025),sustainability of teaching (Leal Filho et al., 2025), sustainability of business higher education(A. T. Nguyen et al., 2025), sustainable development goals and sustainability report (Cumbana & Ventura, 2025), sustainability of doughnut economics (Shao, 2025), sustainability of fashion sector (Bilancia et al., 2025), sustainability of project management (Naeni & Tumpa, 2025), social entrepreneurship and sustainability (Maheshwari & Schrage, 2025), industry 4.0 and sustainability (Fatemi et al., 2025), lean construction and sustainability (Wibowo & Ammar, 2025), real estate sustainability (Máška et al., 2023), sustainability performance of building sector (Zhu & Feng, 2025), corporate sustainability (Gorski & Badea, 2025), social sustainability of supply chains (Bigliardi et al., 2025).

This study was carried out to analyse AI, humanity, and sustainability in terms of trends and opportunities analysis. The study was conducted to answer the following questions: 1) How has the distribution of descriptive information and publications on AI, humanity and sustainability changed? 2) Which are the highly cited publications on AI, humanity, and sustainability? 3) How are the findings of the three field plot, country collaboration analysis, most frequently used word, word cloud, thematic map, thematic evolution and trend topics analyses distributed across publications on AI, humanity and sustainability?

This study aims to analyse trends and opportunities regarding AI, humanity and sustainability within the scope of bibliometric and visualisation analysis. For this purpose, the literature review section is mentioned first. Then the methodology section is explained. Then the findings of the study are mentioned. Finally, the discussion and conclusion sections are mentioned.

LITERATURE REVIEW

Artificial Intelligence

AI was coined to describe AI systems that possess human-like abilities. These abilities include the ability to solve problems, perceive, and learn (McKinsey&Company, 2024). AI is a transformation tool for humanity (Sinha et al., 2025). AI is a tool that can be used in the implementation of sustainability-related strategies (Khan et al., 2025). The types of AI that are widely used today are as follows (Betz, 2024):

- AI (Narrow): A type of AI that can be found in many technological products used daily.
- AI (General): A type of AI designed for performance similar to humans.
- AI (Superintelligence): A type of AI that can outperform humans.
- AI (Reactive Machine): A type of AI that does not create memory and creates real-time responses.
- AI (Limited Memory): A type of AI that can store and use information within its limits.
- AI (Theory): A type of AI with potential that has not yet been realised.
- AI (Self-Aware): A type of AI that is aware of itself and has strong intuition.

Studies have been conducted in the literature on AI in many areas that affect humanity. Among these studies are studies such as management (Dong et al., 2025; Han et al., 2025; Teng et al., 2025; Xie & Wu, 2025), communication and telecommunication (Ertem-Eray & Cheng, 2025; Florea & Croitoru, 2025; Rohrbach & Makhortykh, 2025; Sahebi & Formosa, 2025), logistics and supply chain (Beta et al., 2025; Singh et al., 2025; Wang & Zhang, 2025; Wu & Tai, 2024; Yue et al., 2025), production (Fosso Wamba et al., 2024; May et al., 2024), economics and finance (Akhtar et al., 2025; Maheshwari & Samantaray, 2025; Saba & Monkam, 2025; Zhu et al., 2025), health (Ferreira et al., 2025; Lubowitz et al., 2025; Spencer et al., 2025; Toruner et al., 2025), politics (Mostafaei et al., 2025; Weng, 2025; Xu et al., 2025), law (Bonadio & Trapova, 2024; Chen & Rau, 2024; Vicente, 2024), agriculture (Clay et al., 2024; De la Peña & Granados, 2024; Donfouet & Ngouhouo, 2024; Son et al., 2024), sports (Millington et al., 2025; Sanabria Navarro et al., 2024; Zhang et al., 2024).

AI can be understood to increase efficiency and effectiveness in management, manage environmental innovations, and positively affect decision-making processes (Dong et al., 2025; Murtinu & De Massis, 2025). It is understood that AI can be effective in the optimisation and development of communication processes (Florea & Croitoru, 2025; Rohrbach & Makhortykh, 2025). It can be understood that AI can positively affect the optimisation, effectiveness, efficiency and flexibility of prediction and decision-making in production, logistics and supply chain management processes (Beta et al., 2025; May et al., 2024; Singh et al., 2025). It can be understood that AI is an important factor that can support economic growth, enable the development of payment systems, and positively affect the accuracy of investment decisions (Akhtar et al., 2025; Maheshwari & Samantaray, 2025; Saba & Monkam, 2025). It can be understood that AI can positively impact the development and personalisation of diagnosis and treatment recommendations in the health field (Ferreira et al., 2025; Spencer et al., 2025). AI can also contribute to the development of decision-making, management, and solution-oriented applications in politics and law (Mostafaei et al., 2025; Xu et al., 2025). AI and copyright are among the important issues to consider (Chen & Rau, 2024). AI can also identify potential and existing problems in agriculture and provide more successful solution suggestions (Clay et al., 2024). AI has the potential to undertake some tasks in sports. This means that it can be an important factor in sports (Millington et al., 2025).

AI has the potential to positively impact sustainability through its environmental, social, and governance impacts. AI can have an impact on many issues, including maximising the efficient use of environmental resources, increasing governance effectiveness, ensuring social harmony, and mitigating negative impacts (Xiao & Xiao, 2025). Countries need to implement legal regulations against artificial intelligence. For example, the EU AI Act, enacted in 2024, aims to ensure that AI in the EU is "transparent", "safe", "non-discriminatory", "traceable", and "environmentally friendly"(EU AI Act, 2025). In the United States, an executive order titled "Removing Barriers to American Leadership in Artificial Intelligence" was issued in 2025. Additionally, various legislative proposals that could increase reliability have been passed at the state level (Software Improvement Group, 2025). Labelling Rules, which came into force in China in September 2025, require content generated with artificial intelligence to be labelled (White & Case LLP, 2025).

Sustainability

The term "sustainability" was coined in 1713 by Hans Carl von Carlowitz in his work "Sylvicultura Oeconomica" (Tost, 2025). According to the Brundtland Report, to continue strategic development, it is crucial to ensure a political environment that takes public opinion into account, to prioritise ecological impacts rather than simply increasing productivity and reducing costs in production, to establish an economic and financial structure capable of meeting its own needs with its own resources, to establish an innovative structure capable of constantly solving problems with new ideas, and to have an administrative structure capable of periodic control (United Nations, 1987). Raworth (2017), in his work explaining Doughnut Economics, emphasises that in ensuring sustainability in development, meeting the needs of people to sustain their lives and not damaging the environmental ecological balance are as important as progressing in the economy. Studies have been conducted in the literature on sustainability in many areas that affect humanity. Among these studies are studies such as climate change (Beszedics-Jäger & Buzási, 2024; Gill, 2024; Root, 2025; Savari et al., 2025), agriculture (Eiter et al., 2025; Georgescu et al., 2025; Maharjan et al., 2025; Pillai, 2025), tourism (Lee, 2025; Ramazanova et al., 2025; Yessimova et al., 2025; L. Zhang et al., 2025), transport, logistics and supply chain (Bahri et al., 2025; Bera et al., 2025; El Zein et al., 2025; Fahim et al., 2025; Mahesh & Calvert, 2025; Mogaji, 2025; Ojha & Agarwal, 2025; Pereira et al.,

2025), education (Alexander & Belloni, 2024; Fan, 2025; Haim & Aschauer, 2024; Kent et al., 2025; Quirós-Alpera et al., 2025; Riegel & Ajabnoor, 2024), economic (Bel Hadj Miled, 2025; Hanif & Zheng, 2025; Jiang & Ding, 2025; Li & Imran, 2025; Saini, 2025; Tutar et al., 2025; Xames & Topcu, 2025; Yıldırım et al., 2025).

The level and form of perception of climate change is important in ensuring sustainability. Utilising new technologies at a sustainable level is important in creating solutions for climate change (Root, 2025; Savari et al., 2025). Countries need to follow appropriate policies for sustainability in urban agriculture and protecting agricultural heritage. Ensuring sustainability by protecting agricultural heritage depends on many factors, such as reducing emissions, increasing efficiency, and conducting appropriate analyses (Eiter et al., 2025; Georgescu et al., 2025; Maharjan et al., 2025; Pillai, 2025). For example, the Liquid Prep tool is used to determine the moisture content of the soil and to ensure the most optimal irrigation (Pallardy, 2024). For sustainability in transport, logistics and supply chain, it is important to reduce the carbon released into the atmosphere, ensure high efficiency, determine optimal strategies in line with the demand and supply balance, support it with environmentally friendly investments, etc. (El Zein et al., 2025; Fahim et al., 2025; Mahesh & Calvert, 2025). For example, using artificial intelligence in the DocShipper platform to determine the most optimal route can offer advantages in terms of time and costs (DocShipper, 2025). For sustainability in education, it can be understood that it is important for educational institutions, educators and students to have high environmental awareness, to focus on sustainability, to give importance to feedback in education, to combine theoretical and sectoral education, to meet the food needs in educational institutions and to make optimal use of distance education (Fan, 2025; Kent et al., 2025; Quirós-Alpera et al., 2025; Riegel & Ajabnoor, 2024). For example, the Khanmigo tool can help teachers use their time effectively and improve themselves by helping them with the activities they need to do (Microsoft, 2024). If institutions consider economic sustainability in their activities and planning, they can both be profitable and positively impact sustainability (Hanif & Zheng, 2025; Li & Imran, 2025; Saini, 2025). Sustainability has many important effects in tourism, such as ensuring cultural sustainability and ecological tourism (Lee, 2025; L. Zhang et al., 2025). For example, Marriott International has been able to achieve successful results by using artificial intelligence to achieve emission reduction and automation (Smart Energy Decisions, 2024).

In light of the studies conducted, it can be understood that AI and sustainability for humanity are important in many areas and sectors, and the scope and type of support to be received from AI for the sustainability of humanity is developing day by day.

METHODOLOGY

For this study's trends and opportunities analysis, some descriptive analyses and three field plot, country collaboration analysis, most frequently used word, word cloud, thematic map, thematic evolution and trend topics analyses were conducted.

Research on AI, humanity and sustainability issue was conducted in the WoS, one of the popular databases (Nwagwu, 2025). Bibliometrix Biblioshiny app (Aria & Cuccurullo, 2017) and R (ver. 4.3.2) (R Core Team, 2023) were used in the analyses.

There was no time limit or publication type limitation in the analysis. As a result of the search made on May 13, 2025 in title, abstract and author keywords ("Artificial Intelligence*" or "AI") and ("Human*") and ("Sustainabilit*"), 710 scientific publications suitable for analysis were reached (25 publications were excluded from the analysis because they were not relevant).

FINDINGS

The overview of the analysed publications on the issue of AI, humanity and sustainability is provided in Table 1.

Table 1. Overview of the analysed publications on the issue of AI, humanity and sustainability

Description	Findings
Time interval	2004:2025
Source of Publications	502
Number of Publications	710
References	48908
Authors	3289
Keywords Plus	1394
Keywords of Authors	2801
Publication Types	
Articles	572
Proceedings	123
Editorial Materials	11
Book Chapters	4
Average number of citations per document	13.68
Publication Average Age	33.604

Source: Prepared by the author (with WoS data and Biblioshiny app)

According to the analysis findings on the WoS database, which includes publications on AI, humanity, and sustainability, there were 710 publications, 502 sources, and 3289 authors. The change in the number of publications on AI, humanity and sustainability issue over the years is shown in Figure 1.

Figure 1. Change in the number of publications on AI, humanity and sustainability issue

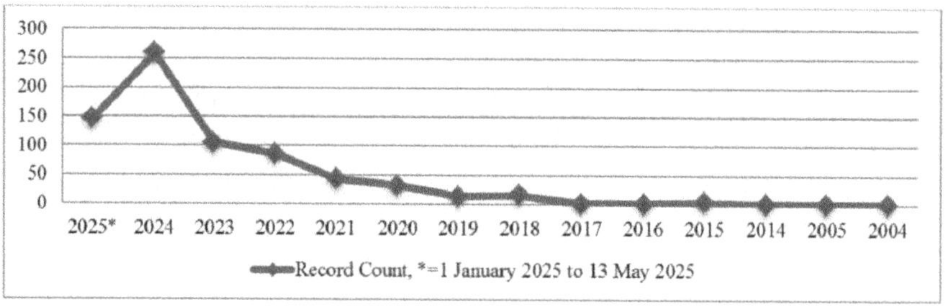

Source: Prepared by the author (with WoS collected data)

It was determined that the highest number of publications on AI, humanity and sustainability issue were in 2024 with 259 publications.

The highly cited publications on AI, humanity and sustainability are listed in Table 2.

Table 2. Highly cited publications on AI, humanity and sustainability issue

Author(s)	Publication of Title	Publication Year	Average per Year	Total Citations
Schwendicke, F. Samek, W. and Krois, J.	Artificial Intelligence in Dentistry: Chances and Challenges	(2020)	73.17	439
Nishant, R., Kennedy, M. and Corbett, J.	Artificial intelligence for sustainability: Challenges, opportunities, and a research agenda	(2020)	67.00	402
Dong, B. W., Shi, Q. F., (...) and Lee, C.	Technology evolution from self-powered sensors to AIoT enabled smart homes	(2021)	45.00	225
Jung, J. H., Maeda, M., (...) and Landivar-Bowles, J.	The potential of remote sensing and artificial intelligence as tools to improve the resilience of agriculture production systems	(2021)	42.20	211
Hassoun, A., Aït-Kaddour, A., (...) and Regenstein, J.	The fourth industrial revolution in the food industry-Part I: Industry 4.0 technologies	(2023)	37.25	149

continued on following page

Table 2. Continued

Author(s)	Publication of Title	Publication Year	Average per Year	Total Citations
Liu, Q., Liu, Z. H., (...) and Pham, D. T.	Human-robot collaboration in disassembly for sustainable manufacturing	(2019)	19.71	138
Schmeisser, S., Miccoli, A., (...) and Tralau, T.	New approach methodologies in human regulatory toxicology-Not if, but how and when!	(2023)	43.00	129
Yigitcanlar, T. and Cugurullo, F.	The Sustainability of Artificial Intelligence: An Urbanistic Viewpoint from the Lens of Smart and Sustainable Cities	(2020)	20.00	120
Delgado, J. A., Short, N. M., (...) and Vandenberg, B.	Big Data Analysis for Sustainable Agriculture on a Geospatial Cloud Framework	(2019)	15.00	105
Liaw, S. Y. Ooi, S. W. (...) and Chua, W. L.	Nurse-Physician Communication Team Training in Virtual Reality Versus Live Simulations: Randomized Controlled Trial on Team Communication and Teamwork Attitudes	(2020)	15.67	94

Source: Prepared by the author (with WoS collected data)

Looking at the most highly cited study on AI, humanity and sustainability issue titled "Artificial Intelligence in Dentistry: Chances and Challenges" published in 2020. This study also examines the effects of AI in the dentistry sector.

The most influential sources on AI, humanity and sustainability issue for Bradford's Law are included in Figure 2.

Figure 2. Influential sources on AI, humanity and sustainability issue for Bradford's Law

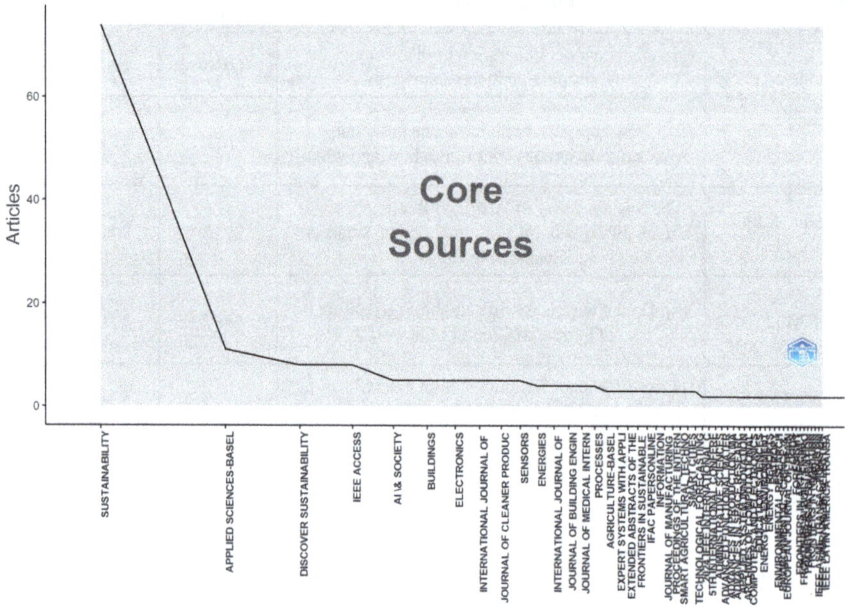

Source: Prepared by the author (with Biblioshiny app and WoS collected data)

It was understood that Sustainability (n=74) was an effective source. It is included in AI, humanity, and sustainability issue' three-field plot analysis Figure 3.

Figure 3. AI, humanity, and sustainability issue' three-field plot analysis

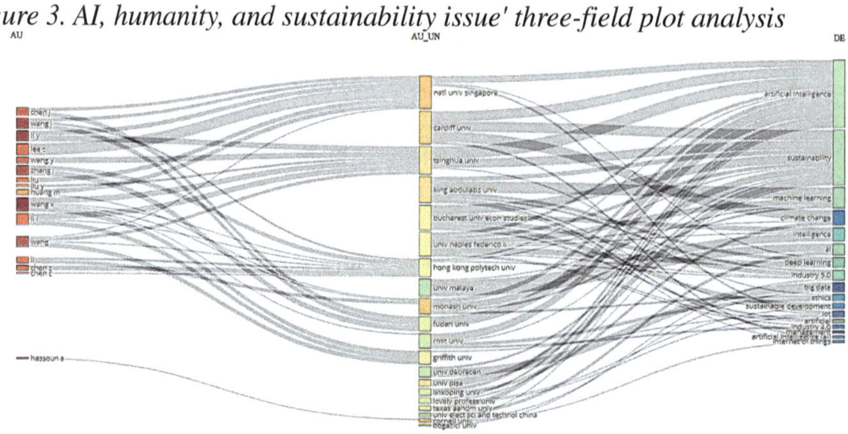

Source: Prepared by the author (with Biblioshiny app and WoS collected data)

The three field plot analysis was conducted within the scope of the left (authors), middle (affiliations) and right (author keywords) fields. According to the findings of the three field plot analysis, it is understood that the author with the most connections is Wang, X. The most connected affiliations is National University of Singapore, and the most connected keyword is artificial intelligence. Figure 4 includes the findings of the country collaboration analysis on AI, humanity and sustainability issue.

Figure 4. AI, humanity and sustainability issue' country collaboration analysis

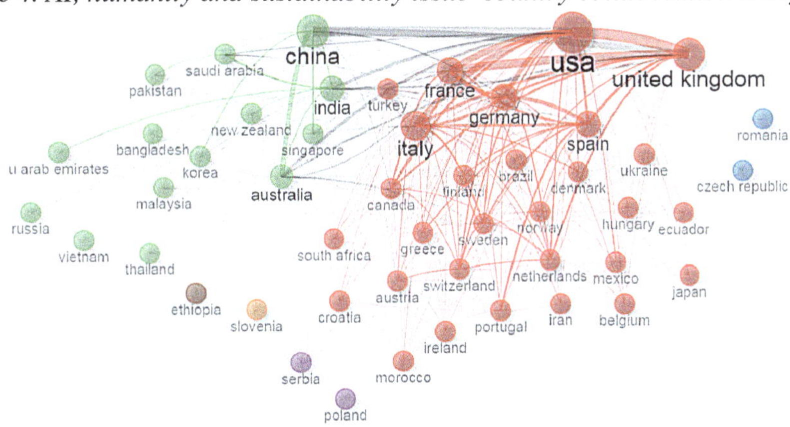

Source: Prepared by the author (with Biblioshiny app and WoS collected data)

According to the findings of AI, humanity and sustainability issue publications' country collaboration analysis, the countries with the most collaborations are China and USA (n=18), USA and United Kingdom (n=18), United Kingdom and France (n=16). It is included in AI, humanity, and sustainability issue' most frequently used word Figure 5.

Figure 5. AI, humanity, and sustainability issue' most frequently used word

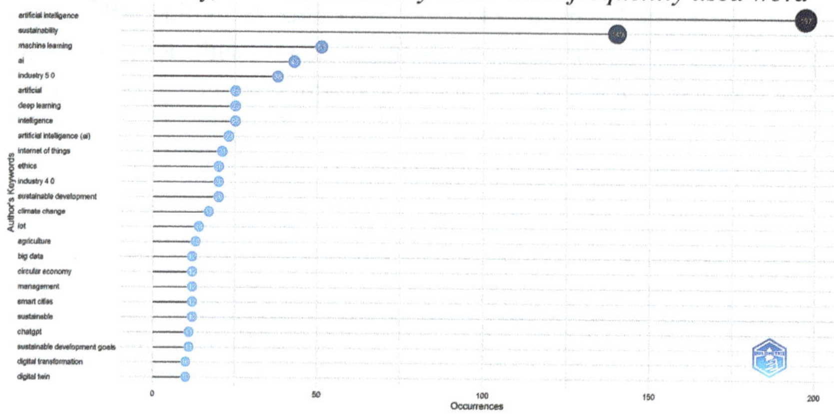

Source: Prepared by the author (with Biblioshiny app and WoS collected data)

According to the findings of the AI, humanity, and sustainability issue publications' most frequently used word analysis, it is understood that the first 5 most frequently used words are artificial intelligence, sustainability, machine learning, AI and industry 5.0. The findings of the AI, humanity, and sustainability issue's word cloud analysis are included in Figure 6.

Figure 6. AI, humanity, and sustainability issue' word cloud

Source: Prepared by the author (with Biblioshiny app and WoS collected data)

The dominant keywords in the word cloud analysis are shown larger in the created figure. According to the findings of the AI, humanity, and sustainability issue' most frequently used word analysis, it is understood that the most dominant author keywords are artificial intelligence, sustainability, machine learning, industry 5.0, deep learning etc. The findings of the AI, humanity, and sustainability issue' thematic map analysis is included in Figure 7.

Figure 7. AI, humanity, and sustainability issue' thematic map

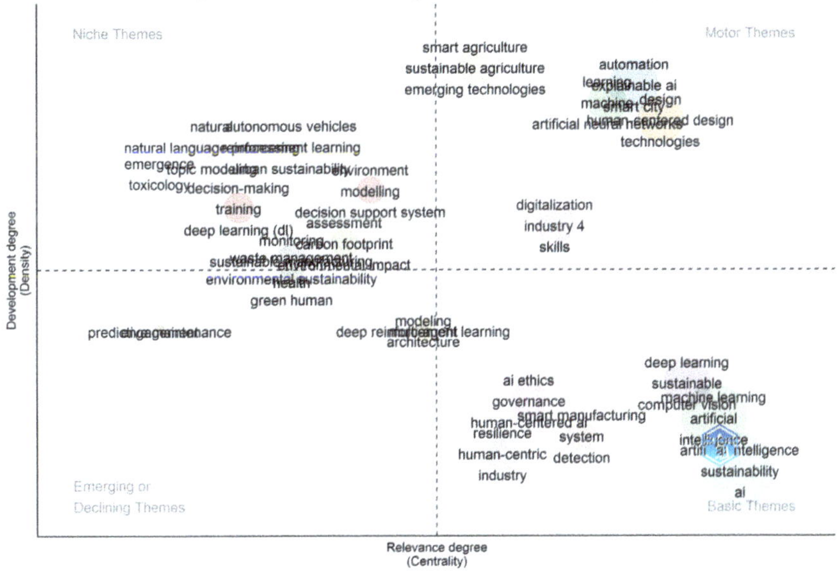

Source: Prepared by the author (with Biblioshiny app and WoS collected data)

According to thematic map analysis findings for keywords, (design, human-centered design, technologies), (automation, explainable AI, smart city), (learning, machine, artificial neural networks), (digitalization, industry 4.0, skills), (smart agriculture, sustainable agriculture, emerging technologies) is included in the distribution of five clusters in motor themes. Among the clusters in niche themes, there are seven clusters: (environment, modelling, decision support system), (assessment, carbon footprint, environmental impact), (autonomous vehicles, reinforcement learning, urban sustainability), (monitoring, sustainable manufacturing, health), (decision-making, training, deep learning (dl)), (natural, natural language processing, topic modeling), (emergence, toxicology).

Among the clusters in the emerging or declining themes, there are four clusters: (modelling, architecture), (multi-agent, deep reinforcement learning), (waste management, environmental sustainability, green human), (engagement, predictive maintenance). Among the clusters in the basic themes, there are six clusters as (artificial intelligence, sustainability, AI), (machine learning, artificial, intelligence), (deep learning, sustainable, computer vision), (smart manufacturing, system, detection), (AI ethics, governance, human-centered AI), (resilience, human-centric, industry). The thematic evolution analysis findings of the AI, humanity, and sustainability issue are included in Figure 8.

Figure 8. AI, humanity, and sustainability issue' thematic evolution

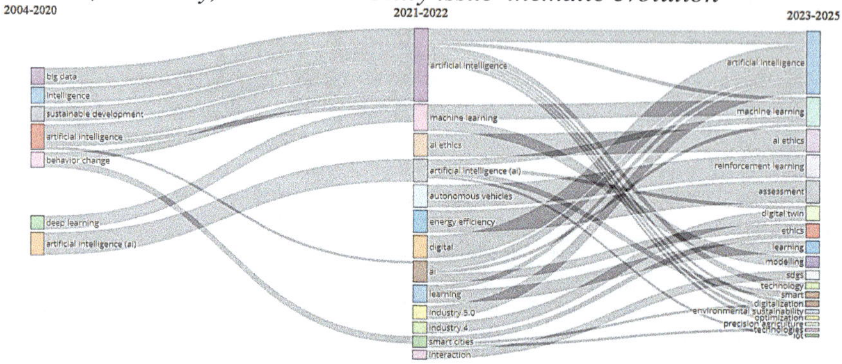

Source: Prepared by the author (with Biblioshiny app and WoS collected data)

It is understood that artificial intelligence was one of the dominant themes between 2004 and 2020. It is understood that the theme of artificial intelligence evolved into artificial intelligence, machine learning, AI, smart cities between 2021 and 2022. The theme of artificial intelligence, which was dominant between 2021-2022, will be artificial intelligence, machine learning, technology, smart, digitalization, environmental sustainability, optimization, precision agriculture between 2023-2025. The findings of the analysis of the AI, humanity, and sustainability issue' trend topics are included in Figure 9.

Figure 9. AI, humanity, and sustainability issue' trend topics

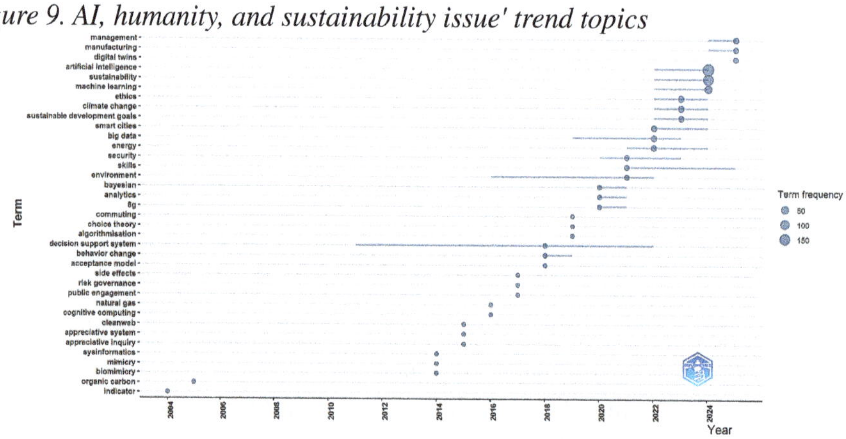

Source: Prepared by the author (with Biblioshiny app and WoS collected data)

According to the trend topics analysis findings, it is understood that artificial intelligence has the highest term frequency in 2024 with 197 term frequency. It is understood that the other highest term frequency in 2024 is sustainability with 139 term frequency and machine learning with 51 term frequency.

DISCUSSION

As a result of the study conducted in the WoS database for the trends and opportunities analysis on AI, humanity, and sustainability, 710 publications related to the issue were identified.

It was understood that the most publications regarding the issue under research were made in 2024. An article has been determined to be the dominant part in the distribution of studies. It can be understood that publications in other types of studies can further enrich the literature on the issue. It was determined that the most cited study was the study titled "Artificial Intelligence in Dentistry: Chances and Challenges". There are many other studies in the literature on AI and its impact on the healthcare sector (e.g., Beltrán-Velasco & Clemente-Suárez, 2025; García et al., 2025; Li et al., 2025; Modi et al., 2025). It has been understood that there are influential sources on AI, humanity and sustainability issue (for Bradford's Law). In the "Sustainability" source, AI, humanity and sustainability issues have been examined from many perspectives (e.g., Fu et al., 2025; Jahangir et al., 2025; Shan et al., 2025).

According to the findings of the three field plot analysis, it is understood that the author with the most connections is Wang, X., while it was determined that the affiliations with the most connections were National University of Singapore. The authors affiliated with this affiliation have done many studies on AI, humanity and sustainability issue (e.g., Huang et al., 2025; Lee et al., 2025; Richards et al., 2024). According to the findings of the publications' country collaboration analysis, the countries with the most collaborations are China and the USA, the USA and the United Kingdom, and the United Kingdom and France. When we look at the countries with the most collaboration, it can be understood that they are among the countries that attach importance to AI and aim to make optimum use of AI.

According to the findings of AI, humanity, and sustainability issue publications' most frequently used words and word cloud analysis, it was understood that the words with the highest repetition frequency were artificial intelligence, sustainability, machine learning, AI and industry 5.0., deep learning. It can be understood that the impact of artificial intelligence on industries in terms of sustainability is high and that it is expected to be high in the future, and the importance of the relationship between machine learning and deep learning and artificial intelligence.

According to the thematic map analysis findings for the keywords of AI, humanity, and sustainability issue, four main themes were created: motor, niche, emerging or declining, and basic. It has been determined that there are five clusters with the highest frequency and development in motor themes. While cluster one contains the keywords design, human-centered design, and technologies. Cluster two contains the keywords automation, explainable AI, and smart city. Cluster three includes the keywords learning, machine, and artificial neural networks. While cluster four includes the keywords digitalization, industry 4.0, and skills. Cluster five includes the keywords smart agriculture, sustainable agriculture, and emerging technologies. When the topics in the motor theme that can be worked together on AI, humanity, and sustainability issue and are thought to have publication potential are evaluated, it is understood that there are topics such as design and human-centered design (Boy & Morel, 2022; El Moussaoui, 2025; Formosa, 2025; Ghafarollahi & Buehler, 2025; Ibrahim et al., 2025; H. Nguyen et al., 2025; Pak, 2023; Tunckaya, 2025), automation (De Alwis & Nam, 2024; Elmousalami et al., 2025; Kaya, 2025; Lo et al., 2024; Sivasankari & Rathika, 2025; Vlacic et al., 2024),, explainable AI (Chakraborty et al., 2021; Heo et al., 2024; Ramakrishnan et al., 2023), smart city (Li et al., 2024; Riedmann-Streitz et al., 2025; Shahrabani & Apanaviciene, 2024; Skubis et al., 2024), learning (Alqithami, 2025; Sun & Hsiao, 2024; Y. Zhang et al., 2025), artificial neural networks(Ahmed et al., 2022; Leonardi et al., 2025), smart and sustainable agriculture (Louta et al., 2024; Mana et al., 2024; Ryo et al., 2023; X. Wang et al., 2025; Xiao, 2025), emerging technologies (Emere et al., 2025; Louta et al., 2024). It can be understood that the topics in the motor themes are suitable for conducting new studies within the scope of previously unexamined or rarely examined factors that can affect human life.

According to the findings of thematic evolution analysis, it is understood that the dominant artificial intelligence theme between 2004-2020 evolved into the themes of artificial intelligence, machine learning, AI and smart cities between 2021-22, and the dominant artificial intelligence theme between 2023-2025 evolved into the themes of machine learning, technology, smart, digitalization, environmental sustainability, optimization, precision agriculture. According to the trend topics analysis findings, it was understood that the themes with the highest frequency in 2024 were artificial intelligence, sustainability and machine learning, respectively. The use of artificial intelligence in various ways for humanity is not a very new situation, its popularity among a wide segment of society can be considered a more recent history. In 2022, with ChatGPT being made available to a wide audience, the popularity of AI began to increase significantly. With the popularity and capabilities of AI being understood by a wide audience, it began to increase its influence in almost all issues affecting humanity, such as sustainability, smart cities, optimisation, and agriculture. It can be understood that this affects the evolution and trending topics in the themes of scientific studies.

It's clear that AI's awareness of its responsibilities to humanity and its commitment to sustainability can be achieved with the support of AI developers, politicians, and the law. It's crucial to develop sensible approaches to ensure that AI's data-hungry attitude and the energy it requires to perform its work do not negatively impact humanity in terms of sustainability. The data used in AI-generated content can pave the way for privacy violations. The potential for misleading information generated by AI-generated content should not be overlooked. It's clear that prioritizing the benefit of humanity is essential when making vital adaptations to utilize AI. The tendency of artificial intelligence to minimise the need for labour in some business lines, the content it creates that may contain biased information and reinforce inequality in social classes indicate that its social impacts must be carefully calculated (Judijanto et al., 2025; Kooli, 2023; Root, 2025; Wen, 2025). Therefore, it can be understood that issues such as privacy, transparency, responsibility, and legal regulations have a high potential to become and remain trends.

CONCULUSION

This study conducted trends and opportunities analysis on the AI, humanity, and sustainability issue. Considering the findings of the analysis, although many studies have been conducted on the AI, humanity, and sustainability issue, it was understood that AI, humanity, and sustainability issue is an issue suitable for new studies in many different scopes and perspectives, considering that AI is constantly developing and the importance of sustainability will continue.

It is understood that with this study, researchers will be able to have an idea about the distribution of publications on the AI, humanity, and sustainability issue, which are the most effective authors, sources, affiliations, countries, and which publications are the most effective with the number of citations. It is evaluated that researchers can make it easier to decide on the subject that can be studied with the most frequently used word, word cloud, thematic map, thematic evolution and trend topics analysis findings.

With this study, practitioners can understand how to make more efficient use of AI in which areas and sectors of the world and human life, based on trends and opportunities on AI, humanity, and sustainability issues, and what can be done. It can be understood that they can have a vision about what can be done in line with AI to ensure sustainability.

The limitations of the study conducted on the AI, humanity, and sustainability issue include the trend and opportunity analysis method used in the study, the database from which the analysis findings were obtained, and the time and scope of the analysis. A different topic can be added to the AI and humanity issue in the future, and a specific effect can be analysed using a different analysis technique.

REFERENCES

Act, E. U. A. I. (2025). *The EU AI Act.* https://www.euaiact.com

Ahmed, M., AlQadhi, S., Mallick, J., Kahla, N. B., Le, H. A., Singh, C. K., & Hang, H. T. (2022). Artificial Neural Networks for Sustainable Development of the Construction Industry. *Sustainability (Basel), 14*(22), 14738. DOI: 10.3390/su142214738

Akhtar, M., Ghafoor, K. A., Maqsood, H., & Murtaza, K. (2025). FinTech payment services adoption among women: the impact of personality, financial services knowledge and artificial intelligence. *International Journal of Accounting & Information Management, ahead-of-print*(ahead-of-print). DOI: 10.1108/IJAIM-09-2024-0355

Alexander, W. R. J., & Belloni, R. (2024). Artificial Intelligence and the Sustainability of the Signaling and Human Capital Roles of Higher Education. *Sustainability (Basel), 16*(20), 8802. DOI: 10.3390/su16208802

Alqithami, S. (2025). Integrating Sentiment Analysis and Reinforcement Learning for Equitable Disaster Response: A Novel Approach. *Sustainability (Basel), 17*(3), 1072. DOI: 10.3390/su17031072

Aria, M., & Cuccurullo, C. (2017). bibliometrix: An R-tool for comprehensive science mapping analysis. *Journal of Informetrics, 11*(4), 959–975. DOI: 10.1016/j.joi.2017.08.007

Bacalhau, L. M., Pereira, M. C., & Neves, J. (2025). A bibliometric analysis of AI bias in marketing: field evolution and future research agenda. *Journal of Marketing Analytics, ahead-of-print*(ahead-of-print), 1-20. DOI: 10.1057/s41270-025-00379-6

Bahri, M. S. S., Shariff, S. S. R., & Yahya, N. (2025). Sustainable port operations and environmental initiatives in Malaysia: A focus on environmental sustainability. *The Asian Journal of Shipping and Logistics, 41*(1), 38–51. DOI: 10.1016/j.ajsl.2025.01.002

Bayakhmetova, A., Rudenko, L., Krylova, L., Suleimenova, B., Niyazbekova, S., & Nurpeisova, A. (2025). Artificial Intelligence in Financial Behavior: Bibliometric Ideas and New Opportunities. *Journal of Risk and Financial Management, 18*(3), 159. DOI: 10.3390/jrfm18030159

Bel Hadj Miled, K. (2025). Nexus between fintech, green finance natural resources, economic growth and environment sustainability: Evidence from BRICS countries. *Future Business Journal, 11*(1), 47. DOI: 10.1186/s43093-025-00469-y

Beltrán-Velasco, A. I., & Clemente-Suárez, V. J. (2025). Harnessing Gut Microbiota for Biomimetic Innovations in Health and Biotechnology. *Biomimetics, 10*(2), 73. DOI: 10.3390/biomimetics10020073 PMID: 39997096

Benabou, A., & Touhami, F. (2025). Empowering human resource management through artificial intelligence: A systematic literature review and bibliometric analysis. *International Journal of Production Management and Engineering, 13*(1), 59–76. DOI: 10.4995/ijpme.2025.21900

Bera, I., Modgil, S., Shrivastava, A. K., Singh, R. K., & Sharma, R. (2025). Data-driven sustainability: advancing supply chain pricing models in B2B. *Journal of Revenue and Pricing Management, ahead-of-print*(ahead-of-print). DOI: 10.1057/s41272-025-00521-0

Beszedics-Jäger, B. S., & Buzási, A. (2024). Evaluating the effectiveness of urban sustainability and climate objectives: A comparative approach. *Discover Sustainability, 5*(1), 269. DOI: 10.1007/s43621-024-00475-0

Beta, K., Nagaraj, S. S., & Weerasinghe, T. D. B. (2025). The role of artificial intelligence on supply chain resilience. *Journal of Enterprise Information Management, 38*(3), 950–973. DOI: 10.1108/JEIM-12-2023-0674

Betz, S. (2024). *7 Types of Artificial Intelligence*. https://builtin.com/artificial-intelligence/types-of-artificial-intelligence

Bhandarkar, V. V., Venkateswaran, K., & Jain, J. (2024). *Will Artificial Intelligence Surpass Human Intelligence? - A Viewpoint*. https://www.infosys.com/iki/techcompass/ai-surpass-human-intelligence.html

Bigliardi, B., Dolci, V., Filippelli, S., Petroni, A., & Pini, B. (2025). Employing innovation for social sustainability in supply chains: A systematic literature review. *Procedia Computer Science, 253*, 2595–2604. DOI: 10.1016/j.procs.2025.01.319

Bilancia, A., Costa, F., & Staudacher, A. P. (2025). Achieving sustainability and circular economy in the luxury fashion industry through lean practices: A systematic literature review. *Computers & Industrial Engineering, 111107*, 111107. Advance online publication. DOI: 10.1016/j.cie.2025.111107

Biswas, B., Gupta, R. P., & Sharma, M. (2025). Parameters of sustainability: A systematic literature review and bibliometric analysis with respect to micro enterprises. *Vilakshan - XIMB. Journal of Management, 22*(1), 116–132. DOI: 10.1108/XJM-03-2024-0049

Bonadio, E., & Trapova, A. (2024). Intellectual property law in gaming and artificial intelligence. In Bevan, C. (Ed.), *Research Handbook on Property, Law and Theory* (pp. 448–462). Edward Elgar Publishing. DOI: 10.4337/9781802202069.00037

Boy, G. A., & Morel, C. (2022). The machine as a partner: Human-machine teaming design using the PRODEC method. *Work (Reading, Mass.)*, *73*(s1), S15–S30. DOI: 10.3233/WOR-220268 PMID: 36214030

Buchari, R. A., Muhtar, E. A., Aiyub, K., Abdillah, A., Miradhia, D., & Muharam, R. S. (2024). Global Research Trends in Sustainability and Environmental Issues: A Sustainable Environment and Future Directions. *Journal of Population and Social Studies*, *33*, 762–783. https://so03.tci-thaijo.org/index.php/jpss/article/view/277440. DOI: 10.25133/JPSSv332025.041

Budhwar, P., Chowdhury, S., Wood, G., Aguinis, H., Bamber, G. J., Beltran, J. R., Boselie, P., Lee Cooke, F., Decker, S., DeNisi, A., Dey, P. K., Guest, D., Knoblich, A. J., Malik, A., Paauwe, J., Papagiannidis, S., Patel, C., Pereira, V., Ren, S., & Varma, A. (2023). Human resource management in the age of generative artificial intelligence: Perspectives and research directions on ChatGPT. *Human Resource Management Journal*, *33*(3), 606–659. DOI: 10.1111/1748-8583.12524

Castonguay, C. (2025). *Why Study Environmental Science and Sustainability Studies?* https://www.educations.com/articles-and-advice/master-studies/why-study-environmental-science-and-sustainability-studies

Chakraborty, D., Başağaoğlu, H., Gutierrez, L., & Mirchi, A. (2021). Explainable AI reveals new hydroclimatic insights for ecosystem-centric groundwater management. *Environmental Research Letters*, *16*(11), 114024. DOI: 10.1088/1748-9326/ac2fde

Che Ghazali, R., Abdul Hanid, M. F., Mohd Said, M. N. H., & Lee, H. Y. (2025). The advancement of Artificial Intelligence in Education: Insights from a 1976–2024 bibliometric analysis. *Journal of Research on Technology in Education, ahead-of-print*(ahead-of-print), 1-17. DOI: 10.1080/15391523.2025.2456044

Chen, P.-H., & Rau, P.-L. P. (2024). Using Artificial Intelligence in Music Creation? a Survey Based on Copyright Consciousness. In Rau, P.-L. P. (Ed.), *Cross-Cultural Design* (pp. 210–225). Springer Nature Switzerland., DOI: 10.1007/978-3-031-60913-8_15

Chusniyah, A., Makruf, I., & Supriyanto, . (2025). Two decades of sustainable development studies in higher education management: A bibliometric analysis. *International Journal of Sustainability in Higher Education*, *26*(3), 614–632. DOI: 10.1108/IJSHE-11-2023-0546

Clay, D. E., Brugler, S., & Joshi, B. (2024). Will artificial intelligence and machine learning change agriculture: A special issue. *Agronomy Journal, 116*(3), 791–794. DOI: 10.1002/agj2.21555

Crăciun, M. A., Domenteanu, A., Dudian, M., & Delcea, C. (2025). Navigating Sustainability: A Bibliometric Exploration of Environmental Decision-Making and Behavioral Shifts. *Sustainability (Basel), 17*(6), 2646. DOI: 10.3390/su17062646

Cumbana, D. A. P. T., & Ventura, J. B. (2025). Sustainability reporting and sustainable development goals: Bibliometric analysis. *Cogent Business & Management, 12*(1), 2444547. DOI: 10.1080/23311975.2024.2444547

De Alwis, N., & Nam, H.-S. (2024). *A way towards port automation: challenges and implications.* WMU Journal of Maritime Affairs., DOI: 10.1007/s13437-024-00350-9

De la Peña, N., & Granados, O. M. (2024). Artificial intelligence solutions to reduce information asymmetry for Colombian cocoa small-scale farmers. *Information Processing in Agriculture, 11*(3), 310–324. DOI: 10.1016/j.inpa.2023.03.001

Delgado, J. A., Short, N. M.Jr, Roberts, D. P., & Vandenberg, B. (2019). Big Data Analysis for Sustainable Agriculture on a Geospatial Cloud Framework. *Frontiers in Sustainable Food Systems, 3*(54), 1–13. DOI: 10.3389/fsufs.2019.00054

DocShipper. (2025). *How AI is Changing Logistics & Supply Chain in 2025?* https://docshipper.com/logistics/ai-changing-logistics-supply-chain-2025/

Donfouet, O., & Ngouhouo, I. (2024). Impact of artificial intelligence on the total productivity of agricultural factors in Africa. *Environment, Development and Sustainability.* Advance online publication. DOI: 10.1007/s10668-024-05528-y

Dong, B., Shi, Q., Yang, Y., Wen, F., Zhang, Z., & Lee, C. (2021). Technology evolution from self-powered sensors to AIoT enabled smart homes. *Nano Energy, 79*, 105414. DOI: 10.1016/j.nanoen.2020.105414

Dong, X., Zhou, N., Zhao, X., & Yang, S. (2025). The impact of artificial intelligence on corporate green innovation: Can "increasing quantity" and "improving quality" go hand in hand? *Journal of Environmental Management, 376*, 124439. DOI: 10.1016/j.jenvman.2025.124439 PMID: 39923623

Dora, M., Kumar, A., Mangla, S. K., Pant, A., & Kamal, M. M. (2022). Critical success factors influencing artificial intelligence adoption in food supply chains. *International Journal of Production Research, 60*(14), 4621–4640. DOI: 10.1080/00207543.2021.1959665

DuPrey Diederichsen, S., Garcia Scherer, M. E., Ribeiro Gandra, T. B., & Sanabria, J. G. (2025). The Relevance of Nearshore Marine Space for Blue Economy Sustainability: A Bibliometric Analysis. *Coastal Management*, *53*(1), 33–48. DOI: 10.1080/08920753.2025.2452035

Eastwood, B. (2025). *When humans and AI work best together — and when each is better alone*. https://mitsloan.mit.edu/ideas-made-to-matter/when-humans-and-ai-work-best-together-and-when-each-better-alone

Eiter, S., Fjellstad, W., & Van Schaik, L. (2025). Monitoring sustainability of urban agriculture: Who is going to do it and how? *Landscape and Urban Planning*, *257*, 105300. DOI: 10.1016/j.landurbplan.2025.105300

El Moussaoui, M. (2025). Architectural practice process and artificial intelligence – an evolving practice. *Open Engineering*, *15*(1), 20240098. doi:10.1515/eng-2024-0098. DOI: 10.1515/eng-2024-0098

El Zein, M., Karimipanah, T., & Ameen, A. (2025). Airports—Energy and Sustainability Perspectives. *Energies*, *18*(6), 1360. DOI: 10.3390/en18061360

Elmousalami, H., Maxy, M., Hui, F. K. P., & Aye, L. (2025). AI in automated sustainable construction engineering management. *Automation in Construction*, *175*, 106202. DOI: 10.1016/j.autcon.2025.106202

Emere, C., Oguntona, O., Ohiomah, I., & Ayorinde, E. (2025). Harnessing Emerging Technologies in the Global Mining Sector from a Bibliometric Standpoint. *Mining (Basel)*, *5*(1), 13. DOI: 10.3390/mining5010013

Ertem-Eray, T., & Cheng, Y. (2025). A Review of Artificial Intelligence Research in Peer-Reviewed Communication Journals. *Applied Sciences (Basel, Switzerland)*, *15*(3), 1058. DOI: 10.3390/app15031058

Fahim, M., Saleh, M., Grida, M., & Gamila, M. A. (2025). Greening the route: Enhancing sustainability and efficiency in omnichannel retailing. *Journal of Cleaner Production*, *500*, 145264. DOI: 10.1016/j.jclepro.2025.145264

Fan, H. (2025). Integrating Ecological Consciousness Into Environmental Art Design Education: Impacts on Student Engagement, Sustainability Practices, and Critical Thinking. *Sustainable Development, ahead-of-print*(ahead-of-print). DOI: 10.1002/sd.3474

Fatemi, S., Smiljic, S., & Behdani, B. (2025). Crossing Paths of Industry 4.0 and Sustainability: A Bibliometric Analysis of Twin Transition Literature. *Procedia Computer Science*, *253*, 1730–1739. DOI: 10.1016/j.procs.2025.01.235

Ferreira, D. D., Ferreira, L. G., Amorim, K. A., Delfino, D. C. T., Ferreira, A. C. B. H., & Souza, L. P. C. e. (2025). Assessing the Links Between Artificial Intelligence and Precision Nutrition. *Current Nutrition Reports*, *14*(1), 47. DOI: 10.1007/s13668-025-00635-2 PMID: 40087237

Florea, N. V., & Croitoru, G. (2025). The Impact of Artificial Intelligence on Communication Dynamics and Performance in Organizational Leadership. *Administrative Sciences*, *15*(2), 33. DOI: 10.3390/admsci15020033

Florence. (2024). *Empower Your Team: The Importance of Sustainability Training.* https://speach.me/blog/empower-your-team-the-importance-of-sustainability-training

Formosa, D. (2025). Design education is too important to be left to designers. *Design Studies*, *98*, 101301. DOI: 10.1016/j.destud.2025.101301

Fosso Wamba, S., Queiroz, M. M., Ngai, E. W. T., Riggins, F., & Bendavid, Y. (2024). The interplay between artificial intelligence, production systems, and operations management resilience. *International Journal of Production Research*, *62*(15), 5361–5366. DOI: 10.1080/00207543.2024.2321826

Fu, C., Chen, C., & Fu, Z. (2025). Seasonal Spatiotemporal Dynamics and Gradients of the Urban Heat Island Effect in Subtropical Furnace Megacity. *Sustainability (Basel)*, *17*(7), 3238. DOI: 10.3390/su17073238

Garcés-Giraldo, L. F., Velasco-Cardona, D. C., Patiño-Vanegas, J. C., Valencia-Arias, A., Rojas-Arias, J., & Sánchez, W. A. (2025). The role of sustainability in university curricula: Trend analysis and research agenda. *International Journal of Education Economics and Development*, *16*(1-2), 172–187. DOI: 10.1504/IJEED.2025.143617

García, G., Carlin, M., & Cano, R. J. (2025). Holobiome Harmony: Linking Environmental Sustainability, Agriculture, and Human Health for a Thriving Planet and One Health. *Microorganisms*, *13*(3), 514. DOI: 10.3390/microorganisms13030514 PMID: 40142407

Georgescu, P.-L., Barbuta-Misu, N., Zlati, M. L., Fortea, C., & Antohi, V. M. (2025). Quantifying the Performance of European Agriculture Through the New European Sustainability Model. *Agriculture*, *15*(2), 210. DOI: 10.3390/agriculture15020210

Ghafarollahi, A., & Buehler, M. J. (2025). Automating alloy design and discovery with physics-aware multimodal multiagent AI. *Proceedings of the National Academy of Sciences of the United States of America*, *122*(4), e2414074122. DOI: 10.1073/pnas.2414074122 PMID: 39854228

Gill, G. N. (2024). Climate Change and India's Cities: Judicial Responses through the Lens of Sustainability Transformations. *Climate Law*, *14*(2), 198–232. DOI: 10.1163/18786561-bja10051

Goralski, M. A., & Tan, T. K. (2020). Artificial intelligence and sustainable development. *International Journal of Management Education*, *18*(1), 100330. DOI: 10.1016/j.ijme.2019.100330

Gorski, A.-T., & Badea, D. (2025). Circular Economy and Corporate Sustainability: Shaping New Business Models for a Resilient Future. *Land Forces Academy Review*, *30*(1), 108–117. DOI: 10.2478/raft-2025-0011

Grand View Research. (2025). *Global Artificial Intelligence Market Size & Outlook*. https://www.grandviewresearch.com/horizon/outlook/artificial-intelligence-market-size/global

Gürdür Broo, D., Kaynak, O., & Sait, S. M. (2022). Rethinking engineering education at the age of industry 5.0. *Journal of Industrial Information Integration*, *25*, 100311. DOI: 10.1016/j.jii.2021.100311

Haim, K., & Aschauer, W. (2024). Innovative FOCUS: A Program to Foster Creativity and Innovation in the Context of Education for Sustainability. *Sustainability (Basel)*, *16*(6), 2257. DOI: 10.3390/su16062257

Han, X., Chen, F., Wang, H., & Xu, S. (2025). Unlocking innovation: Artificial intelligence usage and innovative behavior in the workplace. *Social Behavior and Personality*, *53*(3), 1–13. DOI: 10.2224/sbp.13851

Hanif, M. W., & Zheng, S. (2025). Assessing the economic impact of green finance and renewable energy use on environmental sustainability in high-polluting sectors. *Renewable Energy*, *247*, 123017. DOI: 10.1016/j.renene.2025.123017

Hassan, M., Mahin, H. D., Al Nafees, A., Paul, A., & Shraban, S. S. (2025). Big data applications in intelligent transport systems: A bibliometric analysis and review. *Discover Civil Engineering*, *2*(1), 49. DOI: 10.1007/s44290-025-00205-z

Hassoun, A., Aït-Kaddour, A., Abu-Mahfouz, A. M., Rathod, N. B., Bader, F., Barba, F. J., Biancolillo, A., Cropotova, J., Galanakis, C. M., Jambrak, A. R., Lorenzo, J. M., Måge, I., Ozogul, F., & Regenstein, J. (2023). The fourth industrial revolution in the food industry—Part I: Industry 4.0 technologies. *Critical Reviews in Food Science and Nutrition*, *63*(23), 6547–6563. DOI: 10.1080/10408398.2022.2034735 PMID: 35114860

Heo, S., Nam, K., Kim, S. Y., & Yoo, C. (2024). XRL-FlexSBR: Multi-agent reinforcement learning-driven flexible SBR control with explainable performance guarantee under diverse influent conditions. *Journal of Water Process Engineering*, *66*, 105991. DOI: 10.1016/j.jwpe.2024.105991

Huang, G.-B., Westover, M. B., Tan, E.-K., Wang, H., Cui, D., Ma, W.-Y., Wang, T., He, Q., Wei, H., Wang, N., Tian, Q., Lam, K.-Y., Yao, X., & Wong, T. Y. (2025). Artificial intelligence without restriction surpassing human intelligence with probability one: Theoretical insight into secrets of the brain with AI twins of the brain. *Neurocomputing*, *619*, 129053. Advance online publication. DOI: 10.1016/j.neucom.2024.129053 PMID: 41312528

Hue, T. T., & Hung, T. H. (2025). Impact of artificial intelligence on branding: A bibliometric review and future research directions. *Humanities & Social Sciences Communications*, *12*(1), 209. DOI: 10.1057/s41599-025-04488-6

Ibrahim, K. A., Luk, P. C.-K., Luo, Z., Ng, S. Y., & Harrison, L. (2025). Revolutionizing power electronics design through large language models: Applications and future directions. *Computers & Electrical Engineering*, *123*, 110248. DOI: 10.1016/j.compeleceng.2025.110248

Jahangir, S., Xie, R., Iqbal, A., & Hussain, M. (2025). The Influence of Sustainable Human Resource Management Practices on Logistics Agility: The Mediating Role of Artificial Intelligence. *Sustainability (Basel)*, *17*(7), 3099. DOI: 10.3390/su17073099

Jiang, Y., & Ding, X. (2025). Exploring the Nexus Between Ecosystem Services and Economic Sustainability: A Stakeholder Perspective. *Corporate Social Responsibility and Environmental Management*, *32*(3), 3639–3658. DOI: 10.1002/csr.3110

Jiao, Z., Zhang, C., & Li, W. (2025). Artificial Intelligence in Energy Economics Research: A Bibliometric Review. *Energies*, *18*(2), 434. DOI: 10.3390/en18020434

Judijanto, L., Hardiansyah, A., & Arifudin, O. (2025). Ethics and Security in Artificial Intelligence and Machine Learning: Current Perspectives in Computing. *International Journal of Society Reviews*, *3*(2), 374–380.

Jung, J., Maeda, M., Chang, A., Bhandari, M., Ashapure, A., & Landivar-Bowles, J. (2021). The potential of remote sensing and artificial intelligence as tools to improve the resilience of agriculture production systems. *Current Opinion in Biotechnology*, *70*, 15–22. DOI: 10.1016/j.copbio.2020.09.003 PMID: 33038780

Kaya, C. (2025). Intelligent Environmental Control in Plant Factories: Integrating Sensors, Automation, and AI for Optimal Crop Production. *Food and Energy Security*, *14*(1), e70026. DOI: 10.1002/fes3.70026

Kent, K., Li, L., O'Fee, A., Iyer, A., & Fleming, C. (2025). A multimodal evaluation of an Australian university food environment and sustainability practices through student perspectives and a cross-sectional audit. *International Journal of Sustainability in Higher Education, ahead-of-print*(ahead-of-print). DOI: 10.1108/IJSHE-07-2024-0471

Khan, M. W., Destek, M. A., & Khan, Z. (2025). Income Inequality and Artificial Intelligence: Globalization and age dependency for developed countries. *Social Indicators Research, 176*(3), 1207–1233. DOI: 10.1007/s11205-024-03493-7

Klumpp, M. (2018). Automation and artificial intelligence in business logistics systems: Human reactions and collaboration requirements. *International Journal of Logistics, 21*(3), 224–242. DOI: 10.1080/13675567.2017.1384451

Kooli, C. (2023). Chatbots in Education and Research: A Critical Examination of Ethical Implications and Solutions. *Sustainability (Basel), 15*(7), 5614. DOI: 10.3390/su15075614

Leal Filho, W., Viera Trevisan, L., Sivapalan, S., Mazhar, M., Kounani, A., Mbah, M. F., Abubakar, I. R., Matandirotya, N. R., Pimenta Dinis, M. A., Borsari, B., & Abzug, R. (2025). Assessing the impacts of sustainability teaching at higher education institutions. *Discover Sustainability, 6*(1), 227. DOI: 10.1007/s43621-025-01024-z

Lee, C., Qin, Y., & Wang, Y.-C. (2025). Triboelectric nanogenerators for self-powered sensors and other applications. *MRS Bulletin, 50*(4), 428–438. DOI: 10.1557/s43577-025-00877-z

Lee, Y.-J. (2025). Towards a sustainable future: Analysing meta-competencies in community-based ecotourism on Liuqiu Island. *Journal of Hospitality and Tourism Management, 62*, 96–107. DOI: 10.1016/j.jhtm.2025.01.005

Leonardi, S., Distefano, N., & Gruden, C. (2025). Advancing Sustainable Mobility: Artificial Intelligence Approaches for Autonomous Vehicle Trajectories in Roundabouts. *Sustainability (Basel), 17*(7), 2988. DOI: 10.3390/su17072988

Li, J., & Imran, A. (2025). Sustainable Transitions: Navigating Green Technologies, Clean Energy, Economic Growth, and Human Capital for a Greener Future. *Sustainability (Basel), 17*(8), 3446. DOI: 10.3390/su17083446

Li, J., Liu, Z., Han, G., Demian, P., & Osmani, M. (2024). The Relationship Between Artificial Intelligence (AI) and Building Information Modeling (BIM) Technologies for Sustainable Building in the Context of Smart Cities. *Sustainability (Basel), 16*(24), 10848. DOI: 10.3390/su162410848

Li, N., Yu, X., Yang, D.-P., & He, J. (2025). Natural polysaccharides-based smart sensors for health monitoring, diagnosis and rehabilitation: A review. *International Journal of Biological Macromolecules, 304*, 140966. DOI: 10.1016/j.ijbiomac.2025.140966 PMID: 39952503

Liaw, S. Y., Ooi, S. W., Rusli, K. D. B., Lau, T. C., Tam, W. W. S., & Chua, W. L. (2020). Nurse-Physician Communication Team Training in Virtual Reality Versus Live Simulations: Randomized Controlled Trial on Team Communication and Teamwork Attitudes. *Journal of Medical Internet Research, 22*(4), e17279. DOI: 10.2196/17279 PMID: 32267235

Liu, J., & Chen, J. (2025). Applications and Trends of Machine Learning in Building Energy Optimization: A Bibliometric Analysis. *Buildings (Basel, Switzerland), 15*(7), 994. DOI: 10.3390/buildings15070994

Liu, Q., Liu, Z., Xu, W., Tang, Q., Zhou, Z., & Pham, D. T. (2019). Human-robot collaboration in disassembly for sustainable manufacturing. *International Journal of Production Research, 57*(12), 4027–4044. DOI: 10.1080/00207543.2019.1578906

Lo, W., Yang, C.-M., Zhang, Q., & Li, M. (2024). Increased Productivity and Reduced Waste with Robotic Process Automation and Generative AI-powered IoE Services. *Journal of Web Engineering, 23*(01), 53–88. DOI: 10.13052/jwe1540-9589.2313

Louta, M., Banti, K., & Karampelia, I. (2024). Emerging Technologies for Sustainable Agriculture: The Power of Humans and the Way Ahead. *IEEE Access : Practical Innovations, Open Solutions, 12*, 98492–98529. DOI: 10.1109/ACCESS.2024.3428401

Lubowitz, J. H., Cote, M. P., Ramkumar, P. N., & Kunze, K. N. (2025). Applications of Artificial Intelligence for Health Care Providers. *Arthroscopy, 41*(3), 537–538. DOI: 10.1016/j.arthro.2024.12.006 PMID: 39662852

Machado, C. H., Sousa, M., & Branco, M. C. (2025). Sustainability-Linked Bonds Research: A Bibliometric and Content Analysis Review. *International Journal of Financial Studies, 13*(2), 62. DOI: 10.3390/ijfs13020062

Maharjan, K. L., Gonzalvo, C. M., & Baggo, J. C. (2025). Balancing Tradition and Innovation: The Role of Environmental Conservation Agriculture in the Sustainability of the Ifugao Rice Terraces. *Agriculture, 15*(3), 246. DOI: 10.3390/agriculture15030246

Mahesh, S., & Calvert, S. C. (2025). Decarbonizing airport access: A review of landside transport sustainability. *Transportation Research Part D, Transport and Environment, 140*, 104625. DOI: 10.1016/j.trd.2025.104625

Maheshwari, G., & Schrage, B. (2025). Emerging trends in social entrepreneurship and sustainability: a Southeast Asia analysis. *The Bottom Line, ahead-of-print*(ahead-of-print). DOI: 10.1108/BL-06-2024-0064

Maheshwari, H., & Samantaray, A. K. (2025). Beyond instinct: the influence of artificial intelligence on investment decision-making among Gen Z investors in emerging markets. *International Journal of Accounting & Information Management, ahead-of-print*(ahead-of-print). DOI: 10.1108/IJAIM-10-2024-0371

Mana, A. A., Allouhi, A., Hamrani, A., Rehman, S., el Jamaoui, I., & Jayachandran, K. (2024). Sustainable AI-based production agriculture: Exploring AI applications and implications in agricultural practices. *Smart Agricultural Technology*, *7*, 100416. DOI: 10.1016/j.atech.2024.100416

Máška, J., Janků, J., & Lorencová, I. (2023). Tools and Trends in Real Estate Sustainability Assessment. *Real Estate Management and Valuation, ahead-of-print*(ahead-of-print). DOI: 10.2478/remav-2025-0016

May, M. C., Oberst, J., & Lanza, G. (2024). Managing product-inherent constraints with artificial intelligence: Production control for time constraints in semiconductor manufacturing. *Journal of Intelligent Manufacturing*, *35*(8), 4259–4276. DOI: 10.1007/s10845-024-02472-6

McKinsey&Company. (2024). *What is AI (artificial intelligence)?* https://www.mckinsey.com/featured-insights/mckinsey-explainers/what-is-ai#/

Microsoft. (2024). *Khanmigo for Teachers: Your free AI-powered teaching tool.* https://www.microsoft.com/en-us/education/blog/2024/08/khanmigo-for-teachers-your-free-ai-powered-teaching-tool/

Millington, B., Naraine, M. L., Wanless, L., Safai, P., & Manley, A. (2025). Sport and the Promise of Artificial Intelligence: Human and Machine Futures. *Sociology of Sport Journal, ahead-of-print*(ahead-of-print), 1-10. DOI: 10.1123/ssj.2024-0150

Modi, Z., Dubey, K., & Salunke, P. (2025). Characterization of Fatty Acids and Nutritional Health Indicators of Ghee (Butteroil) Manufactured from Bovine Colostrum and Sweet Cream. *Dairy*, *6*(1), 2. DOI: 10.3390/dairy6010002

Mogaji, E. (2025). Transformative transport services: leveraging sustainability, inclusivity, and technology through marketing management. *Journal of Marketing Management, ahead-of-print*(ahead-of-print), 1-33. DOI: 10.1080/0267257X.2025.2461673

Mostafaei, H., Kordnoori, S., Ostadrahimi, M., & Banihashemi, S. S. A. (2025). Applications of artificial intelligence in global diplomacy: A review of research and practical models. *Sustainable Futures : An Applied Journal of Technology, Environment and Society*, *9*, 100486. DOI: 10.1016/j.sftr.2025.100486

Murtinu, S., & De Massis, A. (2025). Artificial intelligence machines as relational nonhuman actors in entrepreneurial teams. *Journal of Small Business Management, ahead-of-print*(ahead-of-print), 1-27. DOI: 10.1080/00472778.2025.2461031

Naeni, L. M., & Tumpa, R. J. (2025). Digital Technologies and Sustainability in Project Management: Current Trends and Future Perspectives. In Hazır, Ö., & Bruni, M. E. (Eds.), *Tomorrow's Data Empowered Project Management: Agile Decision Making, Sustainability and AI* (pp. 147–168). Springer Nature Switzerland., DOI: 10.1007/978-3-031-84017-3_8

Navarro, G., & Bayona, J. (2025). The Impact of Artificial Intelligence on Quality and Sustainable Development: A Bibliometric Analysis. *Quality Innovation Prosperity*, *29*(1), 81–97. DOI: 10.12776/qip.v29i1.2151

Nguyen, A. T., Latapí, M., Kemper, J. A., P., B., & Lam, H. (2025). Sustainability and sustainable development goals in business higher education research: a systematic literature review. *Environmental Education Research, ahead-of-print*(ahead-of-print), 1-28. DOI: 10.1080/13504622.2025.2482743

Nguyen, H., Nguyen, V., Ludovise, S., & Santagata, R. (2025). Value-sensitive design of chatbots in environmental education: Supporting identity, connectedness, well-being and sustainability. *British Journal of Educational Technology, ahead-of-print*(ahead-of-print). DOI: 10.1111/bjet.13568

Ni, C., & Abdullah, N. L. (2025). Research on absorptive capacity in the green context: A bibliometric and visualization analysis. *Cogent Business & Management*, *12*(1), 2435602. DOI: 10.1080/23311975.2024.2435602

Nishant, R., Kennedy, M., & Corbett, J. (2020). Artificial intelligence for sustainability: Challenges, opportunities, and a research agenda. *International Journal of Information Management*, *53*, 102104. DOI: 10.1016/j.ijinfomgt.2020.102104

Nwagwu, W. E. (2025). Citation analysis of global research on data literacy. *Education and Information Technologies, ahead-of-print*(ahead-of-print), 1-29. DOI: 10.1007/s10639-025-13397-9

Ojha, R., & Agarwal, A. (2025). Examining environmental sustainability in last-mile delivery: a quality function deployment analysis. *The TQM Journal, ahead-of-print*(ahead-of-print). DOI: 10.1108/TQM-07-2024-0249

Pak, L. S. (2023). *Harnessing Design Thinking for Human-Centered Modelling: A tutorial on how designers can pair with data scientists and engineers for modelling* Companion Proceedings of the 28th International Conference on Intelligent User Interfaces, Sydney, NSW, Australia, Pallardy, R. (2024). *How AI and IoT Are Reshaping Agriculture.* https://www.informationweek.com/machine-learning-ai/ai-and-iot-are-reshaping-agriculture

Pereira, M. T., Rocha, N., Silva, F. G., Moreira, M. Â. L., Altinkaya, Y. O., & Pereira, M. J. (2025). Process Optimization in Sea Ports: Integrating Sustainability and Efficiency Through a Novel Mathematical Model. *Journal of Marine Science and Engineering, 13*(1), 119. DOI: 10.3390/jmse13010119

Pillai, S. V. (2025). Urban agriculture: A sustainability guide for developing countries. *Social Responsibility Journal, 21*(4), 725–750. DOI: 10.1108/SRJ-07-2024-0433

Priya, Sharma, K., & Bisht, V. (2025). Moving Towards Sustainable Connectivity: Bibliometric Analysis of IoT-Enabled Financial Sustainability Trends. *E3S Web Conf., 616*, 03033. DOI: 10.1051/e3sconf/202561603033

Quesado, P., Costa Oliveira, H., & Silva, R. (2025). Integrating sustainability goals into the balanced scorecard: a bibliometric analysis of the sustainability balanced scorecard. *Measuring Business Excellence, ahead-of-print*(ahead-of-print). DOI: 10.1108/MBE-09-2024-0139

Quirós-Alpera, S., Roets, A. O. S. B., Robina-Ramírez, R., & Leal-Solís, A. (2025). Bridging Theory and Practice: Challenges and Opportunities in Dual Training for Sustainability Education at Spanish Universities. *Societies (Basel, Switzerland), 15*(2), 32. DOI: 10.3390/soc15020032

R Core Team. (2023). *R: A language and environment for statistical computing. R Foundation for Statistical Computing, Vienna, Austria.* https://www.R-project.org/

Ramakrishnan, J., Seshadri, K., Liu, T., Zhang, F., Yu, R., & Gou, Z. (2023). Explainable semi-supervised AI for green performance evaluation of airport buildings. *Journal of Building Engineering, 79*, 107788. DOI: 10.1016/j.jobe.2023.107788

Ramazanova, M., Silva, F. M., & Vaz de Freitas, I. (2025). Tourists' Views on Sustainable Heritage Management in Porto, Portugal: Balancing Heritage Preservation and Tourism. *Heritage, 8*(1), 10. DOI: 10.3390/heritage8010010

Raworth, K. (2017). *Doughnut Economics: Seven Ways to Think Like a 21st Century Economist.* Chelsea Green Publishing.

Richards, D., Worden, D., Song, X. P., & Lavorel, S. (2024). Harnessing generative artificial intelligence to support nature-based solutions. *People and Nature, 6*(2), 882–893. DOI: 10.1002/pan3.10622

Riedmann-Streitz, C., Streitz, N., Antona, M., Marcus, A., Margetis, G., Ntoa, S., Rau, P.-L. P., & Rosenzweig, E. (2025). How to Create and Foster Sustainable Smart Cities? Insights on Ethics, Trust, Privacy, Transparency, Incentives, and Success. *International Journal of Human-Computer Interaction, 41*(4), 2491–2522. DOI: 10.1080/10447318.2024.2325175

Riegel, C., & Ajabnoor, N. (2024). Investigating the Efficacy and Sustainability of Virtual Education Courses. *Journal of University Teaching & Learning Practice, 21*(1). Advance online publication. DOI: 10.53761/30maba42

Rohrbach, T., & Makhortykh, M. (2025). A matter of mindset? Features and processes of newsroom-based corporate communication in times of artificial intelligence. *Corporate Communications: An International Journal, ahead-of-print*(ahead-of-print). DOI: 10.1108/CCIJ-07-2024-0118

Root, D. (2025). Quantum Technologies in the Context of Climate Change: Emphasizing Sustainability in a Responsible Innovation Approach to Quantum Innovation. *NanoEthics, 19*(1), 4. DOI: 10.1007/s11569-025-00468-x

Ryo, M., Schiller, J., Stiller, S., Rivera Palacio, J. C., Mengsuwan, K., Safonova, A., & Wei, Y. (2023). Deep learning for sustainable agriculture needs ecology and human involvement. *Journal of Sustainable Agriculture and Environment, 2*(1), 40–44. DOI: 10.1002/sae2.12036

Saba, C. S., & Monkam, N. (2025). Artificial intelligence's (AI's) role in enhancing tax revenue, institutional quality, and economic growth in selected BRICS-plus countries. *Journal of Social and Economic Development, ahead-of-print*(ahead-of-print). DOI: 10.1007/s40847-024-00401-0

Sahebi, S., & Formosa, P. (2025). The AI-mediated communication dilemma: Epistemic trust, social media, and the challenge of generative artificial intelligence. *Synthese, 205*(3), 128. DOI: 10.1007/s11229-025-04963-2

Saini, S. (2025). Customer experience and sustainability in social, environmental and economic contexts. *International Journal of Innovation Science, ahead-of-print*(ahead-of-print). DOI: 10.1108/IJIS-03-2024-0054

Sanabria Navarro, J. R., Niebles Núñez, W. A., & Silveira Pérez, Y. (2024). Análisis bibliométrico de la inteligencia artificial en el deporte (Bibliometric analysis of artificial intelligence in sport). *Retos, 54*, 312–319. DOI: 10.47197/retos.v54.103531

Santamaría Ruiz, M. J., Jiménez Calderón, C. E., Osorio Venecia, A. R., Santodomingo, A. A., & Forero, M. P. (2025). Bibliometric behavior of artificial intelligence and digital marketing sustainability. *Procedia Computer Science*, *257*, 1047–1052. DOI: 10.1016/j.procs.2025.03.136

Savari, M., Khaleghi, B., & Sheheytavi, A. (2025). How to reduce the risk of climate change for the sustainability of rural farmers? Based on evidence from Iran. *Environmental and Sustainability Indicators*, *25*, 100581. DOI: 10.1016/j.indic.2025.100581

Schmeisser, S., Miccoli, A., von Bergen, M., Berggren, E., Braeuning, A., Busch, W., Desaintes, C., Gourmelon, A., Grafström, R., Harrill, J., Hartung, T., Herzler, M., Kass, G. E. N., Kleinstreuer, N., Leist, M., Luijten, M., Marx-Stoelting, P., Poetz, O., van Ravenzwaay, B., & Tralau, T. (2023). New approach methodologies in human regulatory toxicology – Not if, but how and when! *Environment International*, *178*, 108082. DOI: 10.1016/j.envint.2023.108082 PMID: 37422975

Schwendicke, F., Samek, W., & Krois, J. (2020). Artificial Intelligence in Dentistry: Chances and Challenges. *Journal of Dental Research*, *99*(7), 769–774. DOI: 10.1177/0022034520915714 PMID: 32315260

Shahrabani, M. M. N., & Apanaviciene, R. (2024). An AI-Based Evaluation Framework for Smart Building Integration into Smart City. *Sustainability (Basel)*, *16*(18), 8032. DOI: 10.3390/su16188032

Shan, D., Qu, F., Wang, Z., Ji, Y., & Xu, J. (2025). A Review of the Application of Computer Vision Techniques in Sustainable Engineering of Open Pit Mines. *Sustainability (Basel)*, *17*(7), 3051. DOI: 10.3390/su17073051

Shao, Q. (2025). Sustainability Evaluation of the Doughnut Economics: A Bibliometric Analysis. *Earth's Future*, *13*(4), e2024EF004638. DOI: 10.1029/2024EF004638

Shunmathy, V., & Selvam, V. (2025). A bibliometric review exploring the nexus between environmental sustainability and electric four-wheeler. *Discover Sustainability*, *6*(1), 219. DOI: 10.1007/s43621-025-01020-3

Siala, H., & Wang, Y. (2022). SHIFTing artificial intelligence to be responsible in healthcare: A systematic review. *Social Science & Medicine*, *296*, 114782. DOI: 10.1016/j.socscimed.2022.114782 PMID: 35152047

Singh, D., Sharma, A., Singh, R. K., & Rana, P. S. (2025). Artificial intelligence enabled supply chain resilience: Insights from FMCG industry. *Journal of Global Operations and Strategic Sourcing*, *18*(2), 414–441. DOI: 10.1108/JGOSS-02-2024-0017

Sinha, A. H., Maurya, A., & Munoz, J. M. (2025). Harnessing the Power of Artificial Intelligence for Sustainable Development. In Dixit, S., Maurya, M., Jain, V., & Subramaniam, G. (Eds.), *Artificial Intelligence-Enabled Businesses: How to Develop Strategies for Innovation* (pp. 391–396). Wiley & Sons Inc-Scrivener Publishing LLC., DOI: 10.1002/9781394234028.ch21

Sivasankari, N., & Rathika, P. (2025). IoT driven building automation systems: A review on energy efficiency, occupant comfort, and sustainability. *Journal of Building Engineering, 104*, 112347. DOI: 10.1016/j.jobe.2025.112347

Skubis, I., Wolniak, R., & Grebski, W. W. (2024). AI and Human-Centric Approach in Smart Cities Management: Case Studies from Silesian and Lesser Poland Voivodships. *Sustainability (Basel), 16*(18), 8279. DOI: 10.3390/su16188279

Smart Energy Decisions. (2024). *Marriott International Implements Data Automation Tools & Artificial Intelligence for Scope 3 Emissions Reporting Enhancements.* https://www.smartenergydecisions.com/columns/marriott-international-implements-data-automation-tools-and-artificial-intelligence-for-scope-3-emissions-reporting-enhancements/

Software Improvement Group. (2025). *AI legislation in the US: A 2025 overview.* https://www.softwareimprovementgroup.com/us-ai-legislation-overview/

Son, N., Chen, C.-R., & Syu, C.-H. (2024). Towards Artificial Intelligence Applications in Precision and Sustainable Agriculture. *Agronomy (Basel), 14*(2), 239. DOI: 10.3390/agronomy14020239

Spencer, B. F.Jr, Sim, S.-H., Kim, R. E., & Yoon, H. (2025). Advances in artificial intelligence for structural health monitoring: A comprehensive review. *KSCE Journal of Civil Engineering, 29*(3), 100203. DOI: 10.1016/j.kscej.2025.100203

Sumarsono, H., Narmaditya, B. S., Rahmawati, F., Prayitno, P. H., & Sahid, S. (2024). Green marketing for sustainability business: A bibliometric analysis. *Multidisciplinary Reviews, 8*(3), 2025078. DOI: 10.31893/multirev.2025078

Sun, Q., & Hsiao, I.-H. (2024). An AI-infused Educational Technology to Cultivate Self-directed Learning in Sustainable Waste Management. *Proceedings of the 2024 International Conference on Information Technology for Social Good*, 127–134. DOI: 10.1145/3677525.3678652

Teng, H.-Y., Li, M.-W., & Chen, C.-Y. (2025). Does smart technology, artificial intelligence, robotics, and algorithm (STARA) awareness have a double-edged-sword influence on proactive customer service performance? Effects of work engagement and employee resilience. *Journal of Hospitality Marketing & Management*, *34*(3), 443–466. DOI: 10.1080/19368623.2025.2449853

Tiyasha, T., Tung, T. M., & Yaseen, Z. M. (2020). A survey on river water quality modelling using artificial intelligence models: 2000–2020. *Journal of Hydrology (Amsterdam)*, *585*, 124670. DOI: 10.1016/j.jhydrol.2020.124670

Toruner, M. D., Shi, V., Sollee, J., Hsu, W.-C., Yu, G., Dai, Y.-W., Merlo, C., Suresh, K., Jiao, Z., Wang, X., Mao, S., & Bai, H. (2025). Artificial Intelligence-Driven Wireless Sensing for Health Management. *Bioengineering (Basel, Switzerland)*, *12*(3), 244. DOI: 10.3390/bioengineering12030244 PMID: 40150708

Tost, M. (2025). Lessons From Assessing Sustainability in The Mining and Resources Sector. In John, M. (Ed.), *The Routledge Handbook of Global Sustainability Education and Thinking for the 21st Century* (pp. 200–217). Taylor & Francis., https://books.google.com.tr/books?id=X29GEQAAQBAJ DOI: 10.4324/9781003171577-16

Tunckaya, Y. (2025). Performance analysis of novel air pollution forecasting system design in a Turkish cement plant via neural and neuro-fuzzy soft computing. *Energy Sources. Part A, Recovery, Utilization, and Environmental Effects*, *47*(1), 395–410. DOI: 10.1080/15567036.2020.1825561

Tutar, S., Tutar, H., Keskin, D. A., Bilan, Y., & Streimikiene, D. (2025). Relationship Between Earnings Quality and Sustainability of Companies. *Corporate Social Responsibility and Environmental Management*, *ahead-of-print*(ahead-of-print). DOI: 10.1002/csr.3211

United Nations. 1987. Report to the World Commission on Environment and Development: Our Common Future (Report A/42/427). New York: United Nations.

Vicente, P. N. (2024). Artificial Intelligence and Freedom of Speech. *European Journal of Communication*, *39*(2), 197–200. DOI: 10.1177/02673231241234766

Vlacic, L., Huang, H., Dotoli, M., Wang, Y., Ioannou, P. A., Fan, L., Wang, X., Carli, R., Lv, C., Li, L., Na, X., Han, Q.-L., & Wang, F.-Y. (2024). Automation 5.0: The Key to Systems Intelligence and Industry 5.0. *IEEE/CAA Journal of Automatica Sinica*, *11*(8), 1723-1727. DOI: 10.1109/JAS.2024.124635

Wang, J., Zhao, W., Ding, J., & Liu, Y. (2025). Shifting research paradigms in landscape ecology: Insights from bibliometric analysis. *Landscape Ecology*, *40*(3), 63. DOI: 10.1007/s10980-025-02082-4

Wang, Q., Sun, T., & Li, R. (2023). Does artificial intelligence promote green innovation? An assessment based on direct, indirect, spillover, and heterogeneity effects. *Energy & Environment, 36*(2), 1005–1037. DOI: 10.1177/0958305X231220520

Wang, S., & Zhang, H. (2025). Enhancing environmental, social, and governance performance through artificial intelligence supply chains in the energy industry: Roles of innovation, collaboration, and proactive sustainability strategy. *Renewable Energy, 245*, 122855. DOI: 10.1016/j.renene.2025.122855

Wang, X., Wu, Q., Zeng, H., Yang, X., Cui, H., Yi, X., Piran, M. J., Luo, M., & Que, Y. (2025). Blockchain-Empowered H-CPS Architecture for Smart Agriculture. *Advanced Science, ahead-of-print*(ahead-of-print), 2503102. DOI: 10.1002/advs.202503102

Wen, D.-L., Liu, X., Deng, H.-T., Sun, D.-H., Qian, H.-Y., Brugger, J., & Zhang, X.-S. (2019). Printed silk-fibroin-based triboelectric nanogenerators for multi-functional wearable sensing. *Nano Energy, 66*, 104123. DOI: 10.1016/j.nanoen.2019.104123

Wen, H. (2025). Artificial Intelligence and Social Ethics: Opportunities, Challenges, and Boundaries — Ethical Reflections in the Age of Technological Waves. *Lecture Notes in Education Psychology and Public Media, 107*(1), 90–96. DOI: 10.54254/2753-7048/2025.LD27419

Weng, M. (2025). Green innovation through artificial intelligence technology: Enhancing environmental, social, and governance performance. *Finance Research Letters, 75*, 106921. DOI: 10.1016/j.frl.2025.106921

White & Case LLP. (2025, Mayıs 29). *AI watch: Global regulatory tracker - China*. https://www.whitecase.com/insight-our-thinking/ai-watch-global-regulatory-tracker-china

Wibowo, M. A., & Ammar, M. A. (2025). Lean construction and sustainability: A review of research trends and implications for the United Nations SDGs. *E3S Web Conf., 605*, 03048. DOI: 10.1051/e3sconf/202560503048

Wu, P.-J., & Tai, Y.-C. (2024). Artificial intelligence-based food-quality and warehousing management for food banks' inbound logistics. *Journal of Enterprise Information Management, 37*(1), 307–325. DOI: 10.1108/JEIM-10-2022-0398

Xames, M. D., & Topcu, T. G. (2025). How Can Digital Twins Support the Economic, Environmental, and Social Sustainability of Healthcare Systems: A Systematic Review Focused on the Triple Bottom Line. *IEEE Access : Practical Innovations, Open Solutions, 13*, 64390–64411. DOI: 10.1109/ACCESS.2025.3559502

Xiao, X. (2025). Sustainable Agriculture with Self-Powered Wireless Sensing. *Agriculture, 15*(3), 234. DOI: 10.3390/agriculture15030234

Xiao, Y., & Xiao, L. (2025). The impact of artificial intelligence-driven ESG performance on sustainable development of central state-owned enterprises listed companies. *Scientific Reports, 15*(1), 8548. DOI: 10.1038/s41598-025-93694-y PMID: 40074861

Xie, H., & Wu, F. (2025). Artificial Intelligence Technology and Corporate ESG Performance: Empirical Evidence from Chinese-Listed Firms. *Sustainability (Basel), 17*(2), 420. doi.org/10.3390/su17020420. DOI: 10.3390/su17020420

Xu, Z., Liu, Z., & Luo, H. (2025). Can Artificial Intelligence Technology Help Achieving Good Governance: A Public Policy Evaluation Method Based on Artificial Neural Network. *SAGE Open, 15*(1), 21582440251317833. DOI: 10.1177/21582440251317833

Yessimova, D., Faurat, A., Belyi, A., Yessim, A., & Sadykov, Z. (2025). Environmental Sustainability and Carbon Footprint of Tourism: A Study of a Natural Park in Northeastern Kazakhstan. *Sustainability (Basel), 17*(4), 1723. DOI: 10.3390/su17041723

Yigitcanlar, T., & Cugurullo, F. (2020). The Sustainability of Artificial Intelligence: An Urbanistic Viewpoint from the Lens of Smart and Sustainable Cities. *Sustainability (Basel), 12*(20), 8548. DOI: 10.3390/su12208548

Yıldırım, F., Ünlü, U., Kuloğlu, A., & Çıtak, Ö. (2025). Modeling and Analysis of the Impact of Quality Growth and Financial Development on Environmental Sustainability: Evidence from EU Countries. *Sustainability (Basel), 17*(2), 774. DOI: 10.3390/su17020774

Yue, X., Kang, M., & Zhang, Y. (2025). The impact of artificial intelligence usage on supply chain resilience in manufacturing firms: a moderated mediation model. *Journal of Manufacturing Technology Management, ahead-of-print*(ahead-of-print). DOI: 10.1108/JMTM-07-2024-0379

Yun, G., Lee, K. M., & Choi, H. H. (2025). Empowering Student Learning Through Artificial Intelligence: A Bibliometric Analysis. *Journal of Educational Computing Research, 62*(8), 1822–1855. DOI: 10.1177/07356331241278636

Zhang, L., Wei, W., Fan, A., Milman, A., & King, B. E. M. (2025). Cultural sustainability in hospitality and tourism: Toward a holistic framework. *International Journal of Contemporary Hospitality Management, 37*(13), 20–38. DOI: 10.1108/IJCHM-10-2024-1551

Zhang, L., Zhao, S., Yang, Z., Zheng, H., & Lei, M. (2024). An artificial intelligence tool to assess the risk of severe mental distress among college students in terms of demographics, eating habits, lifestyles, and sport habits: An externally validated study using machine learning. *BMC Psychiatry*, *24*(1), 581. DOI: 10.1186/s12888-024-06017-2 PMID: 39192305

Zhang, Y., Shi, J., & Huang, Y. (2025). Do artificial intelligence capabilities impact sustainability-oriented innovation performance: exploring the role of green intellectual capital and learning orientation. *Journal of Intellectual Capital, ahead-of-print*(ahead-of-print). DOI: 10.1108/JIC-10-2024-0315

Zhu, Q., Han, C., Liu, S., Li, Y., & Che, J. (2025). Artificial intelligence-driven financial innovation: A robo-advisor system for robust returns across diversified markets. *Expert Systems with Applications*, *274*, 126881. DOI: 10.1016/j.eswa.2025.126881

Zhu, S., & Feng, H. (2025). Construction and demolition waste circulation and its sustainability performance in the building sector: current trend and future directions. *Engineering, Construction and Architectural Management, ahead-of-print*(ahead-of-print). DOI: 10.1108/ECAM-05-2024-0678

KEY TERMS AND DEFINITIONS

Artificial Intelligence: A tool that will become increasingly important for humanity and sustainability as its development continues.

Biblioshiny: An analysis tool frequently used by researchers, including many analysis techniques such as three field plot, thematic map, thematic evolution and trend topics analyses.

Humanity: A living entity conducting research on how to further optimise its sustainability with artificial intelligence.

Opportunities Analysis: An analysis technique for determining specific parts that may be suitable for a new study in the field planned for research in scientific studies.

Sustainability: A factor that is supported by current technologies for the continuation of the universe and humanity.

Trends Analysis: A useful type of analysis to examine in scientific studies to gain information about the current state of the researched field.

Visualisation: An analysis technique that facilitates researchers and practitioners to obtain information about the issue being researched in trend and opportunities analyses.

Web of Science: A database whose popularity has continued from the past to the present and is expected to maintain its popularity in the future.

Chapter 8
Environmental Detreminants of Tuberculosis:
AI as an Innovative Solution

Ismail Ouhammou
https://orcid.org/0000-0003-2340-3438
Laboratory of Natural Resources and Sustainable Development, Faculty of Sciences, Ibn Tofail University, Kenitra, Morocco

Rida Arabi
Laboratory of Natural Resources and Sustainable Development, Faculty of Sciences, Ibn Tofail University, Kenitra, Morocco

Mounia Mezouara
Laboratory of Natural Resources and Sustainable Development, Faculty of Sciences, Ibn Tofail University, Kenitra, Morocco

Fouzia Magmat
https://orcid.org/0000-0001-7513-0879
Laboratory of Natural Resources and Sustainable Development, Faculty of Sciences, Ibn Tofail University, Kenitra, Morocco

Meryem Doubi
https://orcid.org/0009-0000-3812-316X
Laboratory of Natural Resources and Sustainable Development, Faculty of Sciences, Ibn Tofail University, Kenitra, Morocco

Driss Hmouni
https://orcid.org/0000-0001-7598-6204
Laboratory of Natural Resources and Sustainable Development, Faculty of Sciences, Ibn Tofail University, Kenitra, Morocco

ABSTRACT

Tuberculosis (TB) continues to be a major public health issue worldwide, with its prevalence heavily influenced by environmental determinants such as poor living conditions, air pollution, and limited healthcare access. These factors contribute to the spread and persistence of TB, particularly in under-resourced and vulnerable

DOI: 10.4018/979-8-3373-3436-3.ch008

communities. Understanding the environmental influences on TB transmission is key to developing effective prevention and intervention strategies. Artificial Intelligence (AI) offers a groundbreaking solution for analyzing the complex relationships between environmental determinants and TB. This study explores the potential of AI in addressing the environmental determinants of tuberculosis, showcasing how AI can be applied to enhance disease monitoring, improve resource allocation, and support effective policy-making. Integrating AI into public health strategies offers the opportunity to transform the approach to TB control, enabling a more proactive and data-driven response to this global health challenge.

INTRODUCTION

Dramatic reports of rising TB notification rates in poor countries reinforced this view, and the priority was not to identify high-risk groups but to cut the chain of transmission in the community by increasing detection of infectious TB cases and ensuring high rates of complete treatment (Lienhardt, 2001). Subsequently, as case detection remains largely passive, most global public health efforts to combat tuberculosis has focused on treatment. The World Health Organization has set itself the target of successfully treating 85% of tuberculosis cases worldwide. However, this curative approach has shown its limits, especially in areas where health systems are fragile. On the other hand, fortifying preventive measures must be an immediate priority; for instance, the administration of BCG vaccination and the implementation of proactive screening strategies for at-risk populations are essential initiatives to mitigate the incidence of the disease (Kranzer et al., 2013). In addition, elevating community awareness regarding tuberculosis and its modes of transmission is imperative in addressing the stigma associated with the disease and fostering an environment where individuals feel compelled to undergo testing without trepidation (Mathema et al., 2017). Involving community leaders can significantly enhance the promotion of health practices. With this consideration, it is imperative to broaden access to care by integrating tuberculosis services into primary healthcare and coordinating efforts across various sectors to ensure a holistic and comprehensive approach (Holden et al., 2016; Lienhardt, 2001). Tuberculosis ranks among the most prevalent diseases globally, resulting in fatalities and classified as a communicable ailment. In 2021, an estimated 10 million individuals were afflicted with tuberculosis, culminating in approximately 1.6 million deaths. (*Global Tuberculosis Report 2021*, 2021). Tuberculosis is a contagious and airborne affliction, with numerous vectors of transmission, including ambient air, soil, animals, and food. TB transmission is influenced by many factors, including population density, living conditions and hygiene. Therefore, a single factor is difficult to identify as responsible for transmission.

As several studies have shown, the spatial distribution and socioeconomic determinants of tuberculosis are topics that have been the subject of extensive research. Nevertheless, there are still gaps in our knowledge in this area. On the one hand, the precise influence of environmental factors (air quality, local climate, air pollution, and urban environments) is poorly accounted for in epidemiological models. Furthermore, the integration of artificial intelligence (AI) methods into environmental and health data management remains in its infancy in this sector. Furthermore, rigorous assessments of the robustness, interpretability, and transferability of predictive models are rare. In addition, low spatial and temporal resolution or methodological inconsistencies in studies are an obstacle to comparing and generalizing results. Furthermore, the potential of analyzing massive and varied environmental data remains largely untapped. Traditional statistical methods have proven ineffective in understanding nonlinear relationships and complex interactions between variables. It should be noted that these factors may be subject to variation. In addition, these practices limit the effectiveness of local interventions.

In this work, we investigate the environmental determinants of TB, including population density, ambient air quality, socio-economic and poverty status, and access to healthcare. We can learn a great deal by appreciating those two factors, dissemination of TB and to develop appropriate policy options for intervention (prevention and treatment).

UNDERSTANDING TUBERCULOSIS

A few decades later, Tb continues as a worldwide health burden. More than 95% of TB fatalities are in low- and middle-income countries and it is feared they will escalate. Even though it is preventable and curable, Tb killed around 2 million people in 2017. TB, which is transmitted through the air when a Tb patient coughs or sneezes, releases droples with the TB pathogen. TB bacteria adhere to the nasopharynx and respiratory tract, multiplying in the lungs. This disease primarily affects the lungs and is subsequently termed pulmonary tuberculosis (PTB). Extrapulmonary tuberculosis (EPTB) occurs when the TB pathogens enter the bloodstream and affect regions other than the lungs, resulting in disseminated TB (Silva et al., 2021). Accordingly, TB can be divided into common TB, including PTB and EPTB, and two rare types: cavitary tuberculosis and miliary tuberculosis. Extrapulmonary TB can be subdivided into four categories: superficial and deep tissue TB, TB affecting the central nervous system, and TB affecting the abdominal cavity and is categorized as disseminated TB. Also, TB is given descriptors based on the infecting strain, such as drug-sensitive TB (DSTB), multidrug-resistant TB (MDRTB), and extensively drug-resistant TB (XDRTB). Several social, physical, and environmental factors contribute to TB epidemics. Health variables, such as malnutrition, diabetes, and human immunodeficiency virus (HIV) infection, increase susceptibility to TB infection. These behavioral and social determinants interact with widespread bacteriological and ecological factors, such as those related to modernized cities, long-distance migration, occluded air circulation, and the housing of TB cases, contributing to the development of TB epidemics (Sun et al., 2015). With an unimaginable increase in human migration due to economic development and improved transportation systems, countries have become more integrated with the globalization of trade and culture. However, the costs of global expansion include the easy spread of many infectious diseases, such as TB. In the past 20 years, growing TB outbreaks have been reported in many cities where the TB incidence rates were previously classified as low.

ENVIRONMENTAL DETERMINANTS

Infection with Mycobacterium tuberculosis can occur in many body sites, yet the lungs are the preferred niche for an actively replicating infection that can lead to transmission. Determining the optimal environmental conditions for transmission can help eradicate tuberculosis. Increased humidity improves transmission and recommendations for improving ventilation in buildings have long been proposed to increase the air exchange volume. However, large studies that assess both ambient meteorological variables and building conditions against transmission have been lacking. An improved understanding of the effects of humidity and ventilation on transmission mechanisms is critical for arresting the ongoing pandemic of tuberculosis that remains prevalent globally. There is mounting evidence that relative humidity plays an important role in Mycobacterium tuberculosis aerobiology, with subsequent implications for transmission cycle (Chang et al., 2024).

Elaborate on the relevant narratives towards these environmental determinants outline based on the references given. Tuberculosis continues to be a global health threat. Each year up to two billion people are estimated to be infected with Mycobacterium tuberculosis (MTB). It is crucial to identify the hotspots to control TB outbreaks. This study took this idea one step further by gathering demographic data, economic activity, and environmental data to complement the health data. The relationships amongst TB, population, environment and economy were analyzed by different approaches include Spatial Autocorrelation, Ordinary Least Square, Local Indicator of Spatial Association, and Geographically Weighted Regression model. In addition, it showed a conceptual approach to obtain real time epidemiological insights regarding TB active cases, using the deep learning approach, Reinforcement Learning agent and Recurrent Neural Network. A case study was conducted in the city of New York. These results could shed light on epidemiological insights regarding TB spread and hotspots at community level, and pave the ways for the development of active cases prediction system, which could aid public health authorities in TB surveillance and control (Dodd et al., 2021).

Socioeconomic Factors

For many years, health scientists have identified and documented the interaction of socio-economic conditions, population density, geography and climate with the probability of TB transmission or development of disease. Townsend famously developed his 'deprivation index' to quantify such conditions and their relation to health and social factors. He documented a higher incidence of TB in areas of higher deprivation. More recently, however, the introduction of regional national and sub-national incidence rates for TB has paved the way for renewed interest in quantifying the parameters of environmental risk factors that have a global reach, using advanced coding and Data Science techniques. This has included a spatial model for the active tuberculosis incidence rate, parch of deprived households, poverty rate, foreign-born residents and across a 9 km ecological zone that can vary from purely urban to rural. For understanding TB, the literature has provided examples scope for how environmental determinants at a fine resolution can be incorporated into time-dependent data science methods. The spatial-reach synoptic model has been combined with an explanatory factor graph approach to compactly code the synoptic equation and automatically decompose it into a deep neural network of a manageable number of neurons (Nidoi et al., 2021).

The availability of high-quality surveillance data on TB incidence rate and latent social and environmental factors is an essential prerequisite for developing any effective AI-driven model. There have been extensive efforts to standardize the quality and evaluation of data for modeling efforts, which have increased steadily in the USA, Europe and many developed nations. However, these data requirements act as a double-edged sword. So far, active surveillance has been less prevalent or nonexistent in many developing countries. And yet some of the countries with the highest TB burden have been 'modeling-deserving'. Attempts to generate accurate and publicly accessible sub-national data on TB drivers are needed to determine whether environmental determinants also influence TB risks. For many health challenges, the relevant influences can be broadly classified into individual-level and geographical ones (Lansang et al., 2021).

Climate and Weather Conditions

Climate and weather are essential environmental factors concerning its risk of tuberculosis (TB). Studies reported potential associations between average annual temperature and incidence of TB, indicating a positive association (Zhang et al., 2019). The recall time for weather data was shorter than the incubation period of TB, and the association between weather data and TB may result in aggregating immediate and longer-term influences on weather. Daily absolute humidity was identified as one of the potential risk factors of TB transmission in this study and can potentially explain the seasonality of TB for some indirect reasons. Opposite results were observed on its temperature. Nevertheless, analyses on the effect of temperature on TB, a positive association was reported. Future studies splitting weather data on a seasonal/weekly basis or local forecasting date range may reveal important seasonal variation of TB. Data scarcity at finer themes reflects the priority of focusing on the association studies at coarser scales. However, climate is typically treated as a constant in public health studies. As models become well-structured and data become accessible and larger, more extensive climate studies are promising. All comments and suggestions above suggest obvious future work for improvement. Based on the significant results found here, other studies focusing on spatial spread intervention focusing on weather effect, such as 1) intensifying publicity on TB prevention or 2) adopting precautionary health measures can be evaluated. Other environmental/stochastic factors can be incorporated as well thanks to those precursors (Diener & Mudu, 2021). This study also recognized its robustness in both prediction and inference over the coarsest and finest baselines considering yearly and decadal data shortage. The results illustrate the complex structure underlying the climate-disease relationship. Based on data availability in other regions, future studies may consider replicating this work by mentioning reliable estimates of more environmental determinants of disease. This study recognized its contribution to both TB research and public health as well. Unusual TB peaks impacting substantial populations in the next week are standard inputs for prediction, while important weather records, such as temperatures over 32 degrees Celsius, rain in Chengdu during the summertime directly intervene in the public health actions.

Urbanization and Housing

Urbanization significantly influences housing quality and population density, leading to the emergence and resurgence of TB (Cramm et al., 2011; Ren et al., 2022). Countries with accelerating urbanization, especially in low-income settings, are experiencing increased TB risk. Around one billion urban residents in developing countries live in slum-like conditions. These neighborhoods intensify association with TB. Megacities often harbor poor housing, leading to intensify infectious disease spread among urban slum dwellers, including TB. Moreover, a significant fallout quantity is likely to devastate poor housing households due to accommodating large capacity, competing with a high-density population to prevent cross-infection through well-ventilated horizontal spacing. There is an evident positive and significant association between urbanization and TB incidence of countries with different income levels. An increase of 1% urban population proportion leads to 2% TB incidence growth. Prevalent concerns, such as the economic cost, social stigma, insufficient knowledge, falsified information, or the disease being unattended in policy priorities, make promptly written evidence-based documents crucial.

Non-communicable diseases and environmental determinants have received more research attention than airborne infectious diseases. While AI has flourished in COVID-19 tracking and forecasting, it has been scarcely applied in TB outbreak apprehension. Even though a global TB tech revolution occurs, there has been little known on developing a comprehensive and operation-ready data-driven algorithm to provide a neighborhood socio-environmental geography and socio-economic map on TB outbreaks risk and transmit pathways at a blink of an eye in urbanizing regions. Thus, it is valuable to implement AI-derived innovative neighborhood vigilant tools on multi-scale past-detected influencing factors and data-covered cities, including a target megacity at the final stage by fusing open-source data and world-wide used Python packages (Duarte et al., 2021).

Air Quality and Pollution

Air quality and pollution are important components of the environmental determinants of tuberculosis (TB). Research studies on the relationship between air pollution and TB date back to the early 20th century. However, there is insufficient evidence on the non-linear relationship and potential lag effect of air pollution on TB, since most existing studies were based on simple regression models excluding potential confounders and that some risk factors were not analyzed. Many high/burden TB areas are remote and rural, where monitoring data is generally absent. Satellite remote sensing provides an opportunity to monitor air pollution. A data fusion scheme combining chemical transport model simulations, satellite-derived, and ground-based data provides an accurate estimation of NO2, O3, and PM2.5 levels over a global scale. The scheme was successfully applied to study the effects of air pollution on TB in the USA. China has been experiencing a rapid increase in both TB incidence and air pollution, providing an ideal opportunity to study the potential associations and gather insights into tackling the dual epidemic (Glynn et al., 2023).

Compelling epidemiological studies have emerged over the past 2 decades showing the associations between various ambient air pollutants and TB incidence. However, unknown confounding related to the pandemic was not considered in these studies, so it remains to be determined whether the reported effects are robust. Moreover, most studies relied on monitoring data from environmental stations, which usually only cover urban areas and introduce measurement bias in high/burden TB rural areas. Spatial interpolation methods, like riding-based algorithms, have been used to estimate ambient air pollution levels in epidemiological studies to mitigate the issue (Huang et al., 2020). Yet, there is no study in the literature that combined both interpolation methods with geographically weighted regression to investigate the heterogeneous associations between air pollution and TB incidence.

IMPACT OF ENVIRONMENTAL FACTORS ON TUBERCULOSIS TRANSMISSION

Tuberculosis is one of the major global diseases caused by Mycobacterium tuberculosis infection. Tuberculosis is the second-leading infectious disease globally, after Coronavirus Disease 2019 (COVID19). In the near future, TB is expected to be the top virulent disease, given the emergence of multi-drug-resistant tuberculosis (MDR-TB), and is even harder to diagnose as it can co-infect people with human immunodeficiency virus (HIV) or COVID-19. There was 10.6 million people who fell ill with TB in 2021, an increase from 10.4 million in 2020 and as much as 12 million cases are thought to exist. More than 1.4 million people died from TB in 2021, which is an increase of more than 2100 deaths making it 1 of the top infectious disease globally. Prompt diagnosis combined with timely treatment of TB, susceptibility test of the bacteria, and completing treatment is the key to ending TB (Sun et al., 2015).

The transmission of TB is mainly through the environmental path. The 5 environmental factors proposed in this paper are the population density, mean annual temperature, humidity, paroxysmal average atmospheric pressure, and 7-day average PM 10 concentration. Population density is a critical risk factor for TB transmission because it is a representative metric of crowdedness. TB is an infectious disease that is typically spread through droplet transmission. People with active TB expel contagious droplet nuclei into the environment by coughing, sneezing, etc. These droplet nuclei can float in the air for a while and infect people who inhale them. Therefore, cities with high population densities have a higher probability of air exposure to TB. Since densely populated metropolitan areas favor the congregant lifestyle, such as the underground mass transit system, parlors, shopping malls, public bathrooms, etc., they are more susceptible to spread TB (Pinto et al., 2024).

ARTIFICIAL INTELLIGENCE IN PUBLIC HEALTH

The arrival of the AI (artificial intelligence), with its deep neural networks (DNN) technology that implements machine learning (ML) methods, led to an important and very recent paradigm shift regarding its use and application in health and medicine. This technological breakthrough can be divided into Big Data and AI infrastructure development, DNN model development, validation, and benchmarking and different types of intended application in healthcare. Among them all, the application of AI models in Public Health is considered one of the most promising and challenging as they require a collaborative environment among various stakeholders (Fisher & Rosella, 2022). Within this context, TB control provides an excellent laboratory for research using DNN models in nationwide and subnational public health application settings. A large number of devoted experts in terms of manpower and computational resources working together on a well-defined problem have given rise to an abundance of data and knowledge. Given its basic nature, simple epidemiological pen-and-paper models have excelled in matching data-based statistics. Nevertheless, there remains the need to radically improve the understanding of TB control, and an opportunity to hire machine learning experts to develop various advanced AI models for the extrapolation of TB control intelligence that would be otherwise impossible. The following section presents on-going TB and its control activities as well as state-of-the-art collaborative data at the aggregate public health level. Clear strategies and tactics regarding how DNN models can be effectively trained, validated, benchmarked, and used are illustrated. All of these public health controls and DNN models may have a usability component for other similar problems such as COVID-19 or influenza pandemics (Doshi et al., 2017). Tuberculosis has been a significant public health problem worldwide for over 100 years and remains a global top 10 causes of death and the top infectious disease killer. Most of the TB burden is low- and middle-income countries (LMICs). The introduction of DOTS principles has greatly contributed to TB prevention and control and led to a ten-year steady decline of the incidence of smear-positive new TB cases. However, unexpectedly, after a plateau phase, the burdens on case detection and treatment success rates have recently dramatically increased.

Overview of AI Technologies

Artificial intelligence (AI) is steadily gaining momentum across most fields of medicine and the health sciences, especially in radiology and pathology. The use of AI is increasingly being tested and adopted across environmental health, where its potential for assessing and mitigating environmental determinants of health is rapidly being uncovered. One of these reasons is TB, which is why machine-learning algorithms have become so popular so quickly. In the last few years, important AI methods for TB research have got much better and are still helping us learn more. If we can identify where TB is common early on, we can save money and help people who already have TB more easily. By using genotypic markers to accurately divide risk and identify different types of the disease, public health officials can make better decisions about treatments and other matters. These improvements have made it much harder to get the information needed to work out the values in models. The way people act and the places where they live can both change at the same time. This means it's important to understand both of these things completely. More people will need to be able to use AI and data science tools without being technical for AI to be useful for health, both inside and outside of the TB field. Also, standards for data availability in the global south will need to be set by combining data science with other efforts to make health equity better. A research agenda for understanding and mitigating the role of environmental determinants in TB using opportunistic AI has been detailed. The general advancement of machine-learning and AI algorithms in the 2010s catalyzed many downstream applications that leveraged these developments to answer public health questions. Recently harder questions relating to the prevention of TB have begun to be explored: The effective understanding and mitigation of environmental determinants of TB in large populations. Environmental determinants of TB operate through complex and often unmeasured mechanisms, such as poorly ventilated homes or contact with infectious individuals through social networks. Identifying what these mechanisms are and how they contribute to patience is critical for informing public health action. A range of method improvements is needed to enable prevention research to directly re-use data intended for other purposes in this new context. In particular, improved robustness, interpretability and transferability of the modeling methods are important for providing usable insights to public health personnel. Public health action to mitigate environmental determinants typically requires trade-offs between overall effectiveness and equity in wider actions to mitigate poverty, which benefits many diseases. Addressing these trade-offs requires improved ability to marginally increase effectiveness through better targeting or marginally increase equity by increasing treatment of the poorest. Current modeling is unable to fully explore these trade-offs, leaving public health systems with a multi-billion dollar-for-dollar effect on treating active TB (Doshi et al., 2017), which with no false positive can be targeted at the widest environmental determinants of TB as a precursor to eventual treatment.

AI Applications in Disease Surveillance

In recent years, a multitude of AI applications have been developed in conjunction with population-based disease surveillance, including artificial intelligence-based

TB strain typing using genomic data. AI also has a key role in population-based surveillance of disease symptoms through social media content categorization, and AI-based geo-spatial prediction of where disease outbreaks may occur (Doshi et al., 2017). In Spanish-speaking countries, social media surveillance has been used to monitor patterns of hepatitis C drug use outbreaks, models have been applied to find where outbreaks of flu may spread, and data mining of Twitter posts has been used to visualize and map geographic patterns of pertussis outbreaks. For TB, AI technology has been put to good use in TB strain typing and screening for TB-like symptoms from social media video content.

In an era of unprecedented near-worldwide public record-keeping, continent-wide health systems strengthening, and rapid gains in scientifically analyzing vast amounts of data, there exist tools and strategies to monitor these sources. Adding technology that people can understand, like image recognition, statistical natural language processing, and machine learning, can make geospatial analysis better. AI technology lets you keep an overall view of a large group of people's health in a step-by-step way. This skill could help enterprises that use these technologies to manage health systems (Qin et al., 2021).

AI is indispensable for the surveillance of contagious diseases. It looks closely at large amounts of data to find complicated patterns and trends. AI makes it much faster to spread early warnings and makes it easier to guess when outbreaks might happen. This paradigm shift revolutionizes the manner in which public health entities respond. Artificial intelligence employs advanced algorithms to analyze data in real time, discerning early indicators of epidemics through the application of machine learning and deep learning methodologies The amalgamation of demographic data with movement patterns through the application of artificial intelligence has proven to be effective in enhancing the early identification of issues and facilitating proactive interventions (Olaboye et al., 2024).

Predictive Modeling and Risk Assessment

Machine learning has been adeptly employed to develop intricate models aimed at elucidating various health and illness phenomena, thereby underscoring the significant benefits of this innovative methodology (Badawi et al., 2021). Tuberculosis has always been a dangerous disease, and now it is a major threat to health around the world. A lot of work has been done over the years to make tuberculosis less harmful. To make good decisions, you need to know how well epidemiological surveillance works and how diseases spread. These kinds of insights would help stop the spread of tuberculosis and make treatment and control methods better. Figure 5 illustrates the utilization of artificial intelligence and analogous technologies as both a framework and a formidable instrument for the preparation of tuberculosis-related data

(Pariona-Luque et al., 2024). It's very important to use AI tools to keep an eye on infectious diseases. They watch epidemics closely, send out early warnings, and make predictions. For example, better deep learning has made it easier to deal with issues like sparse data and complex nonlinear interdependencies. These issues generally impede conventional statistical methods in assessing public health interventions (Zeng et al., 2021). Natural language processing and machine learning are advanced technologies that can analyze large amounts of data in real time. This method has been demonstrated to enhance early-stage detection and facilitate predictive modeling, enabling the swift identification of health issues and the strategic reallocation of public health resources (Chukwuka Emmanuel Eze et al., 2024; Isiaka et al., 2024). Ultimately, prior research has shown that the utilization of artificial intelligence in scientific fields is distinguished by its ability to monitor and integrate data in real time, exceeding conventional epidemiological monitoring techniques. (Abdallah et al., 2024). The incorporation of advanced big data methodologies into early warning systems significantly enhances monitoring capabilities and predictive modeling, as demonstrated by the source (Hu et al., 2025). Artificial intelligence and machine learning could make it much easier to find and identify infections, which could help control infectious diseases. These new technologies make it easier to predict how people will respond to different treatments (Kherabi & Peiffer-Smadja, 2024). Despite this, AI applications are instrumental in enhancing the precision of diagnoses and facilitating real-time decision-making that aids in the management of pandemics. Nevertheless, numerous challenges remain to be addressed. It is therefore essential to overcome these obstacles in order to fully exploit the potential of AI in the field of public health (Ali et al., 2025).

Despite significant advancements in understanding case transmission in detailed aggregate studies, up-to-date geospatial models of dynamic hypothetical count processes of the disease by discriminating against dominant risk factors are still lacking. Dynamically modeling mechanisms of TB transmission amidst the controversies in dynamics and influence directions, as well as non-availability of strict statistical data is a challenge. By focusing on a few well-sampled regions, creative techniques have been developed. However, they all only indirectly try to address the questions by assessing model performance on predicting epidemiological processes. Moreover, little is known whether and how vastly different environmental, socio-ecological, health, and resources factors or their interdependence emerges. By introducing a generative process for the hypothesized relationship, the proposed model seeks to address these questions (Vyklyuk et al., 2024).

AI SOLUTIONS FOR TUBERCULOSIS CONTROL

More than a quarter of the world's population is estimated to be infected with Mycobacterium tuberculosis (infected individuals). For each one of these infected individuals, the lifetime risk of developing active TB disease is estimated to be 10%. Environmental determinants of TB could be defined as risk factors associated with increased susceptibility to, or exposure of, the mycobactera in settings outside health care (Doshi et al., 2017). Global warming and the warming of the Earth from greenhouse gases, primarily derived from pollution resulting from fossil fuel use, is an example of anthropogenic environmental change. Urbanization, migration-induced population density, and the social-living conditions of informal settlements are examples of natural environmental change outside the health care system. Aside from unique situations of extreme and unprepared social salud, these environmental changes may be quantifiable. For example, state-of-the-art science-society-climate-change models may be used to show the impact of climate change on latitudinal and anthropocentric movements of low- and middle-income countries (LMICs) or on the incidence of pestilences such as tuberculosis. However, these processes are complex, with limited access to data and confounding factors, and thus knowledge gaps and uncertainties in these context-specific data are anticipated. Additionally, because of the extensive intercountry and intercultural variability in etiology, disease spectrum, and social pathogens of TB, the actionability of prediction data is limited. Here human-centered NFT is proposed as a new and innovative approach enabling computationally advanced demand-driven solutions toward "zero TB." It combines quantitative and qualitative data sources of unique TB community perspectives to examine the socio-epidemiological impact of a constantly changing world and the systemic and comprehensive TB control strategies to mitigate the effect of upstream TB determinants and influences. It has been successfully applied in various fields of post-pandemic, climate, and pestilence diseases. It holds the promise of effectively building up required social sharing of knowledge and temporary environment-centric solutions globally to improve the social probability of healthier TB control after the pandemic, climate, and civil wars.

Data Collection and Analysis

Smartphones and mobile devices have allowed significant advances in the delivery of healthcare. The ability to document care easily, transfer, and access images provide leverage for using images and data to assist in better diagnosis. Tuberculosis screening using mobile technology takes advantage of these assets via a comprehensive smartphone-based approach capable of performing general screening and acquiring, transferring, and storing patient data (Doshi et al., 2017). Demographic data is captured via interrogatory screens. Capture controls reduce the likelihood of blurred or poorly acquired images. For study efficiency, images are compressed and image files aggregated for batch transfer at the end of the exam. Interfaces use standardized terminology to elicit responses while voice prompts assist patient engagement. Finally, mobility allows lungs screening in densest areas, other forms of screening can take place in the same community, and follow-up for conversion testing can occur multiple months later in the same location. Offloading computer-hardware limitations to advanced imaging capabilities could be hardware agnostic and better scaled. Storage of image complexity and size for future on-device machine-learning applications could favor multi-model imaging. Another consideration is the pool problem, lawyer problem, and the imbalance of extreme cases, which underline the great need for mined data to enable customized machine-learning algorithms for mobile devices despite limits on a pool.

AI in epidemiological data collection has transformed public health by improving processing, analysis, and decision-making. AI tools, such as machine learning, are used to analyze large and complex data sets, improving epidemic surveillance and risk assessment. This transformation is reflected in improved data processing, where "AI algorithms can quickly analyze large health datasets, accelerating epidemiological research" (Li et al., 2024). In addition, "machine learning algorithms are used for genome sequencing and medical image data analysis for disease diagnosis and risk prediction" (Kaitong et al., 2024). Regarding applications in disease surveillance, "AI has been essential in tracking epidemics, using GIS and predictive models to map and respond to health threats" (Jillahi & Iorliam, 2024; Reinoso et al., 2024).

AI in Diagnostics

In May 2016, the World Health Assembly endorsed a global strategy and set targets on TB to be reached by 2020. This included a target to provide the rapid diagnosis of TB, especially in high-burden settings, with a specific request for countries to make the most use of currently available diagnostic tools. Pioneering work to explore the potential of using AI to detect TB in images began a decade ago. The advent of cheap computers and improved algorithms led to a growing study of literature on the application of AI technologies, and in recent years some initial tools have become available. Image-based screening tests and packages, which incorporate off-the-shelf hardware and some basic AI components, are already being implemented in high-burden countries with limited prior experience of computer processing of chest X-rays (Sheliemina, 2024).

There have been considerable international efforts to both develop and test such tools and, importantly, better capitalize on their availability. Some of this has been technology-focused, with a focus on letting a thousand flowers bloom, which led to an explosion of products that had many potential benefits, but also major challenges in ensuring regulations and brokering access to the best products. We must transition from the technology and innovation phase to the integration phase and begin posing challenging inquiries regarding the distribution of power between clinicians and algorithms (Doshi et al., 2017). Some people have suggested using A) to find tuberculosis outbreaks early on. An intelligent system could monitor an individual's "signature" over time within extensive datasets. This is important for keeping an eye on TB because it can help find people who have signs of the disease or a relapse. This method can find factors that make treatment less likely to work, which could be very helpful for both treating tuberculosis and making medicines that target it. Deep learning algorithms for artificial intelligence are quickly getting better at using chest X-rays to find TB (Qin et al., 2021).

Artificial intelligence is a field that is growing quickly and changing how health care works. It can help doctors make more accurate diagnoses, treat patients better, and give them better care in the medical field. AI is relevant across multiple domains, such as medical imaging, data analytics, and predictive modeling (Galil & Galil, 2023). It aids in the analysis of extensive data sets, the recognition of intricate patterns, and the prediction of disease progression, thereby promoting early detection (Chang et al., 2024; Umapathy et al., 2023).

AI-Driven Public Health Interventions

Recently, AI has been thought of as a possible way to help with TB in global health. AI tools can create strong and representative datasets that are needed to make TB intervention policies work. Nonetheless, they inform a need for comprehensive systematic reviews to facilitate data communication. The development of a diagnostic framework for the use of AI in public health planning will need an investigation of assumptions and identification of the existing knowledge gaps (Doshi et al., 2017). AI is also an important technology to diagnose the disease, improve disease surveillance and develop prediction model for diseases. For example, healthcare related issues related are processed in an assured manner with promptness due to advances in the technologies (Hedayet & Haseen, 2024; Olorunsogo et al., 2024). Hence, healthcare strategies using artificial intelligence are specifically designed and customized, thereby widening the range of healthcare releases and also optimizing the efficiency of health efforts by the government (Ismail et al., 2023; Wang et al., 2024).

DATA COLLECTION AND RESULTS

Data Collection

All within this research, an extensive educational standard was monitored to identify the sociodemographic risk factors, patient history of illness, and territorial extension among tuberculosis cases. The study found that respiratory disease was very common in some areas. It emphasizes the significance of participating in specific awareness initiatives. Epidemiological statistics indicate that most patients had tuberculosis, predominantly affecting young adults. This information helps disease control strategies focus on getting treatment as soon as possible. Furthermore, an analysis of the administered treatment has demonstrated an inconsistency in efficacy, dependent on the protocols followed. It is important for health care workers who diagnose and treat tuberculosis to get the most out of their training. In this case, it is very important to put recurrent screening drives and improving the medical infrastructure at the top of the list. Future research may necessitate a concentration on the assessment of long-term therapeutic effects on patients' pulmonary function. Additionally, patient follow-up methods will aid in the surveillance of recurrence events on a limited scale.

This systematic approach enables an exhaustive analysis of the data, especially focused on patient-specific behaviors affected by tuberculosis. It also helps us learn how bad tuberculosis is in the Moroccan province of Khémisset.

This methodological approach enables a thorough examination of the complexities associated with tuberculosis patients in Khémisset province. You can look at things like the patient's age, sex, and medical history. This in-depth study aims to elucidate the disease's impact on various demographics and to identify potential causative factors. A thorough analysis of the behaviors of tuberculosis patients can clarify the influence of their environment, nutrition, and activities on their health and their vulnerability to contracting the disease. If we look closely at what happens to patients who have trouble getting the healthcare they need, we can understand this better.

To create a survey about tuberculosis in the Khemisset province, we need to collect information about the number of cases, how many people are successfully treated, and what is being done to stop the disease spreading. In-depth analysis of the data collected will highlight emerging trends, assess the effectiveness of public health programs, and formulate recommendations to optimize tuberculosis care in the region.

Data Analysis

1. Socio-Economic Data

A set of 1771 patients, reported in the register, managed of which 1064 (60%) male and 706 (40%) women (sex ratio = 1.5), 56% are urban and 44% rural.

Figure 1. Classification by sex, family status and institutional level

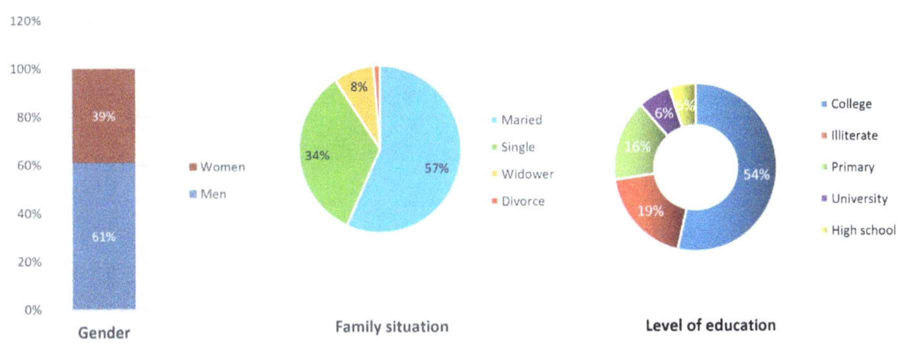

The distribution of respondents to the questionnaire was as follows: 61% male and 29% female, 57% married, 34% single, 8% widowed and 1% divorced. Regarding the institutional level, 54% of the participants have a college level, 19% are illiterate, 16% are primary, 6% are university level and 5% have a high school level. (Figure 1)

Figure 2. Classification of tuberculosis cases

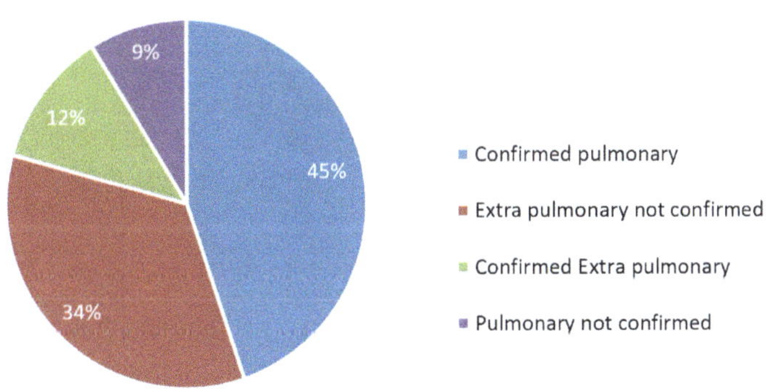

Tuberculosis cases are divided into bacteriologically confirmed pulmonary form (50%) and unconfirmed (7%), and extrapulmonary form with 32% unconfirmed and 11% confirmed. (Figure 2)

2. Environmental Risk Factor

Figure 3. Classification by environment and population density

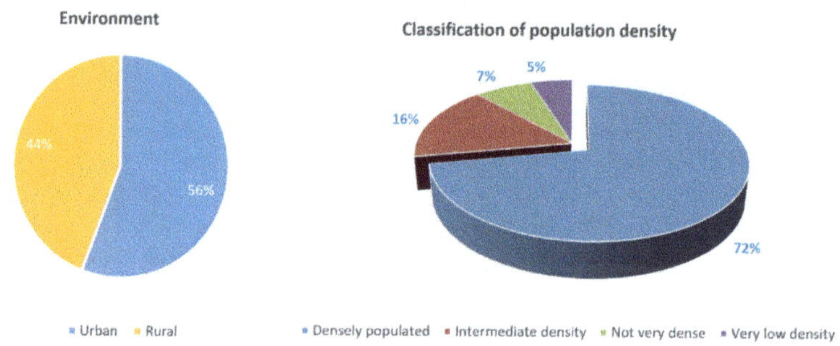

TB appears to affect the urban population (56%) more than the rural population (44%). The most affected participants came from densely populated areas (72%), followed by intermediate density areas (16%), then sparsely populated areas (7%) and 5% lived in very sparsely populated areas. (Figure 3)

Figure 4. Classification according to the mode of travel, attendance and wearing of means of protection.

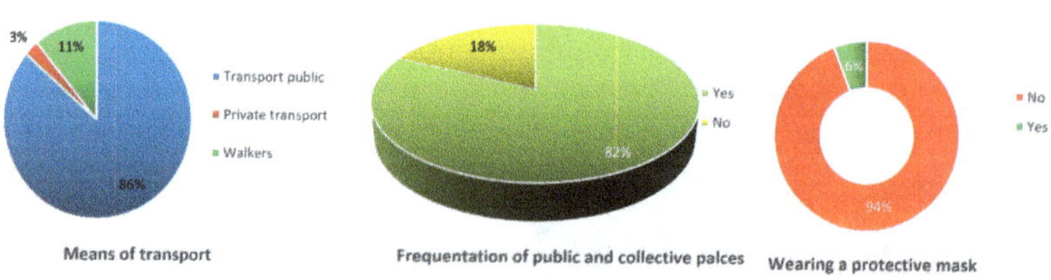

Participating TB patients showed that they can frequent public and communal places in their daily lives (87%). These patients travel to the only TB diagnosis that exists at the provincial level use public transportation (87%), and 11% use their own transportation. The majority of these patients do not use any means of protection (mask) (94%). The average time to get there is 28 minutes. (Figure 4)

In these tobacco smokers we have identified three groups according to the duration of cigarette consumption, the first group uses tobacco for a period that exceeds 20 years, the second group uses it for a period between 10 and 20 years and the last for a period of less than 10 years.

ANALYZING THE INFLUENCE OF HEALTH DETERMINANTS

Impact of Socioeconomic Factors on Tuberculosis Transmission

According to the data from this study, tuberculosis affects a broad category of people, regardless of age or sex, with a male predominance. In this study, it is established that young adults are the most affected by this disease.

The population studied shows that the most affected category is people with professional instability and those who are unemployed and employees in the private sector, the classification of this population according to their income shows that the cases most affected by tuberculosis are patients who have an income of less than 2000 dirhams per month followed by those who have a salary of less than 4000 dirhams. The classification of tuberculosis cases shows that half of the cases are of bacteriologically confirmed pulmonary form, this category presents a risk of transmission of the disease due to its contagious nature. Extrapulmonary forms do not pose a risk to society, but their high rate can be explained by the presence of several factors such as malnutrition, poverty and unhealthy living standards. The urban population develops TB more than the rural population in addition to this urban factor is added to the impact of population density, which is very much seen in the data of this study which shows that the most populated areas (72%) have a high incidence rate of tuberculosis.

The supply of care shows the existence of a single tuberculosis diagnostic center in the provincial territory of Khemisset, place of the study, this work shows that there is an impact of distance between the residences of patients and the diagnostic center, it appears that 40% of tuberculosis patients are far from a distance between 20 and 40 kilometers, 29% are more than 60 kilometers away. Added to this is the average distance that each patient can travel to the nearest health care facility of 10 kilometers. The activities of tuberculosis patients, despite their state of health, but they can frequent, during their daily lives, public and collective places that experience activities and increased circulation of citizens so they can contact other people directly or indirectly with regard to increasing the risk of contagiousness especially since 82% of tuberculosis patients of pulmonary form studied do not use any means of protection to minimize the risk of transmission of this disease. Other factors that increase this risk of contagiousness are the use of public transport without means of protection, especially since more than 95% who travel to the diagnostic center spend an average of more than 28 minutes to get there at the tuberculosis diagnostic center during diagnosis and during check-ups.

Another factor studied is smoking, which is an important risk factor for tuberculosis, as it weakens the immune system and makes the lungs more vulnerable to infections. Smokers are more likely to develop severe tuberculosis diseases and suffer complications during treatment. In this study, it appears that smoking is a characteristic of the male sex in the sample studied, 89% of tuberculosis patients studied are smokers, 93% are smokers for a period exceeding 10 years. Tobacco can therefore be a risk factor for the smoker himself and also his social environment. There is evidence that these environmental factors may influence TB transmission in interaction with other socio-economic determinants. This research gave us an idea of the behavior of tuberculosis patients vis-à-vis their disease and their environmental environment, their movement without means of protection.

Risk Factors and Control Strategies for Tuberculosis: The Importance of Awareness and Access to Care

A body of research has indicated that in circumstances of intensive exposure to airborne tuberculosis, limited contact with a single case of tuberculosis could be sufficient to infect an individual (Regional Committee for Africa, 2017). This idea has been confirmed by recent studies on how tuberculosis is spread in places where people are close together, like airplanes (Lienhardt, 2001).

The bacterium that causes tuberculosis is called Mycobacterium tuberculosis. The most important thing to think about is being around this bacterium. There are many good reasons for this. We know that these people don't know much about the disease or how to stop it. People with tuberculosis are often treated badly, which can make it hard for them to get treatment. People with these kinds of attitudes may not know how to get treatment, may not know how to spread the disease, or may not take the treatment that is given (Sayidah et al., 2018).

If you are poor, sick, or have other problems that make it hard for you to get the care you need, you are still at risk of tuberculosis. The World Health Organization has a plan to help reduce the number of people who get tuberculosis, especially those who are more likely to get it. However, these plans need to include more than just technical reasons why they are needed. It is very important to focus on strategies that involve different sectors of society (Litvinjenko et al., 2023; Spruijt et al., 2023) .

Artificial intelligence has changed how we find, follow, and treat tuberculosis. It has made traditional methods more accurate, faster, and easier to find. AI-based systems are especially good at finding TB in places where there aren't many resources. New technologies are being developed to make sure that healthcare systems are reliable all over the world (Onno et al., 2023).

We can use AI to predict the future by tracking and analysing data. This helps stop outbreaks of tuberculosis (Ahmadi, 2024). AI systems can examine things in more detail, which means that more cases can be solved. These technologies are very important for treating tuberculosis today because they use pattern detection and predictive modelling to help find the disease (Prakash Babu et al., 2024).

Artificial intelligence is changing the way medicine works. This includes the ways doctors diagnose and treat patients, with a focus on treating tuberculosis (Singh et al., 2024).

AI's proactive and real-time monitoring also makes treatment much more effective than older methods (Srivastava et al., 2025). These results show that AI can help fight TB.

AI TECHNOLOGIES APPLIED IN THE FIGHT AGAINST TUBERCULOSIS

The germ that causes tuberculosis TB has spread more recently, making TB more dangerous all over the world, but especially in the Sverdlovsk Oblast (SO) region of Russia. This virus is related to HIV. The plan is to create a useful tool that uses AI to predict how tuberculosis will spread (Cherniaev et al., 2022; Nassimbwa, 2024).

Controlling tuberculosis is hard. There are many obstacles, and there are global goals to reduce the disease. This makes it hard to diagnose and treat patients. Furthermore, prolonged therapeutic protocols have significant physiological and socio-economic repercussions for patients. Applications of AI in the healthcare sector have significantly optimized patient care in terms of diagnosis, treatment and basic research. However, the success of these applications is closely linked to the quality of the technological infrastructure and data.

In the context of today's healthcare systems, the integration of artificial intelligence technologies represents a major challenge. It is imperative to train medical staff in the use of these new technologies to ensure their effective adoption in clinical practice. Artificial intelligence also plays a crucial role in the analysis of epidemiological data, enabling trends to be detected, the progression of epidemics to be modeled and public health resources to be optimized.

The application of artificial intelligence to the early detection of tuberculosis could revolutionize the way the disease is detected and treated. The use of the machine learning algorithms based on the results of medical images would enable infections to be detected more quickly and more accurately. What's more, this approach could also simplify the patient monitoring and assessment of treatment effectiveness, based on real-time data analysis (Abualigah, 2025).

At the same time, there is a need to optimize connectivity and Internet access in remote areas to facilitate the adoption of artificial intelligence-based solutions in hitherto neglected regions. The integration of telemedicine with the above-mentioned technologies could provide patients with easier access to specialist care, thereby facilitating the detection and treatment of tuberculosis.

To design relevant interventions in these contexts, it seems essential to foster interdisciplinary collaborations between public health specialists, artificial intelligence researchers and local communities. A collaborative approach can not only optimize the effectiveness of TB control programs, but also strengthen the resilience of healthcare systems in the face of other emerging infectious diseases (McClean et al., 2024).

The development of artificial intelligence, which is now widely available, is opening up promising prospects for the prevention of epidemics. Indeed, during the pandemic, the rapid spread of diseases with severe respiratory syndromes demonstrated the relevance of using various technologies, such as machine learning models, natural language processing and data analysis, to predict epidemics of infectious diseases. Supervised and unsupervised learning algorithms, such as pattern extraction or relationship modeling models, are frequently used to analyze large sets of medical data, both labeled and unlabeled, in order to predict infectious disease outbreaks (Behara et al., 2022).

There are important questions about ethics that we need to consider when using AI in healthcare. It is essential to implement strict protocols to protect patient data privacy and security. People must agree to their data being collected and used to make decisions, and their name or other identifying information must not be revealed. Always respect what a person wants. Also, the way algorithms are made needs to be fair so that no group has an unfair advantage, which could lead to unfair car.

Adding AI to health systems makes things more complicated. It costs a lot of money to train professionals and buy IT equipment. Healthcare professionals and technical specialists must also work together to create custom solutions that meet the unique needs of different regional health systems (Dutt et al., 2022; Torshizi et al., 2023).

It's very important to check the results that AI gives you. In medicine, these models need to be checked and updated regularly to make sure they work and are correct. What's more, if schools and hospitals work together, they can make better use of artificial intelligence when treating tuberculosis and other diseases that spread from person to person (Jiang et al., 2017).

It is thus important to educate patients about the advantages of new technologies to decrease any reservation and encourage mass use of digital solutions in the healthcare industry. An open and transparent discussion among healthcare professionals, artificial intelligence experts, and civil society can encourage innovation-conducive environment without disrespecting ethical and social requirements (Osnat, 2025).

As we said before, it's more important than ever to be able to process, analyse and make decisions straight away. This is true in many areas, including national defence and security, space agencies and public policy, and mathematical sciences (*A Global Strategy for Tuberculosis Research and Innovation*, 2020). Researchers have been looking at different ways to analyse and explore data (Khalifa & Albadawy, 2024; Stewart et al., 2023), especially because machine learning techniques are so important in these areas. Real-time machine learning is very important in healthcare, especially for diseases that spread easily, like tuberculosis. Successful incorporation of AI requires interdisciplinary collaboration among healthcare workers, data scientists, and software developers. Hybrid designs, combining human knowledge and learning algorithms, promise the most potential in improving diagnostic accuracy and predictions (Natrayan et al., 2024).

To be used in a medical setting, AI still has to get past a few hurdles. Health professionals must make sure that data from artificial intelligence is understood correctly. They also need to create complete rules about how to use the results of algorithms (Stewart et al., 2023). Healthcare professionals must continue their education about AI technologies. They also need to learn about the ethical aspects of using AI to make decisions in healthcare. This will ensure that AI is used in the right way. AI will be very important in helping to control and stop epidemics, especially the fight against tuberculosis. Agencies that make policy need to carefully look at the results of data analysis. This will help them make sure that public health resources are used correctly.

CONCLUSION

Even though there have been policies and programs to fight tuberculosis for many years, it is still a serious public health problem. To control and treat the disease properly, doctors, patients, and the public need to know about the risk factors, how to educate patients, and how to raise awareness. To prevent this, we need to improve air quality, control airborne pollutants, make housing conditions better, and reduce population density in high-risk zones. To help people with tuberculosis, we need to make changes to the environment and work together with screening and treatment programs. The study underscores the profound impact of tuberculosis on vulnerable populations, particularly young adults and individuals in precarious employment situations. The integration of artificial intelligence technologies has the potential to revolutionize diagnostic and therapeutic methodologies; however, it necessitates the development of infrastructure, continuous training, and an interdisciplinary approach. Ethical and social awareness is also crucial for the responsible adoption of AI in healthcare. The integration of environmental determinants into tuberculosis modeling is essential for understanding and mitigating transmission.

Recommendations:

- Longitudinal studies on environmental exposure are essential for understanding the progression of tuberculosis and designing effective strategies to combat the disease.
- The use of transparent AI approaches and the promotion of multi-source data integration are essential.
- The establishment of standards for data governance and the promotion of decentralized learning are imperative for the advancement of knowledge in contemporary society.
- Evaluating environmental interventions through pragmatic trials, using AI for stratified randomization, is essential to improve decision-making and the effectiveness of actions implemented.
- The transdisciplinary research should be encouraged to explore the mechanisms and ethical implications of tuberculosis.

The objective of the present set of recommendations is twofold: first, to enhance the efficacy of future research in this field, and second, to contribute to the global effort to combat tuberculosis.

REFERENCES

A Global Strategy for Tuberculosis Research and Innovation. (2020). 1st ed.). World Health Organization.

Abdallah, R., Abdelgaber, S., & Sayed, H. A. (2024). Leveraging AHP and transfer learning in machine learning for improved prediction of infectious disease outbreaks. *Scientific Reports*, *14*(1), 32163. DOI: 10.1038/s41598-024-81367-1 PMID: 39741160

Abualigah, L. (2025). Enhancing Real-Time Data Analysis through Advanced Machine Learning and Data Analytics Algorithms. *International Journal of Online and Biomedical Engineering (Ijoe)*, *21*(01), 4–25. DOI: 10.3991/ijoe.v21i01.53203

Ali, H. H., Ali, H. M., Ali, H. M., Ali, M. A., Zaky, A. F., Touk, A. A., Darwiche, A. H., Touk, A. A., Ali, H. H., Ali, H. M., Ali, H. M., Ali, M. A., Zaky, A. F., Touk, A. A., Darwiche, A. H., & Touk, A. A. (2025). The Role and Limitations of Artificial Intelligence in Combating Infectious Disease Outbreaks. *Cureus*, *17*. Advance online publication. DOI: 10.7759/cureus.77070 PMID: 39917100

Badawi, A., Liu, C. J., Rihem, A. A., & Gupta, A. (2021). Artificial neural network to predict the effect of obesity on the risk of tuberculosis infection. *Journal of Public Health Research*, *10*(1), 1985. DOI: 10.4081/jphr.2021.1985 PMID: 33849253

Behara, K., Bhero, E., Agee, J. T., & Gonela, V. (2022). Artificial intelligence in medical diagnostics: A review from a South African context. *Scientific African*, *17*, e01360. DOI: 10.1016/j.sciaf.2022.e01360

Chang, M., Emam, M., Chen, X., Lu, D., Zhang, L., & Zheng, Y. (2024). An investigation of the effects of meteorological factors on the incidence of tuberculosis. *Scientific Reports*, *14*(1), 2088. DOI: 10.1038/s41598-024-52278-y PMID: 38267494

Cherniaev, I. A., Chernavin, P. F., Tsvetkov, A. I., Chugaev, Y. P., Cherniaeva, U. I., & Chernavin, N. P. (2022). Forecasting Trends in the Tuberculosis Epidemic Situation in the Region of the Russian Federation by Dynamic Simulation Model. In Blobel, B., Yang, B., & Giacomini, M. (Eds.), *Studies in Health Technology and Informatics*. IOS Press., DOI: 10.3233/SHTI220990

Cramm, M., Koolman, J., Møller, X., & Nieboer, V. (2011). *Socio-economic status and self-reported tuberculosis: A multilevel analysis in a low-income township in the Eastern Cape.*

Diener, A., & Mudu, P. (2021). How can vegetation protect us from air pollution? A critical review on green spaces' mitigation abilities for air-borne particles from a public health perspective - with implications for urban planning. *The Science of the Total Environment, 796*, 148605. DOI: 10.1016/j.scitotenv.2021.148605 PMID: 34271387

Dodd, P. J., Yuen, C. M., Jayasooriya, S. M., Van Der Zalm, M. M., & Seddon, J. A. (2021). Quantifying the global number of tuberculosis survivors: A modelling study. *The Lancet. Infectious Diseases, 21*(7), 984–992. DOI: 10.1016/S1473-3099(20)30919-1 PMID: 33640076

Doshi, R., Falzon, D., Thomas, B. V., Temesgen, Z., Sadasivan, L., Migliori, G. B., & Raviglione, M. (2017). Tuberculosis control, and the where and why of artificial intelligence. *ERJ Open Research, 3*(2), 00056–02017. DOI: 10.1183/23120541.00056-2017 PMID: 28656130

Duarte, R., Aguiar, A., Pinto, M., Furtado, I., Tiberi, S., Lönnroth, K., & Migliori, G. B. (2021). Different disease, same challenges: Social determinants of tuberculosis and COVID-19. *Pulmonology, 27*(4), 338–344. DOI: 10.1016/j.pulmoe.2021.02.002 PMID: 33648891

Dutt, R., Singh, R., Majhi, J., & Basu, G. (2022). Status of drug resistant tuberculosis among patients attending a tuberculosis unit of West Bengal: A record based cross-sectional study. *Journal of Family Medicine and Primary Care, 11*(1), 84–89. DOI: 10.4103/jfmpc.jfmpc_576_21 PMID: 35309659

Chukwuka Emmanuel Eze, Geneva Tamunobarafiri Igwama, Ejike Innocent Nwankwo, & Ebube Victor Emeihe. (2024). AI-driven health data analytics for early detection of infectious diseases: A conceptual exploration of U.S. public health strategies. *Comprehensive Research and Reviews in Science and Technology, 2*(2), 074–082. DOI: 10.57219/crrst.2024.2.2.0038

Fisher, S., & Rosella, L. C. (2022). Priorities for successful use of artificial intelligence by public health organizations: A literature review. *BMC Public Health, 22*(1), 2146. DOI: 10.1186/s12889-022-14422-z PMID: 36419010

Galil, A., & Galil, W. A. (2023). Applications of Artificial Intelligence in the Field of Diagnostic Medicine and Future Prospects. *International Journal of Artificial Intelligence and Emerging Technology, 6*(2), 1–18. DOI: 10.21608/ijaiet.2024.275176.1005

Global Tuberculosis Report 2021. (2021). 1st ed.). World Health Organization.

Glynn, J. R., Khan, P., Mzembe, T., Sichali, L., Fine, P. E. M., Crampin, A. C., & Houben, R. M. G. J. (2023). Contribution of remote M.tuberculosis infection to tuberculosis disease: A 30-year population study. *PLoS One*, *18*(1), e0278136. DOI: 10.1371/journal.pone.0278136 PMID: 36706117

Hedayet, H., & Haseen, F. (2024). Artificial Intelligence in Public Health: A Review Article. *Bangladesh Journal of Bioethics*, *15*(2), 15–19. DOI: 10.62865/bjbio.v15i2.108

Holden, K., Akintobi, T., Hopkins, J., Belton, A., McGregor, B., Blanks, S., & Wrenn, G. (2016). Community Engaged Leadership to Advance Health Equity and Build Healthier Communities. *Social Sciences*, *5*(1), 1. Advance online publication. DOI: 10.3390/socsci5010002 PMID: 27713839

Hu, W.-H., Sun, H.-M., Wei, Y.-Y., & Hao, Y.-T. (2025). Global infectious disease early warning models: An updated review and lessons from the COVID-19 pandemic. *Infectious Disease Modelling*, *10*(2), 410–422. DOI: 10.1016/j.idm.2024.12.001 PMID: 39816751

Huang, S., Xiang, H., Yang, W., Zhu, Z., Tian, L., Deng, S., Zhang, T., Lu, Y., Liu, F., Li, X., & Liu, S. (2020). Short-Term Effect of Air Pollution on Tuberculosis Based on Kriged Data: A Time-Series Analysis. *International Journal of Environmental Research and Public Health*, *17*(5), 1522. DOI: 10.3390/ijerph17051522 PMID: 32120876

Isiaka, A. B., Anakwenze, V. N., Ilodinso, C. R., Anaukwu, C. G., Ezeokoli, C. M.-V., Noi, S. M., Agboola, G. O., & Adonu, R. M. (2024). *Harnessing Artificial Intelligence for Early Detection and Management of Infectious Disease Outbreaks* (SSRN Scholarly Paper No. 4876752). Social Science Research Network. DOI: 10.24940/ijird/2024/v13/i2/FEB24016

Ismail, A., Thakkar, D., Madhiwalla, N., & Kumar, N. (2023). Public Health Calls for/with AI: An Ethnographic Perspective. *Proc. ACM Hum.-Comput. Interact.*, *7*(CSCW2), 354:1-354:26. DOI: 10.1145/3610203

Jiang, F., Jiang, Y., Zhi, H., Dong, Y., Li, H., Ma, S., Wang, Y., Dong, Q., Shen, H., & Wang, Y. (2017). Artificial intelligence in healthcare: Past, present and future. *Stroke and Vascular Neurology*, *2*(4), 230–243. Advance online publication. DOI: 10.1136/svn-2017-000101 PMID: 29507784

Jillahi, K. B., & Iorliam, A. (2024). A Scoping Literature Review of Artificial Intelligence in Epidemiology: Uses, Applications, Challenges and Future Trends. *Journal of Computing Theories and Applications*, *1*(4), 421–445. DOI: 10.62411/jcta.10350

Kaitong, M., Xingtong, L., & Xiaoyan, L., shiyin L., Chenk Z., & Jiangbo D. (2024). Progress in application of machine learning in epidemiology. *epidemiology. Zhonghua Liu Xing Bing Xue Za Zhi, 45*(09), 1321–1326. DOI: 10.3760/cma.j.cn112338-20240322-00148 PMID: 39307708

Khalifa, M., & Albadawy, M. (2024). Artificial Intelligence for Clinical Prediction: Exploring Key Domains and Essential Functions. *Computer Methods and Programs in Biomedicine Update, 5*, 100148. DOI: 10.1016/j.cmpbup.2024.100148

Kherabi, Y., & Peiffer-Smadja, N. (2024). Artificial intelligence in infectious diseases. In *Artificial Intelligence in Clinical Practice* (pp. 151–153). Elsevier. DOI: 10.1016/B978-0-443-15688-5.00020-6

Kranzer, K., Afnan-Holmes, H., Tomlin, K., Golub, J. E., Shapiro, A. E., Schaap, A., Corbett, E. L., Lönnroth, K., & Glynn, J. R. (2013). The benefits to communities and individuals of screening for active tuberculosis disease: A systematic review [State of the art series. Case finding/screening. Number 2 in the series]. *The International Journal of Tuberculosis and Lung Disease : the Official Journal of the International Union against Tuberculosis and Lung Disease, 17*(4), 432–446. DOI: 10.5588/ijtld.12.0743 PMID: 23485377

Lansang, M. A. D., Alejandria, M. M., Law, I., Juban, N. R., Amarillo, M. L. E., Sison, O. T., Cruz, J. R. B., Ang, C. F., Buensalido, J. A. L., Cañal, J. P. A., Castillo-Carandang, N. T., Cordero, C. P., Gaviola, D. M. G., Ladia, M. A. J., Mantaring, J. B. V., Mendoza, M. T., Salamat, M. S. S., Lam, H. Y., Tadolini, M., & Garfin, A. M. C. G.Philippine NTPS 2016 Group. (2021). High TB burden and low notification rates in the Philippines: The 2016 national TB prevalence survey. *PLoS One, 16*(6), e0252240. DOI: 10.1371/journal.pone.0252240 PMID: 34086746

Li, Y., Zou, Y., & Xu, H. (2024). From Data to Decisions: The Integration of AI in Epidemiological Research. *Frontiers in Computing and Intelligent Systems, 9*(1), 23–29. DOI: 10.54097/7jktck77

Lienhardt, C. (2001). From Exposure to Disease: The Role of Environmental Factors in Susceptibility to and Development of Tuberculosis. *Epidemiologic Reviews, 23*(2), 288–301. DOI: 10.1093/oxfordjournals.epirev.a000807 PMID: 12192738

Litvinjenko, S., Magwood, O., Wu, S., & Wei, X. (2023). Burden of tuberculosis among vulnerable populations worldwide: An overview of systematic reviews. *The Lancet. Infectious Diseases, 23*(12), 1395–1407. DOI: 10.1016/S1473-3099(23)00372-9 PMID: 37696278

Mathema, B., Andrews, J. R., Cohen, T., Borgdorff, M. W., Behr, M., Glynn, J. R., Rustomjee, R., Silk, B. J., & Wood, R. (2017). Drivers of Tuberculosis Transmission. *The Journal of Infectious Diseases, 216*(suppl_6), S644–S653. DOI: 10.1093/infdis/jix354 PMID: 29112745

McClean, M., Panciu, T. C., Lange, C., Duarte, R., & Theis, F. (2024). Artificial intelligence in tuberculosis: A new ally in disease control. *Breathe (Sheffield, England), 20*(3), 240056. DOI: 10.1183/20734735.0056-2024 PMID: 39660086

Nassimbwa, K. D. (2024). The Role of Artificial Intelligence in Predicting Epidemics. *RESEARCH INVENTION JOURNAL OF PUBLIC HEALTH AND PHARMACY, 3*(2), 26–29. DOI: 10.59298/RIJPP/2024/322629

Natrayan, L., Kamal, M. D. R., Manivannan, K. K., & Sunil, G. (2024). Machine Learning and Data Mining Approaches for Infectious Disease Surveillance and Outbreak Management in Healthcare. *2024 International Conference on Advancements in Smart, Secure and Intelligent Computing (ASSIC)*, 1–7. DOI: 10.1109/ASSIC60049.2024.10507990

Nidoi, J., Muttamba, W., Walusimbi, S., Imoko, J. F., Lochoro, P., Ictho, J., Mugenyi, L., Sekibira, R., Turyahabwe, S., Byaruhanga, R., Putoto, G., Villa, S., Raviglione, M. C., & Kirenga, B. (2021). Impact of socio-economic factors on Tuberculosis treatment outcomes in north-eastern Uganda: A mixed methods study. *BMC Public Health, 21*(1), 2167. DOI: 10.1186/s12889-021-12056-1 PMID: 34836521

Olaboye, J. A., Maha, C. C., Kolawole, T. O., & Abdul, S. (2024). Innovations in real-time infectious disease surveillance using AI and mobile data. *International Medical Science Research Journal, 4*(6), 647–667. DOI: 10.51594/imsrj.v4i6.1190

Olorunsogo, T. O., Anyanwu, A., Abrahams, T. O., Olorunsogo, T., Ehimuan, B., Reis, O., Olorunsogo, T. O., Anyanwu, A., Abrahams, T. O., Olorunsogo, T., Ehimuan, B., & Reis, O. (2024). Emerging technologies in public health campaigns: Artificial intelligence and big data. *International Journal of Science and Research Archive, 11*(1), 1. Advance online publication. DOI: 10.30574/ijsra.2024.11.1.0060

Onno, J., Ahmad Khan, F., Daftary, A., & David, P.-M. (2023). Artificial intelligence-based computer aided detection (AI-CAD) in the fight against tuberculosis: Effects of moving health technologies in global health. *Social Science & Medicine (1982), 327*, 115949. DOI: 10.1016/j.socscimed.2023.115949

Osnat, B. (2025). Patient perspectives on artificial intelligence in healthcare: A global scoping review of benefits, ethical concerns, and implementation strategies. *International Journal of Medical Informatics, 203*, 106007. DOI: 10.1016/j.ijmedinf.2025.106007 PMID: 40494217

Pariona-Luque, R., Pacheco, A., Vegas-Gallo, E., Castanho, R. A., Lema, F., Pacheco-Pumaleque, L., Añaños-Bedriñana, M., Marin, W., Felix-Poicon, E., & Loures, A. (2024). Assessing Data Analytics Capabilities in Retail Organizations: Insights into Mining, Predictive Analytics and Machine Learning. *WSEAS TRANSACTIONS ON BUSINESS AND ECONOMICS*, *21*, 1546–1556. DOI: 10.37394/23207.2024.21.126

Pinto, P. F. P. S., Teixeira, C. S. S., Ichihara, M. Y., Rasella, D., Nery, J. S., Sena, S. O. L., Brickley, E. B., Barreto, M. L., Sanchez, M. N., & Pescarini, J. M. (2024). Incidence and risk factors of tuberculosis among 420 854 household contacts of patients with tuberculosis in the 100 Million Brazilian Cohort (2004-18): A cohort study. *The Lancet. Infectious Diseases*, *24*(1), 46–56. DOI: 10.1016/S1473-3099(23)00371-7 PMID: 37591301

Prakash Babu, S., Ezhumalai, K., Raghupathy, K., Karoly, M., Chinnakali, P., Gupte, N., Paradkar, M., Devarajan, A., Dhanasekaran, M., Thiruvengadam, K., Dauphinais, M. R., Gupte, A. N., Shivakumar, S. B., Thangakunam, B., Christopher, D. J., Viswanathan, V., Mave, V., Gaikwad, S., Kinikar, A., & Sarkar, S. (2024). Factors Associated With Unfavorable Treatment Outcomes Among Persons With Pulmonary Tuberculosis: A Multicentric Prospective Cohort Study From India. *Clinical Infectious Diseases*, *79*(4), 1034–1038. DOI: 10.1093/cid/ciae367 PMID: 38991034

Qin, Z. Z., Naheyan, T., Ruhwald, M., Denkinger, C. M., Gelaw, S., Nash, M., Creswell, J., & Kik, S. V. (2021). A new resource on artificial intelligence powered computer automated detection software products for tuberculosis programmes and implementers. *Tuberculosis (Edinburgh, Scotland)*, *127*, 102049. DOI: 10.1016/j.tube.2020.102049 PMID: 33440315

Regional Committee for Africa. 67. (2017). *Regional strategy for the management of environmental determinants of human health in the African Region 2017–2021: Report of the Secretariat* (No. AFR/RC67/6). Article AFR/RC67/6. https://iris.who.int/handle/10665/260196

Reinoso, G. P. G., Haro, H. D. P., Madero, J. L. A., Escaleras, L. G. O., Quinquiguano, M. I. A., Pilatasig, W. J. M., & Auqui, L. F. C. (2024). Epidemiological Surveillance Innovative Applications for Community and Public Health: A Systematic Review. *International Journal of Medical Science and Clinical Research Studies*, *4*(03), 546–555. DOI: 10.47191/ijmscrs/v4-i03-32

Ren, H., Lu, W., Li, X., Shen, H., Glynn, J. R., Khan, P., Mzembe, T., Sichali, L., Fine, P. E., Crampin, A. C., & Houben, R. M. (2022). Specific urban units identified in tuberculosis epidemic using a geographical detector in Guangzhou, China. *PLoS One*, *18*(1). PMID: 35428318

Sayidah, D., Sri Rahardjo, S., & Murti, B. (2018). Individual and Environmental Risk Factors of Tuberculosis: A New Evidence from Ponorogo, East Java. *Journal of Epidemiology and Public Health, 03*(03), 353–360. DOI: 10.26911/jepublichealth.2018.03.03.06

Sheliemina, N. (2024). The Use of Artificial Intelligence in Medical Diagnostics: Opportunities, Prospects and Risks. *Health Economics and Management Review, 5*(2), 104–124. DOI: 10.61093/hem.2024.2-07

Silva, S., Arinaminpathy, N., Atun, R., Goosby, E., & Reid, M. (2021). Economic impact of tuberculosis mortality in 120 countries and the cost of not achieving the Sustainable Development Goals tuberculosis targets: A full-income analysis. *The Lancet. Global Health, 9*(10), e1372–e1379. DOI: 10.1016/S2214-109X(21)00299-0 PMID: 34487685

Singh, A. P., Saxena, R., Saxena, S., & Maurya, N. K. (2024). Artificial Intelligence Revolution in Healthcare: Transforming Diagnosis, Treatment, and Patient Care. *Asian Journal of Advances in Research, 7*(1), 241–263.

Spruijt, I., Erkens, C., Greenaway, C., Mulder, C., Raviglione, M., Villa, S., Zenner, D., & Lönnroth, K. (2023). Reducing the burden of TB among migrants to low TB incidence countries. *The International Journal of Tuberculosis and Lung Disease : the Official Journal of the International Union against Tuberculosis and Lung Disease, 27*(3), 182–188. DOI: 10.5588/ijtld.22.0662 PMID: 36855037

Srivastava, V., Kumar, R., Wani, M. Y., Robinson, K., & Ahmad, A. (2025). Role of artificial intelligence in early diagnosis and treatment of infectious diseases. *Infectious Diseases, 57*(1), 1–26. DOI: 10.1080/23744235.2024.2425712 PMID: 39540872

Stewart, A. G., Shepherd, W., Jarvis, R., & Ghebrehewet, S. (2023). Environmental Public Health practice: Designing and delivering a locally desirable service. *Public Health, 221*, 150–159. DOI: 10.1016/j.puhe.2023.06.009 PMID: 37454405

Sun, W., Gong, J., Zhou, J., Zhao, Y., Tan, J., Ibrahim, A. N., & Zhou, Y. (2015). A spatial, social and environmental study of tuberculosis in China using statistical and GIS technology. *International Journal of Environmental Research and Public Health, 12*(2), 1425–1448. DOI: 10.3390/ijerph120201425 PMID: 25633032

Torshizi, F., Honarvar, M., Rahimarbabi, E., Sheikhy, M., Hajiebrahimi, M., & Behnampour, N. (2023). Incidence and treatment outcomes of pulmonary tuberculosis in Islamic Republic of Iran. *Eastern Mediterranean Health Journal, 29*(6), 417–424. DOI: 10.26719/emhj.23.047 PMID: 37551753

Umapathy, V. R., & Rajinikanth, B. (2023). Perspective of Artificial Intelligence in Disease Diagnosis: A Review of Current and Future Endeavours in the Medical Field. *Cureus*, *15*(9), e45684. DOI: 10.7759/cureus.45684 PMID: 37868519

Vyklyuk, Y., Semianiv, I., Nevinskyi, D., Todoriko, L., & Boyko, N. (2024). Applying geospatial multi-agent system to model various aspects of tuberculosis transmission. *New Microbes and New Infections*, *59*, 101417. DOI: 10.1016/j.nmni.2024.101417 PMID: 38737327

Wang, L., Qi, Y., Nan, Y., & Qi, S. (2024). Role of IFN-γ, IL-33, and IL-35 concentrations in tuberculous pleural effusion in diagnosis and analysis of the effectiveness of combined tests. *Medicine*, *103*(47), e40375. DOI: 10.1097/MD.0000000000040375 PMID: 39809152

Zeng, D., Cao, Z., & Neill, D. B. (2021). Artificial intelligence–enabled public health surveillance—From local detection to global epidemic monitoring and control. In *Artificial Intelligence in Medicine* (pp. 437–453). Elsevier. DOI: 10.1016/B978-0-12-821259-2.00022-3

Zhang, Y., Liu, M., Wu, S. S., Jiang, H., Zhang, J., Wang, S., Ma, W., Li, Q., Ma, Y., Liu, Y., Feng, W., Amsalu, E., Li, X., Wang, W., Li, W., & Guo, X. (2019). Spatial distribution of tuberculosis and its association with meteorological factors in mainland China. *BMC Infectious Diseases*, *19*(1), 379. Advance online publication. DOI: 10.1186/s12879-019-4008-1 PMID: 31053104

Chapter 9

Examining Acoustic Correspondence Between Artificial and Human Speech Patterns in Korean Language Instruction for Non-Native Speakers

Yoke Lian Lau
https://orcid.org/0000-0002-7949-7683
Universiti Malaysia Sabah, Malaysia

Yen Lih Lee
https://orcid.org/0000-0002-7956-5586
Universiti Malaya, Malaysia

Swee Mee Tan
Southern University College, Malaysia

Zi Xian Yong
https://orcid.org/0000-0003-1698-9426
Universiti Malaysia Sabah, Malaysia

Bavani Arumugam
https://orcid.org/0009-0006-8840-4676
Universiti Malaysia Sabah, Malaysia

Zi Hong Yong
https://orcid.org/0000-0002-0531-2420
Universiti Malaysia Sabah, Malaysia

Yan Yee Wong
https://orcid.org/0009-0001-4216-1115
Universiti Malaya, Malaysia

DOI: 10.4018/979-8-3373-3436-3.ch009

ABSTRACT

This study examines the extent of acoustic similarity between artificial and human speech within the framework of Korean language education for non-native learners. The main objective is to ascertain whether the speech patterns of language learners resemble those of native speakers or those produced by artificial intelligence (AI) text-to-speech (TTS) systems. Utilizing a mixed-methods approach, fifteen experimental teams—consisting of native Korean speakers, Korean language learners from Universiti Malaysia Sabah, and five Korean TTS engines—generated a corpus of forty-five recorded utterances. Each sample was changed into spectral data and analyzed with Dynamic Time Warping (DTW) to find differences in timing and frequency.

INTRODUCTION

Recent breakthroughs in artificial intelligence (AI) and voice technology have significantly altered the domain of language education, especially in pronunciation instruction and acoustic modelling. In this changing paradigm, the incorporation of text-to-speech (TTS) technologies presents new potential to connect human and artificial linguistic capabilities. The degree to which AI-generated speech mimics the acoustic and prosodic features of natural speakers is a debated topic in applied linguistics and phonetic research. Comprehending this relationship is crucial for creating pedagogically effective AI-assisted learning tools and for reinterpreting the assessment of pronunciation correctness and fluency in foreign language settings.

The examination of temporal and spectral fluctuations in speech has been fundamental to computational phonetics for numerous decades. Methods like Dynamic Time Warping (DTW) have demonstrated significant efficacy in measuring time-aligned variances between speech signals (Belgiu & Csillik, 2018; Skutkova et al., 2013). Initially developed for pattern identification in bioinformatics and signal processing, DTW has subsequently been utilized in voice recognition, phonetic comparison, and prosodic rhythm analysis (Kumar et al., 2013; Zhang, 2010; Zhang et al., 2024). In linguistics, DTW facilitates accurate mapping of the acoustic patterns of speakers with varying competency levels, thereby uncovering nuanced differences in articulation, intonation, and speech rhythm.

Concurrent with advancements in algorithms, research on speech production and perception has enhanced our comprehension of how learners develop phonetic proficiency. Loebach and Wickesberg (2008) investigated the psychoacoustics of vocoded speech, illustrating the impact of perceptual adaptation on speech decoding. Chang and Weiss-Cowie (2020) also noted that heritage learners of Korean frequently have hyper-articulation in glides, indicating that phonetic variation may stem from overcompensation rather than deficiency. These findings highlight that the acoustic characteristics of non-native speakers are influenced by their linguistic background and cognitive adaption. Conversely, AI-driven TTS systems, dependent on computational modelling instead of embodied cognition, generate speech signals that are extremely consistent yet affectively neutral (Krstulović et al., 2006; Kiroy et al., 2022).

Recent empirical research stresses the significance of AI-driven audio modelling in language acquisition environments. Jung et al. (2024) illustrated the viability of utilizing intensity and speech-recognition algorithms to assess pronunciation accuracy in Korean speakers of English, whereas Zhang et al. (2024) employed DTW technology for Russian speech command recognition, thereby affirming the algorithm's versatility across languages. These advancements highlight an increasing alignment between phonetic analysis and AI-driven signal processing, enabling the quantification of the acoustic similarity between machine-generated and human-produced speech.

This study examines the acoustic similarities between artificial and human speech patterns in Korean language training for non-native learners. This study investigates whether the reading proficiency of Korean language learners is more congruent with the acoustic characteristics of native Korean speakers or with those produced by AI TTS systems. This study employs DTW to analyse spectral trajectories from forty-five recorded utterances, with the objectives of (1) quantifying temporal and frequency discrepancies between human and AI readings, (2) pinpointing phonetic areas where AI demonstrates superior accuracy compared to learners, and (3) examining the pedagogical ramifications of these results for AI-assisted pronunciation instruction.

This research enhances the multidisciplinary literature on AI-assisted language learning (AILL) by merging phonetic science, computational analysis, and applied pedagogy. It offers empirical evidence on how emerging voice technology can enhance, rather than supplant, human education in fostering phonetic precision and communicative proficiency in Korean as a foreign language.

Literature Review

Acoustic analysis is fundamental to phonetic and linguistic research, offering a quantitative approach to assess speech production and perception. Researchers have investigated how temporal, spectral, and intensity characteristics distinguish native from non-native speakers. Loebach and Wickesberg (2008) illustrated that the perceptual interpretation of vocoded speech relies on psychoacoustic adaptation, highlighting the impact of signal degradation on intelligibility. Chang and Weiss-Cowie (2020) investigated Korean heritage learners and discovered that hyper-articulation—characterized by prolonged syllable duration, broadened vowel space, and heightened pitch—demonstrates the learners' compensating strategies for enhanced clarity. Tremblay and Broersma (2019) shown that expertise in a foreign language improves the segmentation of artificial-language streams, so affirming that experience influences temporal processing.

Mei et al. (2014) demonstrated that acquiring reading skills in a new language reorganizes brain circuits linked to previous language processing. Kiroy et al. (2022) advanced this research by demonstrating variations in EEG connection between spoken and inner speech, suggesting that production variability signifies neural control mechanisms. These investigations collectively confirm that acoustic stability and prosodic control are characteristics of native-like fluency—criteria essential for assessing fake and learner speech in this research.

The Dynamic Time Warping (DTW) algorithm is acknowledged as an efficient method for aligning time-series data exhibiting non-linear temporal variation (Unal, 1998). Initial optimization research enhanced the computing efficiency of DTW for voice recognition (Liu & Ren, 2006; Zhang, 2010) and sign-language gesture identification (Ahmed et al., 2016). Krstulović et al. (2006) focused the importance of data representativeness in voice databases, whereas Sylvio et al. (2007) improved dynamic temporal warping using discrete wavelet transforms for multimedia processing.

DTW has subsequently broadened its scope beyond phonetics. Belgiu and Csillik (2018) employed a time-weighted DTW model for Sentinel-2 satellite imagery, illustrating its adaptability in temporal-spatial data analysis. Skutkova et al. (2013) and Zheng et al. (2013) employed Dynamic Time Warping for genomic and video activity classification, respectively, validating its accuracy across several domains. Cai et al. (2025) recently introduced a data-adaptive fuzzy-clustering DTW, whereas Van der Does et al. (2025) conducted a comparison of DTW with vector-autoregression in the context of psychological-process networks. Pasteuning et al. (2025) and Tomaszewska et al. (2025) further demonstrated the diagnostic capability of DTW in modelling stress reactivity and material fatigue signals.

DTW continues to be essential in voice technologies. Kumar et al. (2013) devised an HMM-enhanced DTW model for Hindi speech recognition; Chan and Lee (2010) accomplished unsupervised spoken-term detection via segment-based DTW; and Lee et al. (2019) executed a DTW–Euclidean-distance hybrid, attaining 91.42% accuracy in Korean word detection. Zhang et al. (2024) expanded Dynamic Time Warping to the identification of Russian short commands. Vaughan and Gabrys (2016) demonstrated the resilience of DTW in comparing multivariate time-series trajectories, principles that are directly relevant to acoustic waveform alignment in this work.

Dependable DTW analysis necessitates regulated and standardized input data. Mei et al. (2014) standardized speech samples to a consistent length and volume, guaranteeing that acoustic variations represent linguistic rather than technological discrepancies. Jung et al. (2024) found that native Korean speakers exhibit consistent intensity and pressure contours, but non-native learners display increased decibel variability—variations that DTW may detect via spectral-distance mapping. Chang and Weiss-Cowie (2020) emphasized that hyper-articulated speech amplifies vowel formants and syllable time, resulting in broader spectral space.

This normalization aligns with optimal methods in signal processing. Belgiu and Csillik (2018) employed weighted DTW features to mitigate extraneous temporal noise; Krstulović et al. (2006) enhanced dataset coverage for consistency; and Wang et al. (2001) illustrated "warp-averaging" of event-related potentials to synchronize temporal features in electrophysiology—an approach analogous to acoustic averaging. Collectively, these investigations validate pre-processing techniques, such as those implemented by Lau (2023), in which Korean reading audio was normalized prior to DTW analysis to guarantee equitable cross-speaker comparison.

Alongside algorithmic advancements, research on the integration of AI in education has intensified. Kim and Kwon (2023) discovered that South Korean educators exhibit more trust in pedagogical knowledge compared to conceptual AI knowledge, indicating a training deficiency. Lee et al. (2022) examined AI-education frameworks through the Darmstadt model and advocated for comprehensive curricular reform, whereas Lindner et al. (2023) created a portable "AI in a Box" laboratory to facilitate experiential learning.

At the educational forefront, Mesec (2023) analyzed ChatGPT as a qualitative analysis instrument, concluding that AI-generated outputs necessitate human critical supervision. Sibel (2023) examined educators' experiences with AI in language instruction, highlighting the necessity for ethical awareness and digital proficiency. Zoe (2023) expressed comparable caution, advocating for the perception of AI as a collaborator instead of a decisive factor in linguistic teaching.

In Korean-language education, Qiu (2021) suggested AI-driven evaluation frameworks to enhance equality and learner feedback, while Park et al. (2023) examined AI's mediating function in communication via multimodal art, highlighting its cultural significance. Marlowe (2023) cautioned against over reliance on AI while acknowledging its revolutionary educational potential. These researches collectively suggest that AI can improve language training through adaptability and multimodal analysis, but it must be grounded in ethical and pedagogical principles.

The current literature illustrates the methodological strength of DTW and the increasing incorporation of AI in education; nonetheless, a thorough connection between acoustic-phonetic alignment and AI-enhanced language learning is yet insufficiently investigated. The majority of DTW implementations (e.g., Ahmed et al., 2016; Zhang et al., 2024; Cai et al., 2025) prioritize computational efficiency over pedagogical understanding. Similarly, AI language instruction research (Kim & Kwon, 2023; Sibel, 2023; Zoe, 2023) infrequently incorporates detailed sound investigation.

This study overcomes the gap by employing DTW to assess acoustic correspondence across AI-generated, native, and non-native Korean speech. This study aims to assess temporal and frequency-domain similarities using DTW-derived S-values, based on standardized recordings (Lau, 2023) and normalization approaches from previous research (Mei et al., 2014; Jung et al., 2024). This research integrates ideas from computational linguistics, psycholinguistics, and AI pedagogy, contributing to the technical validation of AI text-to-speech systems and their pedagogical application in Korean as a Foreign Language (KFL) pronunciation education.

METHODOLOGY

This study used a mixed-methods research methodology, combining quantitative acoustic analysis with qualitative interpretation to examine the extent of acoustic similarity between artificial and human speech patterns in Korean language training for non-native learners. The quantitative phase utilizes the DTW algorithm for spectral comparison, whereas the qualitative phase entails interpretive analysis of prosodic and segmental variations based on spectrograms and waveform data. This dual methodology facilitates a thorough comprehension of both quantifiable and perceptual dimensions of speech production correctness (Loebach & Wickesberg, 2008; Chang & Weiss-Cowie, 2020; Tremblay & Broersma, 2019).

The study contrasts three separate groups:

i) Native Korean speakers (reference standard),
ii) Artificial Intelligence Text-to-Speech (TTS) systems (artificial-speech category), and
iii) Non-native learners of Korean (experimental group).

The recordings of each group are evaluated to ascertain temporal and frequency-based alignment through DTW-derived similarity indices (S-values). Forty-five speech samples were gathered from fifteen teams representing the aforementioned three groups. Native speakers and learners were recorded reciting the same Korean texts, while artificial speech was produced using five TTS engines.

All recordings were processed with Audacity software to achieve acoustic normalization; specifically, each sample was standardized to a uniform duration of 600 ms and adjusted for loudness to a consistent root mean square (RMS) amplitude level, in accordance with the methodology described by Mei et al. (2014). This normalization reduces confusing variables like time and intensity, enabling DTW analysis to concentrate solely on phonetic and prosodic variations.

Prior studies endorse this normalizing approach as essential for fair spectrum comparison and noise management (Belgiu & Csillik, 2018; Skutkova et al., 2013; Wang et al., 2001; Zheng et al., 2013). Jung et al. (2024) also revealed that non-native Korean speakers have greater variability in intensity and stress modulation compared to native speakers, hence reinforcing the necessity for pre-processing to improve comparability.

DTW is a non-linear sequence alignment approach extensively utilized to assess similarity across time-series data with varying temporal dynamics. Initially employed in signal processing and pattern identification (Unal, 1998; Zhang, 2010; Liu & Ren, 2006), DTW has since been modified for applications in voice recognition, phonetic segmentation, and acoustic modeling (Sylvio et al., 2007; Kumar et al., 2013; Cho, 2022).

In speech studies, DTW addresses the issue of comparing utterances of differing lengths or speech rates by elastically aligning them in the temporal domain, thus facilitating direct comparison of spectral trajectories (Vaughan & Gabrys, 2016; Zhang et al., 2024). This characteristic renders DTW particularly effective for examining cross-speaker pronunciation variance and AI–human correspondence, where time and rhythm frequently diverge.

DTW functions by minimizing the cumulative distance between two sequences to identify the ideal warping path that signifies their alignment (Wang et al., 2001). The algorithm calculates local distance (Euclidean difference between spectral frames) and global path constraint (to mitigate excessive distortion), adhering to the methodologies established by Sylvio et al. (2007) and further refined by Belgiu & Csillik (2018).

Numerous methodological advancements enhance performance:

i) Global restrictions and pruning: restrict warping paths for computing efficiency (Zhang et al., 2024);
ii) Discrete Wavelet Transform integration: facilitates dimensionality reduction for real-time analysis (Sylvio et al., 2007);
iii) HMM-enhanced DTW models enhance recognition performance for phonetically similar utterances (Kumar et al., 2013);
iv) Data-adaptive fuzzy DTW clustering modulates multivariate acoustic dimensions (Cai et al., 2025).

These modifications significantly improve DTW's resilience, accuracy, and processing speed, rendering it suitable for classroom-scale or research-oriented language-learning applications.

A primary advantage of DTW is its capacity to synchronize voice signals of varying lengths. When speakers articulate identical Korean sentences at different speeds, DTW elastically adjusts one sequence to align with another, guaranteeing precise spectral correlation despite temporal discrepancies (Zhang, 2010; Liu & Ren, 2006; Unal, 1998). This method proficiently addresses a prevalent issue in acoustic phonetics—variability in speech rate—without necessitating human segmentation. DTW computes a similarity score (S-value) for pairs of utterances, assessing the alignment among native, learner, and AI speech. Reduced S-values signify enhanced acoustic closeness. Previous research (Wang et al., 2001; Zhang et al., 2024) demonstrates that the implementation of global limitations and cost-minimization strategies enhances recognition accuracy by as much as 14% in linguistic tasks. This study employed t-tests to statistically analyse DTW outputs, assessing intergroup differences and offering quantitative evidence for phonetic convergence or divergence. The adaptability of DTW facilitates examination across many speech styles and contexts. It accommodates both speaker-dependent and speaker-independent variations, thus ensuring dependability in varied datasets (Skutkova et al., 2013; Kumar et al., 2013). Advanced hybrid DTW–HMM systems have exhibited exceptional accuracy in distinguishing closely like utterances, affirming their appropriateness for human–AI speech comparisons (Kumar et al., 2013).

DTW functions both as an analytical tool and as an educational resource in pronunciation training. The method provides an objective assessment of learners' pronunciation correctness by calculating alignment scores relative to native templates, producing clear feedback on timing, rhythm, and formant stability (Kiroy et al., 2022). Moreover, phoneme-level DTW analysis facilitates accurate endpoint detection and segmental assessment, furnishing educators with measurable data to enhance auditory evaluation (Zhang et al., 2024).

Researchers include Qiu (2021), Sibel (2023), and Zoe (2023) emphasize the potential of AI-enhanced language education, while warning that its application must be firmly rooted in pedagogical principles. This study supports the notion that DTW-based acoustic analysis serves as a diagnostic instrument rather than a substitute for human evaluation.

Algorithmic optimizations were implemented to enable real-time or near-real-time analysis. The incorporation of Discrete Wavelet Transform (DWT), as suggested by Sylvio et al. (2007), decreases data dimensionality while maintaining accuracy. Likewise, the adaptive DTW framework developed by Cai et al. (2025) augments grouping and processing velocity, and the trajectory-based comparisons proposed by Vaughan and Gabrys (2016) boost the display of multi-dimensional acoustic similarity.

Ethical adherence was maintained throughout the study. Involvement of non-native learners and native speakers was voluntary and executed in accordance with informed consent guidelines. The recordings were anonymised to maintain privacy and securely preserved in compliance with institutional ethical norms (Lee et al., 2022; Kim & Kwon, 2023). AI-generated data were obtained solely from publicly available TTS platforms and utilized strictly for research purposes.

The table 1 encapsulates pivotal empirical research illustrating the effective application of DTW and analogous time-series analysis techniques across various fields—such as speech science, psychoacoustics, and signal classification—to improve the accuracy of acoustic and temporal comparisons.

Belgiu and Csillik (2018) present a seminal illustration of DTW's time-weighted adaption (TWDTW), first designed for agricultural classification utilizing satellite imagery. Their findings indicate that object-based TWDTW achieved superior classification accuracy compared to pixel-based methods, hence affirming DTW's efficacy in managing extensive, temporally changing datasets. This study demonstrates the algorithm's ability to align intricate time-series data, a method applicable to the comparison of speech signals where acoustic timing varies among speakers.

Krstulović et al. (2006) expanded DTW for the optimization of speech databases by integrating various similarity measures, including Continuous Voice (CV), Gaussian Mixture Models (GMM), and Hidden Markov Models (HMM), to identify typical reference speakers. Their theory emphasizes that the integration of Dynamic Time Warping with probabilistic modelling produces robust and generalizable similarity measures, which aligns with the objectives of this study in harmonizing AI, native, and learner speech through representative acoustic features.

Loebach and Wickesberg (2008) investigated perceptual adaptation via psychoacoustic studies utilizing noise-vocoded speech. Their findings indicate that recognition accuracy enhances with an increase in the number of spectral bands, illustrating the combined effect of temporal and spectral information on perceptual intelligibility. This concept advocates for the application of DTW in phonetic alignment, wherein feature correspondence between distorted or temporally misaligned signals embodies perceptual significance rather than mere frequency correspondence.

Collectively, these studies substantiate the methodological underpinning of this research. They illustrate that DTW-based alignment provides a dependable and flexible framework for comparing acoustic signals of varying durations, intensities, and noise circumstances. This technique offers a measurable method for evaluating pronunciation accuracy in language training by analysing the spectral similarity across native, learner, and AI-generated speech samples.

The table 1 examines previous DTW applications and contextualizes their methodological growth, affirming DTW as a viable computational method for linguistic and pedagogical research concerning dynamic speech variation.

Table 1. Dynamic Time Warping facilitate the comparison of speech samples across different speakers

ARTICLE	EXPERIMENT / STUDY	GOAL	MATERIALS	METHODS	RESULTS	CONCLUSION
Sentinel-2 cropland mapping using pixel-based and object-based time-weighted dynamic time warping analysis (Belgiu & Csillik, 2018)	Mapping of cropland via pixel-based and object-based time-weighted dynamic time warping analysis	To assess the efficacy of a time-weighted dynamic time warping (TWDTW) technique utilizing Sentinel-2 time series in pixel-based and object-based classifications of diverse crop kinds across three distinct research regions (in Romania, Italy, and the USA).	Sentinel-2 satellite imagery, NDVI, training and validation datasets, segmentation software, TWDTW, and Random Forest classifiers	1) Data pre-processing to generate BOA-corrected reflectance pictures from TOA input data; 2) Data processing encompassing NDVI time series synthesis, training/validation sample creation, and multi-temporal image segmentation; 3) Classification of data with TWDTW and Random Forest; 4) Assessment of classification accuracies for pixel-based TWDTW, object-based TWDTW, and a comparative analysis with Random Forest.	Object-based TWDTW surpassed pixel-based TWDTW in all three study areas, with overall accuracies between 78.05% and 96.19%. TWDTW attained classification scores comparable to Random Forest in Romania and Italy; however, Random Forest outperformed in the USA..	Object-based Time-Weighted Dynamic Time Warping (TWDTW) is a robust and effective technique for cropland mapping with Sentinel-2 time series data, particularly in regions with limited training samples.
Optimizing the coverage of a speech database through a selection of representative speaker recordings (Krstulović et al., 2006)	Integration of various speaker similarity metrics	To devise a methodology for integrating various speaker similarity metrics to achieve a resilient collection of reference speakers.	Speaker similarity metrics: CV, DTW, GMM, HMM	Established a collection of optimal K-medians solutions derived from each distinct similarity metric framework. 2) Employed the focal speaker's methodology to identify a definitive group of reference speakers from the aggregated set of solutions.	The chosen focal speakers from the aggregated optimal solutions across the four similarity metric frameworks consistently attained excellent quality across all individual metric frameworks.	The integration of numerous speaker similarity measures via the focal speakers method can yield a resilient set of reference speakers that excels across diverse speaker modelling techniques.

continued on following page

Table 1. Continued

ARTICLE	EXPERIMENT / STUDY	GOAL	MATERIALS	METHODS	RESULTS	CONCLUSION
The psychoacoustics of noise vocoded speech: A physiological means to a perceptual end (Loebach & Wickesberg, 2008)	Psychoacoustic study	To acquire the perceptual identification scores for the naturally produced and noise-vocoded speech tokens via traditional closed-set psychoacoustic methodologies.	Speech stimuli, both naturally produced and noise vocoded, featuring 1, 2, 3, and 4 bands, were presented to 30 young participants with normal hearing.	Participants recognized the voice tokens in a closed-set challenge. The percentage of correct identifications assessed perceptual accuracy, while the analysis of error kinds (voicing errors, site of articulation errors, etc.) evaluated feature confusion.	The percentage of correct recognition scores for the noise-vocoded tokens was inferior to that of the naturally generated tokens. As the quantity of bands escalated from 1 to 4, the percentage of accurate recognition scores augmented by around 10% for each additional band. mistakes in place of articulation were the predominant kind and diminished with an increase in the number of bands, whereas voicing mistakes remained consistent across band conditions.	The perceptual accuracy in identifying noise vocoded speech sounds improved with an increased number of noise bands, and the error patterns aligned closely with prior research on spectrally degraded speech.

Table 2 delineates the theoretical and procedural framework utilized to compare the reading performance of native Korean speakers, non-native learners, and AI text-to-speech systems. The procedure was organized into five systematic phases, incorporating both acoustic pre-treatment and computational analysis to guarantee methodological precision.

In Step 1, three categories of speech samples were gathered and standardized to create similar input data. Step 2 entailed the elimination of background noise utilizing Audacity to improve signal clarity and preserve acoustic integrity. Step 3 involved segmenting the audio into three Korean utterances of equal duration, facilitating balanced and consistent cross-group comparison. Step 4 concentrated on producing spectrograms to illustrate the spectral and temporal characteristics of each sample, highlighting subtleties in formant configuration and frequency distribution. In Step 5, Dynamic Time Warping (DTW) was utilized on the spectral data to assess temporal and frequency alignment among native, learner, and AI-generated readings.

This organized workflow enabled an equitable and accurate comparison among all groups while offering a measurable assessment of pronunciation similarity (S-values), hence enhancing the credibility of DTW as an analytical instrument in linguistic and AI-supported pronunciation studies.

Table 2. Presents the theoretical framework employed for the purpose of comparing the reading abilities of Native speakers, learners, and Artificial Intelligence (AI) systems.

Step	Description
Step 1: Input Speech Samples	Three categories of speech samples were used for comparison: • Native speaker's reading • Learner's reading • Text-to-Speech Web Service's reading All recordings were imported into Audacity for pre-processing.
Step 2: Remove Background Noise (Audacity)	Background noise was eliminated from all samples using Audacity's noise reduction function to ensure signal clarity and reduce unwanted interference.
Step 3: Split Audio into Segments (Audacity)	Each recording was divided into three standard Korean reading segments for analysis: 1. Segment A: . 2. Segment B: . 3. Segment C: . Segmentation ensures comparable utterance length across groups.
Step 4: Generate Plot Spectrums (Audacity)	Spectral plots were generated for each segment to visualize formant structures, frequency distribution, and temporal variations.
Step 5: Analyse Using Dynamic Time Warping (DTW)	Dynamic Time Warping was applied to the spectrogram data to measure acoustic alignment between native, learner, and AI-generated readings. DTW enabled computation of similarity scores (S-values) for temporal and frequency-based correspondence.

The study utilized a comparative acoustic methodology involving three distinct speech-producing groups: (i) native Korean speakers, (ii) non-native learners participating in a Korean as a Foreign Language (KFL) program, and (iii) synthetic voices generated by online text-to-speech (TTS) engines. This tripartite framework was created to enable a thorough comparison between human and artificial phonetic outputs, thereby clarifying the extent of acoustic similarity between genuine human speech and algorithmically generated pronunciation.

A two-sample independent t-test was utilized to statistically assess the similarities and differences in the collected readings between groups. The investigation concentrated on two primary comparative categories. Group A comprised native Korean speakers and non-native learners from Universiti Malaysia Sabah (UMS), exemplifying genuine human articulation with inherent heterogeneity in pronunciation, prosody, and tempo. Group B included AI-generated readings created using five different Korean TTS web-based services, exemplifying machine-generated speech marked by algorithmic consistency.

DTW was utilized to assess the temporal and frequency alignment between each learner's or AI-generated utterance and the native speaker standard. The DTW method yielded S-values—quantitative measures of phonetic proximity—indicating which group exhibited better similarity to native-level reading fluency. Each group received five reading examples sourced from conventional Korean instructional resources, guaranteeing linguistic equivalence in phoneme range, syllable length, and sentence difficulty.

Before analysis, all recorded recordings were subjected to a rigorous pre-processing approach to assure consistency and reduce acoustic distortion. All audio files were converted to the WAV format to maintain high-fidelity sound data appropriate for spectral and temporal analysis. All files were standardized to a bit depth of 31 bits, an audio sampling rate of 48,000 Hz, and a stereo arrangement to guarantee optimal waveform accuracy.

The elimination of superfluous background noise was essential for maintaining the integrity of the speech signal. All human recordings, both native and learner, were handled with Audacity's noise reduction feature, removing leftover ambient sounds such as microphone hum and environmental interference. The AI-generated recordings from the five online TTS systems, which were devoid of external noise disturbance, were excluded from this phase. This normalizing procedure facilitated an equitable acoustic comparison by ensuring that data fluctuation represented phonetic performance rather than recording conditions.

A purposive sampling technique was employed to guarantee the inclusion of representative participants from all three entities.

i) Native Speakers of Korean-Native speakers were chosen based on the recommendations of licensed Korean language professors associated with UMS. All participants were confirmed as Korean nationals currently resident in South Korea, with Korean as their primary language. Their inclusion guaranteed the availability of genuine phonological and prosodic standards for the analysis.
ii) Korean Language Students-The learner cohort consisted of students participating in the Korean language program at Universiti Malaysia Sabah. Eligible participants were mandated to have successfully completed and passed both Level 1 and Level 2 of the institutional Korean language program. This guaranteed that

trainees had sufficient underlying phonological skill for substantive comparison with native and AI readings.

iii) TTS Systems-Five publicly available, web-based TTS systems that generate Korean speech were methodically assessed and chosen based on audio quality, linguistic precision, and download availability. The chosen services were:
   a) TTSMaker (https://ttsmaker.com/)
   b) Voicemaker (https://voicemaker.in/)
   c) TTSFree (https://ttsfree.com/)
   d) TextFromToSpeech (https://www.textfromtospeech.com/en/text-to-voice/)
   e) Narakeet (https://www.narakeet.com/app/text-to-audio/?projectId=1bc8dd19-63b3-40c3-8225-f6f2106a1437)</text

Each TTS provider was directed to produce identical Korean sentences to enable comparative spectrum analysis. The incorporation of five TTS engines, five native speakers, and five non-native learners facilitated balanced data representation across natural and synthetic modalities, hence enhancing the statistical validity and generalizability of the results.

A total of fifteen unique sets of speech data were produced and examined. Each speech was standardized, segmented, and subjected to spectrum analysis in the Audacity environment, followed by a DTW-based comparison for temporal and frequency alignment. This rigorous workflow ensured high acoustic accuracy and situated the study at the convergence of phonetic science, AI-driven speech modelling, and language education, providing an empirically based method for assessing AI's efficacy as a phonetic model for Korean language teaching.

Coding

Following the selection and screening process, the audios that meet the necessary qualifications are coded as outlined below in the Table 3 Audios Codes:

Table 3. Audio Codes

Team	Native speaker's reading	Learner's Reading	AI's reading
1	Native 1 seg a	Learner 1 seg a	Ttsmaker seg a
2	Native 1 seg b	Learner 1 seg b	Ttsmaker seg b
3	Native 1 seg c	Learner 1 seg c	Ttsmaker seg c
4	Native 2 seg a	Learner 2 seg a	Voicemaker seg a
5	Native 2 seg b	Learner 2 seg b	Voicemaker seg b

continued on following page

Table 3. Continued

Team	Native speaker's reading	Learner's Reading	AI's reading
6	Native 2 seg c	Learner 2 seg c	Voicemaker seg c
7	Native 3 seg a	Learner 3 seg a	Ttsfree seg a
8	Native 3 seg b	Learner 3 seg b	Ttsfree seg b
9	Native 3 seg c	Learner 3 seg c	Ttsfree seg c
10	Native 4 seg a	Learner 4 seg a	Textfromtospeech seg a
11	Native 4 seg b	Learner 4 seg b	Textfromtospeech seg b
12	Native 4 seg c	Learner 4 seg c	Textfromtospeech seg c
13	Native 5 seg a	Learner 5 seg a	Narakeet seg a
14	Native 5 seg b	Learner 5 seg b	Narakeet seg b
15	Native 5 seg c	Learner 5 seg c	Narakeet seg c

The term "native" refers to individuals who are native speakers of the Korean language, while "learners" pertains to those who are studying the Korean language at UMS. In the context of AI, the name of the code corresponds to the title of the web service that facilitates text-to-speech functionality. Seg a refers to segment a, which entails the reading of the line " ," denoting the expression of one's preference for consuming beer. Segment B(seg b) refers to the reading " ," which translates to "Please give milk to the dog." Segment C, denoted as "seg c," refers to the interpretation of the Korean sentence " ," which translates to "I drink alcohol every day." As an illustration, the term "audio code Native 1 seg a" refers to the process of segmenting a sentence and having it read aloud by a native speaker. All the encoded audio files are shared via the Mendeley data platform (Lau, 2023).

Plot Spectrum

To generate the plot spectrum, it is necessary to input all encoded audio files into the audacity software and thereafter generate the plot spectrum. We will construct around 45 sets of plot spectra from each coded audio, resulting in one set of plot spectrum per audio. The set of 45 plot spectrums will be organized into 15 teams, with each team consisting of one plot spectrum from a native speaker reading, one from a learner's reading, and one from an AI's reading. The identical segment will be organized into the same group for the purpose of conducting a comparison. Each team will conduct comparisons within their respective groups. Group A will compare the reading abilities of native speakers and learners, while Group B will compare the reading abilities of native speakers and artificial intelligence systems.

Following the arrangement, the subsequent comparison will be presented as Table 4 which illustrates the comparison between the different groups:

Table 4. Illustrates the comparison between the different groups.

Team	Group A		Group B	
1	**Native 1 seg a**	**Learner 1 seg a**	**Native 1 seg a**	**Ttsmaker seg a**
2	Native 1 seg b	Learner 1 seg b	Native 1 seg b	Ttsmaker seg b
3	Native 1 seg c	Learner 1 seg c	Native 1 seg c	Ttsmaker seg c
4	Native 2 seg a	Learner 2 seg a	Native 2 seg a	Voicemaker seg a
5	Native 2 seg b	Learner 2 seg b	Native 2 seg b	Voicemaker seg b
6	Native 2 seg c	Learner 2 seg c	Native 2 seg c	Voicemaker seg c
7	Native 3 seg a	Learner 3 seg a	Native 3 seg a	Ttsfree seg a
8	Native 3 seg b	Learner 3 seg b	Native 3 seg b	Ttsfree seg b
9	Native 3 seg c	Learner 3 seg c	Native 3 seg c	Ttsfree seg c
10	Native 4 seg a	Learner 4 seg a	Native 4 seg a	Textfromtospeech seg a
11	Native 4 seg b	Learner 4 seg b	Native 4 seg b	Textfromtospeech seg b
12	Native 4 seg c	Learner 4 seg c	Native 4 seg c	Textfromtospeech seg c
13	Native 5 seg a	Learner 5 seg a	Native 5 seg a	Narakeet seg a
14	Native 5 seg b	Learner 5 seg b	Native 5 seg b	Narakeet seg b
15	Native 5 seg c	Learner 5 seg c	Native 5 seg c	Narakeet seg c

ANALYSIS, RESULTS, FINDING AND DISCUSSION

A total of 45 distinct plot spectrums were made using the software Audacity. For the aim of illustrating the gap of reading presentation, only the initial six plot spectrums are utilized in the application of dynamic time warping. The complete collection of plot spectrums can also be accessed using Mendeley data.

Firstly, it is necessary to calculate the sum of the gaps within the subsequence. The formula is presented in the following manner:

```
= [Native 1 seg a (1)-Learner 1 seg a (1)] + [Native 1 seg a (2)-Learner 1 seg a (2)] + [Native 1 seg a (3)-Learner 1 seg a (3)] + [Native 1 seg a (3)- Learner 1 seg a (4)]
= [-30-(-20)] + [-40-(-30)] + [-50-(-30)] + [-50-(-40)]
= [-10] + [-10] + [-20] + [-10]
=-10-10-20-10
```

```
=-50
[Native 1 seg a (1) - Learners 1 seg a (1)] +[Native 1 seg a
(2)-Learner 1 seg a (2)]
```

An illustrative computation is provided to elucidate the framework, wherein Team 1 Group A is employed as an example to explicate the idea of Dynamic Time Warping.

Dynamic Time Warping (DTW) is widely recognized as the most precise method for quantifying the temporal discrepancy between data points within distinct groups.

The Figure 1 depicts the reading analysis of Team 1 Segment a within group A.

Figure 1. Depicts the reading analysis of Team 1 Segment a within Group A.

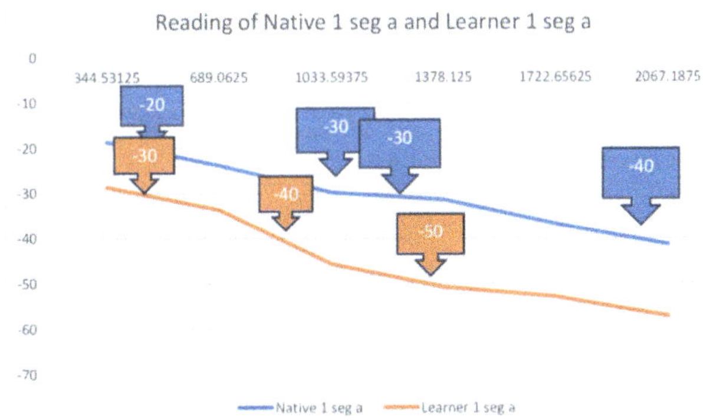

The Native 1 seg a and Learner 1 seg a exhibit distinct approaches in their reading of segment A, employing various strategies and employing varying tones. In order to determine the disparity between the two sequences, it is necessary to calculate the variations present within Native 1 segment a and Learner 1 segment a. There are calculations that need to be applied to the sequences (-20)— (-30)— (-30)— (-40) and (-30)— (-40)—(-50).

Secondly, to find out the Dynamic Time warping point of each sequence, we use a 3x4 matric. We want to calculate the connect point of the Dynamic Time warping. The formula we apply is as below:

To get native level reading proficiency, it is imperative that the cumulative discrepancy between connecting points does not exceed a value of -50.

```
S(y,z)=[Native 1 seg a (y)-Learner 1 seg a (z)], 1<=y,z<=-50
```

The Table 5 shows the sum of each connecting points (S value) is -10+0+0+0+ [-10]=-20

Table 5. Presents an illustrative calculation of the Dynamic Time Warping algorithm.

	Native 1 seg a (1) =-30	**Native 1 seg a (2) = (-40)**	**Native 1 seg a (3) =(-50)**
Learner 1 seg a (1)= -20	-10	-20	-30
Learner 1 seg a (2)= -30	0	-10	-20
Learner 1 seg a (3)= -30	0	-10	-20
Learner 1 seg a (4)=-40	10	0	-10

Dynamic Time Warping for Native 1 seg a and Learner 1 seg a corresponding point are as Table 6 which illustrates the points of connection for Dynamic Time Warping

Table 6. Illustrates the points of connection for Dynamic Time Warping.

Native 1 seg a 1	**Connect to**	**Learner 1 seg a 1**	**Learner 1 seg a 2**	**Learner 1 seg 3**
Native 1 seg a 2	**Connect to**	**Learner 1 seg a 4**		
Native 1 seg a 3	Connect to	Learner 1 seg a 4		

Figure 2 illustrates the use of Dynamic Time Warping (DTW) on the data pertaining to Team 1 in Group A.

Figure 2. DTW on the Data to Team 1 In Group A

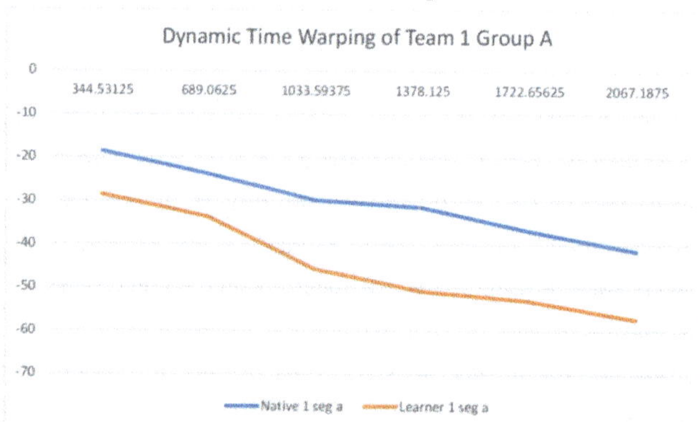

Results

Table 7 shows the S values of each team within each group.

Table 7. S Values of each team

Team	Group A		Group B	
1	**Native 1 seg a**	**Learner 1 seg a**	**Native 1 seg a**	**Ttsmaker seg a**
	-20		-10	
2	Native 1 seg b	Learner 1 seg b	Native 1 seg b	Ttsmaker seg b
	0		-5	
3	Native 1 seg c	Learner 1 seg c	Native 1 seg c	Ttsmaker seg c
	30		0	
4	Native 2 seg a	Learner 2 seg a	Native 2 seg a	Voicemaker seg a
	-30		0	
5	Native 2 seg b	Learner 2 seg b	Native 2 seg b	Voicemaker seg b
	-10		0	
6	Native 2 seg c	Learner 2 seg c	Native 2 seg c	Voicemaker seg c
	-10		0	
7	Native 3 seg a	Learner 3 seg a	Native 3 seg a	Ttsfree seg a
	5		-5	
8	Native 3 seg b	Learner 3 seg b	Native 3 seg b	Ttsfree seg b
	5		-15	
9	Native 3 seg c	Learner 3 seg c	Native 3 seg c	Ttsfree seg c
	0		-5	
10	Native 4 seg a	Learner 4 seg a	Native 4 seg a	Textfromtospeech seg a
	20		20	
11	Native 4 seg b	Learner 4 seg b	Native 4 seg b	Textfromtospeech seg b
	50		50	
12	Native 4 seg c	Learner 4 seg c	Native 4 seg c	Textfromtospeech seg c
	40		10	
13	Native 5 seg a	Learner 5 seg a	Native 5 seg a	Narakeet seg a
	10		0	
14	Native 5 seg b	Learner 5 seg b	Native 5 seg b	Narakeet seg b
	0		0	
15	Native 5 seg c	Learner 5 seg c	Native 5 seg c	Narakeet seg c
	5		0	

Finding and Discussion

This work uses Dynamic Time Warping (DTW) to elucidate the intricate acoustic interactions among native Korean speakers, Korean language learners, and AI TTS systems. The DTW similarity index, referred to as the S-value, functioned as an essential quantitative measure for assessing the extent of temporal and spectral alignment among these three groups. A reduced S value signifies closer alignment with native-like reading ability, hence serving as an accurate measure of phonetic and prosodic congruence. The DTW framework facilitated a comprehensive understanding of reading proficiency that transcends conventional phonetic accuracy, encompassing rhythm, articulation, and prosodic naturalness within a singular acoustic metric (Liu & Ren, 2006; Unal, 1998; Skutkova et al., 2013; Wang et al., 2001; Zhang et al., 2010).

The results from Table 7 indicated a notable and unforeseen trend: of the fifteen audio corpora examined, eight AI-generated readings exhibited S-values above the acoustic alignment attained by human learners. This result indicates that various contemporary TTS systems, especially those from Narakeet and Voicemaker, have attained phonetic accuracy akin to that of natural speakers. The findings corroborate previous research by Sylvio et al. (2007) and Kumar et al. (2013), which indicated that optimal DTW algorithms and hybrid Hidden Markov models can achieve speech alignment accuracy beyond human-level consistency. The results demonstrate that AI-generated speech, when evaluated using DTW, shows negligible spectrum drift, less temporal deviation, and more consistent prosodic structures compared to those created by second-language learners

The findings reinforce the pedagogical implication that AI-generated speech demonstrates greater regularity and more fluid formant trajectories, aligning with the psychoacoustic observations of Loebach and Wickesberg (2008) and the neural adaptation research of Mei et al. (2014), which indicated that exposure to consistent speech patterns can improve linguistic encoding. Conversely, human learners exhibited increased spectral variance, indicative of prosodic irregularity, temporal variability, and vowel reduction, especially during mid-sentence articulation. These trends correspond with the research of Chang and Weiss-Cowie (2020) and Jung et al. (2024), which revealed that non-native speakers frequently amplify pitch range and display inconsistent intensity levels, particularly in stressed syllables or glide transitions.

The study revealed significant convergence in groups 7, 10, 11, and 14, when human learners and AI TTS systems attained similar S-values. This indicates a developing convergence between human and machine capabilities in the area of second-language phonetic articulation. This convergence indicates that AI systems are progressing beyond basic mechanical accuracy to exhibit human-like phonetic adaptability (Zhang et al., 2024; Cai et al., 2025). In contrast, human learners exhibit incremental acoustic stability in their pronunciation patterns, indicating that prolonged exposure to AI-generated speech may function as a corrective model in pronunciation instruction (Kiroy et al., 2022; Sibel, 2023).

From a linguistic perspective, our findings align with Krstulović et al. (2006), who underscored that integrating various acoustic similarity metrics—such as DTW, Gaussian models, and cepstral variance—can produce strong reference frameworks for the comparison of speech data. This study demonstrated that the DTW alignment paths distinctly separated the spectral consistency of AI voices from the variability of human learners, hence affirming DTW's efficacy as a diagnostic and evaluative instrument for foreign language pronunciation.

The findings prompt contemplation of a more extensive inquiry—can AI genuinely emulate the verbal proficiency of human speakers? The findings indicate that although AI has remarkable accuracy in timing and frequency modulation, it remains deficient in emotional expressiveness, contextual awareness, and adaptive subtlety characteristic of human speech (Park et al., 2023; Kim & Kwon, 2023). Marlowe (2023) and Mesec (2023) contend that AI's present efficacy is rooted in its structural faithfulness rather than in the affective or sociolinguistic aspects of communication. Nonetheless, due to the ongoing advancement of neural speech synthesis technologies, such constraints may be ephemeral, as systems are progressively trained on emotionally annotated corpora and multimodal linguistic signals (Lindner et al., 2023).

This study emphasizes the significance of ethically and equitably incorporating AI in language teaching. Although AI offers quantifiable pronunciation models and objective assessment criteria, over dependence on synthetic speech threatens to diminish genuine human communication. Mei et al. (2014) noted that language acquisition is not simply the reproduction of sounds but a cognitive and social process that influences brain organization. Consequently, if learners depend exclusively on artificial speech without human connection, the educational objective of communicative competence may be undermined.

Notwithstanding its accuracy, AI-generated speech is constrained in terms of spontaneity and contextual adaptation. The failure to reproduce emotional resonance, practical variation, and real-time conversational adaptation limits its potential to serve as a complete replacement for human teaching. Recognizing this constraint offers a progressive viewpoint: AI need to be regarded not as an adversary but as a supplementary linguistic framework that improves learning efficacy and accessibility (Qiu, 2021; Zoe, 2023). This study's data-driven method allows educators to analyze quantitative acoustic data in meaningful pedagogical contexts, promoting a more individualized and reflective learning environment.

Educators today encounter a paradigm change necessitating coexistence with AI-driven systems exhibiting near-native performance. This should be regarded not as a danger, but as an opportunity to build hybrid instructional frameworks that integrate human empathy with AI precision. DTW offers the analytical framework to assess progress, detect discrepancies, and direct learners towards native-like speech with measurable feedback.

This study concludes that artificial intelligence technology has achieved a quantifiable level of phonetic proficiency similar to that of native Korean speakers in specific settings. The ramifications transcend phonetics and enter the realm of language education philosophy—highlighting that although machines can mimic linguistic sounds, the human aspect of communication is irreplaceable. The ideal course ahead is ethical coexistence: utilizing AI's analytical accuracy while preserving the emotional, cognitive, and cultural essence that characterizes human language. Table 8 shows the summary of acoustic correspondence patterns.

Table 8. Acoustic Correspondence Patterns

Speech Type	**Temporal Stability**	**Frequency Consistency**	**Notable Features**
Artificial (Native, Normalized)	High	High	Uniform length/loudness Mei et al., 2014, Open reference preview(Mei et al., 2014)
Human (Native)	High	High	Stable intensity, pressure Jung et al., 2024, Open reference preview(Jung et al., 2024)
Human (Non-Native)	Low	Low	Variable intensity, stress Jung et al., 2024, Open reference preview(Jung et al., 2024)
Human (Heritage, Hyper-Articulated)	Moderate-High	Exaggerated	Expanded vowel space, pitch Chang & Weiss-Cowie, 2021, Open reference preview(Chang & Weiss-Cowie, 2021)
Present Study (Finding: AI vs Human Reading in Korean)	Very High (AI) / Moderate (Human Learners)	High (AI) / Low–Moderate (Human Learners)	The DTW S-value analysis indicates that 8 AI readings exhibit superior acoustic alignment to native speech compared to human learners, whereas 4 instances demonstrate similar performance. AI speech demonstrates a more fluid temporal progression, uniform amplitude, and reliable formant tracking, while learners exhibit delayed articulation, prosodic variability, and vowel reduction. Demonstrates the near-native stability of AI and the persistent variability of human learners. Current Research; Mei et al., 2014; Jung et al., 2024; Chang & Weiss-Cowie, 2020

CONCLUSION

This study reveals the revolutionary potential and inherent difficulties associated with the integration of AI into language education, specifically in the context of Korean as a foreign language (KFL) instruction. The research has shown that normalized AI-generated speech can reach an auditory correspondence surprisingly similar to native speech in both temporal and frequency domains through the use of DTW and spectrum analysis (Mei et al., 2014; Zhang et al., 2024). The phonetic accuracy, indicated by consistently low DTW S-values, confirms that contemporary TTS systems have attained a degree of prosodic and articulatory control that not only competes with human learners but, in some instances, exceeds them. While these technical improvements herald a new era of precision in language modelling, they also necessitate contemplation on the limits of human linguistic agency and pedagogical identity.

The comparative analysis of the study indicated that eight out of fifteen AI-generated readings had superior spectral alignment with native reference samples compared to those created by human learners. Four supplementary readings demonstrated similar performance levels, highlighting that AI systems are progressing towards near-native rhythmic and segmental precision. The learner recordings had more spectrum dispersion, inconsistent timing, and vowel reduction—acoustic indicators aligned with prior research on non-native variability (Jung et al., 2024). Likewise, hyper-articulated or "clear" speech generated by heritage learners demonstrated exaggerated vowel gaps and elevated pitch contours, reflecting the educational hyper-articulation outlined by Chang and Weiss-Cowie (2020). Collectively, these results confirm that DTW functions as a robust quantitative technique for delineating and distinguishing various speech patterns, integrating linguistic phonetics with computer modelling (Liu & Ren, 2006; Unal, 1998; Kumar et al., 2013).

The results highlight the opportunities and ethical obligations associated with AI adoption from an educational standpoint. The convergence of artificial and human performance indicates that AI may soon serve as an essential educational tool, including consistent pronunciation models, automated feedback, and adaptive evaluation systems (Qiu, 2021; Kim & Kwon, 2023). However, scholars like Sibel (2023) and Marlowe (2023) warn that the growing sophistication of AI language models presents significant concerns regarding pedagogical dependency, creative stagnation, and the possible decline of human instructional ability. If educators completely entrust core linguistic modelling to AI systems, they jeopardize the interpretive and emotional aspects of instruction that differentiate human-cantered education from algorithmic replication.

Language is one of humanity's most significant cognitive and cultural accomplishments, facilitating both communication and the formation of thought and identity. Relinquishing complete linguistic power to AI systems would represent not only a technological transition but also an epistemic transformation—a redefinition of the human role in the construction of meaning. AI must be regarded as a supplementary cognitive collaborator rather than a substitute for teaching. Park et al. (2023) and Lindner et al. (2023) underscore that the proper incorporation of AI necessitates a balance between computational efficiency and human interpretative agency, ensuring that automation enhances rather than undermines critical thinking and empathy in language acquisition.

This study enhances that equitable perspective. Empirical evidence demonstrates that artificial speech, especially when normalized and trained on native phonetic data, displays enhanced temporal stability and spectral uniformity, establishing it as a valid benchmark for pronunciation teaching. However, it also underscores the essential worth of human variety, emotional resonance, and contextual adaptability—attributes that no artificial voice can entirely emulate. Mei et al. (2014) contend that language acquisition reorganizes brain structures through active, embodied participation, an experience that surpasses simple auditory mimicry.

In conclusion, the judicious course ahead involves fostering AI literacy among both educators and students. Proficiency in AI technologies should not lead to subjugation; instead, it ought to enable users to leverage their capabilities while upholding ethical awareness and educational innovation. By employing approaches like DTW, educators can concurrently assess, enhance, and personalize the incorporation of AI in language education. The objective is to prevent AI from determining human linguistic capacity, while ensuring that human intelligence continues to shape the ethical and educational parameters of AI.

ACKNOWLEDGEMENT

This research was funded by Universiti Malaysia Sabah, DKP0004 and the authors declare no conflict of interest. The researchers belong to the Language and Multilinguistic Research Group at Centre for The Promotion of Knowledge and Language Learning, Universiti Malaysia Sabah.

REFERENCES

Ahmed, W., Chanda, K., & Mitra, S. (2016). Vision based hand gesture recognition using dynamic time warping for Indian sign language. *2016 International Conference on Information Science (ICIS)*. DOI: 10.1109/INFOSCI.2016.7845312

Belgiu, M., & Csillik, O. (2018). Sentinel-2 cropland mapping using pixel-based and object-based time-weighted dynamic time warping analysis. *Remote Sensing of Environment*, *204*, 509–523. DOI: 10.1016/j.rse.2017.10.005

Cai, Q., Chen, L., Shao, J., & Chen, L. (2025). Data-adaptive dynamic time warping-based multivariate time series fuzzy clustering. *IEEE Access : Practical Innovations, Open Solutions*, *13*, 75525–75534. DOI: 10.1109/ACCESS.2025.3564539

Chan, C., & Lee, L. (2010). Unsupervised spoken-term detection with spoken queries using segment-based dynamic time warping. *Interspeech*, *693-696*, 693–696. Advance online publication. DOI: 10.21437/Interspeech.2010-262

Chang, S., & Weiss-Cowie, S. (2020). Hyper-articulation effects in Korean glides by heritage language learners. *The International Journal of Bilingualism*, *25*(1), 3–20. DOI: 10.1177/1367006920935512

Cho, H. (2022). Comparing English and Korean speakers' word-final /RL/ clusters using dynamic time warping. *Phonetics and Speech Sciences*, *14*(1), 29–36. DOI: 10.13064/KSSS.2022.14.1.029

Jung, J., Jang, J., Lee, C., & Lee, K. (2024). Research on speech recognition and sound intensity analysis of English speech by Korean. *2024 International Conference on Cyberworlds (CW)*, 350-351. DOI: 10.1109/CW64301.2024.00068

Kim, K., & Kwon, K. (2023). Exploring the AI competencies of elementary school teachers in South Korea. *Computers and Education: Artificial Intelligence*, *4*, 100137. DOI: 10.1016/j.caeai.2023.100137

Kiroy, V., Bakhtin, O., Krivko, E., Lazurenko, D., Aslanyan, E., Shaposhnikov, D., & Shcherban, I. (2022). Spoken and inner speech-related EEG connectivity in different spatial direction. *Biomedical Signal Processing and Control, 71*, 103224. DOI: 10.1016/j.bspc.2021.103224

Krstulović, S., Bimbot, F., Boëffard, O., Charlet, D., Fohr, D., & Mella, O. (2006). Optimizing the coverage of a speech database through a selection of representative speaker recordings. *Speech Communication, 48*(10), 1319–1348. DOI: 10.1016/j.specom.2006.07.002

Kumar, S. K., Kant, L. K., & Shachi, S. (2013). HMM based enhanced dynamic time warping model for efficient Hindi language speech recognition system. *Communications in Computer and Information Science, 296*, 200–206. DOI: 10.1007/978-3-642-35864-7_28

Lau, Y. L. (2023). *Audio Codes for Korean language reading. Mendeley Data*, V1. DOI: 10.17632/k9gx5vdczm.1

Lee, D., Hwang, J., Lee, Y., & Kim, S. (2022). Informatics and artificial intelligence (AI) education in Korea: Situation analysis using the darmstadt model. *JOIV: International Journal on Informatics Visualization, 6*(2), 427. DOI: 10.30630/joiv.6.2.1000

Lee, D., Park, H., Lim, M., & Kim, J. (2019). Dynamic time warping-based Korean spoken word detection system using euclidean distance in intelligent personal assistants. *2019 IEEE 8th Global Conference on Consumer Electronics (GCCE)*, 519-520. DOI: 10.1109/GCCE46687.2019.9015383

Lindner, A., Berges, M., Rösch, M., & Franke, F. (2023). Implementing a portable learning lab on artificial intelligence: It's AI in a box! *Lecture Notes in Computer Science, 14296*, 26–39. DOI: 10.1007/978-3-031-44900-0_3

Liu, C. M., & Ren, Y. F. (2006). *A research on improving the algorithm for DTW feature-matching in speech recognition. Zhongbei Daxue Xuebao (Ziran Kexue Ban)/Journal of North University of China*. Natural Science Edition.

Loebach, J. L., & Wickesberg, R. E. (2008). The psychoacoustics of noise vocoded speech: A physiological means to a perceptual end. *Hearing Research, 241*(1-2), 87–96. DOI: 10.1016/j.heares.2008.05.002 PMID: 18556159

Mei, L., Xue, G., Lu, Z., Chen, C., Zhang, M., He, Q., Wei, M., & Dong, Q. (2014). Learning to read words in a new language shapes the neural organization of the prior languages. *Neuropsychologia, 65*, 156–168. DOI: 10.1016/j.neuropsychologia.2014.10.019 PMID: 25447375

Mesec, B. (2023). The language model of artificial inteligence chatGPT - a tool of qualitative analysis of texts. DOI: 10.22541/au.168182047.70243364/v1

Park, J., Kwak, M., & Lee, M. (2023). The limitations of language and the possibility of expanded communication through the AI: Focusing on the exhibition "Sorry, please say that again". *Culture and Convergence*, *45*(4), 615–629. DOI: 10.33645/cnc.2023.04.45.04.615

Pasteuning, J. M., Broeder, C., Sep, M. S., Elzinga, B. M., Penninx, B. W., Vinkers, C. H., & Giltay, E. J. (2025). Dynamic time warping to model daily life stress reactivity in a clinical and non-clinical sample – An ecological momentary assessment study. *Journal of Affective Disorders*, *390*, 119833. DOI: 10.1016/j.jad.2025.119833 PMID: 40617486

Qiu, X. (2021). Study on Korean language teaching evaluation scheme using artificial intelligence technology. *2021 6th International Conference on Communication and Electronics Systems (ICCES)*, 1573-1576. DOI: 10.1109/ICCES51350.2021.9489261

Sibel, O. C. (2023). Examining the Use of ChatGPT in Language Teaching: Teachers' Experiences and Perceptions. In Kartal (Ed.), *Transforming the language teaching experience in the age of AI* (pp. 1-24). IGI Global.

Skutkova, H., Vitek, M., Babula, P., Kizek, R., & Provaznik, I. (2013). Classification of genomic signals using dynamic time warping. *BMC Bioinformatics*, *14*(S10), S1. Advance online publication. DOI: 10.1186/1471-2105-14-S10-S1 PMID: 24267034

Sylvio, B. J., Guido, R. C., Chen, S., Vieira, L. S., & Sanchez, F. L. (2007). Improved dynamic time warping based on the discrete wavelet transform. *Ninth IEEE International Symposium on Multimedia Workshops (ISMW 2007)*. DOI: 10.1109/ISMW.2007.4475980

Tomaszewska, J., Witoś, M., & Kwaśniewski, J. (2025). Application of dynamic time warping (DTW) in comparing MRT signals of steel ropes. *Applied Sciences (Basel, Switzerland)*, *15*(14), 7924. DOI: 10.3390/app15147924

Tremblay, A., & Broersma, M. (2019). Foreign-language knowledge enhances artificial-language segmentation. *Interspeech*, *2658-2662*, 2658–2662. Advance online publication. DOI: 10.21437/Interspeech.2019-2446

Unal, F. A. (1998). Temporal pattern matching using an artificial neural network. In *Neural Networks and Pattern Recognition* (pp. 77–104). Elsevier. DOI: 10.1016/B978-012526420-4/50004-5

Van der Does, F., Van Eeden, W., Bringmann, L. F., Lamers, F., Penninx, B. W., Riese, H., Vermetten, E., Van der Wee, N., & Giltay, E. (2025). Dynamic time warp versus vector autoregression models for network analyses of psychological processes. *Scientific Reports*, *15*(1), 11720. Advance online publication. DOI: 10.1038/s41598-025-94782-9 PMID: 40188226

Vaughan, N., & Gabrys, B. (2016). Comparing and combining time series trajectories using dynamic time warping. *Procedia Computer Science*, *96*, 465–474. DOI: 10.1016/j.procs.2016.08.106

Wang, K., Begleiter, H., & Porjesz, B. (2001). Warp-averaging event-related potentials. *Clinical Neurophysiology*, *112*(10), 1917–1924. DOI: 10.1016/S1388-2457(01)00640-X PMID: 11595152

Zhang, J. (2010). Research of improved DTW algorithm in embedded speech recognition system. *2010 International Conference on Intelligent Control and Information Processing*, 73-75. DOI: 10.1109/ICICIP.2010.5564195

Zhang, N., Zhang, S., Wang, W., & Xu, Y. (2024). Implementation of Russian short command speech recognition based on dynamic time warping (DTW) technology. *2024 7th International Conference on Education, Network and Information Technology (ICENIT)*, 129-134. DOI: 10.1109/ICENIT61951.2024.00030

Zheng, H., Li, Z., Fu, Y., Katsaggelos, A. K., & You, J. (2013). Video activity recognition by luminance differential trajectory and aligned projection distance. *Handbook of Statistics*, 300-325. DOI: 10.1016/B978-0-444-53859-8.00012-6

Zoe, M. (2023). Artificial Intelligence's Contribution to English Language Teaching: Are We Asking AI the Right Questions? In Kartal (Ed.), *Transforming the language teaching experience in the age of AI* (pp. 102-114). IGI Global.

Chapter 10
Exploring the Adoption of AI Tools Among PhD Students at Ibn Tofail University: A Quantitative Study

Nouhaila Bentatou
https://orcid.org/0009-0001-0946-0818
Ibn Tofail University, Morocco

Hamid Ait Lemqeddem
https://orcid.org/0009-0007-1270-9286
Ibn Tofail University, Morocco

ABSTRACT

This article explores the use of artificial intelligence (AI) tools among doctoral students at Ibn Tofail University, focusing on their perceived impact on research quality and training needs. A quantitative survey of 30 students revealed high AI adoption: 93.3% use ChatGPT, 50% Grammarly, and 20% QuillBot. Despite these figures, all respondents expressed a strong need for structured training to develop digital literacy and responsible usage. While AI tools assist in writing, paraphrasing, and content generation, their potential is limited by ethical concerns and lack of formal guidance. The study highlights the importance of implementing targeted, discipline-specific programs to ensure effective and ethical integration of AI in doctoral education. These findings contribute to the broader discussion on digital transformation in higher education and illustrate how AI is beginning to reshape academic research practices.

DOI: 10.4018/979-8-3373-3436-3.ch010

INTRODUCTION

Background and Motivation of the Study

Artificial intelligence (AI) is fundamentally transforming the landscape of academic research by automating a range of complex processes, enhancing analytical precision, and accelerating the production of knowledge. Increasingly, AI tools are being integrated at every stage of the research cycle—from literature review to modeling and data visualization—providing researchers across disciplines with unprecedented support. This evolution is part of a broader global trend of digital transformation in higher education, which is reshaping not only how research is conducted, but also how knowledge is disseminated and evaluated.

In higher education institutions, especially at the doctoral level, there is strong pressure on researchers to produce high-quality work in ways that are efficient, especially given the challenges of time and resources. The process of completing research is often laborious and time-consuming. The advent of AI-based solutions are changing traditional components of research (e.g., data collection, analysis, literature synthesis, and even writing papers) and enhancing traditional research processes. AI not only represents a new technological innovation, it serves as a new strategic resource that can improve research productivity and increase research contestedness in a global sense.

The development of generative AI models like ChatGPT coupled with new, AI-based tools like Grammarly, Elicit, and QuillBot, have reduced the barrier to access advanced AI capabilities. These tools support researchers with language, ideas, paraphrasing, summarizing, and discovering literature, and reduce the barrier to access for researchers, especially for those who may not have technical experience. More importantly, these tools allow scholars from non-technical domains, such as the humanities and social sciences, to leverage AI's potential beyond research done in traditional, technical fields like the STEM domains.

Nevertheless, the democratization of AI presents opportunities and challenges. While capabilities in AI tools can lead to improved quality and efficiencies with research, the effective use of these tools requires a baseline of digital literacy and critical literacy. Many doctoral students and early-career researchers lack any structured training or even the development of the basic competencies to be able to interepret and maximize these tools. There is a disconnect from the affordance of AI tools to their optimized use in academic research workflows.

In Morocco, the COVID-19 pandemic necessitated the deployment of digital tools in educational contexts, including at the university level, such as Ibn Tofail University of Kenitra, as well as at the level of students, more broadly. The pandemic catalyzed the need for digital transformation (Baba et al., 2025) on an urgent basis in the context of both teaching and research. In spite of institutional projects underway to use digital technologies, AI tools are incorporated inconsistently and inadequately into doctoral research training. Faculty are realizing interest in AI as are doctoral students, though their support structure development to support practical use continues to lag behind the technology.

Doctoral students occupy a distinctive space in the academic ecology, being early career researchers who are seekers of AI tools, and potentially becoming creators of new innovations. However, many doctoral students lack experience and institutional support, and something as complex as AI-enhanced research practices offers unique challenges. Therefore, it is important to understand how doctoral students perceive, adopt, implement, and integrate AI into their academic practices. This will help institutions to identify enablers and blockers, tailor training courses to actual requirements, and accelerate responsible and effective AI practices.

Research Problem

The utilization of AI tools in doctoral research is a relatively new and under-explored trend. Internationally, there are discussions exploring the ethical, technical, and epistemological issues of AI in higher education, but there is limited empirical research about the experiences of early-career researchers. Doctoral students' requirements to generate original, rigorous knowledge while adhering to tight timelines present specific challenges and opportunities for engaging with AI.

While research teams and doctoral students have access to AI technology, many will not be able to engage with or use this technology to its fullest capacity. A lack of usability skills, doubts about integrity, and absence of formal training will hinder the thoughtful, comprehensive, or cautious application of AI. When AI tools fail to be utilized to their full extent, we lose the advantages that AI could bring to doctoral research quality and efficiency

As such the primary research problem for this study is to consider to what extent doctoral students at Ibn Tofail University are using AI tools in their academic work, and what training considerations are required to optimize this usage?

Study Objectives

The purpose of this study is to investigate the engagement of doctoral students with AI tools through the following specific objectives:

1. Identify the types of AI tools most commonly used by doctoral students at Ibn Tofail University during their research activities.
2. Evaluate the frequency and intensity of AI tool usage among participants.

3. Assess students' perceptions regarding the usefulness and impact of AI tools on research quality.
4. Analyze the specific training needs expressed by doctoral students to enhance their effective use of AI technologies.
5. Test the hypothesis that while students perceive AI tools as beneficial, their adoption is constrained by insufficient training.

Hypotheses

The study is based upon the following hypotheses:

- **H1:** Doctoral students believe that the use of AI tools can improve the quality of their research work.
- **H2:** The adoption of AI tools is limited by a lack of technical skills and appropriate training among doctoral students.

Article Structure

This article has been structured to progress logically from theory to practice.

- The literature review in Section 2 situates study within the more extensive conversation regarding AI in higher education, detailing opportunities and constraints.
- Section 3 explains how the study was developed, including how it was designed, sampling, data collection instruments, and the development of an analytical approach.
- Section 4 reports findings from the survey conducted among 30 PhD students from Ibn Tofail University.
- Section 5 discusses the findings in light of existing literature and with practical implications.
- In Section 6, the article summarizes key takeaways, highlights limitations, and recommends future research and/or action by institutions.

By providing an empirical investigation into AI tool adoption among doctoral students, this article contributes to the expanding body of knowledge on digital transformation in higher education. It also offers practical insights for academic institutions, policymakers, and doctoral programs seeking to support emerging researchers in navigating the evolving digital research environment.

LITERATURE REVIEW

Artificial intelligence (AI) has become a valuable agent for academic research, with the potential to improve research productivity, efficiency, and quality for researchers. This literature review examines the role of AI tools in academic research in relation to doctoral students and the implication of training prerequisites. Although AI technology is more available to many researchers, the literature suggests that optimal use of the technologies has been limited due to lacking training, complexity of the technologies, and ethics. For doctoral students involved in knowledge generation and research competencies, AI is both a challenge and a supported opportunity. AI technology, for instance, can help decrease repetitive tasks, support the overall language quality improvement, and support better analysis of text - but only if the user has the appropriate skills or knowledge to be usefully critical. The following section then attends to three categories; the role of AI technology in academic research, the barriers to use by doctoral students, and the training and needs required to support effective and ethical use. These three categories are informed by recent empirical studies and conceptual work, which will lead to subsequent related fieldwork at Ibn Tofail University.

The Use of AI in Academic Research

In academic research, Artificial Intelligence (AI) is a game-changing occurrence that has altered how researchers search for literature, analyze data, write papers, and distribute scientific content. Researchers across many disciplines are beginning to benefit from the AI capacity to process complex datasets, create new insights, and allow the automation of monotonous tasks. Lu et al. (2018) provide examples of AI in action that speed up the time to discovery and analysis of large datasets in the biomedical sciences, as well as the entire production of academic research. Topol (2019) describes how 'machine learning models' can be used for speedier diagnostics and individualized treatment plans in biomedical research. Learned social scientists or educators, can leverage technology based on AI like natural language processing (NLP) tools including but not limited to sentiment analysis or text mining to provide interpretation of qualitative data (Smutny & Schreiberova, 2020; Zhang et al., 2023).

Many AI-driven initiatives are now ingrained in PhD students' research. Widely-used software, like ChatGPT, provides ideation and summation capabilities, whereas Grammarly and QuillBot eradicate language inaccuracies (Van Dis et al., 2023; Tran, Le, & Tran, 2025). Augmented literature discovery and synthesis for academic writing has allowed AI to reduce the cognitive burden placed on students completing their PhD research, especially for non-native English speakers (Li et al., 2024).

AI is increasingly integrated into the research and publication process via academic databases and publication platforms. This amalgamation can be interpreted as AI transferring from an external support to an integral part of scholars' workflows (Venkatesh & Bala, 2008; Tran, Le, & Tran, 2025).

While AI adoption varies by discipline, STEM disciplines are generally at the forefront in part because those disciplines generally have more digital access and literacy than social sciences, which in turn has more than the humanities, probably due in part to methodological disputes and lack of training (Davis, 1989; Creswell & Creswell, 2017; Popenici & Kerr, 2017; Zawacki-Richter et al., 2019). This variation across disciplines does require specific approaches to AI adoption in research.

Challenges and Barriers to AI Adoption

While the acceptance of AI tools has been encouraging, there are still barriers in the way of them being broadly employed by doctoral students and academic researchers.

The first major barrier is inadequate training. For many researchers, there is a significant gap in their understanding of both the theory and practical application of these AI tools. For instance, in many social science-based fields (where formal training in AI may be limited), researchers may not use the AI functionalities to its fullest extent, or misuse the AI functionality altogether (Creswell & Creswell, 2017; Kasneci et al., 2023). Some doctoral students may use AI tools like ChatGPT or QuillBot without realizing the complexities or limitations of the AI, especially if the students are using the tools without any structure or support (Lund et al., 2023).

The second barrier is the technical complexity of AI. The functionalities of machine learning algorithms, text mining, predictive modeling and data analytics have significant mathematical and programming demands that aren't usually provided in non-STEM curriculums (Hair Jr. et al., 2019; Tran, Le, & Tran, 2025). If institutional support for AI tools isn't present, many researchers decide to abandon the AI tools altogether, simply because they know their familiar traditional methods (Davis, 1989).

Thirdly, ambiguity in ethics poses a significant challenge. AI in content generation and processing sensitive data raises concerns about authorship, originality, and transparency. Doctoral students often raise questions about total use, specifically if there is not an established institutional policy on plagiarism or data protection (Topol, 2019; Floridi & Cowls, 2022; Van Dis et al., 2023). Algorithmic bias and unintended misuse can compromise research integrity (O'Neil, 2016).

Financial and infrastructure limitations create the next barrier to the widespread implementation of AI, especially in developing contexts. Many research institutes have access only to unreliable internet connectivity, lack licensed software, or have limited computing capability, and over 40% of PhD students in these regions report that infrastructure is a significant barrier (Lu et al., 2018; Ade-Ibijola & Okonkwo, 2023).

Finally, cultural dimensions and institutional inertia play a role. Supervisors may display skepticism or be uninformed about AI technologies discouraging students from exploring AI technologies. Therefore, doctoral students are likely to follow the latitudinal practices their supervisors expect on the basis of previous experience, maintaining the status quo and restricting experimentation with AI tools (Venkatesh & Bala, 2008; Kalim et al., 2025).

Training Needs to Optimize AI Adoption

Doctoral students—and researchers more generally—require explicit, context-focused training that not only teaches them what to do (how to use an AI-based tool) but also encourages a critical lens regarding the role of AI and its implications on research. This task is particularly challenging for doctoral students, who need to learn to negotiate the intricacies of conducting original research and the intricacies of applying research design principles and methods using extraordinarily complex digital tools. Preparation for successful training and integration of AI and AI-based tools into research process training is essential and warranted.

According to Creswell and Creswell (2017) training and research methods learning for students must be reframed to include an aspect of AI literacy, which ultimately will help students confidence in their ideas of AI, including what it can do and cannot do. Training students on AI and technology should not be limited to a 30-minute orientation to guide them through using an AI tool, but rather invoke deeper and more layered questions about when, how, and why to use AI when conducting research processes. For students to develop their ability to use AI through a critical lens will help empirically support and immune the shallow, irrational employment of AI and the negative impact that may follow in the quality of their research.

Giving consideration to these types of matters may better support students in utilizing artificial intelligence (AI) in their academic pursuits. From this perspective, experience with, and practical, hands-on, learning is generally more effective than curriculum that is more descriptive, especially in theory-laden learning contexts. Hair Jr, Page, and Brunsveld (2019) discuss facilitating flexibility and inclusive, interactive learning modes of training, such as workshops, seminars, and project-based learning, which may be offered with an open-ended question in mind, recognizing that students learn about learning in their discipline. For instance, a beginning doctoral student might begin with foundational knowledge in AI, such as natural language processing (NLP) methods and data visualization to help ease into AI as a topic for study, whereas a more experienced researcher might contextualize AI in a more complex way, such as thoughtfully integrating AI into a quantitative data analysis or predictive model, or using it for manuscript planning and peer-reviews.

There is also consensus that some sort of convergence of instructional ethics into learning where AI is involved is important. Topol (2019) suggests, one of the best ways to have doctoral students consider principles of AI ethics, is to have students forewarned about the potential for the ethical recruitment of AI into practice. The ethical dilemma includes plagiarism, data privacy, and potential unintentional algorithmic bias. Positioning ethical education around AI enhances a student's ability to engage with AI in a more reliable and transparent way. This positioning strengthens the ethical rigor of well-researched academic standards, as well as providing an opportunity for the student to practice the justification and defense of their methodological decision-making, in an academic context.

Institutional support is again important for the success of engaging in AI education. Venkatesh & Bala (2008) suggest that investment in AI training centers, interdisciplinary mentoring and workgroups, along with access to computing needs through technology and software, can strongly support the prospect of some sustainability and rich integration of AI into doctoral education--or in any structure. Regardless of how much institutional support exists, institutions that enhance students' competencies with AI by providing support for the exploration of experimentation, innovation, and contribution to the ever-changing landscape of research, will support development that comes out of confidence, experimentation, and risk-taking

Finally, it is crucial to consider the disciplinary context in training. As noted earlier, AI tools and applications vary, respectively, by discipline. For social or human sciences disciplines, training might lean into, say, bibliometric mapping and discourse analysis; conversely, a more Stem-like experience might invoke more algorithm design and validation processes. By identifying and adapting to these training distinctions, we maximize relevance needs and experiential impact by allowing and facilitating the doctoral students to meaningfully mobilize AI in a way that fosters a trajectory of their respective research programs.

Conclusion to the Literature Review

We have considered the implications for the increasing use of AI tools in academic research, and in particular notable ways for which AI can be useful (as opposed to simple beneficial) in research i.e. extreme data analysis and extreme complexity bibliographic or referential based research and regarding automating processes (i.e. adding footnotes and managing bibliographic content). Although there is thus an apparent great benefit for AI, and all of that is couched in a potential benefit there are enhancing barriers. These can take the form of poorly trained, complexity of the tools, ethical issues, and lack of and/or poor systems/infrastructural development.

Though many of the students in doctoral programs are more cognizant of the potential benefit and value of AI, they have received insufficient preparation in this regard. The extant reviews of the literature tell us that in order to address those barriers, we need broad structured and discipline specific training programs. Additionally, institutions need to be proactive and supportive of the development of a digital culture, and provide support and ethical understanding to ensure that students engaged in doctoral research can safely and productively use AI.

This literature review provided the theoretical basis for understanding the practices and challenges of AI usage in doctoral research and as an impetus for the empirical analysis of the perspectives and experiences of PhD students at Ibn Tofail University.

METHODS

Type of Research

This study utilizes a quantitative approach as it is particularly useful for measuring exactly how often an observable variable occurs, perceptions of usefulness, and training needs. Data is collected and analyzed objectivity, there is a desire to generalise to a coherent level of patterns and relationships through statistical analysis. The objective of this study is to explore how doctoral students at Ibn Tofail University use AI tools and what barriers and support needs may exist.

Quantitative research enables capturing standardized responses from a relatively large number of participants while minimizing researcher bias; and can offer a numeric description of the possible relationship of variables, in adopting the use of the AI tools, being a consistent use of the AI tool, frequency of using AI tool, preferred AI tools and training needs.

While a range of qualitative methods, such as interviews or case studies, may have provided something of greater descriptive depth; however, remarking as this is an exploratory study and the institutional context necessitates greater foresight and vision, it was likely to be helpful to have quantitative data later as baseline of understanding participant user experience and perceptions in the future mixed-methods literature.

Population and Sampling

The target population consisted of doctoral students who were enrolled at Ibn Tofail University during the 2024–2025 academic year. This population was chosen because they are likely to be engaged in academic research and be more used to digital tools. Their unique position as doctoral students places them as both knowledge producers and customers, and therefore they are an appropriate population to examine the use of AI and other emerging technologies within research workflows.

The study's sampling procedure was non-probability convenience sampling, in that participants were selected based on their availability and willingness to participate in the research. Convenience sampling is often used in exploratory research, particularly during their doctoral journey which had temporal and financial constraints.

The limitation of using this convenience sampling approach means that while the data may not be statistically representative of the entire doctoral student population for generalization, it is useful for the identification of the initial trends and the aspects of interesting patterns. As a sample, a total of thirty participants formed the final sample, which is typical practice in early studies on educational technologies (Hair et al., 2021).

Demographic information (age, gender, field of study, year of doctoral studies) were also collected from participants. This additional measure made it possible for the researchers to cross-tabulate demographic data and analyze the data with subgroup measure, as well.

Data Collection Instrument

The primary means of data collection was an online structured questionnaire, which was intended to collect quantitative and qualitative data. It was divided into sections directed at collecting information about demographics, ways of using AI, perceived advantages and disadvantages, and training needs.

The questionnaire operationalized a range of closed-ended questions (Likert scales, dichotomous yes/no questions, and frequency indicators) along with open-ended questions that allowed respondents to elaborate on their perspectives. The mixed questionnaire structure effectively developed the dataset by collecting informative data on measurable patterns along with personalized experiences.

The tool was devised from well-known models used to evaluate technology, namely the Technology Acceptance Model (Davis, 1989) and later extensions (Venkatesh & Bala, 2008). The items were amended in the context of AI tools in academic research and, appropriately for the doctoral experience.

To ensure validity and clarity, a pilot test was conducted with five doctoral students. Their feedback led to minor adjustments in question wording and sequence. Furthermore, reliability testing was performed using Cronbach's alpha for multi-item scales, confirming acceptable internal consistency.

Data Collection Method

The questionnaire was administered via Google Forms, a secure and widely used online survey platform. The data collection process was conducted over a two-week period, during which doctoral students were invited to participate through institutional mailing lists, WhatsApp groups for doctoral candidates, and faculty research networks.

Participation was entirely voluntary and anonymous. Prior to accessing the questionnaire, each participant was presented with a digital informed consent form, which explained the study's objectives, the confidential nature of responses, and their right to withdraw at any time. No personal identifiers were collected.

The study fully complied with the ethical guidelines of the university's internal research committee and followed General Data Protection Regulation (GDPR) principles to ensure participant confidentiality and responsible data handling.

Three reminders were sent during the collection period to maximize participation, resulting in a complete dataset of 30 responses. There were no missing values, which increased the reliability of the next analyses.

Data Analysis

The data were transferred to SPSS (Statistical Package for the Social Sciences), version 26, where they were cleaned and transformed into coded data to conduct statistical analyses. The analysis occurred through several steps:

1. Descriptive statistics (means, standard deviations, frequency distributions) were used to summarize demographic data and general patterns of AI tool usage.
2. Cross-tabulations allowed for the exploration of relationships between categorical variables, such as gender and tool preference or year of study and training needs.
3. Inferential statistics, including chi-square tests and Pearson correlation coefficients, were applied to test the study's hypotheses regarding perceptions of AI utility and the impact of training availability on tool usage.
4. Thematic content analysis was conducted on open-ended responses to identify recurring themes related to user experiences, perceived obstacles, and preferred training formats.

Using quantitative and qualitative analyses ensured both statistical robustness and contextual relevance. The analysis and results were presented in charts, frequency tables, and graphs for clarity and interpretability.

RESULTS

The results obtained from the questionnaire given to PhD students at the Ibn Tofail University, are descriptively presented in this section relative to usage of artificial intelligence (AI) tools, understanding the perceived benefits and limitations of using these technologies, and what training PhD students need. The results are organized into five sub-sections, which are demographic profile, usage patterns, tool preferences, perceived benefits, and training needs.

Descriptive Analysis of Respondents

Before we present the results of the specific questions, we will briefly outline the characteristics of the sample that we studied. The sample included 30 doctoral students who were enrolled at Ibn Tofail University. The breakdown by gender, field of study and year of study is shown below.

Figure 1. Descriptive Statistics of the Variables Studied.

Statistiques univariées

	N	Moyenne	Ecart type	Manquant		Nombre d'extrêmes[a]	
				Effectif	Pourcentage	Faible	Elevée
Age	30	32,70	10,583	0	,0	0	1
Annéededoctorat	30	2,33	,661	0	,0	0	0
Genre	30			0	,0		
Domainederecherche	30			0	,0		
UtilisationIA	30			0	,0		
OutilChatGPT	30			0	,0		
OutilGrammarlly	30			0	,0		
OutilQuillBot	30			0	,0		
AutresOutils	30			0	,0		
Fréquencedutilisation	30			0	,0		
AméliorationRecherche	30			0	,0		
FormationIA	30			0	,0		

a. Nombre d'observations en dehors de la plage autorisée (Q1 - 1.5*IQR, Q3 + 1.5*IQR).

Source: SPSS

Participants' ages averaged at 32.70 years, with a standard deviation of 10.58, with these indicators reflecting a moderate degree of variability in the age distributions. A supporting finding for the typical profile for doctoral students, sometimes identified as "adult learners", tends to include a wide variety of backgrounds, academically and professionally. The upper outlier will yield one participant, registered at a young sixty-three (63) years of age, which is significantly beyond the mean of the group and reflects the sense of challenges by linear or trajectory based models for doctoral study when people may choose to re-enter an advanced journey of education at any time in their life. There is also not an upper limit of age in doctoral studies, students are not returning from being employed and then pursuing doctoral education after many years, for example, mid-career to take on deficits of education, or having taking time away from education, or simply decided before, or just after, multi-decade long steady workforce. There are challenges in that diversity to evolution and cultivation of rich research study culture, but also indicated there likely will be different rates of digital fluency as well as introductions to AI in those tool.

Years of Doctoral Progression

Average time in the doctoral program was 2.33 years (SD = 0.66), and little variability across the sample was found. Reported average values reflect a greater level of homogeneity in this sense, as this means the majority were at some point in the middle of their doctoral degree or quite close to the end. The absence of outlier values indicates that this group likely provided a consistent representation of student status or academic seniority. This distribution was especially pertinent to the research study because the students in their second or third year would be expected to engage more actively with the research process, and thus would also be more inclined to use more advanced tools such as AI applications for data collection, analysis, writing, and synthesizing literature. Additionally, they still would be appropriately situated in their educational journey, having also engaged with other institutional contexts of knowledge production, in conducting richer ruminations on their utilization of AI tools during their academic work.

Gender and Field of Research

Data regarding gender and field of study of participants were both fully collected; there were no missing responses on either variable. Because we have these variables as categorical variables, we will further examine these two attributes through cross-tabulation analyses to look for any relationships to the patterns of use for AI tools. This analysis will provide valuable insights into the extent to which disciplinary background and/or gender identity, for example, might be related to doctoral students' frequency of use, purpose of AI tools, or type of usage of AI tools. Understanding this data will help shape individualized training and support to ensure equity of access, knowledge of, or comfort with AI tools, depending on student characteristics across demographic and academic lines.

Use of Artificial Intelligence Tools

Variables regarding the use of AI tools, such as ChatGPT, Grammarly, QuillBot, etc. also have no missing data. These will be used to analyze, how often they are used and PhD students' preferences regarding the use of AI technologies.

Frequency of Use and Perception of AI

Variables that relate to the frequency with which AI tools are used, the perceived impact to enhance research, and interest in particular training to engage with the new AI technologies, are complete as well. These responses will help us learn more about PhD students' habits and needs around artificial intelligence.

The age distribution of the participants is represented by the moustache box below. The median age is around 30, with an interquartile range from 25 to 40. An outlier is observed at 69, corresponding to a participant much older than the others. Although this value is extreme, it is consistent with the fact that the doctorate imposes no age limit.

Figure 2. Whisker box: 1D from Age Source: IGI (2014)

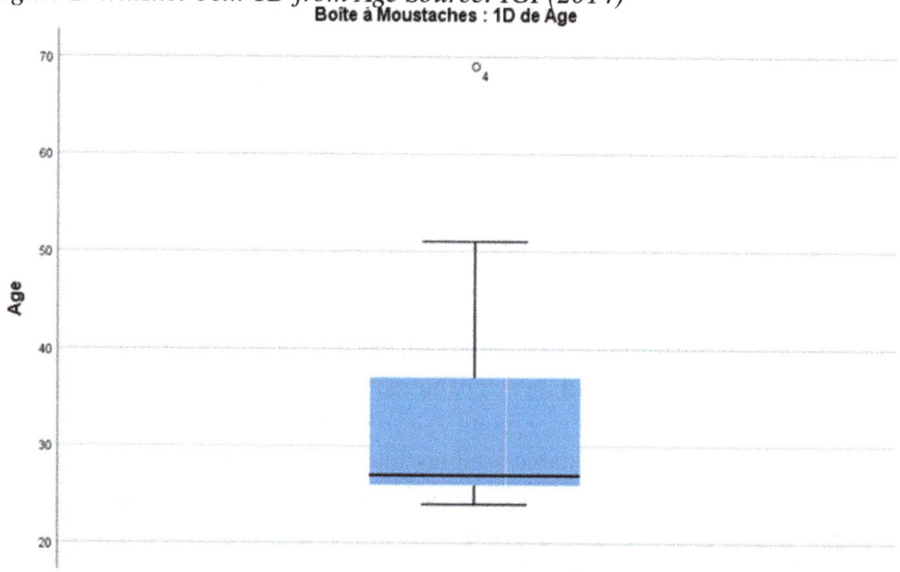

Source: SPSS

Use of Artificial Intelligence Tools

The table below presents descriptive statistics on the frequency of use of artificial intelligence tools and the specific use of certain tools (ChatGPT, Grammarly, QuillBot, and others). The 30 responses collected are complete and valid, with no missing data. This guarantees the reliability of the analyses that follow.

Figure 3. Statistics

Statistiques

		Fréquence d'utilisation	Utilisation de ChatGPT	Utilisation de Grammarly	Utilisation de QuilBot	Utilisation d'autres outils
N	Valide	30	30	30	30	30
	Manquant	0	0	0	0	0

Source: SPSS

The following table shows the breakdown of respondents by frequency of use of artificial intelligence tools. Among the 30 participants:

Analysis of this table reveals that the majority of respondents (56.7%) use AI tools several times a week. This indicates a regular adoption of these technologies, probably linked to their usefulness in improving productivity and quality of work. However, a minority (26.7%) use them only rarely, which may reflect barriers such as lack of training, absence of perceived need or reluctance to use these tools.

On the other hand, 16.7% of respondents report daily use, reflecting a thorough integration of these tools into their usual practices. This includes users with a high level of technology competence, or those people that use these tools as essential elements in their academic or professional activities.

Figure 4. Frequency of use

Fréquence d'utilisation

		Fréquence	Pourcentage	Pourcentage valide	Pourcentage cumulé
Valide	Rarement	8	26,7	26,7	26,7
	Plusieurs fois par semaine	17	56,7	56,7	83,3
	Quotidiennement	5	16,7	16,7	100,0
	Total	30	100,0	100,0	

Source: SPSS

Use of ChatGPT

Table is below to show the proportion of respondents using or not using the ChatGPT tool.

Figure 5. ChatGPT use

Utilisation de ChatGPT

		Fréquence	Pourcentage	Pourcentage valide	Pourcentage cumulé
Valide	Non	2	6,7	6,7	6,7
	Oui	28	93,3	93,3	100,0
	Total	30	100,0	100,0	

Source: SPSS

The analysis demonstrates a significant use of ChatGPT, with 93.3% of respondents, claiming they have used ChatGPT, and only 6.7% indicated no use of ChatGPT. This represents very high use of this tool, likely due to ChatGPT's versatility as well as its capabilities in supporting a diversity of academic and professional needs.

The high use rate observed may also be indicative of the growing popularity of ChatGPT in some research fields, especially for synthesis, writing, grammar checking, and content augmentation tasks that are common in research projects. It is possible the 6.7% respondents had preferences for other technologies or tools, or perhaps these respondents had no familiarity with the technology.

Overall, these results go to illustrate the perceived importance of ChatGPT as a central and relevant tool to current practices associated with artificial intelligence. The significant use reported by the majority of respondents illustrates ChatGPT is likely to continue being an important resource integrated into their work processes.

Use of Grammarly

The table below reveals the breakdown of respondents' use of the Grammarly tool.

Figure 6. Grammarly use

Utlisation de Grammarly

		Fréquence	Pourcentage	Pourcentage valide	Pourcentage cumulé
Valide	Non	15	50,0	50,0	50,0
	Oui	15	50,0	50,0	100,0
	Total	30	100,0	100,0	

Source: SPSS

Results analysis indicates equal distribution of usability: 50% of respondents use it, and 50% do not use it. This equal distribution could represent a moderate level of usage of Grammarly in academic or professional activities overall.

Grammarly usage could be influenced by some factors including respondents' need for grammar or spell checking, proficiency with the language, familiarity with other tools such as ChatGPT or QuillBot, etc.

The fact that one in two respondents does not use it might also reflect a preference for other tools, or that Grammarly is perceived as less compatible with their needs. It may also indicate barriers related to access (ex. a cost or access issue with regard to their language - Grammarly is designed for English primarily).

Using QuillBot

The table below depicts how the respondents utilize the QuillBot tool.

Figure 7. QuillBot use

Utilisation de QuilBot

		Fréquence	Pourcentage	Pourcentage valide	Pourcentage cumulé
Valide	Non	24	80,0	80,0	80,0
	Oui	6	20,0	20,0	100,0
	Total	30	100,0	100,0	

Source: SPSS

Of the 30 participants in the study, 6 (20.0%) said they used QuillBot, while 24 (80.0%) did not. These results indicate that the majority of respondents do not use the tool.

This distribution shows a low adoption of QuillBot among participants, compared with other artificial intelligence tools such as ChatGPT.

Use of Other Tools

The table below shows the breakdown of respondents' use of other tools.

Figure 8. Other tools use

Utilisation d'autres outils

		Fréquence	Pourcentage	Pourcentage valide	Pourcentage cumulé
Valide	Non	23	76,7	76,7	76,7
	Oui	7	23,3	23,3	100,0
	Total	30	100,0	100,0	

Source: SPSS

Among the participants, 76.7% (23 people) say they do not use other artificial intelligence tools in their research. On the other hand, 23.3% (7 people) say they do. The results show that most PhD students in the study are using tools that are familiar and commonly used, with only a small percentage of students looking to other tools as a means to meet a specific need or to diversify their tool usage.

Perceived Benefits of AI in Research

The question on respondents' perception of the possible impact of AI on the quality of their research produced the following findings:

Figure 9. Statistics

Statistiques

l'IA peut-elle améliorer vos recherches ?

N	Valide	30
	Manquant	0

Source: SPSS

Of the 30 participants, 96.7 percent (29 people) felt that AI could aid in improving their research, while 3.3 percent (1 person) did not. These findings demonstrate a primarily positive perception of the potential benefits of AI for academic research and an overall high interest in adopting AI and integrating it into research practices.

Figure 10. Impact perçu de l'IA sur les recherches des doctorants

l'IA peut-elle améliorer vos recherches ?

		Fréquence	Pourcentage	Pourcentage valide	Pourcentage cumulé
Valide	0	1	3,3	3,3	3,3
	1	29	96,7	96,7	100,0
	Total	30	100,0	100,0	

Source: SPSS

The table shows the results of the question concerning the potential impact of artificial intelligence (AI) in the context of research activities. Out of 30 respondents, 29 (96.7%) responded positively, indicating they believe that AI can improve their research. Only one respondent (3.3%) disagreed with the premise.

This suggests a clear consensus amongst respondents with regard to the notion that artificial intelligence has the potential to significantly enhance and positively impact their research practices. This response also demonstrates an alignment with confident attitudes toward advanced digital technologies, as well as a general acceptance of the potential application of AI technologies in research.

Training Needs

Participants were asked about their training needs to effectively use AI tools. The results show:

Figure 11. Impact perçu de l'IA sur les recherches des doctorants

Statistiques

Souhaitez-vous recevoir une formation pour mieux utiliser l'IA ?		
N	Valide	30
	Manquant	0

Source: SPSS

The table indicates that there were 30 participants who answered the question regarding if they wished to receive training to better use artificial intelligence.

Figure 12. Doctoral Students' Interest in Training on AI Utilization

Souhaitez-vous recevoir une formation pour mieux utiliser l'IA ?

		Fréquence	Pourcentage	Pourcentage valide	Pourcentage cumulé
Valide	1	30	100,0	100,0	100,0

Source: SPSS

The table indicates that all the participants (30 out of 30) answered the question and desire training to use artificial intelligence more effectively, represented at 100% for valid responses. As noted, there are no missing responses (0 value in the 'Missing' column).

This indicates consistent readiness among participants to receive training on the use of AI. This also marks strong interest in gaining AI skills, and an acknowledgement of the increasing prominence of AI technology in professional or academic use.

Hypothesis Analysis

We will now test the following hypotheses:

Hypothesis 1: 'Doctoral students at Ibn Tofail University believe that AI could improve the quality of their research.'

Figure 13. Perception of AI's Impact on Improving Research

l'IA peut-elle améliorer vos recherches ?

		Fréquence	Pourcentage	Pourcentage valide	Pourcentage cumulé
Valide	0	1	3,3	3,3	3,3
	1	29	96,7	96,7	100,0
	Total	30	100,0	100,0	

Source: SPSS

As shown in the results, 96.7% of respondents agree that AI could aid in improving the quality of their research. What is shown confirms the hypothesis.

Hypothesis 2: 'Doctoral students at Ibn Tofail University use AI tools, but their usage is limited by a lack of training.'

Figure 14. Cross-tabulation: Use of AI-based Tools in Research and Willingness to Receive Training

Tableau croisé Utilisez-vous des outils basés sur l'intelligence artificielle dans vos recherches ? * Souhaitez-vous recevoir une formation pour mieux utiliser l'IA ?

Effectif

		Souhaitez-vous recevoir une formation pour mieux utiliser l'IA ?	
		1	Total
Utilisez-vous des outils basés sur l'intelligence artificielle dans vos recherches ?	Non	1	1
	Oui	29	29
Total		30	30

Source: SPSS

While most respondents (93.3%) are using AI tools, none (100%) do not feel sufficient in regards to training or do not use these tools, and this lends support to the hypothesis that use is limited by training.

Summary of Results

Results suggest all respondents (100%) use AI tools in their research process; however, their frequency of use appears limited for the majority of PhD students. That said, 96.7% of respondents view AI as a way to have greater quality research outcomes, which underscores the strong potential of these tools in academia. Lastly, 100% of respondents indicated they want more training so they can maximize the use of AI. The findings highlight the importance of laying down appropriate training avenues so that AI tools become a useful part of our academic work.

In the remaining part of this report, we will present a full analysis of the data gathered by the questionnaire addressed to the PhD students at Ibn Tofail University. The results revealed keen interest in AI tools, but also the need for training to maximize use. The research question was, in part, supported by the findings, and support for the assumptions regarding the expected impact AI could have on research quality, and the creation of need for training was confirmed.

DISCUSSION

The research's conclusions provide insightful viewpoints on how doctoral students at Ibn Tofail University employ human recommendations for AI tools. Although the overall results point to high levels of AI usage and optimism about its future, there are notable restrictions on training, frequency, and adoption readiness. This section identifies the strategic and operational implications for post-secondary institutions, provides a more substantial sense of the findings, and places them in relation to the research literature.

General Adoption of AI Tools

The most intriguing finding was that almost all PhD students used AI tools; every respondent used at least one AI-based tool in some capacity for their academic and research endeavors. This reinforces the idea that AI is becoming a part of everyday research projects and supports the global accounts of Lu, Crookes, and McCoy (2018), who argue that AI is becoming essential for researchers worldwide in contexts with limited time and resources.

With a 93.3% uptake rate among all the tools mentioned above, ChatGPT is probably the most popular due to its perceived flexibility, accessibility, and language generation and refinement features. Like other large language models, ChatGPT is intuitive in this regard, and is something people can use without a background in terms of technology or technical knowledge. This may be especially beneficial for researchers in non-STEM fields to take some risk and engage with a new AI tool. Grammarly has a much less lopsided uptake, reflects a 50% uptake while a tool for just paraphrasing like QuillBot has much less use at 20%. This seems to confirm that tools for professional and for paraphrasing experience rather evenly and users may have a preference for a professional word processor. It is also noteworthy that academic researchers selecting academic resources seem to have preference for paraphrasing tools rather than general content generation like ChatGPT.

The fluctuation in the tools indicates a fluctuation in digital maturation of students. Students seem to use AI tools to different depths or levels of engagement (e.g., every day, perhaps, or less careful use). This engagement falls within the types of typologies of user profiles elaborated on by Jarrahi (2018) as AI adopters are domain-specific and depending on certain factors determined by the methodological approach that members of that approach are trained in. Thus, understanding where the students fit in to or between the user profiles delineated above is important for the purpose of building responsive training and support systems.

Positive Perception of AI Benefits

The majority of respondents (96.7%) agree that AI tools are beneficial for their research: they agree that AI tools improve quality in their work. This aligns with Topol (2019), who stated that AI improves efficiency, especially for lengthy processes like data analysis and medical diagnosis, and, by analogy, academic writing. This perception may be influenced by the concrete time savings that AI tools offer, especially in literature synthesis, language correction, and paraphrasing.

Importantly, these positive perceptions transcend disciplines. This points to a paradigm shift in how AI is viewed—not merely as a computational or engineering asset but as a transversal research enabler. AI is no longer confined to technical fields but is increasingly being leveraged in the humanities and social sciences, where it can assist with text analysis, discourse mapping, and bibliographic mining (Jarrahi, 2018).

However, it is important to note that a positive perception does not necessarily equate to competent usage. The difference between perceived usefulness and actual ability to use it provides further credibility to the discussion about using perceived ease of use in this fashion because according to Venkatesh and Bala (2008) perceived ease of use needs training and contextual use to secure technology acceptance and proper use.

Critical Need for Training

A noteworthy takeaway is that all participants expressed some need for training (100%), suggesting that even with access to AI tools, doctoral students frequently do not feel prepared to use them properly. This finding is consistent with the work of Jarrahi (2018) and van Dis et al. (2021), who indicate that access to AI tools is only part of the solution for successfully embedding AI into academic workflows; user competencies and organized learning opportunities are equally important.

The needs students have identified themselves include both lower and higher level skills, including finding and understanding tools, to critically appraising their outputs, to using them ethically. In response, a tiered approach will need to be undertaken in the development of modules for training based on varying proficiency levels and needs based on disciplines. For example, doctoral students in engineering and sciences may wish to have practice training opportunities with algorithmic AI and data modeling, whereas, students in areas of the social sciences may find practice training focused on natural language processing and qualitative data coding and training in ethical use of AI more relevant.

Moreover, the reported training needs not only concern technical skills but also conceptual and ethical skills. According to Floridi and Cowls (2022), responsible AI literacy should also incorporate certain content about fairness, accountability, and transparency. The increasing ubiquity of tools such as ChatGPT and QuillBot to paraphrase and/or write as students increasingly utilize these tools raises serious concerns about the potential for plagiarism, originality, and responsible citation. As universities, administrators, and faculty must proactively address these issues by integrating the ethics of using AI and ChatGPT into their digital pedagogical training and cultivating students' critical literacies to position AI tools, these risks will only grow and/or worsen.

Practical Implications for Academic Institutions

This study's affordability offers doctoral programs, institutional research support services, and university leadership helpful guidance. The use of AI tools in doctoral research, education, and edification has changed from being a stand-alone practice to being a component of a larger systemic change in the way research is conceptualized, conducted, and disseminated. The institutions that do not engage will risk the incommensurability of their doctoral education and training frameworks with the expected practices in the current research context.

In light of our finding and the reasons above, it is recommended that academic institutions develop significant interventions across at least 3 significant strategic areas:

1. Capacity Building

Beyond simple AI awareness or introductory training, we propose that doctoral schools integrate a structured program into their doctoral curriculum or relevant disciplinary training. This program could include practical workshops on technological tools (e.g., ChatGPT, Grammarly, Elicit), following experimental demonstrations and hands-on exercises, as well as discussions on potential applications of these tools in doctoral and post-doctoral research and training. These workshops would be aligned with ongoing initiatives in AI pedagogy, adapted to specific fields (literature, mathematics, science, etc.), and scaled according to user experience and disciplinary context. The ultimate goal is to equip doctoral students with operational and critical competencies to evaluate AI-generated content effectively within their research projects.

2. **Infrastructure Investment**

One major obstacle to the successful adoption of AI is still access. Institutions should invest in obtaining institutional licenses or discounted subscriptions for necessary AI-powered research tools, particularly those that can be used for research management, data analysis, academic writing, and literature discovery. Reachable One important tool for fostering inclusive academic innovation is equity, which in this context means that access to technology and support is not restricted by disciplinary or financial constraints. The lowest level of AI-based research ecosystems is dependable access to software platforms, internet connections, and cloud computing infrastructure.

3. **Policy Development and Ethical Governance**

Universities must have transparent and binding policies addressing the ethical use of AI for academic research in addition to providing helpful assistance. Authorship, academic integrity, plagiarism detection, citing AI-generated content, and what is considered appropriate use to support a particular task in the research workflow are all significant issues. In addition to facilitating responsible use and reducing uncertainty, a clearer (and legal) policy will also give faculty and students more assurance about the worth of work aided by AI.

4. **Interdisciplinary Mentorship and Peer-Led Learning Models**

and use collective learning while applying an equity framework to knowledge. Mentoring models can also help close gaps in formal academic programming, shorten the time it takes to learn useful skills at university, and improve institutional capacity-building education through collective intelligence.

In conclusion, organizations should prepare for the paradigm shift in research that artificial intelligence will bring about. They should prepare to incorporate AI into the academic research methodology, or framework, and view it as more than just an optional smart device. In order to support good researchers and prepare the next generation of academics for a different process and role in research, universities must establish the overt and ethical use of AI by doctoral scholars.

Limitations and Recommendations for Future Research

This study offers valuable understanding of doctoral students' use and understanding of AI tools but it is important to point out several limitations to help provide context for the findings and contribute to future research.

The limitations we discuss are twofold. Firstly, the sample size, (n = 30), and the process of sampling through non-probability convenience sampling techniques limit the generalizability of the findings. Although this is a common approach and suitable for exploratory research, it fundamentally limits the ability to make generalized claims about the research findings being relevant to the greater doctoral student population. Future research should address this limitation by ensuring the use of larger samples and drawing on a more representative sampling method by using stratified or random sampling techniques, to reflect the disciplinary, gender and institutional heterogeneity evident in doctoral research, both within Morocco but also across similar regionally or internationally situated contexts.

Secondly, the study is reliant predominantly on self-reported data, which brings with it the risk of response bias. The participants may have possibly overestimated their engagement with AI tools or perhaps underestimated ethical uncertainty, even if participants did not display any response bias due to social desirability or lack of concrete understanding of what was being measured. The invaluable nature of relying on subjective data tells less about the important insights regarding actual usage behaviours and attitudes that are behind these findings. To strengthen the validity and reliability of future findings, researchers are encouraged to adopt mixed-methods designs, combining surveys with qualitative interviews, focus groups, or direct observational studies. Additionally, usage analytics from AI platforms (where ethically and legally permissible) could offer objective data to triangulate self-reported information and uncover discrepancies between perceived and actual practices.

Another important avenue for future research involves the assessment of the impact of AI tools on concrete academic outcomes. While this study focuses on perceptions and usage patterns, it does not measure how AI affects key performance indicators such as publication output, thesis quality, time-to-completion, or research innovation. Longitudinal studies, in particular, could explore how sustained exposure to AI tools—especially when accompanied by structured training—affects research productivity over time. Such studies would provide empirical evidence for the effectiveness of institutional interventions and inform policy decisions on AI integration in research training.

Moreover, future research should aim to unpack demographic and disciplinary differences in AI adoption and proficiency. Variables such as gender, age, field of study, digital literacy level, and year of doctoral enrollment may shape how students perceive and interact with AI tools. For example, do students in the humanities or social sciences face greater uncertainty about the ethical implications of AI? Are female researchers or older doctoral students less confident in using AI for data analysis or writing assistance? Examining these three dimensions would allow for the development of customized, inclusive, and equitable training experiences to tackle the specific barriers for different student subgroups.

Finally, it would also be useful for future research to explore how the cultural context of the University and supervisions either support or inhibit AI use. It would be of interest to see how the use of AI by students relates to their doctoral supervisors, departmental norms, policies, and other institutional factors in relation to the institutional conditions that promote or inhibit responsible/appropriate use of AI for research.

To conclude, future research should utilize a more expansive, deeper, and more diverse empirical approach to the phenomenon of AI adoption among new researchers. By broadening the focus and consolidating the scope of empirical work in this area, the research community, and supports provided by institutions can assist doctoral students in becoming responsible, ethical, and empowered users of AI technologies.

CONCLUSION

This study provides an empirical examination of the use of artificial intelligence (AI) tools by doctoral students at Ibn Tofail University in their academic research. A quantitative survey was given to 30 participants in the study. The survey, emphasized the widespread use of AI tools, and the generally positive impressions expressed by early-career researchers. However, findings also revealed notable challenges to the utilization of AI tools, especially with regards to training, technical capabilities, and confidence associated with ethical and effective use of AI technologies in research.

The near-universal use of AI technologies such as ChatGPT, Grammarly, and Quillbot make it evident that these tools are not on the fringes of the academic research process, they have become part of the research process itself. ChatGPT, in particular was found to be the most frequently used tool of all of the respondents in the study. This implies the need or demand for tools that offer flexibility, accessibility, and user-friendly interfaces. Further, evidence of respondents' decidedly favorable perceptions of AI for research quality is notable in noting a cultural shift: AI is no longer approaching skepticism or suspicion but is more commonly regarded as an aid to legitimate scholarly productivity.

Nonetheless, the results show a notable discrepancy: while doctoral students may acknowledge the usefulness of AI tools, they have not received adequate training in their use. Everyone involved in this study expressed a desire for more training (in ethics, critical literacy, and/or technical use). Essentially, it seems that researchers and doctoral students are more likely to embrace AI on their own or informally than with institutional support, and many people do not appear to be taking advantage of the advantages of AI technologies, or worse, using them without taking academic integrity into account.

Universities must balance excitement and preparedness if they hope to effectively use AI for high-caliber research. The field of higher education is in a unique position to support the ethical, just, and significant adoption of AI. The first step is to redesign doctoral training programs to incorporate formal AI literacy education that integrates the study of critical, ethical skills with operational or applied skills. For AI training programs, workshops, peer mentoring, and interdisciplinary cooperation may be effective approaches. Second, academic institutions should create institutional guidelines for the moral application of AI in the humanities and make them accessible to all members of the institution. This could offer transparency in using AI tools to help with writing, as well as institutional clarity regarding AI-related issues like plagiarism, attribution, or authorship; bias. Third, we need to make significant investments in digital infrastructure in order to democratize access to AI technologies. In order for the adoption of AI tools to be equitable across fields and student cohorts, meaningful access is also necessary.

The function of academic supervision is another factor to take into account. According to Lee (2008), the research supervisor has a significant impact on the doctoral experience and the student's methodological decisions. In particular, discouraging the use of AI technologies just because a supervisor is ignorant of them or doubts their efficacy may be callous, if not unintentionally harmful. This effectively reduces the opportunities for creative methodology and resource utilization. Whereas supervisors incorporating AI into their research can showcase best practices and help build a culture of digital open practices that engages students. Therefore, universities into consideration the idea of AI training not just for students, but to also supervisors and academics, to help align, link, and develop consistent expectations for research for all.

Importantly, this research impacts the field of educational technology research methodologically as it provides a replicable survey-based approach to understand how doctoral students are adopting AI within a doctoral study. Researchers will be able to follow the approach we have shown here and use it to conduct larger or longitudinal studies in new institutional or cultural contexts as appropriate. It could also contribute to the development of AI-based modules as part of doctoral study curricula or national higher education approaches to developing AI curricula.

Nevertheless, the study is not without limitations. The use of a convenience sample restricts the generalizability of the results, and the relatively small sample size limits the statistical power of hypothesis testing. Additionally, the reliance on self-reported data introduces the possibility of response bias. These limitations point to the need for complementary qualitative approaches—such as in-depth interviews or focus groups—that could explore in more detail the motivations, hesitations, and practical experiences of doctoral students with AI. A mixed-methods design could provide a richer, more nuanced picture of AI adoption dynamics in academia.

Looking forward, several avenues for future research emerge. First, longitudinal studies could examine how training interventions impact the evolution of AI use and proficiency over time. Do students who receive structured training adopt AI more confidently, and do they achieve higher-quality research outputs? Second, comparative studies between institutions—both nationally and internationally—could shed light on contextual factors influencing adoption, such as language, infrastructure, academic culture, or field of study. Third, investigations into the ethical and cognitive implications of AI use—particularly in thesis writing or publication—could help define boundaries and responsibilities in AI-assisted research.

Research could also consider how AI is integrated into academic publishing and peer review. For example, it would be interesting to consider how doctoral students respond to AI-generated essays and the newly introduced feedback from journal submission platforms, as well whether they notice changes in self-efficacy related to coursework or research. A helpful companion would be an interdisciplinary investigation of how AI aids in labor division and teamwork in research groups with authors with varying backgrounds and specialties.

Furthermore, any integration of AI into academic practice must be understood as a cultural and epistemic revolution that challenges long-standing and institutionally accepted standards for authorship, originality, and human judgment in relation to knowledge production. As a result, institutional frameworks must be created to support the development of ethical, reflexive, and critical consciousness in addition to technical awareness. Then and only then will AI be able to help researchers steer clear of blind processes that result in weak, less inclusive, and highly unscientific research processes.

Ultimately, this study has demonstrated how AI tools challenge doctoral research methodologies, but it also clearly demonstrates the need for academics and institutions to be more strategic in their planning procedures. Universities will need to be proactive in developing responsible and equitable AI infrastructures, frameworks for support, training, policies, and leadership in this area of experience. Universities must ensure the next cohort of researchers have the ability to use AI tools, not just efficiently, but ethically and wisely.

ACKNOWLEDGMENT

"This work was carried out with the support of the CNRST under the 'PHD-Associate ScholarShip-PASS' program, for which we express our sincere gratitude."

REFERENCES

Ade-Ibijola, A., & Okonkwo, C. (2023). Artificial intelligence in Africa: Emerging challenges. In *Responsible AI in Africa: Challenges and opportunities* (pp. 101–117). Springer International Publishing. DOI: 10.1007/978-3-031-08215-3_5

Baba, N. E., Anasse, K., & Slimani, N. (2025). Exploring the Relationship Between Artificial Intelligence Awareness and Its Use Among Students: Cadi Ayyad University as A Case Study. *European Journal of Education and Pedagogy*, *6*(4), 22–33. DOI: 10.24018/ejedu.2025.6.4.960

Creswell, J. W., & Creswell, J. D. (2017). *Research design: Qualitative, quantitative, and mixed methods approaches*. Sage publications.

Davis, F. D. (1989). Perceived usefulness, perceived ease of use, and user acceptance of information technology. *Management Information Systems Quarterly*, *13*(3), 319–340. DOI: 10.2307/249008

Floridi, L., & Cowls, J. (2022). A unified framework of five principles for AI in society. *Machine learning and the city: Applications in architecture and urban design*, 535-545.

Hair, J.Jr, Page, M., & Brunsveld, N. (2019). *Essentials of business research methods*. Routledge. DOI: 10.4324/9780429203374

Jarrahi, M. H. (2018). Artificial intelligence and the future of work: Human-AI symbiosis in organizational decision making. *Business Horizons*, *61*(4), 577–586. DOI: 10.1016/j.bushor.2018.03.007

Kalim, U., Kanwar, A., Sha, J., & Huang, R. (2025). Barriers to AI adoption for women in higher education: A systematic review of the Asian context. *Smart Learning Environments*, *12*(1), 38. DOI: 10.1186/s40561-025-00390-5

Kasneci, E., Seßler, K., Küchemann, S., Bannert, M., Dementieva, D., Fischer, F., Gasser, U., Groh, G., Günnemann, S., Hüllermeier, E., Krusche, S., Kutyniok, G., Michaeli, T., Nerdel, C., Pfeffer, J., Poquet, O., Sailer, M., Schmidt, A., Seidel, T., & Kasneci, G. (2023). ChatGPT for good? On opportunities and challenges of large language models for education. *Learning and Individual Differences*, *103*, 102274. DOI: 10.1016/j.lindif.2023.102274

Lee, A. (2008). How are doctoral students supervised? Concepts of doctoral research supervision. *Studies in Higher Education*, *33*(3), 267–281. DOI: 10.1080/03075070802049202

Li, J., Zong, H., Wu, E., Wu, R., Peng, Z., Zhao, J., Yang, L., Xie, H., & Shen, B. (2024). Exploring the potential of artificial intelligence to enhance the writing of english academic papers by non-native english-speaking medical students-the educational application of ChatGPT. *BMC Medical Education*, *24*(1), 736. DOI: 10.1186/s12909-024-05738-y PMID: 38982429

Lu, H., Li, Y., Chen, M., Kim, H., & Serikawa, S. (2018). Brain intelligence: Go beyond artificial intelligence. *Mobile Networks and Applications*, *23*(2), 368–375. DOI: 10.1007/s11036-017-0932-8

Popenici, S. A., & Kerr, S. (2017). Exploring the impact of artificial intelligence on teaching and learning in higher education. *Research and Practice in Technology Enhanced Learning*, *12*(1), 22. DOI: 10.1186/s41039-017-0062-8 PMID: 30595727

Smutny, P., & Schreiberova, P. (2020). Chatbots for learning: A review of educational chatbots for the Facebook Messenger. *Computers & Education*, *151*, 103862. DOI: 10.1016/j.compedu.2020.103862

Topol, E. J. (2019). High-performance medicine: The convergence of human and artificial intelligence. *Nature Medicine*, *25*(1), 44–56. DOI: 10.1038/s41591-018-0300-7 PMID: 30617339

Tran, H. N., Le, T. T. N., & Tran, V. B. U. (2025). AI Tools in Learning Academic Writing: Benefits and Challenges for MA Students in the English Language Studies at the Industrial University of Ho Chi Minh City. *International Journal of AI in Language Education*, *2*(1), 74–91. DOI: 10.54855/ijaile.25215

Van Dis, E. A., Bollen, J., Zuidema, W., Van Rooij, R., & Bockting, C. L. (2023). ChatGPT: Five priorities for research. *Nature*, *614*(7947), 224–226. DOI: 10.1038/d41586-023-00288-7 PMID: 36737653

Venkatesh, V., & Bala, H. (2008). Technology acceptance model 3 and a research agenda on interventions. *Decision Sciences, 39*(2), 273–315. DOI: 10.1111/j.1540-5915.2008.00192.x

Zawacki-Richter, O., Marín, V. I., Bond, M., & Gouverneur, F. (2019). Systematic review of research on artificial intelligence applications in higher education–where are the educators? *International Journal of Educational Technology in Higher Education, 16*(1), 1–27. DOI: 10.1186/s41239-019-0171-0

Zhang, H., Wu, C., Xie, J., Lyu, Y., Cai, J., & Carroll, J. M. (2023). Redefining qualitative analysis in the AI era: Utilizing ChatGPT for efficient thematic analysis. *arXiv preprint arXiv:2309.10771.*

Chapter 11
From Machine Language to Embodied Cognition:
A Paradigmatic Shift in Cognitive Linguistics

Fayçal Agzoum
https://orcid.org/0009-0003-3368-4314
Faculty of Letters and Human Sciences, Sultan Moulay Slimane University, Morocco

Brahim Oumeraouch
Sultan Moulay Slimane University, Morocco

ABSTRACT

This chapter examines the evolution of conceptions of language within the framework of cognitive science, focusing on the shift from a computational paradigm to an embodied approach to cognition. Grounded in a central question — how the mind-as-computer metaphor was gradually replaced by a view of language rooted in lived experience and body–environment interaction — the study adopts a historical, comparative, and critical methodology. The analysis traces major paradigms and compares linguistic models, from Chomskyan formalism to cognitive linguistics. It draws on insights from the philosophy of mind, cognitive psychology, and linguistics to shed light on the epistemological transformations at stake. This chapter, through its historical, theoretical, and practical sections, aims to highlight the continuities, ruptures, and conceptual contributions that have led to a reconfiguration of language as a phenomenon that is at once cognitive, physical, and contextual, from a resolutely interdisciplinary perspective.

DOI: 10.4018/979-8-3373-3436-3.ch011

INTRODUCTION

The study of human language, conceived as a central faculty of the mind, has undergone a significant paradigmatic shift in recent decades, at the crossroads of multiple disciplines. Language processing is now embedded within a broader reflection on the functioning of the human mind, spanning from introspective psychology and behaviorism to classical cognitivist, connectionist, and more recent embodied approaches. These transformations have profoundly renewed our understanding of the cognitive mechanisms involved in natural language.

The cognitive revolution of the second half of the 20th century—described by Ganascia (2006) as "*a thunderclap in a clear sky*"—marks a decisive break. It ushered in the rise of the cognitivist paradigm, based on the idea that the human mind operates as a symbolic processing system, manipulating abstract mental representations through formal algorithms. Strongly influenced by the early developments of cybernetics and artificial intelligence, this paradigm relies on the metaphor of the mind-as-computer, promoting a computational and internalist conception of cognition. This model has, however, been progressively enriched—and at times challenged—by other approaches such as naturalism, functionalism, representationalism, and connectionism. The latter, emerging in the 1980s, introduced more dynamic and distributed models of information processing, based on neural networks inspired by the biological functioning of the brain. Within this evolving landscape, language holds a central position. Initially approached through Chomskyan psycholinguistics—with its focus on syntax and the postulation of a universal grammar—language underwent a major shift from the 1980s onward with the emergence of cognitive linguistics. This new perspective adopts an externalist stance, emphasizing semantic, experiential, and contextual dimensions. It is notably grounded in the principle of embodied cognition, which highlights the constant interactions between language, the body, and the environment. The evolution of language processing thus illustrates a marked paradigmatic transition: from abstract symbolic processing to an embodied cognition, grounded in the metaphor of the "embodied mind." This epistemological shift unfolds within an interdisciplinary and multidimensional dynamic that brings together linguistics, philosophy, psychology, neuroscience, and artificial intelligence.

This chapter aims to examine the main paradigms that have shaped this evolution, analyzing their conceptual foundations, methodologies, and objectives, while highlighting the convergences, divergences, and complementarities between the various approaches. To this end, we will address the following guiding question:

How has the conception of language as a formal system of symbolic processing—grounded in the mind-as-computer metaphor—gradually been supplanted by an embodied view of cognition, integrating lived experience, bodily grounding, and continuous interaction between mind, body, and world in the analysis of language ?

The approach adopted here is at once historical, comparative, and critical. It is rooted in an interdisciplinary perspective, based on a reappraisal of the founding paradigms of cognitive science—introspective psychology, behaviorism, classical cognitivism, connectionism—and a dialogue with linguistic currents, from Chomskyan formalism to contemporary cognitive linguistics. This analysis draws on insights from philosophy of mind, cognitive psychology, and cognitive linguistics to explore how human language is conceptualized. The objective is to demonstrate that theoretical models of language are never neutral: they profoundly shape our understanding of the mind, cognition, and human nature. The shift toward embodied cognition invites us to reconsider the relationships between language, body, and environment within an integrative perspective. This chapter, through its historical dimension (roots and development of cognitive science), theoretical dimension (paradigms and explanatory models), and applicative dimension (contemporary applications in linguistics and cognitive semantics), aims to shed light on the continuities and ruptures that shape the history of cognitive linguistics, to situate the paradigm of embodiment within this trajectory, and to highlight its contributions to the analysis of language as a cognitive, experiential, and contextual phenomenon.

I. HISTORICAL DEVELOPMENTS: FROM ORIGINS TO FOUNDING PARADIGMS

1. The Origins of Cognitive Science: From the Objectification of the Mental to the Modeling of the Mind

In this section, we focus primarily on the evolution of psychology, tracing its path from classical mentalism—an introspective theory often associated with the « Sapir-Whorf hypothesis »—through behaviorism, a psychological paradigm of learning and motivation centered on observable and measurable behaviors, to the emergence of cognitive science. The transition from behaviorism to cognitive science marks a genuine cognitive revolution, driven by scientific disciplines seeking to reconcile two often opposing dimensions in the study of the mind: the psychic and the physiological. From this perspective, we highlight the various approaches within the cognitivist framework: naturalism, functionalism, computationalism, and representationalism. The main objective is thus to explore how information processing operates in human cognition according to each of these paradigms. This will allow for an analysis of their points of convergence and divergence, while also clarifying the contributions and limitations of each orientation.

1.1. From Introspective Psychology to Behaviorism: The Objectivist Turn

The behaviorist paradigm, as a major phase in the evolution of experimental psychology, marks a decisive turning point in the discipline. This shift redirected the focus from consciousness—whose study aims to understand subjective experiences and mental states—to an approach centered on observable and measurable behaviors. In reaction to classical mentalism, behaviorism also sets itself apart from anthropological perspectives, such as those of Sapir and Whorf in the early 20th century.

Known as the « *Sapir-Whorf hypothesis* », this theory posits that human thought is shaped and structured by language, which itself is influenced by the culture of each community. According to these researchers, language plays a fundamental role in shaping human perception and thought, constituting a genuine « *worldview* » specific to its native speakers. In other words, this idea suggests that the language we speak shapes our sensations and our perception of the surrounding world, while also reflecting individuals' daily activities (Meyran, 2017, p. 46). As a result, individuals' relationship to their sensations, as well as their spatial and temporal perceptions, varies according to the language they use. According to Whorf[1], linguistic systems—in terms of both vocabulary and grammar—are not merely tools for conveying pre-existing ideas, but also contribute to the formation of ideas not yet expressed by the speaker. These systems can be seen as frameworks structuring mental activity, guiding the analysis of impressions and influencing individuals' interpretations (Meyran, 2017, p. 46).

Widely influential during the 1950s, the Sapir-Whorf hypothesis was later challenged for various reasons over time. In this context, we particularly highlight the growing influence of Chomsky in the 1960s, as well as the theory of the modularity of mind proposed by Fodor. This theory posits that all human beings possess innate and universal mental structures (Meyran, 2017, p. 47). These authors, whose perspectives emphasize innatism and the universality of cognitive development, postulate the existence of modules dedicated to different cognitive operations, based on genetic foundations common to all humanity.

In short, whereas classical introspective psychology aimed to study consciousness in order to understand internal mental states, and the anthropological perspectives of Sapir and Whorf suggested that language shapes and structures perception while deeply influencing thought, behaviorism refocused attention on the observation of behavior. Indeed, as we shall see later, the behaviorist paradigm is primarily centered on conditioning phenomena and on observable and measurable behaviors.

1.2. Behaviorism: Contributions and Criticisms

Throughout its history, from Watson's early work to post-Skinnerian research, behaviorism—an empirical orientation and experimental study of "*behavior*"—has aimed to explain behavior without reference to "*mental events*" (Kaufmann, 1977, p. 314). In this regard, behaviorism defined itself in contrast to the issue of "mental events," more precisely against the psychology of "*consciousness*" and introspective approaches[2]. The opposition between these two types of psychology—introspective approaches and behaviorism—aimed to distinguish both two kinds of events and two types of descriptions (Kaufmann, 1977, pp. 315–317). What all behaviorist approaches have in common is the use of descriptions referring only to physical events. Thus, for Skinner, behavior is primarily a function of environmental factors—entirely describable in physical terms—rather than a function of internal variables (Kaufmann, 1977). To achieve objectivity, which guarantees scientific validity, the researcher—external to their object of study—relied solely on individual experiments under objectively measurable and controllable conditions, aiming to establish empirical laws linking inputs to outputs (Ganascia, 2006, p. 37). This exclusively behaviorist approach excluded the thinking subject, replacing them with an abstract, opaque substitute, reduced to producing quantifiable responses to quantifiable stimuli, without ever taking into account intrinsic elements such as mental images, motivations, or will. Nevertheless, although behaviorism made significant contributions to experimental psychology, it has also been widely criticized, particularly for neglecting essential aspects of human experience, such as intentionality and mental states. According to Kaufmann (1977, p. 322), Skinner's explanation of verbal behavior—particularly the production of utterances based on similarities, with little regard for "*inner states*"—was criticized by Chomsky. For Chomsky, these similarities, which Skinner failed to account for, should be explained using grammatical or other abstract criteria, involving rules and mental schemas—that is, internal states. In criticizing Skinner's behaviorist theory of language (1957), Chomsky sought to demonstrate that human language learning and behavior could not be reduced to a stimulus-response model. It was necessary to address the mind by recognizing the existence of internal mental life linked to cognitive functioning and to postulate the presence of intermediate representations enabling transitions between a system's inputs and outputs. These representations are essential for explaining and interpreting sensory data (inputs) and the behaviors they produce (outputs) (Steiner, 2005, p. 14).

From a cognitive perspective, we are not reflexive beings: what individuals do fundamentally depends on their beliefs, desires, and the way they interpret language or surrounding objects. In other words, understanding human behavior cannot be limited to the objective properties of the world ; it relies above all on how it is perceived and mentally represented. Humans are therefore sensitive to the information contained in a stimulus, not to its physical format (Steiner, 2005, p. 15).

As for the concept of "*reinforcement*"—whether positive or negative—it refers to the increase or decrease in the likelihood of a response to a stimulus. Reinforcement, as a probabilistic measure concerning behavioral variables, appears to have primarily a metatheoretical meaning (Kaufmann, 1977, p. 323). Furthermore, to modify an individual's behavior, it would suffice to change certain environmental conditions. Reinforcement thus becomes a principle of action determining what should be done in specific circumstances to achieve a predefined objective. In this sense, reinforcement takes the form of a technical imperative (Kaufmann, 1977, p. 324). In fact, experiments are conditioned and guided by factors that direct the experience toward the desired response, while eliminating those that might interfere. In short, the entire trajectory of the experience is steered by its final outcome.

Moreover, in his view, Skinner stated: "I am not interested in explaining why something is reinforcing... I cannot explain why food is reinforcing to a hungry animal..."[3] (Skinner, 1964, p. 104). However, this position is highly questionable, as it provides no real explanation. A theory that explains nothing cannot be considered scientific. For Kaufmann, Skinner appears more like a disguised moralist, given the lack of explanatory grounding in his theory (Kaufmann, 1977, pp. 324–325).

In short, behaviorism overlooked concepts related to higher mental functions such as memory and thinking and neglected the processing of internal phenomena like perception and sensation (Baars, 1986 ; Legrand, 1990). In the 1950s, behaviorism underwent a major crisis, driven by widespread dissatisfaction—especially with its inability to address internal mental processes—which opened the way for new perspectives, particularly those of cognitive science (Legrand, 1990, p. 276). The shift from behaviorism to cognitive science was more than a simple paradigm change ; it redefined psychological approaches and methods. It inaugurated an interdisciplinary crossroads combining the psychic and physiological dimensions of cognition while integrating disciplines such as neuroscience, linguistics, and artificial intelligence. This integrative orientation acknowledges the central role of mental states and brain substrates in better understanding the human being. Its goal is to explore cognition holistically, while still accounting for observable behaviors.

To summarize, behaviorism—dominant until the 1950s under the guise of scientific objectivity—reduced the thinking subject to an opaque hypothetical entity. This view restricted the individual to their interactions with the environment and the mind to a reactive system, blindly responding to external stimuli. As a result, it failed to consider implicit instructions and contextual elements not directly regulated by experience (Ganascia, 2006). However, in the context of cognition—and especially in complex tasks such as reading, writing, speaking, listening, or problem-solving—the subject must collaborate and adhere to certain rules. One cannot be reduced to an entity that mechanically reacts to external stimuli. Cognitive psychology, a discipline focused on the study of cognitive functions as complex processes capable of handling both internal and external information (Ganascia, 2006, p. 61), offers a model-based approach to mental life concerned with how the mind processes information. The emergence of cognitive psychology is thus inextricably linked to the rise of cognitive science (CS).

In general, where behaviorists saw the human mind as an impenetrable "*black box*", cognitivists adopted a radically different view. They conceived of the mind as a "*glass box*", making visible the internal mechanisms governing information processing. Thus, all academic sciences—logic and physics, mathematics and computer science, biology and psychology, sociology and anthropology, among others—came together under the banner of CS. The aim of this "*holy alliance*" of disciplines is to explore cognitive functions, model the mind as an information-processing system, and uncover the mental processes underlying human thought (Ganascia, 2006, p. 7).

By turning our attention to CS, which has emerged and profoundly reshaped the mind sciences, we will seek, in the following sections, to answer the following questions:

- *What conceptual and methodological innovations have cognitivists introduced ?*
- *What are the conceptions, trends, and goals of cognitive science ?*

1.3. The Cognitive Revolution and the Emergence of the Sciences of Mind

1.3.1. Cognitive Sciences: Principles and Development

Emerging in the 1950s and 1960s, cognitive sciences (CS) were established in opposition to behaviorism, strict physicalism, and introspectionism. They adopted a mentalist perspective centered on internal processes. Their aim is to reconcile two dimensions long considered opposed in the study of the mind: the psychic and the physiological. Information processing is thus conceived as an interaction between internal mental mechanisms (the psyche) and observable behavioral or linguistic manifestations. CS are rooted in an interdisciplinary dynamic, relying on collaboration among several fields — psychology, neuroscience, artificial intelligence, linguistics, etc. — which conceive the mind both as a biological entity and an informational structure (Ganascia, 2006). They adopt a theoretical framework that integrates the interdependence between body and mind, matter and symbol, physiological substrate and cognitive activity.

Before precisely defining CS, it is important to clarify a few foundational concepts. The terms *cognitive* and *cognition*, derived from the Latin *cognoscere* (« to know

»), reemerged in the 20th century within scientific reflections on the mechanisms of knowledge (Ganascia, 2006). A discipline is considered cognitive when it focuses on knowledge or on the mental faculties that underlie it (perception, memory, reasoning, etc.). *Cognition* thus refers to the set of mental processes involved in the production, organization, and use of knowledge. The adjective *cognitive* therefore relates to the mental functions engaged in information processing, especially in connection with language, memory, or problem-solving (Neveu, 2004). *Cognitivism*, which appeared in the 1980s, refers to a theoretical approach emerging from psychology, philosophy of language, and computer science, aiming to model cognitive processes using formal and computational tools. A cognitivist is a researcher who adheres to this perspective and develops its methodological and empirical applications. Let us now turn to the question: *what do we mean by cognitive sciences ?*

In ***Invitation to Cognitive Science***, Varela defines CS as "the modern scientific analysis of mind and knowledge in all its dimensions"[4] (1989, p. 9). Their emergence is rooted in the context of World War II and took shape through the alliance of several disciplines — linguistics, cognitive psychology, artificial intelligence, neuroscience, epistemology — converging toward a joint exploration of the human mind. According to Steiner (2005), following Petitot, CS aim to establish a natural science of the mind, understood as the totality of mental functions associated with the central nervous system. CS have profoundly influenced the human and biomedical sciences by introducing a new way of conceiving the mind: a scientific modeling of internal cognitive mechanisms, at the intersection of human and machine (Ganascia, 2006, p. 8). They seek to explain how knowledge is acquired, processed, stored, and used, by integrating psychic, neurobiological, and sociocultural dimensions.

The development of cognitivism can be divided into three major phases (Legrand, 1990):

- The Underground Revolution (from 1956): Initiated by the foundational MIT conference and Miller's article on the limits of short-term memory, this period discreetly marked the beginning of behaviorism's decline.
- Emergence (1960s): Cognitive psychology gained ground and began to achieve academic legitimacy.
- Organization (1970s): The field was consolidated through the creation of dedicated training programs, journals, and conferences.

Concerning their object of study, CS strive to determine the conditions of possibility for knowledge, seeking to answer the question: How do we come to know ? This inquiry unfolds along two complementary lines:

- An approach centered on the conscious individual (psychology, neurobiology) ;
- A broader approach focused on symbolic systems, especially language (linguistics, semantics).

Ganascia (2006) identifies three complementary poles structuring the study of cognition:

- The *psyche*, representing the subjective dimension of knowledge ;
- The *brain*, as the biological substrate of cognitive processes ;
- *Social knowledge*, transmitted and constructed collectively.

These poles intersect across various disciplinary fields:

- Between *psyche* and *brain*: psychopathology, neuropsychology ;
- Between *brain* and *society*: neurolinguistics, connectionism ;
- Between *psyche* and *society*: cognitive anthropology, psycholinguistics, semantics.

This triangular model highlights the interdependence of the mental, biological, and social dimensions in the analysis of cognition. For Ganascia, knowledge constitutes the core of CS — not as a set of contents, but as an object of investigation. This approach — coupled with a marked interest in information-processing machines — is what sets CS apart from traditional disciplines (Ganascia, 2006, pp. 21–23).

Figure 1. Triangular diagram of the interactions between psyche, brain, social knowledge and associated disciplines (Ganascia, 2006, p. 27)

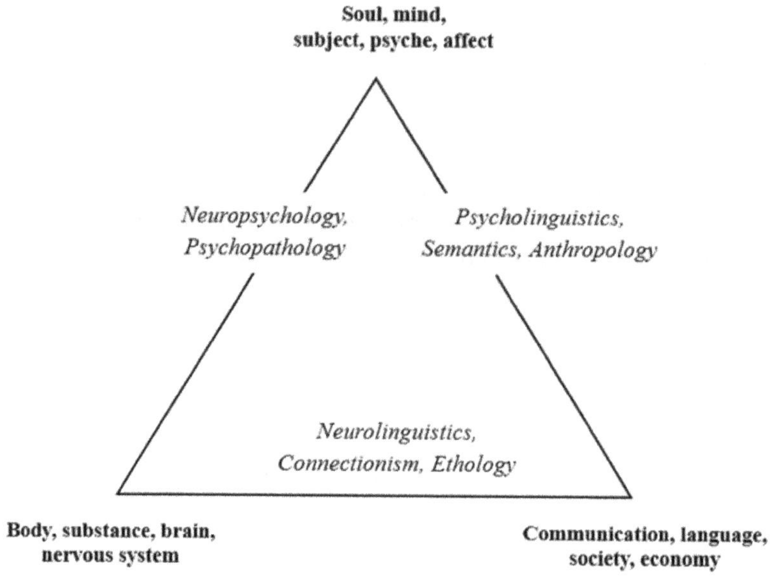

1.3.2. From Cognitive Science and Technology to Cybernetics

Cognitive sciences and technologies (CST) emerged between 1940 and 1956 from exchanges among scientists from diverse disciplines. They[5] constitute an inter-disciplinary hybrid focused on knowledge, information, and communication, while maintaining specific methods (Varela, 1989, p. 21). The accompanying diagram illustrates the major disciplines that converged during this revolution.

Figure 2. The main disciplines contributing to CST

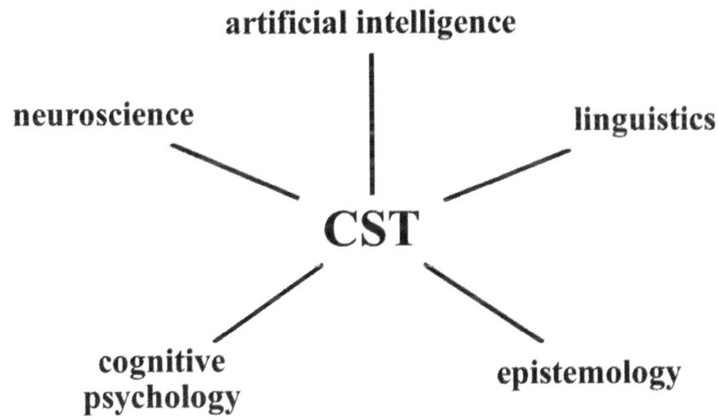

(Varela, 1989, p. 22)

Often regarded as a theory of mind, CST introduced logic and mathematical formalisms into the description of cognitive processes (Varela, 1989, p. 30). Logic was seen as key to understanding the brain, which was conceived as a logical structure composed of neurons (Varela, 1989, p. 30). This revolution fostered the emergence of cybernetics[6].

Developed in the 1940s and 1950s, first-order cybernetics broke away from traditional mechanical automata. Interdisciplinary by nature, it drew on telecommunications, information theory, and concepts such as feedback, simulation, and mathematical logic, applied to the nervous system and human reasoning. It influenced fields such as biology and economics (Varela, 1989, pp. 32–33) by studying[7] the self-organization of complex systems through information processing. These inquiries left a significant mark on psychology and artificial intelligence by integrating computational representations of knowledge with psychological structures.

In natural language processing, progress was driven by the interplay between psychology and the language sciences to create models suited to computational implementation. However, cybernetics revealed its limitations, particularly in machine learning, where algorithms only allowed for simple connections between automata (Ganascia, 2006, p. 88). These limits paved the way for new approaches, notably connectionism, which resurfaced in the 1980s after two decades of neglect. This movement, initially proposed in 1947 by neuropsychologist Hebb (Ganascia, 2006, p. 87), along with other foundational paradigms of CST, will be discussed in this chapter.

II. THEORETICAL FOUNDATIONS: PARADIGMS AND EXPLANATORY MODELS

1. Foundational Paradigms of Cognitive Science

1.1. The Emergence of the Cognitivists

While the 1940s witnessed the birth of cybernetics, a second phase of the cognitive science movement emerged in 1956. During two landmark conferences—one in Cambridge and the other in Dartmouth—researchers such as Herbert Simon, Noam Chomsky, Marvin Minsky, and John McCarthy presented foundational ideas of modern cognitive science, brought together under a common project: the « *cognitivist program* » (Varela, 1989, p. 35 ; Fuchs, 2004, p. 4).

These works introduced a central intuition: intelligence, including human intelligence, is fundamentally comparable to that of a computer. Cognition is thus conceived as the computation of symbolic representations (Varela, 1989, p. 36). At this level, the mind is understood as a form of logic, analogous to computer functioning—laying the groundwork for cognitivism. Presented as the dominant paradigm of cognitive science, cognitivism took shape through various research programs, including psycholinguistics, cybernetics, computer science, and information science. These fields now share a common object of study: the mind, viewed as a cognitive system (Steiner, 2005, pp. 13–14). Their focus lies primarily on the architecture of cognitive functions. Accordingly, the human mind is seen as an information-processing system, akin to a computer. Quoting Miller, Steiner refers to living beings as "*informavores*[8]" (Steiner, 2005, p. 15).

However, while the disciplines[9] within cognitive science coexist, each approaches the study of the human mind according to its own orientations, methodologies, and goals. This disciplinary diversity allows for a richer and more nuanced understanding of the mind.

The following sections will present the cognitivist program by highlighting its main postulates and axioms.

1.2. Classical Cognitivism: Core Postulates

As the founding and dominant paradigm of cognitive science—to the point of being described as « the only game in town » (Steiner, 2005 ; Fodor, 2008) — cognitivism is based on two methodological and philosophical intuitions: *naturalism* and *functionalism*. It also centers on two core hypotheses: *computationalism* and *representationalism*.

1.2.1. Computationalism: The "Mind-as-Machine" Metaphor

We begin with the central hypothesis of cognitivism, as put forward by researchers such as Varela, Thompson, Rosch, and Steiner, according to which:

> *Intelligence — including human intelligence — resembles computation so closely in its essential characteristics that cognition can in fact be defined as operations on symbolic representations [...]. A computation is an operation carried out on symbols, that is, on elements that stand for something else (Varela, 1993, p. 73).*

By highlighting two central notions — computation and symbolic representation — this definition conceives human cognition as a computational process. Indeed, just as in a computer program where the syntax of the code reflects a semantic projection, thought is carried out through the physical manipulation of symbols representing certain aspects of the real world. Thus, in the context of information processing, where representation (or intentionality) is central, semantic operations are expressed through the syntax of the language used (Varela, 1989, pp. 37–39).

Moreover, computationalism[10], which emerged in the 20th century with the work of Turing, conceives cognition as symbolic manipulation based on syntactic properties. In the 1930s, Turing demonstrated that any process sensitive only to these properties — such as calculation — could be imitated by a machine: his famous Turing machine. This intuition laid the groundwork for the computational theory of reasoning. A central theory in cognitive science, also known as symbolic processing (Varela, 1989, p. 37) or computational functionalism (Ganascia, 2006, p. 132), computationalism differs from behaviorism — which reduced the psyche to an inaccessible "*black box*" — by conceptualizing it in terms of information, procedures, and processes, and by comparing its functioning to that of a computer. This analogy is based on the manipulation of symbols according to their syntactic and physical properties, without considering their semantic content (Steiner, 2005, p. 23 ; Ganascia, 2006, p. 132). Thought is modeled here as an information-processing system governed by syntactic algorithms. Mental processes are thus considered independent of biological and semantic dimensions, since they rely solely on syntactic rules. This primacy of syntax is summed up in the maxim: "Take care of the syntax, and the semantics will take care of itself" (Haugeland, 1989, p. 256). More precisely, following a principle of causality, the physical properties of symbols determine their syntactic properties, which in turn indirectly reproduce their semantic properties (Steiner, 2005).

In short, manipulating symbols amounts to reasoning — that is, producing or transforming representations. Thinking, from this perspective, is equivalent to computing according to formal rules based on the syntactic properties of symbols (Steiner, 2005 ; Roux, 2024). The work of the 1960s by Von Neumann, McCarthy, Minsky, and Simon extended this view, leading to the birth of AI. The aim of AI is to design systems capable of manipulating symbolic representations, thereby realizing Turing's intuitions and laying the foundations of modern computational approaches.

As a major research program in cognitive science, computational cognitivism has deeply influenced disciplines such as psychology, linguistics, and especially AI. The latter, described by Varela as "the child of cognitivism," represents its most concrete application (Varela, 1989, p. 44).

However, the rise of AI quickly revealed its limitations. When the goal became to create systems capable of understanding natural language texts (articles, announcements, book chapters, etc.) in order to extract information and update databases, major obstacles arose — beyond the capabilities of mathematicians, logicians, computer scientists, and engineers. It thus became necessary to draw on psychology and language sciences. Among the most complex challenges, natural language processing occupies a central place. Early attempts at machine translation failed due to the lack of adequate grammatical analysis. By reducing translation to a simple lexical substitution, these efforts ignored the complexity of language. This naïve approach — comparable to that of a student translating with a dictionary without discernment — encountered problems such as homography and lexical or syntactic ambiguities (Ganascia, 2006).

Thus, the limits encountered in natural language understanding highlighted the need for interdisciplinary collaboration, bringing to light the importance of semantics and pragmatics. These disciplines provide essential tools for understanding meaning and context — two fundamental dimensions for replicating human cognitive processes on a computer[11] (Ganascia, 2006, p. 69).

Finally, beyond computation, classical cognitivism also relies on the notion of representation, linked to mental states. Mental representations are seen as entities within a formal system, dynamically interpreted as beliefs, desires, or intentions (Varela, 1989, p. 47).

1.2.2. Representationalism and the Role of Mental Representations

The representational theory of mind constitutes a specific approach to mental states. According to representationalism, the human mind processes information by relying on mental and symbolic structures, conceived as internal representations of the external world (Steiner, 2005, p. 22). In other words, this approach is based on the idea of a correspondence between internal mental representations, endowed with symbolic meanings, and the real world.

In examining the levels of analysis on which a cognitive theory should be based, Steiner draws on Marr's (1982) framework, which distinguishes three levels:

- The first level, known as the *computational* level, consists in specifying the cognitive task to be accomplished. In this respect, information processing can be carried out by a cognitive system while taking into account certain constraints. For example, in the case of vision, the cognitive task is to construct a three-dimensional representation of one or more objects from the two-dimensional information received by the retina (Steiner, 2005, p. 25).

- The second level, *algorithmic* level, is fundamental insofar as it defines the algorithms necessary for performing the function identified at the computational level. These algorithms determine the format of the representations used and model the processes through well-defined rules in order to achieve the intended objective.
- The third level, the *implementation* level, concerns the neurophysiological and biological realization of cognitive functions — in other words, their embodiment within the nervous system. For instance, our linguistic or perceptual abilities rely on specific brain structures.

In line with research on the various levels of analysis of cognitive behavior, Pylyshyn (1984) adopts a different perspective and identifies three complementary levels. The first, the *biophysical* level, explains the task through reference to natural laws. The second, the *syntactic*, *symbolic*, or *functional* level, focuses on algorithms, computational capacities, and functional architecture. At this level, syntactic operations interact with representational states. Finally, the third, the *semantic* level, explores the informational content underlying behavior, such as the agent's beliefs[12] or desires.

It is also worth emphasizing that the notions of *function* and *algorithm* play a central role in the analysis of cognitive systems. These systems compute specific functions by manipulating syntactically structured representations using algorithms. According to Fodor, "there is no computation without representation": all cognitive computation requires explicit representations to structure and give meaning to mental content. Without such representations, mental causation cannot occur (Steiner, 2005, p. 26).

In short, through its two main hypotheses — representational and computational — along with its naturalist and functionalist methodological intuitions, classical cognitivism has significantly contributed to the advancement of our understanding of the mechanisms underlying human cognition. These hypotheses aim to explain the workings of the mind and the mental processes involved in information processing and the execution of cognitive functions, particularly by assimilating, within the framework of computational functionalism, the behavior of internal states to that of computer programs. However, these approaches have faced criticism, notably from proponents of connectionism, due to their limitations. Among these is the inability of symbolic computation to account for all dimensions of cognitive systems. It is in this context that the connectionist paradigm emerged, challenging the use of conventional symbols. Connectionism offers a model based on the interconnections of neural networks and self-organization (Varela, 1989, p. 57). It defends the view that cognition emerges from states generated by a network of simple components, where the system's organization is governed by both local and global rules (Varela, 1989, p. 77).

2. Connectionism: The Emergence of Neural Networks

2.1. Critiques of Classical Cognitivism

The cognitivist program has undeniably experienced remarkable development, marked by a multitude of concepts and methods originating from various approaches. It has exerted a crucial influence through hypotheses that integrate both physiological and psychological dimensions. Within the framework of information processing, cognition can be approached through several paradigms: naturalism, functionalism, computationalism, and representationalism. These approaches respectively draw on concepts such as causal laws, cognitive functions, computations and algorithms, as well as mental representations[13]. Nevertheless, these paradigms are not without criticism. For example, computational functionalism has been criticized for its limitations, particularly regarding the distinction between the mental states of a machine and those that are psychologically viable for the human mind (Ganascia, 2006, p. 138).

Connectionism, for its part, challenges two fundamental assumptions of classical cognitivism: computation and representation. It offers an alternative that is more attuned to the intrinsic properties of the cerebral system. This model, based on the notion of *neural networks* and *emergent* or *implicit rules*, takes the brain rather than the computer as its model (Steiner, 2005, p. 28).

Although computationalism accounts for certain complex tasks, such as playing chess, performing calculations, or solving problems, it encounters difficulties with tasks considered more elementary, such as face recognition or the rapid comprehension of linguistic structures. Connectionist models, by contrast, explain these cognitive abilities through systems of interconnected units, analogous to neural networks, where the connections between these units correspond to synaptic connections (Steiner, 2005, p. 28).

2.2. Connectionist Paradigm and Its Core Postulates

After twenty years of dominance by computational orthodoxy (Varela, 1989, p. 54), the orientations of first-order cybernetics—initially based on logical and formal principles—were revived through new connectionist strategies, giving rise to a new form of cybernetics.

The term *connectionism*, sometimes referred to as *neo-connectionism*, reflects the idea that cognitive processes truly emerge at the level of neural connections (Varela, 1989, p. 58).

This approach revitalized cybernetic thinking by deepening the understanding of self-organizing neural networks while promoting interdisciplinarity across fields such as computer science, linguistics, and psychology (Ganascia, 2006, p. 88).

Grounded in the notions of self-organization, emergence, association, and dynamic networks (Varela, 1989, p. 77), connectionism models cognitive processes through connections between neural units. In these models, a neural network adjusts and self-organizes to perform a given cognitive task by configuring the weight of its connections according to the input received and the expected output, without relying on explicit or symbolic representations.

However, despite its significant advances, this paradigm remains subject to criticism. Researchers such as Fodor and Pylyshyn view connectionism as a revival of behaviorism, incapable of fully explaining the systematicity and productivity that characterize human thought. According to them, these models lack coherence and completeness, particularly due to the absence of explicit representations and symbolic rules (Steiner, 2005, p. 30).

In general, throughout this overview of the paradigms that have shaped the cognitive revolution, we have outlined the trajectory of the development of cognitive sciences. This exploration begins with classical mentalism and behaviorism, moves through orthodox cognitivism and its various approaches, and culminates in connectionism.

It provides an essential foundation for understanding how cognitive sciences integrate interdisciplinary orientations and new issues in the study of cognition. Below, we present a summary table outlining the main cognitive approaches, the fundamental principles on which they are based, and their respective limitations.

Table 1. Summary of the Major Assumptions and Limitations of Cognitive Paradigms

Approach	Core Principles	Limitations
Information Processing / Computational Approach	- Information is processed through computational operations, with a mind-machine analogy ; - Cognitive algorithms and modularity of the mind. Primacy of syntax over semantics.	- Lack of causal explanation. - Neglect of bodily embodiment and subjective experience. - The mind is conceived as isolated from the biological and cultural world.
Cognitive Naturalism	- Cognitive processes rely on physical mechanisms and natural laws. - The human mind results from biological evolution. - Interdisciplinary and holistic approach to cognition.	- Neglect of the sociocultural environment's impact. - Difficulty integrating subjective consciousness.
Functionnalism	- Mental states are defined by their functional roles. - Focus on functions rather than brain structure. - Independence from biological substrate.	- Ignorance of subjective experience. - Neglect of internal physical structures. - Underestimation of the role of social interaction and cultural context in cognition.
Representationalism / Symbolic Cognition	- Cognition relies on mental and symbolic representations. - Internal representations correspond to the external world.	- Inability to explain some aspects of cognition, such as perception and emotions. - Neglect of context and social interactions.
Connectionism / Neural Network Approach	- Cognition relies on artificial neural networks inspired by biological neurons. - Information is transmitted and processed through neural connections. - Distributed information processing across neural networks.	- Opacity of internal processes. - Excessive simplification and artificiality of mental operations. - Neural networks are perceived as "black boxes." - Difficulty explaining symbolic cognition.

In sum, this trajectory, illustrating the shift from a reductionist conception to more integrative contemporary approaches, reflects the diversity of assumptions and the constant dynamism that characterize the cognitive sciences. Technological and theoretical advances, the plurality of approaches, the redefinition of methods, and the renewal of disciplinary boundaries have enriched the study of cognitive processes and mental phenomena, providing a deeper understanding of the functioning of the human mind. However, the paradigms examined in this section have also revealed their limits, particularly when confronted with the challenges posed by natural language processing. Between 1980 and 1990, for instance, the field of AI displayed numerous weaknesses: the absence of a pragmatic background and robust non-monotonic reasoning, the static nature of systems, and their limited capacity to adapt to contextual variables.

Among the main avenues for improvement are the lack of embodiment and situatedness (body, environment, real tasks), the insufficient articulation across multiple levels (neural ↔ cognitive ↔ social), the inadequate modeling of contextualization and common sense, as well as the limited treatment of non-literal language (metaphors, implicatures, idiomatic expressions, and pragmatic intentions). These difficulties are particularly evident in handling meaning variability, polysemy, and the figurative and idiomatic dimensions of language. Such challenges call for the contribution of disciplines capable of integrating cognition, language, and human experience, thereby paving the way for the emergence of cognitive linguistics.

Through cognitive semantics, this discipline seeks to analyze natural language by drawing on linguistic, psychological, cognitive, and pragmatic perspectives. In the following section, we will examine the evolution of cognitive linguistics, from its origins in the internalist paradigm of syntax-centered psycholinguistics to its development in more recent externalist approaches. These contemporary perspectives explore cognition in all its complexity, relying on the principle of embodied cognition, according to which knowledge arises from the dynamic interaction between mind and environment.

III. CONTEMPORARY APPLICATIONS: TOWARDS COGNITIVE LINGUISTICS AND SEMANTICS

1. Cognitive Linguistics: Foundations and Contemporary Expansions

1.1. General Linguistics and the Emergence of Cognitive Linguistics

Language, a universal faculty unique to humans, is studied by many disciplines, including psychology, philosophy, anthropology, and above all, linguistics. Linguistics stands out as the only science fully dedicated to the analysis of language.

General linguistics, as the science of human language across time and space, explores its two fundamental dimensions: the social (language as a system) and the individual (speech). It encompasses various schools of thought, including internal approaches such as functionalism, distributionalism, psychosystematics, and generativism, all of which are to varying degrees connected to structuralism. It also integrates enunciative and pragmatic perspectives, which consider the parameters of the speech situation: context, pragmatic intent, modality, etc. Linguistics describes the structure of linguistic systems, from the level of expression (sounds, signifiers) to that of content (meaning, signifieds). This analysis covers all levels of language organization, each corresponding to a specific sub-discipline: phonetics (sounds), phonology (phonemes), morphology (morphemes), lexicology (words), syntax (sentences), and enunciation and pragmatics (utterances). Regardless of the approach — diachronic, synchronic, comparative, or contrastive — and the tools used (commutation, substitution, etc.), linguistic analysis remains descriptive. Its goal is to describe linguistic systems, identify the rules specific to each language, their distinctive features and boundaries, as well as to analyze interlinguistic variation and highlight linguistic universals or invariants through comparative studies.

In the 20th century, numerous theories emerged. Some, like generative grammar or formal grammars, aim to develop modeling formalisms. Others, focused on enunciation or onomasiological and semasiological pathways, emphasize the role of the speaker and the interlocutor in the production and interpretation of utterances.

To these major issues addressed by general linguistics, the emergence of cognitive linguistics in the 1950s–1960s added a new dimension: *cognitive relevance* (Fuchs, 2004). This field seeks to explicitly link the description and analysis of natural languages with the underlying cognitive mechanisms, taking into account the functional architecture of the mind and/or the neural architecture of the brain. This has led to the development of related disciplines such as psycholinguistics and neurolinguistics, which have increasingly converged into what is now called neuropsycholinguistics.

Linguistics becomes cognitive when it moves beyond merely listing words, their uses, and constructing grammars, to examine processes of understanding and memory in language (Ganascia, 2006, p. 10). In this sense, it explores the relationship between thought and language, and the cognitive processes involved in language acquisition, production, and comprehension.

Originating in the syntactocentric psycholinguistic paradigm, this branch focuses on the links between language and cognition. It seeks to describe how the human mind functions with respect to language and the mental processes involved. We now present an overview of cognitive linguistics, from its origins in Chomskyan generativism to contemporary approaches, where language is seen as a window into cognition, and where language, cognition, and human experience are inextricably intertwined.

1.2. From Chomskyanism to Embodiment: A Paradigmatic Shift

Cognitive science, and in particular Cognitive Linguistics (CL), constitutes a relatively recent approach focused on the study of cognition and mental states. This field, which views the human mind as a cognitive system, has profoundly transformed established paradigms.

Within this framework, language comprehension, for instance, is seen as a complex process in which the interlocutor constructs mental representations by combining the information contained in the message with their own knowledge.

To understand is thus to mobilize various mental processes in order to form a representation based on factors such as experience, memory, and linguistic competence, while also drawing on other cognitive functions such as categorization and analogical reasoning.

Moreover, from its classical foundations to its contemporary developments, cognitive Linguistics has undergone two key phases: on the one hand, Chomsky's internalist psycholinguistics, in which the human mind is conceived as disembodied; on the other hand, externalist cognitivist paradigms, in which cognition is embodied and the human being is seen as a thinking body. We will now examine this cognitive shift and its main features in detail.

1.2.1. Syntactocentric Psycholinguistics: Major Postulates

CL emerged in the 1950s, driven by the syntactocentric psycholinguistic paradigm introduced by Chomsky. He rejected behaviorist postulates and advocated for a computational functionalism and a naturalist perspective of the human mind, where mental states are represented by symbolic computations. For Chomsky, a speaker's linguistic competence goes beyond what can be acquired through simple conditioning. In this perspective, syntax holds a dominant position over semantics, and the language faculty is considered autonomous, innate, and independent of any external stimulus. Chomsky's generative grammar is a rationalist approach, in opposition to the inductive methods adopted by behaviorist theories as well as by traditional and structuralist grammars. These, according to Chomsky (1965, pp. 15–16), are limited due to incomplete and defective descriptions, diverging from taxonomic and distributional approaches. He proposed a descriptive and explanatory model based on universal principles and formal rules, promoting a hypothetico-deductive perspective that distances linguistics from sociology and reintegrates psychology into the study of language.

Chomskyan models aim to overcome these limitations and are known as generative grammars (GG), which are capable of enumerating only the grammatical sentences of a language and generating them from an explicit set of rules. This rigorous model also allows each sentence to be assigned a structural description (Chomsky, 1965, p. 15). In other words, GG seeks to describe speakers' competence and explore the unique language faculty of the human species, the foundation of language acquisition. More precisely, GG[14] is based on a system of rules capable of generating an infinite number of structures, following a process that goes from input instructions to the production of sentences (output).

This theoretical framework aims to describe the underlying mechanisms of utterance formation by relying on explicit rules, with the goal of simplifying and unifying language description. Moreover, Chomsky repositions linguistics within a mentalist perspective, conceiving the language faculty as an innate cognitive module. One of the foundations of GG is the distinction between *competence*[15] and *performance*, analogous to Saussure's distinction between « *langue* » and « *parole* », but with an emphasis on the creative aspect of language.

Other key concepts such as *grammaticality*, *acceptability*, and *linguistic universals* are also introduced in this model, which is part of a broader framework known as Universal Grammar (UG). UG posits the existence of innate linguistic structures shared across all languages. This program has gone through several phases in its evolution.

Initially, in its version called the *Standard Theory* (ST[16]), the generative model comprises three main components: the syntactic component, as the model's core element, and the semantic and phonological components, regarded as interpretive. This version aims to explain sentence generation but encounters ambiguities, especially of a syntactic nature. Then, the *Extended Standard Theory* refines this approach by integrating *X-bar theory*, which formalizes universal syntactic structures. Subsequently, the *Principles and Parameters* framework aims to reduce the number of transformational rules by establishing universal principles modifiable across languages through specific parameters. Finally, the *Minimalist Program* continues this pursuit of simplification, positing that the language faculty operates according to principles of economy and optimality, minimizing the mechanisms required to generate sentences.

Regarding language acquisition, Chomsky posits the existence of an innate predisposition that, combined with experience, enables the child to activate the underlying structure of their language acquisition device. This device links primary linguistic data (input) with a generative grammar (output), whose descriptive adequacy is governed by evaluation constraints aimed at explanatory adequacy. In this framework, Chomsky argues that acquisition relies on innate principles and predispositions that shape linguistic knowledge. These latent mental structures are activated through contact with the external world and are thus prepared for interpretation (Chomsky, 1965, p. 74). Accordingly, the study of language learning and the formalization of generative grammars aim to develop a model in which the child, thanks to innate predispositions, discovers the GG of their language through a deductive process where experience plays an indirect role via complex chains of transformations (Chomsky, 1965).

However, the theoretical foundations and implications of GG—based on cognitive algorithms and assuming the modularity of the mind, whereby information processing is carried out through computational mental operations—have drawn criticism (Buyssens, 1969). Indeed, the relevance of the generative model has been contested both internally and externally. Internal contradictions have been noted, particularly in the treatment of syntactic transformations.

Furthermore, some critiques point to the inability of grammatical knowledge to account for the production, interpretation, and comprehension of utterances. Observations include the absence of causal explanation, the neglect of bodily embodiment, the disregard for social and environmental contexts, and the difficulty in accounting for subjective experience. In short, the Chomskyan model is perceived as too abstract and disconnected from the cognitive and empirical reality of language. These significant limitations paved the way for the emergence of CL, which proposes externalist and emergentist approaches. These integrate, for optimal language processing, linguistic, cognitive, and pragmatic parameters, while emphasizing semantics, the embodied nature of cognition, and the continuous mind-body-world interaction.

1.2.2. Towards Embodied Cognition: The Emergence of the Embodiment Paradigm

In the 1960s and 1970s, Cognitive Linguistics (CL) gave rise, within the framework of generativism, to Generative Semantics (GS). This current, which posits that the underlying structure of utterances is based on logical, semantic, and syntactic categories, developed in reaction to certain aspects of Generative Grammar (GG). CL marks a significant break from Saussurean structuralism and generativism by restoring the full range of dimensions inherent in language.

According to Fortis (2012), the development of CL unfolds in three major phases, illustrating its transformation from an internalist, syntax-centered psycholinguistics to an externalist approach favoring semantics and the bodily grounding of human cognition.

- **Crystallization:** From the 1970s to the 1980s, research in CL explored various topics, laying the foundations of cognitive theories. This period also witnessed emerging convergences between GS and CL, particularly around concepts such as prototype theory and frame-type semantic structures.
- **Expansion:** In the 1980s and 1990s, interdisciplinary connections intensified through a network of interrelations linking CL to various semantic domains. Concepts such as construction grammars, collocations, idioms, blending, and prototype theory gained prominence.
- **Recent Developments:** Contemporary perspectives in CL have forged strong connections with pragmatic and enunciative domains. The rapprochement

with functional linguistics highlights the significance of sociocultural factors in the structuring of utterances.

In sum, the relationship between prototype theory and CL, along with the externalist orientation of research—favoring empirical and experimental approaches—challenges the mentalist individualism of syntax-centered GG. The evolution of cognitivism relies on logic, empiricism, and prototype theory, while also emphasizing the pragmatic dimension of utterances. Furthermore, while formal linguistics remains grounded in a computationalist approach based on syntax and mathematical models, contemporary CL places greater emphasis on practices, routines, and bodily interactions with the world. Searle criticizes this computationalist view, asserting that the syntactic system is incapable of accounting for understanding and meaning—essential aspects of our cognitive activities. According to him, "syntax is but an impoverished reduction of semantics" (Steiner, 2005, p. 33). In the same vein, Varela rejects the notion of mental representations in favor of an approach centered on embodiment, consciousness, and phenomenological intuitions.

In summary, cognitive linguistics has evolved from an internalist approach focused on syntax to an externalist perspective emphasizing semantics and bodily embodiment. This new orientation, based on embodied cognition and the idea of a cognitivized body, challenges functionalist and connectionist models that conceive of cognition as disembodied or strictly neural. It emphasizes the construction of meaning from bodily and sensorimotor experience, highlighting the central role of the lived body in intersubjective dynamics. Cognition thus goes beyond the framework of a simple process of mental representation to become a sensory activity, rooted in bodily experience (Apostol, 2021). These advances challenge the mentalist individualism of generative grammar and open up new pragmatic and phenomenological perspectives, particularly through the contributions of thinkers such as Searle and Varela.

Below, we present a table that clearly distinguishes between two cognitive paradigms: psycholinguistics and contemporary cognitive linguistics. This distinction is based on both earlier and more recent works (Handwerker, 1983, 1993 ; Varela et al., 1993 ; Boudon, 1996 ; Victorri, 2000 ; Nyckees, 2007 ; Fortis, 2012 ; Fastrez, 2014). This paradigmatic shift addresses key concepts and foundational principles: on the one hand, psycholinguistics as conceptualized by Chomsky ; on the other, the current trends in cognitive linguistics exploring perspectives such as enaction and embodied cognition. It thus highlights the marked contrast between classical cognitivist approaches and those of contemporary cognitive linguistics. Drawing from this table, we aim to underscore the dividing lines between the innatist and constructivist spheres—conceptually, theoretically, methodologically, and in terms of influential theories. This includes, in particular, the opposition between a formalist and innatist view of language (Chomsky) and an emergentist, embodied approach. This exploration offers valuable insights into the interaction between language and cognition, while underscoring the complexity of language acquisition and the underlying cognitive and mental processes.

Table 2. Summary of Key Concepts in Chomskyan Psycholinguistics and Contemporary Cognitive Linguistics

Criteria	Chomskyan Psycholinguistics	Contemporary Cognitive Linguistics
Cognitif Model	Computational and Symbolic	Embodied and Dynamic
Origin of Language	Innatism: genetically determined linguistic capacity	Constructivism: emerges through interaction and experience
Nature of Cognition	Disembodied mind: abstract symbol manipulation	Embodied mind: cognition integrated with the body and the environment
Role of Experience	Secondary: linguistic structures are innate	Fundamental: cognition develops through experience and interaction
Structure of Language	Autonomy of language: distinct module governed by internal rules	Language integrated with other cognitive functions
Grammar	Universal Grammar: innately specified grammatical structures	Grammar formation influenced by cognition and experience
Advocated Perspective	Centrality of syntax: deep structures and transformations	Importance of semantics and pragmatics
Influential Theories	Generative Grammar Theory	Enactivism, Embodied Cognition, Phenomenology, Gestalt Theory
Methodology	Hypothetico-deductive, objectivist approach	Empirical and experimental, subjectivist approach
Relation to Perception	Independence between linguistic and perceptual processes	Integration of perceptual mechanisms in language comprehension
View of Language	A form of logical computation based on formal rules	A dynamic, adaptive process influenced by environment and experience

1.3. Cognitive Semantics: An Integrative Approach

Cognitive semantics represents a break from the Chomskyan view of language as an autonomous module, focused on syntactic structures and the formal architecture of sentences. Rooted in a modularist conception of cognition, this view tends to marginalize the role of meaning. In contrast, cognitive linguistics regards language as intrinsically connected to other mental faculties and to lived experience, both individual and collective (Geeraerts, 1993). From this perspective, semantics re-engages with certain principles of the pre-structuralist tradition, particularly a psychological approach to meaning: lexical meaning is not autonomous but depends on the speaker's cultural, social, and historical experience. Cognitive semantics thus adopts an empiricist orientation, valuing physical experience as the foundation of abstraction, and takes an interdisciplinary stance, drawing on syntactic, semantic, pragmatic, and cognitive dimensions. It seeks to understand how meaning is constructed through dynamic conceptual structures in constant interaction with the environment.

A central concept in this approach is *experientialism* (Lakoff & Johnson, 1985), which holds that communication relies on an intersubjectivity grounded in embodied and shared experience (Fastrez, 2014). Language, therefore, does not merely verbalize thought—it actively contributes to the formation of human cognition, to the structuring of mental representations, and to the conceptualization of the world (Victorri, 2000 ; Nyckees, 2007).

Cognitive semantics, based on the principle of embodied cognition, posits that interactions between the body and the environment shape mental categories, which translate into abstract representations. It promotes an encyclopedic conception of meaning, the understanding of which is a matter of hermeneutics, seen as a reflection of cognitive activity and activated by networks of contextual knowledge derived from sensory, emotional, and social experience. Based on a close connection between language, thought, and experience, it offers an approach to meaning rooted in experience. From this perspective, thought is neither abstract nor disembodied, but anchored in the body and in sensorimotor interaction with the environment. Concepts such as space, time, and emotions are thus based on bodily schemas and perceptual and motor experiences. Language, through phenomena such as conceptual metaphors and idiomatic expressions, reflects this embodied structuring and manifests the cognitive mechanisms involved in the conceptualization of meaning.

Cognitive linguistics, particularly through cognitive semantics and its models (conceptual metaphor, frame semantics, mental spaces, etc.), explores the representation of meaning. By emphasizing notions such as categorization, prototypicality, conceptual networks, idiomaticity, and analogy, it seeks to address the limitations of AI systems, whether symbolic or statistical, which manipulate abstract representations without embodied grounding.

Although AI is advancing and becoming increasingly multimodal, integrating text, images, graphics, and videos, it remains marked by structural and ethical weaknesses. In this context, Andler (2023) highlights the "missing ingredients" needed to overcome these limitations: consciousness, meaning (understanding, semantic grounding, intentionality), and above all, common sense, regarded as AI's true Achilles' heel. This encompasses difficulties in processing implicit meaning, accessing communicative intentions, and resolving certain translation ambiguities that require contextual interpretation and a pragmatically oriented perspective.

These challenges call for a human–machine complementarity, capable of amplifying human abilities and ensuring progress (Andler, 2023). Such collaboration paves the way for embodied AI, linking language understanding and production to sensorimotor experience, and for robotics in which learning occurs through interaction with the world rather than the application of preprogrammed rules. Multimodal AI thus combines language, vision, gestures, and spatial perception in order to learn not only from textual data but also through experience and action (Mpia et al., 2024).

Finally, the integration of cognitive semantic theories into natural language processing—particularly conceptual metaphor theory (Lakoff & Johnson, 1985)—enables AI to capture the embodied representations underlying linguistic expressions. Frame semantics, in turn, can contribute to the organization of knowledge into conceptual "*micro-worlds*" (Andler, 2023), supporting optimal categorization and a type of processing that simultaneously integrates syntactic, semantic, cognitive, and pragmatic dimensions.

CONCLUSION

The conception of language as a formal system of symbolic processing, derived from the classical cognitivist paradigm and grounded in the mind-as-computer metaphor, long dominated cognitive science. Centered on abstract syntactic rules and symbol manipulation, it emerged from Chomskyan psycholinguistics and early artificial intelligence. While it enabled major advances in the modeling of linguistic reasoning, it also revealed significant limitations, notably its inability to account for the contextual, pragmatic, and figurative dimensions of natural language.

In response, models such as connectionism and cognitive linguistics have shifted attention toward an embodied and externalist view of cognition. Language is understood not as symbolic computation but as a phenomenon rooted in lived experience, perceptual and motor structures, and dynamic interactions between mind, body, and world. Approaches such as conceptual metaphor (Lakoff & Johnson, 1985), frame semantics (Fillmore), and mental spaces (Fauconnier) exemplify this paradigmatic shift, highlighting that meaning arises from sensory and bodily engagement with the world rather than from abstract representations.

The move from a formal model to an embodied approach reflects a profound reconfiguration of the cognitive sciences, placing bodily grounding, environment, and experience at the core of linguistic analysis. It challenges the foundations of generative grammar and calls for a reassessment of cognitive processes in light of empirical data, phenomenological insights, and discursive practices.

Within this framework, cognitive linguistics, particularly through cognitive semantics, clarifies the nature of meaning representation. By drawing on categorization, prototypicality, conceptual networks, idiomaticity, and analogy, it addresses the shortcomings of AI systems, whether symbolic or statistical, which still lack bodily grounding. Although AI is progressing toward multimodal models capable of processing text, images, and video, it continues to face structural and ethical limitations. As Andler (2023) observes, it remains characterized by the absence of consciousness, genuine semantic grounding, intentionality, and, above all, common sense—crucial for pragmatic and contextual understanding of language.

These challenges suggest a complementary relationship between humans and machines, opening the way to embodied AI capable of linking language comprehension and production to sensorimotor experience. Such an approach would foster robotics in which learning arises from interaction with the world, integrating language, vision, gesture, and spatial perception. Finally, incorporating theories from cognitive semantics into natural language processing—whether conceptual metaphor or frame semantics—could enable AI to capture the bodily representations underlying linguistic expressions and to structure knowledge in conceptual frames, supporting richer syntactic, semantic, cognitive, and pragmatic processing.

REFERENCES

Andler, D. (2023). *Intelligence artificielle, intelligence humaine: la double énigme* (Vol. 4, No. 05). Gallimard.

Apostol, P. (2021). De la cognition incarnée au corps cognitivisé. *Studia Universitatis Babes-Bolyai-Philosophia, 66*(2, Suppl.), 15–24. DOI: 10.24193/subbphil.2021.2s.01

Baars, B. J. (1986). *The cognitive revolution in psychology*. Guilford Press.

Boudon, P. (1996). L'inscription corporelle de l'esprit, sciences cognitives et expérience humaine. *Intellectica, 2*(23), 347–370. https://www.persee.fr/doc/intel_0769-4113_1996_num_23_2_1543

Buyssens, E. (1969). La grammaire générative selon Chomsky. *Revue Belge de Philologie et d'Histoire. Belgisch Tijdschrift voor Philologie en Geschiedenis, 3*(47), 840–857. https://www.persee.fr/doc/rbph_0035-0818_1969_num_47_3_2782. DOI: 10.3406/rbph.1969.2782

Chomsky, N. (1965). *Aspects de la théorie syntaxique: Préliminaires méthodologiques.* (M. Braudeau, Trad.) Éditions du Seuil. Retrieved from: https://flum.galexie.com/pdf/Chomsky%201965%20-%20Aspects%20de%20la%20theorie%20syntaxique.pdf

Fastrez, P. (2014). La prise en compte du corps en sémantique cognitive. *Hermès. Law Review, 1*(68), 36–42.

Fortis, J. M. (2012). De la grammaire générative à la linguistique cognitive: retour sur un basculement théorique. *In: Histoire Épistémologie Langage, La linguistique cognitive: histoire et épistémologie., Tome 34, fascicule 1.*, 115-154. Retrieved from: https://hal.science/hal-01417553/

Fuchs, C. (2004). Pour introduire à la linguistique cognitive. *Ophrys/MSH*, 01-24. Retrieved from: https://books.openedition.org/editionsmsh/7059#anchor-fulltext

Ganascia, J. G. (2006). *Les sciences cognitives.* Le pommier.

Geeraerts, D. (1993). Des deux côtés de la sémantique structurale: sémantique historique et sémantique cognitive. *Histoire épistémologie langage, 15*(1), 111-129. Retrieved from: https://www.persee.fr/doc/hel_0750-8069_1993_num_15_1_2370

Handwerker, B. (1983). La linguistique cognitive et le destin de la sémantique. *DRLAV. Documentation et Recherche en Linguistique Allemande Vincennes, 1*(28), 133–151. DOI: 10.3406/drlav.1983.990

Haugeland, J. (1989). *L'esprit dans la machine: Fondements de l'intelligence artificielle*. Odile Jacob.

Kaufmann, J. N. (1977). Psychologie de la «conscience» et science du «behavior». *Philosophiques, 4*(2), 313-326. Retrieved from: https://www.erudit.org/fr/revues/philoso/1977-v4-n2-philoso1313/203082ar.pdf

Lakoff, G., & Johnson, M. (1985). *Les métaphores dans la vie quotidienne*. Les Éditions de Minuit.

Legrand, M. (1990). Du behaviorisme au cognitivisme. *L'année psychologique, 90*(2), 247-286. Retrieved from: https://www.persee.fr/doc/psy_0003-5033_1990_num_90_2_29399

Meyran, R. (2017). Edward Sapir et Benjamin L. Whorf: La langue est une vision du monde. *Les Grands Dossiers des Sciences Humaines.*, (46), 46–47. DOI: 10.3917/gdsh.046.0014

Mpia, H. N., Nzanzu, M. M., & Kasolene, M. K. (2024). *De l'intelligence naturelle à l'intelligence artificielle ou de l'intelligence artificielle à l'intelligence naturelle: Une exploration des liens et des synergies* (Vol. 25). Revue Internationale Multidisciplinaire Etincelle.

Neveu, F. (2004). *Dictionnaire des sciences du langage*. Armand Colin.

Nyckees, V. (2007). La cognition humaine saisie par le langage: de la sémantique cognitive au médiationnisme. *Corela HS-6 - cognition, représentation, langage*, 1-56. DOI: 10.4000/corela.1538

Pylyshyn, Z. (1984). *Computation and Cognition. Toward a Foundation for Cognitive Science*. MIT Press. DOI: 10.7551/mitpress/2004.001.0001

Roux, S. (2024). L'âge classique en sciences cognitives: de la continuité revendiquée à la rupture. (É. D. Sorbonne, Éd.) 101-120. Retrieved from: https://books.openedition.org/psorbonne/114616?lang=fr#anchor-footnotes

Skinner, B. F. (1964). Behaviorism at fifty. *Behavioral and Brain Sciences, 7*(4), 615–621. DOI: 10.1017/S0140525X00027618

Steiner, P. (2005). Introduction cognitivisme et sciences cognitives. *Labyrinthe* (20), 13-39. Retrieved from: https://journals.openedition.org/labyrinthe/754

Varela, F. J. (1989). *Invitation aux sciences cognitives*. Editions du Seuil.

Varela, F. J., & al. (1993). *L'inscription corporelle de l'esprit: sciences cognitives et expérience humaine*. (V. Havelange, Trad.) Éditions du Seuil.

Victorri, B. (2000). Langage et cognition: le malentendu cognitiviste. Retrieved from: https://shs.hal.science/halshs-00009483/

ENDNOTES

1. Whorf exemplifies linguistic relativism through the case of the Hopi, whose language lacks linear temporal markers, and the Inuit, who possess multiple lexical terms for various types of snow. These examples support his view that linguistic structures are incommensurable and shape perception, cognition, and behavior, thus challenging the presumed universality of human thought (Meyran, 2017, p. 47).
2. These approaches, centered on consciousness, seek to describe and explain so-called "mental events" such as intention, attention, and decision-making.
3. [We translate].
4. [We translate].
5. CST mark a conceptual and technological revolution, forming an interdisciplinary network focused on information technology and related fields.
6. Cybernetics is interdisciplinary, involving meetings of computer scientists, linguists, and psychologists to structure knowledge.
7. Quillian proposed a hierarchical knowledge model with access procedures, showing that reaction time grows with each step.
8. This term refers to entities that actively consume information. In SC, it denotes how humans and machines acquire, process, and use information.
9. SC includes cognitive psychology, philosophy, linguistics, AI, and neuroscience, with logic, math, and computer science also playing key roles. Some approaches focus on higher cognitive functions independent of brain structures (Steiner, 2005).
10. Computers serve as functional models of cognition, simulating mental processes. Computational models help us understand the mind (Steiner, 2005, p.16).
11. For a machine to understand language, it must analyze text like a careful student, applying syntax, semantics, and pragmatics.

12 By way of illustration, believing that « *it is raining* » involves maintaining a certain relationship with a symbolic representation of that state of affairs. More generally, to believe, desire, know, or fear that **P** implies having a propositional representation of P in the mind, in the form of a belief, a desire, or another mental state. Similarly, to grasp a concept is to possess a mental representation of that concept (Steiner, 2005, p. 22). Furthermore, representationalists argue that all mental activity is based on symbolic representations that reflect the objects of mental states or facts. Proponents of this paradigm formulate propositional representations such as: **x** believes that **P** ; **x** fears that **P** ; **x** desires that **P**, which are, from a cognitive standpoint, located in specific « *mental boxes* » corresponding to beliefs, fears, or desires.

13 The connectionist paradigm does not completely reject the notion of *representation*, but rather redefines its role within the cognitive system, viewing it as distributed rather than localized in a single physical entity. Representation results from the coordinated activation of certain neurons. Connectionist systems differ from cognitivist-computational systems by their sub-symbolic nature. Indeed, this approach to cognitive science excludes symbols and symbolic computation in favor of numerical operations (Varela, 1989).

14 A grammar is said to be generative if it can produce, from an explicit set of rules, all the grammatical sentences of a language along with their appropriate syntactic structure.

15 Competence refers to the internalized knowledge that an ideal speaker-listener has of their language, enabling them to generate and understand an infinite number of utterances, while performance concerns the actual use of language in concrete contexts (Chomsky, 1965, p. 13).

16 The tripartite structure of the generative model includes the syntactic, semantic, and phonological components. *Syntax*, the system's core, generates the deep structure through syntagmatic and transformational rules that produce the surface structure. The *semantic* component associates the syntactic structure with a meaning representation, while the *phonological* component determines the phonetic form. Chomsky (1965, p. 32) specifies that the deep structure governs semantic interpretation and the surface structure governs phonetic interpretation.

Chapter 12
Inclusive Pedagogy and Artificial Intelligence in the Teaching of Physical Education and Sports

Imane Belmaadadia
https://orcid.org/0009-0004-5942-8500
Faculty of Letters and Human Sciences, Ibn Tofail University, Morocco

Mohamed Meliani
https://orcid.org/0009-0008-5532-0454
Faculty of Letters and Human Sciences, Ibn Tofail University, Morocco

ABSTRACT

This work studies the incorporation of artificial intelligence (AI) as a vector of pedagogical innovation in the teaching/learning of physical education and sports (PE). Based on a systematic literature review of recently published work (2023-2024), this chapter highlights three major advantages of AI devices in PE teaching, including the individualization of educational pathways, the objectivity of evaluation and the development of learners' motivation and commitment, including those with disabilities. The critical analysis highlights challenges to be overcome, namely teacher training, data privacy and educational equity for all. An interdisciplinary conceptual framework is proposed as well as recommendations regarding education policies, digital investment and institutional cooperation. This study aims to establish the foundations for a deontological and continuous integration of AI tools in PE, for innovative, inclusive pedagogical practices adapted to the individual needs of learners.

DOI: 10.4018/979-8-3373-3436-3.ch012

INTRODUCTION

One of the major transformations affecting educational actions today is the integration of artificial intelligence (AI) in teaching. These technological innovations have an impact on all disciplines, including physical education and sports (PE). The digitalization of teaching methods is essential from the outset and traditional approaches are now being redefined through a new lever, AI, which makes it possible to provide innovative solutions to personalize learning paths, analyze performance and optimize feedback for learners. In this dynamic, this work explores the possibility of integrating AI into the teaching/learning of PE in order to overcome the heterogeneity of students' levels, the failures of infrastructure in schools and the ethical problems related to the use of digital technologies. According to Dey (2023), the applications of AI in sports cannot be reduced to a simple measurement of performance; they go beyond it and make it possible to make succinct diagnoses of learners' motor and cognitive abilities. The work of Miao, Zhang and Yan (2023), on the other hand, suggests that the use of deep learning algorithms and intelligent monitoring systems, at the university level, promotes the design of individualized learning paths that meet the needs of each student. Jie, Hou and Hu (2024) show that integrating AI into PE teaching at the university level is a considerable opportunity to optimize traditional pedagogical practices using interactive devices and engaging learning environments. On the other hand, although this progress is promising, several questions need to be analysed in depth with the use of AI. This research explores how PE pedagogical practices can be transformed to improve student engagement, motivation, and learning outcomes. In this context, it is imperative to ensure that AI is able to individualize educational content according to the specific needs of learners and to objectively evaluate their performance, which will reduce disparities between subjects, especially those with disabilities. Similarly, it is essential to manage the potential challenges that hinder the adoption of technologies, namely the still poorly adapted technological infrastructure within educational institutions, the lack of training of educators and the problem of personal data privacy. The present investigation focuses mainly on the ability to improve the motivation and engagement of learners in AI PE, on its ability to personalize learning adapted to the varied profiles of students and on all the operational and ethical challenges that accompany its integration into teaching/learning. This work will therefore examine the extent to which AI can automate performance monitoring, adjust the real time of the proposed exercises and offer immediate feedback to promote the progress of the activity. In addition, it is necessary to highlight the essential conditions for successful integration, including the training of teachers and the installation of suitable technological infrastructures (Castro, Chiappe and Rodríguez, 2024) and careful management of the personal data collected (Ompoc and Aguinaldo, 2024). A main hypothesis can be formulated: the integration of AI into the teaching/learning of PE, through tools allowing individualized monitoring and predictive analysis of performance, could typically increase student engagement and improve their learning outcomes. By optimizing learning paths adapted to the different profiles of the students, AI would not only make it possible to adapt activity methods to the learners' skills, but also to predict future progress. Tian (2024), among others, presents how AI could process data to adjust sports training programs, avoid injuries and increase learner performance, which would give a new dimension to PE teaching that goes beyond subjective and instantaneous assessments towards an inclusive engaging pedagogy. In addition, AI has a positive impact on the entire pedagogical process by changing the teacher/student relationship. The support of virtual tutors and automated assessment systems allows teachers to better manage heterogeneous classrooms, focusing more on individualized assistance and the human dimension of pedagogical practices. From this perspective, pedagogical expertise cannot be substituted by AI, but on the contrary it acts as a complementary tool enriching pedagogical interventions and reinforcing educational practices. This work understands the impact of AI in PE by analyzing technological innovations, integration challenges and ethical requirements. It will explore, through a systematic literature review and case studies, the modalities of a successful integration of AI in PE teaching by considering institutional difficulties and the alarming increase in the rate of physical inactivity (Belmaadadia and Meliani, 2024). This study aims to be able, towards the end, to propose practical suggestions for a harmonious and equitable adoption of AI tools in schools and universities. This research is part of an environment in perpetual transformation, where digital technologies offer new horizons to reconsider the educational act. Indeed, the integration of AI in the teaching/learning of PE is an opportunity that can modernize pedagogical actions subject to personalizing the follow-up of learners and training future PE teachers to benefit from a digital environment in crescendo evolution. By adopting judicious research questions and strong hypotheses associated with a succinct study of contemporary practices, this investigation aspires to set up the foundations of a new vision in pedagogical practices in PE. This work is based on a study that questions the contribution of AI to current methods used in PE via a critical literature review of cases of personalization, evaluation and inclusion. A conceptual framework will then explore hypotheses related to improving student motivation and engagement, with equity in assessment, and with monitoring student progress. The methodology adopted is a mixed approach that aims to assess the impact of the use of AI tools on learning, based on a literature review and case studies. The results presented highlight the effects of AI on the individualization of learning and interaction within the classroom. The discussion will link these findings to the ethical and technical challenges encountered. Finally, recommendations on training, upgrading the technological infrastructure of schools and data management will be issued in order to consider a fair inclusive integration of AI in PE. This chapter presents an educational context combining pedagogy and technology for the teaching of PE, while offering innovative recommendations for the support and inclusion of all students. It lays the foundations for a crescendo of AI integration in PE in Morocco.

APPLYING AI TO PE: STATE OF KNOWLEDGE

Definition and evolution of AI in PE

Many scientific research projects are increasingly interested in the integration of AI in the field of PE and this offers a rich theoretical framework for revisiting usual teaching practices. In this section, it is proposed to examine the theoretical underpinnings of the application of AI to physical education and sport and to highlight the predominant research currents and empirical findings from previous studies while highlighting the challenges and opportunities.

To benefit from the contribution of AI, it is necessary that the capacity of computer systems be similar to certain cognitive functions of the human brain, in particular, including learning, reasoning and adaptation. In line with the pedagogical context, using AI tools means using machine learning algorithms, neural networks and data management processes to analyse student behaviour, generate individualised learning programmes and instant feedback. Through this strategy, it is possible to objectively measure the performance of learners while estimating their progress and thus adapt teaching methods according to the needs of each of them. Dey (2023), for example, presents a detailed assessment of the different applications currently used in the sports field. It states that obtaining accurate diagnoses of students' motor and cognitive abilities is now possible by using smart sensors and accompanying algorithms with a view to individualizing teaching/learning pathways.

Pedagogical individuation and objective evaluation

Several studies have explored the dimensions of the incorporation of AI in the teaching and learning of PE. The first is the personalization of the didactic trajectories of the beneficiaries. In this sense, Miao, Zhang and Yan (2023), emphasize that the use of technological devices based on deep learning promote the development of learning paths adjusted to the specific needs of students. Such a model aimed at personalized learning is particularly judicious in the field of PE, where the disparity in physical, coordination and motivational abilities is typically marked from one student to another. The proposal of tailor-made exercises, adapted according to the instant feedback generated by intelligent and continuous monitoring devices, will radically change the usual, generally standardized, teaching approaches. Jie, Hou and Hu (2024) on the other hand, show that the integration of AI into university teaching can transform the way in which educational content is delivered using interactive and adaptive learning environments.

The second fundamental dimension reported in the research is performance analysis and progress monitoring. The collection and analysis of biomechanical data is done via wearable sensors, combined with motion recognition algorithms. Tian (2024) also mentions this dimension in his work, stating that this technology also makes it possible to evaluate instantaneous sports performance, predict the risk of accidents and suggest personalized adaptations to training programs. Through these analytical approaches, teachers can explore a new perspective on assessment while relying on quantitative and objective information, promoting a better understanding of the learning processes in PE. Moreover, Ompoc and Aguinaldo (2024), through their experimental approach, demonstrate that the integration of AI in a structured way in teaching improves student engagement and academic results, by generating continuous feedback and adjusting exercises to the constantly changing needs of learners.

The experiments and case studies revealed in the literature provide valuable insight into the conditions for the use of AI in the context of PE. For example, Belmaadadia and Meliani (2024) examine the implementation of physical activity and health education in some regions of Morocco, and insist on the need to focus on awareness programs to combat sedentary lifestyles by strengthening campaigns around health education. The integration of digitalization tools could increase the effectiveness of educational programs in schools and develop "health habitus". Omar (2023), on the other hand, also points out that the use of virtual tutors and automated assessment systems will allow teachers to better manage hybrid classrooms by focusing more on personalized follow-up and improving teacher/student interactivity. All this work underlines that AI should not be perceived as a threat to the teacher's function, but rather as an enriching element of pedagogical practice and promoting dynamic and inclusive teaching.

Ethical challenges and inequalities of access

However, the integration of AI in PE also presents exceptional challenges despite the many potential benefits. Teacher training is considered the first obstacle; the application of AI devices requires, in addition to mastery of these technologies, the ability to adapt teaching practices. In this context, in order to ensure the full exploitation of the potential of AI and to ensure quality pedagogical transfer, Castro, Chiappe and Rodriguez (2024) emphasize the importance of developing in-service training programs for teachers. Technical gaps and refusal to change can be barriers to the adoption of these technologies in educational settings. Another major difficulty to overcome is the ethical issues related to the use of AI. By collecting and analyzing students' personal data, the confidentiality of information and the protection of subjects' privacy becomes vulnerable. It is essential that fair protocols to preserve data are put in place by educational institutions to avoid any discrimination or algorithmic bias that can harm fragile students.

Equity in access to digital technologies is also a key issue, particularly in environments where financial and material resources are low. This can create inequality in access to AI devices, further widening the gap between well-equipped and low-capacity facilities. The theoretical and practical challenges related to the adoption of AI in PE encourage us to revisit the entire pedagogical process. The theoretical framework chosen for this study is based on a review of previous work and conceptual strategies adopted in digital education. This framework underlines the importance of individualized learning, continuous performance evaluation and teacher training as strategic mechanisms for the successful integration of AI. The pedagogical transformation brought about by the adoption of AI is not only about the introduction of technology, but requires an update of pedagogical actions, learning paths and their evaluations.

In order to succeed in this transformation, AI must be thought of as an educational ally that complements human know-how with concise and objective analyses of information. Adaptive learning approaches create learning environments where each beneficiary progresses at their own pace, with personalized follow-up and instant feedback. This framework for personalized learning, supported by local investigations, in this case those of Dey (2023), Mia, Zhang AND Yan (2023) proposing innovative solutions to the difficulties due to the heterogeneity of learners' profiles. However, the use of smart technologies to optimize performance and manage injury risk offers unprecedented opportunities for the development of adapted and safe training programs.

Previous studies also reveal that the benefits that PSE can derive from the integration of AI depend largely on the power of institutions to adopt these tools in an appropriate and orderly manner. Thus, to maximize the positive impact of AI on learning, it is essential to put in place a clear and regulated framework, combined with teacher training and investment in the required digital infrastructure. On the other hand, collaboration between researchers, specialists and public good managers is emerging as a key element in prioritizing pedagogical innovation and facilitating the smooth transition to digitalized educational actions.

In short, the theoretical foundation and the literature review presented above prove that the integration of AI devices in the teaching/learning of PE presents promising opportunities to revolutionize pedagogical practices in PE. Contemporary studies underline that AI makes it possible to distinguish learning paths, improve their evaluation and improve student engagement and motivation. However, these benefits come with major challenges, namely teacher training, preservation of personal information, and equitable access. The synthesis of the above-mentioned investigations, mainly due to Belmaadadia and Meliani (2024), Castro, Chiappe and Rodríguez (2024), Dey (2023), Jie, Hou and Hu (2024), Miao, Zhang and Yan (2023), Omar (2023), Ompoc and Aguinaldo (2024) and Tian (2024), offers a global perspective that considers AI as an auxiliary means in the service of an engaging, personalized and ethical approach. This theoretical framework establishes the basis of this study, which aims to explore the necessary provisions for the integration of AI in PE and to issue recommendations for effective implementation.

RESEARCH PROPOSALS AND UNDERLYING THEORY

This study adopts a conceptual scheme that is based on a reflection stipulating that the integration of AI in the teaching/learning of PE represents an essential vector for re-examining and revisiting usual pedagogical practices. This approach is based on the interrelationship between different factors, mainly individualized learning, the objectivity of the assessment and the motivation of the students. This research also highlights that by using digital tools such as machine learning algorithms, smart sensors and instant feedback systems, AI can design clearly adaptive learning environments that respond to the motor, cognitive and socio-emotional specificities of each student and offer a rigorous and objective assessment of their sports skills.

Singular learning

In the same vein, this framework is based on the concept of personalized learning which is qualified by the ability to adapt the pedagogical content and teaching strategies to the individual needs of the learners. Indeed, Miao, Zhang and Yan (2023) postulate that the use of intelligent coaching methods and predictive models using intelligent learning algorithms makes it possible to design adjusted learning trajectories. This adaptation of content is possible through the collection and analysis of biomechanical and behavioral data, which processed by AI devices, provide precise information on the level of competence of each student, hence the identification of his or her needs. This allows AI to become a tool for identifying learners' strengths and weaknesses and consequently the content and difficulty of the proposed exercises.

Objective assessment

Moreover, the incorporation of AI devices offers an objective evaluation of performance in PE. Usually, PE assessment is often subjective, as this process is based on direct observation of teachers. However, the use of motion recognition engineering and biomechanical analysis makes it possible to precisely determine the various performance indicators, including endurance, strength, speed and coordination. According to Dey (2023), the use of AI tools in body movement analysis provides specialists with immediate and objective feedback, leading to a fair and equitable assessment. Such relevance can only improve and guide learning while minimizing the aspects inherent in traditional assessments.

Learner Involvement

This conceptual framework is based on another fundamental dimension, namely, student engagement. The integration of AI tools into learning environments, through the interactivity and individualized feedback it offers, is likely to develop learners' motivation and involvement in PE sessions. Indeed, Jie, Hou and Hu (2024), in their work, point out that the use of engaging technologies such as augmented reality and virtual simulations, can offer engaging learning experiences that stimulate students' interest in physical activity. Omar (2023), for his part, presents in the pedagogical follow-up the contribution of virtual tutors who provide individualized assistance and maintaining a high level of involvement throughout the learning process.

Several hypotheses are necessary based on the different dimensions mentioned above. The first is that the integration of AI in the teaching/learning of PE would significantly promote the development of individualized learning, the improvement of the objectivity of the assessment and the involvement of learners in the process. In this sense, the use of AI would make it possible to optimize performance monitoring, reduce gaps between students' levels and obtain instant feedback. In short, to facilitate a continuous progression of learning. Theoretically, this strategy should lead to better acquisition of sports skills and an increase in motivation among learners. The second hypothesis is to overcome the challenges of integrating digitalization into educational contexts. Certainly, although potential advantages accompany the incorporation of AI devices in PE, this experience can be slowed down by several difficulties, teacher training, technical and ethical constraints in relation to the management of personal data. Continuing education programs are essential according to Castro, Chiappe and Rodriguez (2024) to familiarize teachers with new digital techniques and help them adopt these systems in their pedagogical actions. Thus, an effective integration of AI would greatly depend on the involvement of institutions in the appropriate support and adequate funding to overcome these constraints. The third hypothesis concerns the impact of technological revolutions on the equity of learning. It is true that by offering personalized support, AI would help minimize inequalities between learners, including those from disadvantaged backgrounds or those with specific needs. Although Belmaadadia and Meliani's (2024) work does not directly address AI tools, it argues that any integration of technology must take into account structural, cultural, or socio-economic constraints in order to ensure equity in access to quality physical education. However, without an optimized management of ethical aspects, the use of smart technologies could intensify the already existing disparities. These hypotheses are part of a reference framework where AI is not an objective in itself but a mode for optimising and renovating PE teaching pathways. The idea is that by using AI, the creation of adaptable and responsive learning environments that are adjustable to the needs of students and offer a fair and objective assessment of performance would now be possible. The association between individualized learning, objective assessment and student engagement is the basis of this approach, which is analyzed by case studies and empirical analyses in the work of reference authors (Dey (2023), Miao, Zhang and Yan (2023), Jie, Hou and Hu (2024), Omar (2023).

The successful incorporation of AI in PE will now depend on a set of technological and pedagogical initiatives simultaneously, including modern infrastructure and adapted training programs. At the same time, the design of a rigorous regulatory framework is essential in order to protect personal information and fair access to innovations. These combined strategies will transform PE teaching by maximizing the potential of AI, with a view to ensuring a smooth transition to the optimization of educational practices. The theoretical framework and hypotheses presented in this work aim to prove that AI, integrated in a thoughtful and ethical way, can serve as an effective lever for the improvement of pedagogical actions in PE. These hypotheses will be verified through systematic methodologies and empirical analyses with the aim of offering practical recommendations for the successful implementation of AI in PE, and thus, the birth of a new era in sports teaching/learning.

FOR THE INTEGRATION OF AI IN PE: METHODOLOGICAL APPROACH

To be properly carried out, this research was based on a brief systematic literature review summarizing recent scientific work. This strategy, usually adopted in exploratory studies, ensures a critical and designed review of the existing scientific literature, without having to collect preliminary data. The objective is to explore the contribution of AI to the personalization of learning, the evaluation of sports performance and the involvement of students in the teaching of PE. The selected publications are those published between 2023 and 2024 so that the work is updated and anchored in the most recent innovations, among others, those of Dey (2023), Jie, Hou eu Hu (2024) and Bodemer (2023) which highlight the way in which AI tools are transforming pedagogical approaches.

Sources were collected through academic reference database management systems, specifically Google Scholar, PubMed, Scopus, and journal portals. The keywords used in the search process included: "Artificial Intelligence", "Physical Education and Sports", "Personalisation of Learning", "Diagnostic Assessment", "Innovative Pedagogy", "Inclusion", "Intellectual Disability". The selection of publications was based on the inclusion criteria, among others: relevant topics directly related to AI in PE, contemporary publications (2023/2024) and accessibility of the full text. The selection was made in two different stages. The reading of the titles and abstracts, as a first step, made it possible to make an initial selection to retain the articles that might be appropriate for reading in full. In the second place, a careful reading has favoured the identification of the fundamental theoretical, methodological and empirical elements of each research with a view to an analysis organised around the following dimensions: "individualisation of learning", "performance evaluation", "learner involvement", "technical requirements and ethical constraints". A qualitative thematic content method was used to analyze the data collected. Regularities, discrepancies and gaps were identified for each study. The research was categorized, noting the category of "personalized learning" for the work of Miao, Zhang and Yan (2023), that of Tian (2024) in that of "biomechanical analysis and optimization of training". While the research of Castro, Chiappe and Rodriguez (2024) and Ompoc and Aguinaldo was classified as "institutional challenges". Towards the end, bibliographic management software (Zotero in this case) was used to guarantee the traceability of the data and to distribute the benefits by theme. This method has led to the development of a relevant and sharp synthesis while taking into account the ethical standards of scientific reproducibility.

This strategy offered, in addition to a coherent reference framework, a structuring of the results according to the dimensions previously presented, in order to be able to propose operational recommendations for the application of AI in PE. The personalization of learning, the objectivity of evaluation, the motivation and involvement of students and the anticipation of risks related to sports practice via AI devices are the main contributions highlighted in the research requested.

Finally, the use of such a documentary review is appropriate to the exploratory nature of the study undertaken. It opens the horizons for possible investigations, especially empirical ones, which would enrich the findings highlighted in this work.

PEDAGOGICAL RETURNS AND PUTTING DATA INTO PERSPECTIVE

This research suggests that the adoption of AI in PE has positive effects not only on the individualization of learning pathways, but also on the objectivity of performance evaluation and student involvement. The use of these devices allows, in addition to improving the quality of PE sessions, to raise learners' awareness of health issues by better adjusting sports programs to the different needs of beneficiaries (Belmaadadia and Meliani, 2024). These findings support the idea that AI tools can provide equitable learning opportunities, especially in resource-limited school settings, by urging inclusive PE teaching/learning.

The scope of AI for Education 4.0, based on mechanisms that promote the personalization of learning, has been explored in the work of Castro, Chiappe and Rodriguez (2024). Smart technologies, which can adjust learning content following real-time data collection, have been shown to significantly improve the learning experience. These researchers also confirm that the use of AI makes it possible to individualize learning with immediate feedback facilitating teachers' pedagogical interventions. These findings prove that the singularization of learning, now possible by AI tools, can serve as a central vector for pedagogical efficiency in inclusive PE. Indeed, Dey (2023), by providing a review of contemporary applications used in the field of PE and sport, supports this perspective. According to him, the contribution of AI is not limited to performance monitoring but opens the horizons to innovative methods for assessing skills. Dey emphasizes the ability of AI tools to produce regular objective assessments automatically, which reduces the subjectivity of traditional assessments. The implementation of adapted training pathways, allowing teachers to identify exactly the gaps and the avenues for their improvement in students, is now easy through the adoption of this approach, which makes it possible to offer formative assessments based on accurate data constituting a step forward in planning and personalized pedagogical readjustment. Jie, Hou and Hu (2024) offer a complementary vision by focusing on university teaching and the adoption of AI in PE. They stipulate that the use of digital technologies in PE training courses promotes, in addition to pedagogical innovation, the management of challenges in relation to the heterogeneity of students' profiles and skill levels. They also point out that engaging learning environments and AI-enhanced interactive tools allow for good understanding and better investment on the part of students. As a result, AI devices can contribute to the modernization of academic training in PE, by providing alternatives adjusted to the different needs of learners, thus supporting the evolution towards active and innovative pedagogical practices. The work of Miao, Zhang, and Yan (2023) explores another important dimension in the intelligent teaching of sports activities; the effectiveness of personalized learning paths. They prove that through deep learning algorithms, AI can generate tailor-made programs in which each subject benefits from personalized support with specific performance indicators. Indeed, the results of such a strategy favor a regular development and a good assimilation of sports techniques. However, the work emphasizes the importance of instant feedback that allows students to correct themselves technically and optimize their efforts following the technologically provided guidelines. To support these findings, Omar (2023) highlights the benefits of personalized AI learning. Her research states that the use of virtual tutors and self-directed assessment mechanisms create dynamic and participatory learning contexts, in which learners receive real-time feedback. This innovative approach makes it possible to improve individual performance while promoting a great deal of autonomy in learning. The data collected suggests that AI can transform educational practices in PE by highlighting devices that provide interactive responses to the individualized needs of the subjects. The study highlights that as a result, a strengthening of intrinsic motivation and an improvement in self-evaluation skills will ultimately be in learners. For their part, Ompoc and Aguinaldo (2024) have proven, through their empirical study, the positive impact of the incorporation of AI on students' investment and academic performance in PE. Through a quasi-experimental approach, they show that the integration of AI tools in teaching significantly improves student engagement with better assimilation of knowledge. They also note that the objective assessment offered by AI significantly reduces disparities in grading and allows for relevant support to supervise educational actions. Finally, Tian's (2024) research, focused on the optimization of training and evaluation processes in higher education environments through the use of AI tools, which proves that the analysis of biomechanical and physiological data by technological devices makes it possible to individualize training paths while predicting the risk of injury and adjusting activities according to individual performance. These data offer an innovative vision of performance and health management in PE by adopting an anticipatory and preventive method of risks in relation to sports practice.

Generally speaking, the compilation of the data collected from these various studies specifies that the adoption of AI technological devices is an important resource that can transform pedagogical practices. The results tend towards the personalization of learning, the improvement of the objectivity of evaluation and the strengthening of student involvement and therefore, the challenges of teacher training, the development of digital infrastructure and data ethics. This report presents a solid basis for engaging in future research in this direction, and proposing recommendations for an efficient and ethical application of AI in PE.

CONTRIBUTION OF AI TO PE: REFLEXIVE ANALYSIS

The findings state that the integration of AI into PE teaching has notable interests and major challenges to be overcome. In view of the above-mentioned studies, in particular those of Belmaadadia and Meliani (2024), Castro, Chiappe and Rodríguez (2024), Dey (2023), Jie, Hou and Hu (2024), Miao, Zhang and Yan (2023), Omar (2023), Ompoc and Aguinaldo (2024) and Tian (2024), it seems obvious that AI devices allow for the individualization of teaching programs, an optimization of objective assessment and motivation in learners. Nevertheless, although this innovation is encouraging, it involves methodological, technical and ethical issues that need to be examined in greater depth.

The ability of AI to individualize teaching is an important vector for satisfying the individualized needs of subjects. There is ample research that proves that the use of smart technologies supports the design of personalized education programs by analyzing the motor and cognitive performance of beneficiaries (Miao, Zhang and Yan (2023) and Jie, Hou and Hu (2024) as examples). These technologies use machine learning algorithms to process information retained by motion sensors and other biometric tools instantaneously to proactively adapt educational content and task complexity. This strategy, in addition to being able to adapt pedagogical actions to different profiles, provides immediate feedback that allows for continuous and oriented progress. However, the adoption of these technologies requires colossal investments in digital infrastructure and teacher training. Indeed, the work of Castro, Chiappe and Rodriguez (2024) supports this vision and underlines that the effectiveness of these tools depends largely on the ability of teachers to assimilate and manipulate these devices, hence the need for rigorous in-service training. The investigations of Dey (2023) and Tian (2024) highlight another dimension, that of performance analysis and "the objectivity of evaluation". Usually, PE evaluation is based on the observations of teachers; The likelihood of subjectivity and/or bias in the assessment is obvious. On the other hand, the use of smart sensors, in addition to motion recognition algorithms, allows the quantitative measurement of performance and thus an instantaneous and accurate evaluation. By borrowing this analytical method, the technical weaknesses of each learner are quickly identified and targeted adjustments in the training paths are proposed. In addition, technical objectivity must always be confronted with educational realities; Human expertise is a dimension that must always be considered with caution, in the analysis of data, the contextualization of results and the adaptation of pedagogical follow-ups. As a result, the congruence between automatic analysis and technical appreciation of teachers is essential to best manage the relationship with the machine, which can sometimes not take into account the subtleties related to specific learning environments. Student involvement is another decisive element in the success of innovative pedagogical actions of AI in the teaching/learning of PE. In fact, Omar (2023) and Ompoc and Aguinaldo (2024) attest that the use of digital systems (virtual tutors, interactive assessment tools) allows for optimal student involvement and good assimilation of knowledge. A dynamic and engaging learning environment (e.g. through augmented reality) stimulates learners' intrinsic motivation, which promotes lively participation in sports activities and thus better academic and sporting results. Nevertheless, it is necessary to adapt technological alternatives according to the specific contexts in which they are used in order to foster learner engagement which is highly dependent on cultural differences, Ethically, important issues are raised by the incorporation of AI in PE, particularly those with the collection, analysis and storage of learners' personal information. Privacy and confidentiality issues are emerging given AI's ability to process sensitive data such as student biometrics. As a result, according to Castro, Chiappe and Rodriguez (2024), and Ompoc and Aguinaldo (2024), it is imperative to establish a strict charter to guarantee the confidentiality of this information and to avoid the risks of algorithmic bias or discrimination. In addition, the lack of legislative standards at the global level disrupts the unification of actions, hence the urgency of designing clear guidelines and independent monitoring mechanisms. These procedures are elementary to ensure the responsible and ethical use of AI in an educational setting.

The adoption of AI in PE goes far beyond the direct benefits, it also has indirect benefits, such as the reduction of educational disparities. In addition, Belmaadadia and Meliani (2024) emphasize the importance of turning to disadvantaged areas so as not to reinforce inequalities between facilities and those that are underequipped. In this sense, it is crucial that institutional and political initiatives are mobilized to support the deployment of educational equity on a significant scale by ensuring that all schools have the same opportunities for access to innovative technologies. Overall, the work reviewed states that the incorporation of AI tools into PE will not only improve the performance of subjects, but more importantly, it will transform future pedagogical practices. An integrative method combining objective interpretation by intelligent technologies and subjective interpretation by teachers has proven to be favourable in meeting the challenges of innovative teaching. Indeed, intelligent systems must be seen as a supplementary instrument that can reinforce educational actions without neglecting the indispensable role of the teacher. The combination of digital technology with human know-how will facilitate the achievement of a high level of PE through an individualized and engaging follow-up for all learners.

This systematic literature review based on recent work confirms the hypothesis that the use of AI promotes the personalization of learning, the objectivity of assessments and the motivation and involvement of learners, provided that teachers are trained, the confidentiality of subjects and access to technological devices are guaranteed; tasks that require serious efforts to achieve. Careful consideration should be considered in order to meet the requirements for successful AI integration. Therefore, it will be necessary to plan local research to explore these issues in depth and to highlight the contextual elements that promote the success of innovative technologies in PE. At the same time, these results highlight the interest of choosing a multidisciplinary approach for the integration of AI in PE by taking into account technical and educational aspects in addition to ethical and social aspects. To succeed in such an approach, it would be necessary to design appropriate training programmes, develop sound technological infrastructures and create a clear regulatory framework. In the same sense, it is essential to conduct applied research to test and finalize AI adoption models, while mobilizing the various actors in this innovative project.

To conclude, the findings of the above-mentioned document review prove that the use of AI technologies in the teaching/learning of PE offers an appreciable resource for the transformation of educational actions and the improvement of performance among students. In addition, to fully benefit from this innovation, challenges must be met, such as training, ethics and equal access to these systems. These inferences prepare the ground for possible investigations that will draw even more on criteria that can optimize the long-term use of AI tools in PE by taking into account the disparities and heterogeneity of current educational contexts.

FOR AN ETHICAL INTEGRATION OF AI IN PE: OPERATIONAL PROPOSALS

In order to optimize the benefits of AI in the teaching/learning of PE, it is imperative to make decisive practical recommendations that are based on a strategy combining pedagogy, technology and ethics. These recommendations, based on an analytical reading of the recent work mentioned above (Belmaadadia and Meliani (2024), Castro, Chiappe and Rodríguez (2024), Dey (2023), Jie, Hou and Hu (2024), Miao, Zhang and Yan (2023), Omar (2023), Ompoc and Aguinaldo (2024) and Tian (2024)), aspire to orient educational policies and actions towards a successful and equitable implementation of smart systems in PE.

It seems, above all, that the strengthening of teacher training is essential. The success of such an innovation depends greatly on teachers' skills in mastering technological devices and their appropriate use to individualize educational paths and pedagogical approaches. Specific training, aimed at both the acquisition of technical skills (handling of smart sensors, exploitation of information and understanding of machine learning algorithms) and the creation of personalized programs are fundamental (Castro, Chiappe and Rodriguez, 2024 and Jie, Hou and Hu, 2024). It would be wise for these trainings to be continuous, scalable and delivered by experts in educational technology. Face-to-face or distance seminars, practical workshops or certified modules could be scheduled to allow teachers to share experiences and adopt innovative practices in their pedagogical actions. However, the implementation of pilot projects or practical internships to consolidate teachers' know-how depends greatly on collaboration between academic bodies and technology companies. The development of digital infrastructure in schools is an essential factor in the adoption of AI in PE. Studies by Dey (2024) and Tian (2023) highlight that the optimal use of intelligent systems is based on access to modern technological tools (high-precision motion sensors, instant tracking systems). As a result, educational institutions need to invest in appropriate digital platforms, not only through the installation of ultra-modern devices but above all through the maintenance and updating of equipment. Partnerships between specialized companies and research laboratories, for example, can facilitate their access to new technologies and technical maintenance services. This investment needs to be taken into consideration, especially in institutions with limited resources for an equitable dissemination of new technologies. Another recommendation to consider is to design a concise regulatory framework to ensure confidentiality and transparency when using AI systems in PE. Ompoc and Aguinaldo (2024) emphasize the importance of preserving learners' personal data and managing algorithmic biases that can lead to discrimination. For this reason, the development of clear protocols for collecting, processing and storing information is imperative. Monitoring mechanisms that should be monitored by independent bodies are also to be expected. The responsibilities of each of the actors involved in this process must be well defined to ensure data security. The regulatory approach must take into account the transparency of the algorithms adopted, thus providing all parties involved with the opportunity to understand and discuss the automated assessment criteria. This rigorous management will promote the establishment of confidence in the use of AI, both among teachers and learners. Local research and investigations are also recommended. Recent work is encouraging, but it is necessary to crown these findings with field studies in different educational contexts. To do this, it is preferable to start with pilot projects aimed at a representative sample of institutions to verify the impact of AI devices on learning, motivation, learner involvement and effectiveness in PE. This research would involve, in addition to teachers and students, parents and administrative managers to collect precise feedback and to put forward proposals according to localized realities. The evaluation of these pilot experiments should be carried out according to clear and concise standards via qualitative and quantitative indices to measure the effects of the use of AI on the sports performance, engagement and well-being of beneficiaries. In an ethical vision, access to smart technologies must take into account educational inequalities. Drawing on the outreach work of Belmaadadia and Meliani (2024) focused on health and physical activity promotion, it would be essential to improve health awareness in schools by adapting resources to local needs, which should be a prerequisite for any innovative technology. Hence the importance of designing database programs that ensure access to all beneficiaries, regardless of their socio-economic background and digital skills. In this sense, subsidy or partnership initiatives would be possible to develop technologically disadvantaged schools. Awareness campaigns among the educational community would be beneficial for the promotion of a culture of digital inclusion, which is essential to ensure equity in the benefits gained from the integration of AI. Finally, interdisciplinary and international cooperation is another vector to be taken into consideration for the successful integration of AI into PE. Pedagogy, technology and ethics are closely linked fields, which is why it is desirable to promote collaborative research platforms between universities, research laboratories, technology companies and educational institutions, which will make it possible to centralize resources, exchange knowledge and design joint projects that will benefit the entire education sector. In addition, this international exchange will make it possible to harmonize pedagogical practices and promote the establishment of common standards for the rapid and effective dissemination of innovative technologies.

In short, these proposals aim to create an appropriate environment for the integration of AI in PE by mobilizing several actions, including teacher training, infrastructure development, the design of a clear regulatory framework, the establishment of pilot projects and the encouragement of interdisciplinary collaboration initiatives. The objective is to optimize the benefits of the integration of AI in PE, namely the individualization of teaching/learning pathways, the objectivity of evaluation, student involvement, and the anticipation of the risk of injury, to guarantee equitable and inclusive education.

CONCLUSION

The present work examined the integration of AI in PE teaching/learning and highlighted its main contributions, the major challenges to be met and the possible perspectives to be explored. The analysis of the aforementioned recent research ((Belmaadadia and Meliani (2024), Castro, Chiappe and Rodríguez (2024), Dey (2023), Jie, Hou and Hu (2024), Miao, Zhang and Yan (2023), Omar (2023), Ompoc and Aguinaldo (2024) and Tian (2024)) highlights that intelligent systems present unprecedented opportunities for the individualization of learning trajectories, the objectivity of assessment and the involvement of learners. These findings encourage us to rethink pedagogical approaches in PE, which will have to take into account the individualization of learning paths in order to meet the particular needs of each subject. These approaches should also provide teachers with the tools they need for concise and instantaneous assessment. First, the use of intelligent devices (learning algorithms and intelligent sensors) facilitates the identification, in a meticulous way, of the motor and cognitive abilities of the subjects. The ability of AI tools to make personalized diagnoses has been proven by Dey (2023) and Miao, Zhang Yan (2024). They emphasize that personalized learning paths allow for the harmonious advancement of sports skills. Learning content adapted to the heterogeneous profiles of learners is an essential factor in making it possible, in addition to improving the quality of teaching, to develop student engagement: a very important dimension in a discipline where motivation and physical activity are a matter of course with academic success and general well-being. Similarly, the objectivity of performance evaluation in the strict sense, now possible through AI, represents a considerable evolution compared to the usual approaches where evaluation is inevitably subjective. High accuracy in performance measurement is also possible thanks to intelligent motion recognition systems and instant tracking systems. In this context, Tian (2024) and Omar (2023) stipulate that AI devices identify students' failures and offer personalized adaptations to optimize training sessions. The teacher's wise intervention supported by automated and ongoing evaluation will certainly improve the quality of teaching/learning in PE. At the same time, another aspect should not be neglected, that of learner involvement. The work of Jie, Hou and Hu (2024) and Ompoc and Aguinaldo (2024) shows the positive effect of interactive intelligent systems on motivation in students. The incorporation of engaging learning environments (augmented reality, visual tutors) offers a pedagogical approach that goes beyond the simple sharing of knowledge. Learning becomes more fun, more involved and promotes interaction between learners, which guarantees their commitment to sports activities and sustainable performance. However, while the horizons are promising, there are other challenges in the application of smart technologies in PSA that need to be considered. Teacher training remains one of the obstacles that can hinder the integration of these systems. Castro and Rodriguez (2024) emphasize the importance of setting up continuing education courses to equip teachers with the skills required to ideally exploit the potential of AI. Recommended pedagogical support will make it possible to exploit the advantages of smart technology and avoid the frustration that it can sometimes generate among teachers and even learners. The ethical and legal dimension relating to the secure management of the personal information of these lucky beneficiaries is also to be taken into account. The collection and examination of biometric and motor data, which are essential for the objectivity of assessment and the personalisation of learning, raise privacy and security issues. The development of reliable protocols for data processing is necessary to avoid any bias or algorithmic drift (Ompoc and Aguinaldo, 2024). This is why it is essential to establish a clear regulatory framework and to involve independent control bodies for the responsible and ethical use of these innovations and their requirements. On the other hand, the rehabilitation of the digital infrastructure of schools is therefore imperative. Bodemer (2023) demonstrates that access to intelligent systems and instant monitoring platforms is essential for the application of AI tools. However, in many under-equipped establishments, investment in these devices remains a central issue. AI cannot fully play its role as a pedagogical lever if educational and political decision-makers do not allocate the necessary resources and promote partnerships with technology companies to help them restore the existing infrastructure in their professional institutions. Finally, the integration of AI into PE is conditioned by the power to adopt a collaborative and interdisciplinary approach. The pedagogical, technical and ethical challenges must be overcome by solid collaboration between all actors (researchers, technicians, professors, political decision-makers). Future work should be based on longitudinal and comparative studies to assess the influence of these tools on learners' performance in the long term, and to refine the theoretical and practical models presented in recent studies. This strategy, in addition to optimizing AI adoption methods, will ensure an equitable and fluid popularization of innovative pedagogies. In short, the integration of AI into PE teaching/learning presents encouraging opportunities for the adaptation of educational practices, the improvement of assessment and the involvement of students. Potential benefits, including individualized learning and objectivity of assessments, are moderated by fundamental issues related to teacher training, confidentiality of information, and technological infrastructure. The results of this research, supported by a systematic literature review of recent work by Belmaadadia and Meliani (2024), Castro, Chiappe and Rodríguez (2024), Dey (2023), Jie, Hou and Hu (2024), Miao, Zhang and Yan (2023), Omar (2023), Ompoc and Aguinaldo (2024) as well as Tian (2024) offer a solid basis for proposing practical recommendations and trajectories for future studies. They stipulate that an integrative method combining technical and pedagogical know-how is necessary to fully benefit from the potential of AI with ethical inclusive operationalization.

REFERENCES

Belmaadadia, I., & Meliani, M. (2024). Physical activity and health education in Morocco: The case of the Gharb region. *Podium of Sport Sciences, 2*(2), 79–102. https://revues.imist.ma/index.php/PODIUM/article/view/45752

Belmaadadia, I., & Meliani, M. (2024). Sport, a philosophy for citizenship [Conference paper]. *1st International Conference on Philosophy and Interdisciplinarity: Therapeutic Philosophy, the Key to Researcher's Success (ICPI'24)*, Ibn Tofail University, Kenitra, Morocco.

Castro, G. P. B., Chiappe, A., & Rodríguez, D. F. B. (2024). Harnessing AI for Education 4.0: Drivers of personalized learning. *Electronic Journal of e-Learning, 22*(5), 1–14. DOI: 10.34190/ejel.22.5.3467

Dey, V. (2023). The role of artificial intelligence in physical education and sports: A review of current applications and future potential. *Global Values Journal, 14*(S. Issue, Supplement), 9–14. DOI: 10.31995/jgv.2023.v14iS3.002

Jie, Y., Hou, G., & Hu, X. (2024). The integration of artificial intelligence technology in college physical education: Innovation and challenges. *Curriculum and Teaching Methodology, 7*(3), 175–180. DOI: 10.23977/curtm.2024.070326

Miao, F., Zhang, Q., & Yan, J. (2023). Exploring the effectiveness of individualized learning trajectories in university smart sports education classrooms. *Journal of Social Science Humanities and Literature, 6*(5), 67–73. Advance online publication. DOI: 10.53469/jsshl.2023.06(05).10

Omar, J. (2023). Personalized learning through AI. *Advances in Engineering Innovation, 5*(1), 16–19. Advance online publication. DOI: 10.54254/2977-3903/5/2023039

Ompoc, H. M., & Aguinaldo, J. (2024). The impact of artificial intelligence (AI) integration on student engagement and learning outcomes of tertiary physical education students. *Digital Journal Philippines, 4*(1), 80–86. DOI: 10.62718/vmca.pr-ijetas.4.1.SC-1224-006

Tian, Y. (2024). Empowering college physical education: AI-driven training, teaching, and intelligent information processing. *Molecular & Cellular Biomechanics, 21*(1), 327. Advance online publication. DOI: 10.62617/mcb.v21i1.327

KEY TERMS AND DEFINITIONS

A Diagnostic Assessment: A form of pre-assessment where teachers can assess students' strengths, weaknesses, knowledge, and skills before they are taught

Artificial Intelligence: (AI): All theories and techniques developing complex computer programs capable of simulating certain traits of human intelligence (reasoning, learning, etc.).

Data Ethics: Covers the ethical and moral implications of the collection, sharing, and use of data, especially personally identifiable information. It places particular emphasis on the negative impacts that data projects could have on individuals or society at large. It aims to ensure fair and non-discriminatory use of data.

Inclusion: The action of integrating a person, a group, putting an end to their exclusion (social, in particular.

Objective Assessment: Objective assessment is characterised by the use of measurable, quantifiable criteria that are not influenced by personal opinions to assess an individual's performance, skills or knowledge

Pedagogical Innovation: Also known as innovative pedagogy, it is not exclusively the result of the evolution of teaching devices (serious games or mobile learning). It also refers to "new" methods and ways of working that often put the learner back at the centre of learning. It facilitates memory anchoring and information retention.

Personalization of Learning: A pedagogical approach focused on the needs, interests, goals and abilities of each learner. In this approach, children are encouraged to become active participants in their learning.

Physical Education and Sports (PE): A discipline that aims to develop the physical, cognitive, social and emotional capacities of individuals through the practice of various physical and sports activities. It includes teaching sports techniques, promoting an active and healthy lifestyle, and developing skills such as cooperation, leadership and following the rules.

Chapter 13
Integrating Social AI Into French-Arabic Environmental Translation:
Common Challenges and Solutions

Fatima Chayab
https://orcid.org/0009-0006-8910-0498
Sidi Mohamed Ben Abdellah University, Morocco

Younès Ez-Zouaine
Sidi Mohamed Ben Abdellah University, Morocco

ABSTRACT

The translation of environmental terms from French to Arabic poses significant challenges due to linguistic, cultural, and conceptual differences. These challenges are compounded by the complexity of environmental terminology, which often involves specialized vocabulary related to ecology, climate change, sustainability, and conservation. Common errors in translation include misinterpretations of technical terms. Artificial Intelligence offers a promising solution to these translation challenges. AI can also assist in creating more culturally relevant translations, ensuring that the environmental message is conveyed correctly across linguistic and cultural boundaries. This study explores how AI can improve the translation of environmental terms from French to Arabic, addressing both linguistic and cultural

DOI: 10.4018/979-8-3373-3436-3.ch013

barriers. By applying AI in the translation process, it is possible to bridge gaps between languages and enhance cross-cultural communication on environmental issues, thus contributing to more effective global environmental discourse.

INTRODUCTION

Translating environmental concepts is a complex activity, it represents a major challenge for translators, especially when it comes to switching from French to Arabic. This complexity is amplified by the marked linguistic and cultural differences between these two languages, as well as by the technicality of the terms used in the field of the environment. In a context where awareness and communication on environmental issues are crucial for sustainable development, an accurate and clear translation is essential. Improper translation can lead to misunderstandings, loss of meaning, and even ill-informed decisions that could jeopardize conservation and sustainable development efforts.

Through this study, we will examine the challenges and common mistakes encountered in translating environmental terms from French to Arabic. The audience concerned by translation are not professional translators but graduates in different fields because these terms are increasingly present in our everyday language and have not been used only by specialists. Through examples taken from the book " Les démarches de développement durable, pertinence et apports effectifs dans la gestion de l'air et de l'eau: les exemples de Lille et de Saint-Etienne " (I. Roussel, 2005), we illustrate the complexities of environmental terminology and the potential pitfalls of translation. To support this analysis, we draw on the work of researchers such as Mona Baker, Lawrence Venuti, Myriam Salama-Carr, Jean-Paul Vinay and Jean Darbelnet and Rabab Kandil, whose studies on specialized and scientific translation provide a solid theoretical framework.

It should be noted that the translation of environmental terms remains a field marked by numerous gaps. Examples include the scarcity of empirical studies dealing with translation strategies specific to environmental discourse, the lack of comparative interlinguistic and intercultural analyses related to this field, and the inadequacy of specialized and unified bilingual lexicographical tools. This research is unique in that it combines terminological analysis and translation studies on a contemporary environmental corpus, drawing on linguistic, cultural, and pragmatic aspects. The aim is to highlight the constraints encountered when translating environmental terms from French into Arabic and to propose solutions that enhance their accuracy and acceptability in the target language and culture.

The article is organized according to seven focal points. We will first proceed with the introduction, then we will present the theoretical part followed by the research methodology adopted, then we will present the data collected and the results obtained. And then, we will move on to the discussion of the processes used to translate environmental terms, the aim of which is to explore the linguistic differences between French and Arabic and to propose solutions to improve the accuracy and clarity of translations in the field of the environment. Our intention is to provide tools and recommendations to users of these scientific terms, in order to facilitate better understanding and communication between the French- and Arabic-speaking communities. To conclude, we will present the conclusion to answer the problem of our research. Without forgetting to thank the contributors to the study and to present the list of references.

TRANSLATION THEORY AND ENVIRONMENTAL TERMINOLOGY

Translating environmental texts requires a thorough understanding of specialized terminology and scientific concepts. According to Egyptian translator and professor of translation in Britain, Mona Baker, terminological accuracy is crucial to preserving the integrity of scientific information, she points out that "through the study of terminology, translators can see more clearly the connection between the conscious use of language and our ability to shape the tools we use for communication" (Baker, 1998). Baker warns against translations that do not respect terminological specificities, thus risking distorting the original meaning. She argues that translation must not only convey the literal meaning of words, but also preserve technical and contextual nuances.

Like Baker, Rabab Kandil emphasizes the importance of terminological accuracy. According to her, "Although the comprehension phase is always essential, as in any general or specialized translation, the precision and accuracy of [...] terminology do not allow him or her to adopt exclusively the interpretive theory whose central concern is the question of "meaning" " (Kandil, 2025). She points out that translation is not limited to simply conveying meaning, but requires lexical rigor to avoid ambiguity. For example, the expression " réchauffement planétaire " (Ministère de la Transition écologique, 2025, section Ressources naturelles) is translated in the English version by its equivalent "global warming " instead of translating it literally as "planetary warming". This is an appropriate choice because this expression is common in English and also because the source and target terms refer to the same meaning.

Lawrence Venuti, the American theorist of translation, on the other hand, theorized about translation strategies such as domestication and exoticization, highlighting the cultural implications of these choices. Venuti argues that "A fluent translation is immediately recognizable and intelligible, familiarised, domesticated, not disconcerting foreign, capable of giving the reader unobstructed access to great thoughts, to what is present in the original" (Venuti, 1995). The domestication strategy indicates the naturalization of the target text while erasing the specificities of the source text through the processes of free or indirect translation such as adaptation, modulation, transposition and equivalence explained by Vinay and Darbelnet in their book entitled Stylistique comparé du français et de l'anglais (Vinay and Darbelnet, 1972). For example, the expression "développement durable" (Ministère de la Transition écologique, 2025, section Ressources naturelles), which becomes "sustainable development" in English, has been naturalized through contextual adaptation to the local context.

For the strategy of exoticization, Venuti considers that "a foreignizing method, an ethnodeviant pressure on those values to register the linguistic and cultural difference of the foreign text, sending the reader abroad" (Venuti, 1995). This strategy therefore aims to preserve and preserve the strangeness of the source text within the target text, using the direct translation processes, namely borrowing, tracing and literal translation, according to Vinay and Darbelnet. For example, in the English translation of the following statement: "25 000 hectares artificialisés en moyenne chaque année"(Ministère de la Transition écologique, 2025, section Ressources naturelles) as "25,000 hectares on average of artificial land each year", we note the use of the exotization strategy by retaining the term "artificial ". This approach makes the French original visible without compromising the meaning.

For her part, Myriam Salama-Carr, a researcher at the University of Manchester's Centre for Translation and Intercultural Studies, explored the specific challenges of translation, pointing out that "the notion of conflict is part and parcel of contemporary discourse on translation and interpreting, wherein are frequently couched in terms of dichotomies, tensions and cultural differences, or conflicting allegiances". In this respect, terminological accuracy in specialized areas, such as the environment, is important for a successful transfer from one language to another that are completely opposite.

IMPORTANCE OF ENVIRONMENTAL TRANSLATION

Environmental translation is important for talking to people from other cultures about environmental issues since it helps spread the news about sustainable practices, laws, and Developments in science over the globe (Iwala and Ashiru-Abdulrahman, 2025). Global environmental issues exhibit little regard for country borders or cultural conventions (Karande et al., This shows that we need both literal and metaphorical translations to prevent misunderstandings that might get in the way of efforts throughout the world to tackle these problems. When talking about something like greenhouse gas emissions, people could use various scientific terms in different languages. Temim (2023) says that this might generate uncertainty and make it harder for countries to work together to tackle climate change. On the other side, environmental translation is bringing the world's most important environmental issues to the attention of the general people. Making materials about laws, awareness initiatives, and research available in more than one language is one method to get people talking more about the environment. Important in all countries, but particularly in those with more than one official language, since speakers of minority languages may not have the capacity to change laws that impact their daily life. When people work together, they need to all know about vital factors like biodiversity, the environment, and the circular economy. Precision has two purposes: first, it motivates more engagement (Juillard, 2024). It's also harder to make sure that translations are correct since various cultures have different ideas about environmental issues. The details of each language could shape how people perceive and comprehend environmental concepts. Translators have to deal with all these cultural barriers to ensure their work is helpful and relevant. This translator skill is not as simple as translating languages. It's about knowing the sociopolitical climates of who you're translating for, as well. In a nutshell, environmental translation is an important tool to ensure scientific knowledge is shared in a correct and understandable way. It also raises awareness about the challenges our planet is experiencing and encourages people to work together to solve them (Isidro, 2025).

LANGUAGE CHALLENGES IN TRANSLATION

There are a number of linguistic obstacles that make it hard to communicate French environmental ideals into Arabic. One factor is the effect of cultural nuances. People's opinions toward the environment are more likely to be shaped by cultural ideas and local norms than by technical factors (Oueslati, 2023). For example, the French term "sustainable development" is used a lot, yet there is no one word for it in Arabic. As the political and social climates of Arabic-speaking nations change, the underlying principles that it seems to be based on may also alter. Translators should also consider about these factors (Viviani, 2023) since it's extremely vital to represent culture correctly in translation. Technobabble is also a huge concern. Because of new laws, regulations, and technologies, the environment is continually evolving. To effectively portray the relevance of the links they are addressing, the translator must have first-hand knowledge of the subject matter and the most current breakthroughs in environmental and scientific research. French speakers may find it hard to grasp the Arabic phrases "biodiversity" and "carbon footprint." People who don't speak the same language are more likely to make errors while translating since they don't comprehend each other. There are a lot of Arabic words that mean the same thing, but new ones could be hard to comprehend. Translators may need to use reformulation techniques or “steal” French words from the text to make the already hard job of translating Titans material more harder. It is difficult to translate environmental terms from French to Arabic due to language challenges and the need for cultural and idiomatic comprehension (Markowski, 2024). A skilled translator has to be aware of both the language and the cultural differences. In the end, they are crucial for these two languages to express environmental concerns effectively.

1. Cultural Nuances

When translating from French into Arabic of environmental terms, it is important to consider the cultural factors that shape both appreciation and comprehension of environmental concepts as important as familiarity with language. According to Dubut and Saint-Charles (2025), variations in culture will critically affect people’s interpretation and talk about the environment. For instance, some languages and cultures may be relatively more religious and spiritual in their orientation when interacting with nature (such as Certain Arab cultures); while others (in the instant case, French speaking cultures) may be relatively more aesthetically-oriented towards nature. If you translate these words.word -for word with a similar equivalent, those shades may cause misunderstandings. Therefore, the meaning of sustainability is modified by cultural diversity, something that makes it difficult to interpret words as “sustainable development” (Nguyen, 2024). The word means in French that the economic, social and ecologic parts of life are consonant with one another. In Arabic, however, it carries cultural; historical and religious connotations that could alter its significance (Thiam 2024). It implies that absence of cultural background in the target language could affect the use of biodiversity and climate change terminology which may need adaptations beyond simple translation. I know that translators have a difficult job for the simple reason that each language contains its own cultural references, meanings and values. But getting your point over to local officials generally takes a lot of effort, including reading and talking to people. Arabic readers may find the glossaries and translations in the footnotes and glossaries useful in understanding what could appear like stereotyped arguments that don't take cultural norms into account. When looking at cultural disparities in environmental statements, keep in mind that word choice is just one thing to consider about. To promote cross-cultural understanding and communication and develop enduring solutions to the world's environmental problems, it is just as important to establish a common ground between clashing ideals.

2. Technical Terminology

Translating technical environmental terms is difficult since the language is inherently complicated and you have to pay close attention to every aspect. Kędzia-Klebeko (2024) says that the difficulty comes from the fact that different languages employ different words and ways to group things. For example, the phrase "biodiversity" may mean something different when it is literally translated from French to "Arabic-speaking conditions" than when it is literally translated from Arabic to French, because of the distinct cultural and social contexts of the two languages. Translators need to know a lot about the scientific fields they work in since language differences might change the meaning of things. The translator has a much more difficult job to do here, because certain ideas about the environment may not even exist in one language but would still be extremely important in another. This is also a clear example of the fact that words such as "photovoltaic" do not necessarily have an actual equivalent in target languages (Dalodiere, 2023). So, translators have derived terms or turned to old ones in order to get the technical language correct without losing track of what original speakers need for accuracy and precision. This approach should consider the agreed-upon nomenclature globally as well as the relevant laws and regulations.

COMMON ERRORS IN TRANSLATION

Common mistakes Many common mistakes can make it difficult to translate environmental terms from French into Arabic with accuracy and precision. One of the most hazardous (false) mistakes is to fall for the "false friends" fallacy. For example, the two languages might use words that sound alike but mean very different things (Kotob, 2024). The "sensible" in the Arabic word for sensible is that of the hasas/":حساس" variety, meaning "likely to react strongly to stimuli." This should not be confused with "sensible," which means "of reason and common sense." This is a parallel to the way the ecosystems can be harmed by pollution. What I believe is another problem (to be confirmed) but also has to do with russians speaking english themselves, big issue here we can talk about is people tend to translate 1 on 1. They may not know that Arabic has its own grammar and style, and they could choose to use French dictionaries and grammatical rules. You can't just use technical terminology like "carbon footprint" in a different situation right away. Using these ideas as weapons would be to weaponize them, but it would also stop people from being creative. For translation to work, it's important to know that various languages have distinct rules for grammar and style (Jin & Tu, 2022). But I don't want to think about the issue of meaninglessness. When you translate daily or technical terminology into

Arabic, there is a chance that others may not comprehend what you mean. The term "sustainable development" may possess many interpretations contingent upon the specific cultural and economic framework involved. It would be extremely bad to dismiss these differences and make environmental concerns less relevant because of the continuing dispute (Voyer, 2025). To steer clear of these types of openings, one must be very aware of the words and the world around them. To have a productive conversation on environmental issues in an Arabic-speaking community, you need to know a lot about the language and culture.

1. False Friends

"False friends" are only one of the numerous things that may go wrong for a French to Arabic translator. At first sight, these lines may seem the same, however translators who aren't trained may be misled by the little differences in meaning between the two languages. For example, the French word "assistance." Ibrahim (2023) says that although though it looks like the Arabic term "المساعدة" (al-musa'ada), it means something more official and institutional in French. An unskilled translator could get it incorrect, neglect it, or say it entirely wrong. In the environmental profession, where complicated scientific language is needed, having unreliable friends is a specific problem. Think about the term "reactive." "Reactive" is a frequent English word for describing a chemical molecule that changes as it is tested. "تفاعلي" (tafā'ulī) is an Arabic word that might mean a response, social interaction, or system dynamics. People who don't pay attention to this aspect risk watering down environmental issues and changing the original goal. If you use common sense, you can prevent the grief and suffering that these doppelgangers cause. First, find out how to look at this person to discover whether they are a friend. Translators must be able to understand more than simply the words. They need to know how to utilize these statements in varied situations and with different technology, not only their exact meaning. Using expert glossaries and trustworthy sources of terminology is another technique to make sure the translations are correct (Cardoso Rezende, 2024). There are fake friends that can assist you get the right translation for the setting. We can communicate about global environmental issues in a manner that everyone can understand if we have more accurate and clear translations.

2. Literal Translation

One reason why ecological words translated from French to Arabic don't always work is because they are translated too literally. People think that literal translation is a technique to get meaning from one language to another. They say that this method assumes that exact word-for-word translations can keep the original meaning. But it's preferable to think of the literal as simpler and less significant to other cultures from an ecological point of view. It is well known that translating environmental jargon is hard since the language is specialized and its meaning may alter depending on the situation. The phrase "sustainable development" is more than simply a development; it's a popular and relevant one for this reason. This broad term includes social justice, the idea of a circular economy, and, most importantly, the need to protect resources for future generations. A literal translation of this kind of statement has the inherent risk of being misled by a submissive equivalent that overlooks complexogenically significant nuances. If you ignore them, important talks like sustainability, enacting environmental laws, and teaching people about the environment might become messy. Before their 2023 full analysis came out, Fatima and Boulkhir had already pointed up a similar threat. Even if a literal translation may seem like the best option, it has to be thought about and analyzed carefully before being chosen. Translators should know the cultural standards, legal regulations, and social mores of both languages when they are requested to translate environmental terminology from one language to another. To be a translation, you can't just change the words that mean the same thing. To master the work, you need to be as smart and skilled as the concepts themselves, and you also need to be aware of the cultural and linguistic differences that surround them. VOYER reviewed this important topic in 2025 and gave the following detailed analysis. Before starting environmental or educational projects, it is very important to think about these important things to prevent major misunderstandings and unforeseen consequences. The enticing idea is that having high language skills isn't enough, as evidenced by Mantrach's great work in 2021; you also need a variety of cultural and moral views on damaged environments. Translators have a lot on their plates. They have to find a way to connect ancient and contemporary ways of thinking, as well as all the languages spoken in a given region, including any system whose examples are useful to our job. Translators must assist bridge this information gap and encourage clear communication so that we may get the most up-to-date information and react effectively to the environmental risks that are always changing.

3. Omissions of Meaning

One of the worst things about translating French environmental terminology into Arabic is that you could miss the meaning. Blanchard (2024) strives to make the material seem easier to read by pushing crucial ideas that make sure technical and scientific terms are used correctly. In environmental science, where every word may have a big effect, leaving out terms can make things very confusing. In its broken form, the French word "biodiversity" may mean several things depending on the situation. For example, it might mean the number of species, ecosystems, and the connections between them. The translator makes the Arab people confused by either misinterpreting particular cultural or technical phrases and their context or by changing the meaning of the message. People don't always understand the concepts or there aren't Arabic words that mean the same thing, which is why these differences happen most of the time. It's tempting to leave them out completely when precise matches aren't attainable so that the language doesn't appear too complicated or overpowering (Lucassen, 2024). But this plan might make complicated concepts too simple. Because there are so many different Arabic dialects and words used across the world, Islamic scholars and other translators employ a broad range of methods to translate. This might cause people to misinterpret the original texts.

To avoid this issue, translators must be proficient in both languages and well-versed in the pertinent environmental issues. Translations that prioritize nuanced meaning above literal correctness may benefit from comprehensive resources and cooperation with subject-matter experts. This includes a close look at the phrases used to talk about current environmental challenges and what they signify. in which every word may cause a chain reaction that impacts people and countries. It is vital to keep these gaps in mind while talking about the environment so that you can do it appropriately and effectively (Oueslati, 2023).

STRATEGIES FOR EFFECTIVE TRANSLATION

There are various ways to do it, but translating ecological ideas from French to Arabic is not easy. Using specialized dictionaries is an important part of this process. Viviani (2023) says that translators may find it helpful to have a terminology database with more than a thousand standardized words when they are attempting to make sense of the complicated and ever-changing language used in environmental research. The main purposes of a glossary are to make sure that all terms are consistent and to help readers understand themes by giving English translations of common Arabic words. Using a decent dictionary may also show cultural differences and common phrases, which might make it harder to translate words. Using this kind of technology leads to translations that are more accurate and less likely to make mistakes. You also need help from specialists to translate correctly. Language and environmental specialists may assist speed up the translation process in a variety of ways. First of all, practicing environmentalists may be the best people to set the scene for certain expressions since they know a lot about the problems the world is experiencing now (Prévil & Ortega, 2025). Second, they should learn the local language and culture inside and out so they can communicate better and avoid misunderstandings. Translators may also ask these professionals for help to make sure they are using the right words. This can help you avoid political or legal problems by utilizing precise phrasing. These tips might assist translators understand the topic better and come up with their own opinions about it. This will give them an advantage in talks about the environment throughout the world.

TOOLS AND RESOURCES OF TRANSLATION IN SOCIAL SCIENCES

In using an instrument that has been developed and validated in one culture with people in another culture, there is a need to translate it. Translation should not be a simple swap of words from one language to another, but instead conveys meaning across cultures. This strategy considers issues of direction, lay vs. academic translators, authority and training, a variety of translation conventions, and various types of intercoder agreement. The role of culture and issues around authority will be outlined in relation to the practice of translating. An interpretation of these strategies will be attempted (Drennan, 1992). The first job is to get an educated person to translate into the Cikunda, Kalanga, or Shona, since the master text is in English. It is most preferable if their mother tongue is the language into which they are translating. Even if this is not possible, they should have used their language as their first language for the normal cognitive development of an educated person. The agreed form of translation is direct. This is then taken to a practical person, such as a social worker or teacher. The translator is called the lay translator or the second translator. The person charged with this task reads through each question of the instrument with the translator established in number 1 above. They discuss possible amendments to shorten it. The lay translator suggests wording changes, additional questions they believe to be relevant for their culture, or omissions based upon local knowledge of the use of the instrument and considered opinion of the context and subjects. Thereafter, they discuss the amended version with another group, including a community nurse and an interpreter. They ponder questions of accuracy, semantic matter, and ambiguity. These are iterated through some version of the preceding several steps until they are happy with the final product, which is then typed up. This last step is important to clarify matters of indirection before production. The tedious tidying up of the copy is done. These types of actions are necessary because of the nature of the scoring and potential cross-cultural understanding. Statements by researchers indicate that the individuals involved in this type of translation work fall generally into one of two general categories: "academics" and "lay translators". Academics include university staff and students who are equipped by training and experience in African languages to work with the polysystems theory of language. Translators also take pride in this role, as it represents a prestigious posting in the university system (Bénel & Lacour, 2014). Lay translators include psychologists, psychiatric nurses, social workers, teachers, and university graduates who may have received no systematic training in translation such as academia provides, but for whom as a group it is the first or second language. They presumably learned it while they were youngsters or later in adulthood. As they advanced in their training across several domains of professional expertise, they refined their linguistic abilities to articulate more intricate meanings and subtleties. Different sequences of employing academics and lay translators show what each one prefers and why, which in turn shows how local resources and attitudes toward the task affect the different practice and purpose systems at work.

1. Translation Software

Translation software can be classified into two categories: those whose purpose is to perform translation and those whose aims are to assist the human in the translation task (Bénel & Lacour, 2014). Computer Aided Translation tools (CAT tools) fall into the second category. They do not translate for the user but assist her in the translation task. By including the human in the translation process, they are expected to increase the productivity and quality of translations. Consequently, they are used in many fields, even outside the scientific community, especially in business, where their commercial counterparts now exist.

Unfortunately, in cultural sciences, these tools seem to be carefully avoided. Most scholars, or even reviewers, seem to fear an interaction with a computer aided tool, i.e. the knowledge thought of in human form, with respect to efficiency and precision. The quantized version of knowledge and its associated processing, as it is done by a computer, is not trustworthy nowadays, while the details, applicable only to restricted domains, of the notions underlying it already produce better overall results. The same question is implicitly raised by the existence of translation memories, or TM, used majorly by translating agencies. Translation memories are a kind of database where the human enters her completed texts, be they translations or original, so that, for a new MA thesis or PhD dissertation, she can check whether a sentence or a segment of texts has already been translated.

2. Glossaries and Dictionaries

Building glossaries is one of the basic steps toward effective translation. To translate a text, the first question to ask is, "Is this a new text?" If the text is a new one, then it is useful to build glossaries. In other words, if it has not been translated yet to the target language, it is worthwhile to build a glossary. This glossary should include new words both on the source language (SL) side and the target language (TL) side.

It is important to note that "new" in the above context does not mean that no existing target language (TL) equivalent is available. In contrast, "new" means that no TL equivalent has been used in the fields, contexts, and situations. Therefore, it may be that an existing TL equivalent is; however, this equivalent has not been adopted yet in the relevant field or domain. To build a term glossary on the SL side, it is crucial to understand the text as a whole and, from the perspective of translation, to have close consideration of the translation equivalence of the relevant words.

If this is not the first time to translate this text, then it is extremely important to use the old glossaries. Of course, whether the old translation is used or not is a matter of consideration; however, it is important to use the glossaries. In this case, it may be useful to ask whether existing glossaries help translate accurately or appropriately and whether they are so outdated as to mislead the understanding of the new translation. If existing glossaries hinder translation, then it would be useful not to use them.

3. Online Resources

Technology in general and the Internet, in particular, have significantly changed the landscape of education in general and of translation education in particular. Translation students need extensive knowledge of online resources necessary for improving their translation competence. Teaching translation competence through the use of online bilingual resources requires creative use of technology and adaptation of classroom activities to various technological and pedagogical contexts.

A systematic review of ten research studies focusing on the effectiveness of using online bilingual resources in translation teaching found that more research should be conducted covering a wider geographical area and larger samples. Although many researchers called for conducting more empirical research to investigate this topic, there is little published research on teaching translation competence using online bilingual resources. Personal experience gained over 25 years of teaching both undergraduate and MA students were added to previously published research on the topic to illustrate various strategies conducive to a better understanding of the implications and applications of using online bilingual resources in translation education.

The traditional way of teaching translation competence according to the hierarchical model is too rigid for teaching non-technical written translation. From the review of research studies, observations of contemporary translation practice and news coverage, and translation students' feedback, it was concluded that a combination of both the vertical/sequential and the fl/w model of translation should be used to endow translation students with translation competence that closely resembles the translation process used in practice by professional translators. Translation trainers should adapt the teaching strategies, based on these models, to cater for the requirements of the students taking this course (Elamin, 2023).

THE IMPACT OF TRANSLATION ERRORS

Errors in translating environmental terms may have big implications on formulating and talking about environmental policy. The first and most obvious impact is that the message is changed. Translating technical or legal terms might lead to misunderstandings and wrong assumptions. For example, if people don't grasp how important ecosystems are because of a badly translated phrase like "biodiversity," it might hamper public mobilization and involvement in conservation initiatives. Also, local groups, NGOs, and government organizations may not want to take part since communication isn't working well, which makes it harder to carry out environmental projects. Translation problems may have an influence on environmental policy. An institutional framework that depends on bad translations might make it hard to create, carry out, and enforce environmental rules. For example, when regulatory words are unclear, it may be hard to understand what stakeholders' responsibilities and legal obligations are. Also, it might lead to inaccuracies in the EIA, which would hurt the project's long-term viability and harm biodiversity and natural resources. These kinds of blunders have ramifications that go beyond the issues they cause, such climate change and other problems that are more local.

METHODOLOGY

Our study is based on a qualitative approach that advocates the confrontation of the elements extracted from the source text with their Arabic translation, followed by a description and analysis of the processes used in order to specify the success and failure of the translation.

For the method of data collection and organization we used the services provided by information and communication technologies and applications and software, to send the table of the studied examples to licensees of different ages and genders, in order to translate them, and also for the reading and processing of the data. This study is being carried out in the first half of 2024.

In addition, searches of dictionaries specializing in environmental terminology were also conducted to identify Arabic equivalents of French terms and to assess the adequacy of translations. Common errors have been commented on to determine effective translation strategies and processes based on the words of theorists in this field.

Figure 1. Explanatory diagram of the methodology used in this study

Collection of environmental terms from the book
↓
Translation of terms into Arabic by licensees
↓
Analysis and criticism of translations
↓
Proposal of solutions and recommendations based on results

DATA COLLECTION AND ANALYSIS

For this study, we collected and analysed translations of 13 environmental terms from the book "Les démarches de développement durable, pertinence et apports effectifs dans la gestion de l'air et de l'eau: les exemples de Lille et de Saint-Etienne", they are presented in their context to help translators grasp their exact meaning. The terms and their translations were selected based on their relevance and frequency of use in environmental discussions. They are presented in bold.

Table 1. Environmental terms and their translations (continued on next page)

No.	Original text	Our traduction into English	Page	Translated text	Translatin processes
1	« Une vision hygiéniste de **l'environnement** »	"A hygienist vision of **the environment**"	7	رؤية صحية للبيئة	Translate by equivalence
2	« L'eau et l'air, **ressources naturelles** renouvelables »	"Water and air, renewable **natural resources**"	11	الماء والهواء، موارد طبيعية متجددة	Use of literal translation
3	« **Le développement durable** dans une démarche locale »	"**Sustainable development** in a local approach"	21	التنمية المستدامة في نهج محلي	Use of literal translation
4	« **Le changement climatique** et les incertitudes sur l'équilibre de la Planète »	"**Climate change** and uncertainties about the balance of the planet"	7	التغير المناخي وعدم اليقين بشأن توازن الكوكب	Use of literal translation

continued on following page

Table 1. Continued

No.	Original text	Our traduction into English	Page	Translated text	Translatin processes
5	« Les aléas de **l'atmosphère** peuvent faire varier les quantités d'eau disponible tout en sachant que les réserves accumulées au cours des âges géologiques sont loin d'être épuisées, surtout si la technologie du dessalage de l'eau de mer se généralise »	"The vagaries of **the atmosphere** can vary the quantities of water available, knowing that the reserves accumulated over geological ages are far from being exhausted, especially if seawater desalination technology becomes widespread"	13	المخاطر التي تخص **الهواء** يمكن ان تغير كميات المياه المتوفرة علما ان المواد المتراكمة على مر الحقب الجيولوجية هي بعيدة عن الاندثار خاصة إذا كانت تقنية تحلية مياه البحر ستعمم	Translation by equivalence
6	« Les sécheresses, dans leurs différentes facettes atmosphérique, **hydrologique,** pédologique, peuvent avoir des conséquences dommageables tant sur les vies humaines que sur les récoltes »	"Droughts, in their different atmospheric, **hydrological** and pedological facets, can have harmful consequences on both human lives and crops"	13	يمكن أن تكون حالات الجفاف، بمختلف جوانبها الجوية **والهيدرولوجية** والبيئية، عواقب مدمرة على حياة البشر وعلى المحاصيل على حد سواء.	Translation by borrowing
7	« **L'aérisme,** théorie de la contamination par les miasmes véhiculés par l'air »	"**Aerism**, the theory of contamination by airborne miasmas"	14	**النزعة الهوائية،** نظرية العدوى بسبب الغازات التي ينشرها الهواء	Translation by adaptation
8	« L'air n'est plus seulement le vecteur d'**agents biologiques** pathogènes, c'est sa composition même, modifiée par les rejets anthropiques, qui devient nuisible »	"Air is no longer just the vector of **pathogenic biological agents**, it is its very composition, modified by anthropogenic discharges, that becomes harmful"	16	الهواء ليس فقط موصلا للعوامل **البيولوجية** المتسببة في الأمراض، بل تركيبته في حد ذاتها المعدلة بشريا هي الضارة	Translation by borrowing
9	« **Des aquifères** vulnérables mais précieux pour l'alimentation en eau »	"**Vulnerable aquifers** but precious for water supply"	31	**طبقات المياه** الجوفية ضعيفة، ولكن ثمينة لتوفير الماء	Translation by adaptation
10	« La nappe du calcaire **carbonifère** est captive sous les terrains crétacés	"The Carboniferous **limestone aquifer** is captive under the Cretaceous soils"	31	طبقة الحجر الجيري **الكربوني** محبوسة تحت تضاريس العصر الطباشيري	Translation by borrowing

continued on following page

Table 1. Continued

No.	Original text	Our traduction into English	Page	Translated text	Translatin processes
11	« L'eau est de qualité mais le niveau **piézométrique** ne cesse de diminuer »	"The water is of good quality but the **piezometric level** continues to decrease"	31	ةدوج وذ ءاملا نكل ةيلاع ىوتسملا يف يرتموزيبلا رمتسم ضافخنا	Translation by borrowing
12	« **Les forages** installés dans cette nappe carbonifère ferment les uns après les autres »	"**The boreholes** installed in this carboniferous aquifer are closing one after the other"	31	ةتبثملا رابآلا ةقبط يف ةيفوجلا هايملا هذه ةينوبركلا ةدحاولا قلغت ىرخألا ولت	Translation by equivalence
13	« La surexploitation de la nappe peut induire une réalimentation en eau de surface de qualité inférieure contenant des **nitrates, des chlorures et des sulfates** »	"Overexploitation of the aquifer can lead to a recharge of substandard surface water containing **nitrates, chlorides and sulphates**"	33	لالغتسالا . ةاشرفلل طرفملا نكمي ةيئاملا ىلإ يدؤي نأ ةيذغت ةداعإ ةيحطسلا هايملا ةيعون ب ةضفخنم ىلع يوتحت **رولكلا ،تارتنلا طافلوسلاو**	Translation by borrowing

RESULTS AND DISCUSSION

The comparison of translations with the originals has shown cases of failure and success of the translation, depending on the procedures used by the translators. In example number 1, they used the equivalence process, substituting "environment" with "ةئيب". According to The Dictionary of Biological Diversity and Nature Conservation, this term refers to "a set of elements (biotic or abiotic) that surround an individual or a species, some of which contribute directly to meeting its needs (Patrick, 2015). We find that the Arabic translation is adequate since it reflects the same meaning of the French concept even though there is another Arabic word "طيحم" to translate the term "environment" but the translators were aware of the nuances between the two. The term ةئيب"'" is more accurate for environmental discussions while "طيحم" is broader because it touches on social and cultural dynamics. Similarly, the term "boreholes" in example 12 is rendered by its Arabic equivalent " رابآ" which reflects the intended meaning in the original text.

For example 2, the translators literally conveyed the expression "natural resources" as "ةيعيبط دراوم", this is a motivated choice because it exists in dictionaries such as “The unified dictionary of environment terms” (Arabization Coordination Bureau, 2016). We can say the same for Example 3.

As for example 4, translating the phrase “climate change” as “تغير بيئي” is a common mistake where translators confuse the adjective “climate” and “ecological”. It might be accurate to use a term like “تغير مناخي” to stay true to the context of the climate. We can make the same remark for the translation of the term “Atmosphere” by “هواء”. The latter can be used in a more common discourse, but it does not reflect the breadth and complexity of the atmospheric concept defined as a “560 m cover of air surrounding the earth in which climate and weather phenomena take place” (Patrick, 2015). So, for an accurate and technical translation, it is better to use the term “غلاف جوي” in order to avoid confusion.

For examples 6, 8, 10, 11 and 13, translators have often opted for the borrowing process. It allows you to introduce new terms, and to enrich the vocabulary of the target language. Certainly, it is used to name a new term, coming from another language and which does not yet have a name in the target language, but in cases, the term has an equivalent in the Arabic language as for “biological” translated as “احيائي” (Dictionnaire technique français–arabe, 2004). which relates to biology as the study of life and living organisms. However, the translators' choice to borrow these technical terms is due, on the one hand, to their conformity with terminological standards and conventions in Arabic scientific disciplines, and on the other hand, for “a preventive measure that translators and/or interpreters take in order to avoid any source of controversy” (Constantinescu, 2016). De facto, the borrowing of these terms from the French language to the Arabic language, which are well assimilated and integrated into the target language, contributes to its evolution and diversity, while testifying to the familiarization of technical concepts among a wider audience. However, further clarification may be required depending on the context.

There are cases where linguistic differences between French and Arabic, such as sentence structure and word order, can influence the translation of technical terms. Let's take example 7 where the term “aerisme” in French requires a decomposition in Arabic to preserve the meaning, it is composed of the root “aér” which refers to air and the suffix “ism” which is used to form names indicating doctrines or tendencies. Thus, its translation as “النزعة الهوائية” faithfully captures the meaning of this term. As a result, the translators chose to adapt the term according to the specificities of the Arabic language. The same is true in the translation of the term “Aquifers” in example 9.

From this brief analysis, we can see that the translators faced several challenges. We can cite the non-existence of direct equivalents in Arabic of certain scientific terms, which forces them to create new terms or to borrow them as they are in the source language. In addition, polysemy and semantic nuances can complicate the translation of technical terms, requiring advanced linguistic skills and knowledge in this field to maintain the clarity and precision of the original text.

To overcome these challenges, the translators have resorted to different translation processes in the following proportions:

Figure 2. Processus used

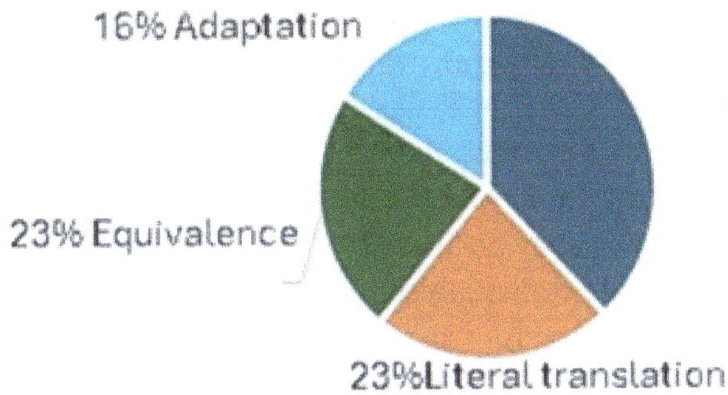

Based on these results, we find that translators proceed in two ways. In the majority of cases, they opted for borrowings and for literal translation as a simple and relevant solution, thus being part of a strategy of exoticization in the sense of Venuti, and by complying with the requirements of terminological accuracy emphasized by Mona Baker. In addition, they have chosen, in some examples, translation by equivalence or adaptation. This approach is part of a domestication whose objective is to produce an effect similar to that of the French term. In any case, the translators have succeeded in most translations in conveying the meaning intended by the author, despite the complexity of translating a scientific term, but they have made mistakes in the translation of some terms such as "climate change" and "atmosphere". There are several reasons why these mistakes could happen.

CONCLUSION

This study raised the complex problems of transfering environmental vocabulary from French to Arabic through insights and examples from "Les démarches de développement durable, pertinence et apports effectifs dans la gestion de l'air et de l'eau: les exemples de Lille et de Saint-Etienne". We demonstrated that when it comes to topics like "sustainable development," "atmosphere" and "climate change," there is plenty of room for mistranslation and misunderstanding thanks to small variations in language and meaning. The findings indicate that although sentences can sometimes be translated directly into Arabic, the translation of their semantics is dependent on such contextual and situational factors. The word “environment” is familiar but has different meanings according to context. Atmosphere” is a powerful word in environmental arguments. It must be written in an appealing form that interests both experts and those unfamiliar with the subject, while maintaining scientific accuracy. “The translator's selection of words is also determined by the recurrence and non-recurrence of expressions in his linguistic environ ment” (Kazumi, 2018). French and Arabic provide significant challenges owing to their divergent syntactic and morphological frameworks, as shown by the examination of linguistic differences. Arabic tends to employ shorter sentences, thus French, which utilizes more words, has to be properly adapted for Arabic. In this adaptation, the ideas must not be too simple, otherwise vital elements may be lost.

One of the most crucial things that affected translation was cognitive ability. Different cultures have different levels of knowledge about environmental notions, which affects how they see and perceive them. To avoid translation errors like using “تغيربيئي” instead of “تغيرمناخي” when “climate change” should be translated as “تغيربيئي,” you need to fully understand the context. A balanced strategy that includes both domestication and foreignization techniques could help translators get over these problems. They also need to employ specialized tools like CAT software and terminology dictionaries to make sure that terms are used consistently. To stay up-to-date on the newest changes in language, you need to train often. To support sustainable development initiatives and improve communication between French- and Arabic-speaking people, environmental ideas need to be translated accurately and in context. Paying careful attention to language differences and employing the correct tools and strategies may help improve translation quality and increase understanding of environmental issues. Our proposals are not only for translators; they are also for teachers and lawmakers who work on environmental communication. We recommend standardizing language, developing and improving bilingual specialized techniques and resources, and advocating for and financing research in this domain. We stress that the limited sample size and the languages being studied are limitations of this study, which is true for every research. So, the results may not work for everything. Concerning this issue, we recommend that further research focus on the integration of multimodal analyses (text, image, sound, etc.) and expand the corpus and linguistic domains.

ACKNOWLEDGMENT

We would like to thank all those who participated in the realization of this research, in particular, the licensees who made efforts in translating the environmental terms studied.

REFERENCES

Arabization Coordination Bureau. (2016). *The unified dictionary of environment terms (English–French–Arabic)* (Series of Unified Dictionaries No. 20, Updated edition). Arabization Coordination Bureau.

Baker, M. (1998). *Routledge encyclopedia of translation studies*. Routledge.

Bénel, A., & Lacour, P. (2014). *Towards a participative platform for cultural texts translators*. In *Cross-Cultural Interaction: Concepts, Methodologies, Tools and Applications* (Vol. 3, pp. 1695–1705). IGI Global. DOI: 10.4018/978-1-4666-4979-8.ch096

Blanchard, C. (2024). *Ecological identity: definition, measurement, and impact on organizational citizenship behaviors for the environment*. [Doctoral dissertation, Université de Montréal]. Université de Montréal Repository. https://umontreal.scholaris.ca/items/eae91f86-fdf7-43a9-b47b-3f941a04a2fe

Cardoso rezende, I. P. (2024). Motives for performance-based substance use among programmers: a qualitative study.

Constantinescu, M. (2016). The cultural dimension of the literary text in translation, biannual review produced by the interlitteras research centre, translation workshop no. 26.

Dalodière, R. (2023, 24 novembre). *Environmental communication: Control of discourse, discourses of control* [Présentation]. *Framing nature: discourses past and present of nature and the environment*, CLAVIER 2023, Milan, Italie. Université de Mons. https://orbi.umons.ac.be/bitstream/20.500.12907/46737/1/Pr%C3%A9sentation%20-%20R.%20Dalodiere.pdf

Dictionnaire technique français–arabe [PDF]. (2004). Dar Al-Kotob Al-Ilmiyah. Consulté sur Scribd : https://www.scribd.com/document/363141080/dictionnaire-technique-francais-arabe-pdf

Drennan, G. (1992). *Aspects of translation in psychological and psychiatric cross-cultural research.* (mémoire de maîtrise, Université de Cape Town, Faculté des Sciences humaines, Département de Psychologie). UCT OpenUCT. https://open.uct.ac.za/server/api/core/bitstreams/017a36d1-a8fc-4793-8b9c-420dc2f58375/conten

Dubut, J. & saint-charles, J. (2025). *Beauty or the beast: promoting unloved wildlife species.* Uqam.ca

Elamin, S. (2023). Investigating the Use of Online Bilingual Resources by Translation Students: The Vertical/Sequential Model Revisited. *Arab World English Journal for Translation & Literary Studies*, 7(4), 48–60. https://www.awej-tls.org/investigating-the-use-of-online-bilingual-resources-by-translation-students-the-vertical-sequential-model-revisited/

Fatima, A. R. I. B., & boulkhir, H. (2023). Circular economy: theoretical foundation and link with sustainable development. *International journal of accounting, finance, auditing, management and economics*, 4(5-1), 111-123.

Ibrahim, H. (2023). The phenomenon of false friends and its impact on translation. طوىسأ ةعماج-بادآلا ةىلكل ةىملعلا ةلجملا.

Iwala, G., & ashiru-abdulrahman, K. (2025). Translation as a means of propaganda on climate change issues in africa. *Concrescence journal of multi-disciplinary research*, 2(1).

Jin, J., & Tu, W. (2025). Study on the limitations of chatgpt in translating political texts according to the "fidelity, clarity and adequacy" criteria. *Canadian Social Science.*

Kandil, R. (2025, janvier). Problématique des hétéronymes dans la traduction juridique : la technologie est-elle un outil d'aide ou un outil de traduction? *Trans-cultural Journal for Humanities & Social Sciences (TJHSS)*, 6(2), 376–...Badr University in Cairo. https://journals.ekb.eg/article_419425_568fe667ba909cee4d56006fbfc8040a.pdf

Kazumi, N. (2018). Environmental terms and the environment of terms, Peter lang gmbh, pp. 201-223.

Kędzia-klebeko, B. (2024). Between duty and pleasure. The challenges of training translators. Annales umcs sectio n educatio nova.

Kotob, C. (2024). … and limitations of open-access machine translation. Analysis of problems related to the bi- or trilingual translation of proper nouns (arabic/french/english) on the internet

Lucassen, F. (2024). *The translation of black humor by the machine translation machine deepl: qualitative analysis of comedians jérémy ferrari, santo cilauro and youp van't hek, from French, English, and Dutch* (Master's thesis, Faculty of Philosophy and Letters, University of Liège). MatheO - Open Access Repository of the University of Liège.

Mantrach, Z. (2021). *Cultural adaptation to the test of diversity: the case of the new metric scale of intelligence (NEMI-2) in the moroccan field* (Doctoral dissertation, Université Sorbonne Paris Nord). HAL. https://theses.hal.science/tel-04032322v1

Markowski, G. (2024). *Jean-claude boulanger, de la conception du lexique à sa dictionnarisation, limoges: lambert-lucas, 2024.* Stylistyka.

Ministère de la Transition écologique, de la Biodiversité, de la Forêt, de la Mer et de la Pêche. (2025). *État de l'environnement en France: Synthèse du rapport 2024. Paris*: CGDD. https://www.notre-environnement.gouv.fr/IMG/pdf/ree2024_rapport.pdf

Nguyen, M. A. (2024). Mirror, mirror, tell me who's the fairest? a cultural analysis of triage protocols for access to intensive care in the context of covid-19.

Oueslati, H. (2023). *Design as a new field of specialized translation. Arabic journal for translation studies.* Atranslationstudies.

Patrick, T. (2015). *Dictionary of biological diversity and nature conservation.*

Prévil, C. & ortega, k. A. (2025). Place-based education and revitalization of indigenous knowledge: perspectives of mapuche cultural facilitators in chile. Ideas. Ideas from the americas.

Roussel, I. (2005). *Les démarches de développement durable, pertinence et apports effectifs dans la gestion de l'air et de l'eau: les exemples de Lille et de Saint-Etienne*, Association pour la prévention de la pollution athmosphérique, Nord-Pas-de-Calais.

Salama-Carr, M. (2007). *Translating and interpreting conflict.* Rodopi. DOI: 10.1163/9789401204385

Temim, S. (2023). Reducing greenhouse gas emissions from wireless networks: improving the performance of artificial intelligence approaches.

Thiam, A. B. (2024). *The social dimensions of agroecological projects in agriculture in senegal: the point of view of field actors.* Scholaris.ca

Venuti, L. (1995). *The translator's invisibility. A history of translation.* Routledge.

Vinay, J.-P., & Darbelnet, J. (1972). *Stylistique comparée du français et de l'anglais.* Didier.

Viviani, C. S. P. (2023). *The national charter for the environment and sustainable development of morocco: a comparative analysis of the arabic and french versions1.* Studi africanistici quaderni di studi berberi e libico-berberi, 101.

Voyer, M. (2025). The "two-eyed seeing" approach and its potential to support the advent of indigenous-led protected areas in quebec.

Chapter 14

Revolutionizing Psychological Methods Through Machine Learning

Meriem Ansari
https://orcid.org/0009-0005-0292-0331
University Hassan II, Morocco

Adil Ghazali
University Hassan II, Morocco

ABSTRACT

This chapter explores the intersection of machine learning and psychology, highlighting how machine learning technologies are transforming both empirical research and the practice of psychology. We provide a comprehensive overview of the innovative applications of machine learning within the field of psychology, including areas such as predictive behavioral analysis and the use of natural language processing techniques to identify emotional indicators in interpersonal communications. This chapter explores sophisticated methodologies, to demonstrate the efficacy of these instruments in the diagnosis of mental health disorders, thereby augmenting objectivity in evaluations and refining intervention strategies. Additionally, we address ethical considerations and concerns related to data confidentiality and interpretation while offering insights into the future development of this interdisciplinary field. This manuscript is designed for scholars and practitioners aiming to comprehend the potentials and constraints of machine learning in the analysis of human behavior.

DOI: 10.4018/979-8-3373-3436-3.ch014

INTRODUCTION

The aim of this book chapter is to identify the relation between psychology and machine learning, the application of machine learning in psychology and its tools in both theoretical and practical psychology.

Machine Learning and psychology are two different sciences. Nevertheless, they have some intersections and influences on each other. Artificial intelligence (AI) has become a revolutionary technology in the 21st century, profoundly influencing numerous sectors. In healthcare, AI systems contribute to diagnosing diseases by analyzing medical images and predicting patient outcomes based on historical data.

In education, AI tools personalize learning experiences, adapt school programs to student needs, and help teachers choose the appropriate teaching method and develop their skills in pedagogy. Furthermore, in scientific research, AI accelerates data analysis, enabling significant progress in areas such as genomics and climate modelling. Social sciences are also embracing AI, using it to analyze social media posts, conduct emotion analysis, study human behavior patterns and also make some diagnoses of their mental health. Overall, artificial intelligence powers a variety of applications, including advanced speech recognition systems that convert spoken language into text, progressive image analysis for different industries, and coherent language translation services that link communication gaps across cultures.

In this chapter, we will explore recent advancements in machine learning, particularly those applied to psychology.

1. MACHINE LEARNING

1.1 Definition

Machine learning is a branch of artificial intelligence that focuses on developing algorithms allowing computers to learn from data without being explicitly programmed. This branch analyses and detects trends within data sets by adopting statistical models and algorithms; as a result, it facilitates predictions or decisions predicated on that information. Machine learning algorithms have the essential capability to boost their performance by facing amplified volumes of data, thus making them able to adapt and enhance their efficacy over time autonomously. The applications of machine learning are wide-ranging, encompassing areas such as image and speech recognition, natural language processing, recommendation systems, and predictive analytics (Jain & Tiwari, 2024).

Some may wonder if machine learning and artificial intelligence are the same or if there is a difference between them. Is it merely a matter of terminology?

In fact, we will explore that topic in the next section.

1.2. Machine Learning and Artificial Intelligence

We begin by defining what Artificial Intelligence (AI) is. AI is about making machines intelligent through diverse methods, while Machine Learning (ML) is specifically founded on only one method: developing computers capable of learning to perform tasks (Rebala et al., 2019).

As an example of an AI method that is not based on learning, we can name expert systems. Even though intelligence is difficult to define, Machine Learning is significantly a subfield of Artificial Intelligence (AI). Many people perceive Artificial Intelligence (AI) and Machine Learning (ML) to be the same thing, and have the belief that Machine Learning is the only applicable way to achieve the goals of AI (Rebala et al., 2019).

We now understand that machine learning is a subfield of artificial intelligence focused on training machines or computers to perform tasks.

1.3. Types of Machine Learning

Machine learning integrates three fundamental types, each with its distinct applications and benefits.

- ***Supervised learning:*** Supervised learning is a type of machine learning that teach a model using labeled data, where the dependent variable is known. In this process, the model generates prediction based on the relationships between the variables and the target variable (Jain & Tiwari, 2024).
- ***Unsupervised learning:*** The model identifies structures and relationships in the data without relying on a predefined target (Jain & Tiwari, 2024).
- ***Reinforcement learning:*** Reinforcement learning is a type of machine learning that teaches a model to make decisions within a context. Based on its actions, the model receives a reward or a punishment, and learns over time to gain more remuneration than punishment (Jain & Tiwari, 2024).

2. PSYCHOLOGY

We have provided an overview of Machine Learning and its benefits. Now, we will focus on another concept in our chapter: Psychology. We will begin by defining Psychology and exploring its theories and methods.

2.1. Definition

APA Dictionary of Psychology defines Psychology as: « the study of the mind and behavior. Historically, psychology was an area within philosophy and emerged from it. It is now a diverse scientific discipline comprising several major branches of research (e.g., experimental, biological, cognitive, lifespan developmental, personality, social), as well as several subareas of research and applied psychology (e.g., clinical, industrial/ organizational, school and educational, human factors, health, neuropsychology, cross-cultural). Research in psychology involves observation, experimentation, testing, and analysis to explore the biological, cognitive, emotional, personal, and social processes or stimuli underlying human and animal behavior. The practice of psychology involves the use of psychological knowledge for any of several purposes: to understand and treat mental, emotional, physical, and social dysfunction; to understand and enhance behavior in various settings of human activity (e.g., school, workplace, courtroom, sports arena, battlefield); and to improve machine and building design for human use » (VandenBos, 2015).

3. MACHINE LEARNING AND PSYCHOLOGY

Machine learning presents a compelling opportunity to enhance the field of psychology. As a scientific discipline, psychology seeks to understand and predict human behavior across a wide range of contexts and environments. The application of machine learning and its tools can significantly benefit this field, offering valuable insights and improving outcomes.

Here are some of the benefits we can highlight:

3.1 Enhanced Predictive Capabilities and Understanding Predictor Variables in Psychological Research

One of the most significant implications of machine learning in psychology is the improved ability to make predictions. As a scientific discipline, one of the main goals of psychology is to predict behavior, understanding whether a specific behavior might occur in different contexts, examining the interactions between various variables, and establishing their correlations. These abilities are essential in the practice of psychology.

Many studies examine the impact of machine learning on psychology and how it develops predictions in the field. Below, we present some funding opportunities for researchers on this topic.

Machine learning algorithms are considered popular tools among researchers thanks to their efficiency in prediction in psychological research. In fact, the use of these techniques makes the researchers more capable to analyze and examining diverse and complex datasets, discovering structures that traditional statistical methods couldn't detect. Moreover, machine learning methodologies have significantly improved the predictive validity of cognitive models. Psychologists are able to develop models that predict human behavior with accuracy and precision, thanks to the exhaustiveness of behavioral data examination from diverse sources. The capacity of prediction is crucial, specifically in complex moral decision-making situations where traditional models can't make an adequate prediction. As an example, researchers can utilize machine learning to predict people's reactions to moral dilemmas, taking into consideration diverse factors that influence these reactions, namely cultural context, emotional state, and situational variables. Moreover, they utilize multiple data sources, such as social media, to generate comprehensive individual profiles. Another virtue of machine learning and its implications is that the science of psychology is its prediction of stress and coping strategies used by individuals during situations of crises, namely the COVID-19 pandemic. In fact, mental health professionals are now able to provide interventions at the right time and reduce the psychological suffering thanks to the use of machine learning. Furthermore, psychologists can create predictive models categorising individuals based on various psychological consequences thanks to supervised machine learning. The adoption of this approach helps in revealing complex behaviors and predicting future mental health issues, enabling adapted treatment plans. A study by Koutsouleris et al. (2018) indicates that machine learning can predict with accuracy and precision how individuals can recover from mental health issues. In this research, they developed a questionnaire that precisely forecasted functional health problems results with over 70% precision by applying support vector machines. These findings highlight the promise of incorporating advanced analytics into mental health assessments, potentially enhancing interventions and outcomes for affected individuals. Essentially, this association between machine learning and psychology is effectively advantageous for the deep comprehension of human behavior, with precise prediction (Henninger et al., 2025; Kliegr et al., 2020; Agrawal et al., 2019; Stachl et al., 2020; Tigga & Garg, 2022; Kliegr et al., 2020; Vélez, 2021; Dehghan et al., 2022) .

The aim of researchers in psychology is more than behavior predictions. Researchers are concentrating on detecting the particular predictor variables that significantly impact their studies. This includes a rigorous exploration of the way these variables are engaged with different outcomes, highlighting their direct and indirect influences. Moreover, researchers dynamically investigate the complex interaction between diverse predictor variables, analyzing the process of this interaction to enhance or reduce their impacts. By exploring these complex relationships, the goal of psychologists is to obtain a deep understanding of the factors that influence human behavior (Henninger et al., 2025).

Furthermore, traditional statistical techniques usually analyze non-linear relationships between different variables with more challenges and difficulties. Nevertheless, machine learning techniques have demonstrated their ability to resolve these complications. By using developed algorithms, researchers can identify and investigate with effectiveness the complex interactions between different psychological factors, for example, the traits of personality, cognitive patterns and emotional reactions can effectively identify and explore the nuanced and intricate interactions that exist among diverse psychological factors, such as personality traits, cognitive patterns, and emotional responses, we add to these factors lifestyle influences such as exercise habits, nutrition and dietary and social interactions. This capacity exposes the process of the interconnection between variables in multifaceted ways, not only enhancing the understanding of these variables in isolation but also revealing how they interconnect in diverse ways, basically ensuring deeper perceptions of human behavior and well-being (Pereira et al., 2025).

Moreover, the integration of eye-tracking technology with machine learning is considered a revolution in studying cognitive processes. Psychology researchers can now use gaze patterns to predict intelligence test scores, shedding light on how eye movements can indicate cognitive performance. By examining where and how long a person looks during tasks, scientists obtain understanding of mental processing speed, attention, and information retrieval capacity. This combination improves our understanding of intelligence and has advantageous applications for educational assessments and cognitive evaluations (Ma & Jia, 2024).

Contrary to traditional statistical models, which usually face challenges with new or unseen data, machine learning (ML) algorithms develop their predictive capacities through a systematic approach. These algorithms are trained on a particular subset of the data, known as the training set, to identify patterns. As we know in psychology, predicting human behavior can be complex. In fact, the use of machine learning algorithms facilitates this procedure, thanks to the evaluation of these algorithms' performance on a separate testing set. Researchers are now able to examine with precision and accuracy the capacity of generalization of the model, guaranteeing its applicability in reality, thanks to the training of these models on unseen data. This capacity to manage unexpected data is essential for evolving effective psychological applications aimed at perfecting treatment strategies (Sterner et al., 2025).

3.2 Advanced Data Analysis in Psychology

Another use of machine learning in psychology is data analysis and its tools. Machine learning now enables the development of models that perform tasks efficiently and accurately, saving both time and effort. As a researcher in psychology, the most stressful procedure is the one of analyzing data, which demands time and a lot of work, and maybe you need additional help from other researchers.

To demonstrate how machine learning can simplify data analysis for psychologists, we present some funding opportunities for researchers in this field.

Machine learning (ML) has advanced psychology by offering developed analytical tools for complex data analysis. These data emerge from mobile sensing technologies, including wearables and apps, as well as digital traces in online contexts. In contrast to conventional statistical methods, ML algorithms efficiently manage high-dimensional datasets with different variables. Thanks to this capacity, psychologists are now able to reveal. This capability enables psychologists to uncover complex relationships between behaviors—such as social interactions and physiological responses—and personality traits like extroversion and emotional stability. As an example, algorithms enable researchers to analyze communication patterns on social media, connecting these behaviors to psychological traits that may, in another way, be ambiguous (Stachl et al., 2020).

Employing exhaustive datasets, machine learning techniques are capable of revealing complex patterns and correlations that may escape conventional statistical analysis. These sophisticated algorithms are able to execute an array of data types, covering neuroimaging results like MRI scans, descriptive clinical assessments through patient examinations, and diverse non-imaging data such as genetic information or behavioral metrics. This multidimensional approach enables researchers to utilize machine learning over a wider spectrum of psychological assessments. As a consequence, as psychology researchers, we gain a deep understanding and comprehension of mental health disorders, significantly deepening our comprehension of mental health disorders, yielding findings that can generate more efficient interventions and treatments personalized to individual patient profiles (Tigga & Garg, 2022; Dehghan et al., 2022).

Methods like Principal Component Analysis (PCA) and Multidimensional Scaling (MDS) are used to illustrate high-dimensional data, which aid psychologists in interpreting relationships between variables and individuals more efficiently. Machine learning (ML) is notably efficient at analyzing extensive and complex datasets. It utilizes general-purpose learning algorithms to reveal ambiguous patterns that traditional statistical methods can't detect. This capability is especially crucial in psychology, where data can be complex and multidimensional. Machine learning techniques such as dimensional reduction participate in handling complex datasets, enabling researchers to reveal patterns and factors that may be immediately obscure. This capacity is essential for improving psychological research (Vélez, 2021; Kovač et al., 2024; Dehghan et al., 2022).

In situations where the number of inputs outpaces the number of subjects, machine learning is proving its ability and advantages. This phenomenon is commonly faced in the branch of psychological research, where researchers usually face datasets that include diverse aspects of variables such as behavioral indicators, cognitive assessments, and demographic factors. In these situations, the adaptability of machine learning enables the development of intricate models that can detect complex relationships and patterns in the data, exceeding the limitations prescribed by conventional statistical tools. Traditional methods usually necessitate a larger number of subjects to guarantee the validity and consistency of their outcomes, whereas machine learning can efficiently utilize the available data, making analysts able to build strong models despite a restricted sample size. This ability unlocked new ways for investigation and understanding of complex psychological phenomena (Kovač et al., 2024).

3.3 Improved Generalizability

One of the key characteristics of science is its ability to generalize results. Therefore, psychology aims to generalize its findings to formulate theories. Machine learning plays a significant role in this capacity. For more details about the implications of machine learning in generalizability in psychology, we present some researches that study this influence.

As we know, in psychology, the small size of the sample impacts the validity of the results; on the other hand, machine learning provides the ability of resampling, which is crucial for evaluating the reliability and generalizability of research results. ML models for categorization can uncover intricate patterns that conventional analyses might ignore, providing new insights into psychological theories. Nevertheless, the evaluation of these models' generalisation capacities is usually ignored, which is essential for validating theories and guaranteeing their real-world validity. By highlighting generalization assessments, researchers are able to improve the robustness of their results in psychological science (Stachl et al., 2020; Zubek & Kuncheva, 2018).

Machine learning (ML) models are often manifested as model-agnostic, which means they contain the capability to provide comparable levels of predictive precision across diverse models, although the fundamental assumptions and systems diverge significantly. This capacity of adaptation enables researchers to carefully examine and choose the most appropriate model based on the unique qualities of their dataset and the particular research questions they plan to address. By doing so, they become able to enhance their analysis, leading to more consistent and generalizable insights. This adaptability not only facilitates a more adapted approach to data analysis but also reinforces the overall reliability of the conclusions inferred from their research (Kovač et al., 2024).

3.4 Enhanced Diagnosis and Prognosis

Clinical psychology, psychopathology, and neuropsychology are branches of psychology that concentrate on diagnosing psychological disorders, classifying them, and determining appropriate treatments. Psychologists employ various tests, questionnaires, and interviews with their clients to accurately diagnose these disorders and decide on the best intervention strategies. *ML* transforms this task from a challenging one to a simple one that does not take much time.

Machine learning methods are capable of significantly improving the diagnosis of mental health disorders by analyzing complex clinical data and biological indicators. By diagnosing indistinct patterns that traditional diagnostic methods may ignore, these creative technologies can guide to more precise and well-timed diagnoses, which are essential for executing effective treatment plans. As an example, machine learning can analyze multiple datasets generated from electronic health records, genetic information, and neuroimaging results to create a comprehensive understanding of an individual's mental health status. This advanced data analysis can demonstrate correlations and tendencies that notify clinicians about the detailed presentation of disorders like depression, anxiety, and psychosis. Furthermore, machine learning algorithms are able to provide comprehensive prognostic findings, which aid mental health professionals in predicting the probable path of a patient's condition. By evaluating multiple variables, including past treatment responses and demographic factors, these algorithms are able to help clinicians in making knowledgeable treatment decisions designed especially for the needs of each patient. As a consequence, the combination of predictive analytics into mental health care opens the way for more adapted approaches, eventually enhancing patient results and promoting a deeper understanding of mental disorders (Dwyer et al., 2018; Vélez, 2021; Dehghan et al., 2022).

Machine learning is making a revolution in psychology, especially in analyzing the Toronto Alexithymia Scale (TAS), which assesses emotional identification and expression. Enhanced algorithms enable clinicians to classify patients based on emotional processing profiles, improve diagnostic precision and offer insights into detailed emotional experiences. This approach allows psychologists to identify singular clinical profiles and patterns that conventional methods might neglect, allowing psychologists to develop personalized treatment plans. By using machine learning intelligence to improve follow-up strategies, clinicians can enhance intervention efficacy, leading to better therapeutic results and improved quality of life for patients (Pegalajar et al., 2023; Vélez, 2021).

In addition to that, another significant value of machine learning is the capacity of analyzing behavioral data and define tendencies that uncover knowledge into mental health issues or cognitive processes, improving our understanding of how people think and behave. By employing these improved computational methods, researchers can acquire a deeper understanding of both physical and psychological phenomena, eventually yielding enhanced diagnosis, treatment, and care (Vélez, 2021).

Moreover, unsupervised machine learning (ML) techniques, especially clustering algorithms, are essential in bringing to light complex, obscured patterns within complex datasets. These techniques demonstrated excellence in detecting groups of individuals who share similar psychological profiles, although these similarities are not easily noticeable through traditional analytical approaches. For example, by employing clustering techniques, researchers can reveal extreme phenotypes—detectable behavioral or psychological characteristics that may indicate implicit disorders or traits. Understanding these extreme phenotypes can significantly improve the development of personalized intervention strategies, guaranteeing that individuals receive more adapted support and treatment based on their singular psychological profiles and needs. This approach not only enriches our understanding of human behavior but also opens the way for creative solutions in mental health and beyond (Vélez, 2021).

3.5 Enhanced Accuracy and Objectivity

Psychology is considered a sensitive science, for its practice with humans and on them. It is not like physics, for example, which requires just material data, and that is all. If we make a diagnosis for a patient, we are responsible for it; we can change their life entirely. We must be careful and have accuracy in our work and results to be sure that we do not trouble someone's life by our diagnosis, for example. This is a simple case where we need accuracy in psychology, and there are many. Machine learning has provided psychology with tools that enhance accuracy; here are some of these enhancements.

Recent enhancements in machine learning, especially in the improvement of advanced models like Deep Super Learner (DSL) and Cascade Deep Forest (CDF), have considerably exceeded traditional analytical techniques in the domain of predicting stress levels and coping mechanisms. These creative models apply complex algorithms to analyze complex data patterns, resulting in remarkable precision rates that can achieve as high as 88.42%. This impressive accuracy emphasizes their eventual benefit in clinical psychology, providing practitioners with new techniques for understanding and managing mental health challenges. By incorporating these developed technologies into psychological evaluations, clinicians can obtain a deeper comprehension of individual stress responses and the effectiveness of diverse coping strategies, eventually improving patient care and results (Tigga & Garg, 2022).

The integration of machine learning in testing processes significantly reduces human biases. By using AI algorithms, subjective elements that obscure judgment are reduced, leading to more equitable, more coherent evaluations. AI-driven evaluations offer a transparent view of performance based on objective data instead of personal opinions. This transition to automation improves validity, making it easier to recognize talent without bias interference (Ma & Jia, 2024).

Recent research has revealed that the scoring capacities of artificial intelligence precisely correspond to those of human evaluators, emphasizing a high degree of validity in evaluations. This technological inclusion not only facilitates the assessment procedure but also improves the accuracy, speed, and general quality of psychological measurements. By employing AI in the scoring of evaluations, organizations can guarantee coherent results, minimize the risk for human error, and enhance the efficacy with which evaluations are managed. Consequently, the integration of AI and conventional assessment methods is a marked improvement in the domain of psychological assessment, ultimately contributing to a more precise understanding of individuals' mental health and cognitive functions (Ma & Jia, 2024).

Recent studies have shown that utilizing Conditional Sequential Learning (CSL) techniques can generate a significant decrease in the average costs related to inaccurate classification in comparison to conventional machine learning algorithms. This is especially important in the domain of psychological research, where inaccurate classification may have deep and extensive consequences. The impact of inexact classification in the field of psychology can have serious consequences on individuals' treatment results, contributing to erroneous therapeutic interventions. Thus, leveraging CSL methods can improve the validity of psychological evaluations and enhance decision-making mechanisms by reducing the chances of such expensive errors (Sterner et al., 2025).

Machine learning models often struggle with generalization, which arises when a model excels at training data but fails to apply its learning to new, unseen data. This situation can generate deceptively high performance metrics during training, while the model faces challenges making precise predictions in real-world scenarios. To cope with this problem, psychologists and data scientists execute a methodology of partitioning their dataset into discrete training and test sets. The training set is used to train the model by enabling it to learn patterns and relationships within the data. Whereas the test set, which is kept intact during the training phase, acts as a reference point to assess the model's performance. By analyzing the model's performance on the test set, researchers can obtain insights into its capability to generalize beyond that dataset. Furthermore, along with evaluating how well the model performs on the test set, researchers can also assess its capacity to generalize beyond the initial training data. This systematic approach guarantees that the advanced models are resilient when applied to new data, improving their predictive abilities in psychological research and other applications (Sterner et al., 2025; Yu, 2023).

Recent developments in machine learning techniques, specifically Support Vector Machines (SVM) and Random Forest algorithms, have proven significant efficacy in the classification of psychological categories in social media content. In a remarkable research, researchers attained a notable general precision rate of 86% when analyzing and categorizing tweets. This funding emphasizes the capacity of machine learning methodologies to improve psychological research by offering valid and accurate classifications of emotional and psychological states based on text data from platforms like Twitter. The results not only demonstrate the abilities of these algorithms but also open the way for more advanced analyses in the domain of psychology (Rizzoli, 2024).

3.6 Innovations in Psychometric Methods

In psychology, we use tests and questionnaires to examine psychological variables. That process requires precision and understanding of the method, its psychometric characteristics, and the specificity of the population. It is hard work that demands knowledge and expertise.

Machine learning participates in that way to make psychometry and the use of tests simpler and flexible.

The rise of "psychometric AI" has remarkably revolutionized the domain of evaluation methodologies. In recent years, researchers have progressively adopted advanced AI algorithms to examine and score multiple testing formats. This creative approach not only improves the precision of scoring but also paves new avenues for understanding test-taker performance. By studying patterns and the fine details in responses, psychometric AI can offer a deeper understanding of cognitive capacities and personality traits, marking a remarkable switch from conventional assessment techniques. This pattern has attracted comprehensive examination and discussion within academic and professional spheres, shedding light on both the eventual advantages and challenges associated with the combination of AI in psychological assessment processes (Ma & Jia, 2024).

3.7 Developing Theories in Psychology

We have presented how ML can change the practice of psychology. Now, we will focus on its theoretical applications in the field of psychology.

Some machine learning techniques have the capacity to independently identify the ideal number of prototypes to maintain, grounded in the patterns and characteristics detected in the data being analyzed. This dynamic learning model suggests that human categorization is not fixed; rather, it is a flexible process influenced by the different stimuli we face in our context. Investigating this essential adaptability provides precious perspectives on cognitive flexibility, highlighting the way individuals manage their thought processes and categorisation strategies in response to various experiences. Understanding these mechanisms can notably enhance our comprehension of cognitive adaptability within the domain of psychology (Zubek & Kuncheva, 2018).

The junction of personality theory and computer science has generated a creative field known as personality computing. This field employs machine learning algorithms to distinguish and analyze personality traits from a large array of data sources, like verbal communication patterns, written text, social media interactions, and digital footprints left by individuals online. Researchers of this domain examine the complex relationships between these data points and the expressions of different personality traits in behaviors, facilitating a deeper understanding of human psychology. By methodically evaluating how traits like extroversion, openness, and conscientiousness impact daily behaviors and decision-making processes, personality computing seeks to offer crucial comprehension that can improve everything from adapted marketing strategies to mental health evaluations (Dehghan et al., 2022).

Inside the field of cognitive psychology, machine learning methods, especially neural networks and deep learning algorithms, play a revolutionary role in modelling and emulating complex cognitive processes. These developed computational methods simplify a deeper investigation of principal domains like perception—how we interpret sensory information—and memory, which includes both the storage and recall of information. Furthermore, these tools help in the analysis of decision-making structures and problem-solving capabilities, enabling researchers to explore the fundamental mechanisms of the way humans think, reason, and learn. By leveraging these sophisticated ML techniques, we gain invaluable insights into the complexities of the human mind, enhancing our comprehension of cognitive processes and their connection (Yu, 2023).

3.8 Developing the Way of Teaching and Learning

Machine learning can also be useful in educational psychology by improving the pedagogy and the ways of teaching.

ML has the potential to significantly enhance both the cognitive and emotional experiences of students during their learning paths. By employing developed algorithms and data analysis, machine learning can generate adapted learning ways designed to the special needs of each student. This personalization allows teachers to detect individual strengths and weaknesses, promoting a more efficient learning environment. Hence, students may experience an improvement in motivation and engagement by interacting with information that connects with their personal preferences and learning styles. For example, adaptive learning platforms can adapt the challenge of tasks in real-time, built on student performance, guaranteeing that each student is properly challenged and supported (Yu, 2023).

This personalized attention fosters better educational results, assuring that each learner is able to develop according to their special needs and capabilities (Yu, 2023).

This aimed approach not only improves academic achievement but also develops a deeper emotional interrelation to the learning procedure, eventually leading to a more fulfilling educational experience (Mutmainnah et al., 2024).

Mutmainnah et al. (2024) explore the deep influence of machine learning (ML) on different psychological dimensions, including motivation, anxiety, and general engagement among students. The study sheds light on how ML-driven systems can play a pivotal role in reducing academic anxiety, especially by offering personalized direction and constructive feedback that is precisely aligned to each learner's individual learning needs. As an example, these developed systems employ algorithms that analyze a student's performance patterns and learning interests, allowing them to adjust educational information in real time. This adapted approach caters to different styles of comprehension, thus promoting a deep sense of competence and self-assurance. As learners connect with these adapted learning environments, they are capable of dealing with academic challenges with enhanced confidence. Furthermore, this flexible support mechanism efficiently minimizes the stress that often accompanies the pressures of academic performance. By reducing feelings of bewilderment, learners tend to develop a profound essential motivation to interact with the subject matter. As a result, students will engage in an enriching educational experience that not only improves academic outcomes but also provides a richer, more fulfilling educational experience that motivates active participation and a continuous enthusiasm for learning (Mutmainnah et al., 2024).

The authors add that the combination of machine learning technology in educational programs contributes to enhancing students' emotional resilience. By employing developed algorithms that analyze patterns in student behavior, teachers can obtain meaningful results about individual emotional reactions. This evidence-based approach enables the ensuring of personalized support and tools, allowing educators to mentor students in efficiently regulating their emotions, especially in the face of academic stress or challenge. For example, if a student is suffering from anxiety during exams, the system could notify teachers to intervene with mindfulness strategies or coping mechanisms adapted to that student's singular needs. Finally, cultivating emotional resilience helps students and prepares them for future challenges, nurturing long-term psychological well-being (Mutmainnah et al., 2024).

Furthermore, Machine Learning (ML) systems are able to significantly improve students' self-confidence by utilizing strategies of positive enhancement. For example, when students receive instant feedback on their progress through interactive evaluations, they tend to feel encouraged by their accomplishments, regardless of how small. This enhancement motivates them to engage more actively in their learning journey. By participating in the material with meaningfulness, the students are more likely to develop a profound understanding of the subject matter; hence, they improve their academic performance and achieve a higher level of self-confidence. The creation of a supportive learning environment which employs positive feedback enables ML systems to aid students in perceiving their capacities, help learners recognize their potential and stimulate a growth mindset (Mutmainnah et al., 2024).

3.9 The Applications of Forensic Psychology

Forensic psychology is a specialized discipline within psychology that employs psychological concepts and knowledge in legal affairs, including criminal and civil cases. Moreover, Machine learning has provided positive results in this dimension of psychology. This employment is progressively enriched by advancements in artificial intelligence (AI) and machine learning (ML), which considerably improve the accuracy and efficacy of forensic explorations. Using predictive analytics, these techniques analyze large datasets to detect patterns and trends that can predict eventual criminal behavior or consequences in legal cases. Furthermore, risk evaluation tools powered by AI allow researchers to examine the probability of returning to crime or the eventual danger posed by individuals, thus helping legal professionals in making evidence-based decisions concerning judgment or reintegration. In the domain of textual analysis, advanced algorithms can perform and interpret vast volumes of written proof, whether it comes from digital communications or psychological assessments, revealing knowledge that might be neglected through conventional methods. Moreover, the technique of data collecting includes obtaining useful information from vast datasets, including criminal records and psychological profiles. This combination of AI and ML not only streamlines the investigative process but also enhances the accuracy of psychological evaluation offered in a tribunal setting, eventually leading to more valid results in legal proceedings. By enhancing the methodologies used in forensic psychology, these technological developments are making a revolution in the field and guaranteeing a higher standard of justice (Yu, 2023).

3.10 The Rise of Artificial Psychology

As artificial intelligence becomes a normal part of our lives, a new subfield of psychology has emerged called artificial psychology.

This upcoming field focuses on the investigation of cognitive architectures—structures that imitate the way the human mind analyzes information—and the advancement of artificial emotions that allow AI systems to present behaviors analogous to emotional responses. By combining notions from traditional psychology with innovative information science, artificial psychology intends to enhance our understanding of both human cognition and the complexities of machine behavior. This multidisciplinary approach highlights essential questions about the ethical implications and eventual applications of emotionally aware AI systems in diverse domains, covering mental health support, user interaction, and social robotics (Yu, 2023).

4. ETHICAL CONSIDERATIONS

As we explored in the previous section, machine learning has offered numerous advantages to the field of psychology, significantly shaping it through a range of tools and applications. However, this branch of artificial intelligence also presents certain risks and can negatively impact individuals, including implications for psychological practice.

4.1 *Bases for Assessments*

When psychologists contemplate using passive testing methods through social media for evaluation purposes, they have to seriously examine whether this method adheres to recognized ethical standards. These norms highlight the need for a comprehensive and exhaustive assessment of individuals before developing any conclusions about their mental health or behavior. There is a notable importance concerning the precision and validity of social media profiles, as these online representations may not totally reflect the complexities of an individual's thoughts, emotions, and behaviors in authentic contexts. Thus, psychologists must be prudent in interpreting the routinely curated content posted on social media platforms, realizing that it might present a biased or incomplete picture of the individual being evaluated (Fleming, 2021).

4.2 *Privacy and Confidentiality*

Assuring the protection of confidential information is of the highest importance in the current digital environment. When utilizing social media-based applications, there is an important risk that client confidentiality may not be totally ensured. Platforms like Facebook often participate in practices that enable them to share user data with third parties, which may lead to personalized advertisements based on personal information. This situation highlights serious fears about privacy, as sensitive client details might unintentionally be revealed. On the other hand, self-content applications have the ability to reduce some of these privacy problems; nevertheless, users must stay prudent and inspect the privacy agreements associated with these applications. It is important to entirely understand how data is managed, retained, and shared to guarantee that users' information is protected. Consistently examining privacy policies and supporting stronger data protection measures can aid in protecting the confidentiality that users deserve (Fleming, 2021).

4.3 *Informed Consent*

Psychologists are necessary to ensure knowledgeable permission before leading any evaluations with users. This process requires offering an exhaustive clarification of all components implicated, such as the roles of any third parties who may obtain the information collected during the evaluation. It is essential for users to be totally conscious of how their personal data, especially information taken from their social media accounts, will be used in the evaluation process. Moreover, users should be aware of the eventual individuals or objects that may have access to this data, assuring they understand the outcomes of their privacy and the boundaries of confidentiality concerning their vulnerable information (Fleming, 2021).

4.4 Record Keeping in the Age of Social Media

The accelerated evolution of data rising from social media platforms offers notable challenges for psychological professionals in efficient record-keeping. Psychologists must explore the complex realm of this digital information, cautiously evaluating which elements of data are pertinent for their medical documentation. This requires not only evaluating the reliability and precision of the information but also understanding how it may refer to individual cases. Furthermore, preserving the confidentiality of private information is highly important. Many social media contents may unintentionally uncover personal information not only about the individuals under a psychologist's treatment but also about third parties mentioned or tagged in those contents. Hence, it is necessary for mental health professionals to apply solid measures to protect this information, guaranteeing that all records follow the ethical policies and legal standards for privacy. For instance, anonymizing data, acquiring voluntary agreement from users about the use of social media content, and advancing clear guidelines for supervising and preserving documents that derive from online interactions. The equilibrium between employing helpful data from social media and safeguarding users' privacy is a sensitive and crucial mission in modern psychological practice (Fleming, 2021).

4.5 Diversity and Justice in Machine Learning

The advancement of many machine learning (ML) tools mainly employs the English language, creating important challenges for individuals who are multilingual or non-English speakers. This language bias can lead to errors in perception and interpretation when these techniques are used over different linguistic groups. Moreover, differences in access to technology can be profoundly related to factors like age, economic status, and geographic location. For example, older adults may face difficulties with using new technology because of ignorance or lack of practice, while poor individuals might have limited access to necessary devices or high-speed internet, making some ML technologies inappropriate for their needs. These challenges emphasize the significant responsibility of psychologists and other professionals in the field to vigorously value most and respect differences. There is a necessary need to advance and promote fair access to psychological evaluation methods and resources that consider the special profiles and situations of all populations. This approach not only promotes integration but also guarantees that the advantages of technological developments get to everyone, regardless of their linguistic or socioeconomic status (Fleming, 2021).

5. CONCLUSION

In this chapter, we explored the dynamic relationship between machine learning and psychology, focusing on how these two fields intersect. We outlined the most significant advantages of machine learning, drawing on both theoretical frameworks and empirical evidence to illustrate its potential impact on psychological research and practice. Additionally, we delved into the various challenges that arise from integrating machine learning techniques into psychological methodologies, discussing issues such as data privacy concerns, the need for interpretability in models, and the ethical implications involved in algorithmic decision-making. Through this comprehensive examination, we aimed to provide a nuanced understanding of

REFERENCES

Agrawal, M., Peterson, J. C., & Griffiths, T. L. (2019). *Using machine learning to guide cognitive modeling: A case study in moral reasoning* [Preprint]. *arXiv*. https://doi.org//arXiv.1902.06744DOI: 10.48550

Dehghan, P., Alashwal, H., & Moustafa, A. A. (2022). Applications of machine learning to behavioral sciences: Focus on categorical data. *Discover Psychology*, *2*(1), 22. DOI: 10.1007/s44202-022-00027-5

Dwyer, D. B., Falkai, P., & Koutsouleris, N. (2018). Machine learning approaches for clinical psychology and psychiatry. *Annual Review of Clinical Psychology*, *14*(1), 91–118. DOI: 10.1146/annurev-clinpsy-032816-045037 PMID: 29401044

Fleming, M. N. (2021). Considerations for the ethical implementation of psychological assessment through social media via machine learning. *Ethics & Behavior*, *31*(3), 181–192. DOI: 10.1080/10508422.2020.1817026 PMID: 34248317

. Henninger, M., Debelak, R., Rothacher, Y., & Strobl, C. (2025). Interpretable machine learning for psychological research: Opportunities and pitfalls.

Jain, V., & Tiwari, S. K. (2024). Overview: Machine learning. In *Machine learning: An art of computer thinking* (Vol. 3, pp. 130–144). IIP Series. DOI: 10.58532/nbennurch183

Kliegr, T., Bahník, Š., & Fürnkranz, J. (2020). Advances in machine learning for the behavioral sciences. *The American Behavioral Scientist*, *64*(2), 145–175. DOI: 10.1177/0002764219859639

Kovač, N., Ratković, K., Farahani, H., & Watson, P. (2024). A practical applications guide to machine learning regression models in psychology with Python. *Methods in Psychology (Online)*, *11*, 100156. DOI: 10.1016/j.metip.2024.100156

Ma, S., & Jia, N. (2024). Measuring Raven's Progressive Matrices combining eye-tracking technology and machine learning (ML) models. *Journal of Intelligence*, *12*(11), 116. DOI: 10.3390/jintelligence12110116 PMID: 39590643

Mutmainnah, I., Shodiq, J., & Faizah, N. (2024). The influence of machine learning on the student learning psychology in Industry 5.0. *Education and Sociedad Journal*, *1*(2), 83–93. DOI: 10.61987/edsojou.v1i2.635

Pegalajar, M. C., Ruiz, L. G. B., Pérez-Moreiras, E., Boada-Grau, J., & Serrano-Fernandez, M. J. (2023). An intelligent approach using machine learning techniques to predict flow in people. *Big Data and Cognitive Computing*, *7*(2), 67. DOI: 10.3390/bdcc7020067

Pereira, M. G., Santos, M., Magalhães, R., Rodrigues, C., Araújo, O., & Durães, D. (2025). Burnout risk profiles in psychology students: An exploratory study with machine learning. *Behavioral Sciences (Basel, Switzerland)*, *15*(4), 505. DOI: 10.3390/bs15040505 PMID: 40282126

Rebala, G., Ravi, A., & Churiwala, S. (2019). Machine learning definition and basics. In *An introduction to machine learning* (pp. 1–17). Springer., DOI: 10.1007/978-3-030-15729-6_1

Rizzoli, V. (2024). The risk co-de model: Detecting psychosocial processes of risk perception in natural language through machine learning. *Journal of Computational Social Science*, *7*(1), 217–239. DOI: 10.1007/s42001-023-00235-6

Stachl, C., Pargent, F., Hilbert, S., Harari, G. M., Schoedel, R., Vaid, S., Gosling, S. D., & Bühner, M. (2020). Personality research and assessment in the era of machine learning. *European Journal of Personality*, *34*(5), 613–631. DOI: 10.1002/per.2257

Sterner, P., Goretzko, D., & Pargent, F. (2025). Everything has its price: Foundations of cost-sensitive machine learning and its application in psychology. *Psychological Methods*, *30*(1), 112–127. DOI: 10.1037/met0000586 PMID: 37561487

Tigga, N. P., & Garg, S. (2022). Prediction of global psychological stress and coping induced by the COVID-19 outbreak: A machine learning study. *Alpha Psychiatry*, *23*(4), 193–202. DOI: 10.5152/alphapsychiatry.2022.21797 PMID: 36425737

VandenBos, G. R. (Ed.). (2015). *APA dictionary of psychology* (2nd ed.). American Psychological Association., DOI: 10.1037/14646-000

Vélez, J. I. (2021). Machine learning based psychology: Advocating for a data-driven approach. *International Journal of Psychological Research*, *14*(1). Advance online publication. DOI: 10.21500/20112084.5365 PMID: 34306575

Yu, C. H. (2023). Artificial intelligence, machine learning, and psychology. In Yu, C. H. (Ed.), *Psychology*. Oxford University Press., DOI: 10.1093/obo/9780199828340-0323

Zubek, J., & Kuncheva, L. (2018). Learning from exemplars and prototypes in machine learning and psychology [Preprint]. *arXiv*. DOI: 10.48550/arXIV.1806.01130

Chapter 15

The Integration of AI and Stakeholders in Citizen Motivation Towards a Sustainable Energy Transition in the Context of a Smart City

Zineb El Assal
https://orcid.org/0000-0002-9470-1531
University Hassan II, Casablanca, Morocco

Hanane Rochdane
University Hassan II, Casablanca, Morocco

ABSTRACT

Citizens' awareness of environmental problems has been strengthened over the past two decades by the publication of a wide dissemination of information and data on the real state of the environment and the dangers likely to arise if corrective actions and measures are not put in place. The integration of AI makes it possible to stimulate personalized solutions adapted to each individual by offering promising prospects and promoting a sustainable lifestyle within Smart Cities. The success of individual awareness programs is related to the growth of the interest in sustainable development in society in order to increase ecological and environmentally friendly behavior. Our study aims to highlight the importance of the integration and motivation of the citizen to use renewable energies in addition to other stakeholders in order to support the smart city project.

DOI: 10.4018/979-8-3373-3436-3.ch015

HISTORICAL CONTEXT OF CITIZEN MOTIVATION

The historical exploration of citizen motivation reveals a complex dynamic, shaped by various socio-political contexts. Over the centuries, citizen participation has been influenced by political movements, technological innovations, and cultural changes. The beginning of modern democracy during the French Revolution reinvented the ideas of participation, restricting citizenship to privileged elites beforehand. This period of upheaval introduced the concept of active citizenship, where civic engagement became essential for the maintenance of freedoms and rights (Bolambuli Bosinga, 2024).

With the emergence of nation-states in the nineteenth century, the idea of motivation was revised by industrialization and urbanization. Major social movements, such as women's suffrage and workers' struggles, have enriched the discourse on what motivates citizens to get involved. Technological revolutions have also played a key role, as they have provided new means of communication and organization, allowing citizens to unite around common goals. However, citizen participation has always been uneven, with structural roadblocks that have stood in the way of the inclusion of diverse voices in the decision-making process (Arellano and Cossi, 2024).

At the dawn of the twenty-first century, the rise of digital technologies has radically transformed the landscape of civic motivation. Social networks and online platforms have not only facilitated the mobilization of citizens but have also generated new forms of engagement, making motivation more accessible. However, they have also raised concerns about disinformation and digital exclusion. In this context, understanding the historical evolution of citizen motivation helps to shed light on modern challenges related to democratic participation and the integration of external actors, including artificial intelligence, in this process. Citizen motivation, while constantly evolving, remains a reflection of the tensions between the individual, the state, and new technologies, each interacting to define what it means to be a motivated citizen in a rapidly changing world (KAZADI, 2025).

AI AND CITIZEN MOTIVATION

In recent years, and following the reports of environmental experts and specifically on climate change, the increase in temperature on Earth from the middle of the twentieth century and the destruction of the environment have become issues related mainly to prosperous economic development. Where does the importance and necessity of implementing awareness-raising policies for all stakeholders that have a direct effect or influence on environmental aggravation and deterioration come from? From a theoretical perspective, our research links different key concepts such as stakeholder theory, sustainable development, smart city, motivation and self-determination theory. We will try to define each concept apart from each apartment to understand our subject.

Stakeholder theory was addressed by Freemane in 1984, he defined a stakeholder as "any group or individual who can affect or be affected by an organization." In other words, it is an entity or actor, whether a natural or legal person, that has the ability to influence the activities of an organization and is also likely to be impacted by the decisions and actions of that organization. The interest of the notion of stakcholders is mainly to decipher the reactions and relationships between an organization and the multiple actors who lock it up and who can influence it. The goal is to build lasting relationships that are beneficial to all parties. In another definition, it was a question of adapting the sphere of responsibility of companies from those who directly benefit from the company's actions, to all those who can affect or are affected by the company's actions.

The concept of sustainable development was first set out in the Brundtland Report, which was also recognized by the report of the World Commission on Environment and Development in 1987. The report highlighted the need to reconcile the needs of present and future generations, highlighting the balance between the social, environmental and economic dimensions of development. It laid the foundation for global awareness of the need to preserve the environment while promoting economic progress and social well-being.

The concept of the Smart City, on the other hand, has emerged more recently and refers to the integration of innovative information and communication technologies (ICTs) to optimize citizens' quality of life, environmental sustainability and the efficiency of urban services. The smart city is determined as much as the harmonious merging of computer, social, physical, human and business systems, with appropriate use of available interconnected data. Its objective is to encourage collective intelligence, thus allowing for better understanding, better control of operations and optimization of limited resources according to the Department of Business Innovation and Skills, 2013. Smart Cities seek to integrate physical infrastructure, communication systems and data to create smarter, connected and sustainable urban environments according to Kummitha and Crutzen, (2017).

Regarding the notion of motivation, according to Graham (2020), motivation is defined as the study of the behavior and reactions of individuals, aimed at explaining the reason that drives them to react in a certain way rather than another. Over the years, the subject of motivation has been evaluated as essential in psychology, prompting a lot of research in this field. Among the most popular theories is the theory of self-determination (DRT) by Ryan & Deci, (2000). Self-determination theory proposes an approach that addresses and unveils the internal and external factors that influence the motivation of individuals. DRT also highlights the importance of social and environmental influences on motivation. Self-determination theory offers a conceptual framework for understanding and explaining human motivation, highlighting the importance of basic needs and social influences.

By combining these concepts, our study leads to the understanding and study of how citizen motivation can be mobilized to support the transition to a smart and sustainable city, highlighting the importance of the use of renewable energy in this context with the integration of different stakeholders.

The fundamental objective of our comprehensive and in-depth study is to highlight the crucial and undeniable importance of the integration and motivation of citizens, without forgetting the unwavering commitment and active contribution of all the stakeholders involved, for the optimal and efficient use of renewable energies in the current context, which is both pressing and promising. This is not only necessary but also vital in order to guarantee the sustainable success and sustainability of a smart city project, thus representing a real step towards a future that is more sustainable, responsible and environmentally conscious. More specifically, our work proposes to explore in depth the various complex factors that influence the motivation of citizens to actively and meaningfully participate in the transition to a smart city, taking into account the different social and economic dynamics that vary from one community to another. We also want to analyse the means, as well as the strategies, to encourage these citizens to adopt sustainable and environmentally friendly practices, in particular through the increasing and essential use of renewable energies which have become indispensable in this era of climate change, marked by major environmental challenges. It is also essential to deepen the understanding of the role and responsibilities of all stakeholders involved, namely government institutions, private sector companies and local communities, as their collective and coordinated engagement is indispensable to make this ambitious and transformative project, which has the potential to redefine the way we live, a success. to consume and interact with our natural and built environment. Our target population is mainly composed of the citizens of the city of Casablanca, who are considered the essential element of the Smart City project. They are the end users of the Smart City's services and infrastructure. Also, all stakeholders who are directly related to the project. However, it is worth noting some limitations of our research. First, there is a lack of a clear government framework for the various stakeholders involved in the monitoring of the Smart City project. This can have an impact on the coordination and collaboration between the actors involved, as well as on the effective implementation of Smart City initiatives. In addition, our research sample is tight and defined on the city of Casablanca, since it is the only Smart City project launched in Morocco so far. This means that the results obtained cannot be generalized to other Smart City contexts in Morocco.

We carried out a field study based on a quantitative survey of the inhabitants of Casablanca to identify their level of integration in the Smart City project and to reveal the determinants of motivation related to the installation of solar panels. This method allowed us to collect data directly from citizens and gain valuable insights into the factors that motivate them to adopt renewable energy sources. Our research objective, which is to raise awareness among citizens of the importance of renewable resources and to encourage them to participate in the Smart City project, is commendable. By identifying the specific motivational determinants that influence their decision to install solar panels, you will be able to better understand how to promote and encourage the use of these resources in the city.

This research is presented and ordered in the following structure: first, we detail the methodology we adopted as well as the target population of our study. Next, we present key statistics from our survey. We then proceed to a discussion of the implications of these results, before giving an overall conclusion to our study. By structuring our paper in this way, we provide a clear and logical framework to present our research, allowing readers to easily follow our argument and understand the scope of our findings.

ROLE OF AI IN MODERN SOCIETY

Artificial intelligence (AI) is playing a pivotal role in the transformation of modern society, redefining the interactions between individuals, institutions, and technologies. Its integration transcends industry boundaries, encompassing varied areas such as health, education, trade and governance. At the heart of this evolution are the capabilities of big data analysis, allowing for the processing and interpretation of information that escapes the human eye. Using advanced algorithms, AI systems discern patterns and trends, making it possible to predict behaviors and optimize decision-making processes. This raises both opportunities and challenges, especially in terms of ethics and responsibility (Modolo, 2025).

In the healthcare sector, for example, artificial intelligence (AI) is revolutionizing not only diagnostic methods but also treatment approaches, analyzing medical images with an accuracy that rivals that of medical professionals, and in some cases can even exceed them. AI systems don't just make a diagnosis; They also personalize treatment plans based on individual and specific patient characteristics, while integrating information generated by different biometric sensors, connected medical devices, and advanced technologies. This ability to analyze and interpret complex data provides unprecedented tooling power that overlays human skills. In education, intelligent learning platforms adapt their pedagogical approaches to the varied and specific needs of students, thus offering a truly personalized learning experience that optimizes not only their engagement and motivational capacities, but also their understanding of content, which is particularly beneficial for very diverse and varied learner profiles (Yanis, 2023). In terms of governance, AI allows for more efficient management of public resources, facilitating the collection and analysis of data on citizens' behaviours. This technological advancement offers decision-makers the opportunity to anticipate the needs of communities and implement proactive strategies to improve overall well-being. However, the increased use of AI raises critical questions about privacy, algorithmic transparency, and equal access to technologies. So, while AI promises to enrich the social fabric, it is essential to establish regulatory and ethical frameworks to guide its integration, ensuring that the benefits reach all levels of society equally. This duality between potential and responsibility will need to be carefully navigated to maximize the positive impact of AI on modern society (Lfarh and Kissami, 2025).

STAKEHOLDERS AND THEIR INFLUENCE

The influence of stakeholders in the process of motivating citizens is crucial in the context of the integration of artificial intelligence (AI). Stakeholders, which include entities as diverse as governments, non-governmental organizations (NGOs), private companies, and citizens themselves, play distinct but interconnected roles in boosting citizen engagement. Their interaction shapes not only the acceptance of AI-based technologies, but also the development of public policies that are based on a collective understanding of citizens' needs and wants. It is therefore imperative to examine how each group influences the perception and adoption of AI in civic motivation (OUBAYOUCEF et al., 2025).

Governments, through their ability to create regulatory frameworks and set policy priorities, exert axiomatic influence on the direction of AI initiatives aimed at motivating citizens. Their role, as regulators and facilitators, can strengthen public trust in technology if appropriate measures are put in place to ensure transparency and data protection. At the same time, NGOs often intervene by providing critical analysis and advocating on behalf of marginalized groups, which can enrich the public debate on the use of AI. Their ability to bring humanistic and ethical perspectives to the table can correct potential biases in algorithms and ensure that civic engagement initiatives remain inclusive and representative (Soguel et al., 2023).

On the other hand, private companies hold resources and expertise that can catalyze AI innovations. They influence the dynamics of citizen motivation by developing products and services that directly meet the expectations of users. Moreover, collaboration between these different actors is becoming essential to create ecosystems of sustainable motivation. Ultimately, the success of citizen engagement initiatives through AI relies on a delicate balance between these stakeholders, whose interests, motivations, and influencers must be skillfully managed to create a synergistic dynamic, where technology respects and values every citizen voice. Thus, understanding how these interactions take shape can offer critical insights for the future development of AI solutions to engage citizens in their communities and beyond (BADDOUH and SOUDANE2024).

MODELS OF CITIZEN MOTIVATION

Citizen motivation is a complex field of study that unfolds around several theoretical and practical models, each offering varied perspectives on the factors that drive individuals to actively engage in societal issues. One of the most influential models is the intrinsic motivation model, which emphasizes the importance of personal satisfaction and the pleasure derived from civic engagement. This model posits that volunteer participation in community initiatives or decision-making processes is often fueled by personal values, the quest for accomplishment, and a sense of belonging to a community. From this perspective, the integration of artificial intelligence can serve to identify and promote these intrinsic motivations, thus strengthening citizens' emotional connection to their environment (Perez-Torrents, 2024). On the other hand, the extrinsic motivation model, often associated with organizational structures and financial or material incentives, also plays a crucial role. This model argues that individuals are likely to become more engaged when they perceive direct benefits such as economic rewards or social recognition. By integrating artificial intelligence into this framework, governments and organizations can develop systems that measure and analyze the impact of incentives on citizen behavior, allowing them to design more tailored and effective mobilization campaigns. Thus, AI could be used to segment the population according to its motivations, allowing for personalization of messages and interventions.

A hybrid model, which combines intrinsic and extrinsic aspects, should also be considered. This more nuanced approach considers that citizens' motivations are not monolithic and that they vary according to the social, economic and cultural context. The synergy between AI and stakeholders can serve to create interconnected engagement platforms, where citizens are encouraged to voice their concerns while receiving tangible recognition for their contribution (Oubayoucef et al., 2025). By recognising the complex dynamics between motivation, engagement and outcome, the strategies developed can aim not only to increase civic participation, but also to forge a more resilient and supportive social fabric. Thus, citizen motivation models, strategically integrated with artificial intelligence tools, represent a fundamental challenge for citizen mobilization and the strengthening of participatory democracy.

INTEGRATION OF AI IN PUBLIC POLICIES

The integration of artificial intelligence (AI) into public policy is a potential revolution, redefining not only the decision-making framework, but also the way governments interact with citizens. Through advanced analytics systems, policymakers can now leverage massive volumes of data to identify trends, anticipate crises, and formulate responses that are more responsive to people's needs. In addition, the integration of AI raises crucial questions about transparency and accountability. As governments rely on automated systems to make decisions that affect the daily lives of citizens, it becomes imperative to ensure that these systems are both understandable and explainable (Zakka, 2025). Public administrations must make a strong and proactive commitment to robust and transparent governance arrangements that carefully monitor the use of AI. This is of paramount importance to ensure that the technologies deployed do not create disastrous social or economic inequalities, but on the contrary, promote greater inclusivity in their use and in the impacts they generate. In this important perspective, the crucial challenge of integrating AI lies not only in the significant technical benefits it can bring to society, but also in the ability of governments to mobilize the various stakeholders involved in an effective and coordinated manner. (Rhattat & Schoch, 2024) This includes, but is not limited to, AI experts, specialized researchers, dedicated public sector employees, as well as the ordinary citizens who experience the consequences of these technologies every day. All these diverse actors must work together in synergy to co-construct informed public policies that truly reflect the diverse perspectives, lived experiences, specific needs, and varied concerns of society as a whole. This will not only prevent potential abuses, but also maximize the benefits that AI can bring to all members of the community.

The interaction between AI and public policies also calls into question the need for enhanced civic education. Citizens need to be informed and trained to actively participate in the debate around emerging technologies and their implications. Awareness-raising initiatives, coupled with participatory platforms, can facilitate this dynamic, allowing citizens to become actors rather than mere receivers of policies. The integration of AI into public policy thus embodies a paradigmatic shift, where the technology is not limited to a technical application, but becomes a catalyst for dialogue and social engagement (Filion, 2025).

METHODOLOGY

In our research work, we adopted a methodology based on a literature review and an empirical study. Concerning the Literature Review part, we carried out an in-depth review of the existing literature on theories of motivation, with particular emphasis on the theory of self-determination developed by Deci and Ryan in 1985. This literature review allowed us to develop a conceptual model that integrates the key concepts of self-determination theory and adapts them to the context of our research. This conceptual model constitutes the theoretical framework of our study and guides our empirical investigation. Whereas the empirical study is based on a quantitative approach and uses an illustrated questionnaire of the conceptual model that we have developed. We chose this method to obtain quantifiable data and allow statistical analysis of the results. Given the size of the market, we opted for a probability sampling method. This means that we gave an equal opportunity to different types of individuals to participate and answer our questionnaire. Our main target population is therefore the citizens of the city of Casablanca, given that this city is directly concerned by the Smart City project. Once we collected the responses to our questionnaire, we conducted a thorough analysis of the results.

Data Collection

To collect data, we developed an interview guide consisting of 20 questions that are asked of the respondents. The questions were formulated in a transparent and understandable way, so that the participants understood the purpose of the survey. We favoured closed-ended questions, using different types of formulations: some required a binary answer (yes or no), others asked to choose a single answer from several proposals, while others allowed one or more answers to be ticked. The questionnaire was disseminated using social media, including through numerous Facebook pages, as well as WhatsApp and email. This dissemination extended over a period of five months, during which we collected the responses. We chose this method of dissemination because of the characteristics of the target population, which is citizens of a smart city. In this context, the use of information and communication technologies (ICTs) is widespread and the digitalization of services is a reality. We have therefore opted for an online approach, which is in line with the profile of the participants. For the data analysis, we used the SPSS software. Once all the data collected was entered into the software, we proceeded to analyze the results it provided. This analysis allowed us to explore participants' responses, calculate descriptive statistics, and highlight significant trends or associations between the variables studied. By using the SPSS software, we were able to conduct a rigorous statistical analysis of the data collected, which will allow us to draw relevant conclusions from the survey results.

Data Analysis

In this section of our article, we will present the main results we obtained from the collection of data for our questionnaire. Here is an overview of the most significant results:

Figure 1. Level of interest of our population in the use of renewable energy

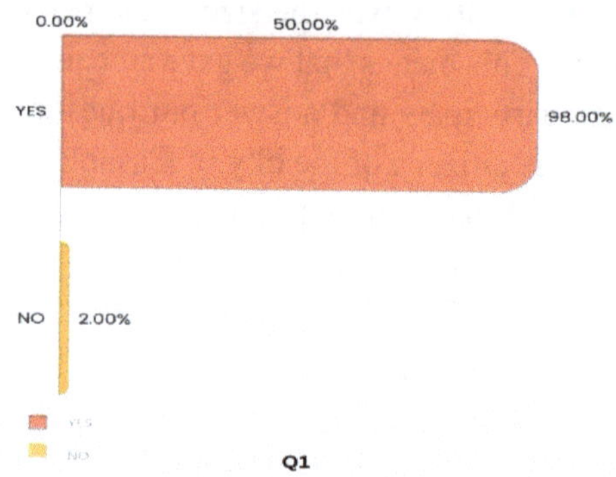

Upon taking a significantly closer overview of the comprehensive and intricate graph displayed above, the detailed statistics that have been meticulously obtained reveal that an impressive and noteworthy 98% of the population surveyed express a strong and genuine interest in the thoughtful and beneficial use of the numerous natural resources that are available to us. In stark contrast, a mere 2% of those surveyed indicate that they have no interest whatsoever in this significant and crucial matter that affects us all directly. This striking and revealing data affirms the remarkably high level of interest that our population collectively demonstrates in the thoughtful and responsible utilization of renewable energies and other vital resources. This, in turn, highlights a shared and growing awareness alongside a commitment towards sustainable practices that can significantly benefit current and future generations alike. The data reflects not just individual preferences but a collective desire to engage in practices that safeguard our environment and ensure a better quality of life.

Figure 2. The level of importance of the use of solar energy among our population

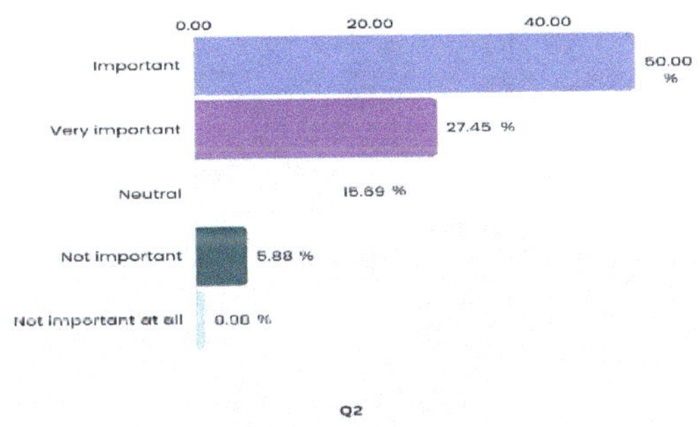

Upon examining the diagram closely and meticulously, it becomes increasingly evident that a significant portion of our target population, specifically about 50% of individuals surveyed, views the use of renewable energies as not only important but also essential for a sustainable future. Furthermore, an additional 27.45% of respondents consider it to be very important, which emphasizes a strong and unwavering commitment to sustainable practices across the board. A smaller segment, accounting for 15.69%, remains neutral on the subject, indicating a mixed level of engagement with various renewable energy initiatives in the market today. Lastly, we have 6% of respondents who express a lack of interest in this particular kind of energy source, signifying an urgent need for increased awareness, educational initiatives, and outreach efforts to engage those who may not recognize the benefits of renewable energy.

Figure 3. The responsibility of protecting the environment according to our interviewees

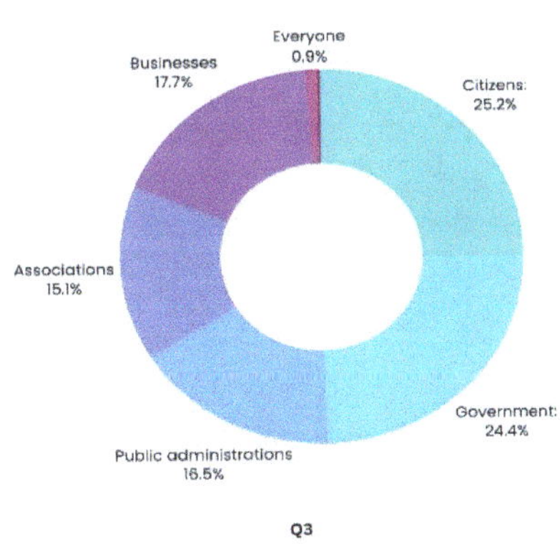

Figure 4. The degree of the target population's sense of responsibility towards their environment.

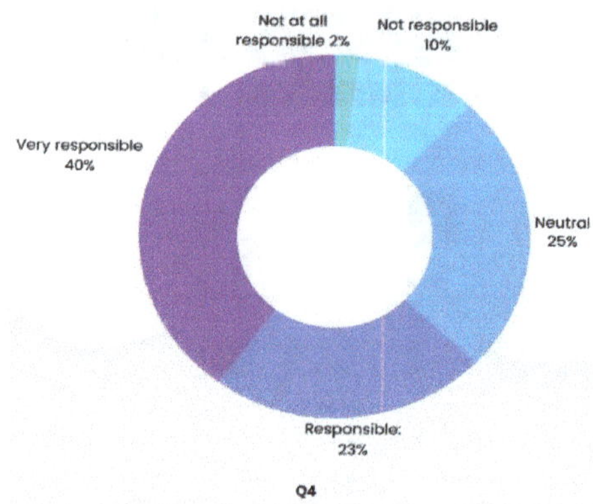

The thorough analysis of the extensive data that has been meticulously gathered and collected reveals that a notable 40% of our surveyed sample identifies itself and expresses a significant sense of responsibility toward its environment, demonstrating a strong and commendable awareness of ecological issues. Furthermore, an additional 23% of our population categorizes itself as responsible, indicating a solid and conscious acknowledgment of their environmental duties among a substantial portion of the participating individuals. Conversely, on the contrasting side of the spectrum, 25% of respondents express a neutral viewpoint, neither feeling particularly responsible for environmental matters nor indifferent to them. Almost 12% of the individuals involved do not regard themselves as carrying any responsibility toward environmental preservation at all. These compelling statistics, when viewed collectively, illustrate that a considerable number of citizens are indeed aware of their personal accountability to protect and preserve their environment for the benefit of future generations. This awareness is crucial in fostering a society that values sustainability and encourages proactive steps toward ecological conservation.

Figure 5. Perspectives on the use of renewable energies for environmental protection.

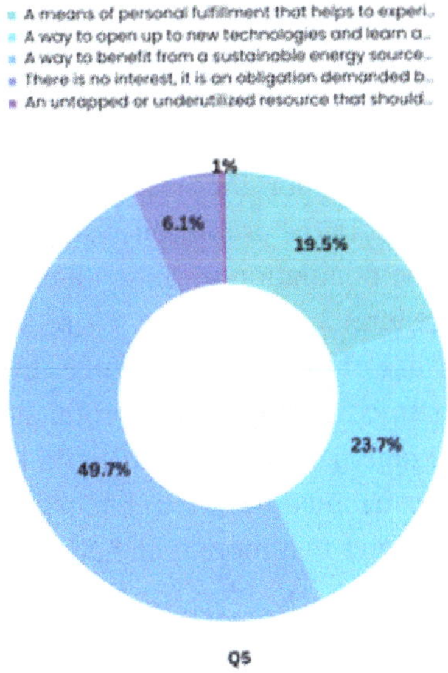

A significant proportion of the individuals questioned in this extensive survey see the utilization of natural resources for the purpose of environmental protection as an immensely valuable and strategically important method to derive meaningful benefits from sustainable, long-term energy solutions. This approach is also perceived as an effective means to dramatically reduce certain operational and resource-related costs in the years ahead, with an impressive response rate of 49.7%. Additionally, a smaller yet notable segment of the respondents, accounting for 23.7%, considers this initiative to be a crucial pathway that opens doors to innovative technologies and facilitates the acquisition of valuable new skills that can enhance and improve their capabilities in various domains. Beyond these practical considerations, a specific portion of individuals regard this endeavor as far more than simply a task to be completed; they view it as a profound means of achieving personal fulfillment that effectively fosters a sense of emotional gratification, thereby creating a stronger bond and feeling of solidarity with our environment and natural world. On the other hand, there exists a minority of respondents who indicate that they feel little genuine personal interest or enthusiasm towards these important matters. They assert that their participation in such activities is simply an obligation dictated by the urgent demands posed by climate change, which they acknowledge cannot be overlooked or ignored any longer.

DISCUSSION

The careful and in-depth analysis of the statistics presented reveals several essential and extremely significant points regarding the growing interest in the use of renewable energies, as well as the crucial responsibility for environmental protection, and the unwavering support for the innovative and ambitious Smart City project. As regards the interest in the use of renewable energies, the results clearly show a strong interest of the population in these alternative energy sources. This demonstrates not only a general and collective awareness, but also a marked and obvious preference for the use of the natural resources available in their immediate environment. This suggests an extremely high and promising potential for the adoption of renewable energy in the region studied, which could lead to significant changes. Regarding the importance attributed to renewable energies, the in-depth analysis of the responses collected shows that more than half of the sample, representing a significant part of the population, considers the use of renewable energies to be of paramount importance and very significant for the future. This trend reinforces the idea that renewable energy is not only fundamental for sustainable development, but also essential to ensure a viable and environmentally friendly future. This highlights the importance given to this form of energy for the protection of the environment. However, it is also noted that a certain percentage does not give importance to this use, which highlights the need for more awareness and information about the benefits of renewable energy. For the responsibility for environmental protection, statistics show that the majority of respondents consider that the responsibility for environmental protection lies with citizens, followed by the government. This underlines the importance of individual and collective involvement in the preservation of the environment. Industrial enterprises, public administrations and environmental protection associations are also considered to have a role to play in this responsibility. On the subject of awareness of environmental responsibility, the data reveal that the majority of the population studied considers themselves to be very responsible towards their environment. This endorses a high awareness of the importance of protecting the environment and adopting responsible ecological behaviors. However, it is also important to note that a significant percentage position themselves as neutral, which may indicate potential for improved environmental awareness and education. Regarding the influencing factors that motivate citizens to use natural resources, the results show that the purchase cost and the installation cost are the elements that represent a concern for individuals on the purchase and installation decision. Finally, looking at the point of support for the Smart City project, the analysis of the results indicates a strong support of the population for the Smart City project. This shows a high level of interest in sustainable development and urban transformation initiatives. Such support can promote the success of the project by engaging a large part of the population and creating positive momentum towards a smarter, more environmentally friendly city.

The analysis of the data collected reveals that citizens of Casablanca demonstrate an increasingly heightened awareness of environmental challenges and the importance of transitioning towards renewable energy. This evolution reflects a broader transformation in the human and social dimensions of urban life, where environmental consciousness is progressively becoming a core element of civic identity. The strong interest in renewable energies observed among respondents signifies that citizens are not merely passive beneficiaries of technological progress but active agents in shaping the city's ecological transition.

However, the data also reveal disparities in levels of awareness and commitment. A portion of the population remains neutral or unengaged regarding environmental protection, signaling a persistent gap between awareness and behavioral adoption. This gap is well-documented in behavioral science and can be explained through the Theory of Planned Behavior (Ajzen, 1991), which emphasizes that intention to act sustainably depends on three determinants: attitudes, perceived behavioral control, and subjective norms. In the Casablanca context, while positive attitudes toward renewable energy are evident, the perception of economic and infrastructural barriers (such as installation costs and limited technical knowledge) may hinder the translation of these attitudes into actual adoption.

In the context of the Smart City, Artificial Intelligence (AI) offers an unprecedented opportunity to address precisely this awareness, behavior gap. AI systems, through their capacity to analyze behavioral data and provide personalized, context-specific feedback, can act as cognitive companions guiding citizens toward more sustainable lifestyles. Smart meters, intelligent home systems, and AI-driven energy management platforms can help individuals visualize their consumption, compare it with community benchmarks, and receive tailored recommendations for reducing waste or adopting renewable sources.

Beyond technical efficiency, the role of AI extends to motivational enhancement. Drawing on Self-Determination Theory (Deci & Ryan, 1985), AI tools can be designed to foster intrinsic motivation by supporting the psychological needs for autonomy, competence, and relatedness. For example, AI-driven gamification interfaces can reward eco-friendly behavior, virtual assistants can support autonomous decision-making, and digital communities can connect citizens around shared ecological goals. Through such design, AI transforms from a purely technological instrument into a social enabler that redefines how citizens engage with sustainability and with one another.

This convergence of human motivation and intelligent technology exemplifies the central theme of this book, the transformation of the humanities and social sciences through AI. Far from reducing the human factor, AI can amplify empathy, collective responsibility, and participatory engagement by making sustainability a co-created experience between humans and machines.

The findings indicate that respondents attribute primary responsibility for environmental protection to citizens themselves, followed by the government. This perception aligns with the principles of Stakeholder Theory (Freeman, 1984), which posits that sustainable transformation depends on the interdependence and collaboration of multiple actors, individuals, public institutions, private enterprises, and civil society organizations.

In the context of Casablanca's Smart City project, this shared responsibility manifests through a triangular relationship between citizens, government, and industry. Citizens provide behavioral engagement and social legitimacy; governments create enabling policies and infrastructures; and industries supply innovative technologies and financial models. The active recognition by respondents of citizen responsibility reflects a promising cultural shift toward participatory environmental governance. Yet, the persistence of "neutral" attitudes within a segment of the population highlights that policy interventions should focus on inclusive communication and equitable access to renewable energy technologies.

AI can again serve as a mediating agent between these stakeholders. Through predictive analytics and participatory digital platforms, AI can help governments anticipate adoption patterns, identify vulnerable populations, and personalize incentive programs. At the same time, it can allow citizens to express feedback and preferences in real time, enabling a more dynamic and responsive model of governance. In this sense, AI does not replace human decision-making but augments the collective intelligence of the Smart City ecosystem.

One of the key issues highlighted in the empirical analysis concerns the financial constraints associated with the purchase and installation of renewable energy technologies. Cost remains a major determinant of adoption decisions, as revealed by the data. This raises a broader ethical and social question about equity in the AI-driven energy transition: who benefits from the Smart City transformation, and who risks being left behind?

AI systems can be instrumental in designing fairer energy ecosystems by simulating cost scenarios, optimizing subsidies, and enabling micro-financing models that adapt to household income levels. However, if poorly governed, AI could also reinforce existing inequalities by favoring digitally literate or affluent groups. This tension underscores the need to integrate ethical AI principles into Smart City governance frameworks, ensuring transparency, inclusivity, and data protection while maintaining citizen trust.

The results show strong public support for Casablanca's Smart City project. This enthusiasm suggests that citizens recognize the transformative potential of technology when aligned with sustainable development objectives. The Smart City, in this sense, is not only a technological innovation but also a new form of citizenship, characterized by co-creation, shared responsibility, and a sense of belonging to a collective environmental mission.

The integration of AI into this vision provides an opportunity to develop what can be termed a Smart Citizenship Model — one that combines technological literacy, ecological awareness, and participatory governance. In this model, citizens are not passive users of AI tools but co-designers of sustainable futures, contributing data, feedback, and creative ideas that shape local environmental policies and urban strategies.

Casablanca's case thus illustrates a broader global trend: cities such as Barcelona, Singapore, and Dubai are increasingly adopting participatory AI systems that balance efficiency with inclusivity. By aligning with these global examples while maintaining cultural and socio-economic specificity, Casablanca can position itself as a leading example of African urban sustainability.

From a theoretical standpoint, this study reinforces the idea that citizen motivation, stakeholder collaboration, and AI integration are mutually reinforcing pillars of the sustainable energy transition. The combination of Stakeholder Theory and Motivation Theory provides a robust conceptual framework for understanding how technological and social dimensions interact in Smart City ecosystems.

Practically, the findings suggest several managerial and policy implications:

- For policymakers, AI-driven participatory platforms can facilitate real-time citizen consultation and adaptive policy design.
- For private enterprises, AI can optimize renewable energy services, predict demand, and design affordable solutions tailored to citizens' financial capacities.
- For citizens, digital literacy initiatives and gamified awareness programs can strengthen engagement and motivation.

Ultimately, achieving sustainable urban transformation requires recognizing that technology and humanity are co-evolving forces. AI's role is not to automate environmental responsibility but to augment human agency in addressing complex ecological challenges.

The chapter's findings affirm that the integration of AI into Smart City strategies can be both a technological and a cultural revolution. The challenge for urban governance is to ensure that this integration remains human-centered, empowering citizens rather than alienating them. By aligning AI innovation with social inclusion, ethical responsibility, and collective motivation, the Smart City can become a living laboratory of human–machine collaboration for sustainability.

Casablanca's experience thus contributes valuable insight into the global dialogue on how AI transforms not only infrastructures but also the values, behaviors, and relationships that define urban life. The transformation of the humanities and social sciences through AI lies precisely here — in understanding that intelligence, whether artificial or human, achieves its highest potential when directed toward shared human and planetary well-being.

FUTURE PROSPECTS FOR AI INTEGRATION

The integration of artificial intelligence (AI) into the intricate and multifaceted social and political dynamics involving citizens opens up an expansive and varied range of promising opportunities and possibilities. However, it simultaneously presents a surprisingly complex set of perspectives and challenges that warrant careful consideration and addressing. As AI technologies continue to evolve and develop, becoming more sophisticated and advanced than ever before, their ability to analyze various behaviors, opinions, and sentiments is not only continuously changing, but also improving at a remarkable and rapid pace. This significant and transformative phenomenon has the potential to fundamentally change the way public authorities engage, communicate, and interact with their citizens across a multitude of contexts and situations (El et al. 2025). For instance, predictive algorithms could be effectively utilized to gain a much deeper and more nuanced understanding of user concerns and needs, which in turn enables the meaningful refinement and enhancement of public policies in ways that are increasingly more attuned and responsive to the populace's diverse aspirations and expectations. In this sense, AI could greatly facilitate and enhance the personalization of government communication efforts, making messages not only far more relevant, but also significantly better adapted to meet the distinct and unique needs of different segments of the population. This targeted and attentive approach could ultimately enhance overall civic engagement and responsiveness, fostering a stronger connection as well as an ongoing dialogue between the authorities and the community they serve effectively. Moreover, utilizing AI in this manner may lead to improved transparency and trust in governmental processes, as citizens may feel more involved and acknowledged in the decision-making processes that affect their lives. Acknowledging the power of data analytics can enable governments to proactively address issues before they become widespread concerns, thus demonstrating a commitment to meeting the evolving needs and expectations of their constituents. As we continue to explore and expand on the implications of AI within the social and political arenas, it is imperative to bear in mind the ethical considerations and potential biases that these technologies may introduce. It is crucial for stakeholders to implement robust and equitable frameworks to ensure that AI acts as a tool for inclusivity, rather than inadvertently reinforcing existing disparities and inequalities. By embracing the potential of artificial intelligence through careful and deliberate governance, we can harness its capabilities to improve citizen engagement and foster a brighter future built on informed and responsive public policy. However, this integration comes with significant challenges. The issue of transparency and accountability must be at the heart of discussions surrounding the use of AI. Citizens need to be informed about the methods and algorithms used to generate analyses that can influence policy decisions. One of the major concerns is the risk of biases inherent in AI models, which can reproduce and amplify pre-existing inequalities if we are not careful. Moreover, to what extent can we allow AI to determine approaches or propose solutions for the common good without eroding the human connection in the decision-making process?

When it comes to collaboration between AI and stakeholders, it is also crucial to promote a multidisciplinary approach. Inclusivity in the development of AI systems must become a norm, with a diversity of voices represented, ranging from technology experts to ordinary citizens, in order to achieve a holistic understanding of the issues. It is essential to adopt adaptable regulations that encourage innovation while protecting the rights of individuals. The search for synergies between AI and citizen engagement is therefore essential, where AI would not only be an analytical tool, but a catalyst for constructive dialogue and real mobilization of society. The future prospects of integrating AI into citizen motivation must be considered with caution, ambition and, above all, a strong commitment to promoting collective well-being (Sahut et al., 2023).

EMERGING TRENDS IN CITIZEN MOTIVATION

In an ever-changing socio-cultural context, civic motivation is the subject of emerging trends that reveal the dynamic interaction between modern technologies and human behaviour. Among these trends, the increased use of digital platforms and artificial intelligence (AI) tools stands out for its ability to engage citizens from diverse backgrounds. Awareness campaigns leverage social media not only to disseminate information, but also to create virtual communities where citizens can share their experiences and concerns (Chedli & Wiliquet, 2023). AI plays a key role in analyzing behavioral data within these platforms, allowing organizations to better understand the intrinsic motivations of individuals and tailor their messages accordingly.

In addition, the integration of AI into citizen motivation raises new ethical and practical questions regarding personalization and inclusion. Elaborate algorithms exist to anticipate the wants and needs of citizens, facilitating the emergence of tailor-made solutions that resonate with local specificities. Nonetheless, this personalization raises concerns about the erosion of privacy and the potential manipulation of behaviors. In addition, inclusivity becomes a central issue in the motivation process: it is essential to ensure that the tools and strategies put in place by organizations are accessible to all, including those who are traditionally marginalized in civic discourse (Okoman, 2024).

In addition, current trends highlight a more collaborative and participatory approach, fostered by innovative technologies such as digital co-creation forums and online consultations. These spaces allow citizens to actively engage in the decision-making process, making their voices and opinions not only visible, but also taken into account. The extension of these democratic methods is a strong signal of a growing willingness to involve citizens at every level of governance. Thus, the emergence of these trends demonstrates a significant potential to reinvent citizen motivation by balancing the use of technology with the core values of participation, transparency and equality.

CONCLUSION

In examining the integration of artificial intelligence (AI) and stakeholder engagement in enhancing citizen motivation, it becomes evident that the intertwining of technology and democratic governance holds significant transformative potential. As societies increasingly rely on digital tools for public administration and civic engagement, the role of AI in facilitating dialogue among stakeholders cannot be overstated. AI's capabilities ensconce a duality of providing personalized communication and analyzing vast amounts of data related to citizen behaviors and preferences. These functionalities can serve as catalysts for motivation by creating tailored interactions that resonate with individual citizens, thus fostering a sense of belonging and active participation in democratic processes.

Moreover, the convergence of AI with stakeholder engagement strategies necessitates a reevaluation of traditional frameworks in civic motivation. For instance, empirical evidence suggests that participatory mechanisms, when augmented with AI, can enhance the efficiency of public consultations, thereby yielding more representative outcomes. Through machine learning algorithms, the sentiment of citizen feedback can be analyzed in real-time, allowing policymakers to adapt their approaches based on the evolving public sentiment. This not only bolsters the responsiveness of governance mechanisms but also empowers citizens, reinforcing their role as co-creators of policies that affect their lives.

The growth of the concept of sustainable development makes it possible to establish a balanced relationship between socio-economic growth, human well-being and growing ecological problems in order to perceive an ambitious improvement in the way citizens treat their natural environment. The aim is to create a sense of responsibility among individuals towards their environment and to be able to limit human activities that have a dangerous impact on the climate as demographic and socio-economic growth in society are constantly increasing. This work is designed to measure the level of integration of the different stakeholders as well as AI in the motivation of Casablanca citizens to use solar energy and participate in the Smart City project. The results obtained indicate that the people in our target population have a strong awareness of their responsibilities and the importance of rational use of natural resources. In other words, the population studied shows a significant interest and concern for environmental protection, the use of renewable energy and support for sustainable initiatives such as the Smart City project. These findings highlight the importance of strengthening environmental education, awareness-raising and civic engagement efforts to promote a transition to a more sustainable lifestyle and increased use of renewable energy. The integration of AI makes it possible to stimulate personalized solutions adapted to each individual by offering promising prospects and promoting a sustainable lifestyle within Smart Cities.

In this sense, by providing data and concrete results on citizens' motivations, our research work can contribute to increasing awareness among the population of Casablanca of the benefits of renewable energies and the importance of their active participation in the Smart City project by integrating AI techniques through intelligent decision support systems, mobile applications and connected platforms, AI technologies applied to the smart management of electricity grids and finally the use of AI to analyse renewable energy consumption and production data to identify trends and levers for action to further engage citizens. It can also help policymakers and Smart City actors to better target their efforts and initiatives to promote the adoption of sustainable technologies.

The increasing attention to environmental issues and the dramatic impact that AI can have, such as in fostering renewable energies within Smart Cities, opens a unique window of opportunity. Yet awareness is not enough; it needs to be translated into enduring behavioral changes through collective action.

For policymakers: Regulate requirements for AI tools to be incorporated into urban sustainability planning (e.g., models of predictive energy demand models, citizen feedback loops). Offer financial incentives (tax breaks, subsidies, low-interest loans) to make renewable power technologies, especially rooftop solar, affordable to low- and middle-income families. And promote inclusive governance instruments facilitating the participation of citizens such as digital citizens' assemblies or AI-based consultation tools to enhance the legitimacy and trustworthiness.

For energy sector stakeholders: Implement personalisation platforms based on AI which offer customised advice to householders on energy consumption, savings vector and adoption routes. Invest in interoperable smart grids that can easily accept decentralized renewable generation (solar panels, EV charging, storage) to better integrate into the city grid. Collaborate with community groups to develop promotional efforts that focus on the benefits to the environment, and the wallet.

For leaders from the community and local organizations: Promote community based, cooperative solar or other peer to peer energy schemes to build social networks and collective ownership. Serve as intermediaries between the public and institutions by making intricate technical and environmental details intelligible in terms of understandable, culturally appropriate accounts. And motivate young and schools to be ambassadors of sustainability introducing renewable energy knowledge into daily life.

This study demonstrates that the integration of AI and stakeholder collaboration plays a decisive role in fostering citizen motivation and facilitating the sustainable energy transition within Smart Cities. By bridging behavioral insights and technological innovation, AI emerges as a transformative tool capable of amplifying environmental awareness, promoting equitable participation, and enhancing collective responsibility. The Casablanca case illustrates that when citizens, governments, and industries co-evolve through intelligent systems, sustainability becomes both achievable and inclusive. Future research should further explore the ethical, cultural, and psychological dimensions of AI-driven sustainability to ensure that Smart City development remains fundamentally human-centered, socially just, and environmentally regenerative.

Overall, the sustainable development of Smart Cities is contingent on matching the innovative policies, the technological applications and the citizen activities. Only when these three realms align, awareness translates into quantifiable gains towards the adoption of renewable energy and a sustainable, resilient environment.

REFERENCES

Arellano, D., & Cossi, C. (2024). Geopolitical construction for the sustainable development of a MERCOSUR metropolitan enclave. Confines. Revue franco-Brésil de géographie/Revista franco-brasilera de geografia, (64).

Baddouh, L., & Soudane, J. A. (2024). The Integration of AI in Human Resources Management: Convergence and Ethical Challenges. International Journal of Accounting, Finance, Auditing. *Management and Economics*, *5*(4), 210–222.

Bolambuli Bosinga, F. (2024). *The Duty of the African Man: Rethinking Democracy and Negro-African Culture with Elie P.* Ngoma-Binda.

Chedli, O., & Wiliquet, C. (2023). *The intercultural and digital experience, essential levers for young people's engagement?* Eclosio.

Deci, E. L., & Ryan, R. M. (1985). *Intrinsic motivation and self-determination in human behavior.* Plenum Press. DOI: 10.1007/978-1-4899-2271-7

Deci, E. L., & Ryan, R. M. (2000). The" what" and" why" of goal pursuits: Human needs and the self-determination of behavior. *Psychological Inquiry*, *11*(4), 227–268.

Filion, M. (2025). PUBLIC INNOVATION POLICIES IN ADVANCED ECONOMIES: THE LIMITS OF EVALUATION AND ORGANIZED ANARCHY

Graham, S. (2020). An attributional theory of motivation. *Contemporary Educational Psychology*, *61*, 101861. DOI: 10.1016/j.cedpsych.2020.101861

KAZADI, C. L. (2025). … INFORMATIONAL: IMPACT OF RADIO FRANCE INTERNATIONALE RFI-AFRIQUE/FACEBOOK ON CITIZEN PARTICIPATION

Lfarh, A., & Kissami, R. (2025). Modernization of Tax Administrations: Digitalization, Artificial Intelligence and Challenges of Tax Governance in Morocco. MANAGEMENT CONTROL, AUDITING AND FINANCE REVIEW (MCAFR), 2(1), 11-27.

Modolo, L. (2025). *Artificial intelligence, an opportunity for higher education?* Management & Datascience.

Okoman, A. A. H. (2024). Integration of the Landscape and Social Acceptability in Infrastructure Projects in Quebec: The Case of the Quebec Interconnection Power Line Project

OUBAYOUCEF, M., ROCHDANE, H., & BEDDAA, M. (2025). The determinants of citizen e-participation: The case of the Casablanca smart city. *Journal of Multidisciplinary Studies in Economic and Social Sciences, 10*(1), 21–44.

Oubayoucef, M., Rochdane, H., & Beddaa, M. (2025). The impact of the use of digital platforms on citizen participation in the smart city: Proposal of a conceptual model. International Journal of Accounting, Finance, Auditing. *Management and Economics*, *6*(3), 295–308.

Perez-Torrents, J. (2024). Managing the collaboration between the business expert and Artificial Intelligence: Two case studies in the healthcare system

Rhattat, R., & Schoch, P. (2024). *Point of view: the integration of a process of legal regulation of AI within companies: challenges and modalities.* Management & Foresight.

Sahut, J. M., Braune, É., & Lissillour, R. (2023). *AI development and ethical issues: moving from a static to a dynamic perspective.* Management & Avenir.

Soguel, N., Bundi, P., Mettler, T., & Weerts, S. (2023). Understand and design public administration. The IDHEAP model.

The World Bank, International Bank for Reconstruction and Development. Global tracking framework 2017: progress towards sustainable energy. 2017. .DOI: 10.1596/978-1-4648-1084-8

United Nations Department of Economic and Social Affairs. (2001). *Indicators of sustainable development: framework and methodologies.*

United Nations General Assembly. (2015). *Transforming our world: the 2030 agenda for sustainable development.*

Yanis, K. (2023). The use of artificial intelligence in oncology: deep learning, a new tool in the diagnosis and optimization of treatments.

Zakka, F. Z. (2025). Open Government Data platforms: from transparency to data governance. Swiss Electronic Journal of Information Science (RESSI), (CIHN24 Special).

Chapter 16
The Role of AI in Facilitating Value Co-Creation in Service Industries

Reda Lharti
https://orcid.org/0009-0001-0880-9264
Ibn Tofail University, Morocco

ABSTRACT

This article investigates the expanding role of artificial intelligence (AI) in value co-creation within service industries. Through a narrative literature review, it highlights four key contributions of AI: enhancing customer engagement through interactive experiences, enabling intelligent automation in collaborative processes, hyper-personalizing offerings via real-time data analytics, and creating new co-creation opportunities with innovative interfaces. Sector-specific examples from hospitality, healthcare, education, and finance illustrate these aspects. Theoretically, the article proposes expanding the co-creation model to include intelligent agents and redefines roles within service systems. Managerially, it stresses the need for hybrid human-AI frameworks and redesigning customer journeys. Limitations include the exploratory nature and reliance on secondary data, pointing to future research on empirical studies, ethical and cultural dimensions, and cross-sector comparisons.

INTRODUCTION

Artificial Intelligence (AI) has emerged as a transformative force across a wide range of service industries, including healthcare, financial services, education, and

DOI: 10.4018/979-8-3373-3436-3.ch016

hospitality (Agarwal et al., 2024). As organizations grapple with the complexities and opportunities of digital transformation, AI is increasingly regarded not merely as a technological tool but as a strategic asset (Omol, 2024). It enables service providers to enhance operational efficiency, develop hyper-personalized offerings, and elevate overall customer experience. This growing reliance on AI aligns with broader trends in automation and digitalization, which have become essential in meeting modern expectations for speed, customization, and service excellence (Radziwill, 2020). (Davenport & Ronanki, 2018) emphasize that AI can facilitate a fundamental rethinking of traditional business models by simultaneously promoting innovation and optimizing operations. As such, the widespread adoption of AI is accelerating a deep and ongoing transformation of the service landscape (Aldoseri et al., 2024).

Concurrently, the conceptual foundation of value creation in service contexts is undergoing a significant shift. Historically, value has been understood within a linear framework in which firms produce offerings that customers consume—a perspective rooted in the Goods-Dominant Logic (GDL) (Popesku, 2015). However, this traditional model is increasingly being challenged by a more interactive and participatory vision of value creation, embodied in the Service-Dominant Logic (SDL) proposed by (Vargo & Lusch, 2004, 2008). Within this new paradigm, value is not embedded in products or services themselves, but instead arises from active engagement and collaborative interactions between multiple actors, including customers, employees, and external stakeholders. The SDL framework provides a robust theoretical lens through which to examine this evolution, emphasizing that value is co-created through the dynamic integration of resources and actor-to-actor interactions (Maghamis, 2018).

In this evolving context, AI is progressively recognized not only as a driver of process efficiency but also as a facilitator of novel modes of value co-creation (J. Paschen et al., 2021). By enabling seamless communication, automating routine tasks, and supporting real-time personalization, AI fosters more meaningful and sustained interactions among stakeholders (Aldoseri et al., 2024). These capabilities have the potential to redefine actor roles within service ecosystems, reshaping how firms engage with customers and how customers participate in the delivery and refinement of services. (Wirtz et al., 2018) underscore the disruptive potential of AI in reshaping value creation mechanisms and altering the structure of service encounters. As AI technologies become more deeply integrated into service delivery, they give rise to new forms of collaboration that blur traditional boundaries between providers and consumers.

These developments prompt critical questions about the changing nature of value co-creation in an AI-driven environment. How are intelligent systems transforming the dynamics of value creation? What roles do human and non-human actors now assume in service interactions? And how do these changes affect customer expectations and experiences? (Huang & Rust, 2021) argue that we are witnessing a paradigm shift, one in which AI not only enhances service efficiency but also redefines the essence of customer engagement and collaborative service creation. Understanding these changes is especially important, as organizations must navigate both the benefits and the ethical, regulatory, and organizational implications of incorporating AI into service ecosystems.

Against this backdrop, the central research question addressed by this study is: In what ways is AI transforming the mechanisms of value co-creation in service industries? This overarching inquiry encompasses several more specific lines of investigation. For instance, how does AI influence the frequency and quality of actor interactions? How does it shape service personalization and customer involvement in co-creating their own experiences? And to what extent does it enhance—or potentially hinder—the inclusivity and effectiveness of collaborative processes? As (U. Paschen et al., 2020) suggest, the intersection of AI and value co-creation offers both unprecedented opportunities for innovation and complex challenges that warrant careful analysis.

This article investigates how Artificial Intelligence (AI) transforms value co-creation in service ecosystems. It explores AI's capacity to foster customer engagement, personalize interactions, and enhance collaboration among stakeholders. By examining the evolving roles of companies, customers, employees, and AI systems, the study highlights how non-human agents are becoming integral to service co-creation. Through a narrative literature review, it synthesizes insights from service management, information systems, and AI ethics to provide an interdisciplinary understanding of AI's impact. The analysis identifies structural shifts in service delivery, including new technological interfaces and hybrid human–machine configurations, which reshape customer journeys and organizational processes. The findings reveal that AI enhances personalization, improves engagement, and streamlines interactions across sectors such as hospitality, healthcare, and education. However, the discussion also underscores challenges such as data privacy, algorithmic bias, and the risk of depersonalized service. The study calls for extending existing theoretical models, notably Service-Dominant Logic, to include AI as an active co-creator. It concludes by emphasizing that AI should be viewed not merely as a tool for automation but as a strategic partner capable of generating new forms of value and innovation within service ecosystems, while highlighting future research opportunities for empirical validation.

1. METHODOLOGY

For the purpose of this research, a narrative literature review was selected as the primary method of analysis. This methodological choice is justified by the multidisciplinary and evolving nature of the field under study, situated at the intersection of artificial intelligence (AI), value co-creation, and service industries. Unlike systematic reviews, the narrative review allows for a more flexible and exploratory approach, which is well-suited to the complexity of ongoing transformations and the diversity of available sources (Greenhalgh et al., 2018). It enables critical synthesis while facilitating the integration of perspectives from a variety of disciplines, including marketing, management, information technology, and the social sciences (Baumeister & Leary, 1997).

To build the literature corpus, three major academic databases were utilized: Scopus, Web of Science, and Google Scholar. These databases were selected for their complementarity and extensive coverage of international publications. The search process was refined using combinations of relevant keywords such as "artificial intelligence," "value co-creation," "service industries," "customer engagement," and "digital transformation."

A variety of document types were included in the review: peer-reviewed journal articles, industry reports from specialized organizations, and empirical case studies published in academic or professional outlets. This diversity was intended to reflect the hybrid reality of the field, which encompasses both theoretical research and practical applications.

With respect to the selection criteria, the included publications were required to address at least two of the following three dimensions: AI as an operant resource, value co-creation, and service industries. Particular attention was given to recent studies, especially those published within the last ten to fifteen years—a period characterized by a significant acceleration in the adoption of AI in service contexts (Huang & Rust, 2021).

2. LITERATURE REVIEW: KEY CONCEPTUAL FRAMEWORKS

This literature review aims to build the theoretical foundations for understanding the relationship between artificial intelligence (AI) and value co-creation within service industries. It explores how AI technologies influence service interactions, reshape actor roles, and enable new forms of collaboration and personalization. To structure the analysis, the review is organized around three complementary thematic axes, each addressing a key aspect of the AI–value co-creation nexus. This approach allows for a comprehensive examination of both the opportunities and challenges presented by AI in service contexts, while also identifying gaps in the existing literature and directions for future research.

The first axis examines the concept of value co-creation through the lens of Service-Dominant Logic (Vargo & Lusch, 2004, 2008), highlighting the active participation of customers and stakeholders in value creation via engagement, interaction, and the integration of resources within service ecosystems. The second axis examines various types of AI used in service contexts, such as chatbots, recommendation systems, and generative AI, and analyzes their influence on customer journeys and service experiences (Kumar et al., 2025). The third axis investigates the convergence between AI and co-creation, highlighting how AI is reshaping interaction mechanisms, enabling personalized engagement, and redefining actor roles within service ecosystems (Peruchini et al., 2024).

2.1. Value Co-Creation in Services

The concept of value co-creation has significantly reshaped the theoretical foundations of marketing and service management. This shift was largely driven by the Service-Dominant Logic (SDL) introduced by (Vargo & Lusch, 2004), which departs from the traditional Goods-Dominant Logic (GDL). Rather than viewing value as something produced solely by the firm, SDL emphasizes that value emerges through interactive processes involving customers and other stakeholders. In this perspective, services are not seen as isolated activities but as a logic of exchange centered on collaboration, resource integration, and continuous dialogue. This paradigm shift places relational and participatory dimensions at the core of value creation in service ecosystems.

In this paradigm, actors—including firms, customers, and partners—are conceptualized as resource integrators engaged in reciprocal value creation dynamics (Vargo & Lusch, 2008). Co-creation thus entails a participatory logic, where each actor contributes distinct value through their competencies, knowledge, and interactions. The customer is no longer a passive recipient but becomes a co-producer of perceived value (Prahalad & Ramaswamy, 2004). This shift in perspective requires a reconfiguration of traditional roles within value chains and calls for a deeper understanding of interaction, engagement, and coordination mechanisms.

Three fundamental mechanisms underpin the process of value co-creation. The first is interaction, which constitutes the relational foundation of co-creation. Beyond simple transactional exchange, interaction in services is multidimensional and often involves symbolic, emotional, and experiential dimensions (Grönroos & Voima, 2013). The second mechanism is engagement, referring to the motivation, frequency, and intensity of stakeholder participation, particularly that of the customer (Brodie et al., 2019). The third is resource integration—encompassing material, informational, and human resources—which enables the production of contextualized and personalized value through co-production processes (Chandler & Vargo, 2011).

2.2. Artificial Intelligence in Service Industries

The integration of artificial intelligence (AI) into service industries represents a major technological disruption (Bock et al., 2020). AI extends beyond mere task automation; it enhances the capabilities of both systems and human actors by providing simulated cognitive functions such as perception, natural language understanding, decision-making, and learning (Siemens et al., 2022).

The typologies of AI applied in service contexts are diverse and continuously evolving. Key categories include:

- **Chatbots and conversational agents**, which enable real-time, continuous interaction with customers (Adam et al., 2021);
- **Recommendation systems**, which analyze user preferences and behaviors to deliver personalized product or service suggestions (Ricci et al., 2021);
- **Generative AI**, capable of producing original content, thereby opening new possibilities for creative services and communication (Amankwah-Amoah et al., 2024);
- **Service robotics**, deployed in sectors such as hospitality, healthcare, and logistics to deliver hybrid experiences that combine automation with human-centered service (Fusté-Forné & Jamal, 2021).

One of AI's central contributions lies in its increasing level of autonomy and its capacity to adapt to various contexts. Through techniques such as machine learning and natural language processing (NLP), AI systems can now manage complex, contextualized, and even emotionally nuanced interactions in real time (Nag et al., 2023). This significantly reshapes the nature of customer journeys by embedding intelligent, seamless, and often predictive service moments throughout the experience lifecycle.

In this context, service processes themselves become "augmented": AI takes on analytical, decision-making, and even relational functions in collaboration with human employees. This hybridization of roles redefines service production and organizational logics, shifting toward a customer-centric perspective. Organizations that successfully align AI capabilities with co-creation expectations are thus positioned to offer service experiences that are innovative, engaging, and differentiated (Manser Payne et al., 2021).

2.3. AI–Value Co-Creation Convergence

The convergence of artificial intelligence (AI) and value co-creation represents a major strategic evolution for service industries. AI functions not only as a technological tool but also as a facilitator of co-creation by enriching interactions, enhancing personalization, and expanding opportunities for customer engagement.

First, AI enables dynamic personalization of interactions. Through predictive analytics and continuous learning, intelligent systems can adapt services in real time to individual preferences, thereby creating experiences that are perceived as more relevant and engaging (Rane, 2023). For instance, in sectors such as banking or healthcare, intelligent platforms recommend personalized solutions while iteratively integrating customer feedback.

Second, AI enhances active customer participation in the service process. By offering intuitive, accessible, and interactive interfaces—such as voice assistants or conversational platforms—it lowers technological barriers and stimulates engagement. The customer becomes an augmented co-producer, capable of interacting with AI agents to co-design offerings, co-solve problems, or co-evaluate services (Kot & Leszczyński, 2022). This AI-assisted co-creation approach aligns with a participatory and evolving service experience.

Third, AI contributes to the reinvention of roles and spaces of interaction. It enables the development of intelligent digital platforms that orchestrate multi-actor co-creation ecosystems involving customers, companies, developers, and institutions. These platforms, by combining algorithmic intelligence with user-centered design, facilitate the networking of resources, the emergence of communities of practice, and collaborative innovation (Perälä, 2024). In sectors such as tourism, education, and retail, AI transforms customer interfaces into spaces for value co-construction.

This convergence also raises ethical and relational challenges: How can algorithmic transparency be ensured? What about the reliability of automated decisions and the quality of human–machine experience? These issues must be addressed through an inclusive approach to co-creation—one that integrates human, technological, and social dimensions (Kohlgrüber et al., 2021).

3. RESULTS: AI'S CONTRIBUTION TO VALUE CO-CREATION

The literature review reveals that artificial intelligence is profoundly transforming value co-creation dynamics within service industries. It acts as a catalyst for engagement, a lever for efficiency, a driver of personalization, and a generator of innovation in terms of interfaces and user journeys. These contributions manifest across multiple levels of customer-provider interaction, significantly impacting service practices, processes, and relationships.

3.1. Strengthening Customer Engagement

One of the major contributions of Artificial Intelligence (AI) in service industries lies in its ability to enhance customer engagement by fundamentally transforming interaction and experience modalities. AI enables the creation of interactive, personalized, and continuous environments that foster active, voluntary, and sustained user participation in value co-creation processes (Chandra & Rahman, 2024).

In the hospitality sector, for example, the integration of conversational chatbots and virtual assistants ensures 24/7 customer service, providing instant and personalized responses to client requests before, during, and after their stay (Vashishth et al., 2024). These intelligent systems, powered by machine learning capabilities, adapt to user profiles and preferences while offering proactive recommendations (Janiesch et al., 2021). This not only improves service efficiency but also fosters lasting relational engagement by extending customer interaction beyond traditional touchpoints.

In healthcare, AI enables personalized patient monitoring through mobile apps, diagnostic chatbots, and telemedicine platforms (Leone et al., 2021). These interactive tools facilitate continuous communication between patients and healthcare providers while enhancing user autonomy in managing their health. For instance, intelligent conversational agents can remind patients to take medication, collect symptom data, or provide tailored advice (Schachner et al., 2020). Such constant and contextual interaction encourages patients to actively engage in their own care journeys.

In education, AI is transforming learning methods through adaptive learning environments, intelligent tutoring platforms, and immersive interfaces such as augmented and virtual reality. These tools create highly personalized learning experiences tailored to each learner's pace, needs, and cognitive style. The dynamic adaptation of educational content, supported by predictive algorithms, fosters deep engagement, particularly by stimulating intrinsic motivation through gamification and interactive storytelling (Holmes et al., 2022). AI thus becomes a catalyst for knowledge co-construction among teachers, learners, and intelligent systems.

In logistics, AI improves customer experience by making processes more transparent, interactive, and predictable. For example, delivery companies use intelligent assistants that allow customers to track parcels in real time, modify delivery options, or interact with automated support services. These tools provide fast and seamless service while also encouraging a form of transactional engagement based on trust, transparency, and perceived control (Dubey et al., 2021). By placing the customer at the heart of logistics operations through smart interfaces, AI promotes a new form of service co-production.

Moreover, AI strengthens emotional engagement through immersive mechanisms such as gamification or augmented reality, which transform ordinary experiences into playful, interactive, and emotionally rich journeys. As suggested by (Hoyer et al., 2020), the scripting of service journeys combined with contextual personalization elicits positive emotions that enhance memorability and customer loyalty. With its ability to process behavioral data and anticipate expectations, AI adjusts the content, channel, and timing of interaction, thereby creating a seamless, proactive, and engaging experience (Lemon & Verhoef, 2016).

3.2. Augmented Automation and Efficiency of Collaborative Processes

Artificial Intelligence (AI), far from merely substituting human tasks, now plays a fundamental role in augmenting human capabilities and optimizing collaborative processes. In a value co-creation logic, AI is no longer just an automated tool; it acts as a co-actor in service delivery, actively collaborating with customers and employees to generate value (Dave et al., 2023). This dynamic introduces a new era of augmented automation, where AI supports human cognitive processes such as understanding, decision-making, and contextual adaptation (Mohamed, 2025).

In the hospitality sector, this augmented automation is reflected in the use of intelligent operational management systems, such as room management optimization platforms or chatbots integrated into the Property Management System (PMS) (Dasgupta et al., 2024). These technologies not only accelerate request processing but also streamline coordination between departments (front desk, housekeeping, food and beverage). For instance, AI can automatically reallocate human resources based on occupancy rates or customer preferences, thereby improving both operational efficiency and perceived service quality (Tussyadiah, 2020).

In healthcare, AI serves as a decision-making partner. Tools like diagnostic support systems help healthcare professionals jointly analyze large volumes of medical data with AI to refine diagnoses, personalize treatments, and co-create care pathways. (Meyer et al., 2024) emphasizes that this tripartite collaboration between doctors, patients, and algorithms introduces an innovative form of co-delivery in healthcare, where each actor—human or artificial—contributes to the quality and accuracy of care while accelerating treatment timelines.

In education, AI enhances the efficiency of collaborative teaching processes by supporting instructors in managing heterogeneous classrooms and offering personalized learning paths (Ayeni et al., 2024). Intelligent tutoring systems automatically adapt educational content to each learner's level, while providing real-time analytics dashboards to educators (Lin et al., 2023). This human–machine complementarity improves the relevance of educational interventions and strengthens collaboration between teachers, learners, and intelligent systems (Holmes et al., 2022). Rather than replacing teachers, AI empowers them to better orchestrate the learning process, enabling more inclusive and responsive education.

In logistics, augmented automation is embodied in intelligent supply chain management systems that forecast demand, optimize delivery routes, and facilitate coordination among stakeholders (Temitayo Oluwadamilola Adesoga et al., 2024). For example, Amazon and DHL use predictive algorithms and collaborative robots (cobots) in their warehouses to streamline operations, allowing employees to focus on higher value-added tasks (Winkelhaus & Grosse, 2020). This human–AI complementarity significantly reduces friction in logistics processes and improves responsiveness to demand fluctuations (Wamba et al., 2023).

This human–machine collaboration model is not about displacing human actors but about enhancing their capacity for interaction, responsiveness, and innovation in service relationships. This results in a smoother division of roles, where AI handles routine or data-intensive tasks, while humans focus on interpretation, empathy, and creativity. According to (Huang & Rust, 2018), such complementarity is essential for the success of augmented services, ensuring continuity between technical efficiency and human meaning.

Augmented automation is transforming collaborative service processes by making them more efficient, agile, and personalized (Huang & Rust, 2021). By becoming integrated into service co-production, AI redefines collaboration methods and paves the way for a new generation of intelligent services, where humans and machines interact in a logic of mutual enhancement. This evolution calls on researchers and practitioners to develop hybrid organizational models capable of fully leveraging this extended collaborative intelligence (Daugherty & Wilson, 2018).

4. DISCUSSION

The findings of this narrative review highlight how artificial intelligence (AI) is reshaping value co-creation dynamics in service industries. This transformation operates at multiple levels: micro (customer-machine interaction), meso (design of service offerings and user journeys), and macro (organizational logics and platform ecosystems).

4.1. Redefining Actor Roles in Co-Creation

Artificial intelligence is fundamentally reshaping the traditional roles of actors within service systems. Historically, firms were viewed as the primary creators of value, while customers were positioned as passive recipients (Prahalad & Ramaswamy, 2004). This perspective was challenged by the Service-Dominant Logic (SDL), which emphasized co-creation as a dynamic and reciprocal process involving continuous interaction between providers and consumers (Vargo & Lusch, 2008). Today, AI introduces a new dimension by acting not only as a facilitator but as an active participant in value creation, thereby blurring the boundaries between human and machine contributions (Waardenburg & Huysman, 2022).

This integration of AI into service delivery calls into question the perceived legitimacy of machines as co-creative agents. Users do not universally accept AI as a neutral or equivalent actor. Some customers may actually trust chatbots more than human agents, appreciating their efficiency and objectivity, while others exhibit strong resistance to automated interactions (Jiang et al., 2024). These divergent attitudes have a direct impact on the effectiveness and acceptance of AI-enabled co-creation processes, highlighting the importance of user perception in the success of hybrid service systems. Moreover, these dynamics raise broader concerns around the social acceptability and ethical deployment of AI in service settings (Manser Payne et al., 2021). Consequently, redefining actor roles in AI-mediated co-creation demands not only structural and technological transformation but also a nuanced understanding of the socio-emotional responses of users within these emerging ecosystems.

4.2. Hybridization of Service Processes

Service co-creation is increasingly characterized by hybrid processes that strategically integrate human input with artificial intelligence. Although the concept of hybrid service models is not entirely new, AI considerably enhances their scope and flexibility. It performs dual roles: automating repetitive or low-value tasks—such as sorting queries or conducting predictive analyses—while simultaneously enhancing user engagement through adaptive, intelligent interfaces (Huang & Rust, 2018). This dual functionality allows for a more sophisticated and responsive service infrastructure.

Within this emerging paradigm, service processes are no longer conceived as linear or static. Rather, they evolve according to a co-evolutionary logic, where user behavior, AI system responses, and contextual factors continuously interact and shape each other (Song & Bonanni, 2024). This dynamic foster mechanism of organizational learning, allowing companies to fine-tune their value propositions and service experiences in near real-time, based on data-driven insights across the entire customer journey.

The idea of "AI as a co-deliverer of service" is becoming increasingly salient. AI is no longer just a support tool—it acts as a responsive partner capable of reshaping customer interactions based on principles of personalization, continuity, and operational efficiency. A clear illustration of this can be found in the financial services sector, where robo-advisors analyze investor profiles in real time and propose ongoing portfolio optimizations (Onabowale, 2024). Such applications exemplify how hybrid service processes lead to more adaptive, collaborative, and context-aware service ecosystems, reshaping the fundamentals of co-creation.

4.3. Skills, Expectations, and the Evolving Role of the Customer

AI-enabled co-creation depends significantly on the customer's ability to actively participate in technology-mediated service processes. This participation is shaped by the customer's technological, cognitive, and emotional competencies, which directly influence the extent and quality of the co-created value. In essence, co-creation with AI is not only about what technology can do, but also about how effectively users can understand, interpret, and engage with it.

The customer's agency—their ability to act meaningfully within the service interaction—is closely linked to their digital literacy (Parasuraman & Colby, 2015). A customer who possesses higher digital competence is more likely to collaborate effectively with AI systems. However, this capacity is not uniform. Variations in digital readiness are observed across generational, cultural, and professional lines. For instance, in the education sector, AI-powered tutoring tools have the potential to support personalized learning experiences, but their success relies on students' ability and motivation to engage with these tools (Luckin & Holmes, 2016).

At the same time, customer expectations are evolving alongside technological advancements. AI systems, particularly in domains like e-commerce, have set high benchmarks for speed, relevance, and personalization. These expectations are now transferring to other sectors such as healthcare, education, and hospitality, where clients increasingly demand consistent, intelligent, and responsive interactions. Consequently, firms are compelled to raise and harmonize their service standards across channels and industries, ensuring that the promise of AI-driven co-creation meets or exceeds the heightened expectations it has helped to create.

4.4. Ethical, Social, and Strategic Issues

While artificial intelligence enhances co-creation by offering efficiency, personalization, and scalability, it also brings forward a series of ethical, social, and strategic concerns that organizations must confront. One of the foremost challenges is algorithmic transparency. For customers to participate meaningfully and trustfully in AI-enabled co-creation, they must be aware of how AI systems function, the types of data they process, and the intended outcomes of their use (Chandra & Rahman, 2024). When algorithmic decision-making remains opaque or difficult to interpret, it can foster distrust, leading to resistance and the erosion of the customer–firm relationship.

Another pressing issue is algorithmic bias. AI systems are often trained on historical datasets, which may contain embedded social biases. If left unaddressed, these biases can be perpetuated or even magnified through AI-generated decisions, thus compromising fairness and equity in customer interactions (Afreen et al., 2025). In the context of co-creation, this means that some user segments may systematically receive suboptimal recommendations or services, creating disparities in perceived service quality.

Strategically, the integration of AI is reshaping how firms conceive of and manage service delivery. The deployment of AI in customer journeys, employee training, and service design requires a shift toward platform-based ecosystems where customer experience is co-constructed and continuously optimized. Firms must now view AI not merely as a support tool but as a core strategic asset around which value creation processes are reconfigured.

Lastly, the proliferation of AI in services raises questions about the human element. As more tasks become automated, organizations must carefully consider how to preserve empathy, warmth, and authenticity in their interactions. Delegating responsibilities to machines should not come at the cost of relational richness. This calls for the ethical design of AI systems that uphold human values and foster emotionally intelligent engagement (Haenlein & Kaplan, 2019). The future of co-creation will thus depend not only on technological capacity but on the responsible, inclusive, and value-driven deployment of AI.

5. IMPLICATIONS, PERSPECTIVES, AND LIMITATIONS

This section, dedicated to implications, perspectives, and limitations, offers a critical analysis of the results in order to highlight the theoretical contributions, managerial implications, and future research avenues. It emphasizes the need to expand traditional co-creation models by incorporating the mediating role of artificial intelligence in interactions between service actors.

From a practical standpoint, it underscores the importance of designing hybrid human–AI systems and rethinking customer journeys to foster smooth and effective collaboration. This section also revisits the limitations of the study, particularly its exploratory nature and reliance on secondary literature. Finally, it opens promising research avenues, such as conducting empirical studies on AI-driven co-creative experiences, performing cross-sectoral comparisons, and integrating ethical and cultural dimensions into the analysis of emerging practices.

5.1. Theoretical Implications

The integration of AI in services challenges traditional Service-Dominant Logic by introducing AI as an active actor in value co-creation. This shift calls for revisiting theoretical models to understand how AI reshapes co-creation mechanisms, actor roles, and collaboration dynamics within evolving, technology-mediated service ecosystems.

5.1.1 Toward an Expanded Model of AI-Mediated Co-Creation

The integration of artificial intelligence (AI) into service systems fundamentally challenges and extends traditional theoretical paradigms, particularly the Service-Dominant Logic (SDL) proposed by (Vargo & Lusch, 2004). SDL traditionally centers on the idea that value is co-created through human interaction, mutual service exchange, and resource integration among various actors within a service ecosystem. It treats value not as something delivered unilaterally by a provider, but as collaboratively produced through dynamic interactions and relationships. However, the increasing presence of AI technologies in service delivery systems introduces new, non-human actors into the value co-creation equation, raising important theoretical questions about their role, agency, and impact.

AI systems, particularly those powered by machine learning, natural language processing, and automation, are no longer passive tools or background technologies. They actively interact with customers, employees, and other stakeholders, often performing functions traditionally reserved for human agents. In this evolving landscape, AI assumes the role of an operant resource—a term used in SDL to describe entities capable of acting on other resources to create value (Huang & Rust, 2018). Unlike operand resources, which are acted upon (e.g., raw materials), operant resources contribute directly to value creation by processing information, making decisions, and adapting to users' preferences in real-time.

This shift necessitates a conceptual expansion of SDL to include AI as a value co-creator rather than a mere facilitator. Theorizing AI as a service actor leads to important reconceptualizations of agency and interaction within service ecosystems. For instance, AI may autonomously respond to customer needs, personalize offerings, or coordinate complex service tasks—thereby participating meaningfully in the co-creation process. In many cases, customer engagement and satisfaction increasingly depend on how well AI systems understand and respond to individual preferences, expectations, and behaviors.

Emerging conceptual models advocate for a hybrid co-creation framework in which human and non-human actors (including AI systems) collaborate within dynamic, digitally enabled environments. These frameworks recognize that AI can both substitute for and augment human actors, creating new forms of interaction and value exchange that were previously unattainable. Consequently, the boundaries between human agency and machine agency are becoming more fluid, and the theoretical focus must adapt accordingly.

Moreover, this evolution calls for the development of multilayered interaction models that can accommodate not just the dyadic relationships between providers and customers, but also the triadic or networked configurations involving AI. These models must address how trust is built between users and machines, how transparency and explainability affect value perceptions, and how responsibilities are distributed in co-created outcomes.

5.1.2 Redefining Roles in the Service System

The growing integration of artificial intelligence (AI) into service systems is not merely an operational or technological shift—it represents a profound transformation in the configuration and interaction of actors within the service ecosystem. Traditional role boundaries between service providers, employees, and customers are being redefined as AI systems increasingly mediate, support, and even drive value co-creation. This evolution calls for a reconsideration of existing theoretical assumptions about actor roles, agency, and collaboration in service delivery.

In this emerging landscape, customers are no longer passive recipients of standardized services. Instead, they are becoming active co-designers, engaging directly with intelligent systems to customize their experiences in real-time. Whether through conversational agents, recommendation engines, or adaptive interfaces, customers interact with AI to influence the form, content, and timing of service outputs. This participatory role enhances the depth of their engagement and repositions them as key contributors in the co-creation process. From a theoretical standpoint, this challenges traditional consumer behavior models and highlights the need for frameworks that can account for interactive, AI-mediated personalization dynamics.

Simultaneously, the role of employees is shifting from that of direct service providers to that of facilitators and orchestrators of AI-enabled service encounters (Larivière et al., 2017). Rather than delivering services alone, employees increasingly collaborate with AI tools—such as decision support systems or predictive analytics platforms—to co-deliver value in more efficient, consistent, and scalable ways. This transformation necessitates the development of new skills and competencies, particularly in managing AI outputs, interpreting algorithmic suggestions, and ensuring a seamless human-machine interface. It also invites theorists to revisit concepts like employee empowerment, job satisfaction, and role clarity in hybrid work environments.

Most notably, AI itself emerges as a multifaceted actor within the service system. Depending on the context, it can function as a virtual assistant, a content curator, a problem-solver, or even an expert advisor—each role involving different degrees of autonomy, adaptability, and interaction with human stakeholders. This multiplicity complicates traditional classifications of actors in service ecosystems and demands a broader conceptualization of agency. Theoretical models must therefore evolve to incorporate AI as a semi-autonomous service actor, capable of co-performing tasks, learning from interactions, and influencing service outcomes.

These role reconfigurations also surface critical questions about human–machine collaboration, particularly regarding governance, ethics, and accountability. As AI becomes increasingly embedded in frontline service processes, determining who is responsible for decisions and outcomes becomes less clear. Theoretical frameworks must begin to address these ambiguities, integrating ethical considerations and control mechanisms into models of service interaction. Issues such as trust, transparency, and user consent become central to understanding how AI-mediated relationships are formed and sustained.

5.2. Managerial Implications

This study contributes theoretically by expanding value co-creation models to include AI as a mediator and engagement catalyst. It also redefines roles within service systems, where customers, employees, and AI agents interact in dynamic, distributed ways, reshaping influence, responsibility, and value creation within service ecosystems.

5.2.1 Need to Design Hybrid Human-AI Systems

As artificial intelligence (AI) becomes increasingly integrated into service ecosystems, organizations are confronted with a crucial managerial challenge: how to effectively design and implement hybrid human-AI systems that capitalize on the distinct yet complementary capabilities of both human workers and intelligent machines. Rather than viewing AI as a replacement for human labor, forward-looking organizations must adopt a collaborative approach, wherein AI augments human performance and vice versa, ultimately enhancing value co-creation.

To do so, it is essential to recognize that AI excels at processing large volumes of data, identifying patterns, and automating repetitive or rule-based tasks. These capabilities make AI particularly useful for improving operational efficiency, decision-making accuracy, and responsiveness in real time. Conversely, human employees bring irreplaceable qualities to the table—such as empathy, ethical reasoning, contextual understanding, and creative problem-solving—that are vital in maintaining trust, emotional connection, and nuanced service delivery. The real managerial opportunity, therefore, lies not in replacing humans, but in designing systems that orchestrate a symbiotic relationship between people and AI (Afreen et al., 2025).

Building such hybrid systems is not merely a technical undertaking—it demands a reconfiguration of organizational structures, processes, and cultures. From a practical standpoint, this requires substantial investment in training and upskilling employees to work alongside AI technologies. Employees need to develop digital literacy, learn to interpret algorithmic insights, and acquire soft skills to navigate increasingly complex service interactions that involve both machines and people. Organizations must also foster a mindset shift among staff, encouraging openness to innovation and collaboration with non-human agents.

In addition, effective change management is critical to ensuring a smooth integration of AI systems. Resistance to technological change is common, especially when roles and routines are being redefined. Managers must therefore proactively communicate the purpose and benefits of hybrid systems, engage employees in the transformation process, and provide support mechanisms to address concerns related to job security, role ambiguity, and loss of autonomy.

Ethical considerations are also central to the managerial design of hybrid systems. As AI takes on more prominent roles in decision-making and customer interaction, issues of transparency, accountability, and fairness become increasingly important. Managers must ensure that AI tools operate in alignment with organizational values and stakeholder expectations. This includes implementing mechanisms for algorithmic oversight, explaining AI-driven decisions to customers, and safeguarding privacy and data security.

Moreover, cross-functional collaboration is necessary to design systems that are technically robust and human-centered. This implies that AI integration should not be confined to the IT department but involve inputs from HR, operations, customer service, and compliance teams. The goal is to build service environments where AI empowers human actors and reinforces, rather than undermines, the relational and experiential aspects of service delivery.

5.2.1 Rethinking Customer Journeys to Integrate Human-Machine Collaboration

The integration of artificial intelligence (AI) into customer journeys is reshaping how organizations deliver experiences and co-create value with their users. To fully harness the benefits of AI, managers must fundamentally rethink customer journeys, designing them to support seamless collaboration between human and machine actors. This involves more than automating isolated touchpoints—it requires a holistic redesign of the entire customer experience, centered on fluid and intelligent interactions.

A key managerial task is to identify where AI can meaningfully enhance the customer journey. This means mapping out the different stages of interaction and determining where AI can add the most value, either by providing information, increasing personalization, or streamlining processes. Rather than replacing human actors, AI should be positioned as a complementary force—handling repetitive, data-driven tasks while humans focus on emotional, creative, or judgment-intensive aspects of the service.

Equally important is the design of user-friendly and trustworthy interfaces that facilitate the transition between AI-powered and human-led interactions. Customers should be able to move effortlessly from a chatbot to a human agent, or from an AI-generated recommendation to a personalized consultation. This demands thoughtful orchestration of service flows, ensuring continuity, transparency, and responsiveness. These transitions are critical moments that can make or break the overall customer experience.

Consider the healthcare sector: AI-enabled chatbots can serve as the first point of contact, offering basic guidance, triaging symptoms, and directing patients to appropriate care pathways. Healthcare professionals then step in to handle complex clinical decisions, leveraging the initial data collected by the system. This collaboration increases efficiency while maintaining the empathy and expertise that only human providers can offer. In retail, a similar model can be applied, where AI delivers tailored product suggestions, and human sales staff provide added value through face-to-face engagement and advisory services.

Such reimagined customer journeys also require cross-functional coordination within the organization. Marketing, IT, service design, and frontline teams must collaborate to align their efforts and ensure the integrated system functions cohesively. Training employees to interact effectively with AI systems is essential, as is equipping them with new digital skills and a clear understanding of their evolving roles in this hybrid environment.

Moreover, these redesigned journeys must respect customer expectations around ethics, data privacy, and transparency. Managers need to address concerns related to algorithmic decision-making, ensure compliance with data protection standards, and maintain a clear boundary between machine automation and human accountability. Building trust in AI-enabled services is crucial, and transparency about where and how AI is involved in the customer journey plays a vital role in that process.

5.3. Study Limitations

This study offers valuable insights into the role of artificial intelligence (AI) in facilitating value co-creation within service industries. However, several limitations must be acknowledged to appropriately frame the scope and applicability of its findings. These limitations are inherent to the study's exploratory nature and methodological choices and point to opportunities for future research to build on and refine the present analysis.

Firstly, the exploratory scope of the study inherently constrains the generalizability of its conclusions. The primary aim was not to provide definitive answers or universally applicable models but rather to identify key themes, conceptual developments, and emerging dynamics at the intersection of AI and value co-creation. As such, the insights offered should be viewed as preliminary, laying the groundwork for deeper investigation rather than representing conclusive evidence. The diversity and complexity of service industries—from healthcare and hospitality to education and retail—mean that AI's role in co-creation may vary significantly across contexts. Generalizing findings across these sectors without empirical substantiation risks oversimplifying the nuanced ways in which AI impacts different service ecosystems.

Secondly, the methodological reliance on secondary literature represents another limitation. The study is based on a narrative review of existing academic and conceptual contributions, which, while offering a rich theoretical foundation, does not provide empirical validation of the phenomena discussed. This reliance means the analysis is somewhat abstract and may lack the contextual specificity that field-based research would offer. Real-world practices, stakeholder experiences, and implementation challenges in AI-mediated co-creation processes remain underexplored due to this limitation.

By not incorporating primary data—such as interviews, surveys, or case studies—the study does not capture the lived experiences, perceptions, or behaviors of service employees, customers, or AI system designers. Consequently, the findings should not be interpreted as reflective of actual practices within specific organizational or sectoral settings. This theoretical orientation also makes it difficult to assess the practical feasibility or effectiveness of proposed AI-mediated interactions in value co-creation, including potential obstacles and unintended consequences.

Moreover, the exclusive focus on literature may unintentionally introduce biases linked to the existing body of knowledge, which itself may underrepresent certain geographical areas, industries, or minority perspectives. For instance, much of the current research on AI in service industries is concentrated in technologically advanced economies, which may not reflect the realities of emerging markets or resource-constrained environments.

5.4. Future Research Directions

As artificial intelligence (AI) becomes increasingly embedded in service systems, future research must evolve to capture the complexity of AI-mediated value co-creation. Although this study provides a conceptual foundation, further investigations are essential to empirically validate and contextualize its propositions. Three major directions emerge as particularly promising: empirical exploration of user experiences, comparative sectoral analysis, and the integration of ethical and cultural considerations into the study of AI-enabled services.

First, there is a critical need for empirical studies that examine real-life co-creation experiences involving AI. While conceptual models help structure our understanding, they must be substantiated through observation of actual interactions between humans and intelligent systems. Future research should focus on how customers and employees perceive and engage in AI-mediated co-creation processes. This includes exploring their attitudes toward AI, the emotional and cognitive dimensions of their experiences, and the behavioral outcomes associated with these interactions. Key constructs such as trust, perceived usefulness, perceived competence, and ease of use can be assessed to understand what drives or hinders the successful integration of AI into service relationships (Gursoy et al., 2019). Additionally, empirical studies can shed light on how the human-machine collaboration dynamic evolves over time, particularly as users become more familiar with AI tools and their capabilities.

Second, adopting comparative approaches across different service industries can help uncover how contextual factors shape the implementation and effectiveness of AI in value co-creation. AI is not used uniformly across sectors; its applications and implications vary depending on the nature of the service, customer expectations, regulatory environments, and technological readiness. For instance, in healthcare, ethical considerations and data privacy are critical, whereas in retail, personalization and speed of service might be more dominant concerns. Research comparing sectors such as finance, hospitality, education, and tourism can generate a richer understanding of industry-specific challenges, best practices, and innovation trajectories. Such comparative insights can inform sector-tailored strategies for AI adoption and foster cross-sector learning and benchmarking.

Third, future research must take seriously the ethical and cultural dimensions of AI-mediated value co-creation. The increasing presence of AI in services raises pressing questions about data governance, algorithmic transparency, fairness, and user autonomy. Researchers should investigate how different ethical concerns influence the design, deployment, and acceptance of AI technologies across contexts. Moreover, cultural variables—such as norms, values, and beliefs—shape individuals' perceptions and expectations regarding AI. These factors may affect not only the success of AI adoption but also the inclusivity and social legitimacy of AI-driven service systems. Exploring cross-cultural variations in user attitudes toward AI can help ensure that technological innovations are aligned with local needs and values, promoting more equitable and human-centered service ecosystems (Nkwo et al., 2025).

CONCLUSION

The increasing integration of artificial intelligence in services marks a significant transformation in the dynamics of value co-creation. Traditionally, value creation relied on a unilateral production logic, where the company provided a service or product to a passive customer. However, the Service-Dominant Logic (SDL), developed by (Vargo & Lusch, 2004, 2008), introduced an alternative perspective, emphasizing that value is co-created through interactions between providers and customers, focusing on "value-in-use" rather than "value-in-exchange." Within this theoretical framework, the customer becomes an active participant in the service process, and value creation emerges from the synergies among resources, skills, and relationships.

Artificial intelligence, as an enabling technology, strengthens this logic by allowing richer, personalized, and real-time interactions between companies and their customers. For example, chatbots, virtual assistants, and intelligent recommendation systems enable continuous, adaptive, and contextualized communication, significantly enhancing customer engagement and the relevance of responses provided. As highlighted by (Chandra & Rahman, 2024), AI increases company responsiveness while smoothing access to information and services, directly contributing to improved user experience and stronger customer relationships.

Moreover, AI does not merely automate repetitive tasks or support technical operations: it now plays an active role in the service process. It becomes a genuine co-actor in value co-creation, capable of contributing to the production of new and enriched experiences. This evolution requires redefining roles within the service system. Customers, employees, and intelligent agents now interact within an expanded and interconnected ecosystem where boundaries between human functions and technological capabilities are increasingly permeable. From this perspective, AI-mediated co-creation calls for revising classical theoretical models to integrate new modes of interaction, coordination, and value contribution.

For management actors, these transformations call for concrete responses. Companies must design hybrid systems that leverage both human skills — such as empathy, creativity, and judgment — and AI capabilities — such as speed, precision, and big data analysis. It becomes essential to rethink customer journeys to harmoniously integrate human-machine collaboration, ensuring that AI complements and enriches the human experience rather than replacing it. This also involves investing in continuous employee training so they can effectively use AI tools and adopt new collaborative roles. Furthermore, attentive organizational change management is indispensable to promote technology acceptance and prevent internal resistance.

However, this study presents some limitations. Its exploratory nature, combined with an approach mainly based on a narrative literature review, restricts the scope of its conclusions. Generalization of results should therefore be cautious. To go further, empirical research will be necessary. These could include in-depth case studies in specific sectoral contexts, or quantitative surveys measuring the effects of AI on the value co-creation perceived by customers. Such empirical work would help validate and enrich the concepts presented in this research framework.

Additionally, exploring sector-specific particularities in the analysis of AI-mediated co-creation appears relevant. Interaction modalities and value dynamics may vary significantly depending on whether the sector is healthcare, education, finance, or hospitality. A comparative cross-sector approach would better explain the success conditions for AI integration in services, as well as levers for optimizing the co-creative experience. Finally, integrating ethical and cultural dimensions in the analysis is an unavoidable challenge. AI usage in service interactions raises many issues related to personal data protection, algorithm transparency, decision-making accountability, and social acceptability of intelligent interfaces. These dimensions are especially sensitive in intercultural contexts where customer expectations of AI may differ considerably.

REFERENCES

Adam, M., Wessel, M., & Benlian, A. (2021). AI-based chatbots in customer service and their effects on user compliance. *Electronic Markets*, *31*(2), 427–445. DOI: 10.1007/s12525-020-00414-7

Adesoga, T. O., Ajibaye, T. O., Nwafor, K. C., Imam-Lawal, U. T., Ikekwere, E. A., & Ekwunife, D. I.Temitayo Oluwadamilola AdesogaTolulope Olusola AjibayeKenneth Chukwujekwu NwaforUmmulikhaeri Temitope Imam-LawalEmmanuel Ayobamidele IkekwereDaniel Ikechukwu Ekwunife. (2024). The rise of the « smart » supply chain : How AI and automation are revolutionizing logistics. *International Journal of Science and Research Archive*, *12*(2), 790–798. DOI: 10.30574/ijsra.2024.12.2.1304

Afreen, J., Mohaghegh, M., & Doborjeh, M. (2025). Systematic literature review on bias mitigation in generative AI. *AI and Ethics*, *5*(5), 1–53. DOI: 10.1007/s43681-025-00721-9

Agarwal, P., Swami, S., & Malhotra, S. K. (2024). Artificial intelligence adoption in the post COVID-19 new-normal and role of smart technologies in transforming business : A review. *Journal of Science and Technology Policy Management*, *15*(3), 506–529. DOI: 10.1108/JSTPM-08-2021-0122

Aldoseri, A., Al-Khalifa, K. N., & Hamouda, A. M. (2024). AI-powered innovation in digital transformation : Key pillars and industry impact. *Sustainability (Basel)*, *16*(5), 1790. DOI: 10.3390/su16051790

Amankwah-Amoah, J., Abdalla, S., Mogaji, E., Elbanna, A., & Dwivedi, Y. K. (2024). The impending disruption of creative industries by generative AI: Opportunities, challenges, and research agenda. *International Journal of Information Management*, *79*, 102759. DOI: 10.1016/j.ijinfomgt.2024.102759

Ayeni, O. O., Al Hamad, N. M., Chisom, O. N., Osawaru, B., & Adewusi, O. E. (2024). AI in education : A review of personalized learning and educational technology. *GSC Advanced Research and Reviews*, *18*(2), 261–271. DOI: 10.30574/gscarr.2024.18.2.0062

Baumeister, R. F., & Leary, M. R. (1997). Writing narrative literature reviews. *Review of General Psychology*, *1*(3), 311–320. DOI: 10.1037/1089-2680.1.3.311

Bock, D. E., Wolter, J. S., & Ferrell, O. (2020). Artificial intelligence : Disrupting what we know about services. *Journal of Services Marketing*, *34*(3), 317–334. DOI: 10.1108/JSM-01-2019-0047

Brodie, R. J., Löbler, H., & Fehrer, J. A. (2019). Evolution of service-dominant logic : Towards a paradigm and metatheory of the market and value cocreation? *Industrial Marketing Management, 79*, 3–12. DOI: 10.1016/j.indmarman.2019.03.003

Chandler, J. D., & Vargo, S. L. (2011). Contextualization and value-in-context : How context frames exchange. *Marketing Theory, 11*(1), 35–49. DOI: 10.1177/1470593110393713

Chandra, B., & Rahman, Z. (2024). Artificial intelligence and value co-creation : A review, conceptual framework and directions for future research. *Journal of Service Theory and Practice, 34*(1), 7–32. DOI: 10.1108/JSTP-03-2023-0097

Dasgupta, S., Dasgupta, D. S., & Jamader, A. R. (2024). AI The Future of Hotel. *Available at SSRN* 4992038.

Daugherty, P., & Wilson, H. (2018). *Human+ machine : Reimagining work in the age of AI; 2018*. Harvard Business Review Press.

Dave, D. M., Mandvikar, S., & Engineer, P. A. (2023). Augmented intelligence : Human-AI collaboration in the era of digital transformation. *International Journal of Engineering Applied Sciences and Technology, 8*(6), 24–33. DOI: 10.33564/IJEAST.2023.v08i06.003

Davenport, T. H., & Ronanki, R. (2018). Artificial intelligence for the real world. *HBR'S 10 MUST*, 67.

Dubey, R., Gunasekaran, A., Childe, S. J., Fosso Wamba, S., Roubaud, D., & Foropon, C. (2021). Empirical investigation of data analytics capability and organizational flexibility as complements to supply chain resilience. *International Journal of Production Research, 59*(1), 110–128. DOI: 10.1080/00207543.2019.1582820

Fusté-Forné, F., & Jamal, T. (2021). Co-creating new directions for service robots in hospitality and tourism. *Tourism and Hospitality, 2*(1), 43–61. DOI: 10.3390/tourhosp2010003

Greenhalgh, T., Thorne, S., & Malterud, K. (2018). Time to challenge the spurious hierarchy of systematic over narrative reviews? *European Journal of Clinical Investigation, 48*(6), e12931. DOI: 10.1111/eci.12931

Grönroos, C., & Voima, P. (2013). Critical service logic : Making sense of value creation and co-creation. *Journal of the Academy of Marketing Science, 41*(2), 133–150. DOI: 10.1007/s11747-012-0308-3

Gursoy, D., Chi, O. H., Lu, L., & Nunkoo, R. (2019). Consumers acceptance of artificially intelligent (AI) device use in service delivery. *International Journal of Information Management*, *49*, 157–169. DOI: 10.1016/j.ijinfomgt.2019.03.008

Haenlein, M., & Kaplan, A. (2019). A brief history of artificial intelligence : On the past, present, and future of artificial intelligence. *California Management Review*, *61*(4), 5–14. DOI: 10.1177/0008125619864925

Holmes, W., Persson, J., Chounta, I.-A., Wasson, B., & Dimitrova, V. (2022). *Artificial intelligence and education : A critical view through the lens of human rights, democracy and the rule of law*. Council of Europe.

Hoyer, W. D., Kroschke, M., Schmitt, B., Kraume, K., & Shankar, V. (2020). Transforming the customer experience through new technologies. *Journal of Interactive Marketing*, *51*(1), 57–71. DOI: 10.1016/j.intmar.2020.04.001

Huang, M.-H., & Rust, R. T. (2018). Artificial intelligence in service. *Journal of Service Research*, *21*(2), 155–172. DOI: 10.1177/1094670517752459

Huang, M.-H., & Rust, R. T. (2021). A strategic framework for artificial intelligence in marketing. *Journal of the Academy of Marketing Science*, *49*(1), 30–50. DOI: 10.1007/s11747-020-00749-9

Janiesch, C., Zschech, P., & Heinrich, K. (2021). Machine learning and deep learning. *Electronic Markets*, *31*(3), 685–695. DOI: 10.1007/s12525-021-00475-2

Jiang, P., Niu, W., Wang, Q., Yuan, R., & Chen, K. (2024). Understanding Users' Acceptance of Artificial Intelligence Applications : A Literature Review. *Behavioral Sciences (Basel, Switzerland)*, *14*(8), 671. DOI: 10.3390/bs14080671

Kohlgrüber, M., Maldonado-Mariscal, K., & Schröder, A. (2021). *Mutual learning in innovation and co-creation processes : Integrating technological and social innovation*. *6*, 498661.

Kot, M., & Leszczyński, G. (2022). AI-activated value co-creation. An exploratory study of conversational agents. *Industrial Marketing Management*, *107*, 287–299. DOI: 10.1016/j.indmarman.2022.10.013

Kumar, A., Shankar, A., Behl, A., Chakraborty, D., & Gundala, R. R. (2025). Anthropomorphic generative AI chatbots for enhancing customer engagement, experience and recommendation. *Journal of Consumer Marketing*, *42*(4), 472–483. DOI: 10.1108/JCM-06-2024-6922

Larivière, B., Bowen, D., Andreassen, T. W., Kunz, W., Sirianni, N. J., Voss, C., Wünderlich, N. V., & De Keyser, A. (2017). "Service Encounter 2.0" : An investigation into the roles of technology, employees and customers. *Journal of Business Research*, *79*, 238–246. DOI: 10.1016/j.jbusres.2017.03.008

Lemon, K. N., & Verhoef, P. C. (2016). Understanding customer experience throughout the customer journey. *Journal of Marketing*, *80*(6), 69–96. DOI: 10.1509/jm.15.0420

Leone, D., Schiavone, F., Appio, F. P., & Chiao, B. (2021). How does artificial intelligence enable and enhance value co-creation in industrial markets? An exploratory case study in the healthcare ecosystem. *Journal of Business Research, 129*, 849–859. DOI: 10.1016/j.jbusres.2020.11.008

Lin, C.-C., Huang, A. Y. Q., & Lu, O. H. T. (2023). Artificial intelligence in intelligent tutoring systems toward sustainable education : A systematic review. *Smart Learning Environments*, *10*(1), 41. DOI: 10.1186/s40561-023-00260-y

Luckin, R., & Holmes, W. (2016). *Intelligence unleashed : An argument for AI in education.*

Maghamis, F. (2018). *Service dominant logic (SDL), service exchange and mutual value creation–a case study from Middle-East's telecommunication industry.*

Manser Payne, E. H., Dahl, A. J., & Peltier, J. (2021). Digital servitization value co-creation framework for AI services : A research agenda for digital transformation in financial service ecosystems. *Journal of Research in Interactive Marketing, 15*(2), 200–222. DOI: 10.1108/JRIM-12-2020-0252

Meyer, L. M., Stead, S., Salge, T. O., & Antons, D. (2024). Artificial intelligence in acute care : A systematic review, conceptual synthesis, and research agenda. *Technological Forecasting and Social Change*, *206*, 123568. DOI: 10.1016/j.techfore.2024.123568

Mohamed, N. (2025). *Augmented Intelligence : A Comprehensive Review of the Flexibility Between Human and Artificial Intelligence. Journal of The Institution of Engineers*. Series B.

Nag, P. K., Bhagat, A., Priya, R. V., & Khare, D. K. (2023). *Emotional intelligence through artificial intelligence : Nlp and deep learning in the analysis of healthcare texts. 1*, 1-7.

Nkwo, M., Ikwunne, T., Adejoro, C., & Anuyah, O. (2025). Exploring Usability of AI Systems in the Global South—Toward Responsible Human-Centered AI for Sustainable Cities and Communities. In *Usability for the World : Building Better Cities and Communities* (p. 125-165). Springer.

Omol, E. J. (2024). Organizational digital transformation : From evolution to future trends. *Digital Transformation and Society*, *3*(3), 240–256. DOI: 10.1108/DTS-08-2023-0061

Onabowale, O. (2024). The rise of AI and Robo-Advisors : Redefining financial strategies in the digital age. *International Journal of Research Publication and Reviews, 6*.

Parasuraman, A., & Colby, C. L. (2015). An updated and streamlined technology readiness index : TRI 2.0. *Journal of Service Research*, *18*(1), 59–74. DOI: 10.1177/1094670514539730

Paschen, J., Paschen, U., Pala, E., & Kietzmann, J. (2021). Artificial intelligence (AI) and value co-creation in B2B sales : Activities, actors and resources. *Australasian Marketing Journal*, *29*(3), 243–251. DOI: 10.1016/j.ausmj.2020.06.004

Paschen, U., Pitt, C., & Kietzmann, J. (2020). Artificial intelligence : Building blocks and an innovation typology. *Business Horizons*, *63*(2), 147–155. DOI: 10.1016/j.bushor.2019.10.004

Perälä, K. (2024). *The role of user-centric design in global platform economy value creation.*

Peruchini, M., da Silva, G. M., & Teixeira, J. M. (2024). Between artificial intelligence and customer experience : A literature review on the intersection. *Discover Artificial Intelligence*, *4*(1), 4. DOI: 10.1007/s44163-024-00105-8

Popesku, M. (2015). *Clarifying value in use and value creation process.*

Prahalad, C. K., & Ramaswamy, V. (2004). Co-creation experiences : The next practice in value creation. *Journal of Interactive Marketing*, *18*(3), 5–14. DOI: 10.1002/dir.20015

Radziwill, N. (2020). *Connected, intelligent, automated : The definitive guide to digital transformation and quality 4.0.* Quality Press.

Rane, N. (2023). Enhancing customer loyalty through Artificial Intelligence (AI), Internet of Things (IoT), and Big Data technologies : Improving customer satisfaction, engagement, relationship, and experience. *Internet of Things (IoT), and Big Data Technologies: Improving Customer Satisfaction, Engagement, Relationship, and Experience (October 13, 2023).*

Ricci, F., Rokach, L., & Shapira, B. (2021). Recommender systems : Techniques, applications, and challenges. *Recommender systems handbook*, 1-35.

Schachner, T., Keller, R., & v Wangenheim, F. (2020). Artificial intelligence-based conversational agents for chronic conditions : Systematic literature review. *Journal of Medical Internet Research, 22*(9), e20701. DOI: 10.2196/20701

Siemens, G., Marmolejo-Ramos, F., Gabriel, F., Medeiros, K., Marrone, R., Joksimovic, S., & de Laat, M. (2022). Human and artificial cognition. *Computers and Education: Artificial Intelligence, 3*, 100107.

Song, X., & Bonanni, C. (2024). AI-driven business model : How AI-powered try-on technology is refining the luxury shopping experience and customer satisfaction. *Journal of Theoretical and Applied Electronic Commerce Research, 19*(4), 3067–3087. DOI: 10.3390/jtaer19040148

Tussyadiah, I. (2020). A review of research into automation in tourism : Launching the Annals of Tourism Research Curated Collection on Artificial Intelligence and Robotics in Tourism. *Annals of Tourism Research, 81*, 102883. DOI: 10.1016/j.annals.2020.102883

Vargo, S. L., & Lusch, R. F. (2004). Evolving to a new dominant logic for marketing. *Journal of Marketing, 68*(1), 1–17. DOI: 10.1509/jmkg.68.1.1.24036

Vargo, S. L., & Lusch, R. F. (2008). Service-dominant logic : Continuing the evolution. *Journal of the Academy of Marketing Science, 36*(1), 1–10. DOI: 10.1007/s11747-007-0069-6

Vashishth, T. K., Sharma, V., Sharma, K. K., Kumar, B., Kumar, A., & Panwar, R. (2024). Artificial intelligence (AI)–powered chatbots : Providing instant support and personalized recommendations to guests 24/7. In *Technology and Luxury Hospitality* (pp. 211–236). Routledge. DOI: 10.4324/9781003488248-15

Waardenburg, L., & Huysman, M. (2022). From coexistence to co-creation : Blurring boundaries in the age of AI. *Information and Organization, 32*(4), 100432. DOI: 10.1016/j.infoandorg.2022.100432

Wamba, S. F., Queiroz, M. M., Jabbour, C. J. C., & Shi, C. V. (2023). Are both generative AI and ChatGPT game changers for 21st-Century operations and supply chain excellence? *International Journal of Production Economics, 265*, 109015. DOI: 10.1016/j.ijpe.2023.109015

Winkelhaus, S., & Grosse, E. H. (2020). Logistics 4.0 : A systematic review towards a new logistics system. *International Journal of Production Research, 58*(1), 18–43. DOI: 10.1080/00207543.2019.1612964

Wirtz, J., Patterson, P. G., Kunz, W. H., Gruber, T., Lu, V. N., Paluch, S., & Martins, A. (2018). Brave new world : Service robots in the frontline. *Journal of Service Management*, *29*(5), 907–931. DOI: 10.1108/JOSM-04-2018-0119

Chapter 17
Transforming Education With Artificial Intelligence: Tools, Challenges, and Future Directions

F. Sammy
SRM Institute of Science and Technology, India

J. Antony Vijay
RMK College of Engineering and Technology, India

P. Gopika Priya
Vel Tech Multi Tech Dr. Rangarajan Dr. Sakunthala Engineering College, India

P. Lokesh
Vel Tech High Tech Dr. Rangarajan Dr. Sakunthala Engineering College, India

Srikanth Lakumarapu
CVR College of Engineering, India

M. G. Dinesh
https://orcid.org/0009-0009-7643-5338
EASA College of Engineering and Technology, India

G. Belshia Jebamalar
SA Engineering College, India

ABSTRACT

Artificial intelligence (AI) is rapidly reshaping education by enhancing teaching methods, personalizing learning experiences, and fostering critical thinking skills. This chapter reviews key AI technologies such as intelligent tutoring systems, adaptive learning platforms, and natural language processing tools and their applications in improving instruction, assessment, and learner engagement. It also examines AI's role in developing higher-order cognitive skills through collaborative learning and argumentation support. The chapter discusses challenges including data privacy,

DOI: 10.4018/979-8-3373-3436-3.ch017

algorithmic bias, and equitable access, alongside ethical considerations vital for responsible AI integration. Finally, it outlines future research directions, emphasizing emerging technologies and interdisciplinary collaboration. This comprehensive overview highlights AI's transformative potential to create inclusive, personalized, and effective educational environments that prepare learners for complex real-world challenges.

1. INTRODUCTION

1.1 Background and Motivation

One of the biggest transformations seen in teaching is introducing Artificial Intelligence (AI) into schools. In recent years many industries have been transformed by the fast advances in AI technologies, especially in machine learning, natural language processing and computer vision(Chen et al 2020). AI has helped healthcare, finance and manufacturing sectors to improve how they operate, how accurate their work is and the decisions they make. Because education is so important for society and individuals, it can use AI's advantages more than most fields. AI is being used in education to replace the old, single-method approach with adaptive and personalized teaching for everyone's benefit. Traditional education systems have regularly encountered the same set of problems. One serious problem is that it's not personalized enough. Using the same curriculum and way of teaching often misses the differences in how fast, in what way and what students already know. As a consequence, a lot of students either miss out on important skills or become uninterested, reducing their chances for success. Besides, not all people have the same chance to receive quality education. Because of a lack of resources, rural areas, underfunded schools and marginalized communities often cannot give all students the same level of education. In addition, traditional ways of assessing students find it challenging to measure abilities such as thinking critically, being creative and solving problems. In this situation, AI can greatly help education by solving the problems mentioned above. With the use of advanced algorithms and data, AI systems give students personalized learning. For example, intelligent tutoring systems make changes to instruction as it happens, so the content and speed match the learner's level. Because of this level of customization, students understand the lessons better, remember them and stay interested. AI also makes it possible for underserved people to access quality online learning whenever and wherever they need it. The spread of learning opportunities closes achievement gaps and supports learning throughout life.

AI also helps by giving students feedback they can use right away. AI-powered tools check student data at all times and provide useful feedback to teachers and students, making it easier than traditional ways to watch each student's progress. They can show if a learner has misunderstood something, suggest how to correct it and observe improvement, allowing better support. AI also helps strengthen important skills from the 21st century, for example critical thinking, by providing interactive simulations, learning by solving problems and using natural language tools that make students think, evaluate and design answers rather than simply recall information. The motivation behind the chapter is to look at how AI technologies are being used in education and to see what effect they have on teaching and learning. This chapter looks at both improving teaching and boosting critical thinking, in order to present a complete picture of AI in education. Understanding these factors helps educators, policymakers and researchers use AI to improve how education works for everyone(Engelbrecht et al 2025).

1.2 Importance of AI in Modern Education

Artificial Intelligence (AI) helps to improve education by matching the needs of different students with the resources available. Because of COVID-19, there was a faster than normal move to digital and remote education and this helped reveal the good and bad parts of traditional education systems. Because of this, AI was used to help customize and improve the way people learn. AI can help education by adjusting what is taught, how fast the lessons are delivered and how they are explained to match the way each student learns. AI can observe how students do in real time using adaptive learning platforms and make changes to the curriculum accordingly. It enables students to learn at the right level which makes their progress more certain and helps them feel more confident. AI is playing a big part in intelligent tutoring systems which help students get similar guidance and instant feedback that a human tutor would give(Suresh et al 2025). Also, AI-based tools that grade assignments automatically help teachers by taking care of repetitive work and leaving them time to give more attention to students. Teachers can rely on AI-powered chatbots to give scientifically supported ideas for running the classroom and planning lessons. Along with helping in administration and giving information, AI supports the development of thinking skills. By using simulations, group projects and solving problems, it promotes critical thinking, creativity and logical reasoning. Having these capabilities helps students get ready for employment in modern, technology-based companies where being flexible and innovative matters a lot. With AI, education becomes more flexible, more efficient and open to everyone. It supports learning in school and also gives students the skills they need for the 21st century. If AI is incorporated into education, students and teachers are able to work in an engaging and efficient way that adapts to new changes in the world of work.

1.3 Objectives and Scope of the Chapter

The purpose of this chapter is to systematically review the current situation of AI in education, mainly to see how it improves teaching, learning and helps develop critical thinking. The purpose of the research is to (1) describe the AI tools and techniques in use in schools, (2) examine their effects on teaching and learning, (3) look at how AI helps develop critical thinking skills and (4) review the ethical, social and technical problems related to using AI in education. The applications included in the scope are intelligent tutoring systems, systems for automated assessment, personalized learning platforms, virtual assistants and AI-assisted collaborative learning environments. The chapter combines information from computer science, educational psychology and instructional design to give a broad view helpful for researchers, educators and policymakers wanting to make use of AI in education.

1.4 Structure of the Chapter

The rest of this chapter is arranged as follows. In Section 2, the chapter covers the main AI technologies used in education, pointing out machine learning, natural language processing and recommender systems. Intelligent tutorial systems, automated marking and tools that help teachers are covered in Section 3. In Section 4, we discuss how AI makes learning more personal, engaging and accessible. Section 5 looks at how AI helps students build critical thinking skills and faces certain challenges. Section 6 looks at how privacy, fairness and bias are considered in ethics. Section 7 discusses the ways AI is evaluated in education using supporting research data. Section 8 discusses new trends and the future research.

2. OVERVIEW OF AI TECHNOLOGIES IN EDUCATION

2.1 Definition and Key Concepts of AI Relevant to Education

AI is the term used when computers are used to mimic human thinking processes. In education, AI is the collection of tools and systems that allow computers to do what people used to do. Understanding people's language, identifying patterns, choosing actions and adapting to different information, they consist of. The important ideas in AI for education are automation, personalization and interactivity.

Now machines can do tedious things that take a lot of time such as grading and administrative work. Personalized system can change lessons, the speed at which learners learn and feedback depending on the needs of a learner. Learners or educators can interact with the AI and receive real time replies and the AI can adjust the learning plan. These all help to create a more interesting, successful and more expandable learning experience.

2.2 Types of AI Techniques Used in Education

Many educational activities have been improved by using different AI methods. Machine learning (ML) is considered one of the main examples because it allows systems to improve on their own after studying data, without having to be programmed(Prabhu et al., 2025). Educational ML algorithms help by studying student results to predict their performance, find areas they are lacking and suggest personal ways of learning. Many people use natural language processing (NLP) to allow machines to understand and use human language(Chowdhary, K., & Chowdhary, K. R. 2020). NLP enables chatbots in education to answer student questions right away, allows for the quick assessment of writing through automated scoring and supports learning languages by using speech recognition and talking software(Fanni et al 2023). Schools use computer vision to read handwriting, spot student interest from their faces and check how involved they are in the lesson. In education, recommender systems which are widely used in online shopping, now help by recommending suitable learning resources, exercises or people to collaborate with a learner. Other important AI methods are knowledge representation and reasoning which help organize difficult educational content and guide students in solving problems.

2.3 Historical Development and Recent Trends in AI Educational Tools

AI has been used in education in many new ways as time has passed. The first AI educational tools which emerged in the 1960s and 1970s, were mainly expert systems based on rules to help students learn specific subjects. In their initial phase, ITS guided users with detailed feedback and directions, but their advice was fixed by the rules the programmers wrote. Because of new developments in machine learning and more online educational data, the 1990s and early 2000s saw a move towards using data to guide decisions. At this time, learning platforms appeared that would change content and difficulty depending on how learners interacted with them(Hilbert et al 2021). Recent years have seen quick growth in many areas due to deep learning, huge data and cloud services(Dhinakaran, D et al., 2025; Ponnuviji,

N. P et al., 2025). Today's AI educational tools are designed to make learning easier, as they allow students to learn using text, audio, video and interactive simulations together. A focus on explainable AI is increasing, so that AI's decisions can be understood by both educators and students. Using AI, AR and VR technologies together is creating new ways for students to learn. Because of AI, chatbots and virtual assistants, students can now get help and support for learning outside of school. In general, AI in education has moved from fixed, rule-based methods to more lively, student-focused and context-aware systems that might help change education around the world(Jain et al 2024).

3. AI FOR ENHANCING TEACHING

AI is completely changing education with new tools and ways of working that help teachers, get rid of the paperwork and give the students personal learning plans. Large changes are being brought by its skill in studying data, tailoring instruction for each individual and handling common tasks. In this article, we look at some important areas that AI has a big impact on teaching such as ITS, auto grading, AI based curriculum design and AI based tools for teachers that help with classroom control and response to students.

3.1 Intelligent Tutoring Systems (ITS) and Personalized Instruction

The most important use of AI in education is in Intelligent Tutoring Systems (ITS). Better than traditional computer learning, they provide students the same sort of interactive and adaptive help that people can give(Lin et al 2023). ITS use advanced AI tools like machine learning, cognitive science models and real time data analysis to customize instruction for each learner while conventional teaching uses the same method for all (Luan & Tsai, 2021). ITS sits at its center, allowing teachers to check student progress and adjust lessons in real time. Take for example, if a student is having trouble understanding something, the system will be able to tell because of how they respond to problems or the errors they keep making. As a result, the ITS can adjust the course content by adding further notes, using examples that are simpler or changing the type of problem. If a student proves skilled, the program speeds up or adds tougher subjects to prevent boredom and help the student gain more knowledge. There are many good things about this kind of instruction model. It first helps students learn better by focusing on their different strengths and weaknesses. With ITS, students can follow their own learning paths instead of being required to move through the same content as a group. As a result, students are less likely to lose interest since the learning is always adapted to their abilities and learning preferences. Besides, ITS allows education to be scaled easily. Availability and price often make it difficult to use human tutors. With intelligent systems, a lot of students can benefit from personalized tutoring that was previously available only to a small group. Also, ITS take the workload off educators so they don't have to handle instructional differentiation on their own. Teachers can use these systems to manage the basics of adapting their teaching, so they can focus on mentoring, giving social and emotional support and teaching advanced thinking skills. The combination of ITS and human teaching in classrooms makes education more effective.

3.2 Automated Grading and Assessment

Assessment and grading are important parts of teaching since they tell teachers what students have learned and how to continue their education. Even so, grading essays and projects can be a slow process and is sometimes affected by human mistakes. Such systems are now being used to speed up and ensure fair grades for students. Currently, programs for grading use NLP, pattern recognition and machine learning to assess many student submissions. Objective questions such as multiple-choice and fill-in-the-blank, are easily marked by AI systems which offer quick results that help students realize what they got wrong and adjust their knowledge(Mir et al 2023). Today, AI can handle the difficult task of evaluating essays, short answers and programming assignments by recognizing and understanding their content. These systems test the text for how well it is organized, grammatically correct and relevant to the topic, as well as how well it answers the prompt. Although there is still room for growth, NLP keeps helping automated graders get better at assessing complex and creative student assignments. An important advantage of using AI in assessment is that students get feedback instantly. If feedback comes swiftly, students can address their mistakes right away and easily keep what they've learned in mind. With automated systems, the same grade is given to every student, as there are no differences caused by human tiredness, mood or hidden biases. Automated grading helps teachers by handling a large number of assignments which gives them more hours to work on curriculum, lesson plans and supporting students. Because of technology, teachers can evaluate students' progress more often and step in early when students have difficulties. Even so, there are still some obstacles. Many automated graders find it hard to review creative or context-related answers which is why human help is still vital. At the same time, questions about openness, justice and protecting data need to be considered as more of these systems are put into use. Still, the future of AI in assessment is looking good. When algorithms and data are improved, they will often help score papers alongside teachers, making assessment better, fairer and more thorough.

3.3 AI-Driven Content Creation and Curriculum Design

It is no easy or cheap task for teachers to design lessons and curricula that are effective for different learners and that follow new educational standards. AI is here to help creating data based content and improving the curriculum and providing the learning materials more suitable, relevant and flexible for each student. AI technology can process a huge amount of educational materials like books, notes, articles and videos and put that knowledge together to create new teaching material. For example, it can make quizzes that match what a student already knows, make short summaries of large texts or make videos to make hard ideas easy to understand. Teachers use AI tools to create content but AI tools are also used to spot areas of curriculum that need to change. Student scores can be analyzed to see where a large number of students are having problems and changes in the curriculum or additional support materials may be necessary. This loop ensures that program content is relevant to what students need and to what the program wants to accomplish. Also, AI makes it easier to study a complex area of study by providing information in manageable bits that suit each learner. However, with this personalized approach, students learn their knowledge slowly and they don't get overwhelmed. At the system level, AI powered analytics reveal to teachers which instructional methods and teaching approaches 'work'. AI is used to look at the effects of curriculum design on student results to improve the way learning is presented and used. The use of evidence in the curriculum design is an assurance that the learning programs are productive and beneficial. Also, AI generated content can be inclusive by showing many different views and backgrounds that suit various learning options. Responsive schools build classrooms that feel inclusive to everyone. All in all, AI in education gives teachers new tools that enable them to teach better, more creatively and faster which is a win for everyone in the classroom.

3.4 Teacher Support Tools

A large part of teaching is managing classroom situations, looking after student interest and giving helpful feedback. Artificial intelligence is really helping teachers deal with the different teaching challenges and to make decisions on the best approaches. Classroom management is one of the important uses of AI. Computer vision, audio analysis and behavior study are what they use to track what happens in the classroom. By studying the students' facial expressions, body language and how much they are interacting, artificial intelligence can tell if students are not paying attention, are bored or are struggling. If teachers are alerted to these signals in real time, they can give students the help they need before things get serious. AI platforms also examine how students collaborate in the classroom. Gaining insight into these social factors allows teachers to support a classroom that encourages learning for all students. It is also important that AI support tools can produce customized feedback reports. When AI combines information on how students perform, join in and behave, it can create detailed reports that explain what each student has achieved and what they could improve. The information in these reports helps teachers plan lessons and connect with both students and parents more openly. Besides, numerous AI tools link easily with Learning Management Systems (LMS) and automate common administrative duties including attendance, submission of assignments and communication. With this integration, teachers have less to do, so they can focus better on teaching and helping students. They allow teachers to learn from data by pointing out frequent classroom challenges and useful ways to address them. Educators can use these findings to make their teaching better and better as time goes on. AI in teacher support helps to improve the overall way teachers teach. Thanks to actionable insights, easy-to-manage admin and prompt interventions, these tools help create a more efficient, helpful and supportive learning environment. AI is changing the way teaching is done and this goes further than just using automated tools. Learning is customized in new ways with Intelligent Tutoring Systems, grading is done quickly and fairly by AI, content is improved by AI and support tools for teachers help manage and provide feedback in classrooms. All of these AI applications support teachers in making their lessons more effective, interact better with students and organize their work more productively. As AI improves, it will play a more important role in education, encouraging new ideas that make teaching and learning fairer, more flexible and effective.

4. AI FOR ENHANCING LEARNING

4.1 Personalized Learning Paths and Adaptive Learning Systems

AI making learning more personalized is one of its most valuable additions to education today. Adaptive learning systems guide instruction based on how fast every learner moves, what they already know and what they like to learn. The systems are always gathering and studying information from student quizzes, how long they work on assignments and their mistakes. They use machine learning to find the learner's strong and weak points and suggest content and exercises that help the learner improve. A student who needs help with algebra might do extra exercises and get different explanations and an advanced student could try more in-depth tasks. Because they meet students' needs, adaptive learning systems reduce stress, encourage them to learn more and help them do better. It also helps people from different backgrounds and learning abilities because it is tailored to each student's needs.

4.2 Virtual Learning Environments and AI-Driven Simulations

Using AI in VLEs has changed regular classrooms into spaces where students can learn by doing. Because of AI, learners can take part in simulations that represent situations that are hard to experience in person. Medical students can carry out surgical tasks in a virtual operating room and engineering students may test virtual models. Thanks to these simulations, learners receive instant feedback and the program changes the challenge level based on their progress, encouraging them to be more active and think critically. With AI, group activities and discussions in VLEs are made possible, balanced participation is promoted and conflicts are mediated. Because AI-enhanced virtual environments are flexible and detailed, students can understand and keep information better by working with it in practice(siva subramanian et al., 2024).

4.3 AI-Powered Educational Chatbots and Virtual Assistants

Customers can rely on chatbots and virtual assistants for fast and continuous help day and night. With these tools, students can get answers, be led through the content and receive hints whenever they ask. By using natural language processing, chatbots help students understand lessons in a natural way and can quickly clear up their questions (Maheswari, B., & Nagarajan, R. 2024). Virtual assistants may also serve as study planners, inform students of important dates and give encouraging messages to keep them interested. Thanks to their quick and individualized help, these agents make tutoring available to many students in large classrooms or those learning from home(Mathew et al 2021). They also record information on regular challenges faced by learners which educators can use to know which areas to focus on.

4.4 Gamification and Engagement Through AI

AI plays a major role in helping gamification succeed in education. AI makes gamified learning better by automatically changing the challenges, prizes and feedback to keep the learner motivated(Pedro et al 2019). So, AI may review how a player is doing to decide on the game's difficulty or set new tasks that fit the learner's skills which avoids making the game too easy or hard. Thanks to AI, avatars, leaderboards and interactive narratives can be personalized to enhance learning and encourage learners to interact with each other. When gamification uses AI to make learning interesting, people want to learn more, try new things and think creatively. This works very well with young learners and in subjects that repeat over and over such as learning languages and math.

4.5 Accessibility and Inclusivity Improvements via AI

AI is important for helping learners with different needs access and use education more easily. Thanks to speech recognition and synthesis, students who are hard of hearing can watch or listen to spoken words using captions or sign language avatars. Computer vision and image recognition technology allow visually impaired learners to understand visuals and move around learning platforms without seeing them. With the help of AI, translation tools make it easier for people who don't speak a language well to join global education programs. AI also helps by spotting learning disabilities and by making changes to the way content is presented and offering targeted intervention. When AI addresses physical, language and thinking problems, it makes sure all students can succeed at school.

5. AI TO FOSTER CRITICAL THINKING AND HIGHER-ORDER SKILLS

5.1 AI Tools That Encourage Problem-Solving and Reasoning

Educational institutions value critical thinking because it includes problem-solving, reasoning and analysis. These tools are helping students by giving them tough problems that encourage them to think deeply. For example such systems can guide learners by explaining steps one at a time and offering hints relevant to their thought process. With AI, learners can face scenarios from real life that need them to use their knowledge creatively and decide on different solutions which helps them experiment and think deeply. Since the problem difficulty is adjusted based on the student's responses, these tools ensure the student is helped to grow without being overloaded. They also typically supply detailed hints about what was wrong and how to improve the way they think.

5.2 AI in Collaborative Learning and Peer Interaction

Working together helps develop critical thinking by introducing different ideas, teaching negotiation and encouraging people to solve problems as a unit. Artificial intelligence helps promote group learning by managing how peers communicate and by supporting group activities. One way AI is used is by grouping people who have different skills and are looking to learn the same thing, so everyone participates equally. AI can watch for how engaged individuals are and can support quieter students by suggesting things they might share and by helping to address conflicts. These intelligent tools make it possible for students to learn together safely and productively by discussing and building knowledge. AI analyzes information on how students work together and communicate, so teachers can use that information to guide students in teamwork and important discussions.

5.3 Natural Language Processing for Argumentative Writing and Debate Analysis

Natural language processing (NLP) helps people improve their critical thinking by encouraging writing and debate. With the help of AI, students can get feedback on their essay structure, how well they make their arguments and how easy it is for readers to understand their points. With these tools, learners are shown where their arguments have errors, helping them to fix them. To help with debate analysis, NLP algorithms examine arguments to point out important points, opposing arguments and the methods used, giving instant feedback as practice takes place. By helping students think about their language choices and the arguments they build such tools improve their analytical and critical skills. They also help make it possible for everyone to get high-quality feedback which may be rare in regular classrooms because of time limits.

5.4 Challenges and Opportunities for Cultivating Critical Thinking with AI Support

Even though AI can help with critical thinking, a few challenges need to be resolved to get the most out of it. Making certain that AI tools truly involve students in thinking, rather than only getting them to finish simple tasks, is a major challenge. The problem is that giving too much help can weaken students' individuality and make them less willing to discover new ideas. There is still much research being done on AI that supports exploration, questioning and thinking about one's own thinking. Besides, critical thinking changes with the situation and culture which makes it difficult to create AI that works everywhere. A further worry is making sure that AI does not misuse or share personal information about learners. Thanks to explainable AI and multimodal learning analytics, we can now help students learn both the recommendations and the reasons behind them from AI. If you use technology and human coaching together with peer collaboration, it can result in learning models that make the most of each strength. With the growth of AI, it can help improve critical thinking education by offering learning experiences that scale up, are personalized and interactive.

6. CHALLENGES AND ETHICAL CONSIDERATIONS

6.1 Data Privacy and Security in AI Educational Applications

Data privacy and security are some of the biggest problems when trying to use AI in education. Most AI in education uses a lot of sensitive student information which covers personal details, how they study and their achievements. Making sure this data is safe from anyone who should not access it is very important for the trust between learners, educators and parents. Even so, there are complex concerns when it comes to people agreeing to their data being collected, stored and shared on different platforms. Secure encryption, anonymization and proper handling of data should all be used. Students and teachers must be told clearly what information is taken, how it is applied and what they can do about accessing or removing their details. If privacy issues are not dealt with, education AI could lose its ethical credibility and not be used by many.

6.2 Bias and Fairness in AI Algorithms

An AI algorithm will be unbiased only if its training data is unbiased. If data in education reflects old inequalities or cultural beliefs, it can result in unfair situations for some learners and help keep stereotypes alive. As an example such systems can favor certain styles or vocabulary used by people in dominant social groups. In a similar way, recommendation tools tend to favor materials that fit with traditional curricula and ignore diverse topics. Ensuring AI models are free from bias means testing and validating them with many types of people and situations. Various studies are underway to find ways to prevent AI from being biased. When people involved in the system are transparent about their decisions and when they work with stakeholders, bias can be spotted and corrected more easily. The absence of these controls could actually make educational differences worse instead of better.

6.3 Teacher and Student Acceptance and Trust Issues

AI will bring benefits to education mainly if both teachers and students accept and trust it. Skepticism can result from worries about losing their jobs, not being able to make decisions or interacting less with people. There is a possibility that teachers worry AI tools may be used to replace them or prove their decisions wrong. Students could avoid using AI because they are afraid of being watched all the time. One must prove that AI systems are dependable, correct and helpful in teaching to build trust. Educators will be able to use AI tools properly if they learn about both their strengths and weaknesses. Likewise, having clear explanations of how AI is used and safe can put students' minds at ease about data and the fairness of the recommendations. Sharing the process of designing and reviewing AI systems with educators and learners helps everyone feel a connection to what they are taught.

6.4 Impact on Educational Equity and Digital Divide

Even though AI can boost both learning opportunities and standards, it could make existing differences between people even worse. Learners in schools or communities with limited internet may find it hard to use technology-enabled learning. It is also true that not all have the necessary digital skills needed for making good use of these technologies. Since not everyone has access to AI, people are concerned about who profits and who doesn't. It is necessary for decision-makers and groups to focus on creating inclusive infrastructure, offering low-cost technology and training people to use AI to ensure fairness in using AI. In addition, AI systems ought to be made with an eye to many cultural and economic backgrounds so they are relevant and easy to use. AI can be truly helpful in education only if the digital gap is closed.

6.5 Ethical Frameworks and Policy Guidelines

Having clear guidelines and detailed frameworks is necessary to face the ethical issues in AI in education. They ought to include rules about transparency, accountability, fairness, privacy and inclusivity. International groups, governments and schools are coming up with guidelines for ethical AI to respond to these problems. The document, for instance, UNESCO Recommendation on the Ethics of Artificial Intelligence, outlines a worldwide standard that stresses human rights and sustainable development. At an institutional level, AI policies are needed to manage the buying, setting up and testing of AI to comply with ethical and legal rules. Robust governance models can only be developed when educators, technologists, ethicists, policymakers and learners join forces. Committees that watch over ethics and keep monitoring can find unintended results and help with actions to fix them. As a result, including ethics in the development process helps the educational mission and ensures safety for all parties.

7. EVALUATION AND IMPACT OF AI IN EDUCATION

7.1 Metrics and Methodologies for Assessing AI Tools Effectiveness

It's important to test how well AI tools work in education so they help students and teachers reach their goals. Both metrics and various methodologies are used to examine AI-powered applications for education. Typical quantitative measures for students are their test scores, how well they complete assignments, how much time they spend on tasks and their rate of retention. They allow us to assess if using AI helps students improve their learning or improve their abilities. Student and teacher surveys, along with observing how much they use the tools and like them, give us information about how AI is being accepted. Besides, learning analytics give detailed information about learners' actions such as their movements through modules and reactions to personalized help. Scientists use RCTs as the best method to confirm that AI systems cause certain outcomes by comparing groups given the treatment and those who are not. Case studies and longitudinal studies tell us about how programs are implemented and the results they have over time. Besides, using usability testing and expert opinions helps uncover both good and bad aspects of the design. When different methods are combined, we can see the full results of AI in education.

7.2 Empirical Findings from Studies and Experiments

Many research studies have studied AI in schools and found it can help, but there are some points to keep in mind. Studies on Intelligent Tutoring Systems have regularly demonstrated that students do better when learning math and science subjects that require stepwise problem solving. Using adaptive learning platforms has been shown to interest learners more and close the gap between learners by offering specially designed content. Automated systems make grading quicker and offer timely feedback, but researchers say that detailed open-ended problems should still be checked by people. Learning environments that use AI encourage students to work harder and better grasp the main ideas through simulations. AI chatbots are useful for providing support on a large scale which is needed in many large or remote classes. Yet, it is also clear from studies that how a learning program is implemented, the learners' features and the environment can influence its success. It has been pointed out that technology cannot achieve its full potential unless it is used along with teaching methods and teacher involvement.

7.3 Long-Term Impacts on Student Learning Outcomes and Teaching Practices

AI doesn't only help students do well right away; it also affects teaching methods and student learning styles. Over a period, AI can guide students to control their own learning by providing individualized routes and feedback in real time. Because of this shift, students can learn to plan, monitor and review their own development. AI tools give teachers the ability to spot and address student needs, offer differentiated support and automate regular tasks in the classroom. This frees teachers up to work more on creative and people-focused parts of teaching such as mentoring and encouraging critical thinking. Even so, the real impact comes from building teachers' skills to use AI in their teaching. At the same time, people are more interested in how AI helps create equal access to education and if the challenges of bias and digital gaps are solved, AI may make high-quality education accessible to everyone. Since AI is being integrated into education more and more, it is important to constantly watch and adjust our methods to ensure we get the most benefits while avoiding problems.

8. FUTURE DIRECTIONS AND RESEARCH OPPORTUNITIES

8.1 Emerging AI Technologies with Potential in Education

With AI technology progressing rapidly, many recent developments are likely to bring big changes to education. XAI seeks to make the way AI makes decisions easy for users to grasp. In schools, XAI helps teachers and students by explaining the reasons behind personalized suggestions, comments or grades. Showing this information can help students feel more confident and think more about how they learn. AI is also being used in multimodal learning to assess and blend information from various forms—including text, speech, facial expressions and gestures to fully understand a learner's condition. Using multimodal AI can allow teachers to see more clearly a student's engagement, emotions and mental load, helping them intervene when needed. AI's skills in talking with humans will improve as natural language understanding gets better. AI technologies in development give us new ways to make learning more engaging, flexible and focused on the learner.

8.2 Integration of AI with Other Technologies (AR/VR, IoT)

Now, the use of AI in education is tied more and more to technologies such as augmented reality (AR), virtual reality (VR) and the Internet of Things (IoT) (Ponnuviji, N. P et al., 2024; Ganesan, I et al., 2024). Together, these technologies enable creating rich and engaging learning environments on the job. AI makes it possible for VR simulations to develop practical scenarios for learners in medicine, engineering and environmental science where they can practice and learn with no risk. AR allows the addition of information to physical items so students can see abstract ideas in real time(Ponnuviji, N. P et al., 2023; Kokila, M. S et al., 2024). IoT devices can gather real information (e.g. from classroom sensors and wearable gadgets) to make AI systems constantly aware of what affects learning. Information and pacing can change thanks to the integration which keeps students more involved and interested. Research is needed to explore the best ways to combine these technologies and to overcome issues of cost, accessibility and user experience.

8.3 Personalized Critical Thinking Skill Development Frameworks

The goal of providing students with the opportunity to think critically and use higher order skills is still the main goal in education. The new research should search for ways to help all learners develop these skills in their own ways. System should be able to judge each learner's critical thinking and find their weaknesses and assign activities that suit their capability. When AI is married with education psychology and cognitive science, the result is improved and supported intervention strategies. Also, with AI, students should learn to be conscious of how they think, what their biases are and how they decide. Moreover, personalized frameworks could include collaborative and social activities such as talking about, reviewing each other's work and solving problems together, with the assistance of AI. These thorough strategies will be a major part in helping students deal with real world problems requiring thinking, analyzing and combining information.

8.4 Interdisciplinary Research and Collaboration Needs

AI in education will move ahead only if researchers and stakeholders from different fields join forces. Having computer science, education, psychology, ethics and sociology experts join forces is necessary to ensure that AI tools are good for teaching, dependable and benefiting society. It is important that educators work together in making sure AI systems fit what happens in classrooms and what is taught. At the same time, people working in ethics and policy need to deal with fresh concerns about privacy, fairness and accessibility. Together with collaborative research, AI educational tools may be developed to be relevant and accessible in many parts of the world. Academic, industrial and government agencies working together can help bring innovation faster and support the adoption of standards. Sharing educational data and AI models in open repositories could help increase both transparency and growth for everyone. When different areas of education cooperate and communicate, AI can be used to raise teaching, learning and critical thinking around the world.

9. CONCLUSION

The chapter has reviewed the many ways artificial intelligence is changing education, especially by influencing teaching, learning and critical thinking skills. The study shows that AI-based intelligent tutoring, adaptive learning systems and AI chatbots greatly improve how learners interact with their lessons and teachers. Because AI can review a lot of data, students with different learning styles and needs can experience learning that is better suited to them. In addition, using AI encourages students to think critically, solve problems, learn with others and get ready for the challenges they will face in the future. AI can greatly improve education by making it possible to change how we teach and help everyone, no matter where they live, get better education. But we must also pay attention to problems such as privacy, bias in algorithms and the digital gap. In addition, we should help educators and learners trust and accept each other by ensuring there is transparency, strong ethics and meaningful teamwork with AI. We can make the most of AI by doing more research, working together between different fields and making sure designs are inclusive. Suggestions for stakeholders are that teachers should use AI to assist their teaching, rather than rely on it to replace their instruction and that technology should be added to lessons carefully. AI solutions are better when developers place importance on fairness, make them easy to understand and design them with users in mind. Authorities should form detailed rules and ensure fair spending on infrastructure to maintain privacy, teach digital skills and solve access problems. By working together, these efforts can make use of AI to support learning that is both interesting, personalized and important for all students.

REFERENCES

Chen, L., Chen, P., & Lin, Z. (2020). Artificial intelligence in education: A review. *IEEE Access : Practical Innovations, Open Solutions, 8*, 75264–75278. DOI: 10.1109/ACCESS.2020.2988510

Chowdhary, K., & Chowdhary, K. R. (2020). Natural language processing. Fundamentals of artificial intelligence, 603-649.

Dhinakaran, D., Kumar, N. J., & Ponnuviji, N. P. (2025). Safeguarding confidentiality and privacy in cloud-enabled healthcare systems with spectrasafe encryption and dynamic k-anonymity algorithm. *Expert Systems with Applications, 279*, 127584. DOI: 10.1016/j.eswa.2025.127584

Engelbrecht, J., Oates, G., & de Carvalho Borba, M. (2025). *Artificial intelligence and social media in mathematics education. In social media in the changing mathematics classroom*. Springer Nature Switzerland.

Fanni, S. C., Febi, M., Aghakhanyan, G., & Neri, E. (2023). Natural language processing. In *Introduction to artificial intelligence* (pp. 87–99). Springer International Publishing. DOI: 10.1007/978-3-031-25928-9_5

Ganesan, I., Ponnuviji, N. P., Kumar, A. S., Nithya, M., Jambulingam, U., & Lalitha, S. D. (2024). Real-Time Event Detection and Predictive Analytics Using IoT and Deep Learning. In Industry Applications of Thrust Manufacturing: Convergence with Real-Time Data and AI (pp. 1-41). IGI Global Scientific Publishing. DOI: 10.4018/979-8-3693-4276-3.ch001

Hilbert, S., Coors, S., Kraus, E., Bischl, B., Lindl, A., Frei, M., Wild, J., Krauss, S., Goretzko, D., & Stachl, C. (2021). Machine learning for the educational sciences. *Review of Education, 9*(3), e3310. DOI: 10.1002/rev3.3310

Jain, V., Singh, I., Syed, M., Mondal, S., & Palai, D. R. (2024). Enhancing educational interactions: A comprehensive review of AI chatbots in learning environments. In 2024 11th international conference on reliability, infocom technologies and optimization (trends and future directions)(ICRITO) (pp. 1-5). IEEE. DOI: 10.1109/ICRITO61523.2024.10522392

Kokila, M. S., Fenil, E., Ponnuviji, N. P., & Nirmala, G. (2024). Securing cloud-based medical data: An optimal dual kernal support vector approach for enhanced EHR management. *International Journal of System Assurance Engineering and Management, 15*(7), 3495–3507. DOI: 10.1007/s13198-024-02356-1

Lin, C. C., Huang, A. Y., & Lu, O. H. (2023). Artificial intelligence in intelligent tutoring systems toward sustainable education: A systematic review. *Smart Learning Environments, 10*(1), 41. DOI: 10.1186/s40561-023-00260-y

Luan, H., & Tsai, C. C. (2021). A review of using machine learning approaches for precision education. *Journal of Educational Technology & Society, 24*(1), 250–266.

Maheswari, B., & Nagarajan, R. (2024). EduChatbot: Implementing educational Chatbot for assisting the teaching-learning process by NLP-based hybrid heuristic adopted deep learning framework. *Kybernetes.*

Mathew, A. N., Rohini, V., & Paulose, J. (2021). NLP-based personal learning assistant for school education. *International Journal of Electrical and Computer Engineering, 11*(5), 4522–4530. DOI: 10.11591/ijece.v11i5.pp4522-4530

Mir, T. A., Lawaye, A. A., & Khanday, A. M. U. D. (2023). NLP techniques and challenges to process social media data. In *Advanced applications of NLP and deep learning in social media data* (pp. 171–218). IGI Global. DOI: 10.4018/978-1-6684-6909-5.ch009

Pedro, F., Subosa, M., Rivas, A., & Valverde, P. (2019). Artificial intelligence in education: Challenges and opportunities for sustainable development.

Ponnuviji, N. P., Elangovan, G., Sujatha, K., Jambulingam, U., Ganesan, I., & Lalitha, S. D. (2024). IoT-Enabled Assistive Technologies Approach for Personalized Geriatric Health Monitoring and Safety. In Future of AI in Biomedicine and Biotechnology (pp. 125-146). IGI Global. DOI: 10.4018/979-8-3693-3629-8.ch007

Ponnuviji, N. P., Nirmala, G., Kokila, M. S., & Priyadharshini, S. I. (2025). Optimizing Image Retrieval in Cloud Servers with TN-AGW: A Secure and Efficient Approach. Journal of The Institution of Engineers (India): Series B, 106(2), 459-473.

Ponnuviji, N. P., Sumaiya Begum, A., Gnanasekaran, T., Rajendiran, M., & Shenbaga Ezhil, S. (2023, April). Leveraging Random Forest for Intelligent IoT Systems in Industrial Environments. In International Conference on Internet of Things (pp. 46-57). Cham: Springer Nature Switzerland.

Prabhu, D., Tejasri, M. V. S. L., Saratha, B., & Anish, T. P. (2025, April). Future Horizons: Key Trends Shaping the Evolution of Machine Learning. In *2025 8th International Conference on Trends in Electronics and Informatics (ICOEI)* (pp. 1091-1099). IEEE.

Siva Subramanian, R., Nalini, M., & Aswini, J. (Eds.). (2024). *Navigating the Augmented and Virtual Frontiers in Engineering*. IGI Global. DOI: 10.4018/979-8-3693-5613-5

Suresh, D., Lokesh, P., Yamini, B., Yuvasri, B., Sathya, V., Girija, P., & Siva, S. R. (2025). AI Driven Personalization in Education: Transformative Practices and Emerging Trends. *Transformative AI Practices for Personalized Learning Strategies*, 27-46.

Chapter 18
Unfolding the Ethical and Philosophical Implications of AI in Shaping Human-Centered Fields

A. Rahmath Nisha
https://orcid.org/0009-0001-5146-2411
Saveetha School of Management, Saveetha Institute of Medical and Technical Sciences, Chennai, India

A. K. Subramani
https://orcid.org/0000-0003-0783-7113
Saveetha School of Management, Saveetha Institute of Medical and Technical Sciences, Chennai, India

S. Harini
https://orcid.org/0000-0002-3856-7390
Saveetha School of Management, Saveetha Institute of Medical and Technical Sciences, Chennai, India

ABSTRACT

The integration of Artificial Intelligence (AI) into humanist areas in the profession such as healthcare, education, law, and arts provokes significant ethical and philosophical dilemmas. The use of AI in human centered disciplines has a significant contribution in the fast-evolving environment. The philosophical and ethical issues of the implementation of AI as well as human-centered sciences are problematic and multidimensional. Ethics is one of the most urgent philosophical problems of

DOI: 10.4018/979-8-3373-3436-3.ch018

AI in the anthropocentric fields. In AI systems, especially in the health and legal decision-making processes, some ethical issues should be included in the programming of AI systems as it is the bias in the AI decision-making that is responsible of the AI-driven results. Morally, in the delicate and supreme consideration that should take place in these areas, the input of AI causes influence on human creativity, and raises issues regarding the essence of intelligence and authorship; it lessens human reasoning, and decision-making.

1. INTRODUCTION

1.1. Overview of AI's Growing Role in Human-Centric Professions

Artificial Intelligence (AI) has become one of the transformers in any human-related field that redesigns different areas of human life, including education, healthcare, social work, and even the future of the human species. The role of AI is highlighted in the human-centered disciplines and reducing the human control and automating the routine operations. Applications of AI and its effects in these areas highlight the way AI can supplement the human abilities by being ethically and socially responsible.

1.2. Emphasis on AI's Dual Potential

AI has the potential to play very important role in advancing the sustainable development. By aligning the AI systems with human values and to make sure the inclusive access, it can achieve the global objectives. Advancements in generative AI and human-AI collaboration will be vital role for unlocking a wide range of opportunities. These applications can develop the domains like data visualization, healthcare, and legal counsel, which encourages the reliability, safety, and trust. Eventually, they will enhance the human performance while promoting the creativity and accountability (Secinaro et al., 2021). AI's applications in the field of human-centered disciplines, highlights its potential benefits for economic growth and social development and also mentions the ethical concerns like data privacy, biases, and job displacement, entailing ethical frameworks for responsible AI deployment (Tran et al., 2019).

In order to improve energy efficiency, low operating costs, and guarantee sustainability, this chapter investigates the application of artificial intelligence (AI) in monitoring power systems for SMEs. It provides information regarding the existing energy problems, such as SMEs face, emphasizes the real-time observation, and elaborates the advantages of AI integration. It examines AI approaches to identifying trends in energy consumption, including machine learning, deep learning, and predictive analytics (Kumara et al., 2024). The HR executives are changing the leadership style, applying less rigid leadership style, facilitating the independence of the employees, and enhancing the communication channels within the new AI-empowered system of HRM. The research article is an effort of bridging the gap between the theoretic and the real by offering a practice-based guidance to the business owners and human resource managers (Baruah et al., 2024). Artificial intelligence is the intelligence that is exhibited by the robots and resembles the human capabilities of learning and solving problems (Ganta et al., 2023).

2. BACKGROUND OF AI IN HUMAN-CENTERED DISCIPLINES

2.1. Traces AI's Evolution and Scholarly Contributions Over the Last Two Decades

Hasty development and growing aspirations to introduce Artificial Intelligence (AI) into different spheres has characterized the development of AI. In the last twenty years, AI has been witnessing an impressive expansion in the number of contributions and scholarly interest (Shao et al., 2021). The need for AI has become uppermost in addressing global barriers, particularly in the field of human centered development However, the integration of AI faces significant barriers, including data scarcity, restricted technical infrastructure, regulatory deficiency, and socio-economic unevenness (Turyasingura et al., 2024). Moreover, the development of AI has given the opportunity to concentrate the power of research and make the interaction between AI and social sciences difficult (Frank et al., 2019). With the continued development of AI, it is essential to have AI literacy and this is why urgently requires AI literacy, technical expertise, and improved logic in the educational sector to equip society with the AI-based future (Walter, 2024). It provides a summary of the interactions between AI and various fields of interest involving humans and points out some of the primary ethical and philosophical issues, as presented as Table 1.

3. PERSPECTIVES OF AI IN HUMAN CENTERED DISCIPLINES

3.1. AI and Human Intelligence

AI and Human Intelligence: It remains a central argument in the integration of AI in the human centric fields as an extension of human abilities or a possible depiction of human skills. Nonetheless, researchers believe that AI does not possess human intuition, moral thinking, and emotional intelligence (Dreyfus, 1992; Brynjolfsson and McAfee 2017; Luckin, 2018) and this lack of qualities is quite detrimental in such human areas as psychology, social work, and education.

3.2. AI and Ethical Concerns

AI systems are highly trained and include historical information which becomes most urgent ethical issue unless thoroughly elaborated. These prejudices are able to be enhanced and causes unequal results in the sector such as law, healthcare and employment. Transparency and accountability in the area of healthcare like misdiagnosing a patient or unfairly sentencing a patient to legal penalties cause significant ethical issues (Floridi et al., 2018).

Table 1. AI approaches for the Human- Centered Discipline

HUMAN-CENTERED DISCIPLINE	AI APPROACHES	KEY CONSIDERATIONS
Healthcare	AI-driven diagnostics, robotic surgeries, predictive analytics for disease prevention	Patient consent, bias in medical AI, ethical accountability in AI-driven decisions
Education	Personalized learning systems, AI tutoring, automated grading	Data privacy, fairness in AI assessment, teacher-AI collaboration
Law & Justice	AI legal assistants, predictive policing, automated case analysis	Bias in legal AI models, fairness in sentencing, human oversight in legal decisions
Arts & Creativity	AI-generated music, literature, and visual art	Authenticity, authorship, impact on human creativity
Social Sciences	AI in behavioral research, sentiment analysis, policy recommendation	Ethical data collection, bias in AI-driven social studies, transparency in policy-making
Workforce & Economy	AI automation in workplaces, decision-support systems	Job displacement, workforce adaptation, ethical AI deployment in businesses

3.3. AI and Human Centered Decision Making

Evolution of AI, has much to answer the question: to what extent does humans leave the decision making to the AI judgment? In other cases, humans can be inclined to neglect their expertise decision or moral aspects because of excessive confidence in AI predictions that are very high (Rahwan, 2018). The human-oriented approaches to AI suggest a paradigm in which AI is presented as a decision-support system and not as an independent authority in critical areas.

4. THE ETHICS OF AI IN HUMAN CENTERED DISCIPLINES

4.1. Ethical Aspects of AI

The case of an ethical AI in human-related fields that dwell upon the tenets such as transparency, fairness, accountability, and privacy. It emphasizes the measures to reduce the risks like bias and discrimination, when technology is merged with the values of the society and human wellbeing (Balayogi et al., 2025). Ethical systems should be created to make sure that AI technologies are designed and applied in a manner that upholds human rights and is transparent and, in addition, to interpret human emotions, know social clues that will make sure robots allow people to engage and interact meaningfully in their different environments (Zhang et al., 2024). Fairness, transparency, accountability, and privacy are examples of ethical concerns in human-centered AI protection that makes AI systems respect human rights, be free of biases, and empower users, gaining their trust and improving user experiences and aligned with human values and the welfare of society (Usmani et al., 2023).

Table 2. Ethical principles in the AI

ETHICAL PRINCIPLE	DESCRIPTION	REFERENCES
Fairness and Non-Discrimination	AI should avoid biases by ensuring equitable treatment	**(Floridi, 2023)**
Privacy and Data Protection	Users must be informed when the AI is handling the data. AI must ensure security, confidentiality, encryption and must be regulated under proper compliance	**(Pflanzer et al., 2023)**
Transparency and Explainability	Model of Black box should be avoided and decisions should be explainable to users by offering and ensuring trust and ethical accountability	**(Pflanzer et al.,2023)**
Accountability and Governance	Deployment of AI in an organization must take responsibility for its legal liability and ethical issues	**(Ricci, 2023)**
Human Oversight and Control	AI need to assist the human decision making rather than replacing them completely. For the sensitive fields human intervention must remain possible	**Pflanzer et al., (2023)**
Sustainability and Societal Impact	AI design must be energy consumption and zero societal impacts with environmental sustainability	**Pflanzer, et al., (2023)**

4.2. Architecture, Engineering, and Construction (AEC)

AI in the AEC sector area improves architectural processing, the performance of design and engineering, data driven project management, collaboration, and safety, and subsequently boosts human capabilities and aligns systems with human interests and preferences (Rafsanjani and Nabizadeh, 2023).

4.3. Workplace Well-Being

The use of AI in human-related fields, especially in reducing employee burnout, is meaningful when applied with extensive training, high customization, and frequent feedback, resulting in the reduction of burnout rates and enhancement of employee well-being in stressful environments (Meduri et al., 2024).

4.4. Human-Robot Interaction

AI supports social sciences by working towards allowing robots to recognize emotions, comprehend social involvement, and have moral communications. This promotes the quality of communication and cooperation, which eventually enhance the social experience and quality of life in areas such as healthcare, education and customer service (Zhang et al., 2024).

4.5. Complexity and Autonomy of AI

The heightened dangers of AI in the complexity and autonomy, which can provoke weaknesses that exposes human consumers. Such difficulties might have had a serious effect on the technical, regulatory, and societal environment, and provided the crucial consideration of human-centered AI design (Cheruvu, 2022). In another research (Mohan and Ramkumar, 2024), they found out that the best way to manage CP is to identify it in its early stage and thus apply the Artificial Intelligence Assisted Learning Methodology (AIALM) along with a cascaded LeNet architecture. The given strategy enhances the accuracy and efficiency of CP prediction due to the advances in deep learning and artificial intelligence. The Cascaded LeNet architecture was inspired by convolutional neural networks (CNNs) that are supposed to provide the relevant knowledge of CP-related brain images. This is one example of the application of AI to solve complexity in medicine.

5. ALGORITHMIC BIAS AND SOCIETAL IMPACT

The issues of privacy, control, and the possible negative impact on the human life and mental abilities. Perpetuation of societal inequalities, division aggravation with the help of algorithm decision-making, and false expectations are some of the risks of AI in human-centered disciplines. As a technology centered researcher (Xu and Dainoff, 2023), this researcher is prone to failures and accidents, as they are recorded in the AI Incident Database. Human-centered AI solution is necessary to reduce such risks and support interdisciplinary collaboration (Ozmen et al., 2023).

6. HUMAN VS. MACHINE INTELLIGENCE: REDEFINING COGNITION AND CREATIVITY

6.1. Philosophical Debate: Can AI be Creative?

The human capital is described as flexible, emotionally conscious, and self-efficacy to design and generate ideas based on novelty using complex concepts (Gardner, 2011). Unlike, machine intelligence is based on data-driven learning, historical pattern recognition and optimization, which are more efficient but do not have intrinsic self-consciousness and human values context (Russell and Norvig, 2021). Creativity as a factor of human capital which was also thought of as a standard of the quality of human capital is quickly becoming disputed by AI-produced art, music and literature (Boden, 2004). In the meantime, AI is capable of producing copies of human imaginations, by making multiple recombination and rendering probabilistic modelling instead of inspirational or personal experience (Colton and Wiggins, 2012).

There is some doubt in this argument that machine-generated works can be the original or rather, it is just an extrapolation of existing works by humans, produced by the machine. Human and machine intelligence with each other implies that cognition and creativity should be redefined. Instead of displacing human thought, AI can be considered as an augmentative tool, which can be used to expand the human potential. The next discussion should be based on ethical issues and cooperation between the human intuition and machine effectiveness to achieve the greatest benefits of each (Floridi, 2023).

7. THE ROLE OF AI IN SHAPING THE HUMAN IDENTITY AND SOCIAL STRUCTURES

7.1. AI and Identity Formation

The role of AI in the formation of the human identity and social structures through the process of automating the routine tasks as well as offers instant feedback, which improves the self-perception and collective identity. The research emphasizes that although AI has the potential to boost identity formation, it can also pose identity threats under specific task alignment, which will impact the individual and organizational identities (Canbul, 2024). When discussing the idea that AI should not be perceived as its own entity, (Hipolito,2023) points out that this reality is used to dodge ethical designs and bolstered prejudices. It, instead, proposes a vision of AI as a part of human self-determination agencies and emphasizes the effect of AI and identities formation, which is shaping social relations and cultural environment.

7.2. Social Structures and AI

The robotic aspect of AI that can transform human identity and social structures is the opportunity to enhance capabilities and alter functionality and relations. The coexistence of the AI and the society simultaneously present the appearance of the social needs and struggles to the world, limit the changes of the societal patterns. As a result of automation of intellectual labor, intellectual process replacement, and work redistribution, AI shifts in the economic roles, and this aspect has led to creation of the stratification of the society and the creation of the network of high-skilled communities. Ethical and Philosophical Implications: AI is actively re-forming the human identity and social structures by influencing the social relations and agency.

7.3. Ethical and Philosophical Implications

AI is actively reconstructing the human identity and social structures through the impact on social relations and agency. It emphasizes that AI technologies are capable of giving rise to new types of social death that affects human dignity and how people reflect on themselves in the society. Critical phenomenological approach the study highlights the risk of these changes being both ethical and philosophical and calls to reconsider the concept of agency in the world, which is becoming mediated by technology (Arocha,2024). As well, the effects of AI on the working population, such as job displacement, and the necessity to resort to upskilling, further influence social orders. This chapter explores the necessity of responsible AI development to make it beneficial to the entire society (Ashraf and Mustafa, 2025).

8. ETHICAL BOUNDARIES IN AI DECISION-MAKING

8.1. Importance of Ethical Considerations in AI Development

Imaging and electronic medical record (EMR), laboratory diagnosis and treatment, augmentation of intelligence of physicians, new drug discovery, preventive and precision medicine, biological extensive data analysis, acceleration of processes, and data storage availability are some of the roles of AI in healthcare to the health organizations. However, this field of science0020faces number of ethical and legal issues. Despite of these significant advances in the field of AI in communities is not available to all civilizations. Emerging and low-income based countries experiencing lack of access to cutting-edge technology. It should be highlighted that deploying AI presents a number of obstacles which includes ethical boundaries, privacy and data protection, informed permission, social gaps, medical consultation, empathy, and sympathy. Before incorporating artificial intelligence into the healthcare system, practitioners and experts should address the four medical ethics principles, including autonomy, beneficence, nonmaleficence, and justice in all aspects of healthcare (Jahn, 2011; Farhud et al., 1999; Farhud, 2019)

Figure 1. Tommy, the robot nurse, helps keep flesh-and-blood doctors and nurses safe from coronavirus at the Circolo Hospital in Varese, Italy

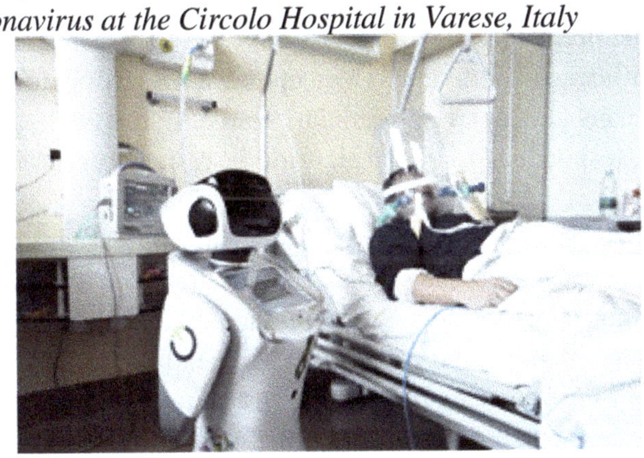

Source: (Pasquale, 2020)

9. KEY ETHICAL PRINCIPLES FOR AI DECISION-MAKING

Artificial intelligence (AI) is quickly invading all aspects of civilization. Algorithms are rapidly making decisions that were traditionally performed by humans, such as determining who is hired, fired, granted a loan, or how long an individual spends in prison (O`neil, 2017). For example, someone could be falsely marked for a crime based on an incorrect yet confident misidentification of the victim using surveillance camera footage analysis. Many AI systems, such as face recognition software, rely on machine learning algorithms which are trained on labeled data. It has recently been demonstrated that algorithms trained on biased data exhibit algorithmic discrimination (Bolukbasi et al., 2016)

10. CHALLENGES IN IMPLEMENTING HUMAN CENTERED AND ETHICAL AI TECHNICAL CHALLENGES

As noted by (Shin, 2023), algorithms ought to be viewed and examined as sociotechnical systems that embody and perpetuate social dynamics, including biases and disparities. The issue of algorithmic bias has received extensive attention. For example, media platforms that utilize biased algorithms can amplify the spread of false information (Giansiracusa, 2021; Shin and Shin, 2023). Such bias in algorithms can stem from flawed human choices. A case in point is a healthcare algorithm, implemented nationally in the United States, that consistently prioritized enrolling White patients into intensive-care programs over Black patients who were in worse health, due to the reliance on medical cost data from insurance claims as a stand-in for healthcare requirements (Obermeyer et al., 2019). Research investigating the factors that might influence individuals' perceptions and reactions to algorithmic bias through experiments and interviews remains scarce. (Parra et al., 2021) examined how participants responded to a biased algorithmic result, specifically whether they would scrutinize the outcome in various everyday situations.

In other words, benefits from a biased algorithm might cause individuals to overlook or dismiss bias negatively impacts other demographic groups (Eslami et al., 2019). This study focuses on specifically race-related algorithmic bias, which often garners more attention and discussion than gender bias, by evaluating facial recognition algorithms known for their improved accuracy with lighter-skinned users and lower performance for those with dark skin tones. This type of skin color-related algorithmic bias has been documented and widely disseminated through the Gender Shade project, which assessed commercial facial recognition technologies developed by leading AI companies like IBM and Microsoft (Buolamwini and Gebru, 2018). Similar concerns in the medical field have also evaluated by the researchers and raised the concerns regarding the absence of transparency and representation in the training datasets used by AI algorithms for diagnosing skin cancer and various diseases (Daneshjou et al., 2021).

10.1. Explainable AI (XAI)

The beauty industry has adopted facial recognition technology as tools for skin analysis and product recommendation based on the analysis, exemplified by L'Oréal's Skin Genius. To explore how the role of Explainable AI (XAI) in aiding bias detection supports colorism, a bias system that favors individuals with lighter skin tones, which is prevalent in both facial recognition algorithms and the beauty industry (Childs, 2022).

The primary objective of the XAI is to assist users in understanding the reasons behind an outcome from the system and help them recognize the system may succeed or fail, and help them to determining when to trust the system or acknowledge its mistakes through clear explanations, user-friendly interfaces, and human-centered around the user, (Gunning, 2019). Increasing research on user evaluation in XAI has generally validated the effectiveness in improving users' understanding of AI systems (Kenny et al., 2021).

This method showcases examples from the training model's dataset that bears similarity to the user input within the model's representation. Such an explanation may be more intuitive and easier to grasp, because it is similar to the way human beings explain processes (Arrieta et al., 2020). The explanation by example method can help create an awareness of the diversity and inclusion problems in the AI systems as it allows the users to consider whether the examples provided are similar or related to their own experiences.

Figure 2. Experiment stimuli is created in line with the AI Skincare site assists in detecting various variables of skin congruency.

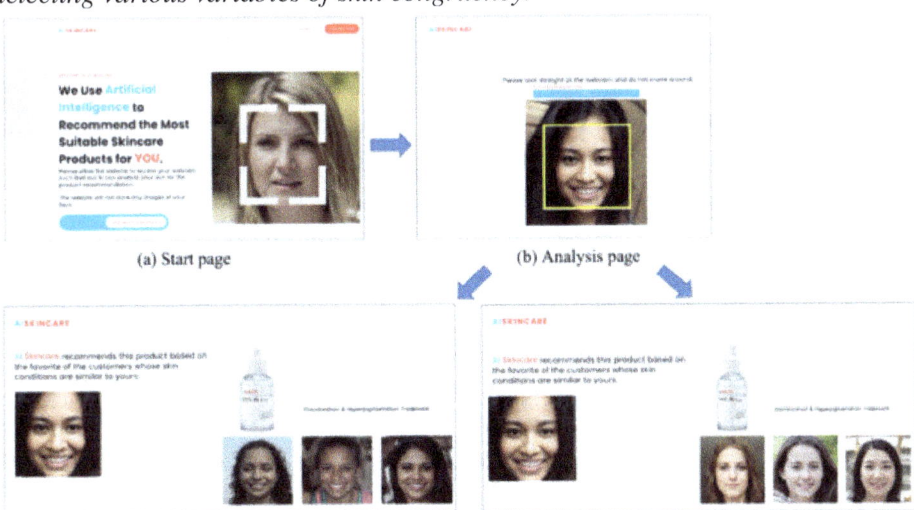

Source: (Wang et al., 2024)

11. STRATEGIES FOR ADDRESSING THE CHALLENGES IN THE ORGANIZATION

The transforming potential of AI is that it will automate the jobs that need to be performed, such as the data categorization, compliance monitoring, and identification of threats that will result in the growth in the productivity of the organization. However, (Dwivedi et al., 2021) not only discusses significant advantages of the possibilities of the AI but also the implementation presents the real-time issue of the balance between automation and human control, as a result, (Díaz-Rodríguez et al., 2023) argues that achieving the balance between the automation and the human control is actually complicated to make sure that the applications of the AI can match the ethical standards, preserve the quality of data, and reduce biases, thus, building an efficient information governance frameworks. It is worth noting that according to (Diaz-Rodriguez et al.,2023) emphasis should be put on an equilibrium approach that bridges the efficiencies of AI with human supervision so that ethical and effective information control are achieved: although AI can significantly enhance efficiency in a way that properties of large data volumes are handled faster and more precisely than by human labor force, enabling quick decision-making and low-cost operations; it is sometimes the advantage of AI and it must be moderated with the potential risks. They argue that the problems regarding data quality can arise in case the information used to construct AI systems is erroneous or biased and leads to detrimental decision-making (Chen et al., 2023). This transition may require an employee to develop the new skills to effectively collaborate with the AI systems, and the organizational culture might need to support automation and AI-centric decision-making (Chen et al., 2023; Wirtz et al., 2020)

11.1. Balancing Automation and Human Oversight

Automation and human oversight should be balanced for making an effective, ethical, and trustworthy decisions in the information governance. While AI excels in processing the large volume of data and detecting the patterns that may be ignored by the humans which makes judgment remains indispensable particularly in AI-generated insights. As highlighted by (Olaniyi et al., 2023), human oversight is crucial in the strategic decisions, as it guarantees that AI's support rather than not completely replacing the human judgment. Similarly, (Díaz-Rodríguez et al., 2023) also emphasizes that, AI is effective in handling day to day tasks, which requires human inputs for decision making for understanding the context, ethics, and long-term ramifications; thus, enhancing a collaborative dynamic between AI and human oversights.

11.2. Societal Challenges

Unbeknownst to the public, algorithms are substituting traditional public servants in various frontline services (Gaozhao et al., 2024). The shift to modern algorithms in place of public servants has altered citizen perceptions regarding the performance and quality of public institutions (Gaozhao et al., 2024; Quinn et al., 2021). In certain instances, algorithms can give biased decisions which impacts citizen's government benefits. Such incidents lead to emotional distress and unnecessary frustration for both citizens and public servants (Eubanks, 2018; Gaozhao et al., 2024). It is clear that the earlier model of public organizations, which heavily depended on human resources, must be revised to meet the increasing citizen demand for electronic services and to adapt to changing conditions (Kemper and Kolkman, 2019).

11.3. Public Attitudes Towards AI

Public sentiment often goes overlooked when it comes to AI governance and policy execution (Wilson 2022). The implementation of AI in the public sector is expected to enhance public value (Criado and Gil-Garcia, 2019; Kieslich et al., 2021), yet advancements in technology bring both beneficial and adverse effects. Both governments and the private sector maintain the perspective that "people might willingly embrace new technologies, even if they do not engage with or utilize them" (Kieslich et al., 2021). This general public is skeptical about the adequacy of the evidence backing the incorporation of AI technology in public organizations and the provision of public services. As a matter of fact, increasing pressure is mounted on public agencies to provide the public values as quickly as possible on limited resources (Criado and Gil-Garcia, 2019; Kieslich et al., 2021). At the same time, the tech sector still puts pressure on the public bodies purporting that the challenges of offering public services and goods in a short time frame can be resolved by using AI. Depending on different conditions, people are molded to have a certain attitude towards AI-managed government services. However, in some cases, AI algorithms are unpredictable, make discriminatory and biased decisions, and require additional changes to reduce legal problems (Wenzelburger et al., 2024). Most people find AI useful in information processing; nevertheless, some groups of people, especially belonging to the marginalized sections, experience racial discrimination and see no ethical concerns of AI (Gaozhao et al., 2024).

12. STRATEGIES FOR ADDRESSING CHALLENGES

12.1. Ethical AI Design Principles and Human-Centered AI Approaches

The ethical implications of the AI systems development are highly significant to make sure that they are based on the principles of fairness, transparency, and accountability. The problem of impartiality may arise when the datasets are biased or algorithmic judgments are somehow unfair towards particular populations. The AI transparency should be understandable and explicable to users which generates trust and allows checking the results of algorithm work. The measures of accountability play a crucial role in making sure that both developers and users are liable to the outcomes of AI systems.

The ways of minimizing bias, how to make AI explainable and regulatory systems are examples of how to address ethical issues in AI development. The trends of the current time suggest that the interdisciplinary cooperation of ethicists, technologists, policymakers, and other interested parties is possible to develop ethical principles and rules in relation to AI usage. The ethical concerns should be guaranteed with the development of AI including fairness, transparency, and accountability. Such important works are (Jobin et al., 2019) a detailed overview of the ethical concerns of AI and (Floridi and Sanders, 2004) a discussion of the ethical implications of AI and data science. To be user-centric on the AI systems feature the introduction of multimodal interfaces, personalization of the user experiences, and the introduction of AI to daily devices and applications all is the new trend. Designing AI UX The principles of user-centered design are increasingly becoming crucial and AI systems can be enhanced with references to the methods of iterative design and user testing are enhanced with references to the feedback of users. Among the valuable readings, there is the book by Norman "The Design of Everyday Things" (2013) and the book by Nielsen Usability Engineering (1993).

12.2. Developing Transparent, Accountable AI Systems

The moral component of AI systems responsibility and visibility is also a critical aspect especially in matters of bias mitigation. Since AI is increasingly integrated into our society, it is critical to make sure the implementation process is fair and accountable (Mensah, 2023). The possible fears of biasness in the AI systems have been alarming as they are likely to mirror the prejudices in the training data. Amazon's recruitment tool, designed using machine learning to evaluate resumes and identify the top candidates for job openings is one of the notable examples for this (Dastin, 2022).

Transparency in AI algorithms helps in building users' trust. By delivering clear insights about the algorithms, developers can trust that users grasp and trust the decisions made by AI systems. (Rajkomar et al.,2018) explored that doctors were more ready to trust an AI system when they could follow the foundational protocol and reasoning behind its suggestions which enables healthcare professionals to make well-informed decisions, which ultimately leads to improved patient care.

Moreover, the companies are reluctant to disclose proprietary information, as it could lead them to lose the trade secrets. This lack of transparency leads to distrust among the users and blocks the acceptance of AI in human centered disciplines. Researchers have been investigating possible solutions, including explainable AI models and open-source platforms to overcome these obstacles with explainable AI models that seek to provide understandable outputs (Caruana et al., 2015).

12.3. Policy and Regulatory Frameworks to Ensure Fairness and Equity

Fairness metrics are the preliminary technical frameworks for designing the fair AI which indicates that it is impossible to satisfy multiple fairness standards simultaneously (Chouldechova, 2017; Kleinberg et al., 2016). These fairness AI not only do multiple fairness standards conflict with each other (Alves et al., 2023), but they also clash with other critical aspects of AI systems, such as predictive accuracy (Menon and Williamson, 2018), calibration (Pleiss et al., 2017), impact (Jorgensen et al., 2023), and privacy (Cummings et al., 2019), for which Pareto optimality must be considered (Wei and Niethammer, 2022).

Additionally, selecting a fairness metric necessitates accounting for several competing goals: stakeholders' utility, alignment with human values (Friedler et al., 2021), the general public's actual perception of fairness (Saha et al., 2020), and legal as well as normative constraints (Xenidis, 2020; Kroll, 2015). The manner in which various objectives and requirements are pursued, articulated, and formalized influences the selection of fairness metrics and, consequently, the design of an AI system (Passi and Barocas, 2019)—an illustration of the framing effect bias, as demonstrated. Even when focusing on a specific fairness standard, there arises the challenge of measuring the extent of unfairness. Actually, even the most obvious choices related to algebraic operations (such as the difference or ratio of proportions) may bear a lot of consequences. According to (Pedreschi et al., 2012), the largest risk difference of top-k protected subgroups by law are not equal to the largest risk difference of top-k with the largest selective risk ratio. As such, the choice of options to emphasize discrimination in one way might not identify or prevent discrimination in a different way.

13. CONTRIBUTION

13.1. Ethical Artificial Intelligence in Decision Making Fields

In identifying the ethical dilemma that exists in the interaction of AI and various fields of study. As it has been heard, AI technologies, simulating human intelligence and performing the tasks that require human cognitive skills, raise numerous ethical issues that span beyond the boundaries of disciplines. In the center of these dilemmas lies the debate over the potential benefits of AI and also some demerits it poses to people and society. The possibilities of AI in healthcare are enormous, along with improvements in the educational process and efficient optimization of the resource allocation. It also augments the ethical considerations linked with the bias in the algorithm, invasion of privacy and losing of work, as well as destruction of the autonomy of human beings (Jack et al., 2012). We have the cross functional approach that is based on the crucial inter-relatedness of the technological advances, ethical issues, and social responsibility. Moreover, it emphasizes the need to solve the ethical dilemma before its emergence as a way of making sure that AI is beneficial to the entire society and to improve the lives of people (Muniandi et al., 2019; Nazat, 2024).

13.2. Philosophical Discussions on AI Cognition and Creativity

The artificial intelligence (AI) has opened new possibilities of creative activities in the period of the fast-changing digital era. Advanced generative deep learning systems have not only been shown to be able to solve complex problems, such as drug and protein synthesis (Jumper et al., 2021), but also in artistic areas, such as poetry writing and narration (Franceschelli and Musolesi, 2024). The need to study creativity was heightened as the generative capabilities of AI tend to blur the boundaries between human-created and machine-created creations, which is why the need to study creativity is even more significant, especially in relation to AI.

The history of humanity has seen human creativity being studied in-depth in several areas, such as psychology, philosophy, and cognitive science (Kirkpatrick, 2023). Nevertheless, there is still no consensus on the definition of what constitutes creativity, which is mostly related to the subjective features of various definitions in the academic literature (Runco and Jaeger, 2012; Sawyer 2012). Besides, more sophisticated AI models are pre-programmed to generate results that resemble the data they were trained on (Foster, 2022). It raises such essential questions about authenticity of their work as whether they are genuine, or merely a collection of pieces (Somepalli et al., 2023).

Figure 3. Relative Creativity (a) and Statistical Creativity (b). (a): Relative Creativity measured based on the ability of AI to create artwork that is similar to the work of a fictional human being due to the same biographical factors. (b): Statistical Creativity measured based on the ability of AI to generate responses to prompts that are similar to the work of a fictional human artist as identified with a distribution distance metric.

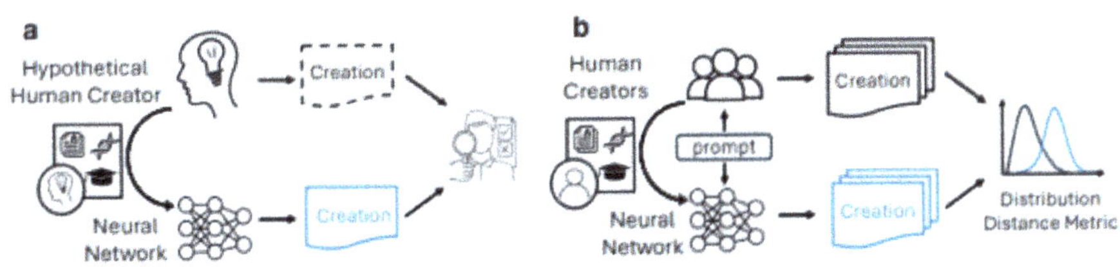

Source: (Wang et al.,2024)

This research aims at building a strong paradigm on researching creativity in artificial intelligence. Our starting point is a hypothetical situation: imagine an AI creates a work of art, and he has not seen anything like it before. This art produced by AI was not noticed during the past 20 years. A human artist makes the same work and is acclaimed independently many years later, which is a question that is very intriguing. In the case the previous invention by the AI has to be treated as a creative invention, since it pre-dates the identification of the human artist, even before this new artist was born? The rational response would be yes. This mind experiment pushes us out of the conventional approaches to answering the question, Is AI capable of creativity? --question that is mired in the difficult and unclear task of defining creativity in some certain way--to a more concrete one: Can AI be compared to human creativity?

13.3. Policy Recommendation for Responsible AI Governance

The AI governance has been born as a result of the need to understand, control, and manage, direct, and determine AI technology, as well as the institutions and settings in which its surrounds. development (Dafoe, 2018). Donations to the AI governance of people may be categorized into three. major categories (Sigfrids et al., 2022). The former type includes contributions that suggest large-scale governance regimes and are aimed at developing the holistic view on the broad systemic socio-technical phenomenon and can provide larger groups of integrated means and measures to govern such phenomena. Such contributions differ with regards to the focus on either soft governance mechanisms (not legal like informational approaches) and hard governance (legal regulations). In some of those works, a more lenient approach to the self-organization of AI developers is provided, and the regulation of the population is described by the provision of public governance in the framework of which development must take place (Wirtz et al., 2020; de Almeida et al., 2021).

The second category will focus on how the AI should be governed by the people. The specific contributions which relate to these efforts are those which deal with the practical governance processes and principles that should be the guiding principle of these efforts. It has focused on how to plan stakeholder interaction and social discussion (Sun and Medaglia, 2019; Ulnicane et al., 2021), the character of the regulatory and steering process, and the need to implement long-term and adaptable governance strategies and practices (Liu and Maas, 2021). Altogether, the articles in this section hold the position that governance ought to support the use of good governance and AI ethics principles (Sigfrids et al., 2022).

The third group directly concerns the issue of the ways in which the principles of ethics and human rights may be integrated into policy making using tangible instruments and mechanisms. To some extent, this category coincides with the second category. The third category (Contributors (Yeunget al., 2019)) emphasizes a major problem namely, the lack of applicability of proposed AI ethics principles and frameworks into real-world AI policy and development practices. However, when the rules and principles of AI ethics are applied as the basis of governance, the political aspect of the matter is frequently overlooked during the discussions. The authors have mentioned that it is common to view ethical guidelines as a distraction in the context of working conditions, environmental impact, and significant cultural changes (Crawford et al., 2016).

14. PRACTICAL RELEVANCE

14.1. Healthcare Educators

The present situation in the sphere of clinical activity in healthcare, which is determined by the increased use of AI, indicates one alarming aspect of the situation development, the lack of knowledge of physicians about the new technology. Although the use of AI in the field of health becomes more and more popular, many clinicians have insufficient knowledge of its features, constraints, and implications (Rajpurkar et al., 2022). Clinicians will have more chances to evaluate and implement the AI tools in a moral context and promote the appropriate practice with safety measures by developing a solid presence in the AI (Gilbert, 2024). This plan may be compared to the ongoing initiatives that are geared toward the optimization of clinical activity to address antimicrobial resistance (AMR) or to implement antimicrobial stewardship (Chetty et al., 2024).

14.2. Opportunities in Legal Sector

Table 3. AI impact on legal sector

BENEFITS	DESCRIPTION	IMPACT ON LEGAL PRACTICE
Efficiency in Case Management	AI can systematically organize and categorize case files, schedule tasks, and automatically track deadlines.	It alleviates the administrative workload, allowing legal professionals to concentrate on strategy.
Streamlined Legal Research	AI-driven tools can sift through extensive legal databases to pinpoint pertinent precedents and statutes.	This speeds up research, ensuring that lawyers have access to the most relevant information.
Enhanced Decision-Making	AI technologies offer predictive analytics to evaluate potential case outcomes based on historical data.	This empowers lawyers and clients to make well-informed choices regarding litigation strategies.

15. CONCLUSION

This chapter introduces a person to the fact that the merging of AI is linked to profound ethical and philosophical issues. The paper also points at the necessity of striking a balance between the capabilities of the AI and the human centered disciplines in order to make the AI implementation responsible. Ethical concerns in AI include minimization of biases, belief in transparency, and responsibility legitimation in the decision-making process. The issue of AI on human cognition, creativity, and social organization should be carefully considered to avoid the negative implications. With these difficulties, there should be a moderate way with human moral sense and supervision. Besides, there must be an improvement in public awareness and knowledge of AI to make people responsible to work with it. To conclude, AI should not be viewed as a complement to human intelligence, but rather as a tool that will complement its capabilities. The inclusion of AI in human centered disciplines will also require a keen management team, ethical insights and a low tolerance to compromising the human life conditions. These are the factors that we can deal with in advance to help us create a future where AI and humans live side by side and foster the innovation.

REFERENCES

. Alves, G., Bernier, F., Couceiro, M., Makhlouf, K., Palamidessi, C., & Zhioua, S. (2023). Survey on fairness notions and related tensions. *EURO journal on decision processes, 11,* 100033. DOI: 10.1016/j.ejdp.2023.100033

Arocha, J. G. (2024). Artificial Intelligence and the New Dynamics of Social Death: A Critical Phenomenological Inquiry. https://doi.org/DOI: 10.31219/osf.io/vnfmj

Arrieta, A. B., Díaz-Rodríguez, N., Del Ser, J., Bennetot, A., Tabik, S., Barbado, A., & Herrera, F. (2020). Explainable Artificial Intelligence (XAI): Concepts, taxonomies, opportunities and challenges toward responsible AI. *Information Fusion, 58,* 82–115. https://arxiv.org/abs/1910.10045. DOI: 10.1016/j.inffus.2019.12.012

Ashraf, Z. A., & Mustafa, N. (2025). Role of AI in Transforming Society. In Qidwai, M. (Ed.), *Intersection of Human Rights and AI in Healthcare* (pp. 431–452). IGI Global Scientific Publishing., DOI: 10.4018/979-8-3693-7051-3.ch018

Balayogi, G., Vijaya Lakshmi, A., & Sophie, S. L. (2025). Human-Centric Ethical AI in the Digital World. In Bhattacharya, P., Hassan, A., Liu, H., & Bhushan, B. (Eds.), *Ethical Dimensions of AI Development* (pp. 175–196). IGI Global Scientific Publishing., DOI: 10.4018/979-8-3693-4147-6.ch008

Baruah, A., Shaikh, M., Kumar, R. M., Shaikh, I. A. K., & Thomas, S. N. (2024, April). Artificial Intelligence Influence on Leadership Styles in Human Resource Management for Employee Engagement. In *2024 Ninth International Conference on Science Technology Engineering and Mathematics (ICONSTEM)* (pp. 1-5). IEEE. DOI: 10.1109/ICONSTEM60960.2024.10568819

Boden, M. A. (2004). *The creative mind: Myths and mechanisms.* Routledge. DOI: 10.4324/9780203508527

Bolukbasi, T., Chang, K. W., Zou, J. Y., Saligrama, V., & Kalai, A. T. (2016). Man is to computer programmer as woman is to homemaker? debiasing word embeddings. *Advances in Neural Information Processing Systems,* •••, 29.

Brynjolfsson, E., & McAfee, A. (2017). *No. 1* (Vol. 4). Machine, platform, crowd: Harnessing our digital future. WW Norton & Company.

Buolamwini, J., & Gebru, T. (2018). Gender shades: Intersectional accuracy disparities in commercial gender classification. In *Conference on fairness, accountability and transparency* (pp. 77-91). PMLR. https://proceedings.mlr.press/v81/buolamwini18a.html.

Caruana, R., Lou, Y., Gehrke, J., Koch, P., Sturm, M., & Elhadad, N. (2015, August). Intelligible models for healthcare: Predicting pneumonia risk and hospital 30-day readmission. *In Proceedings of the 21th ACM SIGKDD international conference on knowledge discovery and data mining* (pp. 1721-1730). DOI: 10.1145/2783258.2788613

Chen, P., Wu, L., & Wang, L. (2023). AI Fairness in Data Management and Analytics: A Review on Challenges, Methodologies and Applications. *Applied Sciences (Basel, Switzerland), 13*(18), 10258. DOI: 10.3390/app131810258

Cheruvu, R. (2022). Unconventional concerns for human-centered artificial intelligence. *Computer, 55*(7), 46–55. DOI: 10.1109/MC.2022.3170423

Chetty, S., Swe-Han, K. S., Mahabeer, Y., Pillay, A., & Essack, S. Y. (2024). Interprofessional education in antimicrobial stewardship, a collaborative effort. *JAC-Antimicrobial Resistance, 6*(2), dlae054. Advance online publication. DOI: 10.1093/jacamr/dlae054

Childs, K. M. (2022). "The shade of it all": How Black women use Instagram and YouTube to contest colorism in the beauty industry. *Social Media + Society, 8*(2), 20563051221107634. DOI: 10.1177/20563051221107634

Chouldechova, A. (2017). Fair prediction with disparate impact: A study of bias in recidivism prediction instruments. *Big Data, 5*(2), 153–163. DOI: 10.1089/big.2016.0047

Colton, S., & Wiggins, G. A. (2012). Computational creativity: The final frontier? In *ECAI 2012* (pp. 21–26). IOS Press.

Crawford, K., Whittaker, M., Elish, M. C., Barocas, S., Plasek, A., & Ferryman, K. (2016). The Social and Economic Implications of Artificial Intelligence Technologies in the Near-Term. *In AI Now Public Symposium.*

Criado, J. I., & Gil-Garcia, J. R. (2019). Creating public value through smart technologies and strategies: From digital services to artificial intelligence and beyond. *International Journal of Public Sector Management, 32*(5), 438–450. DOI: 10.1108/IJPSM-07-2019-0178

Cummings, R., Gupta, V., Kimpara, D., & Morgenstern, J. (2019). On the compatibility of privacy and fairness. In *Adjunct publication of the 27th conference on user modeling, adaptation and personalization* (pp. 309-315). DOI: 10.1145/3314183.3323847

Dafoe, A. (2018). AI governance: a research agenda. *Governance of AI Program, Future of Humanity Institute, University of Oxford: Oxford, UK, 1442,* 1443. http://www.fhi.ox.ac.uk/govaiagenda

Daneshjou, R., Smith, M. P., Sun, M. D., Rotemberg, V., & Zou, J. (2021). Lack of transparency and potential bias in artificial intelligence data sets and algorithms: A scoping review. *JAMA Dermatology, 157*(11), 1362–1369. DOI: 10.1001/jama-dermatol.2021.3129

Dastin, J. (2022). Amazon scraps secret AI recruiting tool that showed bias against women. In *Ethics of data and analytics* (pp. 296–299). Auerbach Publications. DOI: 10.1201/9781003278290-44

De Almeida, P. G. R., dos Santos, C. D., & Farias, J. S. (2021). Artificial intelligence regulation: A framework for governance. *Ethics and Information Technology, 23*(3), 505–525. DOI: 10.1007/s10676-021-09593-z

Díaz-Rodríguez, N., Del Ser, J., Coeckelbergh, M., de Prado, M. L., Herrera-Viedma, E., & Herrera, F. (2023). Connecting the dots in trustworthy Artificial Intelligence: From AI principles, ethics, and key requirements to responsible AI systems and regulation. *Information Fusion, 99*, 101896. DOI: 10.1016/j.inffus.2023.101896

Dreyfus, H. L. (1992). *What computers still can't do: A critique of artificial reason.* MIT press.

Dwivedi, Y. K., Hughes, L., Ismagilova, E., Aarts, G., Coombs, C., Crick, T., & Williams, M. D. (2021). Artificial Intelligence (AI): Multidisciplinary perspectives on emerging challenges, opportunities, and agenda for research, practice and policy. *International Journal of Information Management, 57*, 101994. DOI: 10.1016/j.ijinfomgt.2019.08.002

Eslami, M., Vaccaro, K., Lee, M. K., Elazari Bar On, A., Gilbert, E., & Karahalios, K. (2019, May). User attitudes towards algorithmic opacity and transparency in online reviewing platforms. In *Proceedings of the 2019 CHI Conference on Human Factors in Computing Systems* (pp. 1-14). DOI: 10.1145/3290605.3300724

Eubanks, V. (2018). *Automating inequality: How high-tech tools profile, police, and punish the poor.* St. Martin's Press.

Farhud, D. (2019). Epigenetic and Ethics: How are Ethical Traits Inherited? . *International Journal of Ethics and Society, 1*(3), 1–4. http://ijethics.com/article-1-53-en.html

Farhud, D. D., Nickzat, N., & Mahmoodi, M. (1999). VIEWS OF GROUP OF PHISICIANS, NURCES AND MIDWIVES ON ETHICAL PRINCIPLES IN MEDICAL GENETICS, IN TEHRAN. *Iranian Journal of Public Health, 28*(1-4), 193–198.

. Floridi, L. (2023). The ethics of artificial intelligence: Principles, challenges, and opportunities.

Floridi, L., Cowls, J., Beltrametti, M., Chatila, R., Chazerand, P., Dignum, V., Luetge, C., Madelin, R., Pagallo, U., Rossi, F., Schafer, B., Valcke, P., & Vayena, E. (2018). AI4People—an ethical framework for a good AI society: Opportunities, risks, principles, and recommendations. *Minds and Machines*, *28*(4), 689–707. DOI: 10.1007/s11023-018-9482-5

Floridi, L., & Sanders, J. W. (2004). On the morality of artificial agents. *Minds and Machines*, *14*(3), 349–379. DOI: 10.1023/B:MIND.0000035461.63578.9d

Foster, D. (2022). *Generative deep learning*. O'Reilly Media, Inc.

Franceschelli, G., & Musolesi, M. (2024). On the creativity of large language models. *AI & Society*, •••, 1–11. DOI: 10.1007/s00146-024-02127-3

Frank, M. R., Wang, D., Cebrian, M., & Rahwan, I. (2019). The evolution of citation graphs in artificial intelligence research. *Nature Machine Intelligence*, *1*(2), 79–85. DOI: 10.1038/s42256-019-0024-5

Friedler, S. A., Scheidegger, C., & Venkatasubramanian, S. (2021). The (im)possibility of fairness: Different value systems require different mechanisms for fair decision making. *Communications of the ACM*, *64*(4), 136–143. DOI: 10.1145/3433949

Ganta, L., Sinduja, P., & Priyadharshini, R. (2023, March). Knowledge And Awareness Of the Use of Artificial Intelligence In Digital Pathology. In *2023 International Conference on Business Analytics for Technology and Security (ICBATS)* (pp. 1-6). IEEE. DOI: 10.1109/ICBATS57792.2023.10111238

Gaozhao, D., Wright, J. E.II, & Gainey, M. K. (2024). Bureaucrat or artificial intelligence: People's preferences and perceptions of government service. *Public Management Review*, *26*(6), 1498–1525. DOI: 10.1080/14719037.2022.2160488

Gardner, H. E. (2011). *Frames of mind: The theory of multiple intelligences*. Basic books.

Giansiracusa, N. (2021). Crafted by Computer: Artificial Intelligence Now Generates Headlines, Articles, and Journalists. In *How Algorithms Create and Prevent Fake News: Exploring the Impacts of social media, Deepfakes, GPT-3, and More* (pp. 17-39). Berkeley, CA: Apress. DOI: 10.1007/978-1-4842-7155-1_2

Gilbert, S. (2024). The EU passes the AI Act and its implications for digital medicine are unclear. *NPJ Digital Medicine*, *7*(1), 135. DOI: 10.1038/s41746-024-01116-6

Gunning, D., & Aha, D. (2019). DARPA's explainable artificial intelligence (XAI) program. *AI Magazine*, *40*(2), 44–58. DOI: 10.1609/aimag.v40i2.2850

. Hipólito, I. (2023). The Human Roots of Artificial Intelligence.

Jack, G., Greenwood, M., & Schapper, J. (2012). Frontiers, intersections and engagements of ethics and HRM. *Journal of Business Ethics, 111*(1), 1–12. DOI: 10.1007/s10551-012-1427-y

Jahn, W. T. (2011). The 4 basic ethical principles that apply to forensic activities are respect for autonomy, beneficence, nonmaleficence, and justice. *Journal of Chiropractic Medicine, 10*(3), 225–226. DOI: 10.1016/j.jcm.2011.08.004

Jobin, A., Ienca, M., & Vayena, E. (2019). The global landscape of AI ethics guidelines. *Nature Machine Intelligence, 1*(9), 389–399. DOI: 10.1038/s42256-019-0088-2

Jorgensen, M., Richert, H., Black, E., Criado, N., & Such, J. (2023, August). Not so fair: The impact of presumably fair machine learning models. In *Proceedings of the 2023 AAAI/ACM Conference on AI, Ethics, and Society* (pp. 297-311). DOI: 10.1145/3600211.3604699

. Jumper, J., Evans, R., Pritzel, A., Green, T., Figurnov, M., Ronneberger, O., ... & Hassabis, D. (2021). Highly accurate protein structure prediction with AlphaFold. *nature, 596*(7873), 583-589.

Kemper, J., & Kolkman, D. (2019). Transparent to whom? No algorithmic accountability without a critical audience. *Information Communication and Society, 22*(14), 2081–2096. DOI: 10.1080/1369118X.2018.1477967

Kenny, E. M., Ford, C., Quinn, M., & Keane, M. T. (2021). Explaining black-box classifiers using post-hoc explanations-by-example: The effect of explanations and error-rates in XAI user studies. *Artificial Intelligence, 294*, 103459. DOI: 10.1016/j.artint.2021.103459

Kieslich, K., Lünich, M., & Marcinkowski, F. (2021). The threats of artificial intelligence scale (TAI) development, measurement and test over three application domains. *International Journal of Social Robotics, 13*(7), 1563–1577. DOI: 10.1007/s12369-020-00734-w

Kirkpatrick, K. (2023). Can AI demonstrate creativity? *Communications of the ACM, 66*(2), 21–23. DOI: 10.1145/3575665

Kleinberg, J., Mullainathan, S., & Raghavan, M. (2016). Inherent trade-offs in the fair determination of risk scores. *arXiv preprint arXiv:1609.05807*. https://doi.org//arXiv.1609.05807DOI: 10.48550

Kroll, J. A. (2015). Accountable algorithms (Doctoral dissertation, Princeton University).

Kumara, V., & Sharma, M. D., Samson Isaac, J., Saravanan, S., Suganthi, D., & Boopathi, S. (2024). An AI-Integrated Green Power Monitoring System: Empowering Small and Medium Enterprises. In V. Jain, M. Raman, A. Agrawal, M. Hans, & S. Gupta (Eds.), *Convergence Strategies for Green Computing and Sustainable Development* (pp. 218-244). IGI Global Scientific Publishing. DOI: 10.4018/979-8-3693-0338-2.ch013

Liu, H. Y., & Maas, M. M. (2021). 'Solving for X?'Towards a problem-finding framework to ground long-term governance strategies for artificial intelligence. *Futures*, *126*, 102672. DOI: 10.1016/j.futures.2020.102672

. Luckin, R. (2018). *Machine Learning and Human Intelligence. The future of education for the 21st century.* UCL institute of education press.

Meduri, K., Nadella, G. S., Gonaygunta, H., Kumar, D., Addula, S. R., Satish, S., Maturi, M. H., & Rehman, S. U. (2024). Human-centered AI for personalized workload management: A multimodal approach to preventing employee burnout. *Journal of Infrastructure. Policy and Development*, *8*(9), 6918. DOI: 10.24294/jipd.v8i9.6918

Menon, A. K., & Williamson, R. C. (2018). The cost of fairness in binary classification. In *Conference on Fairness, accountability and transparency* (pp. 107-118). PMLR. https://proceedings.mlr.press/v81/menon18a.html.

. Mensah, G. B. (2023). Artificial intelligence and ethics: a comprehensive review of bias mitigation, transparency, and accountability in AI Systems. *Preprint, November, 10*(1), 1.

Mohan, P. P., & Ramkumar, G. (2024, April). Experimental evaluation of brain cerebral palsy disease prediction using artificial intelligence assisted learning methodology. In *2024 Ninth International Conference on Science Technology Engineering and Mathematics (ICONSTEM)* (pp. 1-7). IEEE. DOI: 10.1109/ICONSTEM60960.2024.10568758

Muniandi, B., Huang, C. J., Kuo, C. C., Yang, T. F., Chen, K. H., Lin, Y. H., Lin, S.-R., & Tsai, T. Y. (2019). A 97% maximum efficiency fully automated control turbo boost topology for battery chargers. *IEEE Transactions on Circuits and Systems. I, Regular Papers*, *66*(11), 4516–4527. DOI: 10.1109/TCSI.2019.2925374

Nazat, S., Arreche, O., & Abdallah, M. (2024). On evaluating black-box explainable AI methods for enhancing anomaly detection in autonomous driving systems. *Sensors (Basel)*, *24*(11), 3515. DOI: 10.3390/s24113515

Obermeyer, Z., Powers, B., Vogeli, C., & Mullainathan, S. (2019). Dissecting racial bias in an algorithm used to manage the health of populations. *Science*, *366*(6464), 447–453. DOI: 10.1126/science.aax2342

Olaniyi, O. O., Abalaka, A., & Olabanji, S. O. (2023). Utilizing big data analytics and business intelligence for improved decision-making at leading fortune company. *Journal of Scientific Research and Reports*, *29*(9), 64–72. https://ssrn.com/abstract =4571876. DOI: 10.9734/jsrr/2023/v29i91785

Ozmen Garibay, O., Winslow, B., Andolina, S., Antona, M., Bodenschatz, A., Coursaris, C., Falco, G., Fiore, S. M., Garibay, I., Grieman, K., Havens, J. C., Jirotka, M., Kacorri, H., Karwowski, W., Kider, J., Konstan, J., Koon, S., Lopez-Gonzalez, M., Maifeld-Carucci, I., & Xu, W. (2023). Six human-centered artificial intelligence grand challenges. *International Journal of Human-Computer Interaction*, *39*(3), 391–437. DOI: 10.1080/10447318.2022.2153320

Parra, C. M., Gupta, M., & Dennehy, D. (2021). Likelihood of questioning ai-based recommendations due to perceived racial/gender bias. *IEEE Transactions on Technology and Society*, *3*(1), 41–45. DOI: 10.1109/TTS.2021.3120303

Pasquale, F. (2020). Liability for Medical Robot Malfunctions: Adapting Malpractice Principles. https://coilink.org/20.500.12592/kv8m95

Passi, S., & Barocas, S. (2019, January). Problem formulation and fairness. In *Proceedings of the conference on fairness, accountability, and transparency* (pp. 39-48). DOI: 10.1145/3287560.3287567

Pedreschi, D., Ruggieri, S., & Turini, F. (2012, March). A study of top-k measures for discrimination discovery. In *Proceedings of the 27th Annual ACM Symposium on Applied Computing* (pp. 126-131). DOI: 10.1145/2245276.2245303

Pflanzer, M., Traylor, Z., Lyons, J. B., Dubljević, V., & Nam, C. S. (2023). Ethics in human–AI teaming: Principles and perspectives. *AI and Ethics*, *3*(3), 917–935. DOI: 10.1007/s43681-022-00214-z

Pleiss, G., Raghavan, M., Wu, F., Kleinberg, J., & Weinberger, K. Q. (2017). On fairness and calibration. *Advances in Neural Information Processing Systems*, •••, 30.

Quinn, T. P., Senadeera, M., Jacobs, S., Coghlan, S., & Le, V. (2021). Trust and medical AI: The challenges we face and the expertise needed to overcome them. *Journal of the American Medical Informatics Association : JAMIA*, *28*(4), 890–894. DOI: 10.1093/jamia/ocaa268

Rafsanjani, H. N., & Nabizadeh, A. H. (2023). Towards human-centered artificial intelligence (AI) in architecture, engineering, and construction (AEC) industry. *Computers in Human Behavior Reports, 11*, 100319. DOI: 10.1016/j.chbr.2023.100319

Rahwan, I. (2018). Society-in-the-loop: Programming the algorithmic social contract. *Ethics and Information Technology, 20*(1), 5–14. DOI: 10.1007/s10676-017-9430-8

Rajkomar, A., Oren, E., Chen, K., Dai, A. M., Hajaj, N., Hardt, M., Liu, P. J., Liu, X., Marcus, J., Sun, M., Sundberg, P., Yee, H., Zhang, K., Zhang, Y., Flores, G., Duggan, G. E., Irvine, J., Le, Q., Litsch, K., & Dean, J. (2018). Scalable and accurate deep learning with electronic health records. *NPJ Digital Medicine, 1*(1), 18. DOI: 10.1038/s41746-018-0029-1

Rajpurkar, P., Chen, E., Banerjee, O., & Topol, E. J. (2022). AI in health and medicine. *Nature Medicine, 28*(1), 31–38. DOI: 10.1038/s41591-021-01614-0

Ricci, A. (2023). *The Geography of Uncertainty: A Conceptual Model of Early Modern Globalization and the Current Crisis*. Routledge., DOI: 10.4324/9781003394204

Runco, M. A., & Jaeger, G. J. (2012). The standard definition of creativity. *Creativity Research Journal, 24*(1), 92–96. DOI: 10.1080/10400419.2012.650092

Russell, S. J., & Norvig, P. (1995). *Artificial intelligence: A modern approach* [the intelligent agent book]. Prentice hall.

Saha, D., Schumann, C., Mcelfresh, D., Dickerson, J., Mazurek, M., & Tschantz, M. (2020, November). Measuring non-expert comprehension of machine learning fairness metrics. In *International Conference on Machine Learning* (pp. 8377-8387). PMLR. https://proceedings.mlr.press/v119/saha20c.html.

Sawyer, K. (2012). Extending sociocultural theory to group creativity. *Vocations and Learning, 5*(1), 59–75. DOI: 10.1007/s12186-011-9066-5

Secinaro, S., Calandra, D., Secinaro, A., Muthurangu, V., & Biancone, P. (2021). The role of artificial intelligence in healthcare: A structured literature review. *BMC Medical Informatics and Decision Making, 21*(1), 1–23. DOI: 10.1186/s12911-021-01488-9

Shao, Z., Yuan, S., Wang, Y., & Xu, J. (2022). Evolutions and trends of artificial intelligence (AI): Research, output, influence and competition. *Library Hi Tech, 40*(3), 704–724. DOI: 10.1108/LHT-01-2021-0018

Shin, D., & Shin, E. Y. (2023). Data's impact on algorithmic bias. *Computer, 56*(6), 90–94. DOI: 10.1109/MC.2023.3262909

Shin, D. D. (2023). *Algorithms, humans, and interactions: How do algorithms interact with people? Designing meaningful AI experiences*. Taylor & Francis.

Sigfrids, A., Nieminen, M., Leikas, J., & Pikkuaho, P. (2022). How should public administrations foster the ethical development and use of artificial intelligence? A review of proposals for developing governance of AI. *Frontiers in Human Dynamics*, *4*, 858108. DOI: 10.3389/fhumd.2022.858108

Somepalli, G., Singla, V., Goldblum, M., Geiping, J., & Goldstein, T. (2023). Diffusion art or digital forgery? investigating data replication in diffusion models. In *Proceedings of the IEEE/CVF conference on computer vision and pattern recognition* (pp. 6048-6058). DOI: 10.1109/CVPR52729.2023.00586

Sun, T. Q., & Medaglia, R. (2019). Mapping the challenges of Artificial Intelligence in the public sector: Evidence from public healthcare. *Government Information Quarterly*, *36*(2), 368–383. DOI: 10.1016/j.giq.2018.09.008

Tran, B. X., Vu, G. T., Ha, G. H., Vuong, Q. H., Ho, M. T., Vuong, T. T., La, V.-P., Ho, M.-T., Nghiem, K.-C. P., Nguyen, H. L. T., Latkin, C. A., Tam, W. W. S., Cheung, N.-M., Nguyen, H.-K. T., Ho, C. S. H., & Ho, R. C. (2019). Global evolution of research in artificial intelligence in health and medicine: A bibliometric study. *Journal of Clinical Medicine*, *8*(3), 360. DOI: 10.3390/jcm8030360

Turyasingura, B., Ayiga, N., Byamukama, W., Kayusi, F., Tumuhimbise, M., & Tumushabe, T. (2024). Application of Artificial Intelligence (AI) in Environment and Societal Trends: Challenges and Opportunities. *Babylonian Journal of Machine Learning*, *2024*, 177–182. DOI: 10.58496/BJML/2024/018

Ulnicane, I., Eke, D. O., Knight, W., Ogoh, G., & Stahl, B. C. (2021). Good governance as a response to discontents? Déjà vu, or lessons for AI from other emerging technologies. *Interdisciplinary Science Reviews*, *46*(1-2), 71–93. DOI: 10.1080/03080188.2020.1840220

Usmani, U. A., Happonen, A., & Watada, J. (2023, June). Human-centered artificial intelligence: Designing for user empowerment and ethical considerations. In *2023 5th international congress on human-computer interaction, optimization and robotic applications (HORA)* (pp. 1-7). IEEE. DOI: 10.1109/HORA58378.2023.10156761

Walter, Y. (2024). Embracing the future of Artificial Intelligence in the classroom: The relevance of AI literacy, prompt engineering, and critical thinking in modern education. *International Journal of Educational Technology in Higher Education*, *21*(1), 15. DOI: 10.1186/s41239-024-00448-3

Wang, H., Zou, J., Mozer, M., Goyal, A., Lamb, A., Zhang, L., & Kawaguchi, K. (2024). Can AI be as creative as humans? *arXiv preprint arXiv:2401. 01623.*https://doi.org//arXiv.2401.01623DOI: 10.48550

Wei, S., & Niethammer, M. (2022). The fairness-accuracy Pareto front. *Statistical Analysis and Data Mining, 15*(3), 287–302. DOI: 10.1002/sam.11560

Wenzelburger, G., König, P. D., Felfeli, J., & Achtziger, A. (2024). Algorithms in the public sector. Why context matters. *Public Administration, 102*(1), 40–60. DOI: 10.1111/padm.12901

Wilson, C. (2022). Public engagement and AI: A values analysis of national strategies. *Government Information Quarterly, 39*(1), 101652. DOI: 10.1016/j.giq.2021.101652

Wirtz, B. W., Weyerer, J. C., & Sturm, B. J. (2020). The Dark Sides of Artificial Intelligence: An Integrated AI Governance Framework for Public Administration. *International Journal of Public Administration, 43*(9), 818–829. DOI: 10.1080/01900692.2020.1749851

Xenidis, R. (2020). Tuning EU equality law to algorithmic discrimination: Three pathways to resilience. *Maastricht Journal of European and Comparative Law, 27*(6), 736–758. DOI: 10.1177/1023263X20982173

Xu, W., & Dainoff, M. (2023). Enabling human-centered AI: A new junction and shared journey between AI and HCI communities. *Interactions (New York, N.Y.), 30*(1), 42–47. DOI: 10.1145/3571883

. Yeung, K., Howes, A., & Pogrebna, G. (2020). AI governance by human rights–centered design, deliberation, and oversight: An end to ethics washing.

Zhang, Y., Kassem, K., Gong, Z., Mo, F., Ma, Y., Kirjavainen, E., & Häkkilä, J. (2024, December). Human-centered AI Technologies in Human-robot Interaction for Social Settings. In *Proceedings of the International Conference on Mobile and Ubiquitous Multimedia* (pp. 501-505). DOI: 10.1145/3701571.3701610

KEY TERMS AND DEFINITIONS

Artificial Intelligence: Artificial Intelligence (AI) refers to the capability of a computer systems to perform the critical tasks that typically needs human intelligence, such as learning, reasoning, analysing, interpreting, problem-solving, and decision-making.

Human Centered Disciplines: Human-centered design refers to user-centered design, that prioritizes understanding and addressing the needs of human throughout the design process and ensuring that its products, services, and systems are usable and effective.

Ai Decision-Making: AI decision-making which effectively utilizes the AI techniques to analyze the data, identifying patterns, and make informed choices offering benefits like faster, accurate, and data-driven decision-making across diverse fields.

Ai Ethics: AI ethics refers to the principles and guidelines that addresses artificial intelligence technology is developed and used focusing on responsibly, safety, security, human values.

Human Intelligence: Human intelligence refers the cognitive abilities that allow individuals to learn, adapt, understand the abstract concepts, and use that knowledge to navigate their environment. It involves complex constructs like reasoning, problem-solving, and memory.

Technology: Technology is the practical application of the scientific knowledge, tools, and techniques in order to create solutions to solve the problems or improve human life.

About the Contributors

Salmane Bourekkadi is a Moroccan academic specializing in computer science and philosophy (holding two PhDs). He is affiliated with the Faculty of Human and Social Sciences in Kenitra, Morocco. In collaboration with other researchers, he has co-authored books such as "Science and Technology at the Service of the Environment: Doctoral Students' Club" and "Standardized Management of Information Technology Between the Strategic Approach and the Operational Approach". He has also contributed to academic articles, including on "Computational Psychology and its Impact on Human Behavior", exploring the intersection between computer science, psychology, and neuroscience to solve problems related to human behavior in the digital world.

***

Rahmath Nisha is a dedicated professional with comprehensive, hands-on experience in Human Resource Management (HRM), having successfully managed the entire employee life cycle—from recruitment and onboarding to performance management and employee engagement. She holds an MBA in Human Resource Management, where she was recognized as a Gold Medalist and awarded the title of Best Outgoing Student. Her academic journey began with a Bachelor's degree in Electronics and Communication Engineering, showcasing her diverse educational foundation. Currently serving as an Assistant Professor, she combines industry expertise with academic insight to mentor and inspire the next generation of HR professionals.

Hamid Ait Lemqeddem is a Research Professor at the National School of Commerce and Management (ENCG) of Ibn Tofail University in Kenitra, Morocco. He holds a PhD in Economic Sciences from the Faculty of Economic Sciences, Rabat-Agdal. His research interests include environmental governance, sustainable development, logistics, digitalization of public procurement, territorial economic intelligence, big data, customer relationship management, SME performance, social entrepreneurship, crowdfunding, and the application of artificial intelligence in management. He has published numerous articles in these fields and participated in several international conferences.

Bavani Arumugam Seiyalu is a senior lecturer at the Centre for the Promotion of Knowledge and Language (PPIB), Universiti Malaysia Sabah. She holds a PhD in Language Education from the University of Malaya. Her research interests include language education, linguistics, literature, and qualitative studies.

Nouhaila Bentatou is a doctoral researcher at Ibn Tofail University, Kenitra, Morocco. She holds a Master's degree in International Trade and Logistics and is currently pursuing a PhD in Management Sciences, focusing on the impact of digital transformation on the optimization of logistics costs in the Moroccan automotive sector. Her research interests include digital transformation, Industry 4.0, sustainable logistics, and ethical artificial intelligence applied to supply chain management. She has contributed to several academic publications and international conference presentations, reflecting her commitment to research on sustainability and responsibility in contemporary logistics systems.

Mehmet Fatih Burak holds a PhD in business administration from Istanbul Beykent University, Türkiye. His research interests include strategic management, organizational development, information systems, e-business, e-commerce, international trade, leadership, and corporate social responsibility.

Sammy F is an Assistant Professor in the Department of Computing Technologies, School of Computing, at SRM Institute of Science and Technology, Kattankulathur. He is actively involved in teaching and mentoring students in the field of computing and technology. His academic interests include software development, data analytics, and emerging computing paradigms

Belshia Jebamalar is an Assistant Professor in the Department of Computer Science and Engineering at S A Engineering College. She is dedicated to teaching core computer science subjects and mentoring students for academic excellence. Her interests focus on strengthening technical foundations and practical problem-solving skills.

Vijay J is an Assistant Professor in the Department of Computer Science and Engineering at R M K College of Engineering and Technology, RSM Nagar, Puduvoyal. He is involved in teaching core computer science subjects and mentoring students in their academic growth. His interests include enhancing programming proficiency and applying engineering concepts to real-world challenges.

Srikanth Lakumarapu is an Associate Professor in the Department of Computer Science and Engineering at CVR College of Engineering, Telangana, India. He is actively involved in teaching, research, and guiding students in core and advanced areas of computer science. His academic interests emphasize quality education, innovation, and practical application of engineering concepts.

Yoke Lian Lau serves as a lecturer at the Centre for the Promotion of Knowledge and Language Learning (PPIB) at Universiti Malaysia Sabah (UMS). Her research centers on language education, artificial intelligence in linguistics, and inclusive pedagogy. She has extensively published and presented on subjects pertaining to AI-assisted language acquisition, phonetic analysis, digital literacy, and language teaching for those with special needs. In addition to her academic pursuits, she is a distinguished author of children's books and a pioneer in bilingual education innovation. Her ongoing efforts involve the creation of an AI-based pronunciation training model for learners of Mandarin.

Dinesh M. G. is a faculty member at EASA College of Engineering and Technology, Coimbatore, Tamil Nadu, India. He specializes in engineering education and research, contributing to advancements in his field.

Gopika Priya P is an Assistant Professor in the Department of Artificial Intelligence and Data Science at Vel Tech Multi Tech Dr. Rangarajan Dr. Sakunthala Engineering College, Avadi, Chennai. She is dedicated to teaching and mentoring students in AI, data science, and emerging intelligent systems. Her academic interests focus on developing analytical thinking and practical skills among engineering students.

Lokesh P is an Assistant Professor in the Department of Computer Science and Engineering (Artificial Intelligence and Machine Learning).He is associated with Vel Tech High Tech Dr. Rangarajan Dr. Sakunthala Engineering College. His academic interests include teaching and research in AI and machine learning technologies.

Harini S is an accomplished academic with dual postgraduate degrees-MBA and M.Com-as well as a Post Graduate Diploma in Business Management (PGDBM). Worked as an Assistant Professor with four years of teaching experience, Harini is recognized for her research-oriented mindset and dedication to academic innovation. During her MBA, Harini was honored as the Best Outgoing Student and received a coveted gold medal, reflecting her commitment to excellence and leadership. Her passion for research is evident in her extensive work with various scholarly articles, particularly those employing quantitative approaches. Harini's innovative spirit and analytical skills have earned her the prestigious Young Researcher Award. In addition to her research contributions, Harini has reviewed several research chapters, further establishing her reputation as a meticulous and insightful scholar. She is driven by a passion for advancing knowledge, fostering academic innovation, and inspiring the next generation of researchers.

A.K. Subramani is a distinguished academic with a PhD in Business Administration from Manonmaniam Sundaranar University, Tirunelveli, India. With 18 years of teaching experience, he has made significant contributions to the field of human resource management and organisational behaviour. He has an impressive publication record with 80 articles in international journals, including two papers in the ABDC-A category, eight in the ABDC-B category, three in the ABDC-C category, 30 in Scopus-indexed journals, and eight in Web of Science journals. He has served as a resource person for various training workshops on SPSS and AMOS software packages.

Karim Tabaa is a PhD student at Ibn Tufail University, Faculty of Humanities and Social Sciences, currently working within civil society as a social worker and assistant in humanitarian issues. His research interests, based on academic training, focus on digitisation, health, medicine, gender issues, development policies, and other topics that fall within the core competencies of sociology.

Swee Mee Tan currently works at the Department of Languages and Linguistics, Southern University Colloge. Swee Mee does research in Literary Theory, Applied Linguistics and Discourse Analysis.

Zi Hong Yong currently a Mandarin language teacher of Universiti Malaysia Sabah.

Yong Zi Xian is currently a Mandarin language teacher at the Centre for the Promotion of Knowledge and Language, Universiti Malaysia Sabah (UMS). She completed her master's degree in teaching Chinese to Speakers of Other Languages (TCSOL) at Peking University, China. Her research interests include Chinese language teaching and learning and Chinese character studies. She can be contacted via email at: zixian.yzx@ums.edu.my.

Index

A

C

D

E

N

O

P

R

S

T

U

V

www.ingramcontent.com/pod-product-compliance
Lightning Source LLC
LaVergne TN
LVHW062340300926
849161LV00007B/1771